Civil Rights

Pearson
Education

Civil Rights
New Labour, Freedom and the Human Rights Act

Helen Fenwick

An imprint of Pearson Education

Harlow, England · London · New York · Reading, Massachusetts · San Francisco
Toronto · Don Mills, Ontario · Sydney · Tokyo · Singapore · Hong Kong · Seoul
Taipei · Cape Town · Madrid · Mexico City · Amsterdam · Munich · Paris · Milan

Pearson Education Limited
Edinburgh Gate
Harlow
Essex CM20 2JE
England

and Associated Companies throughout the world

Visit us on the World Wide Web at:
http://www.pearsoneduc.com

First published 2000

ISBN 0 582 29818 0 PPR

British Library Cataloguing-in-Publication Data
A catalogue record for this book is available from the British Library

10 9 8 7 6 5 4 3 2 1
05 04 03 02 01

Typeset by 35 in 10/12pt New Baskerville
Printed in Great Britain by Henry Ling Ltd.,
at the Dorset Press, Dorchester, Dorset

Contents

Preface

This book was completed a few days before the Human Rights Act 1998 came fully into force. It was therefore written at a time of unprecedented change in the human rights field in the UK. It reflects the resulting redirection of academic debate in that field that is now occurring. The argument about the merits of adopting 'a Bill of Rights' has now moved on and instead is focusing on the new issues arising from the reception of the Convention into domestic law, particularly the extent to which the Convention will have real efficacy. This is a central concern of this book since the alternative would lead, it argues, to a *lower* standard of protection for freedom than we had in the pre-Human Rights Act era. There is a danger that the Human Rights Act will be utilised in Parliament to give the impression that a process of human rights auditing has occurred, stifling political discourse and obscuring the rights-abridging effects of legislation. Its effects may be marginalised due to the reduction or exclusion of judicial scutiny which tends to accompany the provision of a statutory basis for interferences with rights.

These comments indicate the ambivalence which this book seeks to capture. While the contribution of the New Labour government to the protection of liberty must be acknowledged, doubts about its commitment to such protection are already emerging. The stance of the government towards human rights issues is revealed in its willingness to introduce protection for rights to a fair trial, to the freedoms of expression and assembly, and yet to introduce a new statutory framework for the use of coercive state power which will tend to undermine those rights. The government, having introduced the Human Rights Act, then went on to re-write state surveillance and counter-terrorist measures in the Terrorism Act 2000 and the Regulation of Investigatory Powers Act 2000. An intriguing interaction between that new framework and the Human Rights Act was thereby set in motion, providing part of the impetus for this book. It has therefore concentrated selectively on human rights concerns, choosing to focus on the coercive use of power by state agents in order to make the argument that at the very beginning of the Human Rights Act era the danger of a decrease in state accountability and the creation of merely empty guarantees through a minimalist interpretation of the Convention, is apparent. Such an interpretation, to which the Convention is particularly susceptible, may be reflected not only in legislation, but in the judicial approach to the Act. The differences between the position of the Strasbourg Court and the domestic one, especially in criminal justice matters, may go unrecognised and therefore the Convention jurisprudence may appear to legitimise established illiberal common law tendencies.

This book seeks therefore, at this turning point for individual liberty in the UK, to make a contribution to the debate that is currently under way. It argues for an understanding of the dangers of a minimalist interpretation of the Convention and for the full realisation in domestic law of its underlying principles in order to ensure state accountability. In tracing the adherence of the new statutory framework to the models introduced under the Conservative governments of 1989–1997, it seeks to indicate the difficulties of creating such accountability that lie ahead.

This book is written for those with an interest in the influence of the Human Rights Act on the use of coercive state power, especially by the police and the Intelligence Services. The links of this subject to criminal justice theories, judicial review, and constitutional concepts are so strong that a legal analysis of this field, in a book of this length, must assume a familiarity with these matters. It covers legislation that affects England, Wales, Northern Ireland and Scotland but concentrates on its impact in England and Wales. It includes the full text of the Human Rights Act, for ease of reference. The main body of the text was completed by the end of May 2000, but it was possible to add some later material in September 2000.

A number of people have helped me in formulating the ideas expressed in this book. My thanks are especially due to my colleagues at Durham, Professor Colin Warbrick, Professor Ian Leigh and Gavin Phillipson who offered a number of very valuable criticisms and suggestions. Pat Bond and Elaine Richardson of Pearson Education responded to the difficulties of producing the book at a time of such constant change in an unfailingly helpful and flexible fashion.

The book is dedicated with love and affection to my father and mother, my husband Paul and children Clare, Daniel and Patrick.

Durham
September 2000

Table of Cases

European Court of Justice

Germany

New Zealand

United Kingdom

United States

Table of Legislation

Table of International Instruments

Human Rights Act 1998

1998 Chapter 42

An Act to give further effect to rights and freedoms guaranteed under the European Convention on Human Rights; to make provision with respect to holders of certain judicial offices who become judges of the European Court of Human Rights; and for connected purposes.

[9th November 1998]

BE IT ENACTED by the Queen's most Excellent Majesty, by and with the advice and consent of the Lords Spiritual and Temporal, and Commons, in this present Parliament assembled, and by the authority of the same, as follows: –

Introduction

1. The Convention Rights

(1) In this Act 'the Convention rights' means the rights and fundamental freedoms set out in –

(a) Articles 2 to 12 and 14 of the Convention,

(b) Articles 1 to 3 of the First Protocol, and

(c) Articles 1 and 2 of the Sixth Protocol,

as read with Articles 16 to 18 of the Convention.

(2) Those Articles are to have effect for the purposes of this Act subject to any designated derogation or reservation (as to which see sections 14 and 15).

(3) The Articles are set out in Schedule 1.

(4) The Secretary of State may by order make such amendments to this Act as he considers appropriate to reflect the effect, in relation to the United Kingdom, of a protocol.

(5) In subsection (4) 'protocol' means a protocol to the Convention –

(a) which the United Kingdom has ratified; or
(b) which the United Kingdom has signed with a view to ratification.

(6) No amendment may be made by an order under subsection (4) so as to come into force before the protocol concerned is in force in relation to the United Kingdom.

2. Interpretation of Convention rights

(1) A court or tribunal determining a question which has arisen in connection with a Convention right must take into account any –

(a) judgment, decision, declaration or advisory opinion of the European Court of Human Rights,
(b) opinion of the Commission given in a report adopted under Article 31 of the Convention,
(c) decision of the Commission in connection with Article 26 or 27(2) of the Convention, or
(d) decision of the Committee of Ministers taken under Article 46 of the Convention,

whenever made or given, so far as, in the opinion of the court or tribunal, it is relevant to the proceedings in which that question has arisen.

(2) Evidence of any judgment, decision, declaration or opinion of which account may have to be taken under this section is to be given in proceedings before any court or tribunal in such manner as may be provided by rules.

(3) In this section 'rules' means rules of court or, in the case of proceedings before a tribunal, rules made for the purposes of this section –

(a) by the Lord Chancellor or the Secretary of State, in relation to any proceedings outside Scotland;
(b) by the Secretary of State, in relation to proceedings in Scotland; or
(c) by a Northern Ireland department, in relation to proceedings before a tribunal in Northern Ireland –

(i) which deals with transferred matters; and
(ii) for which no rules made under paragraph (a) are in force.

Legislation

3. Interpretation of legislation

(1) So far as it is possible to do so, primary legislation and subordinate legislation must be read and given effect in a way which is compatible with the Convention rights.

(2) This section –

(a) applies to primary legislation and subordinate legislation whenever enacted;

(b) does not affect the validity, continuing operation or enforcement of any incompatible primary legislation; and
(c) does not affect the validity, continuing operation or enforcement of any incompatible subordinate legislation if (disregarding any possibility of revocation) primary legislation prevents removal of the incompatibility.

4. Declaration of incompatibility

(1) Subsection (2) applies in any proceedings in which a court determines whether a provision of primary legislation is compatible with a Convention right.
(2) If the court is satisfied that the provision is incompatible with a Convention right, it may make a declaration of that incompatibility.
(3) Subsection (4) applies in any proceedings in which a court determines whether a provision of subordinate legislation, made in the exercise of a power conferred by primary legislation, is compatible with a Convention right.
(4) If the court is satisfied –
(a) that the provision is incompatible with a Convention right, and
(b) that (disregarding any possibility of revocation) the primary legislation concerned prevents removal of the incompatibility,
it may make a declaration of that incompatibility.
(5) In this section 'court' means –
(a) the House of Lords;
(b) the Judicial Committee of the Privy Council;
(c) the Courts-Martial Appeal Court;
(d) in Scotland, the High Court of Justiciary sitting otherwise than as a trial court or the Court of Session;
(e) in England and Wales or Northern Ireland, the High Court or the Court of Appeal.
(6) A declaration under this section ('a declaration of incompatibility') –
(a) does not affect the validity, continuing operation or enforcement of the provision in respect of which it is given; and
(b) is not binding on the parties to the proceedings in which it is made.

5. Right of Crown to intervene

(1) Where a court is considering whether to make a declaration of incompatibility, the Crown is entitled to notice in accordance with rules of court.
(2) In any case to which subsection (1) applies –
(a) a Minister of the Crown (or a person nominated by him),
(b) a member of the Scottish Executive,
(c) a Northern Ireland Minister,
(d) a Northern Ireland department,

is entitled, on giving notice in accordance with rules of court, to be joined as a party to the proceedings.

(3) Notice under subsection (2) may be given at any time during the proceedings.

(4) A person who has been made a party to criminal proceedings (other than in Scotland) as the result of a notice under subsection (2) may, with leave, appeal to the House of Lords against any declaration of incompatibility made in the proceedings.

(5) In subsection (4) –

'criminal proceedings' includes all proceedings before the Courts-Martial Appeal Court; and

'leave' means leave granted by the court making the declaration of incompatibility or by the House of Lords.

Public authorities

6. Acts of public authorities

(1) It is unlawful for a public authority to act in a way which is incompatible with a Convention right.

(2) Subsection (1) does not apply to an act if –

(a) as the result of one or more provisions of primary legislation, the authority could not have acted differently; or

(b) in the case of one or more provisions of, or made under, primary legislation which cannot be read or given effect in a way which is compatible with the Convention rights, the authority was acting so as to give effect to or enforce those provisions.

(3) In this section 'public authority' includes –

(a) a court or tribunal, and

(b) any person certain of whose functions are functions of a public nature, but does not include either House of Parliament or a person exercising functions in connection with proceedings in Parliament.

(4) In subsection (3) 'Parliament' does not include the House of Lords in its judicial capacity.

(5) In relation to a particular act, a person is not a public authority by virtue only of subsection (3)(b) if the nature of the act is private.

(6) 'An act' includes a failure to act but does not include a failure to –

(a) introduce in, or lay before, Parliament a proposal for legislation; or

(b) make any primary legislation or remedial order.

7. Proceedings

(1) A person who claims that a public authority has acted (or proposes to act) in a way which is made unlawful by section 6(1) may –

(a) bring proceedings against the authority under this Act in the appropriate court or tribunal, or

(b) rely on the Convention right or rights concerned in any legal proceedings,

but only if he is (or would be) a victim of the unlawful act.

(2) In subsection (1)(a) 'appropriate court or tribunal' means such court or tribunal as may be determined in accordance with rules; and proceedings against an authority include a counterclaim or similar proceeding.

(3) If the proceedings are brought on an application for judicial review, the applicant is to be taken to have a sufficient interest in relation to the unlawful act only if he is, or would be, a victim of that act.

(4) If the proceedings are made by way of a petition for judicial review in Scotland, the applicant shall be taken to have title and interest to sue in relation to the unlawful act only if he is, or would be, a victim of that act.

(5) Proceedings under subsection (1)(a) must be brought before the end of –

(a) the period of one year beginning with the date on which the act complained of took place; or

(b) such longer period as the court or tribunal considers equitable having regard to all the cicumstances,

but that is subject to any rule imposing a stricter time limit in relation to the procedure in question.

(6) In subsection (1)(b) 'legal proceedings' includes –

(a) proceedings brought by or at the instigation of a public authority; and

(b) an appeal against the decision of a court or tribunal.

(7) For the purposes of this section, a person is a victim of an unlawful act only if he would be a victim for the purposes of Article 34 of the Convention if proceedings were brought in the European Court of Human Rights in respect of that act.

(8) Nothing in this Act creates a criminal offence.

(9) In this section 'rules' means –

(a) in relation to proceedings before a court or tribunal outside Scotland, rules made by the Lord Chancellor or the Secretary of State for the purposes of this section or rules of court,

(b) in relation to proceedings before a court or tribunal in Scotland, rules made by the Secretary of State for those purposes,

(c) in relation to proceedings before a tribunal in Northern Ireland –

(i) which deals with transferred matters; and

(ii) for which no rules made under paragraph (a) are in force,

rules made by a Northern Ireland department for those purposes, and includes provision made by order under section 1 of the Courts and Legal Services Act 1990.

(10) In making rules, regard must be had to section 9.

(11) The Minister who has power to make rules in relation to a particular tribunal may, to the extent he considers it necessary to ensure that the tribunal can provide an appropriate remedy in relation to an act (or proposed act) of a public authority which is (or would be) unlawful as a result of section 6(1), by order add to –

(a) the relief or remedies which the tribunal may grant; or

(b) the grounds on which it may grant any of them.

(12) An order made under subsection (11) may contain such incidental, supplemental, consequential or transitional provision as the Minister making it considers appropriate.

(13) 'The Minister' includes the Northern Ireland department concerned.

8. Judicial remedies

(1) In relation to any act (or proposed act) of a public authority which the court finds is (or would be) unlawful, it may grant such relief or remedy, or make such order, within its powers as it considers just and appropriate.

(2) But damages may be awarded only by a court which has power to award damages, or to order the payment of compensation, in civil proceedings.

(3) No award of damages is to be made unless, taking account of all the circumstances of the case, including –

(a) any other relief or remedy granted, or order made, in relation to the act in question (by that or any other court), and

(b) the consequences of any decision (of that or any other court) in respect of that act,

the court is satisfied that the award is necessary to afford just satisfaction to the person in whose favour it is made.

(4) In determining –

(a) whether to award damages, or

(b) the amount of an award,

the court must take into account the principles applied by the European Court of Human Rights in relation to the award of compensation under Article 41 of the Convention.

(5) A public authority against which damages are awarded is to be treated –

(a) in Scotland, for the purposes of section 3 of the Law Reform (Miscellaneous Provisions) (Scotland) Act 1940 as if the award were made in an action of damages in which the authority has been found liable in respect of loss or damage to the person to whom the award is made;

(b) for the purposes of the Civil Liability (Contribution) Act 1978 as liable in respect of damage suffered by the person to whom the award is made.

(6) In this section –
'court' includes a tribunal;
'damages' means damages for an unlawful act of a public authority; and
'unlawful' means unlawful under section 6(1).

9. Judicial acts

(1) Proceedings under section 7(1)(a) in respect of a judicial act may be brought only –

(a) by exercising a right of appeal;

(b) on an application (in Scotland a petition) for judicial review; or

(c) in such other forum as may be prescribed by rules.

(2) That does not affect any rule of law which prevents a court from being the subject of judicial review.

(3) In proceedings under this Act in respect of a judicial act done in good faith, damages may not be awarded otherwise than to compensate a person to the extent required by Article 5(5) of the Convention.

(4) An award of damages permitted by subsection (3) is to be made against the Crown; but no award may be made unless the appropriate person, if not a party to the proceedings, is joined.

(5) In this section –
'appropriate person' means the Minister responsible for the court concerned, or a person or government department nominated by him;
'court' includes a tribunal;
'judge' includes a member of a tribunal, a justice of the peace and a clerk or other officer entitled to exercise the jurisdiction of a court;
'judicial act' means a judicial act of a court and includes an act done on the instructions, or on behalf, of a judge; and
'rules' has the same meaning as in section 7(9).

Remedial action

10. Power to take remedial action

(1) This section applies if –

(a) a provision of legislation has been declared under section 4 to be incompatible with a Convention right and, if an appeal lies –

(i) all persons who may appeal have stated in writing that they do not intend to do so;

(ii) the time for bringing an appeal has expired and no appeal has been brought within that time; or

(iii) an appeal brought within that time has been determined or abandoned; or

(b) it appears to a Minister of the Crown or Her Majesty in Council that, having regard to a finding of the European Court of Human Rights made after the coming into force of this section in proceedings against the United Kingdom, a provision of legislation is incompatible with an obligation of the United Kingdom arising from the Convention.

(2) If a Minister of the Crown considers that there are compelling reasons for proceeding under this section, he may by order make such amendments to the legislation as he considers necessary to remove the incompatibility.

(3) If, in the case of subordinate legislation, a Minister of the Crown considers –

(a) that it is necessary to amend the primary legislation under which the subordinate legislation in question was made, in order to enable the incompatibility to be removed, and

(b) that there are compelling reasons for proceeding under this section, he may by order make such amendments to the primary legislation as he considers necessary.

(4) This section also applies where the provision in question is in subordinate legislation and has been quashed, or declared invalid, by reason of incompatibility with a Convention right and the Minister proposes to proceed under paragraph 2(b) of Schedule 2.

(5) If the legislation is an Order in Council, the power conferred by subsection (2) or (3) is exercisable by Her Majesty in Council.

(6) In this section 'legislation' does not include a Measure of the Church Assembly or of the General Synod of the Church of England.

(7) Schedule 2 makes further provision about remedial orders.

Other rights and proceedings

11. Safeguard for existing human rights

A person's reliance on a Convention right does not restrict –

(a) any other right or freedom conferred on him by or under any law having effect in any part of the United Kingdom; or

(b) his right to make any claim or bring any proceedings which he could make or bring apart from sections 7 to 9.

12. Freedom of expression

(1) This section applies if a court is considering whether to grant any relief which, if granted, might affect the exercise of the Convention right to freedom of expression.

(2) If the person against whom the application for relief is made ('the respondent') is neither present nor represented, no such relief is to be granted unless the court is satisfied –

(a) that the applicant has taken all practicable steps to notify the respondent; or

(b) that there are compelling reasons why the respondent should not be notified.

(3) No such relief is to be granted so as to restrain publication before trial unless the court is satisfied that the applicant is likely to establish that publication should not be allowed.
(4) The court must have particular regard to the importance of the Convention right to freedom of expression and, where the proceedings relate to material which the respondent claims, or which appears to the court, to be journalistic, literary or artistic material (or to conduct connected with such material), to –
(a) the extent to which –
(i) the material has, or is about to, become available to the public; or
(ii) it is, or would be, in the public interest for the material to be published;
(b) any relevant privacy code.
(5) In this section –
'court' includes a tribunal; and
'relief' includes any remedy or order (other than in criminal proceedings).

13. Freedom of thought, conscience and religion
(1) If a court's determination of any question arising under this Act might affect the exercise by a religious organisation (itself or its members collectively) of the Convention right to freedom of thought, conscience and religion, it must have particular regard to the importance of that right.
(2) In this section 'court' includes a tribunal.

Derogations and reservations

14. Derogations
(1) In this Act 'designated derogation' means –
(a) the United Kingdom's derogation from Article 5(3) of the Convention; and
(b) any derogation by the United Kingdom from an Article of the Convention, or of any protocol to the Convention, which is designated for the purposes of this Act in an order made by the Secretary of State.
(2) The derogation referred to in subsection (1)(a) is set out in Part I of Schedule 3.
(3) If a designated derogation is amended or replaced it ceases to be a designated derogation.
(4) But subsection (3) does not prevent the Secretary of State from exercising his power under subsection (1)(b) to make a fresh designation order in respect of the Article concerned.
(5) The Secretary of State must by order make such amendments to Schedule 3 as he considers appropriate to reflect –

(a) any designation order; or

(b) the effect of subsection (3).

(6) A designation order may be made in anticipation of the making by the United Kingdom of a proposed derogation.

15. Reservations

(1) In this Act 'designated reservation' means –

(a) the United Kingdom's reservation to Article 2 of the First Protocol to the Convention; and

(b) any other reservation by the United Kingdom to an Article of the Convention, or of any protocol to the Convention, which is designated for the purposes of this Act in an order made by the Secretary of State.

(2) The text of the reservation referred to in subsection (1)(a) is set out in Part 11 of Schedule 3.

(3) If a designated reservation is withdrawn wholly or in part it ceases to be a designated reservation.

(4) But subsection (3) does not prevent the Secretary of State from exercising his power under subsection (1)(b) to make a fresh designation order in respect of the Article concerned.

(5) The Secretary of State must by order make such amendments to this Act as he considers appropriate to reflect –

(a) any designation order; or

(b) the effect of subsection (3).

16. Period for which designated derogations have effect

(1) If it has not already been withdrawn by the United Kingdom, a designated derogation ceases to have effect for the purposes of this Act –

(a) in the case of the derogation referred to in section 14(1)(a), at the end of the period of five years beginning with the date on which section 1(2) came into force;

(b) in the case of any other derogation, at the end of the period of five years beginning with the date on which the order designating it was made.

(2) At any time before the period –

(a) fixed by subsection (1)(a) or (b), or

(b) extended by an order under this subsection,

comes to an end, the Secretary of State may by order extend it by a further period of five years.

(3) An order under section 14(1)(b) ceases to have effect at the end of the period for consideration, unless a resolution has been passed by each House approving the order.

(4) Subsection (3) does not affect –

(a) anything done in reliance on the order; or

(b) the power to make a fresh order under section 14(1)(b).

(5) In subsection (3) 'period for consideration' means the period of forty days beginning with the day on which the order was made.

(6) In calculating the period for consideration, no account is to be taken of any time during which –

(a) Parliament is dissolved or prorogued; or

(b) both Houses are adjourned for more than four days.

(7) If a designated derogation is withdrawn by the United Kingdom, the Secretary of State must by order make such amendments to this Act as he considers are required to reflect that withdrawal.

17. Periodic review of designated reservations

(1) The appropriate Minister must review the designated reservation referred to in section 15(1)(a) –

(a) before the end of the period of five years beginning with the date on which section 1(2) came into force; and

(b) if that designation is still in force, before the end of the period of five years beginning with the date on which the last report relating to it was laid under subsection (3).

(2) The appropriate Minister must review each of the other designated reservations (if any) –

(a) before the end of the period of five years beginning with the date on which the order designating the reservation first came into force; and

(b) if the designation is still in force, before the end of the period of five years beginning with the date on which the last report relating to it was laid under subsection (3).

(3) The Minister conducting a review under this section must prepare a report on the result of the review and lay a copy of it before each House of Parliament.

Judges of the European Court of Human Rights

18. Appointment to European Court of Human Rights

(1) In this section 'judicial office' means the office of –

(a) Lord Justice of Appeal, Justice of the High Court or Circuit judge, in England and Wales;

(b) judge of the Court of Session or sheriff, in Scotland;

(c) Lord Justice of Appeal, judge of the High Court or county court judge, in Northern Ireland.

(2) The holder of a judicial office may become a judge of the European Court of Human Rights ('the Court') without being required to relinquish his office.

(3) But he is not required to perform the duties of his judicial office while he is a judge of the Court.

(4) In respect of any period during which he is a judge of the Court –

(a) a Lord Justice of Appeal or Justice of the High Court is not to count as a judge of the relevant court for the purposes of section 2(1) or 4(1) of the Supreme Court Act

1981 (maximum number of judges) nor as a judge of the Supreme Court for the purposes of section 12(1) to (6) of that Act (salaries etc.);

(b) a judge of the Court of Session is not to count as a judge of that court for the purposes of section 1(1) of the Court of Session Act 1988 (maximum number of judges) or of section 9(1)(c) of the Administration of Justice Act 1973 ('the 1973 Act') (salaries etc.);

(c) a Lord Justice of Appeal or judge of the High Court in Northern Ireland is not to count as a judge of the relevant court for the purposes of section 2(1) or 3(1) of the Judicature (Northern Ireland) Act 1978 (maximum number of judges) nor as a judge of the Supreme Court of Northern Ireland for the purposes of section 9(1)(d) of the 1973 Act (salaries etc.);

(d) a Circuit judge is not to count as such for the purposes of section 18 of the Courts Act 1971 (salaries etc.);

(e) a sheriff is not to count as such for the purposes of section 14 of the Sheriff Courts (Scotland) Act 1907 (salaries etc.);

(f) a county court judge of Northern Ireland is not to count as such for the purposes of section 106 of the County Courts Act (Northern Ireland) 1959 (salaries etc.).

(5) If a sheriff principal is appointed a judge of the Court, section 11(1) of the Sheriff Courts (Scotland) Act 1971 (temporary appointment of sheriff principal) applies, while he holds that appointment, as if his office is vacant.

(6) Schedule 4 makes provision about judicial pensions in relation to the holder of a judicial office who serves as a judge of the Court.

(7) The Lord Chancellor or the Secretary of State may by order make such transitional provision (including, in particular, provision for a temporary increase in the maximum number of judges) as he considers appropriate in relation to any holder of a judicial office who has completed his service as a judge of the Court.

Parliamentary procedure

19. Statements of compatibility

(1) A Minister of the Crown in charge of a Bill in either House of Parliament must, before Second Reading of the Bill –

(a) make a statement to the effect that in his view the provisions of the Bill are compatible with the Convention rights ('a statement of compatibility'); or

(b) make a statement to the effect that although he is unable to make a statement of compatibility the government nevertheless wishes the House to proceed with the Bill.

(2) The statement must be in writing and be published in such manner as the Minister making it considers appropriate.

Supplemental

20. Orders etc. under this Act

(1) Any power of a Minister of the Crown to make an order under this Act is exercisable by statutory instrument.

(2) The power of the Lord Chancellor or the Secretary of State to make rules (other than rules of court) under section 2(3) or 7(9) is exercisable by statutory instrument.

(3) Any statutory instrument made under section 14, 15 or 16(7) must be laid before Parliament.

(4) No order may be made by the Lord Chancellor or the Secretary of State under section 1(4), 7(11) or 16(2) unless a draft of the order has been laid before, and approved by, each House of Parliament.

(5) Any statutory instrument made under section 18(7) or Schedule 4, or to which subsection (2) applies, shall be subject to annulment in pursuance of a resolution of either House of Parliament.

(6) The power of a Northern Ireland department to make –

(a) rules under section 2(3)(c) or 7(9)(c), or

(b) an order under section 7(11),

is exercisable by statutory rule for the purposes of the Statutory Rules (Northern Ireland) Order 1979.

(7) Any rules made under section 2(3)(c) or 7(9)(c) shall be subject to negative resolution; and section 41(6) of the Interpretation Act (Northern Ireland) 1954 (meaning of 'subject to negative resolution') shall apply as if the power to make the rules were conferred by an Act of the Northern Ireland Assembly.

(8) No order may be made by a Northern Ireland department under section 7(11) unless a draft of the order has been laid before, and approved by, the Northern Ireland Assembly.

21. Interpretation etc.

(1) In this Act –

'amend' includes repeal and apply (with or without modifications);

'the appropriate Minister' means the Minister of the Crown having charge of the appropriate authorised government department (within the meaning of the Crown Proceedings Act 1947);

'the Commission' means the European Commission of Human Rights;

'the Convention' means the Convention for the Protection of Human Rights and Fundamental Freedoms, agreed by the Council of Europe at Rome on 4th November 1950 as it has effect for the time being in relation to the United Kingdom;

'declaration of incompatibility' means a declaration under section 4;

'Minister of the Crown' has the same meaning as in the Ministers of the Crown Act 1975;

'Northern Ireland Minister' includes the First Minister and the deputy First Minister in Northern Ireland;

'primary legislation' means any –

(a) public general Act;
(b) local and personal Act;
(c) private Act;
(d) Measure of the Church Assembly;
(e) Measure of the General Synod of the Church of England;
(f) Order in Council –
(i) made in exercise of Her Majesty's Royal Prerogative;
(ii) made under section 38(1)(a) of the Northern Ireland Constitution Act 1973 or the corresponding provision of the Northern Ireland Act 1998; or
(iii) amending an Act of a kind mentioned in paragraph (a), (b) or (c); and includes an order or other instrument made under primary legislation (otherwise than by the National Assembly for Wales, a member of the Scottish Executive, a Northern Ireland Minister or a Northern Ireland department) to the extent to which it operates to bring one or more provisions of that legislation into force or amends any primary legislation;

'the First Protocol' means the protocol to the Convention agreed at Paris on 20th March 1952;
'the Sixth Protocol' means the protocol to the Convention agreed at Strasbourg on 28th April 1983;
'the Eleventh Protocol' means the protocol to the Convention (restructuring the control machinery established by the Convention) agreed at Strasbourg on 11th May 1994;
'remedial order' means an order under section 10;
'subordinate legislation' means any –

(a) Order in Council other than one –
(i) made in exercise of Her Majesty's Royal Prerogative;
(ii) made under section 38(1)(a) of the Northern Ireland Constitution Act 1973 or the corresponding provision of the Northern Ireland Act 1998; or
(iii) amending an Act of a kind mentioned in the definition of primary legislation;
(b) Act of the Scottish Parliament;
(c) Act of the Parliament of Northern Ireland;
(d) Measure of the Assembly established under section 1 of the Northern Ireland Assembly Act 1973;
(e) Act of the Northern Ireland Assembly;
(f) order, rules, regulations, scheme, warrant, byelaw or other instrument made under primary legislation (except to the extent to which it operates to bring one or more provisions of that legislation into force or amends any primary legislation);
(g) order, rules, regulations, scheme, warrant, byelaw or other instrument made under legislation mentioned in paragraph

(b), (c), (d) or (e) or made under an Order in Council applying only to Northern Ireland;

(h) order, rules, regulations, scheme, warrant, byelaw or other instrument made by a member of the Scottish Executive, a Northern Ireland Minister or a Northern Ireland department in exercise of prerogative or other executive functions of Her Majesty which are exercisable by such a person on behalf of Her Majesty;

'transferred matters' has the same meaning as in the Northern Ireland Act 1998; and

'tribunal' means any tribunal in which legal proceedings may be brought.

(2) The references in paragraphs (b) and (c) of section 2(1) to Articles are to Articles of the Convention as they had effect immediately before the coming into force of the Eleventh Protocol.

(3) The reference in paragraph (d) of section 2(1) to Article 46 includes a reference to Articles 32 and 54 of the Convention as they had effect immediately before the coming into force of the Eleventh Protocol.

(4) The references in section 2(1) to a report or decision of the Commission or a decision of the Committee of Ministers include references to a report or decision made as provided by paragraphs 3, 4 and 6 of Article 5 of the Eleventh Protocol (transitional provisions).

(5) Any liability under the Army Act 1955, the Air Force Act 1955 or the Naval Discipline Act 1957 to suffer death for an offence is replaced by a liability to imprisonment for life or any less punishment authorised by those Acts; and those Acts shall accordingly have effect with the necessary modifications.

22. Short title, commencement, application and extent

(1) This Act may be cited as the Human Rights Act 1998.

(2) Sections 18, 20 and 21(5) and this section come into force on the passing of this Act.

(3) The other provisions of this Act come into force on such day as the Secretary of State may by order appoint; and different days may be appointed for different purposes.

(4) Paragraph (b) of subsection (1) of section 7 applies to proceedings brought by or at the instigation of a public authority whenever the act in question took place; but otherwise that subsection does not apply to an act taking place before the coming into force of that section.

(5) This Act binds the Crown.

(6) This Act extends to Northern Ireland.

(7) Section 21(5), so far as it relates to any provision contained in the Army Act 1955, the Air Force Act 1955 or the Naval Discipline Act 1957, extends to any place to which that provision extends.

Schedules

Section 1(3)

Schedule 1
The Articles

Part I
The Convention

Rights and Freedoms

Article 2
Right to life

1. Everyone's right to life shall be protected by law. No one shall be deprived of his life intentionally save in the execution of a sentence of a court following his conviction of a crime for which this penalty is provided by law.

2. Deprivation of life shall not be regarded as inflicted in contravention of this Article when it results from the use of force which is no more than absolutely necessary:

(a) in defence of any person from unlawful violence;

(b) in order to effect a lawful arrest or to prevent the escape of a person lawfully detained;

(c) in action lawfully taken for the purpose of quelling a riot or insurrection.

Article 3
Prohibition of torture

No one shall be subjected to torture or to inhuman or degrading treatment or punishment.

Article 4
Prohibition of slavery and forced labour

1. No one shall be held in slavery or servitude.

2. No one shall be required to perform forced or compulsory labour.

3. For the purpose of this Article the term 'forced or compulsory labour' shall not include:

(a) any work required to be done in the ordinary course of detention imposed according to the provisions of Article 5 of this Convention or during conditional release from such detention;

(b) any service of a military character or, in case of conscientious objectors in countries where they are recognised, service exacted instead of compulsory military service;
(c) any service exacted in case of an emergency or calamity threatening the life or well-being of the community;
(d) any work or service which forms part of normal civic obligations.

Article 5
Right to liberty and security

1. Everyone has the right to liberty and security of person. No one shall be deprived of his liberty save in the following cases and in accordance with a procedure prescribed by law:
(a) the lawful detention of a person after conviction by a competent court;
(b) the lawful arrest or detention of a person for non-compliance with the lawful order of a court or in order to secure the fulfilment of any obligation prescribed by law;
(c) the lawful arrest or detention of a person effected for the purpose of bringing him before the competent legal authority on reasonable suspicion of having committed an offence or when it is reasonably considered necessary to prevent his committing an offence or fleeing after having done so;
(d) the detention of a minor by lawful order for the purpose of educational supervision or his lawful detention for the purpose of bringing him before the competent legal authority;
(e) the lawful detention of persons for the prevention of the spreading of infectious diseases, of persons of unsound mind, alcoholics or drug addicts or vagrants;
(f) the lawful arrest or detention of a person to prevent his effecting an unauthorised entry into the country or of a person against whom action is being taken with a view to deportation or extradition.

2. Everyone who is arrested shall be informed promptly, in a language which he understands, of the reasons for his arrest and of any charge against him.

3. Everyone arrested or detained in accordance with the provisions of paragraph 1(c) of this Article shall be brought promptly before a judge or other officer authorised by law to exercise judicial power and shall be entitled to trial within a reasonable time or to release pending trial. Release may be conditioned by guarantees to appear for trial.

4. Everyone who is deprived of his liberty by arrest or detention shall be entitled to take proceedings by which the lawfulness of his detention shall be decided speedily by a court and his release ordered if the detention is not lawful.

5. Everyone who has been the victim of arrest or detention in contravention of the provisions of this Article shall have an enforceable right to compensation.

Article 6
Right to a fair trial

1. In the determination of his civil rights and obligations or of any criminal charge against him, everyone is entitled to a fair and public hearing within a reasonable time by an independent and impartial tribunal established by law. Judgment shall be pronounced publicly but the press and public may be excluded from all or part of the trial in the interest of morals, public order or national security in a democratic society, where the interests of juveniles or the protection of the private life of the parties so require, or to the extent strictly necessary in the opinion of the court in special circumstances where publicity would prejudice the interests of justice.

2. Everyone charged with a criminal offence shall be presumed innocent until proved guilty according to law.

3. Everyone charged with a criminal offence has the following minimum rights:

(a) to be informed promptly, in a language which he understands and in detail, of the nature and cause of the accusation against him;

(b) to have adequate time and facilities for the preparation of his defence;

(c) to defend himself in person or through legal assistance of his own choosing or, if he has not sufficient means to pay for legal assistance, to be given it free when the interests of justice so require;

(d) to examine or have examined witnesses against him and to obtain the attendance and examination of witnesses on his behalf under the same conditions as witnesses against him;

(e) to have the free assistance of an interpreter if he cannot understand or speak the language used in court.

Article 7
No punishment without law

1. No one shall be held guilty of any criminal offence on account of any act or omission which did not constitute a criminal offence under national or international law at the time when it was committed. Nor shall a heavier penalty be imposed than the one that was applicable at the time the criminal offence was committed.

2. This Article shall not prejudice the trial and punishment of any person for any act or omission which, at the time when it was committed, was criminal according to the general principles of law recognised by civilised nations.

Article 8
Right to respect for private and family life

1. Everyone has the right to respect for his private and family life, his home and his correspondence.

2. There shall be no interference by a public authority with the exercise of this right except such as is in accordance with the law and is necessary in a democratic society in the interests of national security, public safety or the economic well being of the country, for the prevention of disorder or crime, for the protection of health or morals, or for the protection of the rights and freedoms of others.

Article 9
Freedom of thought, conscience and religion

1. Everyone has the right to freedom of thought, conscience and religion; this right includes freedom to change his religion or belief and freedom, either alone or in community with others and in public or private, to manifest his religion or belief, in worship, teaching, practice and observance.

2. Freedom to manifest one's religion or beliefs shall be subject only to such limitations as are prescribed by law and are necessary in a democratic society in the interests of public safety, for the protection of public order, health or morals, or for the protection of the rights and freedoms of others.

Article 10
Freedom of expression

1. Everyone has the right to freedom of expression. This right shall include freedom to hold opinions and to receive and impart information and ideas without interference by public authority and regardless of frontiers. This Article shall not prevent States from requiring the licensing of broadcasting, television or cinema enterprises.

2. The exercise of these freedoms, since it carries with it duties and responsibilities, may be subject to such formalities, conditions, restrictions or penalties as are prescribed by law and are necessary in a democratic society, in the interests of national security, territorial integrity or public safety, for the prevention of disorder or crime, for the protection of health or morals, for the protection of the reputation or rights of others, for preventing the disclosure of information received in confidence, or for maintaining the authority and impartiality of the judiciary.

Article 11
Freedom of assembly and association

1. Everyone has the right to freedom of peaceful assembly and to freedom of association with others, including the right to form and to join trade unions for the protection of his interests.

2. No restrictions shall be placed on the exercise of these rights other than such as are prescribed by law and are necessary in a democratic society in the interests of national security or public safety, for the prevention of disorder or crime, for the protection of health or morals or for the protection of the rights and freedoms of others. This Article shall not prevent the imposition of lawful restrictions on the exercise of these rights by members of the armed forces, of the police or of the administration of the State.

Article 12
Right to marry

Men and women of marriageable age have the right to marry and to found a family, according to the national laws governing the exercise of this right.

Article 14
Prohibition of discrimination

The enjoyment of the rights and freedoms set forth in this Convention shall be secured without discrimination on any ground such as sex, race, colour, language, religion, political or other opinion, national or social origin, association with a national minority, property, birth or other status.

Article 16
Restrictions on political activity of aliens

Nothing in Articles 10, 11 and 14 shall be regarded as preventing the High Contracting Parties from imposing restrictions on the political activity of aliens.

Article 17
Prohibition of abuse of rights

Nothing in this Convention may be interpreted as implying for any State, group or person any right to engage in any activity or perform any act aimed at the destruction of any of the rights and freedoms set forth herein or at their limitation to a greater extent than is provided for in the Convention.

Article 18
Limitation on use of restrictions on rights

The restrictions permitted under this Convention to the said rights and freedoms shall not be applied for any purpose other than those for which they have been prescribed.

Part II
The first protocol

Article 1
Protection of property

Every natural or legal person is entitled to the peaceful enjoyment of his possessions. No one shall be deprived of his possessions except in the public interest and subject to the conditions provided for by law and by the general principles of international law.

The preceding provisions shall not, however, in any way impair the right of a State to enforce such laws as it deems necessary to control the use of property in accordance with the general interest or to secure the payment of taxes or other contributions or penalties.

Article 2
Right to education

No person shall be denied the right to education. In the exercise of any functions which it assumes in relation to education and to teaching, the State shall respect the right of parents to ensure such education and teaching in conformity with their own religious and philosphical convictions.

Article 3
Right to free elections

The High Contracting Parties undertake to hold free elections at reasonable intervals by secret ballot, under conditions which will ensure the free expression of the opinion of the people in the choice of the legislature.

Part III
The sixth protocol

Article 1
Abolition of the death penalty

The death penalty shall be abolished. No one shall be condemned to such penalty or executed.

Article 2
Death penalty in time of war

A State may make provision in its law for the death penalty in respect of acts committed in time of war or of imminent threat of war; such penalty shall be applied only in the instances laid down in the law and in accordance with its provisions. The State shall communicate to the Secretary General of the Council of Europe the relevant provisions of that law.

Schedule 2
Remedial orders

Orders

1.—(1) A remedial order may –
(a) contain such incidental, supplemental, consequential or transitional provision as the person making it considers appropriate;
(b) be made so as to have effect from a date earlier than that on which it is made;
(c) make provision for the delegation of specific functions;
(d) make different provision for different cases.
(2) The power conferred by sub-paragraph (1)(a) includes –
(a) power to amend primary legislation (including primary legislation other than that which contains the incompatible provision); and
(b) power to amend or revoke subordinate legislation (including subordinate legislation other than that which contains the incompatible provision).
(3) A remedial order may be made so as to have the same extent as the legislation which it affects.
(4) No person is to be guilty of an offence solely as a result of the retrospective effect of a remedial order.

Procedure

2. No remedial order may be made unless –
(a) a draft of the order has been approved by a resolution of each House of Parliament made after the end of the period of 60 days beginning with the day on which the draft was laid; or
(b) it is declared in the order that it appears to the person making it that, because of the urgency of the matter, it is necessary to make the order without a draft being so approved.

Orders laid in draft

3.—(1) No draft may be laid under paragraph 2(a) unless –
(a) the person proposing to make the order has laid before Parliament a document which contains a draft of the proposed order and the required information; and

(b) the period of 60 days, beginning with the day on which the document required by this sub-paragraph was laid, has ended.

(2) If representations have been made during that period, the draft laid under paragraph 2(a) must be accompanied by a statement containing –

(a) a summary of the representations; and

(b) if, as a result of the representations, the proposed order has been changed, details of the changes.

Urgent cases

4.—(1) If a remedial order ('the original order') is made without being approved in draft, the person making it must lay it before Parliament, accompanied by the required information, after it is made.

(2) If representations have been made during the period of 60 days beginning with the day on which the original order was made, the person making it must (after the end of that period) lay before Parliament a statement containing –

(a) a summary of the representations; and

(b) if, as a result of the representations, he considers it appropriate to make changes to the original order, details of the changes.

(3) If sub-paragraph (2)(b) applies, the person making the statement must –

(a) make a further remedial order replacing the original order; and

(b) lay the replacement order before Parliament.

(4) If, at the end of the period of 120 days beginning with the day on which the original order was made, a resolution has not been passed by each House approving the original or replacement order, the order ceases to have effect (but without that affecting anything previously done under either order or the power to make a fresh remedial order).

Definitions

5. In this Schedule –

'representations' means representations about a remedial order (or proposed remedial order) made to the person making (or proposing to make) it and includes any relevant Parliamentary report or resolution; and

'required information' means –

(a) an explanation of the incompatibility which the order (or proposed order) seeks to remove, including particulars of the relevant declaration, finding or order; and

(b) a statement of the reasons for proceeding under section 10 and for making an order in those terms.

Calculating periods

6. In calculating any period for the purposes of this Schedule, no account is to be taken of any time during which –

(a) Parliament is dissolved or prorogued; or
(b) both Houses are adjourned for more than four days.

Schedule 3
Derogation and reservation

Part I
Derogation

The 1988 notification

The United Kingdom Permanent Representative to the Council of Europe presents his compliments to the Secretary General of the Council, and has the honour to convey the following information in order to ensure compliance with the obligations of Her Majesty's Government in the United Kingdom under Article 15(3) of the Convention for the Protection of Human Rights and Fundamental Freedoms signed at Rome on 4 November 1950.

There have been in the United Kingdom in recent years campaigns of organised terrorism connected with the affairs of Northern Ireland which have manifested themselves in activities which have included repeated murder, attempted murder, maiming, intimidation and violent civil disturbance and in bombing and fire raising which have resulted in death, injury and widespread destruction of property. As a result, a public emergency within the meaning of Article 15(1) of the Convention exists in the United Kingdom.

The Government found it necessary in 1974 to introduce and since then, in cases concerning persons reasonably suspected of involvement in terrorism connected with the affairs of Northern Ireland, or of certain offences under the legislation, who have been detained for 48 hours, to exercise powers enabling further detention without charge, for periods of up to five days, on the authority of the Secretary of State. These powers are at present to be found in Section 12 of the Prevention of Terrorism (Temporary Provisions) Act 1984, Article 9 of the Prevention of Terrorism (Supplemental Temporary Provisions) Order 1984 and Article 10 of the Prevention of Terrorism (Supplemental Temporary Provisions) (Northern Ireland) Order 1984.

Section 12 of the Prevention of Terrorism (Temporary Provisions) Act 1984 provides for a person whom a constable has arrested on reasonable grounds of suspecting him to be guilty of an offence under Section 1, 9 or 10 of the Act, or to be or to have been involved in terrorism connected with the affairs of Northern Ireland, to be detained in right of the arrest for up to 48 hours and thereafter, where the Secretary of State extends the detention period, for up to a further five days. Section 12 substantially re-enacted Section 12 of the Prevention of Terrorism (Temporary Provisions) Act 1976 which, in turn, substantially re-enacted Section 7 of the Prevention of Terrorism (Temporary Provisions) Act 1974.

Article 10 of the Prevention of Terrorism (Supplemental Temporary Provisions) (Northern Ireland) Order 1984 (SI 1984/417) and Article 9 of the Prevention of Terrorism (Supplemental Temporary Provisions) Order 1984 (SI 1984/418) were both made under Sections 13 and 14 of and Schedule 3 to the 1984 Act and substantially re-enacted powers of detention in Orders made under the 1974 and 1976 Acts. A person who is being examined under Article 4 of either Order on his arrival in, or on seeking to leave, Northern Ireland or Great Britain for the purpose of determining whether he is or has been involved in terrorism connected with the affairs of Northern Ireland, or whether there are grounds for suspecting that he has committed an offence under Section 9 of the 1984 Act, may be detained under Article 9 or 10, as appropriate, pending the conclusion of his examination. The period of this examination may exceed 12 hours if an examining officer has reasonable grounds for suspecting him to be or to have been involved in acts of terrorism connected with the affairs of Northern Ireland.

Where such a person is detained under the said Article 9 or 10 he may be detained for up to 48 hours on the authority of an examining officer and thereafter, where the Secretary of State extends the detention period, for up to a further five days.

In its judgment of 29 November 1988 in the Case of *Brogan and Others*, the European Court of Human Rights held that there had been a violation of Article 5(3) in respect of each of the applicants, all of whom had been detained under Section 12 of the 1984 Act. The Court held that even the shortest of the four periods of detention concerned, namely four days and six hours, fell outside the constraints as to time permitted by the first part of Article 5(3). In addition, the Court held that there had been a violation of Article 5(5) in the case of each applicant.

Following this judgment, the Secretary of State for the Home Department informed Parliament on 6 December 1988 that, against the background of the terrorist campaign, and the over-riding need to bring terrorists to justice, the Government did not believe that the maximum period of detention should be reduced. He informed Parliament that the Government were examining the matter with a view to responding to the judgment. On 22 December 1988, the Secretary of State further informed Parliament that it remained the Government's wish, if it could be achieved, to find a judicial process under which extended detention might be reviewed and where appropriate authorised by a judge or other judicial officer. But a further period of reflection and consultation was necessary before the Government could bring forward a firm and final view.

Since the judgment of 29 November 1988 as well as previously, the Government have found it necessary to continue to exercise, in relation to terrorism connected with the affairs of Northern Ireland, the powers described above enabling further detention without charge for periods of up to 5 days, on the authority of the Secretary of State, to the extent strictly required by the exigencies of the situation to enable necessary enquiries and investigations properly to be completed in order to decide whether criminal proceedings should be instituted. To the extent that the exercise of these powers may be inconsistent with the obligations imposed by the Convention the Government has availed itself of the right of derogation conferred by Article 15(1) of the Convention and will continue to do so until further notice.

Dated 23 December 1988.

The 1989 notification

The United Kingdom Permanent Representative to the Council of Europe presents his compliments to the Secretary General of the Council, and has the honour to convey the following information.

In his communication to the Secretary General of 23 December 1988, reference was made to the introduction and exercise of certain powers under section 12 of the Prevention of Terrorism (Temporary Provisions) Act 1984, Article 9 of the Prevention of Terrorism (Supplemental Temporary Provisions) Order 1984 and Article 10 of the Prevention of Terrorism (Supplemental Temporary Provisions) (Northern Ireland) Order 1984.

These provisions have been replaced by section 14 of and paragraph 6 of Schedule 5 to the Prevention of Terrorism (Temporary Provisions) Act 1989, which make comparable provision. They came into force on 22 March 1989. A copy of these provisions is enclosed.

The United Kingdom Permanent Representative avails himself of this opportunity to renew to the Secretary General the assurance of his highest consideration.

23 March 1989.

Part II
Reservation

At the time of signing the present (First) Protocol, I declare that, in view of certain provisions of the Education Acts in the United Kingdom, the principle affirmed in the second sentence of Article 2 is accepted by the United Kingdom only so far as it is compatible with the provision of efficient instruction and training, and the avoidance of unreasonable public expenditure.

Dated 20 March 1952. Made by the United Kingdom Permanent Representative to the Council of Europe.

Schedule 4
Judicial pensions

Duty to make orders about pensions

1.—(1) The appropriate Minister must by order make provision with respect to pensions payable to or in respect of any holder of a judicial office who serves as an ECHR judge.

(2) A pensions order must include such provision as the Minister making it considers is necessary to secure that –

(a) an ECHR judge who was, immediately before his appointment as an ECHR judge, a member of a judicial pension scheme is entitled to remain as a member of that scheme;

(b) the terms on which he remains a member of the scheme are those which would have been applicable had he not been appointed as an ECHR judge; and

(c) entitlement to benefits payable in accordance with the scheme continues to be determined as if, while serving as an ECHR judge, his salary was that which would (but for section 18(4)) have been payable to him in respect of his continuing service as the holder of his judicial office.

Contributions

2. A pensions order may, in particular, make provision –

(a) for any contributions which are payable by a person who remains a member of a scheme as a result of the order, and which would otherwise be payable by deduction from his salary, to be made otherwise than by deduction from his salary as an ECHR judge; and

(b) for such contributions to be collected in such manner as may be determined by the administrators of the scheme.

Amendments of other enactments

3. A pensions order may amend any provision of, or made under, a pensions Act in such manner and to such extent as the Minister making the order considers necessary or expedient to ensure the proper administration of any scheme to which it relates.

Definitions

4. In this Schedule –

'appropriate Minister' means –

(a) in relation to any judicial office whose jurisdiction is exercisable exclusively in relation to Scotland, the Secretary of State; and

(b) otherwise, the Lord Chancellor;

'ECHR judge' means the holder of a judicial office who is serving as a judge of the Court;
'judicial pension scheme' means a scheme established by and in accordance with a pensions Act;
'pensions Act means –
   (a) the County Courts Act (Northern Ireland) 1959;
   (b) the Sheriffs' Pensions (Scotland) Act 1961;
   (c) the Judicial Pensions Act 1981; or
   (d) the Judicial Pensions and Retirement Act 1993; and
'pensions order' means an order made under paragraph 1.

Chapter 1

Introduction

It would not be too much of an exaggeration to say that May 1997, when New Labour came to power, looked like a new dawn for civil liberties. Relief seemed to be at hand, after many years of seeing the country condemned at Strasbourg and elsewhere, during the Conservative years, for its human rights record. Ronald Dworkin said, famously, of the Thatcher years, 'Liberty is ill in Britain'.[1] Ewing and Gearty wrote in 1989: 'It should now be clear that civil liberties in Britain are in a state of crisis'.[2] The New Labour government came to power with a manifesto which promised a radical programme of Constitutional change and, most significantly, the introduction of the Human Rights Act 1998 as the means of receiving the European Convention on Human Rights into domestic law, 50 years after it was signed. Rights were, finally, to be 'brought home'.[3] There were expectations that the Human Rights Act would prove to be something akin to a panacea for all that is wrong with fundamental freedoms in the UK or, at the least, commentators perceived that civil liberties had been re-energised. With the creation of positive rights, there was a sense of a break with the erosions of liberty of the past.[4]

This book seeks to examine the reality behind the rhetoric of 'bringing rights home'. It does not seek to defend a particular political philosophy – to examine the *merits* of receiving the Convention into domestic law. That issue has been exhaustively debated.[5] Rather, it assumes that the argument

[1] R Dworkin *Index on Censorship* (1988) pp7–8.

[2] *Freedom under Thatcher* (1989) OUP p255.

[3] See *Bringing Rights Home: Labour's plans to incorporate the ECHR into UK Law*: A Consultation Paper December 1996 (1997) and the White Paper *Rights Brought Home* October 1997 CM 3782; see also J Straw and P Boateng (1997) 1 EHRR 71.

[4] See Cooke 'The British Embracement of Human Rights' [1999] EHRLR 243; D Feldman 'The Human Rights Act and Constitutional Principles' (1999) 19 (2) LS 165.

[5] See M Zander *A Bill of Rights?* (1996) London: Sweet and Maxwell; P *Craig Public Law and Democracy in the UK and USA* (1990); J Waldron 'A Rights-based Critique of Constitutional Rights' [1993] 13 OJLS 18; D Oliver 'A Bill of Rights for the UK' in *Government in the UK* (1991); A Lester 'Fundamental Rights: the UK Isolated?' [1984] PL 46.

has moved on and that a number of new issues arise from the reception of the Convention which should now redirect the debate. The placing of further power in the hands of the judiciary, as an unaccountable and, in general, a politically conservative group unrepresentative of society as a whole, raised concerns among leftist scholars.[6] However, the Parliamentary override power[7] seems to have satisfied the fears of at least one of the prominent critics of Bills of Rights.[8] Since the dangers of excessive judicial activism in pursuit of a conservative agenda have been at least partially answered, the focus of the debate should be, it is argued, on the dangers of minimalism, as indicated below.

This book takes the Convention as its starting point and argues that as it has been received into domestic law it should be afforded a genuine efficacy since the alternative would be likely to lead to a decrease in state accountability and an obscuring of political discourse as to the nature of state power and countervailing civil rights. That alternative might be more damaging than the previous Constitutional position. As Chapter 2 explains, the Convention creates a moral structure which incorporates a set of values into UK law. Some are absolute; some have presumptive priority over competing social interests.[9] The Convention jurisprudence employs concepts recognised and developed across the world by judges who may be viewed as defending a particular set of liberal values. These may be employed in a counter-majoritarian fashion in the sense that they aid in the protection of the rights of unpopular groups. But in the case of the Human Rights Act their judicial use is subject to the possibility of using the Parliamentary override.

As Chapter 2 explains, the Act therefore achieves a compromise between Parliamentary and judicial power in that Parliament may pass legislation incompatible with the Convention[10] and could ultimately repeal or modify

[6] See notes 53 and 58, and associated text below, regarding reform of the composition of the judiciary.

[7] The power arises owing to the provisions of ss3, 6 and 19 of the Human Rights Act, as Chapter 2 explains. See also the full text of the HRA at the beginning of this book.

[8] See K Ewing 'The Human Rights Act and Parliamentary Democracy' [1999] 62(1) MLR 79.

[9] The rights fall into three groups: those which are absolute: Articles 3, 4, 6(2), 6(3), 14 and First Protocol Article 3; those which are very narrowly qualified: Articles 2, 5, 6(1), 7, Sixth Protocol Article 1 (read with Article 2) and those which are materially qualified: Articles 8–12, First Protocol Article 1. See further Chapter 2 pp22–24.

[10] The ability of Parliament to do so is, of course, subject to the ability of the judiciary to disapply domestic law which is incompatible with EC law. The position is as set out in the leading case *Elliniki Rasdio Phonia TilesRassi AE* v *Dimotiki Etaria* (1991) ECR I-2925: 'as soon as any [national] legislation enters the field of application of Community law, the [ECJ] as the sole arbiter in this matter, must provide the national court with all the elements of interpretation which are necessary in order to enable it to assess the compatibility of that legislation with the fundamental rights – as laid down particularly in the European Convention on Human Rights – the observance of which the Court ensures'. Thus any national law within the field of application of EC law can be assessed as to its compliance with the Convention rights. The courts can disapply legislative provisions

the Act itself.[11] Within this compromise previous and future erosions of liberty may be countered. Moreover, the process of protecting rights could be afforded a transparency which it previously lacked. The judiciary will be affording such protection by a means – the Human Rights Act – which was subject to full Parliamentary debate. The process has been made explicit, in contrast to the obscurities and inconsistencies which arose from the development of a common law of human rights[12] and from the tradition of residual liberty. Citizens' areas of liberty could only be ascertained by an exhaustive scrutiny of restrictive legislation with its accompanying jurisprudence.[13]

However, this book contends, two possible dangers arise. The Convention rights might be minimised and undermined in Parliament and in the courts. In Parliament the rights might become merely empty guarantees which cast a legitimising cloak over rights-abridging legislation and executive action.[14] As Chapters 3 and 9, in particular, argue, the New Labour government used the Convention in debate on the Terrorism Bill 2000 and the Regulation of Investigatory Powers Bill 2000 as a means of affording an appearance of credibility to draconian legislation and thereby curbing or pre-empting a fully normative debate as to the merits of the legislation and the balance struck between state power and civil rights. In effect, the debate became a legalised as opposed to a political one. Both Bills were accompanied by statements declaring their compatibility with the Convention, and during debate Parliament was given the reassurance that the Bills met human rights standards. The values underlying the Bills were not subjected to the full rigour of political analysis owing, it will be argued, to the appearance of rectitude afforded to them by the statements and by such reassurance. Thus the rights can be used to 'legalise' political discourse in a manner which obscures their own erosion. However, as Chapter 2 argues, judicial activism in response to the Convention could ameliorate the effects of such

which appear to conflict with EC law as interpreted in reliance on those rights. This applies in particular where a member state is seeking to carve out an exception to the general principles of EC law. In such instances the review of the European Court of Justice is most intensive. Thus the Convention rights are not directly justifiable since they are not free-standing rights. The position under *Ellinki* was not therefore changed by the Amsterdam Treaty Article 6(2) which provides that the Union 'shall respect the fundamental rights' under the Convention as 'general principles of Community Law'. For enforcement of the Convention by this means, see Craig and G De Burca *European Law: Text and Materials* 2nd edn, Chapter 7 (1998) OUP.

[11] Parliament is of course also free to reply to judicial activism in interpreting domestic law in order to comply with the Convention by passing legislation which unambiguously abridges rights.

[12] See Chapter 2 p35.

[13] Admittedly, such trawling through legislation will continue in the era after the Human Rights Act. But a consideration of s3 of the Human Rights Act (see Chapter 2 p43) together with the Convention rights will afford an improved guidance.

[14] This danger was pointed out by Conor Gearty in 'Terrorism and Human Rights' [1999] 19(3) LS 367 at 379.

legislation and could also alert Parliament to the possibility that it has been misled.[15]

The other danger which, as indicated, relates to the first is that an activist approach will be eschewed. Under the model which Chapter 2 terms 'minimalist' judges could duck the hard issues, purporting to review government actions under the Convention standards but adopting a deferential stance which fails to create any real accountability. An appearance of human rights auditing might be created which was belied by the reality. As this book argues at a number of points, this has occurred at Strasbourg owing to the doctrine allowing a degree of discretion to be afforded at times to the member states.[16] A lack of understanding of the effect which this doctrine has had could underpin both judicial and Parliamentary minimalism. In other words, the development of a minimal domestic version of the Convention could undermine the protection it could, potentially, offer.

The intention of this book is to take these dangers as a central concern and to reveal the extent to which they are already becoming evident. It will seek essentially to contrast them with the impact which the Convention, potentially, could have, as a means of protecting vulnerable minorities and generally curbing executive encroachment on freedom.

From Dicey to Thatcher

As indicated, the traditional Constitutional position was that where other jurisdictions recognised civil rights the UK recognised only civil *liberties*.[17]

[15] This is a complex issue since if judges adopt a creative interpretation of such legislation, compatibility with the Convention will be achieved, albeit in a manner probably not intended by the executive. It could therefore appear that the statements of compatibility were well-founded. On the other hand, if they issue declarations of incompatibility injustice may be done to particular citizens, although at the same time Parliament will be alerted to the possibility that the Convention has been used in a misleading fashion. As Chapter 2 argues, adoption of the minimalist model would mean 'reading down' the Convention rights in order to achieve compatibility. That course would not appeal to a more activist-minded judge. But even if, therefore, such declarations are rare, it may eventually become apparent that statements of compatibility and assertions regarding compatibility in Parliamentary debate must be viewed with scepticism. See further Chapter 2 pp44 and 47.

[16] The affording of such discretion is termed the 'margin of appreciation' doctrine; see Chapter 2 p27.

[17] This terminology is based on the analysis of Wesley Hohfeld (*Fundamental Legal Concepts as Applied in Judicial Reasoning* (1920), particularly pp35–41). Hohfeld attempted to demonstrate the way that claims of rights in everyday language can in fact be broken down into more specific claims. First, if it is claimed that X has a right proper or 'claim right' to A then this means that persons, generally or particularly, are under some specific corresponding duty to ensure that X has access to A. Second, X may be said to have an immunity as against a particular person or body; this means that they are disabled from interfering with the exercise by X of the interest (A) protected by the immunity. Third,

This position was viewed by the influential Constitutional writer, Dicey, as advantageous. Under the Diceyan model of the Constitution, civil liberties are protected by individual judicial decisions; a document termed a Bill or Charter of Rights is both unnecessary and undesirable as a means of protecting them.[18] Under this model, citizens in a state in which everyone is free to do all which the law does not forbid, enjoy greater liberty than those whose liberty is protected by such a document since by being delineated rights would be more limited. Under the UK Constitution citizens would know with absolute confidence that where there was no relevant law they could exercise their liberty as they pleased without fear of incurring any sanction.

The Diceyan model underpinned the view expressed in the post-war years that a Constitution embodying a presumption of liberty provided a protection for rights that could not be achieved by basing them on a Constitutional document such as a Bill of Rights. Although it would be problematic to argue that there was ever a 'golden age' of civil liberties in the UK,[19] the post-war years appeared to a number of commentators to come closer to one than the Thatcher and Major years,[20] in comparison with the records in other European countries. Some historians and political scientists, although by no means all, consider that there was a post-war consensus in UK politics until the Thatcher government 'dismantled much of the consensus'.[21] 'Old Tory statecraft based on patriotism, social cohesion, Union and Empire disintegrated in the face of . . . alternative visions of post-Imperial Conservative nationhood. Enoch Powell's free economy . . . prevailed as the basis of Thatcherite strategy'.[22] Under this view of the consensus, high Tory values underpinned respect for political freedoms, but under Conservative rule since 1979 liberty suffered and the UK began to lag behind many other democracies in respect of its human rights record. The Thatcher government was said to have demonstrated a 'mundane and corrupting insensitivity to

if X has only a liberty (what Hohfeld calls a privilege) to do A, this far weaker claim merely means that X does no wrong in exercising his liberty – the rights of others are not thereby infringed. However, no one has a duty to allow him to exercise A or to assist him in exercising it.

18 Dicey *The Law of the Constitution* (8th edn) (1959).

19 Ewing and Gearty argue that there is a misconception that the first half of the twentieth century constituted such an age in *The Struggle for Civil Liberties: Political Freedom and the Rule of Law in Britain 1914–1945* (1999) OUP.

20 See P Thornton *Decade of Decline: Civil Liberties in the Thatcher Years* (1989) London: NCCL. Ewing and Gearty, writing in 1989, found: 'In recent years there has been a marked decline in the level of political freedom enjoyed in Britain'. They found that the turning point and beginning of the decline might be said to have occurred in the 1970s but that 'the process of erosion became more pronounced' after the Conservative election victory in 1979 (Preface to *Freedom under Thatcher* (1989) OUP).

21 D Fraser 'Post-War Consensus: A debate not long enough' [2000] 53(2) Parliamentary Affairs 2000 347.

22 D Baker in [2000] 6(2) Party Politics 250 commenting on D Lynch *The Politics of Nationhood, Sovereignty, Britishness and Conservative Politics* (1999) Basingstoke: Macmillan.

liberty'.[23] Although the Major government showed in certain respects a greater awareness of the value of individual rights,[24] in its central criminal justice Act, the Criminal Justice and Public Order Act 1994, it demonstrated a similar insensitivity. The Conservative years from 1979 to 1997 were marked by the attempts of outside bodies – the European Court of Justice and the European Court of Human Rights – to protect liberties in the UK, attempts which were met, increasingly, by hostility among sections of the Conservative party.[25]

Contrary, therefore, to the Diceyan thesis, liberty was receiving a significant measure of protection from international courts and under international documents rather than being the result of decisions of the judiciary applying the common law. In *Freedom under Thatcher*[26] Ewing and Gearty pointed out that Thatcher had exposed the precarious nature of the Constitutional means of protecting liberty. Their central criticism was not that she had changed the Constitutional structures to her advantage; she 'merely utilised to the full the scope for untrammelled power latent in the British constitution but obscured by the hesitancy and scruples of previous, consensus-based political leaders'.[27] In other words, she exposed and exploited the weakness of the UK Constitution. As David Feldman puts it: 'few of the values of our society find expression in constitutional form . . . This was not too serious a problem when politics was dominated by a high Tory willingness to restrain individualism in order to further communal goods, coupled with an hierarchical model of society in which the elite understood that their position carried obligations with it: the belief that *noblesse oblige*. However that belief has been eroded. Thatcherite belief in the market as the supreme arbiter of human worth marginalised the values of traditional Toryism.'[28]

In the context of fundamental rights, then, Thatcherism exposed the flawed nature of the Diceyan model.[29] Since, under that model, the Constitution provides no effective check to untrammelled Parliamentary sovereignty, a government determined to push through a legislative programme extending the reach of state power which – almost incidentally – erodes the residual areas of liberty, is able to do so. While it is important not to allow the record of the Conservative governments of

[23] R Dworkin *Index on Censorship* (1988) pp7–8. See also P Thornton *Decade of Decline: Civil Liberties in the Thatcher Years* (1989) London: NCCL.

[24] The 'Open government' initiatives were introduced under this government: see the White Paper 'Open Government' Cm 2290 and the Code of Practice on Access to Government Information. The Secret Intelligence Service was placed on a statutory basis under the Intelligence Services Act 1994 (see Chapter 8 p295).

[25] The reaction of senior Cabinet members, particularly Michael Heseltine, to the decision of the European Court of Human Rights in *McCann* v *UK* (1995) 21 EHRR 97 that the UK had breached Article 2 (right to life) was particularly hostile.

[26] (1989) OUP.

[27] Ibid at p7.

[28] 'The Human Rights Act 1998 and Constitutional Principles' [1999] 2 LS 165 at p166.

[29] Dicey *The Law of the Constitution* (8th edn).

1979–1997 to distort debate as to the efficacy of the democratic process in protecting civil liberties, it is also important to bear in mind the lessons which have been learnt as to the Constitutional weaknesses which those governments exposed. A Constitution based on the twin notions of Parliamentary supremacy and negative liberties provides no reliable protection against the erosion of a liberty to the point where it exists largely as an exercise of police discretion.[30]

Thatcherism demonstrated that the democratic process, as operating within the UK Constitution, could not be relied upon to protect civil liberties. In so doing Thatcher influenced the long-running debate between those commentators and policy-makers who had always wanted to leave liberties to the protection of that process[31] and those in the liberal tradition who had wished to entrust them, for the most part, to the judiciary.[32] The Labour Opposition of the time, now the Labour government, changed sides in that debate, apparently in the main as a response to Thatcherism.

Constitutional transformation: the Human Rights Act

In the general election in 1992 Labour officially opposed adoption of a Bill of Rights on the ground that government reforms would be endangered if power were transferred from government to the judiciary.[33] In the late 1990s this was still, broadly speaking, the position of the left.[34] In 1993 John Smith, the new leader, committed the Party to incorporation of the European Convention on Human Rights;[35] this policy was continued when Tony Blair took over the leadership in 1994 and it formed part of the 1997 election manifesto. The Green Paper *Bringing Rights Home*,[36]

[30] Chapter 4 argues that freedom of expression by means of public protest provides an example of such a liberty: pp115–116.

[31] See, for example, Griffiths 'The Political Constitution' [1979] MLR 1; K Ewing 'Human Rights, Social Democracy and Constitutional Reform' in *Understanding Human Rights*, A Tomkin and C Gearty (eds) (1996) Mansell.

[32] Leading exponents of this position include: M Zander *A Bill of Rights?* (1996) London: Sweet and Maxwell; G Robertson *Freedom, the Individual and the Law* (1993) Penguin; Lord Lester of Herne Hill QC 'Fundamental Rights: the UK Isolated?' [1984] PL 70; Lord Scarman *English Law. The New Dimension* (1974) London: Stevens.

[33] See *The Charter of Rights: Guaranteeing Individual Liberty in a Free Society*, Labour Party document 1990. This document contained a list of 40 human rights topics on which Labour wished to legislate; a Bill of Rights was not mentioned.

[34] See, for example, K Ewing and C Gearty 'Rocky Foundations for Labour's New Rights' [1997] 2 EHRLR 149 and M Tushnet 'Living with a Bill of Rights' in Tomkin and Gearty (eds) ibid, note 31.

[35] See *A New Agenda for Democracy: Labour's Programme for Constitutional Reform* (1993). The Labour Party Conference in 1993 adopted a policy of incorporating the Convention, but setting up a commission to draft a tailor-made Bill of Rights for the UK.

[36] J Straw and P Boateng *Bringing Rights Home: Labour's plans to incorporate the ECHR into UK Law*: A Consultation Paper, December 1996 (1997).

published in 1996, concluded: 'We aim to change the relationship between the state and the citizen, and to redress the dilution of individual rights by an over-centralising government that has taken place over the past two decades.' This aim was to be achieved by means of the European Convention on Human Rights as afforded further effect in UK law under the Human Rights Act 1998. Once Labour came to power the White Paper *Rights Brought Home* was published in 1997[37] and the Bill was introduced into Parliament in 1997. The Act came fully into force on 2 October 2000.

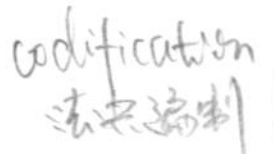

The Convention thus received into domestic law creates a transformation in Constitutional terms since it provides positive rights in place of negative liberties. The codification of the rights of citizens, regarded by Dicey as endangering liberty, has occurred. A cultural change from complacency regarding liberty to a consciousness of rights is under way. While the Diceyan tradition demanded a basis in law for interference with liberties by public authorities, this demand is clarified and confirmed in respect of interferences with the guarantees.[38] It obliges public authorities, in particular the police, not only to discharge duties such as the duty to keep the peace, but to uphold human rights. It asks the judiciary to consider matters such as the 'quality' of law, not merely its formal existence.[39] It asks the judiciary to examine the necessity in a democracy of interfering with a right, the proportionality of the means used with the aim in question, and to inform Parliament, if necessary, that on one or more of these matters it has breached the Convention.

These are bold, imaginative Constitutional changes. However, such boldness had limits, which are reflected in the Human Rights Act. The choice of model for the reception of the Convention might be viewed as reflecting old Labour suspicion of the liberal, individualist, rights-based tradition, especially the enhancement of judicial power, or, more cynically, as indicating authoritarian leanings on the part of New Labour. A seminal Constitutional decision involving a choice between judicial and Parliamentary checks on executive power, and therefore as to the allocation of power, had to be taken regarding the choice of model for the enforcement of the Convention. The choice made was, as indicated above, to leave the ultimate task of curbing executive power to Parliament; the judiciary would remain subject to primary legislation. As Chapter 2 indicates, the Human Rights Act therefore seeks to reconcile a transfer of power to the judiciary with Parliamentary sovereignty. It is readily apparent, then, that there is a contradiction between the liberal aim of affording the Convention rights efficacy in domestic law in order to aid in reversing the effects of over-centralisation of power, and the aim of preserving the key feature of the Constitution which gave rein to that power.

[37] October 1997 CM 3782.
[38] See Chapter 2 p23.
[39] See Chapter 2 p25.

This contradiction gives rise to one of the central themes explored throughout this book – the search for a means of giving efficacy to the rights in the face of hostile primary legislation, particularly New Labour legislation.

Freedom in the post-Human Rights Act era

In the sense indicated, the Human Rights Act was Thatcher's legacy. From the liberal 'individual rights' standpoint,[40] the Act was the right response. But in the view of many commentators, especially those on the left, including Ewing and Gearty, the wrong lessons were learnt. The right response to Thatcherism, in their view, would have been to reform the democratic process in order to render it effective in protecting liberty.[41] Rejecting the 'solution' of a Bill of Rights, they argued in 1989: 'The need is for major surgery to the body politic to reduce the load on an already overworked House of Commons and to introduce some real and effective constraints on the power of the Prime Minister.'[42] Since those words were written immense Constitutional changes have occurred under the New Labour government, in particular devolution and the (partial) reform of the House of Lords, but the effects of such constraints in terms of protecting civil rights and liberties are likely to be indirect and uncertain. It is still unclear that the democratic process can be trusted to afford such protection. The voting system for the Westminster Parliament is still unreformed. Centralising aspects remain evident even in the devolution legislation since Westminster is in theory entirely free to legislate in the devolved areas.[43] This is not to argue that devolution will not affect fundamental rights and freedoms. On the contrary – devolution will create plurality which may tend to foster them.[44] In particular, it may well be that a distinctive Scottish human rights culture will emerge which will influence that in England.[45] The partially reformed House of Lords currently sees itself as having greater credibility than its predecessor and

40 The stance sometimes referred to by the label 'liberal normativism': see Martin Loughlin *Public Law and Political Theory* (1992).

41 See 'Rocky Foundations for Labour's New Rights' [1997] 2 EHRLR 149 and Ewing and Gearty *Freedom under Thatcher* (1989) Chap 8.

42 Ibid at p275.

43 See Chapter 2 pp42–43. It has, however, been argued that devolution will in practice create a quasi-federal structure: see A Bradley 'Constitutional Reform, the Sovereignty of Parliament and Devolution' in *Constitutional Reform in the UK: Practice and Principles*, Hare and Forsyth (eds) the University of Cambridge Centre for Public Law (1998).

44 See M O'Neill 'Great Britain: From Dicey to Devolution' [2000] 53(1) Parliamentary Affairs 69.

45 For very early signs of the emergence of such culture, see A O'Neill 'The European Convention on Human Rights and the Independence of the Judiciary: the Scottish Experience' [2000] 63 (3) MLR 429.

as a result is more interventionist.[46] Clearly, the fully reformed House may take the same or a more radical view.[47] But the Westminster Parliament is still dominated by the executive and still has an untrammelled power to introduce rights-abridging legislation throughout the UK.[48] In this context it cannot yet be said that radical Constitutional reform which would genuinely constrain the power of the Westminster executive has occurred.

Moreover, reform of Parliament and of the voting system may be largely irrelevant in a period in which the prevailing stance on both government and Opposition benches is a largely anti-liberal one. It is particularly pertinent, in 2000, to consider Parliament's discharge of its central responsibility for protecting individual rights from the mid-1990s onwards, and the probabilities in the immediate future. During the last Conservative years, Labour in Opposition under Blair took a stance that could hardly be viewed as civil liberties oriented. A number of political scientists observed that in the 1990s there was a general policy convergence, with the front-benchers of the Labour and Conservative Parties closer on many issues than at any point since the 1970s.[49] In the civil liberties context two key examples are provided by the Opposition impact on the Criminal Justice and Public Order Act 1994 and the Police Act 1997. Despite protests against the 1994 Bill and the far-reaching nature of many of the new provisions, the Bill went through Parliament relatively intact. As A T H Smith observes, 'Presumably for fear of being seen to be soft on crime . . . the Labour Party declined to oppose the Bill on Second Reading, leaving the serious opposition to the Bill to the Peers [although] . . . the prospects of serious opposition were negligible'.[50] As Chapter 10 explains, the Liberal Democrats took the lead in proposing the more far-reaching amendments to the 1997 Bill.[51]

[46] See Lord Cranborne HL Deb 22 February 2000 cols 151–152 and cols 163–164. The Lord Privy Seal stated in the House Magazine on 27 September 1999 that the new House of Lords will 'be more legitimate because its members have earned their places and therefore more effective . . .'. In the Committee stage in the Lords of the Criminal Justice (Mode of Trial) Bill the first amendment put down was a 'wrecking' amendment which was carried by the Lords and resulted in the immediate withdrawal of the Bill (HL Deb 20 Jan 2000 col 1246ff). The House of Lords Act 1999 removed the automatic right of hereditary peers to sit in the House of Lords. An 'interim' House of Lords of 90 members, elected by the peers, is currently sitting, until the reform is completed.

[47] See the Wakeham Report of the Royal Commission published in January 2000, *A House for the Future* Cm 3534 (available on the web: http://www.official-documents.co.uk/document/cm45/4534/4534.htm). The Report suggested a mainly appointed House of 550 with a minority of elected representatives; the government is pledged to act on the proposals: HL Deb 7 March 2000 col 912.

[48] See Chapter 2 p42. The government can, of course, use the Parliament Act procedure in order to get its legislation through the Lords and it may be that it will have to resort to this in future if the Lords tend to refuse to accept the conventional restraints in which they previously acquiesced. Note the view of Bradley, note 43 above.

[49] A Seldon, 'The Consensus Debate' [1994] 14 Parliamentary Affairs 512.

[50] A T H Smith (1995) Crim LR 19 at p27.

[51] P374.

At the present time, this book will argue, the Conservative Opposition under Hague has adopted a stance which is more authoritarian and even less civil rights minded than the Labour government. It also seems clear that the Conservative approach is likely to remain unchanged after the next general election. The stance of the Labour government is indicated in the two central 'state power' measures it has introduced, the Terrorism Act 2000 and the Regulation of Investigatory Powers Act 2000, discussed fully at various points in the following chapters. It will be contended that the consensus which some commentators viewed as 'shaping the politics of the 1990s'[52] is continuing post-2000. It may be argued, then, that there has been little effective opposition in the Commons on human rights matters for the last six years and at present little prospect of any.

The role of the judiciary as the protector of the individual rights of citizens is therefore currently especially significant and the means of carrying it out is potentially provided by the Convention under the Human Rights Act. The Convention, therefore, can be looked to as one means, within a number of Constitutional changes, of seeking to curb executive power, and its ability to do so is the central concern of this book. As argued above, now that the Act is in force, the Bill of Rights debate between left and liberals need not be revisited.[53] But it may take a new direction. It is legitimate to attack the Human Rights Act as an instrument which has not enshrined 'second generation' rights, which has instead selected and elevated 'first generation' civil rights, ignoring the social and economic ones which might give those civil rights some substantive rather than formal value. That argument could now, however, be utilised to press for introducing second generation rights to future Protocols to the Convention,[54] for giving further effect to the European Social Charter 1961 in domestic law,[55] and for affording binding effect to

[52] D Dutton *British Politics since 1945* 2nd edn (1997) Blackwell p155.

[53] The liberal view is generally sympathetic to the notion of protecting civil rights in a Bill of Rights (see note 32 above and J Rawls *A Theory of Justice* (1972) and *Political Liberalism* (1990); R Dworkin *Taking Rights Seriously* (1977) Chap 6 and *A Bill of Rights for Britain*), in contrast to the leftist view (see M Tushnet 'An Essay on Rights' (1984) 62 *Texas Law Review* 1363; D Herman 'Beyond the Rights Debate' (1993) 2 *Social and Legal Studies* 25). While the left therefore opposed adoption of a Bill of Rights in the UK (see Ewing and Gearty *Freedom under Thatcher* (1989) OUP p275; Waldron 'A Right-based critique of constitutional rights', 13 OJLS 18 pp49–51; Loughlin *Public Law and Political Theory* (1992), especially pp220–227) a number of liberal commentators, although not all, supported it. For an attack on such adoption from a liberal point of view see J Allan 'Bills of Rights and Judicial Power – A Liberal's Quandary' OJLS 16(2) 337–352.

[54] With a view to adding such Protocols to Schedule 1 of the Human Rights Act. This is of particular significance in relation to the draft Discrimination Protocol, Protocol 12, which will provide a guarantee of freedom from discrimination extending beyond the civil rights arena; see Chapter 2 p23.

[55] Liberty campaigned for this possibility at the time when the Human Rights Bill was proposed but at the present time the Labour government has shown no interest in it.

elements of the recently published EU Charter of Fundamental Rights, which includes a number of social and economic rights.[56]

Chapter 2 indicates the key part that the judiciary has to play in the enterprise of the Human Rights Act, in affording the guarantees the efficacy which, it is argued, they currently lack. Unless the judiciary takes a creative, activist stance the enterprise is unlikely to succeed. However, the argument that the domestic judiciary cannot be trusted to protect the interests of minorities and/or unpopular groups but will tend rather to protect property and national security interests must be acknowledged.[57] It is a powerful argument even to those who do not accept the conclusion that the left has drawn from it. As indicated above, that conclusion constituted the main argument against a Bill of Rights. In 2000 it can be utilised to argue *inter alia* for a more radical reform of the judicial appointments system than the one which is currently under contemplation.[58]

This book identifies a number of points at which a choice between deferential minimalism and its converse, creative activism, will arise. It will be argued that a central influencing factor will be the response of the domestic judiciary to the international doctrine of the margin of appreciation – the notion that the national authorities should be allowed a variable degree of discretion in determining matters peculiarly within their purview. As Chapter 2 indicates, the judiciary is not minded to import that doctrine wholesale into domestic decision-making under the Human Rights Act (HRA). But the growth of an equivalent doctrine in domestic law is possible as is a determination to maintain traditional common law deference in areas of national security or policing decisions. Such stances might have the same diluting impact on the Convention rights as has occurred at Strasbourg.

In contrast, a creative, muscular response would be able to overcome that effect by a determined rejection of the margin of appreciation aspects of Strasbourg decisions, and, where necessary, by a reliance in so doing on Strasbourg principles rather than Strasbourg outcomes. The paucity

[56] The Charter, published in May 2000 (available from the European Commission web-site and from the web-site of the House of Lords Select Committee on the European Parliament), contains those rights recognised under the European Convention on Human Rights together with a number of new social rights, including the right to strike, guarantees of maximum working hours, worker consultation and trade union membership. The rights could, potentially, bind the EU institutions. Certain member states and the European Commission are proposing that the Charter should be included in a proposed Treaty of Nice in December 2000. The UK considers that the Charter should not become part of the Treaty, and therefore have binding effect, but should have a merely declaratory status.

[57] J Griffiths *The Politics of the Judiciary* 4th edn (1991) esp at p327.

[58] The Peach Report Dec 1999 www.open.gov.utc/lcd/judicial/Peach/reportfr.htm. The Judicial Appointments and Training Commission: see *Access to Justice Labour Party* (1995). Under the current proposals the Commission would have an advisory role only. See R Brazier 'The Judiciary' in *Constitutional Reform: The Labour Government's Constitutional Reform Agenda* R Blackburn and R Plant (eds) (1999) 329 Harlow, Essex: Longman. In the first 20 months of the government the Lord Chancellor made 17 (exclusively male) appointments to higher judicial office: see Legal Action February 1999 5.

or the elusiveness of the Strasbourg jurisprudence is indicated throughout this book. Speaking of compatibility with 'the Convention rights' may therefore be empty rhetoric in a number of central areas. At a number of points, therefore, methods of forging a creative approach to the rights by reliance on those principles are explored. The application of Strasbourg principles in the domestic context may mean that the Convention under the HRA will represent a response to Thatcherism, a means of infusing substantive values into the Constitution to replace the consensus-based notion of *noblesse oblige* which she rejected.

The argument as to the propriety of judicial activism will no doubt constitute one of the focuses for debate arising from the HRA. But in the classic arenas of state power with which this book is concerned – the use of power by the police and the security and intelligence services – perhaps a reasonable consensus between leftist and liberal commentators may exist regarding the need to defend civil rights[59] by subjecting the agents of the state to rigorous accountability based on the rule of law. In Dicey's view, 'the rule of law' demanded the prohibition of wide discretionary powers; it insisted instead on 'The absolute supremacy of regular law as opposed to the influence of arbitrary power [therefore excluding] the existence of . . . wide discretionary authority on the part of the Government'.[60] Dickinson, writing in 1927, insisted that there were two fundamental aspects of the rule of law, namely that 'every citizen is entitled, first, to have his rights adjudicated on in a regular common-law court, and, secondly, to call into question in such a court the legality of any act done by an administrative official'.[61] The more recent attack on these propositions as a prescription for modern government was not, broadly speaking, directed at their applicability to curbing coercive state power in the arenas with which this book is concerned.[62] As Chapter 2 indicates, these propositions underpin the conception of the rule of law developed at Strasbourg, which the UK has in effect received into domestic law by means

[59] This perspective sees the ruling bourgeoisie as having 'a pre-disposition to anti-democratic and anti-civil libertarian positions', and therefore hard-won rights, which are constantly in danger of being snatched away, must be defended by the working classes; see Hunt *Politics and Power* (1981) Vol 4.

[60] Dicey *The Law of the Constitution* (8th edn) p198. See also J Jowell 'The Rule of Law today' in Jowell and Oliver (eds) *The Changing Constitution* (3rd edn 1994); P Craig *Public Law and Democracy in the United Kingdom and the United States of America* (1990) esp Chap 2 and (1997) PL 467 esp pp470–474; M Loughlin *Public Law and Political Theory* (1992) pp140–162.

[61] *Administrative Justice and the Supremacy of Law* (1927) p35.

[62] Essentially, these propositions were attacked mainly on the basis that they underpinned a particular conception of government, one in which the application of the rule of law would impede progressive social policies involving schemes of public provision for health, education and welfare. See Murray Hunt 'Constitutionalism and Contractualisation' in Taggart (ed) *The Province of Administrative Law* (1997) Hart Publishing p24; B J Hibbits 'The Politics of Principle: Albert Venn Dicey and the Rule of Law' (1994) 23 Anglo-Am LR 1.

of the HRA.[63] While they had a particular and immediately evident applicability to a Constitution based on negative liberties, they are also central to the protection of positive rights, particularly in the context of the preservation of Parliamentary sovereignty. Ironically, Dicey's conception of the rule of law, central to his attack on continental assertions of rights, is almost indistinguishable from Strasbourg's.

Recent commentaries suggest that there is no enthusiasm from leftist scholars for the vesting of broad discretionary powers in the police or the ousting of the jurisdiction of the ordinary courts in protecting individuals from the abuse of powers by the police or the security and intelligence services.[64] Both are matters which, this book argues, may be addressed under the HRA. But a school of leftist thought remains highly critical of reliance *solely* on traditional legal remedies against the police, or other state bodies.[65] Further, the view may be taken that a narrow doctrinal legal analysis is at best incomplete and at worst positively misleading. Thus critical analysis of, for example, the theoretical protection for individuals under the HRA or any particular enactment is of little value without an awareness of the influence of wider societal factors. There should be an awareness of how much that theoretical protection is in reality available to the underprivileged individuals who are often in most need of asserting their rights (in particular working class black men, the most likely target of police harassment or misuse of police powers, such as stop and search).

This argument can be applied to the whole enterprise of the HRA. Reliance should be placed not only on the judiciary and on traditional legal remedies, but on the other bodies which can contribute to its success, based on the notion of seeking to afford *substantive* efficacy to the rights, taking the social context into account. The government which introduced the HRA has a responsibility to ensure compliance with it and, as this book indicates, the government sought – in a somewhat flurried manner – to achieve this in advance of 2 October 2000, when the Act came fully into force. A Parliamentary Committee on Human Rights is to be set up which will *inter alia* advise on legislation.[66] Scotland

[63] See pp25–26.

[64] See Ewing and Gearty *Freedom under Thatcher* (1989) OUP p255; Sanders and Young *Criminal Justice* (1994); Baldwin 'Taking Rules to Excess: Police Powers and the Police and Criminal Evidence Bill 1984' in M Brenton and C Jones (eds) *The Year Book of Social Policy in Britain 1984–5* (1985) pp9–29; Phil Jones 'Police Powers and Political Accountability: the Royal Commission on Criminal Procedure'; P Hillyard 'From Belfast to Britain: Some critical comments on the Royal Commission on Criminal Procedure' both in *Politics and Power* Vol 4 (1981); T Jefferson 'Policing the Miners: Law, Politics and Accountability' in Brenton and Ungerson (eds) *The Year Book of Social Policy in Britain 1985–6* (1986) pp265–286.

[65] See, for example, Ewing and Gearty ibid at 255–262.

[66] See R Blackburn 'A Parliamentary Committee on Human Rights' in *Constitutional Reform: The Labour Government's Constitutional Reform Agenda* R Blackburn and R Plant (eds) (1999) Harlow, Essex: Longman.

will have a Human Rights Commission[67] as does Northern Ireland.[68] The experiment in Northern Ireland will be worth watching in this respect and could provide a partial model for a future Human Rights Commissioner, although the Northern Ireland Commissioner has particular concerns regarding religious discrimination which are not applicable in England and Wales. Developments may be triggered by these Commissions which may increase the pressure for setting up such a body in England. The decision not to set up a Human Rights Commission, as proposed in the Green Paper,[69] created, however, a weakness in the extra-judicial enforcement of the Act. The responsibility for such enforcement will tend to devolve to existing bodies such as the Police Complaints Authority, the Parliamentary Intelligence and Security Committee, the Interception of Communications and Surveillance Commissioners.[70] The responsibility in this regard of such protective and enforcement bodies forms a key theme throughout this book. The extent to which they are able to discharge it and the stance taken towards them in this respect by the New Labour government will be a particular focus of concern.

Conclusions

The intention of this book is to concentrate centrally on the opportunities offered by the HRA of reversing the erosion of fundamental freedoms which occurred under Thatcher and Major, and which, it will argue, is currently occurring under New Labour. Such erosion has occurred, unsurprisingly, in the central arenas of state power – the points at which the state, through the agency of the police and the security and intelligence services, can deploy coercive powers against the citizen. In these arenas the New Labour government is currently putting in place its own unique and extensive legislative framework which will not only build on and extend the one established during the Thatcher and Major years, but will largely rewrite state surveillance and counter-terrorist measures. The new framework is intended to constitute in many respects a response

[67] The Justice Minister Jim Wallace has stated that he is in favour of a Scottish Human Rights Commission: The Scottish Executive: An Open Scotland SE/1999/51 November 1999.

[68] The Belfast Agreement promised that Northern Ireland would have such a Commission. For discussion, see C Harvey and S Livingstone 'Human Rights and the Northern Ireland Peace Process' [1999] EHRLR 162 esp at pp168–174.

[69] *Bringing Rights Home: Labour's plans to incorporate the ECHR into UK Law*: A Consultation Paper December 1996 (1997). See S Spencer 'A Human Rights Commission' in *Constitutional Reform: The Labour Government's Constitutional Reform Agenda* R Blackburn and R Plant (eds) (1999) at p395, Harlow, Essex: Longman.

[70] See Chapters 9 and 10 for discussion of the Commissioners; their role, under different titles, will be similar to the previous one.

to the HRA, as this book explains. Therefore a central concern will be the compatibility between the new legislation and the Convention. This book explores the ironic possibilities of using the Convention to temper the excesses of a government which, it will be contended, appears in some respects to be as wedded to authoritarianism as the Thatcher one. Most significantly, it considers the attachment of New Labour, as indicated in its own 'state power' legislation, to the principles it itself has introduced under the HRA – those of legality, necessity, proportionality. Jack Straw, the New Labour Home Secretary, has written: 'The Human Rights Act is the most significant statement of human rights since the 1689 Bill of Rights'.[71] It will 'increase individual rights'[72] and, according to the Prime Minister, aid in 'restoring trust in the way we are governed'.[73] The reality behind these claims will be evaluated, not only in terms of the Act itself, but in relation to both the established and the new, far more comprehensive, framework for the exercise of coercive and intrusive powers by state agents.

Conclusion.

[71] See Foreword to Wadham and Mountfield *Guide to the Human Rights Act 1998* (1999) Blackstones.
[72] Preface by Tony Blair to the White Paper *Rights Brought Home* October 1997 CM 3782.
[73] Conclusion to *Bringing Rights Home: Labour's plans to incorporate the ECHR into UK Law*: A Consultation Paper December 1996 (1997).

Chapter 2

The Human Rights Act

Introduction

The Human Rights Act 1998, which affords the European Convention on Human Rights 'further effect' in domestic law, represents a dramatic shift in rights protection in the UK, away from residual freedoms towards positive rights. It provides the UK with something very close to a modern Bill of Rights, for the first time. Under s3 of the Act (HRA) the judiciary must interpret legislation, if at all possible, so as to comply with the Convention rights and under s2 it must take the Strasbourg jurisprudence into account. S6 provides that public authorities, including courts, and private bodies acting publicly are bound by the rights.[1]

The impact of the HRA will be strongly influenced by the stance taken by the judiciary to the duty encapsulated under s6 and the interpretative obligation of s3. The courts can seek to give the rights genuine efficacy – an approach which can be termed activist – or they can adopt the interpretation which will cause the least disturbance to the existing order – a minimalist stance.[2] But, as this book indicates, Parliament,[3] government ministers, bodies such as the Police Complaints Authority, the Intelligence

[1] Thus in Hohfeldian terms the 1998 Act provides claim rights – against public authorities only – rather than a set of immunities since it can be overridden by primary legislation: see W Hohfeld *Fundamental Legal Concepts as Applied in Judicial Reasoning* (1920).

[2] These terms are discussed further below. These terms or equivalent ones such as 'muscular or interventionist' as opposed to deferential, timorous and restrained are scattered across writings about the stances of courts adjudicating on human rights matters: see, for example, D Beatty 'The Canadian Charter of Rights: Lessons and Laments' [1997] MLR 481 at p487; Lord Irvine in the 1999 Paul Sieghart Memorial Lecture 'Activism and Restraint: Human Rights and the Interpretative Process', published [1999] EHRLR 350; Sir John Laws 'The Limitations of Human Rights' [1998] PL 254 at p259.

[3] Parliament, as indicated below, is not bound under s6 HRA. But since, traditionally, it sees itself as a guardian of freedom, it might be expected that a view on activism would eventually be taken.

Services Commissioner and other public and quasi-public authorities also have the opportunity of adopting an activist or a minimalist approach.

The aim of this chapter is to provide a frame of reference for the discussion of the HRA and the Convention rights which permeates this book. It argues, as Chapter 1 indicates, that the New Labour government has carried on the illiberal traditions of the previous Conservative governments in showing, in its 'state power' legislation, a 'corrupting insensitivity to liberty'.[4] Since the Constitution has been based on the notion of negative liberties only it has been unable to counter the creeping erosion of freedom which has occurred under successive governments. This book traces the potential countering effect of the Convention and its jurisprudential accretions under the HRA. The role of this chapter is to show that in so doing the inadequacies and contradictions inherent in both instruments will be pivotal.

The European Court of Human Rights has sought to adopt a dynamic approach, but it has also deferred to the national authorities; a number of applications which, commentators agree, raised highly significant human rights issues never reached the Court since the Commission declared them inadmissible, frequently in furtherance of a deferential approach.[5] Equally, the HRA itself is seeking to reconcile conflicting aims under ss3 and 6 – to preserve national sovereignty but to counter its impact on human rights. The profound inadequacies of the remedial system, discussed below, reflect, it will be contended, the compromise adopted. S2 of the Act allows the judiciary to develop a domestic Convention jurisprudence free from the more deferential decisions of the Commission and Court, and yet leaves the way open for the courts to apply the bare document itself, which without its accumulated jurisprudence may be unable to address the pressing human rights concerns of the UK post-2000, many of which, as this book seeks to show, are raised by New Labour legislation. Most fundamentally of all, the Convention, despite its strong concern with procedural values, reflects substantive norms. A central theme of this book concerns the reconciliation between infusing such norms into a 'constitution which is almost entirely procedural'[6] with maintaining a separation of powers which requires the judiciary to deal with the Convention 'as law and not as moral idealism'.[7] This chapter therefore devotes some space to considering the possible approaches which public and quasi-public bodies, including the judiciary, might take

[4] R Dworkin *Index on Censorship* (1988) pp7–8. See also R Dworkin *A Bill of Rights for Britain?* (1988) pp9–10.

[5] See Ewing and Gearty 'Rocky Foundations for Labour's New Rights' [1997] 2 EHRLR 149. One of the clearest examples of such applications is *Council of Civil Service Unions* v *UK* (1988) 10 EHRR 269 in which the ban on unions at GCHQ was not found to breach Article 11.

[6] See D Feldman 'The Human Rights Act and Constitutional Principles' (1999) 19 (2) LS 165 at p166.

[7] See Sir John Laws 'The Limitations of Human Rights' [1998] PL 254 at p257.

in seeking a way within these conflicting provisions and principles to realise the lofty aims of the government in 'bringing rights home'.[8] The possibilities represented by such approaches form one of the key themes of this book.

Strasbourg principles and the evolution of the Convention rights

Introduction

The Convention, the Strasbourg control mechanism and Strasbourg concepts have been discussed in an extensive literature.[9] The limited concern of the discussion below is to focus on those issues which are especially pertinent in the domestic context. From today's perspective the 50-year-old Convention looks very much like a creature of its period[10] with its provision against slavery and its long lists of exceptions to certain fundamental rights. Its out-of-date feel has led a number of commentators to echo the plea put forward five years ago by Tomkins and Rix for 'a document of principle for the 1990s and not a document of exceptions from the 1950s'.[11] It might appear that the present structure of the Convention is simply not adequate to the task of bringing about far-reaching reforms and thereby fulfilling the Constitutional role which a number of commentators have enthusiastically mapped out for it.[12] As Feldman puts it, 'the Convention rights are by no means a comprehensive basis for a modern system of protection for [individualistic and public] values'.[13]

[8] See *Bringing Rights Home: Labour's plans to incorporate the ECHR into UK Law*: A Consultation Paper December 1996 para 2.4 (1997) and the White Paper *Rights Brought Home* October 1997 CM 3782; see also J Straw and P Boateng (1997) 1 EHRR 71.

[9] See Merrills and Robertson *Human Rights in Europe* 3rd edn (1993); R Beddard *Human Rights and Europe* 3rd edn (1980); J E S Fawcett *The Application of the European Convention on Human Rights* 2nd edn (1987); F G Jacobs *The European Convention on Human Rights* (1975); Z Nedjati *Human Rights under the European Convention* (1978); Harris, O'Boyle and Warbrick *Law of the European Convention on Human Rights* (1995); B Dickson and A Connelly *Human Rights and the European Convention* (1996); S Livingstone *The European Convention on Human Rights* (1999); P Van Dijk and F Van Hoof *Theory and Practice of the European Convention on Human Rights* 3rd edn (1998).

[10] The Convention was drafted in 1949 and based on the United Nations Declaration of Human Rights. The Declaration was adopted on 10 December 1948 by the General Assembly of the UN.

[11] 'Unconventional Use of the Convention' 55(5) MLR 721 at p725. See also Professor Ashworth 'The European Convention on Human Rights and English Criminal Justice: Ships which pass in the Night?', chapter in *English Public Law and the Common Law of Europe* Dr M Andenas (ed) (1998) Keyhaven Publications p215.

[12] See, for example, D Feldman 'The Human Rights Act 1998 and constitutional principles' (1999) 19 (2) LS 165; Lord Lester of Herne Hill QC 'First Steps Towards a Constitutional Bill of Rights' [1997] 2 EHRLR 124.

[13] D Feldman ibid at p170.

The far more thorough South African Bill of Rights, which covers certain social, economic and environmental rights, provides an example of such a system.

However, the decisions of the European Court of Human Rights documented in this book suggest that the Convention is sufficiently open textured to be able to cover circumstances not envisaged when it was created[14] and to adapt to changing social values. The Convention with its associated jurisprudence comes close to comprising a modern 'document of principles' due largely to the enterprise of the Court which has insisted upon the dynamic nature of the Convention and has adopted a teleological or purpose-based approach to interpretation which has allowed the substantive rights to develop.[15] But those principles cannot always be sought in the *outcomes* of applications. The traditional approach of the doctrine of precedent in UK courts will not therefore always be appropriate to the development of the domestic jurisprudence. Since traditionally the Constitution recognised only negative liberties as opposed to positive rights, the judicial focus of concern always tended to be on the content and nature of the restrictions in question rather than on the value and extent of the right. In other words, despite proud traditions of upholding certain fundamental rights, Constitutional inadequacy became, inevitably, apparent. This approach will no longer be appropriate. Below, various approaches to the Convention are considered as the basis for allowing a subtle infusion of Strasbourg principles into UK law.

Influence of the Strasbourg control mechanism

As indicated at a number of points in this book, the European Commission on Human Rights has had a strong influence on the Strasbourg jurisprudence since until recently it determined the admissibility of an application.[16] An application which *inter alia* had not exhausted domestic remedies or was manifestly ill-founded would be declared inadmissible.[17] The manifestly ill-founded admissibility condition afforded a very significant power to the Commission. Formally speaking it was excluded from the role of determining on the merits of the application, although it could give an Opinion. Yet when it declared an application manifestly ill-founded it was in fact pronouncing on the merits because it was determining whether or not a *prima facie* violation had taken place. This condition therefore created an extension of the role of the Commission behind the cloak of merely determining admissibility and meant that it frequently took the final decision on the merits. The Commission was generally

[14] See, for example, *Soering* v *UK*, judgment of 7 July 1989, A.161; (1989) 11 EHRR 439.
[15] See P Van Dijk and F Van Hoof *Theory and Practice of the European Convention on Human Rights* 3rd edn (1998).
[16] Under (old) Article 27.
[17] Article 27(2).

characterised as an administrative rather than judicial body; however, when it found that an application was manifestly ill-founded it was taking a decision on a question of law which had a binding effect. Thus, in respect of such decisions it was acting judicially. Disquiet as to its discharge of this judicial function was a factor in the decision of the Parliamentary Assembly of the Council of Europe to merge the Commission with the Court, under Protocol 11.[18] The Committee of Experts for the improvement of procedures for the protection of human rights (DH-PR) put forward as one argument for reform the fundamental need to reinforce the judicial character of the control machinery.[19] The main danger was, as a number of commentators have pointed out, that a lower standard of human rights than that allowed by the Convention was at times enabled to prevail.[20]

Once Protocol 11 was ratified and came into force[21] judges of a Chamber of the Court began to take decisions on admissibility under Articles 27 and 28 and to conduct the examination of the merits with a view to reaching a friendly settlement.[22] The authority of the Convention could be viewed as enhanced since its jurisprudence was no longer influenced by the decisions of an administrative body. These developments suggest that in applying the Strasbourg jurisprudence under s2 of the HRA the courts and other public authorities should take account of the variable quality of the admissibility decisions undertaken by the Commission, especially the older ones. Commentators have viewed the Court as becoming more activist in the late 1990s,[23] a development which is likely to continue now that the diluting tendency of the Commission has been removed. Any such development will be of significance, bearing in mind the provision of s2 HRA to the effect that the Strasbourg jurisprudence, 'whenever made or given', should be taken into account if relevant. The Court is not bound by its own decisions; therefore a cautious decision of the Court which was followed by the House of Lords in the post-HRA era might be found, after a more activist later decision at Strasbourg, to be out of accord with the development of the Convention. A lower court, under s2, could then depart from the decision in the Lords.

[18] Recommendation 1194, adopted on 6 October 1992.

[19] See 'Reform of the Control System' (1993) HRLJ 31 para 12.

[20] See Harris, O'Boyle and Warbrick *Law of the European Convention on Human Rights* (1995) at pp627–628. The Committee of Experts for the improvement of procedures for the protection of human rights (DH-PR) put forward as one argument for reform the fundamental need to reinforce the judicial character of the control machinery; see 'Reform of the Control System' (1993) HRLJ 31 para 12. See, further, T Jones 'The Devaluation of Human Rights under the European Convention' [1995] PL 430; P Mahoney 'Marvellous Richness or Invidious Cultural Relativism?' (1998) 19 Human Rights Law Journal 1.

[21] On 1 November 1998.

[22] See *Rules of Procedure of the European Court of Human Rights* 4 November 1998, rules 53, 55 and 62, and Article 35.

[23] See Chapter 5 p200 and p209.

Convention rights and exceptions

Sl of the HRA only gives 'further effect' to a particular version of the Convention, although further Protocols may be added in future, under s1(4), by the Secretary of State. Article 1, which provides that the member states must secure the rights and freedoms to their subjects,[24] is omitted as is Article 13 which provides that there must be an effective remedy in national law for breach of the rights. The rights covered at present by s1 are listed in Schedule 1 which is set out, with the full text of the HRA, at the beginning of this book. They are: Articles 2–12 and 14, Articles 1–3 of the First Protocol, Articles 1 and 2 of the Sixth Protocol. The rights must be read with Articles 16–18. The omission of Article 13 was said in Parliament to be justified on the basis that its function is covered by s8 of the Act, which provides for a remedy where a public authority breaches a Convention right. Lord Irvine said in Parliament on this point that had Article 13 been included the courts might have been tempted to create further remedies, going beyond those created under s8; in particular they might have created forms of horizontal effect.[25] Article 13 can, however, be considered since it, and Article 1, are part of the Convention jurisprudence under s2.[26]

The substantive rights covered fall into two groups. Articles 2 to 7 cover a number of fundamental rights: the right to life under Article 2 with limited exceptions in which deprivation of life is permissible; the absolute, non-derogable guarantee against torture or inhuman or degrading treatment under Article 3;[27] the right to liberty under Article 5;[28] the right to a fair hearing under Article 6;[29] the presumption of innocence under Article 6(2); minimum rights applicable to everyone charged with a criminal offence under Article 6(3), including the rights to 'legal assistance of his own choosing' and to 'examine or have examined witnesses against him and to obtain the attendance and examination of witnesses on his behalf under the same conditions as witnesses against him';[30] the right to

[24] They are free to decide how this should be done. This was affirmed by the Irish Supreme Court in *The State (Lawless)* v *O'Sullivan and the Minister for Justice*; see Yearbook of the Convention on Human Rights Vol II (1958–9) at pp608–622.

[25] Lord Irvine, HL Official Report 18 November 1997 Vol 583 col 475. See further below on the question of horizontal effect.

[26] It was accepted by Lord Irvine that Article 13 could be taken into account: HL Deb Vol 583 cols 475–477 18 November 1997.

[27] Article 3 treatment may be justifiable where its object is to satisfy the demands of Article 2, the right to life: *Herczegfalfy* v *Austria* A 244 (1992).

[28] See further on these three Articles, Chapter 6 esp pp229–232 and pp247–255.

[29] See further on Article 6 Chapters 5, 6 and 7.

[30] In investigating a fair hearing Strasbourg has found that a number of rights may be implied into the fairness requirement of para 1, either read alone or in conjunction with the para 3 guarantees. Since Article 6(3) contains minimum guarantees the Article 6(1) protection of a fair hearing goes beyond that of para 3. In investigating a fair hearing Strasbourg is not confined to the Article 6(3) guarantees; it has considered a number of further requirements of fairness. Thus, the Court has added a number of specific rights to Article 6(1) through the fair hearing guarantee.

freedom from slavery under Article 4 and to freedom from retrospective criminal sanctions under Article 7. Articles 8–11 may be said to cover a more developed conception of human rights; they provide the right to respect for privacy under Article 8,[31] and rights to the freedoms of expression, association and assembly under Articles 10 and 11[32] and to thought, conscience and religion under Article 9. Article 12 provides a right to marry and to found a family. In the First Protocol, Article 1 provides a right to the peaceful enjoyment of property, Article 2 to education and Article 3 to free elections. Articles 1 and 2 of the Sixth Protocol abolish the death penalty except in time of war or the threat of war. Article 14 provides a prohibition against discrimination in the enjoyment of the Convention rights. If no violation of the substantive right taken alone is found, and even if that claim is manifestly ill-founded, there can still be a violation of that Article and Article 14 taken together so long as the matter at issue is covered by the other Article.[33] Article 14 covers differential treatment which is unjustifiable, either in the sense that it relates to no objective and reasonable aim or in the sense that there is no reasonable proportionality between the means employed and the aim sought to be realised.[34] Although the Court has granted more autonomy to Article 14 than appeared to be intended originally,[35] it remains of limited value since it is not free standing and does not cover social and economic matters lying outside the protected rights. But these weaknesses will be addressed by Protocol 12 which will provide a free-standing right to freedom from discrimination in relation to rights protected by law.[36] Since Protocol 12 addresses a central flaw in the Convention there is a strong case for adding it to the rights protected by the HRA.

One of the key aims of the Convention is procedural – where interferences with the guarantees are allowed, they must have a basis in law. This demand is found in para 2 of Articles 8–11, in Article 2 in respect of the circumstances in which deprivation of life is permitted, and in respect of Article 5[37] and the First Protocol, Article 1 exceptions. The view of the Convention as primarily a procedural instrument is supported by the lack of qualifications to the 'due process' guarantees. All the Articles except Articles 3, 4(1), 6(2), 7 and Article 3 of the First Protocol are subject to certain specified restrictions, and general restrictions – albeit of limited

[31] See further on Article 8 Chapter 6 at p254, and 9 at pp364–368.

[32] See further on Articles 10 and 11 Chapter 3 esp at pp61–64 and Chapter 4 at pp124–130.

[33] In *X* v *Federal Republic of Germany* Appl 4045/69 (1970) Yearbook XIII it was said: 'Article 14 . . . has no independent existence; nevertheless a measure which in itself is in conformity with the requirement of the Article enshrining the right or freedom in question, may however infringe this Article when read in conjunction with Article 14 for the reason that it is of a discriminatory nature'.

[34] *Geïllustreerde Pers NV* v *the Netherlands* D and R 8 (1977).

[35] For comment on the increasing autonomy of Article 14 see S Livingstone (1997) 1 EHRR 25.

[36] For further discusssion of the draft Discrimination Protocol see G Moon (2000) 1 EHRLR 49.

[37] See further Chapter 6 pp229–231.

scope – are allowed under Articles 16 and 17. Restrictions are allowed on the political activity of aliens (Article 16) and on any activity aimed at the destruction of the Convention rights or their limitation to a greater extent than is provided for in the Convention (Article 17).[38] Article 18 places a limitation on the restrictions in providing that the motives of the national authority in creating them must be the same as the aims appearing behind the restrictions when the Convention was drafted. Bearing Article 18 in mind, the restrictions introduced by Articles 16 and 17 do not introduce qualifications, except possibly in the most exceptional emergency circumstances, to the guarantees unqualified on their face.

Significantly, no general qualifying clause on the lines of the New Zealand Bill of Rights, the Canadian Charter or the South African Bill of Rights was included. General qualifications on those lines were confined to para 2 of Articles 8–11. A broad range of exceptions to the primary right are provided covering a range of societal interests: national security, public safety, the prevention of disorder or crime, the protection of health or morals or the rights of others. Articles 8–11 therefore present a strong contrast to the less qualified or unqualified guarantees since, while the latter operate as rules, the former may be said to operate as principles.[39] Rules and principles may be distinguished in the sense that a principle has weight in a particular set of circumstances, while a rule will determine the response to them.[40] These rights may be viewed as a bundle of competing principles in which the primary norm is weighted above the exceptions. Externally, from the point of view of figuring in the legal system, Articles 8–11 act as rules, in that they may determine an issue without reference to other legal rules, but internally they represent principles. Griffiths viewed them as statements of conflict masquerading as the resolution of it.[41] In seeking to resolve the conflict, these Articles indicate a structured approach to state interference with the guarantees. To be justified, such interference must be prescribed by law, have a legitimate aim, be necessary in a democratic society and be applied in a non-discriminatory fashion (Article 14). Strasbourg's main concern has been with the 'necessary in a democratic society' requirement; the notion of 'prescribed by law' has been focused upon to some extent but usually with the result that it has been found to be satisfied.[42] The 'legitimate

[38] Restrictions are allowed on the political activity of aliens (Article 16) and on any activity aimed at the destruction of the Convention rights or their limitation to a greater extent than is provided for in the Convention (Article 17). Article 17 was used by the Commission to allow the banning of the German Communist Party: *Kommunistische Partei Deutschland* v *Federal Republic of Germany* Application 250/57 Yearbook I (1955–57) Vol 6 p222.

[39] See G Phillipson 'The Human Rights Act, "Horizontal Effect" and The Common Law: A Bang or a Whimper?' [1999] 62 MLR 824 at p831.

[40] A distinction of this sort was suggested by R Dworkin *Taking Rights Seriously* 2nd impression (1978).

[41] *The Political Constitution* (1979).

[42] See the discussion of *Malone* v *UK* (1985) 7 EHRR 14 in Chapter 9 and of *Hashman and Harrup* v *UK* (1999) Chapter 4 p147.

aim' requirement will normally be readily satisfied; as Harris, O'Boyle and Warbrick point out, the grounds for interference (under para 2 of Articles 8–11) are so wide that 'the state can usually make a plausible case that it did have a good reason for interfering with the right'.[43]

Interpreting 'prescribed by law' in *Sunday Times* v *UK*,[44] the European Court of Human Rights found that 'the law must be adequately accessible' and 'a norm cannot be regarded as a "law" unless it is formulated with sufficient precision to enable the citizen to regulate his conduct'. In *Malone* v *UK*[45] the European Court of Human Rights found that there should be some correlation between the significance of a rule, in terms of its interference with human rights, and its legal force, and that where such correlation is lacking it would be prepared to find that the rule is not 'law'. The Court has also paid some attention to the democratic legitimacy of rules in determining whether they are 'law'.[46] Thus, two questions arise: is there something recognisable as law and is it of the right 'quality'? Merely providing a statutory basis for an interference with a Convention right may be insufficient. As Harris, O'Boyle and Warbrick put it, 'Wholly general, unfettered discretion will not satisfy the Convention no matter what the formal validity of the delegating rule'.[47]

The requirements of 'prescribed by law' confirm and clarify the rule of law requirement that the government is not placed in the same position as a citizen in being able to do anything which the law does not forbid.[48] These requirements therefore clearly call into question the use of quasi-legislation and administrative guidelines authorising interference with civil liberties. At the present time the Labour government is seeking to address this concern by placing a number of such rules on a statutory basis, especially in the Regulation of Investigatory Powers Act 2000. However, as Chapter 6 indicates, certain aspects of police powers may continue to have an insufficient legal basis.[49] Further, ironically, the largely unfettered executive discretion provided for in that Act for the issuing of surveillance

[43] See Harris, O'Boyle and Warbrick *Law of the European Convention on Human Rights* (1995) at p290.

[44] (1979–1980) 2 EHRR 245 at paras 46–53.

[45] (1985) 7 EHRR 14 at paras 66–80.

[46] P Van Dijk and F Van Hoof argue that the Court has not paid enough attention to the democratic legitimacy of a rule, citing laws of the European Union; see *Theory and Practice of the European Convention on Human Rights* 3rd edn (1998). Harris, O'Boyle and Warbrick argue that such criticism should be levelled equally at the Court's acceptance of the common law as having sufficient democratic legitimacy: *Law of the European Convention on Human Rights* (1995) at p286.

[47] Ibid at p287.

[48] Megarry VC in *Malone* v *MPC* [1979] Ch 344 considered that the government *was* placed in this position. On the other hand it is a basic principle of judicial review that a public authority must have a basis in law for its actions. The inquiry into 'prescribed by law' is, under the Convention, prior to the enquiry into the exceptions and therefore at Strasbourg the outcome of *ex parte Ruddock* [1987] 1 WLR 1482 would have been avoided. In *Ruddock* the fact that national security considerations arose, prevented review in an instance in which no satisfactory basis in law for the interference was available.

[49] See Chapter 6 p218 and p228.

warrants may not provide a legal basis of sufficient quality. This may also be true of other statutory provisions within the same model, discussed in Chapters 3 and 8.

The Court has interpreted 'necessary in a democratic society' as meaning that 'an interference corresponds to a pressing social need[50] and, in particular, that it is proportionate to the legitimate aim pursued'.[51] The requirements to consider necessity and proportionality are highly significant; when criminal law interferes with Convention guarantees, the courts must not only apply the law, but consider whether the interference is proportionate to the aim of, for example, preserving public order. The application of these principles in that field is considered further in Chapters 3 and 4. In the field of judicial review the requirements of proportionality will be likely to lead to a more intensive review of the decision in question and a more structured analysis. The difference between *Wednesbury* unreasonableness and proportionality is illustrated by Simon Brown LJ in *ex p Smith*: 'if [the Convention] were part of our law . . . then clearly the primary judgement . . . would be for us and not for others; the constitutional balance would shift. But that is not the position. In exercising merely a secondary judgement this court is bound, even though acting in a human rights context to act with some reticence'.[52] Under the traditional *Wednesbury* doctrine the decision-maker had to act with a high degree of unreasonableness before the decision could be interfered with[53] although under later formulations more was required in order to justify violations of human rights.[54] It can be said, then, that the concept of proportionality was already filtering into UK law, but that under the Convention this process will be accelerated and affirmed, with the result, as various examples given in this book indicate, that the judiciary will be empowered to call ministers, officials and other public bodies to account, in requiring them to live up to the Constitutional duty to respect fundamental rights, which the HRA imposes on them under s6. In this sense in particular the HRA allows a shift from form to substance[55] to occur. But the extent to which this is the case depends on the approach taken by the judiciary to the requirements of proportionality which will in turn determine the intensity of the review.

The doctrine of proportionality is strongly linked at Strasbourg to the principle of the margin of appreciation: the Court has found, 'the margin of appreciation extends in particular to the choice of the reasonable and appropriate means to be used by the authority to ensure that lawful

[50] See *Handyside* v *UK* judgment of 7 December 1976 A.24.
[51] *Olsson* v *Sweden* A 130 para 67 (1988).
[52] *R* v *Ministry of Defence ex p Smith* [1996] QB 517 at p541.
[53] See Lord Diplock in *Council of Civil Service Unions* v *Minister for the Civil Service* [1985] AC 375 at p410.
[54] See *R* v *Ministry of Defence ex p Smith* [1996] QB 517.
[55] The phrase is used by the Lord Chancellor in 'The Development of Human Rights in Britain under an Incorporated Convention on Human Rights' [1998] PL 221 at p235.

manifestations can take place peacefully'.[56] In *Markt intern Verlag* v *FRG*[57] the Court found: 'the European Court of Human Rights should not substitute its own evaluation for that of the national courts in the instant case, where those courts, on reasonable grounds, had considered the restrictions to be necessary'.

The Strasbourg doctrine of the margin of appreciation

The European Court of Human Rights has stated that the role of the Convention in protecting human rights is subsidiary to the role of the national legal system[58] and that since the state is better placed than the international judge to balance individual rights against general societal interests, Strasbourg will operate a restrained review of the balance struck. The doctrine of the margin of appreciation conceded to states was first adopted in respect of emergency situations but it was allowed to affect the application of all the Articles although it has a particular application with respect to para 2 of Articles 8–11. It has now reached the stage where it can be said that it permeates the Convention jurisprudence. If a broader margin is allowed, Strasbourg review will be highly circumscribed. A narrow margin conceded to the state means that a rigorous or intensive review of the proportionality between the aim of an interference and the extent and nature of the interference will be undertaken.[59]

It is not easy to predict when each approach will be taken but it seems to depend on a number of identifiable factors. The Court and Commission consider that in certain sensitive matters, most notably national security[60] but also the protection of morals[61], states are best placed to determine what is needed within their own particular domestic situation. In considering the imposition of positive obligations placed on the state a broad margin will be allowed.[62] Emergency situations and the invocation of threats to national security also invite deference. In *Council of Civil Service Unions* v *UK*[63] the European Commission, in declaring the Unions' application inadmissible, found that national security interests should prevail over freedom of association even though the national security interest was weak while the infringement of the primary right was very clear: an absolute ban on joining a trade union had been imposed. The high (or low) point of deference was perhaps reached in *Brannigan and*

56 *Chorherr* v *Austria* Series A 266-B para 31 (1993).
57 Series A 165 para 47 (1989).
58 *Handyside* v *UK* A 24 para 48 (1976).
59 See, for example, the *Sunday Times* case Series A 30 (1979); 2 EHRR 245. The width allowed depends on a number of factors including the aim of interference in question and its necessity.
60 See *Leander* v *Sweden* Series A 116 para 67 (1987).
61 See *Handyside* v *UK* Series A 24 para 48 (1976).
62 See *Plattform Arzte fur Das Leben* v *Austria* (1988) 13 EHRR 204.
63 No 11603/85, 50 DR 228 (1987); 10 EHRR 269.

McBride v *UK*[64] in which the European Court of Human Rights upheld a derogation entered by the UK after the decision in the case of *Brogan and Others* v *UK*.[65] The Court found that 'a wide margin of appreciation [on the question] of the presence of an emergency . . . and on the nature and scope of derogations necessary to avert it [should be allowed]'[66].

The common standards doctrine will be influential – the lack of a uniform standard among the member states will tend to mean that a wide margin will be conceded. The lack of such a standard was a key factor in the ruling in *Otto-Preminger Institut* v *Austria*.[67] The decision concerned the seizure of a film likely to offend religious feeling. The European Court of Human Rights found that the film would receive protection under Article 10 but that its seizure fell within the 'rights of others' exception. In considering whether its seizure and forfeiture was 'necessary in a democratic society' in order to protect the rights of others to respect for their religious views (under Article 9), the Court took into account the lack of a uniform conception within the member states of the significance of religion in society and therefore considered that the national authorities should have a wide margin of appreciation in assessing what was necessary to protect religious feeling.

On the other hand, where a principle has received general acceptance in the member states and in particular where it is closely linked to the notion of democracy, the Court will afford a narrow margin only. For example, in *Socialist Party and Others* v *Turkey*[68] the Court found that the dissolution of the Socialist Party of Turkey had breached Article 11 since: 'there can be no democracy without pluralism . . . It is of the essence of democracy to allow diverse political programmes to be proposed and debated . . . Taking these matters into account . . . In determining whether a necessity existed, the Contracting state was found to possess only a limited margin of appreciation'. The picture is more confused where a principle may be said to have received some general acceptance within the contracting states and where the Court itself appears to have espoused it in the past but where it cannot clearly be said that a common standard can be found. Such confusion appears to underlie the remarks in *Cossey* v *UK*[69] of Judge Martens in his dissenting Opinion: 'this caution [in allowing a wide margin of appreciation based on a strict application of the common standards doctrine] is in principle not consistent with the Court's mission to protect the individual against the collectivity[70] . . . in

[64] Series A 258-B (1993).
[65] Judgment of 29 November 1988 (1989) Series A 145-B (1988); 11 EHHR 117. See further Chapter 6 p250.
[66] Para 207.
[67] Series A 295-A (1994); 19 EHRR 34.
[68] Judgment of 25 May 1998 (1999) 27 EHRR 51, paras 41, 47, 50.
[69] A 184 (1990).
[70] At para 5.6.3.

this context [of legal recognition of gender reassignment] there simply is no room for a margin of appreciation'. Thus, even within the Court there is disagreement as to the interferences which fall within the margin conceded to the state. In the only decision of the Court finding a violation of the freedom of assembly guarantee of Article 11, *Ezelin* v *France*,[71] two of the partly dissenting judges considered that the interference in question fell within that margin,[72] although the majority found that the state had exceeded it.

As the findings in these decisions suggest, the margin of appreciation doctrine may tend to undermine the Convention and its growth has therefore attracted criticism. Van Dijk and Van Hoof have written of it as 'a spreading disease. Not only has the scope of its application been broadened to the point where in principle none of the Convention rights or freedoms are excluded, but also has the illness been intensified in that wider versions of the doctrine have been added to the original concept.'[73]

Responses to the Convention: activism or restraint?

A central issue under the HRA concerns the domestic application of the margin of appreciation. Since the doctrine has probably been the key dilutant of Convention standards, it is essential that UK judges and other public authorities should reject it as a relevant factor in their own decision-making under the Convention. As indicated, the doctrine is a distinctively international law doctrine, based on the need to respect the decision-making of nation states within defined limits. Therefore it would not appear to have any application in national law.[74] However, under s2 HRA the domestic judiciary 'must take into account' any relevant Strasbourg jurisprudence, although it is not bound by it.[75] A central

[71] A 202-A (1991).

[72] Judges Ryssdal and Pettiti, at pp26 and 28–30.

[73] Van Dijk and Van Hoof *The Theory and Practice of the European Convention on Human Rights* (1990) p604. For further discussion of the doctrine see O'Donell 'The Margin of Appreciation Doctrine: Standards in the Jurisprudence of the European Court of Human Rights' 4 Human Rights Q (1982) 474; Morrisson 'Margin of Appreciation in Human Rights Law' 6 Human Rights J (1973) 263; T Jones 'The Devaluation of Human Rights under the European Convention' [1995] PL 430; P Mahoney 'Marvellous Richness or Invidious Cultural Relativism?' (1998) 19 Human Rights Law Journal 1.

[74] As Sir John Laws puts it: 'The margin of appreciation doctrine as it has been developed at Strasbourg will necessarily be inapt to the administration of the Convention in the domestic courts for the very reason that they are domestic; they will not be subject to an objective inhibition generated by any cultural distance between themselves and the state organs whose decisions are impleaded before them.' 'The Limitations of Human Rights' [1998] PL 254 at p258.

[75] The term exhaustively covers any 'judgement, decision, declaration or advisory opinion of the Court', any 'opinion of the Commission given in a report adopted under Article 31', any 'decision of the Commission in connection with Article 26 or 27(2)' or any

concern is therefore the reconciliation of s2 HRA with the development of the margin of appreciation doctrine, taking into account its international character. Below three possible models which the domestic judiciary might adopt in responding to the HRA, and in particular to this doctrine, are indicated. The discussion concerns the responses of the judiciary since it has the primary responsibility for interpretation of the Convention rights under s3. But the models indicated may also be reflected in the decision-making of public and quasi-public bodies which are seeking to discharge their obligations under s6.

S2 creates quite a weak obligation since it is open to the judiciary to consider but disapply a particular decision. Only the Convention rights themselves are binding under s6. As pointed out above, the rights appear, in many respects, quite out of date today. But since 1950 they have been subject to a rich and extensive jurisprudence. The domestic judiciary may view a number of the Articles as far too bald and imprecise unless their interpretation at Strasbourg is taken into account.[76] But where little or no guidance was provided by the Strasbourg jurisprudence, except in a very general sense, it would be open to the judiciary to develop its own version of the doctrine of the margin of appreciation (under a different name) based upon common law acceptance of judicial deference to Parliament and to aspects of executive power. Conversely, it would also be open to the judiciary to consider whether it is possible and desirable to avoid applying the margin of appreciation aspects of the jurisprudence.[77] While it is clear that the doctrine itself has no application in national law,[78] the obligation to disapply it may be viewed as going much further than merely refusing to import it into domestic decision-making. There are some clear indications from the judiciary that it is not minded to import the doctrine wholesale into domestic law, but that it may be prepared to rely on decisions at Strasbourg which have been influenced by the doctrine. To an extent this was the approach adopted in the leading pre-HRA case of *R* v *DPP ex p Kebilene*:[79] although the doctrine itself was rejected, the outcomes of applications at Strasbourg were taken into account without adverting to the influence the doctrine had had on them.[80]

'decision of the Committee of Ministers taken under Article 46'. The words 'in connection with' appear to mean that all findings which may be said to be linked to the admissibility procedure, including reports prepared during the preliminary examination of a case, could be taken into account.

76 It may be noted that this is not necessarily the case; the Strasbourg jurisprudence may have the effect of 'reading down' the right; see the discussion of *Salabiaku* v *France* A 141-A (1988) in Chapter 3 pp105–106.

77 See Hunt, Singh and Demetriou [1999] 'Is There a Role for the Margin of Appreciation in National Law After the Human Rights Act?' EHRLR 15.

78 In *R* v *Stratford Justices ex p Imbert*, *The Times* 21 February 1999, Buxton LJ confirmed obiter that the doctrine had no such application. This is also the advice currently given by the Judicial Studies Board.

79 [1999] 3 WLR 372.

80 Such applications included *H* v *UK* App No 15023/89 and *Bates* v *UK* App No 26280/95.

These considerations make it apparent that the HRA and the Convention itself leave open a great deal of leeway for diverse judicial approaches, ranging from a minimal response to a more intrusive jurisdiction. Below, three broad approaches, termed the 'review' or minimalist, 'traditionalist' and 'activist' models are indicated, but this should not be taken to imply that they are entirely discrete, that any particular judge could be said to exemplify, consistently, one of these approaches, or that other variations are unlikely to arise. For example, from a leftist perspective, an 'activist' approach would tend to differentiate between interference in socio-economic matters, including the allocation of public resources, and protection for suspects' rights.[81]

The 'review' or minimalist model

One feature of this approach would be a full reliance on the margin of appreciation aspects of the Strasbourg jurisprudence, resulting in the operation of a restrained review jurisdiction only, in determining issues covered by any 'relevant' jurisprudence. This would not mean openly importing the margin of appreciation doctrine into domestic decision-making; rather, it would mean applying such aspects regardless of the influence it had had on them. In a sense it would mean importing the doctrine by the back door. An example of adoption of this model in the pre-HRA era was provided by *R* v *Khan*;[82] the House of Lords relied on an exclusion of evidence decision at Strasbourg, *Schenk* v *Switzerland*,[83] where a very wide margin of appreciation had been allowed, without acknowledging that this was the case. For example, it was said in the Lords in *Kahn*, 'the discretionary powers of the trial judge to exclude evidence march hand in hand with article 6(1) of the Convention . . . the decision of the Court in *Schenk* . . . confirms that the use at a criminal trial of material obtained in breach of privacy enshrined in article 8 does not of itself mean that the trial is unfair'.[84] The House of Lords therefore appeared impliedly to reassure itself that sufficiently high standards would be maintained by following *Schenk*. But the decision in *Schenk* in fact confirms that admitting evidence obtained from such a breach is within the margin of appreciation conceded to the national courts; it does not therefore confirm that a *domestic* practice of so doing meets internationally and nationally recognised standards of procedural justice.

There appears to be at present some judicial readiness to adopt the 'review' approach under the cloak of a domestic doctrine of deference. Signs of judicial adherence to this approach were found in *ex p Kebilene*.[85]

[81] See, for example, Mark Tushnet 'An Essay on Rights' (1984) 62(8) *Texas Law Review*.
[82] [1997] AC 558.
[83] (1988) 13 EHRR 242. See further Chapter 5 pp201–6.
[84] Ibid at p583 per Lord Nicholls.
[85] [1999] 3 WLR 172. See Chapter 3 pp103–107.

Lord Hope said: 'This technique [the margin of appreciation] is not available to the national courts when they are considering Convention issues arising within their own countries [but] . . . In some circumstances it will be appropriate for the courts to recognise that there is an area of judgement within which the judiciary will defer, on democratic grounds, to the considered opinion of [the democratic body or person] whose act or decision is said to be incompatible with the Convention.' In the context of the case, which concerned the compatibility of primary terrorist legislation with the Convention, these findings were used to justify a deferential approach. Indeed, they sought to introduce qualifications into a guarantee which on its face was unqualified. The term used by Lord Hope to describe the area in which choices between individual rights and societal interests might arise was 'the discretionary area of judgement';[86] he found that it would be easier for such an area of judgment to be recognised 'where the Convention itself requires a balance to be struck, much less so where the right [as in Article 6(2)] is stated in terms which are unqualified . . . But even where the right is stated in [such] terms . . . the courts will need to bear in mind the jurisprudence of the European Court which recognises that due account should be taken of the special nature of terrorist crime and the threat which it poses to a democratic society.'[87] In support of his balancing approach Lord Hope referred to Lord Woolf's findings in *Attorney-General of Hong Kong* v *Lee Kwong-kut*.[88] Lord Woolf considered the Canadian approach when applying the Canadian Charter of Rights and Freedoms, section 1 of which states that the rights and freedoms which it guarantees are: 'subject only to such reasonable limits prescribed by law as can be demonstrably justified in a free and democratic society'. He said: 'In a case where there is real difficulty, where the case is close to the borderline, regard can be had to the approach now developed by the Canadian courts in respect of section 1 of their Charter'.

The approach of Lord Hope towards the development of a broad domestic doctrine of deference was therefore based on a watering down of the Convention rights since a provision equivalent to s1 of the Charter was, as indicated above, omitted from the basic Convention rights under Articles 2–7. A somewhat similar approach was taken in *R* v *Chief Constable of Sussex ex parte International Ferry Traders Ltd*.[89] Lord Slynn, in a speech with which the other Law Lords agreed, found: 'the courts have long made it clear that . . . they will respect the margin of appreciation or

[86] First coined by D Pannick 'Principles of interpretation of Convention rights under the Human Right Act and the Discretionary Area of Judgement' (1998) PL 545, 549–551.

[87] He gave the example of the ruling of the Court in *Murray* v *United Kingdom* (1994) 19 EHRR 193, 222, para 47.

[88] [1993] AC 951, 966.

[89] [1999] 1 All ER 129. The decision was taken in the context of EC, not Convention, law but the principles referred to were the same.

discretion which a Chief Constable has', and in this instance that margin had not been exceeded. Lord Hoffman found: 'on the particular facts of this case the European concepts of proportionality and margin of appreciation produce the same result as what are commonly called *Wednesbury* principles . . . in this case I think that the Chief Constable must enjoy a margin of discretion that cannot differ according to whether its source be found in purely domestic principles or superimposed European principles'. In other words, it is possible to discover, as in *Kahn* and *Kebilene*[90] that traditional notions of deference to the executive and to Parliament may be coterminous and perhaps ought to be coterminous with the expression of the margin of appreciation doctrine, or that Strasbourg principles happen to yield the same result as *Wednesbury* ones.

This approach could be justified on the basis that a balance has always been struck in UK law between particular civil liberties and societal and other concerns by reference either to common law principle or Parliamentary restraint. In the particular context it is probable that that balance has been found to accord with the Convention at Strasbourg[91] (either in a specific or more general sense) even though the Convention was ratified by the UK 50 years ago, and therefore there is no reason to disturb it now. On this view the national legal system has already achieved the requisite balance within the margin it is allowed at Strasbourg. Having reviewed aspects of the balance struck by the national law, Strasbourg is satisfied with it and therefore it is necessary only to ensure that that margin is not exceeded in any particular instance.

The 'review' approach would provide a little more protection for human rights than would be provided under current judicial review principles, since the domestic courts will have to consider proportionality: an interference will be disproportionate where it goes beyond the aim in question or where little or no evidence of the need for it is advanced by the state. Where the Strasbourg jurisprudence allows different views to be taken of the need for a particular restriction, a domestic court fully applying it, including its margin of appreciation aspects, would tend to defer to the judgment of the executive. Clearly, this approach is distinguishable from that of heightened *Wednesbury* unreasonableness[92] but it would often lead to the same outcome.[93] This approach would be most problematic where it was confronted by a clearly analogous decision at Strasbourg adopting a stance opposed to the previous general trend of

[90] [1999] 3 WLR 172; discussed below and in Chapter 3 pp103–107.

[91] For example, in the public order and freedom of assembly context this could be said, in a broad sense: see Chapter 4 pp129–130.

[92] See *R* v *Secretary of State for Defence ex parte Lustig-Prean, Smith and Others* [1996] 1 All ER 257, 263.

[93] It might collapse into it if, in effect, a general test of 'reasonableness' rather than necessity and proportionality is adopted as Beatty suggests it has been in Canada under the Charter: see 'The Canadian Charter of Rights: Lessons and Laments' 60 MLR 481 at p493.

UK law.[94] This will not arise very frequently, as this book indicates, but the example of *Saunders* v *UK*[95] discussed more fully in Chapter 7,[96] comes to mind. Following *Saunders*, if a penalty formally attaches to silence in questioning by police, or other analogous bodies, and the coerced statements are then used in evidence, a breach of Article 6 is almost bound to occur. S172 of the Road Traffic Act (RTA) 1988 makes it an offence for motorists not to tell police who was driving their vehicle at the time of an alleged offence. The coerced statement can then be used in evidence at trial for the RTA offence in question. As a result of the domestic application of *Saunders*, s172 has already been rendered virtually nugatory in *Brown*[97] in Scotland, but this may have been due to the different arrangements there for the reception of the Convention[98] which made such a result more readily achievable. Now that the HRA is fully in force, a court could rely, in a case analogous to *Brown*, on s6(2)(b) HRA, discussed further below, which provides that where primary legislation is incompatible with the Convention rights a public authority (the court) can act incompatibly with the Convention if it 'is acting so as to give effect to or enforce those provisions'. One possibility, which would seem to be in accordance with s3 HRA and would not breach s6(2)(b), would be to exclude the evidence under s78 of the Police and Criminal Evidence Act on the basis that admitting it would breach Article 6. Without considering all the arguments on this matter, it can be said that such exclusion would be unlikely to recommend itself under this approach since it would be opposed to the general trend of UK law, as the decision in *Kahn* itself indicated, unless the coerced statement could be viewed as an involuntary admission.[99]

Three further courses are available which would be more in accord with a minimalist stance. A court could rely on s6(2)(b) and simply give effect to s172 RTA, regardless of the requirements of Article 6 as indicated in *Saunders*. In the circumstances envisaged, that is what the HRA may allow. It would of course have the unpalatable effects of convicting a person in breach of Convention standards and inviting an application to Strasbourg. A variant of this approach would be to find a means of distinguishing the RTA case in the particular circumstances, from *Saunders*. Reliance on s6(2)(b) would still be necessary, on the assumption that the legislation itself is incompatible. A further possibility would be to find a

[94] This occurred in *Osman* v *UK* (2000) 29 EHRR 245. In criticising the Strasbourg decision, Lord Hoffman has made it clear that he views the House of Lords as having a limited role in adjudicating on human rights issues: 'Human Rights and the House of Lords' [1999] 62(2) MLR 159, 161.

[95] (1997) 23 EHRR 313; No 19187/91.

[96] See pp281–282.

[97] *Brown* v *Procurator Fiscal* (2000) see Guardian News Report 9 February 2000 and [2000] 5(2) J.CIV.LIB 193.

[98] Under the Scotland Act s57.

[99] See further Chapter 5 pp202–203, 206.

means of distinguishing s172 from s437 of the Companies Act 1985, the provision at issue in *Saunders*, and then to argue that s172 does not create incompatibility, in which case it would not be necessary to rely on s6(2)(b). But perhaps the most attractive course for the determined minimalist would be to argue that Article 6 *itself* does not expressly require that coerced statements should be excluded from evidence. The obligation under s6 HRA applies only to the guarantees themselves, not to the jurisprudence, which need only be taken into account under s2. Having taken *Saunders* into account it could then be disapplied, possibly by distinguishing it on the facts, or on the basis of distinctions between the purposes underlying the two statutes in question. S172 of the RTA could be seen as satisfying a more pressing social need in curbing traffic accidents.

The 'traditionalist' model

A further approach, which may be termed 'traditionalist', would, it is contended, show, in certain contexts, strong differences from the minimalist one. The terminology adopted relies on the Diceyan notion that the common law recognises and upholds fundamental human rights and that therefore an approach which at times takes an activist stance towards such rights is in accordance with UK legal tradition. Such an approach may be found in *Derbyshire CC* v *Times Newspapers*[100] in which it was found that local (or central) government cannot sue for libel. In the House of Lords Lord Keith said, 'I find it satisfactory to be able to conclude that the common law of England is consistent with the [freedom of expression] obligations assumed under [the Convention]'.[101] Butler-Sloss LJ said in the Court of Appeal: 'I can see no inconsistency between English law upon this subject and Article 10 . . . This is scarcely surprising, since we may pride ourselves on the fact that freedom of speech has existed in this country perhaps as long, if not longer than . . . in any other country in the world'.[102] S3 of the HRA is prefigured in certain judicial review decisions that have recognised common law rights which cannot be abrogated except by express words or necessary implication – where there is only one way of reading the legislation in question. These include, so far, the rights of access to the courts,[103] to free speech,[104] and to life.[105] In identifying common law traditions of upholding fundamental rights,

[100] [1993] AC 534.
[101] Ibid at p551.
[102] [1992] 3 WLR 28 at p60.
[103] *R* v *Lord Chancellor ex parte Witham* [1998] QB 575.
[104] *R* v *Secretary of State for the Home Dept ex p Simms* [1999] 3 All ER 400.
[105] *R* v *Secretary of State for Social Security ex p Joint Council of Welfare of Immigrants* [1996] 4 All ER 835.

therefore, academic lawyers would look to such decisions rather than to those of more minimalist judges.[106]

The traditionalist approach would therefore underpin trends in decision-making that would not always be coterminous with those arising under the minimalist approach, which might, albeit without acknowledging it, follow more readily the contours of the margin of appreciation doctrine. This approach might take a more rights-affirming stance than Strasbourg in certain *selected* contexts since common law traditions of deference were particularly apparent only in certain areas of executive decision-making, areas which do not fully coincide with areas covered by the margin of appreciation doctrine.[107] Where Strasbourg activism coincided with common law activism this approach would lead to greater protection for rights, not least because the traditionalist would derive reassurance from the Convention underpinning provided for the preferred approach. S11 of the HRA affords recognition to the protection for fundamental rights already achieved under the common law, in providing that reliance on a Convention right does not restrict existing rights or freedoms, or a person's right to make any claim 'which he could make or bring apart from ss7–9'. This provision may have great significance in certain contexts.[108]

But where common law tradition had diverged from Strasbourg in developing in a *less* rights-oriented manner, the traditionalist might seek for a means of remaining within it. Thus a more interventionist approach to the exercise of rights of political expression would not preclude a deferential approach to matters which the executive might be viewed, traditionally, as peculiarly well placed to determine.[109] Following this approach a court would refuse to apply the margin of appreciation doctrine and yet would adopt a restrained stance in some circumstances. The court following notions of common law restraint expressed in a manner similar to the *Kebilene* 'area of discretionary judgement' doctrine might find that it could afford a limited interpretation to Strasbourg decisions if to do so would be in accordance with common law tradition. Obvious examples in which this stance might be taken are in respect of the exclusion of improperly or illegally obtained non-confession evidence, where

[106] Examples of such non-rights-based decisions discussed in this book which in the view of the writer could be called 'minimalist' include: the Divisional Court decisions in *DPP* v *Jones and Lloyd* v *DPP* [1997] 2 All ER 119, *DPP* v *Moseley, Woodling and Selvanayagam* Judgment of 9 June 1999; reported [1999] J.Civ.Lib 390 (Chapter 4 p149 and p167, respectively); *Chalkley* [1998] 2 Cr App R 79 (Chapter 5 p199).

[107] For example, the decision of *R* v *Samuel* [1988] QB 615 on exclusion of evidence may be viewed as more 'activist' than the decision in the same context at Strasbourg in *Schenk* v *Switzerland* A 140 (1988).

[108] Where statutory provisions seek to curb reliance on s7 HRA in the ordinary courts, s11 may have a countering effect. See Chapter 3 p88 for discussion and Chapter 10 p409.

[109] On this point see, further, D Pannick 'Principles of interpretation of Convention rights under the Human Right Act and the Discretionary Area of Judgement' (1998) PL 545, 549–551.

the common law tradition may be termed 'amoral',[110] or in public protest decisions where the common law approach has not fully reflected the Convention since the focus of concern has been, broadly speaking, on proprietorial rather than protest rights.[111] Where Strasbourg and the rights themselves leave leeway to do so, and even perhaps where they do not, the traditionalist might in such contexts take a stance as narrow as that of the minimalist, although in other instances this approach might be indistinguishable from an activist one. Ultimately, if the traditionalist is open, under the HRA, to the infusion of Strasbourg jurisprudence, together with jurisprudence from other jurisdictions, into the common law, this approach may merge with an activist one. This is the most probable course and the most desirable in that it would recognise and promote common law strengths, while at the same time revivifying them.

The 'activist' model

A further possible approach would be to adopt a more intrusive jurisdiction. This approach might be termed 'activist' in the sense that it would tend to lead to greater interference with executive decision-making, and would depart, to an extent, from common law tradition in so doing. It would tend to require consideration to be given primarily to the principles developed at Strasbourg for the interpretation of the Convention rights, rather than following specific decisions, whether as to admissibility or otherwise. But, in contrast to Lord Hope's approach in *ex p Kebilene*, it would use such principles to enhance rather than constrain the utilisation of the rights.[112]

Strasbourg has found that the purpose of the Convention is to 'maintain and promote the ideals and values of a democratic society'[113] which include tolerance of views offensive to the majority,[114] and to provide 'rights that are practical and effective' rather than 'rights that are theoretical

[110] M Zander *The Police and Criminal Evidence Act 1984* 3rd edn (1995) at p236. See further Chapter 5 pp202–203.

[111] See Gray and Gray 'Civil Rights, Civil Wrongs and Quasi-Public Places' [1999] 1 EHRLR 46, and see further Chapter 4 pp158–160.

[112] Such an approach was evident in the Divisional Court in *R* v *DPP ex p Kebilene* [1999] 3 WLR 175. The Lord Chief Justice, Lord Bingham, found that the provisions in question undermined the presumption of innocence under Article 6(2) 'in a blatant and obvious way' owing to the use of presumptions and the possibility of conviction on reasonable suspicion falling short of proof under s16A PTA, as amended. See further Chapter 3 p103.

[113] *Kjeldsen* v *Denmark* (1976) 1 EHRR 711, 731; see also the comments of the Court in *Socialist Party* v *Turkey* (1998) Case 20/1997/804/1007 (1999) 27 EHRR 51 as to the need for pluralism in a democracy.

[114] In *Handyside* v *UK* 1 EHRR 737 para 49 (1976) the Court said: '[Article 10] . . . is applicable not only to "information" or "ideas" that are favourably received or regarded as inoffensive . . . , but also to those which offend, shock or disturb the State or any sector of the population. Such are the demands of that pluralism, tolerance and broadmindedness without which there is no "democratic society"'.

or illusory'.[115] These concepts have not always found expression in practice, partly because of the diluting effect of the margin of appreciation doctrine. But in support of the 'activist' approach it might be pointed out that much of the more deferential Strasbourg jurisprudence is very heavily influenced by decisions of the Commission, which, as indicated above, is not a fully judicial body[116] and therefore has less authority than the Court. It would be in accordance with Strasbourg principles to have regard to the balance struck between individual rights and societal interest in other European courts, and perhaps also to that struck by the International Covenant on Civil and Political Rights and in other jurisdictions, including the USA or Canada. By so doing it might be possible to determine what the outcome of a decision at Strasbourg would have been had a lesser or no margin been conceded to the state. Human rights jurisprudence from other jurisdictions will clearly prove very valuable where the Strasbourg jurisprudence is exiguous, which is frequently the case. Indeed, the domestic courts are already showing a willingness to take such jurisprudence into account.[117] Thus activism would occur in accordance with a synthesis of Strasbourg and national Constitutional principles. As D Beatty puts it, 'the same set of principles and analytical framework . . . are used by [the judiciary] in Washington, Tokyo, New Delhi, Strasbourg, Rome, Karlsruhe . . . [principles] which lie at the core of the concept of constitutional rights that allow judges to act out their role as guardians of the constitution in an objective, determinate and ultimately very democratic way'.[118]

A national court which afforded *greater* protection to the substantive rights would never exceed the margin conceded to the state unless two fundamental Convention rights came into conflict. The rejection in the Lords during debate on the Human Rights Bill of a Conservative amendment which would have required that the Strasbourg jurisprudence should be binding on the UK courts also lends support to this argument. In rejecting the amendment the government spokesperson, the Lord Chancellor, implied that the possibility would thereby be left open of applying higher standards than those applied at Strasbourg.[119] A further Conservative amendment to the Bill, which was also rejected, sought to ensure that the domestic judiciary would be obliged to adhere to the margin of appreciation doctrine in interpreting and applying the Convention. Any

[115] *Airey* v *Ireland* (1979) 2 EHRR 305, 314.

[116] At pp20–21.

[117] In *Albert Reynolds* v *Times Newspapers and others* [1999] 4 All ER 609 the House of Lords took into account authorities from Canada, Australia and New Zealand, although in this instance they found that the Strasbourg jurisprudence was more influential.

[118] 'The Canadian Charter of Rights: Lessons and Laments' D Beatty [1997] 60 (4) MLR 481 at p481. This assertion of judicial objectivity would of course be attacked in certain quarters: see R Unger *The Critical Legal Studies Movement* (1986).

[119] 'The Bill would of course permit UK courts to depart from existing Strasbourg decisions and upon occasion it might well be appropriate to do so and it is possible they might give a successful lead to Strasbourg.' HL Debs 18 November 1997 col 514.

domestic judge uncertain whether to disregard a Commission decision on admissibility or a deferential decision of the Court would therefore be able to find some justification under the *Pepper* v *Hart*[120] doctrine for so doing.

The rejection of these two amendments suggests that the legislation is not intended to place the judiciary under an obligation to afford greater weight to the Convention rights than Strasbourg has previously required, but that they are afforded a discretion to do so. It follows, it may be argued, that this approach would allow the HRA to recognise the difference between the roles of a national and an international court, and in particular the need for the latter but not the former to take common European standards into account.

However, before accepting that activism is necessary in order to realise the full benefits of the Convention, it is essential to consider both what activism means and what its effects may be. The main concern of this book is with vertical effects in the classic arenas of state power and therefore it avoids the most problematic issues since activism is usually welcomed by most commentators in such arenas.[121] Indeed, as indicated in Chapter 1, some, although by no means all, commentators look to the HRA as a means of undoing the effects in such contexts of years of untrammelled Parliamentary sovereignty.[122] As this book indicates, especially in relation to state surveillance in Chapters 9 and 10, counter-terrorist measures in Chapter 3, the security and intelligence services in Chapter 8, and public order measures in Chapter 4, such effects are readily evident. But unbridled judicial activism might have less desirable effects in other contexts and it is therefore necessary to explain the liberal democratic version of activism which is being advocated. The example of abortion was used by the Lord Chancellor in Parliamentary debate in order to illustrate the possibilities which might arise. If activism was simply taken to mean a requirement to 'read up' the Convention rights and if necessary to 'read down' the domestic statute, the ideological views of particular judges might be given expression by means of the HRA. This could mean affording the Abortion Act 1967 as amended a very restrictive interpretation (which would not be difficult given its apparently limited application) and reading up the right to life under Article 2. The government would probably subsequently bring forward legislation to restore the broader application of the Act[123] but there might be a period of time during which

[120] [1993] AC 593; [1993] 1 All ER 42.

[121] See, for example, K Ewing and C Gearty *Freedom under Thatcher* (1989).

[122] See Chapter 1 p1, note 4. Some commentators, however, continue to view the allocation of any further power to the judiciary as a dangerous step and therefore consider that the protection of civil liberties should be left to Parliament; see J Griffiths 'The Brave New World of Sir John Laws' [2000] March MLR 159.

[123] It may be noted that if the government brought forward such legislation it would not need to issue a declaration of incompatibility (although it might be safer to do so to protect the legislation) since it would be overruling a precedent of the House of Lords, not the Convention guarantees themselves.

the social effects of the judgment were strongly apparent, bearing especially on women.

Adoption of such a stance would not, however, be warranted since this would be an instance in which, it is argued, the principles underlying and justifying activism would not be engaged. At Strasbourg Article 2 does not prevent abortion since the Commission has declined to find that the foetus is protected.[124] This is not an instance where it could readily be said that had Strasbourg refused to show deference to the member state it would have decided differently in the relevant decisions. The stance adopted, which allowed a wide margin of appreciation, appeared to be taken partly because in those decisions a conflict of rights, between Articles 8 and 2, arose. Where there is such a conflict it may be appropriate to look at the principles underlying them (as in the apparent clash between privacy and press freedom)[125] in an effort to resolve the conflict at the level of principle, but where the underlying principles are probably entirely opposed, as in this instance, it would be incumbent on the judiciary to defer to Parliament since refusing to do so would mean making a moral choice in an area of irreconcilable conflict. The proper role of activism is to uphold individual rights in the face of state interference or state neglect of the right, not to substitute judicial for state interference, in intruding on rights, even in the name of upholding competing rights. Judicial activism is justified where it results in an enhancement of the fairness and justice of public policy-making, rendering public authorities accountable by reference to Constitutional principle.[126] It is unjustified as a means of imposing particular views of morality on individuals. As Sir John Laws puts it, that is a matter 'upon which the judges have no special voice'.[127]

A further fear frequently expressed is that activism may seek to constrain the exercise of state power used in order to serve collective ends.[128] As Chapter 1 indicates, the Convention, as a deeply ideological document, may be viewed as elevating individualistic, atomistic goals over socialist collective ones,[129] although the jurisprudence does not provide many

[124] *Paton* v *UK* (1980) 3 EHRR 408; *H* v *Norway* No 17004/90 (1992) unrep.

[125] See C Emerson 'The Right to Privacy and the Freedom of the Press' (1979) 14 (2) Harvard Civil Rights–Civil Liberties Law Review 329 esp at p331. See further H Fenwick and G Phillipson 'The Doctrine of Confidence as a Privacy Remedy in the Human Rights Act Era' [2000] 63(5) MLR 660–693.

[126] See D Feldman 'The Human Rights Act and Constitutional Principles' (1999) 19 (2) LS 165; Sir John Laws 'The Limitations of Human Rights' [1998] PL 254.

[127] Sir John Laws ibid. For the view that the judiciary, and Sir John Laws in particular, are, in effect, claiming the power to determine moral and political matters see Griffiths 'The Brave New World of Sir John Laws' [2000] 63(2) MLR 159.

[128] For example, to effect the abolition of grammar schools with a view to enhancing choice for a wider range of pupils. As is well known the US Supreme Court in the 1920s and 1930s used the Bill of Rights to strike down progressive employment legislation resulting from the New Deal.

[129] See Ewing and Gearty 'Rocky Foundations for Labour's New Rights' (1997) EHRLR 149, but cf D Feldman 'The Human Rights Act and Constitutional Principles' (1999) 19 (2)

examples of denial of such goals. An activist approach to it might merely be seen as exacerbating this tendency. The judiciary in other jurisdictions has often pursued what may be termed a differentiated activist approach; it may have appeared to be activist in areas with which it had sympathy but deferential in areas with which it did not, such as trade unionism.[130] Differentiated activism may merely mean arbitrary activism. However, it may be argued that the Convention recognises collective values in the sense of seeking to underpin the democratic process and of affording recognition to a wide range of public interests under para 2 of Articles 8–11. An activist judge should therefore seek to give such values full effect as key aspects of the underlying Strasbourg principles.[131] In so far as an irresolvable conflict between individualism and collectivism may nevertheless arise,[132] it is suggested that where the matter in question is one which involves a clash of moral principles *and* the judiciary is not well placed to assess the social and economic implications of the choice, the issue may be seen as falling within a discretionary area of judgment. This would be a much narrower area than that indicated by Lord Hope, by the margin of appreciation doctrine or by traditional common law deference, which, as indicated, tended in certain contexts to allow abrogation of fundamental rights. It would perhaps allow the boundaries of permissible activism to be delineated with reasonable clarity while still affording efficacy to the rights.[133]

The HRA itself clearly represents a choice as to the responsibility for resolving moral and political issues. Under it judicial activism has limits; a government determined to advance collectivist goals can do so through primary legislation which cannot be struck down by the judiciary under the Act, while the response to a finding that legislation is incompatible with the Convention is in executive and Parliamentary hands. This is due to the determination to preserve Parliamentary sovereignty under the Act, which is discussed below. The other side of this coin is of course that a government determined to push through classic civil-rights-abiding legislation, such as the Terrorism Act 2000, can also succeed in doing so. These dual and conflicting aspects of judicial activism and of sovereignty arise from the attempt to reconcile conflicting Constitutional aims which lies at the heart of the HRA.

LS 165 at pp173–178; see also Review by G Phillipson (1998) PL 538 of F Dobson's chapter 'Can the Common Law Really Protect Rights?' in Leyland and Woods (eds) *Administrative Law Facing the Future* (1998) Blackstones.

[130] See, for example, *Re Public Service Employee Relations Act* [1987] 1 SCR 313.

[131] See further Chapter 4 p120 and p170. See also D Feldman ibid note 129 at pp173–176; A Mowbray 'The Role of the European Court of Human Rights in the promotion of democracy' [1999] Winter PL 703.

[132] See *Young, James and Webster* v *UK* (1981) 4 EHRR 38.

[133] This approach appears to be in accord with that originally put forward by D Pannick in 'Principles of interpretation of Convention rights under the Human Rights Act and the Discretionary Area of Judgement' (1998) PL 545, 549–551.

The Constitutional status of the Convention under the HRA

As indicated, the choice made in determining the Constitutional status of Bills or Charters of Rights is a political one. Such instruments may be afforded (or may acquire) some special protection from express or implied repeal which may at its highest involve their entrenchment. In Germany, for example, no method of repealing parts of the German Basic Law is provided. In the USA the amendments to the Constitution cannot be amended without a two-thirds majority in Congress. The model chosen in the USA and the response of the US Supreme Court is generally viewed as representing the triumph of liberal individualism over socialism.[134] The model chosen in order to give the Convention further effect in domestic law seeks, as indicated above, to reconcile a transfer of power to the judiciary with Parliamentary sovereignty.[135] In contrast to the US model, it creates a more subtle reallocation of power which, formally speaking, does not compromise Parliamentary sovereignty. Not only was the Convention given no special Constitutional status, in the sense of entrenchment, it was not simply incorporated into domestic law as a statute. The model utilised is based on the model adopted for the New Zealand Bill of Rights 1990, but there are subtle differences, which a number of commentators[136] view as positive and advantageous ones.

The devolution legislation places the Scottish Parliament and the Welsh Assembly in a different position. The Welsh Assembly is not able to pass primary legislation and it is bound by the Convention under s107(1) of the Government of Wales Act 1988. The Scottish Parliament cannot act incompatibly with the Convention under s29(2)(d) Scotland Act 1998. The executive and law officers in Scotland are also bound.[137] But under s3 HRA any primary legislation within the reserved areas[138] passed by the Westminster Parliament and applicable to Scotland and Wales will be binding, even if it is not compatible with the Convention. These arrangements mean that Scotland has, in effect, a Bill of Rights in the traditional sense since the Parliament is bound by the Convention and

[134] The phrase was used by Ewing and Gearty of the HRA in 'Rocky Foundations for Labour's New Rights' (1997) EHRLR 149. On anti-collectivist decisions of the US Supreme Court see B L Strayer 'Life under the Canadian Charter' [1988] PL 347 at pp366–367.

[135] See further K Ewing 'The Human Rights Act and Parliamentary Democracy' [1999] 62(1) MLR 79.

[136] See, for example, D Feldman ibid note 129, above, at p180; F Bennion 'What interpretation is possible under s3(1) HRA?' [2000] PL 77. Cf G Marshall 'Patriating Rights – with reservations: the Human Rights Bill' in University of Cambridge Centre for Public Law *Constitutional Reform in the UK: Practice and Principles* (1998) Chap 8 p76.

[137] See Scotland Act s57. Thus in Scotland and Wales the Convention became binding from 1 July 1999, when the devolution legislation came into force, over a year before the HRA came fully into force.

[138] S29(2)(b) of the Scotland Act 1988 and Schedule 5, and Schedule 2 of the Government of Wales Act 1988.

therefore cannot pass primary legislation which conflicts with it. The references to 'legislation', below, are to legislation emanating from the Westminster Parliament.

In one respect the Convention has a lower status than pre-existing law since it cannot impliedly repeal other statutes. But under s3 HRA the judiciary is placed under an obligation to ensure that primary and subordinate legislation is compatible with the Convention rights 'so far as it is possible to do so'. If it is not possible to do so the court must merely apply the primary legislation under s3(2)(b) or the subordinate legislation if 'primary legislation prevents the removal of the incompatibility' under s3(2)(c). These provisions preserve not only Parliamentary but executive power since they allow Orders in Council as well as primary legislation to override the Convention.[139]

But s3 creates a very strong interpretative obligation. It goes well beyond resolving ambiguity in statutory provisions by adopting the Convention-based interpretation which was already occurring in the pre-HRA era.[140] Lord Lester has observed, on this point: 'Would [the courts use the incorporating measures] to go much further than the traditional position in which the courts seek to interpret ambiguous legislation so as to be in accordance with rather than breach treaty obligations undertaken by the UK? I hope and believe that they would indeed do so.'[141] S3 appears to place the judiciary under an obligation to render legislation compatible with the Convention if there is any loophole at all allowing it to do so, even if this means departing from precedent, twisting to an extent the natural meaning of the statutory words, or reading words into the statute. As Lord Irvine puts it, the courts will be expected to use 'strong interpretative techniques' which may include 'the implication of appropriate language into an apparently unambiguous provision'.[142] The Home Secretary, however, said at the Committee stage of the Bill in the Commons: 'It is not our intention that the courts . . . should contort the meaning of words to produce implausible or incredible meanings'.[143] In other words, the judiciary is being asked to adopt an activist approach which will not rely, as in the past, on carrying out Parliament's presumed intention as encapsulated in other, prior legislation. The position will differ as regards prior and subsequent legislation. Prior legislation passed after 1950 may be subject to a 'legislative intention plus compatible construction rule'[144]

[139] Under s21(1)(f)(i) the term 'primary legislation' includes Orders in Council.

[140] See *AG* v *BBC* [1981] AC 303, 354; *Derbyshire CC* v *Times Newspapers Ltd* [1993] AC 534.

[141] 'First Steps Towards A Constitutional Bill of Rights' (1997) 2 EHRLR 124 at p127. On similar lines Lord Cooke argues: 'The Act could become a dead letter if the canon of interpretation laid down by s3(1) were not followed in spirit' [1999] EHRLR 243 at p256.

[142] 'The Development of Human Rights in Britain under an Incorporated Convention on Human Rights' Lord Irvine of Lairg [1998] PL 221 at p228; cf G Marshall 'Two kinds of compatibility: more about s3 of the HRA 1998' [1999] P 377.

[143] HC 3 June 1998 col 421.

[144] See F Bennion 'What interpretation is possible under s3(1) HRA?' [2000] PL 77.

while subsequent legislation may be subject only to the legislative intention rule since it may be presumed that Parliament will already have sought to bring it into conformity with the Convention, especially as it is likely to be accompanied by a statement of its compatibility under s19. It has been argued that therefore a purposive construction, based on the Dworkinian view of law as integrity, will be adopted.[145] Such a construction would be fully in keeping with an activist approach to the Convention. Possibly, the inability of the Convention to effect implied repeal will not therefore prove to have a significant inhibiting effect on its impact.

The interpretative obligation is arguably rendered stronger in respect of subsequent legislation under s19, a provision which bears some similarity to a 'notwithstanding' clause, on the Canadian model.[146] When a minister introduces a Bill into either House of Parliament he or she must make and publish a written statement to the effect either that in his or her view the provisions of the Bill are compatible with the Convention rights, or that although unable to make such a statement the government wishes nevertheless to proceed with the Bill.[147] Use of the latter statement would be bound to cause political embarrassment and, almost certainly, successful applications to Strasbourg. It is therefore likely to be a very rare occurrence, probably arising only in time of war or national emergency.

The status of a statement of compatibility is not entirely clear since it is not part of the statute it accompanies, but the courts will probably see it as evidence of Parliament's intention. Therefore if a minister makes a statement to the effect that the legislation is compatible with the Convention, but subsequently it appears that there is incompatibility, the judiciary would be likely to do its utmost to ensure compatibility, especially where Parliamentary debate had proceeded on the assumption that the Bill was indeed compatible. The judiciary could be said to be under a dual adjuration to do so, arising from both s3 and the statement. It may be noted that the Terrorism Act 2000 was accompanied by a statement of compatibility made by the Home Secretary, Jack Straw, although, as Chapter 3 argues, it contains a number of provisions of doubtful compatibility. This was pointed out by the Liberal Democrats' spokesman, Simon Hughes MP, at the second reading of the Bill, although since the amendments he put forward intended to ensure such compatibility were defeated, the majority view may be taken to have been that compatibility had already been achieved.[148] The obligation to ensure compatibility will therefore be very strong in respect of such provisions.

[145] Ibid note 144.

[146] Under this model legislation can include a clause stating 'this statute is to be given effect notwithstanding the provisions of the Canadian Charter'. This is the model favoured by Sir William Wade 'The United Kingdom's Bill of Rights' in University of Cambridge Centre for Public Law *Constitutional Reform in the UK: Practice and Principles* (1998) Chap 6 p65.

[147] S19 came into force under Commencement Order 1998 SI No 2882.

[148] HC Debs 15 March 2000 col 368.

If a court is unable to ensure compatibility it can, if of sufficient authority,[149] make a declaration of incompatibility under s4. Under s5(1) when a court is considering making a declaration the Crown must be given notice so that it can, under s5(2), intervene by being joined as a party to the proceedings. S3 provides that the interpretative obligation does not affect the validity, continuing operation or enforcement of any incompatible primary legislation, and this is equally the case under s4(6) if a declaration of incompatibility is made. S4 may seem to come close to allowing an infringement of Parliamentary sovereignty since, 'For the first time Parliament has invited the judges to tell it that it has acted wrongly by legislating incompatibly with a Convention right'.[150] But the court is not informing Parliament that it has acted *unlawfully*, since, as explained below, Parliament is not bound by the Convention.

If a declaration is made s10 will apply which, in a departure from the New Zealand scheme, allows a minister to make amendments to the offending legislation by means of the so-called 'fast track' procedure. S10 may also be used where a decision of the European Court of Human Rights suggests that a provision of legislation is incompatible with the Convention. Therefore campaigning groups could lobby government to make amendments under s10 following any such decision. However, the minister is under no obligation to make the amendment(s) and may only do so if there are 'compelling reasons'. In other words, the fact that a declaration of incompatibility has been made will not in itself provide a compelling reason.

Schedule 2 provides two procedures for making a 'remedial order' which must, under s20, be in the form of a statutory instrument. Sch 2 para 2(a) and para 3 provide for a standard procedure whereby the minister must lay a draft of the Order before Parliament, together with the required information – an explanation of the incompatibility and a statement of the reasons for proceeding under s10 – for at least 60 days, during which time representations can be made to the minister. It must then be laid before Parliament again and does not come into effect until it is approved by a resolution of each House within 60 days after it has been laid for the second time. The emergency procedure under sch 2 para 2(b) and para 4 follows the same route, apart from the very significant provision for allowing the minister to make the Order before laying it before Parliament. Thus, the amendment can be made outside the full Parliamentary process which would be required for primary legislation, but otherwise the responsibility for amending primary legislation remains

[149] S4(5) provides that this applies to the House of Lords, the Judicial Committee of the Privy Council, the Courts-Martial Appeal Court; in Scotland the High Court of Justiciary sitting otherwise than a trial court, or the Court of Session; in England and Wales the High Court or the Court of Appeal.

[150] D Feldman 'The Human Rights Act and Constitutional Principles' (1999) 19 (2) LS 165 at p187.

firmly in Parliamentary hands retaining 'Parliament's authority in the legislative process'.[151]

These arrangements mean that the HRA itself is subject to express and implied repeal. But the Act is likely to acquire such a high iconic status as a symbol of the UK's commitment to human rights that its express repeal or repeal of significant parts of it will probably become increasingly unlikely. Arguably the Act of Union with Scotland 1706 and the European Communities Act 1972 provide precedents. Implied repeal will remain, theoretically, a possibility. The Convention itself appears to be subject to express repeal, but also, highly significantly, to have a higher status than a statute in that it is not subject to implied repeal. This is implicit in the procedure under s4. If Parliament passed any incompatible legislation, although accompanied by a statement of compatibility, or a court found that prior legislation was incompatible, it would be expected that the Convention guarantee would be impliedly repealed, under the normal convention regarding subsequent legislation and, as regards the prior legislation, due to the special status of the Convention. But it is not envisaged that this would occur under the HRA since otherwise the s4 procedure would be redundant: the Convention right would have been repealed impliedly to the extent of its incompatibility which could not therefore be declared.

If legislation is found to be incompatible in a lower court, it remains valid; there would be a period of time, whether or not a declaration of incompatibility was subsequently made, during which the Convention provision in question could be utilised in respect of other relevant non-incompatible provisions. Indeed, the HRA leaves open the possibility of finding compatibility in respect of the incompatible provision itself since it could be revisited in a subsequent suitable case. In other words, a different court might take a different view on incompatibility. Possibly in so doing it might be aided by jurisprudential developments occurring at Strasbourg, after the initial finding of incompatibility. If in such circumstances compatibility could not, however, be achieved, the provision could nevertheless be viewed as a source of principle, until and if compatibility was achieved via the ss4 and 10 procedure. It would not appear to suffer a diminution of status except, to an extent, in relation to the incompatible legislative provision itself.

This would also appear to be the case where Parliament passes inconsistent legislation, accompanied by a statement that the minister wishes to proceed with it despite being unable to make a statement of compatibility. A court faced with this apparently contradictory adjuration – the s3 obligation in the face of such a statement – should follow s3 in striving to render the legislative provision compatible with the Convention right

[151] K Ewing 'The Human Rights Act and Parliamentary Democracy' [1999] 62(1) MLR 79 at p93.

in question. Ministers may underestimate the powers of judges to find compatibility, just as they may overestimate them when issuing a statement of compatibility under s19. S3 makes no mention of the approach which should be taken when a statement of compatibility is not made. Therefore, the s3 obligation would still apply in such circumstances, although the court might look to Parliamentary debate on the Bill in question for guidance as to Parliament's intention. If compatibility cannot in fact be achieved, the court should issue a declaration under s4, since the courts, not the executive, are the final arbiters as to the interpretation of legislation. Further, since the HRA applies to itself, adoption of this course would appear to satisfy the interpretative obligation under s3 in respect of ss4 and 19.

In terms of its Constitutional status, the Convention is therefore a chimera-like creature. It cannot impliedly repeal statutes, but it cannot itself be impliedly repealed. In this sense its status is the exact converse of that of the instrument receiving it into UK law. It provides guarantees to individuals which they may not be able to rely on, under s3, but which may continue to exist in a form of limbo, as principles, perhaps indefinitely. The litigant who can show that his or her rights have been violated owing to primary legislation will lose the case, gaining only the 'booby prize'[152] of a declaration of incompatibility. The external status of an incompatible guarantee as a rule would be held in abeyance, or no longer figure as a rule in the legal system but, in Dworkinian terms, its internal character as a bundle of principles would be unchanged.[153] The Convention is intended to leave Parliamentary sovereignty intact and yet it asks judges to depart from clear statutory words, laying upon them, in relation to virtually all statutes passed from 2000 onwards, a dual adjuration to do.

In conscientiously seeking to fulfil the interpretative obligation a court might unwittingly adopt a minimalist interpretation in 'reading down' the rights, as Lord Hope seemed poised to do in *ex p Kebilene*, rather than 'reading down' the domestic legislation, affording it a rights-based interpretation in order to find compatibility, as Lords Lester and Irvine advocate. Further, as the discussion of possible models above sought to indicate, the Convention guarantees are frequently elusive. Even a rights-minded court, seeking to impose an 'activist' interpretation on a legislative provision, might find that the Convention jurisprudence provides no firm anchor for so doing. Examples of uncertainty are scattered throughout this book and at present they are beginning to emerge in Parliament.[154]

[152] As Marshall puts it in 'Two kinds of compatibility: more about s3 of the HRA 1998' [1999] PL 377 at p382.

[153] See G Phillipson 'The Human Rights Act, "Horizontal Effect" and The Common Law: A Bang or a Whimper?' [1999] 62 MLR 824 at p831.

[154] Simon Hughes proposed an amendment to cl 56 of the Terrorism Bill 2000, which went to a vote; it was overwhelmingly defeated by a combination of Labour and Conservative

Such lack of clarity renders the task of Parliament and the drafters of legislation even more formidable in placing an incompatible law on the statute book, one which will survive interpretation under s3. If that task comes to appear very burdensome without repeal of the Act or Convention, it may be argued that although formally Parliamentary sovereignty will remain intact, it will have suffered, *de facto*, a degree of compromise.

The other, more likely, possibility is that lack of precision will encourage the government to introduce legislation which complies with a minimal version of the Convention. And compliance may be achieved on the balance of probabilities, even in relation to such a version. The hallmark of the two pieces of legislation considered in this book which have been accompanied by statements of compatibility, the Terrorism Act 2000 and the Regulation of Investigatory Powers Act 2000, is that they raise profound questions about their compatibility. The task of the courts in 'reading up' Convention rights in relation to these two Acts, which are, it is argued, based on such a version of the Convention, forms one of the key themes in the following chapters.[155]

Obligations of public and private bodies

S6 of the HRA creates what may be viewed as an arbitrary division between public and private bodies. Bodies such as nursery schools which have little power, ability or desire to infringe human rights are covered, while corporate bodies, such as Shell or media oligopolies, which may have immense ability and means to do so, are not. Some bodies are bound in respect of certain functions but not others. In other words, there is an imperfect correlation between the rights-infringing ability of a body and the extent to which, if at all, it is bound by the Convention rights. These criticisms could be and are levelled at Bills of Rights in general on the basis that they identify the elected government as the enemy, not recognising that the elected government is the protector of the people, who need protection not from it but from massive multinational corporations.

But, contrary to this argument, when the elected government does act as the enemy in that it uses coercive state power arbitrarily against citizens through the medium of state agents, s6 does not necessarily provide a curb. The classic rights-infringing public authorities, in particular the security and intelligence services, may be formally but not substantively bound, as Chapter 8 indicates.

members. One of Hughes' arguments was that the clause was incompatible with Article 6 and he wanted to see the legal advice of the government on the point which apparently was to the effect that the two are compatible. The advice was not forthcoming. Compatibility will be left to be tested in the domestic courts and perhaps at Strasbourg.

155 See in particular Chapter 3 pp75–81 and Chapter 9 p344, respectively.

Public authorities

Under s6 Convention guarantees are binding only against public authorities. Under s6(3)(a) the term 'public authority' includes a court or tribunal, and under (b) 'any person certain of whose functions are functions of a public nature' but does not include Parliament 'or a person exercising functions in connection with proceedings in Parliament'. This refers to the Westminster Parliament; the Scottish Parliament and the Welsh Assembly will clearly be public authorities. Not only is the definition under s6(3)(b) non-exhaustive, it also leaves open room for much debate on the meaning of 'functions of a public nature'. Under s6(5) 'in relation to a particular act, a person is not a public authority by virtue only of s6(3)(b) if the nature of the act is private'. Thus, private bodies which cannot be brought within the definition are not bound by the guarantees, although this does not mean that they are entirely unaffected by them; see the discussion of 'horizontal effect' below. Quasi-public bodies are in the same position when acting in relation to their private as opposed to their public function. A GP, for example, would be exercising a public function in relation to NHS patients, a private one in relation to private patients.

S6 therefore creates two categories of body against which the Convention can be directly enforced: 'pure' public authorities which can never act privately, even in respect of matters governed by private law, such as employment relations, and quasi-public authorities which have a hybrid function. The third category, falling outside s6, contains private bodies which have no public function at all. 'Pure' public authorities include bodies which are self-evidently of a public nature, such as the police, government departments, local authorities, the security and intelligence services. Classic hybrid bodies include Railtrack, privatised water companies and other contracted-out services. 'Pure' private bodies would include individual citizens, newspapers and other private companies. These distinctions are clearly going to give rise to an enormous amount of litigation.

Obviously an exception had to be made under s6 in order to bring it into harmony with s3 and to realise the objective of preserving Parliamentary sovereignty, but it is argued that the method adopted may not fully succeed in so doing. S6(2) provides: 'sub-section(1) does not apply to an act if, (a) as the result of one or more provisions of primary legislation, the authority could not have acted differently; or (b) in the case of one or more provisions of, or made under, primary legislation which cannot be read or given effect in a way which is compatible with the Convention rights, the authority was acting so as to give effect to or enforce those provisions'. S6(2)(a) creates a strong obligation requiring public authorities to do their utmost to act compatibly. But it is not easy to reconcile s3 with s6(2)(b), especially where the authority is under a dual adjuration, as it will be, increasingly, in future. If s3 is applied to s6(2)(b), it would suggest that where an authority has a discretion to act to give effect to or enforce incompatible provisions, it should exercise its discretion against so doing, since otherwise it would not appear to satisfy s3. It may be noted that s6(2)(a) applies to primary legislation only, whereas s6(2)(b) applies also to subordinate legislation made under incompatible primary legislation. This is implicit in the use of the words 'or made under' used in the latter subsection but not the former.

The exception under s6 applies to statutes only. If a common law provision conflicts with the duty of a public body under s6, the duty will prevail. Therefore certain common law reforms under s6 may occur more readily: the limited meaning of 'victim' will still have some restrictive effect,[156] but no provision has been included in the Act allowing the common law to override the Convention or creating restrictions as to those courts which can find incompatibility between the two.

Bodies able to invoke Convention rights

Under s7(1) the Act allows a person who is (or would be) the victim of a breach of a Convention right by a public authority to bring proceedings against the authority or rely on the Convention in any legal proceedings. S7(7) provides: 'a person is a victim of an unlawful act only if he would be a victim for the purposes of Article 34 of the Convention if proceedings were brought in the European Court of Human Rights in respect of that act'. It was accepted in Parliament that the Strasbourg interpretation of 'victim' would be used, rather than the wider test for standing under judicial review domestic.[157] The UK group *Liberty* had argued for adoption of the latter as the test. Under the Strasbourg test, contained in Article 34, a person (or group or non-governmental organisation) may not bring an application unless he or she has been personally affected by the alleged violation.[158] This provision means that pressure groups cannot in general bring actions claiming breach of Convention rights. In particular it appears to mean that although such groups may currently be able to challenge public bodies by way of judicial review, on the test of 'sufficient interest' they will be unable to do so in reliance on Convention rights.[159]

In this respect, although the definition of the bodies covered under s6 is wide and brings a large number within its scope, the application of the Convention is narrowed by adopting quite a limited definition of a 'victim'. Since, as s11 makes clear, nothing prevents the raising of Convention points in judicial review applications based on the wider standing rules,

[156] Under S7(7), see below.

[157] See the ruling of Rose LJ in *Secretary of State for Foreign Affairs ex p the World Development Movement* [1995] 1 All ER 611, 618–620.

[158] *X* v *Austria* No 7045/75, 7 DR 87 (1976); *Knudsen* v *Norway* No 11045/84, 42 DR 247 (1985).

[159] S11 would bar the way to any narrowing of those rules.

pressure groups and others may be able to raise such points outside the HRA, but not within it. A court, bound by s6, confronted by a Convention issue in such an application, would have to consider whether to scrutinise proportionality or apply traditional review principles only. A common law of human rights – in some respects of a more protective nature – might continue to develop. A dual system of judicial review might arise, with stronger standing rules but weaker scrutiny, outside the HRA, while the reverse applied under s7(1).[160] In order to avoid such a development, which would be bound to create arbitrariness, the judiciary may be minded to break down distinctions between cases based on the s7(1) standing rules, and those outside them but raising Convention points, by relying on s6 once an application is in court. In other words, the old standing rules may eventually prevail.

From a different perspective, it may be said that the definition of both victims and public and quasi-public authorities does not allow the HRA to have an impact that correlates fully with the location of power in the UK. Where power exists it may be used in a manner which infringes human rights. But the HRA will be unable to address a number of instances of abuse of rights, while allowing certain powerful bodies to use it to enhance their power. For example, corporate media bodies may be able both to use the Act and to continue to rely on rights-based arguments for the enhancement of their power. The Act will not limit what has been termed 'the ability of corporate media giants to further their own commercial ends while acting in ways that run counter to maximising the provision of information upon which the claim is premised'.[161] In other words, certain powerful bodies may be able to use the Act for rights-abridging ends or in order to curb the expression of the values that underlie the Convention guarantees.

Invoking the Convention under s6

In the contexts covered by this book the Convention would frequently be invoked in criminal proceedings. In such instances the 'weak' position of certain groups in seeking to rely on the rights is not as relevant as it is in relation to other methods, in particular judicial review.[162] But the possibility of using judicial review arises, especially in the context of police powers, as indicated in Chapters 4, 5, 6 and 7 and 9. The practical limitations of judicial review in human rights matters are indicated below. But it should be pointed out here that, substantively speaking, some groups are

[160] See K Steyn and D Wolfe 'Judicial Review and the Human Rights Act: Some Practical Considerations' (1999) EHRR 614.

[161] See M Feintuck *Media Regulation, Public Interest and the Law* Part 1 Chap 3 (1999), Edinburgh University Press.

[162] See A McColgan *Women under the Law: The False Promise of Human Rights* (2000) Pearson Education.

virtually precluded from taking this course owing to its inaccessibility, the fact that judicial review may only be initiated in the High Court in London and the extent to which most solicitors/law centres or advisers on legal help-lines have awareness of the availability or appropriateness of such review in any particular instance.[163]

Formally speaking, then, there are a number of possible methods of using the Convention against a public authority or a hybrid body acting in its public capacity[164] under s7(1) which provides: 'A person who claims that a public authority has acted or proposes to act in a way which is made unlawful by s6(1) may (a) 'bring proceedings against the authority under this Act in the appropriate court or tribunal or (b) rely on the Convention right or rights concerned in any legal proceedings'. The individual could seek to bring judicial review proceedings under s7(1)(a). The ground of review would be on the basis of illegality in that the authority has breached s6.[165] The alternative ground would be *ultra vires* on the basis that once the legislation in question was interpreted compatibly with the Convention under s3 it did not give the authority the right to breach it as it has done.[166] It is also possible that proceedings could be brought for breach of statutory duty – the duty under s6. The possibility of creating what has been termed a 'constitutional tort' of breach of Convention rights has been left open by the HRA and by the Lord Chancellor in Parliamentary debate.[167] Other existing tort actions, such as false imprisonment, which are coterminous with Convention rights (in that instance, Article 5) could be brought against public authorities under s7(1)(b) with a view to expanding the scope of the action by reference to the right.[168] The possibilities presented by the use of tort actions are discussed at various points in this book, but most extensively in Chapter 5.[169] Under s7(1)(b) the Convention guarantees could afford a defence in criminal proceedings where it could be argued that a public authority had acted unlawfully under s6. They could also be used to afford a defence in civil proceedings where the plaintiff was a public authority.

If proceedings are brought against a public authority under s7(1)(a) they must brought, under s7(5), within one year 'beginning with the date on which the act complained of took place' or 'such longer period as the court or tribunal considers equitable having regard to all the circumstances, but that is subject to any rule imposing a stricter time limit

[163] See A P Le Sueur and M Sunkin *Public Law* (1997) Pearson Education, Chaps 21–28 esp Chap 21 'Access to Judicial Review'.

[164] The term 'public authority' will be used to encompass both types of body for the purposes of the rest of the discussion.

[165] See P Craig *Administrative Law* 4th edn (1999) pp556–9 London: Sweet and Maxwell.

[166] The approach adopted in *R* v *Lord Chancellor ex parte Witham* [1998] QB 575.

[167] HL Deb Vol 585 cols 853–856 24 November 1997.

[168] Such actions would also of course be available against purely private bodies. See further G Phillipson 'The Human Rights Act and The Common Law' [1999] 62 MLR 824 esp at pp834–840, and discussion below of horizontal effects. See also Bamforth [1999] CLJ 159.

[169] Pp194–197.

in relation to the procedure in question'. The implications of the time limits relating to s7(1)(a) proceedings are considered below. But they should be contrasted with the provision in respect of s7(1)(b), under s22(4)(b): 'para (b) [of s7(1)] applies to proceedings brought by or at the instigation of a public authority *whenever the act in question took place*; but otherwise that subsection does not apply to an act taking place before the coming into force of that section' (emphasis added). Thus, where the Convention is used as a 'shield' against public authorities, pre-commencement action is covered. Thus, before the Act came fully into force public authorities were seeking to abide by it in bringing proceedings, including prosecutions, against citizens.

On the face of it, the vast majority of actions brought under s6 against public authorities contemplated in this book would raise purely public law issues and would therefore arise by way of proceedings for judicial review[170] due to the procedural exclusivity principle.[171] The discussion below will very briefly indicate, in this context, the issues raised by this principle, which have been the subject of a number of commentaries.[172] It means that litigants will not benefit from the procedural advantages of bringing an action by way of writ or an originating summons. If proceedings were begun in this way they would be struck out since they should have been brought by way of judicial review. Under the Supreme Court Act 1981 s31(3) judicial review requires leave (now termed 'permission') and around half of judicial review actions fail at the leave stage.[173] The leave requirement is therefore controversial and has been severely criticised.[174] It will of course have to be interpreted compatibly with the Convention rights under s3 HRA, taking, as indicated above, the Article 13 jurisprudence into account.

Most significantly, the limitation period of three months for judicial review proceedings would operate for most cases alleging a breach of the Convention instead of the one year period under s7(5)(1)(a), unless s7(1)(a) creates a new cause of action. A *Pepper* v *Hart* statement supports the possibility that this is the case, and that the one-year period would apply: 'someone with a genuine grievance will be able to pursue it under s7(1)(a) whether or not within the judicial review time limit'.[175] This arguable possibility means that applicants raising arguments based on

[170] See in particular Chapter 3 at p94, Chapter 10 at pp388–9.

[171] The reasoning behind the 'exclusivity principle', requiring that public law actions should proceed by way of judicial review (see *O'Reilly* v *Mackman* [1983] 2 AC 237 at p283), was based on a need to protect public authorities in the exercise of their duties; they would be protected by the procedural limitations built into Order 53.

[172] See for example S Fredman and G Morris 'The Costs of Exclusivity: Public and Private Re-examined' [1994] PL 69 at pp70–71 and 80–81.

[173] See A P Le Suer and M Sunkin 'Application for Judicial Review' [1992] PL 102; Law Commission Consultation Paper No 226/HC 669 *Administrative Law: Judicial Review and Statutory Appeals.*

[174] See the JUSTICE–All Souls Report *Administrative Law: Some Necessary Reforms* 1988.

[175] HC Deb Vol 314 col 1099.

rights recognised under common law could not normally be brought if outside the three-month time limit. On the other hand, such applicants could take advantage of the 'sufficient interest' standing test rather than the stricter 'victim' test under the HRA. Applicants raising Convention points under s6(1) the HRA would have to comply with both the 'victim' test and the one-year rule. An applicant raising a mixture of Convention and common law points would be in a complex position. In respect of the Convention the applicant would be subject to the stricter standing rules, but the broader time limit. In respect of the common law grounds, the reverse would be the case. It has been pointed out that these arrangements create complex procedural obstacles leading to unfairness between applicants.[176]

As Leigh and Lustgarten have pointed out, on the assumption that actions under s7(1)(a) would generally take the form of judicial review, the procedure may not be adequate as a means of determining the crucial issue of proportionality.[177] It is far less likely in judicial review proceedings that discovery would be ordered or cross-examination allowed. Therefore there are inadequacies in its fact-finding role. Possibly if a perception arises among the judiciary that judicial review is simply inadequate to the task it is required to undertake under the HRA, the courts will take an activist approach in using their discretion, for example, to require cross-examination.

The principle of procedural exclusivity clearly leads to effects which run counter to the aims underlying the HRA since it may mean that public authorities are not called to account when they breach the Convention rights. The more relaxed approach to the principle evident in *Roy* v *Kensington and Chelsea Family Practitioner*[178] may avoid the striking out of actions on the ground that they should have been brought by way of an application for judicial review. Since that decision further relaxation has occurred.[179] If the courts are prepared to adopt an activist stance towards rendering the rights efficacious, they may be prepared to go further in this direction. This is a matter which is currently under review and eventually a single procedure may be adopted in public and private law cases.[180]

Remedies

Under s8(1) a court which has found that an act or proposed act of a public authority is unlawful, is authorised to grant 'such relief or remedy

[176] D Nicol 'Limitation periods under the HRA and Judicial Review' [1999] LQR 216.

[177] I Leigh and L Lustgarten 'Making Rights Real: the Courts, Remedies and the Human Rights Act' [1999] 58 (3) CLJ 509.

[178] [1991] 1 All ER 705.

[179] See *Mercury Communications Ltd* v *Director General of Telecommunications* [1996] 1 WLR 48.

[180] The Woolf reforms set out in Lord Woolf's Report *Access to Justice* 1996 were given effect under the Civil Procedure Act 1997. The Civil Procedure Rules came into force in April 1999 but the Rules Committee set up under the 1997 Act has not yet finished the task of revising the procedures by which applications for judicial review are made.

or . . . order within its powers as [the court] considers just and appropriate'. The term 'unlawful' clearly does not mean 'breach of a Convention guarantee' where such a breach is 'lawful' due to incompatible primary legislation or secondary legislation made under such legislation. In such circumstances no remedy is available other than a declaration of incompatibility and the ability to make such a declaration is, as indicated, confined to certain higher courts. A litigant in a lower court or tribunal, in such circumstances, appears to be completely remediless since even the empty remedy of a declaration is unavailable. The forum at the next level might be equally powerless. In the circumstances covered by this book the picture is mixed as regards the ability of litigants to get into a court which can issue a declaration.[181] The litigant has little or no incentive to appeal in the hope of eventually reaching a court able to make a declaration, assuming that permission (where required) would be granted where clear incompatibility is present, especially as there is no provision requiring the Crown to bear its own costs where it intervenes in accordance with s5(2) HRA. In criminal proceedings, however, the courts may take the view that to convict a defendant in breach of the Convention would be an abuse of process.[182]

It is impossible not to conclude that this system of remedial action is inadequate to the task of providing a domestic remedy for violation of Convention rights.[183] Further, it may undermine the remedy at Strasbourg. Assuming that Strasbourg would view it as an effective remedy, which is doubtful,[184] the availability of the 'remedy' of a declaration is likely to make the task of exhausting domestic remedies in order to take an application to Strasbourg even more difficult. In any event, if legislation is not forthcoming within the next few years to amend s4 HRA with a view to allowing lower courts to make declarations, the pressure on the judiciary to find compatibility will become increasingly severe.

[181] For example, an appeal from a magistrate's court to the Crown Court would require a further appeal in order to obtain a declaration. A declaration could be obtained using only one level of appeal if an appeal was by way of case stated to the Divisional Court. Appeals from the Proscribed Organisations Appeal Commission are, by leave, to the Court of Appeal in England and Wales, and to the equivalent courts in Scotland and Northern Ireland (see further Chapter 3 p87).

[182] See the views of Lord Steyn *R* v *DPP ex p Kebilene and others* [1999] 4 All ER 801.

[183] See I Leigh and L Lustgarten 'Making Rights Real: the Courts, Remedies and the Human Rights Act' [1999] 58 (3) CLJ 509 at p543. They conclude that rights may be less well protected than previously as a result of the HRA.

[184] The applicant only needs to exhaust those possibilities which offer an *effective* remedy, so if part of the complaint is the *lack* of a remedy under Article 13 then the application is not likely to be ruled inadmissible on this ground: *X* v *UK* (1981) Appl 7990/77, D and R 24. A remedy will be ineffective if according to established case law there appears to be no chance of success: Appl 5874 172, Yearbook XVII (1974). Strasbourg has not yet had the opportunity to rule on the question whether a Declaration of Incompatibility could amount to an effective remedy since no analogous procedure exists in the contracting states. Since it offers nothing which has previously been recognised as a remedy to the individual in question, it is suggested that there are strong grounds for considering that the system would not be viewed as offering an effective remedy.

Assuming that a breach of the Convention is found which is not the result of incompatible legislation, all the familiar remedies including certiorari, a declaration or mandamus are available so long as they are within the jurisdiction of the relevant court or tribunal. Under s8(2) damages cannot be awarded in criminal proceedings but this leaves open the possibility that they could be awarded in judicial review as well as other civil proceedings. However, traditionally the courts have been reluctant to award damages in public law cases and s8(3) HRA encourages the continuance of this tradition in requiring consideration to be given first to any 'other relief or remedy granted or order made', the consequences of the court's decisions and the necessity of making the award.

Under s8(4) the court in deciding to award damages must take into account the principles applied by the European Court of Human Rights. This suggests that awards are likely to be low. The court can award compensation under what is now Article 41.[185] The purpose of the reparation is to place the applicant in the position he or she would have been in had the violation not taken place. Compensation will include costs unless the applicant has received legal aid, although where only part of a claim is upheld the costs may be diminished accordingly.[186] It can also include loss of earnings, travel costs, fines and costs unjustly awarded against the applicant. Compensation is also available for intangible or non-pecuniary losses such as loss of future earnings[187] or opportunities,[188] unjust imprisonment,[189] stress or loss of personal integrity.[190] But there are two difficulties in following the principles of the European Court. One is, as Mowbray has pointed out, that the method of determining the award in any particular judgment is frequently unclear.[191] The other is that the Court, prior to the changes introduced under Protocol 11, had no independent fact-finding role[192] and therefore where it was unclear that the breach had occasioned the effect in question it has at times refused to award compensation. This is a clear instance in which domestic courts can create higher standards than those maintained at Strasbourg, both in terms of dealing with this issue of causality and in creating a clearer

185 Previously Article 50 under the old numbering of the Articles.

186 *Steel* v *UK* (1998) 28 EHRR 603 para 125.

187 For example, in *Young, James and Webster* v *UK* judgment of 13 August 1981, A 44 (1981) pecuniary and non-pecuniary costs, taking such loss into account, were awarded: the Court ordered £65,000 to be paid.

188 *Weekes* v *UK* A 145-A (1988).

189 In *Steel* v *UK* (1998) 28 EHRR 603 para 122 the three successful applicants were each imprisoned for seven hours. The Court, without giving reasons, awarded them £500 each in compensation for non-pecuniary damage.

190 See further A Mowbray 'The European Court of Human Rights' Approach to Just Satisfaction' [1997] PL 647; D Feldman 'Remedies for Violation of Convention Rights under the HRA' [1998] EHRLR 691; Amos 'Damages for breach of the HRA' [1999] EHRLR 178. The question of the level of damages is addressed further in Chapter 5 pp196–7.

191 Ibid at p650.

192 As I Leigh and L Lustgarten point out in 'Making Rights Real: the Courts, Remedies and the Human Rights Act' [1999] 58 (3) CLJ 509 at p529.

rationale for awards, although they will be able to derive guidance from post-1998 decisions taken under the Protocol 11 reforms.

The use of injunctions under the HRA is discussed in Chapter 4 in the context of public protest. The discussion considers in particular the use of the Convention rights as a defence, taking into account s12 HRA, which provides special protection for freedom of expression, where interim injunctions are obtained in *civil* proceedings against protesters, an increasingly significant phenomenon.[193] Injunctions could also be sought in certain circumstances by groups or individuals claiming that the decision of a public authority had breached the Convention. Their use would be especially appropriate in the context of public protest. As Chapter 4 points out and, as indicated above, in relation to the *International Ferries* case, courts have shown deference to decisions of the police regarding public protest. However, there may well be circumstances in which a strict approach to proportionality would lead to a finding that bans or orders affecting protesters had gone further than necessary to achieve the ends in view.[194] In such an instance issuance of an injunction would be appropriate. It may be noted that the decision at Strasbourg most in point in respect of such bans, *Christians against Racism and Fascism* v *UK*,[195] is a classic example of a decision which, while according with a traditionalist stance in public protest matters, would be disapplied under the activist approach. It is a relatively elderly decision of the Commission alone, in which the margin of appreciation doctrine[196] was strongly influential in leading to the conclusion that the application was manifestly ill-founded.

'Horizontal' effect

Statutes which affect the legal relations between private parties are affected by s3 HRA and therefore in this sense the Act clearly creates horizontal effects. The position is less clear in relation to the common law. This is the area of greatest uncertainty under the Act and it has therefore proved to be a focus for academic debate.[197] The main concern of

[193] See pp166–9. S12 does not apply to 'relief' in criminal proceedings.

[194] See Chapter 4 p168.

[195] Application No 8440/78 21 DR 138.

[196] Ibid, at pp149 and 151.

[197] See, for example, M Hunt 'The "Horizontal" Effect of the Human Rights Act' (1998) PL 423; C B Graber and G Teubner 'Art and Money: Constitutional Rights in the Private Sphere?' (1998) 18(1) OJLS 61; I Leigh 'Horizontal Rights, The Human Rights Act and Privacy: Lessons from the Commonwealth' [1999] 48 ICLQ 57; W Wade, University of Cambridge Centre for Public Law 'The UK's Bill of Rights' *Constitutional Reform in the UK: Practice and Principles* (1998 Oxford) pp62–64, and on the Convention generally: A Clapham *Human Rights in the Private Sphere* (1993 Oxford: Clarendon Press); A Clapham 'The Privatisation of Human Rights' (1995) EHRLR 20; G Phillipson 'The Human Rights Act, "Horizontal Effect" and The Common Law: A Bang or a Whimper?' [1999] 62 MLR 824; Buxton LJ 'The HRA and Private Law' [2000] LQR 48.

this book is with vertical liability – the relations between citizen and state – and therefore this issue will be outlined only. The Act will affect the legal relations between private persons and bodies (horizontal effects) although, since they are outside the scope of s6, they will not be bound by it directly. The academic debate is currently polarised, Professor Wade perceiving no distinction between the obligations of private and public bodies[198] and Lord Justice Buxton taking the stance that no horizontal effects are created.[199]

This chapter takes the middle ground, where commentators are beginning to cluster[200] in perceiving a limited degree of horizontal effect. A citizen wishing to sue a private body under the HRA alleging breach of a Convention right could explore various possibilities. The citizen could identify a statute affecting the matter in question and then invoke s3, claiming that the court as a public authority under s6 must afford a remedy itself for the breach.[201] This is problematic. To begin with, the litigant would have to find a cause of action in order to get into court at all.[202] Even if this was possible (e.g. a very weak claim in reliance on an uncertain area of the common law), the court might not accept that Parliament could have intended to allow the distinction between private and public bodies under s6 to be destroyed by this means.[203] Even if the court was prepared to find a breach of the Convention it appears that it would be unable to afford a remedy to the litigant under s8 HRA since remedies are only to be given in respect of 'acts of public authorities.'[204] Therefore only those remedies already available under the common law could be granted.

A litigant could argue that the court as a public authority is under a duty to interpret the common law so as to render it compatible with the Convention. A court is already under a duty to do this where the common law is unclear,[205] but the litigant could argue for an obligation in respect of the common law resembling that under s3 in respect of legislation.

198 'The United Kingdom's Bill of Rights' in Hare and Forsyth (eds) *Constitutional Reform in the United Kingdom: Practice and Principles* (1998 Oxford: Hart) pp62–63.

199 'The Human Rights Act and Private Law' [2000] LQR 48. Wade, having set out his position in favour of full direct horizontal effect, as indicated in note 198 above, then returned to the attack, replying to Buxton in 'Horizons of Horizontality' [2000] Summer LQR 217.

200 G Phillipson 'The Human Rights Act, "Horizontal Effect" and the Common Law: A Bang or a Whimper?' [1999] MLR 62 824; M Hunt 'The "Horizontal" Effect of the Human Rights Act' (1998) PL 423.

201 There is a strong consensus that the courts' inclusion within the definition of those bodies bound not to infringe Convention rights is the key to the horizontal effect of the Act upon the common law (note 200 above). See also M Hunt ibid.

202 Phillipson, note 200 above, pp828–829.

203 M Hunt ibid at p840.

204 For discussion of this point see Phillipson ibid fn 83.

205 See note 201 above.

There is as yet no consensus on how this point will be received,[206] although the majority view is that the HRA will at the least heighten the impact of the Convention on the common law.

Conclusions

The HRA represents, in Constitutional terms, a shift from form to substance – a movement away from procedure to merits. But if the rhetoric about the infusion of normativism into the Constitution, albeit under the constraint of developed Constitutional principles, is to become reality, Parliament, the executive and the judiciary will have to confront the difficulties, inconsistencies and contradictions revealed by these arrangements. The discussion above illustrates the immense scope afforded to the judiciary, other public and quasi-public authorities[207] either to minimise or to afford efficacy to the rights. Parliament has deliberately left a number of central matters to be determined by the judiciary, especially in the remedial field. That is why its stance will be so significant. But the responsibility for making this enterprise work lies with many bodies outside the judiciary. A central theme of this book concerns the extent to which the ordinary courts will be prevented from applying the HRA, by New Labour legislation, in contexts where it is most needed. As Chapter 1 mentions, the government has asked both Houses of Parliament to appoint a Joint Committee on Human Rights.[208] The Committee's recommendations might be expected to address this tendency as an aspect of a continuing process of reform, probably requiring legislation, which has been begun but far from completed under the HRA.

[206] Hunt argues for an absolute duty on the courts to render the common law compatible with the Convention rights; Phillipson suggests that the obligation will be only to have regard to the Convention rights as guiding principles, having a variable weight depending on the context; Leigh considers that the HRA 'does not formally change the approach to Convention questions in the common law, although there may be a chance of atmosphere post-incorporation' (ibid note 183 pp82–83).
[207] Acting in their public function; see s6(5) discussed above at p49.
[208] House of Commons Hansard col 604 14 December 1998.

Chapter 3

Extending 'Emergency' Legislation

Introduction

Terrorism and democracy

If a democracy readily abandons its democratic ideals, including adherence to the rule of law, in the face of terrorist activity, it lays itself open to the charge that its attachment to them was always precarious and qualified. In defending the introduction of new counter-terrorism legislation, the Terrorism Act 2000, with immense potential to extend the impact of the previous legislation, Jack Straw, the Home Secretary, claimed in 1999 that he was 'simply protecting democracy' and that extensive measures were needed since 'by its nature terrorism is designed to strike at the heart of our democratic values'.[1] In justifying similar, if far less wide-ranging, extensions of such legislation in the face of high levels of IRA activity during the 1970s and 1980s, Mrs Thatcher famously said in 1988: 'We do sometimes have to sacrifice a little of the freedom we cherish in order to defend ourselves from those whose aim it is to destroy that freedom altogether'. Although this is a powerful argument, it must confront the paradox that in seeking to defend democracy, counter-terrorist measures may undermine it: they may themselves strike at democratic values if they become disproportionate to the aim of protecting them. As Tony Blair, the then Shadow Home Secretary, observed in 1993: 'if we cravenly accept that any action by the government and entitled "prevention of terrorism" must be supported in its entirety and without question we do not strengthen the fight against terrorism, we weaken it'.[2] As J Wadham of *Liberty* has said: 'Draconian anti-terrorist laws . . . have a far greater impact on human rights than they ever will on crime'.[3]

[1] See the *Guardian* 14 November 1999.
[2] Hansard House of Commons 10 March 1993 col 975.
[3] See the *Guardian* 14 November 1999.

Without a full commitment to the rule of law the difference between the terrorist and the state vision of power begins to diminish. It follows that in a democracy steps taken in abandonment of such a commitment should be subject to the most rigorous tests for proportionality: an immediate and very serious threat should be evident; the measures adopted should be effective in combating it and should go no further than necessary to meet it. This chapter, and certain of those succeeding it,[4] will suggest that in a number of respects the new counter-terrorist Act of 2000 fails to live up to these democratic ideals. It will therefore come into conflict with a number of Convention rights under the HRA since the notion of preserving and fostering such ideals is crucial to the Convention. It will be argued that it comes into conflict with Article 6 which affords great prominence to the right to a fair trial 'in a democratic society within the meaning of the Convention'.[5] Its detention provisions may not be fully compatible with the Article 5 guarantees, also of central importance in a democracy.[6] Since the new legislation will, as argued below, tend to stifle the expression of a vast range of groups representing minority interests, such as animal rights activists, and outlaw the very existence of many such groups, while at the same time largely preventing or curbing journalistic investigation of their activities or media debate regarding them, it comes directly into conflict with the Article 10 and 11 guarantees of expression, assembly and association, generally viewed as essential in a democracy. This is most clearly the case given that the aims of the groups likely to be affected by the new Act are, broadly speaking, political ones, and the expression in question is underpinned by the free speech justification often termed the 'argument from democracy'. This justification has been described by Barendt as 'probably the most attractive . . . of the free speech theories in modern Western democracies' and as 'the most influential theory in the development of twentieth century free speech law',[7] an assertion which has received strong support from domestic judges and at Strasbourg. Associated primarily with the American writer Meiklejohn,[8] its basic thesis is that citizens cannot participate fully in a democracy unless they have a reasonable understanding of a range of political issues; therefore open debate on such matters is necessary to ensure the proper working of a democracy. As Lord Steyn has put it, 'freedom of speech is the lifeblood of democracy . . . The free flow of information and ideas informs political debate'.[9] In so far as democracy rests upon ideas both of participation *and* government accountability, the argument from

[4] Chapters 5, 6 and 7.
[5] *De Cubber* v *Belgium* A 86 para 30 (1984).
[6] See *Winterwerp* v *Netherlands* A 33 para 37 (1979). See further Chapter 6 pp240–242.
[7] *Freedom of Speech* (1986) pp20 and 23 respectively.
[8] See for example 'The First Amendment is an Absolute' (1961) Sup Ct Rev 245 and *Political Freedom* (1960) esp 115–124.
[9] *R* v *Home Secretary ex parte Simms* [1999] 3 All ER 400, 408.

democracy may be seen to encompass also the function which a free press fulfils.

The high regard in which freedom of speech and of the press, as 'essential foundations of a democratic society',[10] is held by the Strasbourg institutions is well known and need not be rehearsed in any detail here. It has been emphasised that the freedom extends to ideas that 'offend, shock or disturb'.[11] Particular stress has been laid upon 'the pre-eminent role of the press in a State governed by the rule of law which has a duty "to impart information and ideas on matters of public interest" which the public "has a right to receive"'.[12] It is a marked feature of the Strasbourg Article 10 jurisprudence that clearly political speech, which may be seen as directly engaging the participation rationale, receives a particularly high degree of protection. The 'political' speech cases of *Sunday Times* v *UK*,[13] *Jersild*,[14] *Lingens* v *Austria*,[15] *Thorgeir Thorgeirson* v *Iceland*,[16] all resulted in findings that Article 10 had been violated; all were marked by an intensive review of the restriction in question in which the margin of appreciation was narrowed almost to vanishing point. Where national security was raised as an issue in *Observer and Guardian Newspapers* v *UK*[17] the margin of appreciation conceded was broader but a violation of Article 10 was found. Where the speech directly concerns government actions the stance taken is particularly robust, even where issues of national security appear to arise. In *Incal* v *Turkey*,[18] finding a breach of Article 10, the Court said that 'the limits of permissible criticism are wider with regard to the Government than in respect of private citizens', and that the dominant position the government occupies should persuade it to display restraint in resorting to criminal proceedings. The Court found that although the argument had been raised that the measures in question were counter-terrorist, the links of the applicant to terrorism were uncertain.[19] This stance reflects values endemic in the Convention: it is clearly difficult to show that an interference with democracy-supporting speech is 'necessary in a democratic society'.[20]

[10] *Observer and Guardian* v *the United Kingdom* judgment of 26 November 1991, Series A No 216 pp29–30 para 59.

[11] See, for example, *Thorgeirson* v *Iceland* (1992) 14 EHRR 843 para 63.

[12] *Castells* v *Spain* judgment of 23 April 1992, Series A No 236 p23 para 43.

[13] 26 April 1979, A 30.

[14] *Jersild* v *Denmark* (1994) 19 EHRR 1 concerned an application by a Danish journalist who had been convicted of an offence of racially offensive remarks after preparing and broadcasting a programme about extreme racists which included overtly racist speech by the subjects of the documentary.

[15] (1986) 8 EHR 407; the case concerned the defamation of a political figure.

[16] (1992) 14 EHRR 843. The speech concerned consisted of newspaper articles alleging reporting allegations of brutality against the Reykjavik police.

[17] (1991) 14 EHRR 153.

[18] (2000) 29 EHRR 449.

[19] The conviction of the applicant was found to be disproportionate to the aim of countering terrorism pursued.

[20] Article 10(2).

Determination to protect political expression is also evident in UK courts, particularly in cases where journalistic material raises political issues,[21] although deference to widely drafted primary legislation[22] or governmental arguments from national security[23] have resulted in the ready upholding of restrictions on directly political speech. Earlier findings to the effect that 'The media . . . are an essential foundation of any democracy'[24] have recently been reinforced by pronouncements in the House of Lords' decision in *Reynolds*[25] which afforded an explicit recognition to the duty to inform the people on matters of legitimate public interest.[26] Press freedom in relation to political expression has clearly been recognised as having a particularly high value in UK and Convention jurisprudence, and therefore the inclusion of journalists in the new and wide net of counter-terrorist liability requires a very strong justification, particularly as it may extend to a range of groups covering such divergent issues as animal rights, environmental matters, abortion and militant fundamentalist religious beliefs.

Strasbourg has further found that freedom of association is closely linked to freedom of expression. While earlier Strasbourg jurisprudence was more protective of state interests,[27] the recent 'association' jurisprudence of the Court is more interventionist. In *Socialist Party and Others* v *Turkey*[28] the Court allowed only a very narrow margin of appreciation in finding that the dissolution of the Socialist Party of Turkey had breached Article 11. The Court said that democracy demands that diverse political programmes should be debated, 'even those that call into question the way a state is currently organised'. The Court did not accept that the message of the group, that a federal system should be put in place which would ensure that Kurds would be put on an equal footing with Turkish citizens generally, amounted to incitement to violence. The dissolution of the Party was disproportionate to the aim in view – the preservation of national security. This stance is in accordance with the Convention jurisprudence which has quite consistently recognised the need to protect

[21] *Reynolds* v *Times Newspapers* (1999) HL (see note 25 below); *Derbyshire County Council* v *Times Newspapers* [1993] AC 534.

[22] *Secretary of State for Home Affairs ex parte Brind* [1991] 1 AC 696.

[23] *Attorney-General* v *Guardian Newspapers* (No 2) [1990] 1 AC 109.

[24] *Francome* v *Mirror Group Newspapers* [1984] 1 WLR 892, 898, per Sir John Donaldson.

[25] *Reynolds* v *Times Newspapers* HL [1999] 4 All ER 609, judgment of 28 October available from the House of Lords web-site: http://www.publications.parliament.uk/pa/ld/ldjudinf.htm.

[26] As Lord Nicholls put it: 'freedom to disseminate and receive information on political matters is essential to the proper functioning of the system of parliamentary democracy cherished in this country. This freedom enables those who elect representatives to Parliament to make an informed choice, regarding individuals as well as policies, and those elected to make informed decisions'.

[27] See *Glasenapp* v *FRG* A 104 (1986); *Kosiek* v *FRG* A 105 (1986); *CCSU* v *UK* (1988) 10 EHRR 269.

[28] Judgment of 25 May 1998 (App No 20/1997/804/1007); (1999) 27 EHRR 51 paras 41, 47, 50.

the interests of minority and excluded groups.[29] Similar findings were made in *Sidiropoulos* v *Greece*.[30] The Court said that one of the most important aspects of freedom of association was that citizens should be able to form a legal group with the aim of acting collectively in their mutual interest. Similarly, in *Vogt* v *Germany*[31] the Court held that a woman dismissed from her teaching post because of her membership of an extreme left wing group had suffered a violation of both Articles 10 and 11. Counter-terrorist provisions, therefore, which extend to groups putting forward a wide range of political messages – using that term in the broad sense which Strasbourg has endorsed – interfere with the flow of information and ideas. Such provisions will come into conflict with the expression, association and assembly of a very wide and divergent range of groups and persons and therefore call into question their compatibility with democratic values.

Groups which adopt the use of direct action create the possibilities of disorder, of violence to citizens and damage to property. They may, if sufficiently resourced and well organised, threaten national security. Clearly, the state has a duty to protect citizens from their attentions. The need to give weight to such interests explains the general acceptance of the freedoms of expression, assembly and association as non-absolute rights,[32] even though it may be that violent protest is most likely to bring about change. The ordinary criminal law exists, however, in order to punish members of such groups for specific actions. It will be argued below that the impact of the new legislation on those freedoms, and on the right to a fair trial, is disproportionate to the aims pursued and in a number of respects is, therefore, contrary to the claims of the Home Secretary, unnecessary in a democratic society.

The legal and historical context

This chapter will focus centrally on the break with the UK's counter-terrorist response of the 1970s, 1980s and 1990s which has occurred under the New Labour government with the introduction of the Terrorism Act 2000. The recent history of the UK's counter-terrorism legislation – essentially the Prevention of Terrorism (Temporary Provisions) Act 1989 (the PTA) and the Northern Ireland (Emergency Provisions) Act 1996 as

[29] Such groups have included criminals: *Soering* v *UK* A 161 (1989); prisoners: *Ireland* v *UK* A 25 (1978), *Golder* v *UK* A 18 (1975); racial minorities: *East African Asians* cases 3 EHRR 76 (1973), *Hilton* v *UK* No 5613/72, 4 DR 177 (1976) (no breach found on facts); sexual minorities: *Dudgeon* v *UK* A 45 (1981), *B* v *France* A 232-C (1992); political minorities: *Arrowsmith* v *UK* No 7050/75, 19 DR 5 (1978); religious minorities: *Kokkinakis* v *Greece* A 260-A (1993).

[30] (Chamber) (1998) available from the Court's web-site, www.dhcour.coe.fr.

[31] (1995) 21 EHRR 205.

[32] See the leading US case, *Hague* v *Committee for Industrial Organisation* 307 US 496 (1938). For further discussion see Williams, DGT [1987] Crim LR 167.

amended by the Northern Ireland (Emergency Provisions) Act 1998 – revealed some acceptance of the principle that emergency measures should be adopted only in the face of immediate and severe need. When the then Home Secretary Roy Jenkins (now Lord Jenkins of Hillhead) introduced the first Prevention of Terrorism (Temporary Provisions) Act in 1974, he referred to the powers it granted as 'unprecedented in peace-time' but 'fully justified to meet the clear present danger'. The Act was introduced soon after the Birmingham pub bombings that same year, in which 21 people died and over 180 were injured.

Despite pronouncements such as that of Lord Jenkins, which are scattered across the Parliamentary debates of the 1970s, 1980s and 1990s on extensions of the counter-terrorist legislation, it cannot be said that Parliament has shown a genuine commitment to the principle that such legislation must be introduced only to meet a clear and present danger. In the 1990s Parliament quite frequently showed a marked readiness to accept claims that a number of proposed statutory measures would lead to the curbing of terrorist activity. Although such measures were likely to represent an infringement of civil liberties, they did not in general encounter determined criticism from the Opposition. For example, the debate in the House of Commons on the Prevention of Terrorism (Additional Powers) Act 1996, which was guillotined, failed to consider in depth either the efficacy of the measure in terms of curbing terrorist activity or its likely impact on civil liberties. The debate provided, in microcosm, a good instance of the debasement and impoverishment of Parliamentary criminal justice debate in the mid-1990s. The Labour Party supported the proposals partly on the narrow ground that they represented only a small increase on the extended police powers to combat terrorism, which were included in the Criminal Justice and Public Order Act 1994, and which were not challenged on grounds of principle at the Committee stage of that Bill.[33] Issues as to the real value of these powers were raised only by certain back-benchers owing to pressure of time and to the stance of the Labour leadership.

The incremental extension of the PTA, which was originally intended in 1974 to be a temporary measure, reluctantly adopted as an unpalatable but necessary response to an emergency, is charted below. Many of the measures discussed in this chapter clearly indicate a willingness to abandon the rule of law in the face of terrorism despite uncertainty as to the need to adopt them. The pattern, as this chapter indicates, has been one of steady additions to those 'temporary' provisions, meaning, inevitably, that provisions originally viewed as draconian began to look normal and acceptable compared with their successors. Thus, what may be termed the old model for counter-terrorist legislation – temporary, incrementally developed in the face of particular emergencies, with localised effect

[33] See J Straw HC Deb 2 April 1996 col 221.

– was viewed in many quarters as deeply flawed, not least in that the legislation became more far reaching as the terrorist activity diminished. As explained below, it was at its most extensive, as a temporary measure, in 1998, although the peace process was in being. Nevertheless, it had not entirely lost touch with the values espoused by Lord Jenkins in 1974, in the sense that additions to the original legislation were relatively minor and usually had at least an apparent justification as a response to a genuine danger. The Criminal Justice (Terrorism and Conspiracy) Act 1998, for example, was passed in the wake of the Omagh bombing, carried out by the splinter group, the Real IRA, which caused the deaths of some 22 people.

The new permanent counter-terrorist scheme under the current Labour government, which will probably come into force in late 2000, will represent, this chapter will contend, a dramatic break with those values. At the time of writing the peace process in Northern Ireland culminating in the *British Irish Agreement reached in the multi-party negotiations*[34] is still in existence.[35] The process and the Agreement, which has included releasing those imprisoned on terrorist charges, recognise that criminalisation of persons engaging in a struggle largely viewed in Republican communities in Northern Ireland as political, was counter-productive. It gave the impression to those communities that no real alternative other than violence was available to them. The Agreement has, to an extent, marginalised those Republican splinter groups which rejected the possibility of a peaceful solution, preferring to continue the use of para-military tactics. By the end of 1999 some of these groups had also declared a cease-fire, although some remain adamantly opposed to the peace process. As the 1998 Labour government Consultation Paper *Legislation Against Terrorism*[36] puts it: 'subsequent progress including elections to the Northern Ireland Assembly mean that the outlook in Northern Ireland is changing, and suggest that the days of widespread violence and terrorism may soon be gone for good'.

Repeal of the Prevention of Terrorism (Temporary Provisions) Act 1979 which, in its original form, was introduced after the IRA pub bombings in Birmingham in 1974, might therefore have been expected. This would probably have been the expectation in 1974. The PTA embodies the paradoxical nature of the measures adopted for use against the IRA over the last 20 years. As Ewing and Gearty have pointed out, it and its predecessors were adopted as emergency anti-terrorist measures, but were then

[34] Cm 3883 (1998).

[35] In November 1999, after Senator Mitchell had negotiated a settlement, Sinn Fein announced the beginning of decommissioning. However, at the present time decommissioning has not yet occurred and the IRA shows no sign of undertaking it. Failure to decommission is viewed as the main stumbling block to the process.

[36] Home Office and Northern Ireland Office *Legislation Against Terrorism. A Consultation Paper* Cm 4178 prepared 17 December 1998 (1998 London: Stationery Office).

applied as ordinary criminal legislation.[37] Since the 'criminalisation' approach has largely been abandoned, repeal of much of the legislation that accompanied it would appear to be appropriate. In so far as a threat from 'international terrorism' remained, it could have been met by powers graduated to levels of threat. In fact, the counter-terrorism provision post-2000 under the Terrorism Act 2000 will be more extensive than in the worst years of Irish terrorist violence. They will be graduated only in respect of the two different regimes for proscribed and other terrorist groups. This chapter will argue that the New Labour government shows little recognition of the need to repeal provisions viewed as tolerable only for a short period of time in the face of a pressing emergency, and which were accompanied by a conscious acceptance of an abandonment of democratic ideals. Flawed as were the justifications used in the past for the extension of emergency legislation, the current government has largely abandoned the need for them, adhering instead to a more illiberal version of authoritarianism. The justifications in the past were based on actual threats; the justifications underpinning the present scheme are based largely on speculation.

Ironically, the only development which may tend to temper the excesses of the new statute is the Human Rights Act. Indeed, as the findings of the Divisional Court and House of Lords in *ex parte Kebilene*[38] (discussed below) indicate, it has already shown its potential to do so. Interestingly, the Consultation Paper which preceded the legislation[39] appears to assume that most of its proposals would not lead to conflicts with the Convention, under the HRA. At certain points this issue is explicitly addressed; at others the relevant Convention Articles are simply not mentioned. When the Home Secretary introduced the Terrorism Bill to Parliament in December 1999 he made a declaration of its compatibility with the Convention rights under s19(1)(a) HRA, but obviously the courts remain at liberty to find incompatibility.[40]

This is an instance in which the courts will have the key role to play in tempering the potential of the new legislation. This is apparent, bearing in mind the role played by Parliament in debating the new Bill, which was circumscribed – in civil liberties' terms – owing to the very large majority of the Labour government and the stance of the main Opposition party. Parliament as currently composed had already shown itself willing to pass draconian legislation, the Criminal Justice (Terrorism and Conspiracy) Act 1998, with no significant amendment, although during

[37] *Freedom under Thatcher* (1989) p213.

[38] Divisional Court [1999] 3 WLR 372; HL [1999] 4 All ER 801, available from the Lords' web-site. It may be noted that *ex p Kebilene* concerned legislation, the Criminal Justice and Public Order Act 1994 s82, passed under the Major government. But the provisions at issue have been reproduced in the Act of 2000 in ss57 and 58 (see below).

[39] Cm 4178, prepared 17 December 1998.

[40] See further Chapter 2.

debate concerns were strongly expressed in certain quarters.[41] In debate on the Bill of 2000 the main proposals made by the Conservative Opposition were more draconian than those of the government. They included the reintroduction of internment[42] and the extension of detention by executive, not judicial authorisation.[43] The stance of the courts may also be of indirect significance in shaping the response of the executive itself to the new powers. As discussed below, at many points the new powers leave overt discretion to the executive. For example, the Attorney-General currently has powers to give consent to prosecutions for the offence of conspiracy in the UK to commit offences abroad. It is to be expected that where the conspirators are seeking to overthrow a dictatorship, the consent would be withheld, even though technically the offence has been committed. Clearly, the police will always have a discretion in determining when to arrest. It is a hallmark of terrorist legislation that it is often marginalised in favour of the use of ordinary criminal provisions.[44] If, when prosecutions are brought, the judiciary takes a robust line as regards HRA standards, the willingness to rely on the new provisions may be diminished further. Most simply, it might be said that robust use by the judiciary of those standards may have an educative effect on those who must administer the new Act and even on government ministers.

The temporary counter-terrorism legislation

Incremental extension

Although the level of Irish terrorist violence was at its highest between 1968 when the Troubles began and the early 1970s, extension of the Prevention of Terrorism (Temporary Provisions) Act 1974 and then of the 1989 Act continued to occur over the succeeding 25 years, under Thatcher, Major and Blair. The 1974 Act was passed at a time when the level of IRA violence was very high: in 1973 there were 86 explosions; before the Birmingham pub bombs 20 people had been killed in 1974 and over 150 injured. In 1972 103 soldiers and 321 civilians died. The argument in favour of adopting extreme rights-abridging measures looked fairly plausible in the early 1970s. The Report of Lord Diplock's

[41] See, for example Mr Sayeed 'The government are used to using their very large majority to bully through inadequate legislation' (HC Debs 2 September 1998 col 726); Mr McNamara: 'The Bill is dangerous and we have been rushed into it without any proper thought' (HC Debs 2 September 1998 col 786).

[42] A new Schedule 2 and a new clause which would have effected this was proposed: HC Debs 15 March 2000 cols 331–337. Both were defeated, Labour and Liberal Democrat MPs voting together: HC Debs 15 March 2000 col 347.

[43] HC Debs 15 March 2000 col 431.

[44] See C Walker *The Prevention of Terrorism* (1986) at p183.

Commission led to the passage of the Northern Ireland (Emergency Provisions) Act 1973 (the EPA). As well as providing special powers for the security forces, the 1973 Act established different arrangements, including mode of trial, for terrorist cases. It was also made subject to annual review and to renewal by Parliamentary debate. Features of the earlier pre- and post-war anti-IRA measures were found in the EPA which provided a model for the 1974 Act and was similarly extended:[45] 'One of [the EPA's] features has been a steady increase in size and scope'.[46] As noted at various points below, the more draconian measures were confined to Northern Ireland. Where the threat was perceived to be most obvious, therefore, the measures were more far reaching. This is not to suggest that the measures were justified or effective. It has been said: '[the EPA's] real purpose is to placate the electorate, as well as some of the elected, who demand that some steps must be taken by the law to counteract terrorism, regardless of how effective these might prove in practice'.[47]

The original emergency provisions under the 1974 Act had a renewal period of six months. This was soon extended to one year under the Prevention of Terrorism (Temporary Provisions) Act 1976. The Prevention of Terrorism (Temporary Provisions) Act 1984 included 'international terrorism' for the first time among its provisions. It was to be regularly reviewed and was to expire in five years. It was replaced by the Prevention of Terrorism (Temporary Provisions) Act 1989, also subject to annual renewal, but without the five-year time limit. By 2000 the PTA had been in existence for 11 years and was extended again throughout the 1990s. It was renewed for the last time,[48] ironically, immediately after the Second Reading on the Terrorism Bill 2000.

Since 1989 additional powers have been added by subsequent statutes – the Criminal Justice Act 1993, the Criminal Justice and Public Order Act 1994, the Prevention of Terrorism (Additional Powers) Act 1996 and the Criminal Justice (Terrorism and Conspiracy) Act 1998. The Northern Irish provisions followed a similar pattern, culminating in the passing of the Northern Ireland (Temporary Provisions) Act 1998. Paradoxically, although the level of violence has dropped over the 25 years since the first Act was passed, its current successor represents a much enlarged version of the first Act. Extension was not discouraged by the cease-fire in September 1994 (which broke down in 1996) or the peace process in 1998. Thus, the notion that only a severe emergency, such as the one which appeared to be in being in 1974, could justify such far-reaching provisions has gradually been abandoned. The reality behind the 'temporary'

[45] It was amended in 1975, consolidated in 1978, amended again in 1987 and consolidated with further amendments in 1991 and 1996.

[46] Bailey, Harris and Jones *Civil Liberties: Cases and Materials* (1995) at p283.

[47] B Dickson 'Northern Ireland's Emergency legislation' [1992] PL 592 at p597.

[48] The Prevention of Terrorism (Temporary Provisions) Act 1989 (Continuance) Order 2000. See HC Debs 15 March 2000 col 474.

provisions appears to be that for much of the twentieth century governments have kept emergency legislation on file or in suspension, ready to be brought into law at short notice under a supine Parliament.

This governmental stance has persisted, despite the fact that the efficacy of the PTA remains in doubt. Walker has found that the Act is 'largely peripheral in effect'[49] and that the ordinary criminal law has on the whole been used against terrorism. The fact that the level of violence has tended to drop over the last 25 years (albeit inconsistently) does not appear to be attributable to the operation of the 1974 Act or its successors, but to changes in policy at governmental level and within the Republican organisations themselves. The level of violence was in fact particularly high in the two years immediately after the 1974 Act was passed. It may therefore be said that Parliament has demonstrated not only that it is willing to move quickly to cut down freedoms in situations perceived as emergencies, but that it then shows little inclination to repeal the measures adopted, preferring instead a process of normalisation, extension and accretion.

The Criminal Justice (Terrorism and Conspiracy) Act 1998

Once the peace process in Northern Ireland was placed on a formal basis under the *British Irish Agreement reached in the multi-party negotiations*[50] the fear became that splinter groups such as the Continuity IRA and the Real IRA, which, for various reasons, deplored the abandonment of paramilitary tactics, would seek to disrupt it. This occurred in the Omagh bombing carried out by the Real IRA, in August 1998. It prompted the introduction in the 1998 Act of new draconian anti-terrorist measures to be inserted into the PTA. The Criminal Justice (Terrorism and Conspiracy) Bill 1998 was rushed through both Houses in two days (in fact 27 hours) in the wake of the bombing. The argument for the speed was that the powers it contained were needed immediately for operational reasons. The Bill was only published to MPs at 6 pm on the day before the debate. A two-line whip was imposed on Labour MPs and the Opposition parties supported the Bill. Nevertheless, a number of MPs opposed it on the basis that even in the face of terrorism the freedom to discuss the legislative response should not be abandoned.[51]

The Act was intended to make it easier to convict members of proscribed groups; it introduced new ss2A and 2B into the PTA for that purpose (discussed below). In fact no immediate action at all was taken in reliance on the powers the new Act conferred. After two months the UK Act had still not been used (the equivalent legislation in Northern

[49] C Walker *The Prevention of Terrorism* (1986) at p183.

[50] Cm 3883 (1998).

[51] See, for example, comments of Richard Shepherd MP Hansard House of Commons 2 September 1998 cols 714, 715.

Ireland had been) although persons had been arrested in respect of the bombing. It appeared that the Act was passed more as a propaganda exercise than because the powers were genuinely needed. The Act ensured 'symmetry' with Ireland since the Dail was passing a similar Act on the same day. It was suggested in Parliament that the Act had in reality been passed in order to win the approval of President Clinton who was visiting Belfast in the same week.[52] Apart from such 'political' motivation, the curtailment of Parliamentary debate and its debatable efficacy in practice, a frequent hallmark of 'emergency' legislation is that other, unrelated controversial provisions which have been awaiting an opportune moment to get onto the statute book are added,[53] and are also able to take advantage of the stifling of Parliamentary debate which occurs in apparent response to the 'emergency'. The Criminal Justice (Terrorism and Conspiracy) Act 1998 exhibits all these characteristics.

The Act brought together two entirely separate and controversial matters – provisions related to proscribed terrorist organisations and to conspiracies. Only the first of these was clearly concerned with the threat and use of violence for political ends (terrorism as defined in the 1989 Act s20(1)). S5 of the Act adds a new s1A to the Criminal Law Act 1977, making it a criminal offence to conspire in any act 'or other event' which would also be an offence under the law of a foreign country so long as the offence in question would also be unlawful in the UK.[54] It is not therefore confined to terrorist offences as defined in s20 of the 1989 Act, although it was introduced in terrorist legislation. The conspiracy can be to commit any offence, however trivial, so long as it is an offence in both the UK and the 'target' country. The new s1A offence opens up the possibility that politically active refugees discussing possible means of overcoming repressive regimes abroad might fall foul of s5.[55] It was pointed out in Parliament that the provisions could also apply to 'an environmental pressure group organising a peaceful protest in Germany against the dispatch of some toxic material to Britain'.[56] This would be the case, assuming that the protest would be likely to infringe criminal law in both the UK and Germany.

The government considered that sufficient safeguards were introduced in providing that the offence plotted must be a crime in both countries and by requiring that, in most cases, the Attorney-General must give his

[52] Mr J Sayeed HC Debs 2 September 1998 col 726.

[53] The Bill substantially reproduced provisions in an earlier Bill on conspiracy which the Major government had been forced to drop in 1996.

[54] It may be noted that Crown servants are exempted from these provisions, presumably on the ground that otherwise they would catch some activities of the security and intelligence services.

[55] It is ironic to note that plans to assassinate Hitler during World War II by, for example, dissident Germans in England would have been covered by s5.

[56] By Mr Alan Beith Deputy Leader of the Liberal Democrats, HC Debs 2 September 1998 col 735.

or her personal consent, having regard to the public interest, for the prosecution. The government stated its belief that: 'these provisions strike the right balance between ensuring it is possible to take decisive action against those plotting terrorist and other criminal acts elsewhere from the UK while building in safeguards . . . these provisions on conspiracy will continue to play an important role in deterring international terrorists from using this country as a base for their operations'.[57] These arguments and those used in Parliament were, however, disingenuous in their indications that the new provisions were necessary in order to curb international terrorism. The new s1A of the 1977 Act makes no mention of terrorism and although the new provisions may curb terrorist activity, they leave a disturbingly broad discretion to the Attorney-General as to their use against non-terrorist groups.

This Act represented the final extension of the temporary legislation and, in terms of the proscription-related provisions, indicated the willingness of the Labour government to depart from previously accepted criminal justice standards – a characteristic which found a much fuller expression in the Terrorism Act 2000. The 1998 Act was the forerunner of the Act of 2000 and in some respects it foreshadowed the developments of that Act since it introduced a far-reaching and controversial change to standards of criminal evidence[58] and brought an unprecedented range of groups within its ambit.

The single, permanent anti-terrorism statute

The government published a Consultation Paper on the future of anti-terrorism laws in December 1998.[59] It was intended to address the question of the rationale of retaining 'emergency' anti-terrorism laws in the face of the peace process[60] and therefore to counter the argument that the current version of the PTA with its various later accretions should be repealed and not replaced. The 1998 Paper was based on a Report prepared by Lord Lloyd of Berwick in 1996.[61] In 1995 Lord Lloyd had been asked by Michael Howard, the then Home Secretary, to consider the future of anti-terrorist legislation on the assumption that a lasting peace was achieved. He recommended in his Report that a new permanent anti-terrorist law should replace the temporary provisions. The policy adopted in his Report formed the background to the Consultation Paper and in

[57] *Legislation Against Terrorism: a consultation paper* Cm 4178, prepared 17 December 1998, at para 4.18.

[58] The provisions inserting s2A into the PTA.

[59] *Legislation against Terrorism. A Consultation Paper* Cm 4178 (1998 London: Stationery Office).

[60] See the Introduction to the Paper, and in particular para 6.

[61] Lord Lloyd of Berwick's *Inquiry into legislation against terrorism* (Cm 3420), published in October 1996.

turn to the Terrorism Bill 2000. Once the Act of 2000 comes into force, it will repeal the PTA and EPA.[62] The new Bill has four key hallmarks. It is far more extensive, covering a much wider range of groups; it is permanent; its main provisions will apply equally across the UK, although there are special transitional provisions for Northern Ireland; and it will retain almost all the draconian special powers and offences adopted under the previous 'temporary' counter-terrorist scheme, while adding new incitement offences.

The justification for the new provisions is that they are needed at the present time to combat the threat from three groups. The first of these comprises those Irish splinter groups opposed to the peace process.[63] The second comprises 'international terrorists'. The Paper notes that across the world there has been a rise in terrorism motivated by religious idealism.[64] Both these groups are already covered under the existing legislation, although not all the special provisions are applied equally to international terrorism. The threat is apparently from the new, third, group, on which the case for new legislation must largely rest. This group comprises a wide and disparate range of domestic groups other than those connected with Irish terrorism, such as animal rights or environmental activists[65] and, possibly, anti-abortion groups.[66] The Paper accepts that

[62] As noted below, the PTA was renewed for the last time on 15 March 2000. The EPA was renewed for the last time on 24 August 2000. The special measures it provides for Northern Ireland will be provided in Part VII of the Act of 2000.

[63] In the Paper the government finds: 'there are small numbers who remain opposed to peace and wedded to violence. So, even though the context is of a general movement towards lasting peace in Northern Ireland, it is too soon to be confident that all terrorism has been abandoned' (ibid para 2.3).

[64] Lord Lloyd's Report draws attention to 'possible future changes in the terrorist threat' and to lives and property in the UK; changes which mirror what is happening across the world' (ibid para 2.4). Examples are given of the rise of 'Islamic extremism' and the use of Sarin nerve gas on the Tokyo underground in 1995 by the Aum Shinrikyo religious cult, which killed 12 people and affected up to 5,500.

[65] 'The threat from some marginal but extreme elements of the animal rights movement continues to be of more concern to the Government [than Scottish or Welsh nationalist groups]'. The Paper notes that animal rights extremists have in the past sent letter bombs to the leaders of major political parties, attacked Bristol University's Senate House with a high-explosive bomb, targeted a veterinary surgeon and a psychologist with car bombs and caused millions of pounds' worth of damage. 'The shape of new counter-terrorist legislation needs to reflect the possible threat from indigenous groups too' (Chap 2 of the Paper, at para 2.5). In Chap 3 of the Paper the concerns regarding these groups are given some further substance. It is noted that in 1997 more than 800 incidents were recorded by the Animal Rights National Index (ARNI) and 'these included attacks on abattoirs, laboratories, breeders, hunts, butchers, chemists, doctors, vets, furriers, restaurants, supermarkets and other shops' which resulted in injuries although not in deaths and in damage done in 1997 estimated at more than £1.8 million (ibid para 3.10).

[66] The Paper speculates as to the possibility that anti-abortion groups will adopt terrorist methods in the UK: 'In the United States, for example, there is an increasing tendency by individuals and groups to resort to terrorist methods. Some of those opposed to the USA's laws on abortion have bombed clinics and attacked, and, in a number of cases, killed doctors and nursing staff employed by them. Although there have been no comparable attacks in the United Kingdom, the possibility remains that some new group or individual could operate in this way in the future' (ibid para 3.12).

the level of violence associated with such groups is low compared with the level of IRA violence in the early 1970s. However, it argues that these groups pose a continuing threat and that other single issue groups may be set up and may use violent methods 'to impose their will on the rest of society'.[67] Thus, the Paper switches the focus of concern from the need for measures to combat a high and rising level of violence to the need to be ready to combat the possibility of violence in the future. The threat of violence from environmental, animal rights or anti-abortion activists may be a real possibility but it has not yet materialised on anything like the scale previously thought of as necessary to justify the draconian anti-terrorist laws. Moreover, it is unclear that the ordinary criminal law would be inadequate as a response to the activities of such groups. The Paper merely provides assertions rather than evidence as to the need for special counter-terrorist measures, as opposed to a more effective use of the existing criminal law. No effort is made to analyse the need for the extension of the special provisions to a very wide range of new groups. It does not, for example, draw on experience from other countries, including European ones, which are equally faced with extremist groups. The problems experienced in the USA are mentioned, but no study is made of the efficacy of the means used to combat them.

The conclusion of the government in the Consultation Paper is that a threat comparable with that existing in 1974 can be discerned: 'In the language of the then Home Secretary introducing the PTA legislation in 1974, the Government believes that there exists now a clear and present terrorist threat to the UK from a number of fronts'.[68] But if these examples of group violence are compared with those available in 1974, it is immediately apparent that they are far more uncertain and speculative. The keynote of the Paper is the need to safeguard the UK from future threats from indigenous groups, most of which have not yet arisen and may not do so. The unquestioned assumption is that the new legislation will counter any future threat before it materialises. No attention is paid to the possibility of counter-productivity – that the designation of some indigenous groups as terrorist may encourage a growth in extremism within such groups which may perceive themselves as unable to use the normal channels of political campaigning. In comparison with the climate in 1974 or even, to a lesser extent, in 1998, in the wake of the Omagh bombing, the case for new legislation based on the threats indicated, has not, it is argued, been made out.

The intention is that the new Terrorism Act 2000 will be permanent; this has the advantage, as the Paper points out,[69] of being 'transparent', that is, no pretence is made that the legislation will be repealed. This is

[67] Para 3.12.
[68] Ibid at para 2.7.
[69] Ibid para 2.8.

a strong argument, given the spurious nature, indicated above, of claims that the legislation was temporary and passed only in response to a current emergency. But it abandons even the pretence that temporary and regrettable emergency measures, involving an ordinarily unacceptable infringement of civil liberties, are in contemplation. The Paper notes that the vast majority of criminal law is permanent, implying that this provides a reason for abandoning the temporary nature of the counter-terrorism legislation and thereby blurring past distinctions between criminal law and special measures adopted to meet specific emergencies.

Parliamentary scrutiny of the new legislation is also virtually abandoned, although the government did accept concerns expressed in the Second Reading of the Bill, to the extent of agreeing to an annual report to Parliament.[70] A new clause supported by the Liberal Democrats making the legislation renewable was rejected by the government[71] and no provision for the full review of the legislation was included. Therefore the permanent powers will receive even less scrutiny than the temporary ones did. The clause was withdrawn after the Home Office Minister had pointed out that the HRA would provide 'an important new safeguard'.[72] The justification offered for abandoning the review process is that it: 'does not reflect the current reality that such powers are likely to be needed for the foreseeable future'.[73] This bland statement, based on little evidence, fails to take account of the fact that these powers were adopted and extended over a long period of time (apparently) to meet the serious threat posed by a particular group of highly organised terrorists, commanding a range of arms. It also fails to take account of the need for Parliamentary scrutiny to oversee the workings of the new powers. It leaves their use far more overtly in executive as opposed to Parliamentary hands. If certain of the new powers are not in practice used they should be repealed; an annual review would provide a forum for arguing for such repeal. This appears to be precisely what the government is seeking to avoid, presumably in the interests of saving Parliamentary time and avoiding political controversy. In other words, human rights appear to be viewed as a commodity which can be afforded value only when convenient. While it may be argued that the previous review process achieved little, it is at least possible in the post-HRA era that some MPs would have used such a process to afford a stricter scrutiny.

The main provisions of the Terrorism Act 2000 will apply equally across the UK. This on its face represents a more satisfactory approach than passing more draconian legislation for Northern Ireland, which has in the past been the case, or, in effect, trying out such legislation in Northern Ireland first and then transferring it to Britain. But once again it erodes

[70] See HC Debs 15 March 2000 col 360. This provision is now s126.
[71] See HC Debs 15 March 2000 cols 352–356.
[72] See HC Debs 15 March 2000 col 363.
[73] Ibid para 2.8.

the principle that special powers should be as narrow as possible; if the threat is greater in one locality it may therefore provide a justification for more draconian powers confined to that locality. Although that justification has been attacked as doubtful, in the sense that counter-terrorist legislation appears to have been adopted in Northern Ireland for reasons other than its efficacy in countering terrorism,[74] it is undeniable that the threat of terrorism has been greater in Northern Ireland than in the rest of the UK.

The universal application of the new legislation is in any event only an aspiration of the new statute, since under Part VII of the Act it will retain for five years a number of differentials between the powers applicable to Northern Ireland and to Britain.[75] The new counter-terrorism legislation includes in Part VII a number of temporary provisions specific to Northern Ireland. The government stated that its objective is: 'progressively to transform the security environment as appropriate, and achieve complete normalisation as part of the implementation of the [Belfast] Agreement as a whole'. Once that is achieved, the government's position is that there will be no need for any temporary Northern Ireland specific powers.[76] The temporary provisions will be subject to annual review and to Parliament's approval of the Home Secretary's orders of renewal.[77]

Extending the definition of terrorism under the Terrorism Act 2000

Terrorism is currently defined in section 20(1) of the Prevention of Terrorism (Temporary Provisions) Act 1989 as 'the use of violence for political ends and includes any use of violence for the purpose of putting the public, or any section of the public in fear'. But this does not mean that the PTA powers apply to all activities which fall within this definition. The special powers conferred apply only to 'terrorism connected with the affairs of Northern Ireland' or (in certain instances) to international terrorism. Non-Irish domestic terrorism, that is terrorism having its origins in the affairs of any part of the UK other than Northern Ireland, is excluded from the scope of the Act. The s20 definition of terrorism is in fact extraordinarily wide and imprecise since the use of the word 'includes' means that the requirement of putting a section of the public in fear is not an essential ingredient of it. The terms 'violence' and 'political ends' are undefined. Arguably, therefore, 'the use of violence for political ends' could include some public protest. It is unclear whether s20 is confined to violence against persons. The definition might therefore

[74] See B Dickson 'Northern Ireland's Emergency legislation' [1992] PL 592 at p597.
[75] Under s112(4) the additional temporary measures for Northern Ireland only are time-limited to five years.
[76] Ibid para 1.3.
[77] This was promised in the Paper (ibid para 1.4) and is now contained in s123(4)(f).

be unworkable in practice were it not for the current qualified application of the powers. Even bearing those qualifications in mind, the definition means that the special powers can be used against a very wide range of activities so long as a connection with Northern Irish affairs or, even more vaguely (in the case of certain powers), an 'international' aspect can be found. The definition of terrorism in the EPA is identical to that in s20 of the PTA. The EPA does not impose any limitations on the kinds of terrorism to which it applies. But there appears to be official agreement that in practice the powers have only been used to combat Irish terrorism.[78]

In his Report Lord Lloyd criticised the definition of terrorism in s20 and the restrictions imposed throughout that Act limiting the use of the powers to certain terrorist groups. He suggested that there is no difference in principle between the activities of those groups and those of domestic 'terrorist' groups unconnected with Irish affairs.[79] Presumably Lord Lloyd, in using the term 'terrorist' in relation to such groups, was relying on the very wide s20 definition. This, however, fails to address the possibility that this definition would be unsatisfactory were it not in practice unused in determining the application of the special powers. If that definition is relied upon, many groups fall within it and in principle should therefore be subject to the special powers. In other words, once a group or person is labelled 'terrorist', powers applicable to terrorists should be applied to them. But this begs the question whether a much narrower definition of terrorism should be used in order to justify a broader use of such powers. The government in proposing the new legislation agreed with Lord Lloyd, arguing that the suffering of the victims would be the same, whether caused by 'a republican or loyalist paramilitary, an international terrorist or an animal rights activist'.[80] But the argument which seeks to extend the definition of terrorism on the basis that the experience of the victims is the same whether the group in question is officially designated terrorist or not is flawed. The experience of a person who is attacked for motives of jealousy or greed is the same as that of one who is killed for a political motive. Most grave and prolonged of all may be the suffering of the victim of the sexually motivated killer. On this argument either all serious crimes against the person should be designated terrorist or no crimes should be. It has been argued that it is the quality of indiscriminate public violence (hence, terror) which is fundamental.[81] However, it is suggested that the fear experienced by many women of

[78] Ibid para 3.2.

[79] Ibid para 3.5.

[80] '[T]he methods which ['terrorists'] employ are those in common currency amongst terrorists everywhere – bombs, incendiaries, shootings, arson and so forth. Nor is there any difference in the fear, pain or despair felt by the victims or their families . . . The injuries and the destruction of life and property are the same' (ibid para 3.6).

[81] *Terrorism* (1996) 'What is Terrorism?' I Primoratz p130 in C Gearty (ed) Aldershot, Dartmouth.

being randomly selected for sexual attack is of a similar quality. The reason for treating so-called terrorist activity differently from 'ordinary' crime is not the suffering of the victim but the potentially profound effect on the established order which terrorism may have but which ordinary crime (unless it reaches certain levels)[82] does not. Thus, the definition of terrorism should only encompass groups which seek to overthrow that order.

Proceeding from its doubtful premise, the government found in the Consultation Paper that the special powers were needed to combat all forms of 'terrorism', indigenous or otherwise, and that therefore the restricting qualifications under the PTA should be abandoned.[83] But it rejected the option of simply adopting the s20 definition, without any qualification as to the use of the powers. It agreed with Lord Lloyd in finding the definition too wide in that it could cover the use of trivial violence which should be dealt with by the ordinary criminal law, and too narrow because it might not cover adequately the activities of religiously inspired groups.[84] Lord Lloyd recommended that the definition of terrorism used by the FBI in the USA should be adopted. Its definition is: 'the use of serious violence against persons or property, or the threat to use such violence, to intimidate or coerce a government, the public, or any section of the public in order to promote political, social or ideological objectives'. The government, however, rejected this definition as too broad since it includes the use of serious violence for 'social' objectives,[85] and too narrow in that it does not cover forms of damage to property.[86] The government stated that its proposed new definition was: 'the use of serious violence against persons or property, or the threat to use such violence, to intimidate or coerce a government, the public, or any section of the public for political, religious or ideological ends'.[87]

The proposed definition was an extraordinarily wide interpretation of 'terrorism'. Clearly, it was intended to include forms of direct action adopted by environmental groups or animal rights activists. This definition was in some respects wider than that under s20, since it clearly

[82] It may be pointed out that once ordinary crime reaches certain levels it probably has as destabilising an effect on society as terrorism has. For example, in certain parts of the UK ordinary crime has had a localised, profoundly destabilising effect in terms of the encouragement of vigilantism and the infringement and undermining of the enjoyment of the benefits of a civilised society, such as personal security, freedom of movement, privacy, etc.

[83] Ibid para 3.13.

[84] Ibid para 3.14.

[85] The latter could, for example, include crimes committed by criminals other than terrorists such as blackmail or extortion for gain (ibid para 3.16).

[86] 'It appears not to cover the damage and serious disruption which might result from a terrorist . . . contaminating a public utility system such as a water or sewage works [or] . . . hacking into some vital computer installation and, without using violence, altering, deleting, or disrupting the data held on it' (ibid para 3.16).

[87] Ibid para 3.17.

applied to property as well as persons and covered serious disruption as well as violence. In its *application* it would also have been far wider. It was, however, narrower than that under s20 in that it made it clear that intimidating or coercing a government, the public, or any section of the public was an essential ingredient. The definition actually adopted under s1 of the new Act is significantly wider even than the proposed one or that under s20. S1 provides, in essence, that 'terrorism' means the use or threat, 'for the purpose of advancing a political, religious or ideological cause', of action 'designed to influence the government or to intimidate the public or a section of the public' (s1(1)(b)) which involves serious violence against any person or serious damage to property, endangers the life of any person, or 'creates a serious risk to the health or safety of the public or a section of the public' 'or is designed seriously to interfere with or seriously to disrupt an electronic system'. The Act will also apply wherever terrorist action takes place under s1(4). The requirement of a threat to the established order contained in the words 'to intimidate or coerce a government', the key limiting factor under the proposed definition, has been watered down to 'influence'. But the key point is that in its potential effect the s1 definition is far wider in practice than s20 since the new legislation, unlike the PTA, allows the *definition itself* to determine the application of the special powers. The government assumes that such application will, owing to the decisions of police officers, the DPP and CPS, in practice affect only the most extremist groups. But, given the lack of effective, independent control over the day-to-day decision-making of such bodies, this is not, it is argued, a satisfactory position in civil liberties' terms.

The definition was attacked in Parliament as creating a 'fatally flawed' Bill. It was also said: 'it is utterly perplexing that we should apparently be wedded to a definition that threatens to undermine so sweepingly civil liberties and the credibility of governance itself'.[88] However, the amendments put forward by the Liberal Democrats, which would have narrowed it down, were overwhelmingly defeated, Labour and Conservative MPs (with a few exceptions) voting together.[89] (The limiting words of s1(1)(b) were added as a Lords' amendment, reluctantly accepted by the government.) The new definition will tend to allow many activities, currently criminal, to be re-designated as terrorist. The definition now expressly covers threats of serious disruption or damage, to, for example, computer installations or public utilities. The definition is therefore able to catch a number of forms of public protest. Danger to property, violence or a serious risk to safety that can be described as 'ideologically, politically, or religiously motivated' may arise in the context of many demonstrations and other forms of public protest, including some industrial disputes.

[88] Mr Simpson MP HC Debs 15 March 2000 cols 399 and 394.
[89] HC Debs 15 March 2000 col 415.

The government stated in the Paper that it had 'no intention of suggesting that matters that can properly be dealt with under normal public order powers should in future be dealt with under counter-terrorist legislation'.[90] But once special arrest and detention powers are handed to the police they can be used, at their discretion, if a particular person or group falls, or appears to fall, within the new definition. Some direct action against property by animal rights or environmental activists may well fall within it. As Chapter 4 points out, some 'direct action' by such groups may be viewed as forms of expression and as having, to varying extents, the same role as political speech.[91] Some direct action, such as the destruction of genetically modified crops, may be intended both to disrupt and to draw attention to a cause. Direct action forms of protest going beyond persuasion may provide a substantive means of engaging in the more *effective* means of communicating with others (since such forms are most likely to attract media attention). To label forms of such action 'terrorist', as the new legislation does, is not only to devalue that term but to take a stance towards forms of protest more characteristic of a totalitarian state than of a democracy.

The new definition will also allow the currently non-criminal actions of a number of persons to be redesignated terrorist since the special terrorist offences, discussed below, will apply to a wide range of persons, including those who have some contact with persons designated 'terrorist'. Thus, technically speaking, the Home Secretary is right in stating, as he has done, that the definition *itself* will not create any new offences.[92] But it will, potentially, lead to the criminalisation of the actions or omissions of a wide range of persons, many of whom do not themselves fall within the definition. The response of some groups to their redesignation as terrorist may be to exacerbate any threat they pose. Within such groups the more moderate activists may tend to become extremists since legitimate avenues of protest will largely be closed to them, especially if they are eventually proscribed. If they are not proscribed, groups may be uncertain whether their actions will be labelled terrorist, given the imprecision and breadth of the definition. In fact, the strong likelihood, as indicated below, is that only a minority of the groups which could fall within s1(1) will be proscribed, at least in the initial years. Unlike the PTA and EPA regimes, in which the special powers were used in practice against proscribed groups only, the special powers (apart from those specifically linked to proscription) can be used against any group falling within the broad definition of terrorism. Therefore a number of persons may unwittingly fall within the ambit of the special terrorist offences.

[90] Ibid para 3.18.

[91] Such action is likely to be already tortious or criminal but, as Chapter 4 argues, defendants can raise Article 10 and 11 arguments in defence.

[92] See the *Guardian* 14 November 1999.

Application of the PTA offences under the new Act

The intention is that virtually all the extensive range of special terrorist offences will be retained under the new statute and that most of them will apply to the vast range of groups which could, potentially, fall within the new definition. Under Part VII some will continue to apply only to Irish rather than international terrorist groups, while, depending on additions to the list of proscribed groups under Schedule 2, some proscription-related offences may initially apply only to Irish groups. Once the range of terrorist offences available are considered in relation to, for example, environmental or animal rights groups, the potentially immensely broad impact of the new legislation becomes apparent, as does the possibility that parts of it may infringe certain of the Convention rights, most notably Articles 10, 11, 6 and 5, under the HRA.

One controversial power, of exclusion, is, however, to be abolished. Section 5 of the PTA currently provides for exclusion from Great Britain, section 6 for exclusion from Northern Ireland and section 7 for exclusion from the whole of the UK. In effect, these powers meant that Northern Irish citizens could be forced to go back to Northern Ireland; there was little reciprocity in terms of excluding Irish citizens to Britain.[93] These provisions were reviewed by Lord Jellicoe in 1983;[94] he concluded that the exclusion power should be allowed to lapse as soon as circumstances suggested that it was not strictly necessary.[95] The powers have been used with increasing infrequency: there were 248 orders in force in 1982; by the end of 1996 there were 24. In 1997 the Home Secretary considered that they were no longer effective in combating terrorism and revoked the 12 which remained. The exclusion powers are not currently in force: they were lapsed with effect from midnight on 21 March 1998, although until repeal of the PTA by the Act of 2000 they could be reactivated. These powers would clearly be entirely irrelevant in relation to the new domestic groups to be designated as terrorist and probably largely irrelevant to the small Irish splinter groups, such as the Real IRA. They would be extremely complex to operate in respect of 'international terrorists'. Thus, even if they were retained, these powers would probably remain largely unused under the new statute. Nevertheless, their repeal is to be welcomed on the principle that such laws should be repealed rather than left to lie on the statute book with the possibility that they could be arbitrarily reactivated in future.

[93] Walker *The Prevention of Terrorism* 2nd edn (1992) pp84–85; only four persons have been excluded to Britain.

[94] *Report on the Operation of the Prevention of Terrorism (Temporary Provisions) Act 1978.*

[95] Jellicoe (1983) para 200; however, the review by Lord Colville recommended on this basis that power to make exclusion orders should be repealed (*Report on the Operation in 1990 of the Prevention of Terrorism Act 1989*).

Proscription

Under section 1 of the PTA, the Secretary of State could by order proscribe any organisation which appeared to him to be concerned in Irish terrorism, or in promoting it or encouraging it. No provision was made under the PTA for proscribing international terrorist organisations active in the UK. The organisations currently proscribed are listed in Schedule 1 to the Act; at present the IRA and INLA are proscribed and these powers are extended to Northern Ireland by virtue of s28 of the Northern Ireland (Emergency Provisions) Act 1991.[96] Proscription of the IRA is taken to include splinter groups such as the Continuity IRA and the Real IRA. Equivalent provisions in Northern Ireland are set out in sections 30 and 31 and Schedule 2 to the EPA. Twelve organisations, including the IRA, the INLA, the UDA, the UVF, the UFF, and most recently the LVF and the Continuity Army Council, are currently proscribed. 'Organisations' were widely defined as 'any association or combination of persons' (s1(6) of the PTA). Further, an organisation did not need to engage in terrorism itself; it was enough if it promoted or encouraged it.

Proscription may be seen as providing a legitimate means of expressing outrage at certain activities, thereby tending to prevent illegitimate expressions of public anger. It has been argued that it may discourage supporters of terrorist organisations and may signal political strength.[97] But it has also been contended that these benefits are minimal and that it is 'a cosmetic part of the PTA' which is in fact 'counter productive as it impedes criminal investigation and political discussion'.[98] Lord Jellicoe's review of the operation of the PTA doubted the value of proscription, considering that its detrimental effects in terms of constraining the free expression of views about Northern Ireland outweighed its benefits.[99] In response, a Home Office circular was issued[100] giving guidance to the police as to the proper use of ss1 and 2, bearing in mind the possible effect on freedom of expression.

There have been no convictions for proscription-related offences in Britain since 1990 although, in the same period, 195 convictions were obtained in Northern Ireland. Therefore the need to retain the power to proscribe in relation to Britain under the new legislation is unclear. However, under the Terrorism Act 2000 the current power of proscription and all the proscription-related offences are retained, and their impact is greatly extended. S3(1) provides: 'For the purposes of this Act an

[96] For commentary on the predecessor to the 1991 Act see *Review of the Operation of the Northern Ireland (Emergency Provisions) Act 1978* Cmnd 9222; D Bonner [1984] PL 348.

[97] P Wilkinson *Terrorism and the Political State* (1986) p170.

[98] See C Walker *The Prevention of Terrorism in British Law* 2nd edn (1992) p64. See also D Bonner [1989] PL 440.

[99] Cmnd 8803, 1983; the review did not, however, recommend deproscription, since it would create public resentment.

[100] On 9 August 1983 (Current Law Statutes 1984 note to s1(1)).

organisation is proscribed if it is listed in Schedule 2, or it operates under the same name as an organisation listed in that Schedule'. The power to add to or delete groups from the Schedule is exercised under s3(3) by the Secretary of State, by order. Under s3(4) the power may be exercised 'only if he believes that [the organisation] is concerned in terrorism' and under s3(5) it will be concerned in terrorism if it '(a) commits or participates in acts of terrorism, (b) prepares for terrorism, (c) promotes or encourages terrorism, or (d) is otherwise concerned in terrorism'. In other words, groups which do not themselves fall within the s1 definition but which are in any way 'concerned' in terrorism can be proscribed. The addition of the term 'concerned in terrorism' makes this provision wider than that under the PTA. Parliament's approval is required for additions to, or deletions from, the list as it was under the PTA provisions.[101]

Difficult decisions will have to be taken concerning the new 'terrorist' groups (under the new definition) to be proscribed. At present under Schedule 2 of the new Act the groups listed were already proscribed under the EPA; they will now be proscribed throughout the UK.[102] But the key issue under the new Act will be whether all or most of the other groups falling within the new definition will eventually be proscribed. There appear to be three options for the trend of proscription over a period of time. First, the current proscriptions could be retained, merely adding further Irish splinter groups if necessary. Second, both Irish and international groups could be proscribed, leaving domestic groups which fall within the definition unproscribed. Third, all groups falling within the definition could be proscribed. This will clearly be a very significant matter; whichever option is chosen the government is likely to leave itself open to severe criticism. Choosing the first or second would mean that while the members of certain domestic groups are, in effect, redefined as 'terrorists', the groups would remain openly able to engage in various public activities such as advertising for members, fund-raising, holding marches or possibly even putting up members to stand for elections.[103] This would seem bizarre and would aid in devaluing the concept of

[101] Under s123(4) of the Act of 2000, 'An order or regulations under any of the following provisions shall not be made, subject to subsection (4), unless a draft has been laid before and approved by resolution of each House of Parliament'. The provisions listed include s3(3). S123(5) covers cases of urgency, in which case an order may be made without approval; if so it will lapse after 40 days unless approved.

[102] The following groups are listed in Schedule 2: The Irish Republican Army, Cumann nam Ban, Fianna nah Eireann, The Red Hand Commando, Saor Eire, The Ulster Freedom Fighters, The Ulster Volunteer Force, The Irish National Liberation Army, The Irish People's Liberation Organisation, The Ulster Defence Association, The Loyalist Volunteer Force, The Continuity Army Council, The Orange Volunteers, The Red Hand Defenders.

[103] All these activities might in certain respects fall within the terrorist offences discussed below, but they do not in themselves either constitute offences or lead almost inevitably to liability under the proscription-related offences.

terrorism. Such a stance could come to undermine the whole legislation and provides an argument for returning to the qualifications of the PTA, rather than for proscribing all the new 'terrorist' groups.

Lord Lloyd recommended adoption of the third option. This option would be highly problematic in practical terms and deeply objectionable at the level of principle. The government is attracted to it since it would provide 'a mechanism to signal clearly condemnation of any terrorist organisation whatever its origin and motivation'.[104] The government also saw advantages in criminalising fund-raising activity of any kind for a particular group since that would remove the requirement to prove end use of funds. But it recognised the practical problem that the provisions could be circumvented by changing the group's name. It is unlikely to put this option into practice for some years.[105]

If the third option is eventually adopted, the list, if it is to have any credibility, would have to be exhaustive: it would clearly be inequitable to proscribe one group falling within the definition while failing to proscribe another which was equally within it. Given its width, the definition potentially covers a vast range of organisations. There would clearly be practical difficulties in drawing up and then maintaining an up-to-date list of international and domestic groups to be proscribed. The list would be of immense scope; it would probably include hundreds of names and it would quickly become out of date. Clearly, it might come to appear ludicrously broad and simply unworkable. It is likely that the list will be built up gradually, beginning with the addition of international groups.[106]

Proscription-related offences

S2(1)(a) of the PTA made it an offence to belong to a proscribed organisation and this provision is reproduced in s11 of the 2000 Act. Under s11(1) a person commits an offence if he or she belongs or professes to belong to a proscribed organisation; a maximum penalty of 10 years' imprisonment is imposed. It is notable that there is no *mens rea* requirement. There is a limited defence under s11(2): 'it is a defence for a person charged with an offence under subsection (1) to prove that the organisation was not proscribed on the last (or only) occasion on which he became a member or began to profess to be a member, and that he

[104] 'The current provisions, under which only Irish terrorist groups can be proscribed, could be construed by some as indicating that the Government does not take other forms of terrorism as seriously. Furthermore a wider provision could deter international groups from establishing themselves in the UK' (the 1998 Consultation Paper *Legislation on Terrorism* at para 4.14).

[105] At the Committee stage in the House of Commons the government said that in the immediate future it would not add domestic groups to the list; see HC Debs 15 March 2000 col 431.

[106] The explanatory notes to the Act state: 'The Government is considering which organisations involved in international terrorism might be added to the Schedule'.

has not taken part in the activities of the organisation at any time while it was proscribed'. But it is not a defence to prove that the defendant did not know that the organisation was proscribed or that it was engaged in activities covered by ss1(1) and 3 of the Act.

Under s2(1)(a) of the PTA it was also an offence to solicit support, other than money or other property, for a proscribed organisation. This is reproduced in s12(1) and it is also an offence under s12(2) for a person to arrange, manage or assist in arranging or managing a meeting which he knows is: '(a) to support a proscribed organisation, (b) to further the activities of a proscribed organisation, or (c) to be addressed by a person who belongs or professes to belong to a proscribed organisation'. It is an offence under s12(3)(a) to address such a meeting in order to encourage support for a proscribed organisation or 'further its activities'. These are broadly drawn offences, although they do include a *mens rea* ingredient. Their impact on speech, association and assembly is clearly far reaching bearing in mind the wide range of meetings, including very small, informal ones, covered. The fact that the majority of speakers at a meeting were opposed to the methods or aims of a proscribed group would not affect the liability of the organiser, so long as he was aware that a speaker was a member, or professed member, of such an organisation, speaking in support of it. A meeting is defined as one at which three or more persons are present and there is no need for it to be open to the public. The maximum punishment for this offence is 10 years' imprisonment.

Restrictions on the use of badges or uniforms as signals of support for certain organisations are intended to have the dual effect of preventing communication – by those means – of the political message associated with the organisation and of tending to minimise the impression that the organisation is supported, thereby denying reassurance to its members, lowering their morale and preventing them from arousing public support. Under s3 of the PTA 1989 it was an offence to 'wear any item which arouses a reasonable apprehension that a person is a member or supporter of a proscribed organisation'. This provision is reproduced in s13 which makes it an offence to wear an item of clothing, or wear, carry or display an article 'in such a way or in such circumstances as to arouse reasonable suspicion [that the person in question] is a member or supporter of a proscribed organisation'. Again it is notable that no element of *mens rea* is included. The offence can be established on the basis of proof of reasonable suspicion alone and no defence is provided.

Clearly, a number of objections of principle arise in respect of the application of the proscription-related offences to a wider range of groups. The key objection is that, by making it possible to proscribe a wide range of groups, the legislation potentially curtails proscription-related activities which previously would not have been conceived of as related to terrorism. Some examples are illustrative. A group which did not itself engage in terrorism but which, for example, expressed support for the 'serious disruption' of a computer system could be proscribed as falling within the definition. It would be an offence to wear a badge expressing support for a proscribed environmental activist group or to carry a leaflet which aroused reasonable suspicion that such support was being expressed, although the leaflet was in fact that of a similar but more moderate and non-proscribed group. If a person who opposed the use of violence to further the cause of animal rights organised a meeting to express such views in private with two other people, one of whom was a member of a proscribed animal rights group, who spoke in its favour, she would commit an offence carrying a maximum penalty of 10 years' imprisonment, unless she could disprove the mens rea element. The proscription-related evidence provisions will exacerbate these possibilities. S2A of the PTA made it possible to convict a person of membership of a proscribed organisation on the unsubstantiated opinion of a police officer combined with adverse inferences drawn from the silence of the accused person. These highly controversial provisions, which were inserted by ss1–4 of the Criminal Justice (Terrorism and Conspiracy) Act 1998, were reproduced in the Act of 2000 in ss108 and 9 but applied only to Northern Ireland, with the intention that they should be repealed within five years. The new provisions are discussed below.

Deproscription

Under the previous scheme if an organisation was proscribed on insufficient grounds there was little possibility of challenge to the order. There was no right of appeal against proscription, and judicial review, while theoretically available, was likely to be extremely limited. In *McEldowney* v *Forde*[107] an order was made under statutory instrument banning Republican clubs or any like organisation, thus potentially outlawing all Nationalist political parties. Nevertheless, the House of Lords preferred not to intervene, Lord Diplock stating that he would do so only if proscription were extended to bodies obviously distanced from Republican views.

The new Act sets up, under s5, a new body known as the Proscribed Organisations Appeal Commission (POAC). It is modelled on the Special Immigration Appeals Commission which also provided the model for the new Tribunal set up under the Regulation of Investigatory Powers Act 2000, discussed in Chapter 10.[108] The Commission also appears to have certain parallels with the Security and Intelligence Service Tribunals, discussed in Chapter 8, which have never upheld a complaint. Under s4, if an individual is affected by proscription, or an organisation considers that it should not be proscribed, the first step is to ask the Secretary of State to deproscribe; the Secretary of State is obliged to consider such applications within a period of time specified in regulations to be made under

[107] [1971] AC 632.
[108] At p401 *et seq.*

s4(3). If the Secretary of State refuses to deproscribe, then the organisation or individual may appeal to the POAC as set out in s5 and Schedule 3.[109] Under s5(3) the Commission 'shall allow an appeal against a refusal to deproscribe an organisation if it considers that the decision to refuse was flawed when considered in the light of the principles applicable on an application for judicial review'. Clause 9 of the original Bill provided that the reference to those principles allows the appellant to raise points concerning those rights under the European Convention on Human Rights which are 'Convention rights' under the HRA. After amendment this provision was removed, but the Commission would be expected to apply Convention principles as a court would in judicial review proceedings, now that the HRA is in force. If the Commission finds in favour of an applicant and makes an order to that effect, this has the effect of requiring the Secretary of State either to lay a draft deproscription order before Parliament or to make a deproscription order on the basis of the urgency procedure. Such a finding is to be treated, under s9(4)(b), as determining that 'an action of the Secretary of State is incompatible with a Convention right'. Rules may be made under s9 providing that the POAC is the forum in which proceedings under s7HRA can be brought. If the POAC finds against the applicant under s5, s6 allows a further appeal from its decision to a court, on a point of law, and – depending on the rules made – in relation to s7HRA, if leave is given by the POAC or the court in question. Under s7, if an appeal to the POAC is successful, and an order has been made deproscribing the organisation, anyone convicted of one of the offences listed in subsection (1)(c) in respect of the organisation may appeal against his or her conviction to the Court of Appeal or Crown Court which must allow the appeal,[110] so long as the offence was committed after the date of the refusal to deproscribe. This provision includes persons, other than members of the organisation itself, who have been convicted of proscription-related offences at a point after a refusal to deproscribe, who have already exhausted ordinary avenues of appeal.

The procedure before the POAC may be far removed from that which would be applicable in an ordinary court. Under Schedule 3 para 5(1) the Lord Chancellor has the power to make rules regulating the exercise

[109] It may be noted that under s10 immunity from criminal proceedings is conferred upon a person who seeks deproscription by way of application or appeal under ss4 or 5, either on behalf of the proscribed organisation or as the person affected. Clearly, otherwise, such a person would be discouraged from pursuing either course, or from instituting proceedings under section 7 of the HRA, by the risk of prosecution for certain offences, for example the offence of membership of a proscribed organisation. Section 10 provides that evidence of anything done, and any document submitted for these proceedings, cannot be relied on in criminal proceedings for such an offence except as part of the defence case.

[110] Under s7(2), once deproscription has occurred, if the convicted person appeals to the Court of Appeal under section 1 of the Criminal Appeal Act 1968 (appeal against conviction on indictment) 'the court shall allow the appeal'.

of the right of appeal to the Commission and prescribing practice and procedure to be followed in its proceedings. Its members are to be appointed by the Lord Chancellor. Three members must attend the proceedings and one must be a person who holds or has held high judicial office (within the meaning of the Appellate Jurisdiction Act 1876). Under Schedule 3 the Lord Chancellor's rules may provide that proceedings may be determined without an oral hearing in specified circumstances; provision may be made regarding the burden of proof; full particulars of the reasons for proscription or refusal to deproscribe may be withheld from the organisation or applicant concerned; the Commission may exclude persons, including legal representatives, from all or part of the proceedings and permit proceedings for leave to appeal to a court under section 6 to be determined by a single member. Thus, although the procedure may appear adversarial, its procedural limitations are likely to handicap one side so greatly that the Commission may be unable to discharge its fact-finding role effectively. It may therefore prove ineffective in protecting bodies from unjustified proscription.[111]

Bearing these comments in mind, a further feature of the proceedings is significant. Under Schedule 3 para 8, s9(1) of the Interception of Communications Act 1985 'shall not apply in relation to (a) proceedings before the Commission, or (b) proceedings arising out of proceedings to which paragraph (a) applies'.[112] Thus, the Commission may take its decision on the basis of secret intercept evidence. But such evidence cannot be disclosed to the organisation concerned, its legal representatives or the applicant under para 8(2). Therefore the applicant or the legal representatives would have no means of challenging it or of bringing forward other evidence which might be relevant to it; Article 8 or Article 6 arguments could not be made. A complaint (or, in future, an appeal) to the Interception of Communications Tribunal could not be mounted, unless on speculative grounds only.[113]

This procedure is clearly designed to keep deproscription claims, for the most part, out of the ordinary courts. The courts could have heard such claims in judicial review proceedings and could have applied Convention principles to them under the HRA. Recourse to a court is not, however, entirely prevented; an avenue of appeal from a decision to refuse leave is provided, and the Act does not contain an ouster clause. However, the remedy provided by the POAC may mean that judicial review of decisions to refuse leave and to refuse to make a deproscription order is found to be unavailable. S9 appears to be intended to keep proceedings based on s7HRA largely in the POAC, thereby, apart from the appeals

[111] For discussion of the similar limitations in respect of the new Tribunal set up under the Regulation of Investigatory Powers Act 2000 see Chapter 10 pp404–6.

[112] This will have to be amended to refer to the equivalent provision under the Regulation of Investigatory Powers Act 2000, once that Act comes into force. See Chapter 9 p358.

[113] See Chapter 10 p405.

procedure, preventing the ordinary courts from hearing points raised under s7 HRA. Various features of the deproscription procedure raise Convention issues which are considered below.

Special 'terrorism' offences

As indicated, the new Act will apply all the special 'terrorism' offences which were developed in the context of the PTA or EPA to an extremely wide range of organisations. Unless and until the Home Secretary proscribes a range of domestic animal rights and environmental groups, the proscription-related offences will not apply to them. But all the special terrorist offences, which have no equivalents in ordinary criminal law, will apply, as will the special criminal justice regime for terrorists, affording them lesser rights within the criminal justice system than 'ordinary' criminals.[114]

Section 29 of the EPA made it an offence to direct 'at any level' a terrorist organisation. The maximum sentence which could be given on conviction for the offence was life imprisonment. The PTA contained no equivalent provision. The term 'directing' was not defined in the EPA but it clearly had the meaning of taking some authority for actions to be carried out, or playing some part in giving orders in relation to them.[115] The Consultation Paper noted that there have only been two convictions for this offence, pointing out that its nature means that it is difficult to get evidence to support a charge; witnesses are particularly reluctant to make statements implicating people who hold positions of authority within terrorist organisations. But where a conviction is obtained, 'it is likely to be of some significance and to have a major impact on the terrorist organisation in question'.[116] Lord Lloyd considered that the offence had been of real value. He recommended that it should be retained in permanent legislation and it should be extended to cover the whole of the UK and all forms of terrorism. The government agreed with his recommendation,[117] which is fully reflected in s56 of the new Act. Thus, the leaders, and all with some authority within the vast range of groups within the UK which may fall within the definition, will become liable to a sentence of life imprisonment simply by virtue of their position once the Act comes into force.

A very wide range of other people, who are not part of any of these groups, may also suddenly be criminalised. Section 18 of the PTA made it an offence to fail to report information to the police which might be

[114] See further Chapters 6 and 7.

[115] In the Consultation Paper the government explained: 'The offence is aimed at the strategists – those who plan campaigns and order them to be carried out, but who do not normally themselves take any part in the detailed planning or execution of the individual attacks which make up the campaign' (ibid para 12.9).

[116] Ibid para 12.9.

[117] Ibid para 12.10.

of material assistance in preventing an act of terrorism or in arresting someone carrying out such an act. It applied only to Irish terrorism and it extended throughout the UK. Lord Lloyd questioned the practical value of this offence and recommended that an offence of this sort should not be included in any permanent legislation.[118] However, the government considered that its existence gave a 'clear signal' to citizens regarding the abhorrence of terrorism, and included it in the Act, in s19, in a somewhat modified form. Suspicions arising in home life are no longer covered, but the offence is nevertheless of extremely wide application.[119] S19 goes well beyond requiring banks and other businesses to report any suspicion they might have that someone is laundering terrorist money or committing any of the other terrorist offences in ss15–18. It applies to all employees or employers and means that if, during the course of their work, a person comes across information about, or become suspicious of, someone whom he or she suspects may be using money or property to contribute to the causes of terrorism, that person will commit a criminal offence carrying a maximum penalty of five years' imprisonment if he or she does not report them. This offence is currently one of the most controversial in the PTA, but it will clearly appear even more draconian when applied to a much greater range of people. Anyone working with someone who is active in the manner now designated terrorist, or someone whose work happens to bring them into contact in some way with information related to activities linked to terrorism, will be placed in an invidious position. Such people may suffer a conflict of loyalties, especially if they have sympathy with the activities of the animal rights or environmental group in question, while not wishing to become a member of it. They may also fear reprisal and may therefore be forced to face the dilemma of the choice between risking violence or committing an offence. S19 does not necessarily exempt family members from the duty since many small businesses employ other members of the family, including teenagers.

The new offence will also place journalists investigating the activities of certain groups, such as animal rights campaigners, in a very difficult position, especially where they had contacts within the group. It would appear almost impossible for any investigative journalism to occur in such circumstances, without risk of incurring a five-year prison sentence. The provision requiring the surrender of information might mean that the identity of sources could not be protected. A defence is provided under s19(3) which appears to be aimed *inter alia* at journalists: 'it is a defence

[118] Ibid para 12.7.

[119] S19(1) provides: 'this section applies where a person – (a) believes or suspects that another person has committed an offence under any of sections 15 to 18, and (b) bases his belief or suspicion on information which comes to his attention in the course of a trade, profession, business or employment. (2) The person commits an offence if he does not disclose to a constable as soon as is reasonably practicable – (a) his belief or suspicion, and (b) the information on which it is based'. Subsection (5) preserves the exemption in respect of legal advisers' privileged material.

for a person charged with an offence under subsection (2) to prove that he had a reasonable excuse for not making the disclosure'. This defence would allow a journalist to raise Convention points. But it is clear that s19 would be likely to have a strong deterrent effect on investigative journalism in relation to extremist groups. This might have the counter-productive effect of helping to keep the activities of the more secretive of such groups out of the public eye.

A further wide range of people will be criminalised under the new clause relating to the collection of information, which is based on section 16B of the PTA. S16B made it an offence in England, Wales and Scotland to collect, record or possess any information which might be useful to terrorists; it applied to both Irish and international terrorism. Equivalent provision was made for Northern Ireland in s33 of the EPA. This offence was designed principally to catch those compiling or possessing targeting information. Lord Lloyd found that the police considered the offence to have been particularly useful in Northern Ireland. He recommended its retention, and it is included in s58(1) which provides: 'A person commits an offence if (a) he collects or makes a record of information of a kind likely to be useful to a person committing or preparing an act of terrorism, or (b) he possesses a document or record containing information of that kind'. This is another extremely wide offence, particularly since, in common with the one arising under s56, it lacks any requirement of knowledge regarding the nature of the information or any requirement that the person intended to use it in order to further the aims of terrorism. It could catch, for example, a journalist who possessed information as to the location of fur farms which might be targeted by animal rights groups. The provisions would also cover the retention of notes relating to such locations, regardless of the intention in possessing them. They could even catch, theoretically, a retailer selling fur products who possessed a list of such locations. A defence of proving that 'he had a reasonable excuse for his action or possession' is provided. But the deterrent effect on journalism is likely to be severe, especially as the maximum penalty is imprisonment for 10 years.

S16A(1) of the Prevention of Terrorism Act 1989, as inserted by s82 of the Criminal Justice and Public Order Act 1994, provided that a person is guilty of an offence if he or she has an article in his or her possession in circumstances giving rise to a reasonable suspicion that the article is in his or her possession for a purpose linked to terrorism. Under s16A(3) the accused could rebut this presumption of guilt by proving that the article was not in his or her possession for the purpose mentioned in s16A(1). Under s16A(4) if it is proved that the article and the accused were both present on the premises or that the article is present on premises which the accused occupies or habitually uses, this may be sufficient evidence of possession, unless the accused proves that he or she did not know of its presence or had no control over it. This offence is reproduced in s57 of the new Act. An amendment put forward by the

Liberal Democrats, which would have removed the presumption that proof of the presence of the article on the occupier's premises is sufficient to establish the offence, was overwhelmingly defeated by a combination of Labour and Conservative MPs.[120]

The new legislation does not only act as the 'trigger' applying the old offences to a wider range of groups; it will also create new offences of inciting terrorism abroad, which apply under ss59, 60 and 61 to England and Wales, Northern Ireland and Scotland, respectively. In the Consultation Paper the government expressed concerns as to the effect on free speech: 'the incitement offence could be difficult in practice to prove and ... the effect of [its creation] could be to constrain freedom of expression. On the other hand ... considerable concern can be caused by ... statements ... encouraging and glorifying acts of terrorism'.[121] The government came down on the side of inclusion of the offence. Under s59(1), 'A person commits an offence if (a) he incites another person to commit an act of terrorism wholly or partly outside the United Kingdom, and (b) the act would, if committed in England and Wales, constitute one of the offences listed in subsection (2)'. Under s59(2) the offences are the more serious offences against the person: murder, an offence under sections 18, 23, 24, 28 or 29 of the Offences against the Person Act 1861 (OAPA) and an offence under section 1(2) of the Criminal Damage Act 1971. Under s59(3), the penalty for conviction under this section will be the penalty 'to which he would be liable on conviction of the offence listed in subsection (2) which corresponds to the act which he incites'. Ss60 and 61 create equivalent provisions relating to Scotland and Northern Ireland.

In defending the introduction of the new offence Jack Straw has pointed out that existing legislation which has implemented various international covenants means that it is already an offence to incite anyone abroad to hijack an aircraft or to invite someone in Turkey or India to commit murder. Therefore, extending the offence to other countries, such as Japan or Australia, is logical: 'Every terrorist attack represents a violation of our democratic values ... our response must be sufficiently robust to challenge and defeat these ... activities. I think we have got the balance right'.[122] This claim is presumably based on the restriction of the offence to incitement to commit the serious offences listed. Nevertheless, it is open to question. It means that a person who encouraged another to assassinate a terrorist dictator would commit an offence punishable with a mandatory sentence of life imprisonment. The offence might also be committed during a demonstration at which words spoken denouncing such a dictator could be construed as amounting to incitement to

[120] HC Debs 15 March 2000 col 435.
[121] Ibid para 4.19.
[122] J Straw in a *Guardian* article 14 December 1999.

assassinate the dictator. S59 also creates doubtful distinctions between offences. Sometimes very little separates the person who commits grievous bodily harm (s18 of the OAPA) from the person who commits serious bodily harm (s20 OAPA) and this is more clearly the case where the attack need not in fact have been committed. But the s20 offence is not listed in s59(2). Therefore, determination that a person is subject to a penalty of a maximum of life imprisonment or to no penalty at all may rest on a very fine distinction.

The offences discussed above could probably only have been introduced in the context of the threat from Irish terrorism, in some instances, as indicated above, at a time when the number of deaths from bomb attacks had been very high in the preceding years. At the time MPs obviously could not know that in 2000 they would be asked to apply all these offences to groups which, in terms of their ability to create a serious threat to life and their willingness to do so, cannot be compared with the IRA. Moreover, certain of these offences appeared only in the EPA, partly on the basis, as indicated above, that the threat was greatest in Northern Ireland and that without some apparently strong justification, they should not be included in the PTA.

Requirements of the Convention under the HRA

Clearly, a number of the provisions above may have been of doubtful compatibility with the Convention when they were only applied in practice to certain Irish terrorist groups. But once they are applied far more widely, the issue of compatibility, on a domestic level under the HRA, becomes far more problematic. It is not possible to consider all the instances in which the new legislation may give rise to conflicts with the Convention; the focus will be on certain of its key aspects. Walker has argued in relation to the PTA and EPA provisions that *prima facie* proscription breaches Articles 10 and 11 of the European Convention on Human Rights but that, apart from exceptions contained in those Articles, Article 17 might justify it since it limits Convention guarantees to activity in harmony with its aims and this could not be said of IRA methods.[123] This Article states that the Convention is not to be interpreted so as to imply a right 'for any State, group or person to engage in any activity . . . aimed at the destruction of any of the [Convention rights] or at their limitation to a greater extent than . . . provided for in the Convention'. Clearly, a number of groups might be proscribed under the current provisions, taking s1 into account, which cannot so readily be viewed as out of harmony with the aims of the Convention, and therefore the exceptions under the relevant Articles will frequently have to be relied on if compatibility with the Convention is to be found. This could be said *a fortiori* of the much wider

[123] C Walker *The Prevention of Terrorism in British Law* (1992) pp49–50.

range of persons potentially affected by the special terrorist offences which also *prima facie* breach Articles 10 and 11 of the Convention.

There are a number of possible methods of seeking to ensure that the HRA is complied with in this context. They depend mainly on court action, but, as pointed out in Chapter 2, the Home Secretary and other relevant members of the executive are bound by s6 HRA to abide by the Convention. Articles 10 and 11 should therefore be taken into account in taking decisions to add groups to the list of those proscribed under the new Act. Their requirements in relation to such groups are discussed below. Since the police and the Home Secretary are subject to the Convention under s6, judicial review could be sought of decisions taken by them under the new Act. But, as indicated above, decisions to proscribe may be found to be unsusceptible to review. The POAC itself, as a public authority, must apply the Convention rights in its adjudications and therefore, in relation to the question of deproscription, it should take the relevant Convention rights into account. The courts will be able to apply those rights in hearing appeals from the POAC, on points of law. There would also be the possibility of considering whether the POAC provides an effective remedy for the citizen.[124] The rules made by the Lord Chancellor under s9 with the intention that proceedings under section 7(1)(a)HRA are brought in the POAC would have to be interpreted compatibly with the Convention under s3HRA.

In judicial review proceedings or on an appeal on a point of law to a court against a refusal to deproscribe, it could be argued that the POAC does not meet the requisite standards of independence under Article 13 since *inter alia* the Lord Chancellor appoints its members.[125] The ability of the Lord Chancellor to regulate its procedure would also be relevant. This argument would depend on the view taken of the role of the Lord Chancellor, and in particular whether it could be said that in appointing the POAC and regulating it he should be viewed as acting as part of the executive. It could also be argued that the POAC fails to comply with Articles 6(1) and (3) since the applicant may be in such a weak position before it. Article 6 guarantees a fair hearing in the determination of a criminal charge.[126] It provides basic guarantees under Article 6(3) of a fair hearing, including the right to cross-examination and to legal representation. These requirements are discussed further in Chapters 5 and 7.[127] The POAC's appeal function might be viewed as the 'determination of a criminal charge' since proscription carries criminal implications going

[124] As Chapter 2 points out at p22, this possibility is open due to the *Pepper* v *Hart* statement of the Lord Chancellor in Parliament to the effect that although Article 13 was omitted from the rights protected by the HRA, the courts may be able to view acceptance of the need to allow an effective remedy under Article 13 as an aspect of the intention behind the Act. See Hansard HL 18 November 1997 col 477, Hansard HC 20 May 1998 col 980.

[125] See *Govell* v *UK* (1997) 4 EHRLR 438, discussed further in Chapter 5 at p192.

[126] For further discussion as to the field of application of Article 6 see Chapter 5 pp191–2.

[127] At pp184–5 and pp287–292.

beyond those relating to terrorism alone. It is arguable that the POAC may not provide a fair hearing for the appellant, bearing in mind the procedure which can be followed, described above. The actual procedure followed will depend on the rules made by the Lord Chancellor; those rules will presumably be applied at the discretion of the POAC itself. But the 2000 Act suggests that the new rules should provide for various features of the proceedings, such as exclusion of the appellant from all or part of them, and the direct and secret reception of evidence from phone intercepts which may breach the requirements of fairness.[128] Depending on the procedure adopted in a particular instance it is possible that, apart from any of the other requirements of fairness, the minimal safeguards of Article 6(3) might be unobserved or not fully observed. The impartiality and independence requirements of Article 6(1) could also be raised. It is suggested that the appointments procedure for the POAC complies with the Article 6 requirements in these respects,[129] but that it is debatable whether this is the case in relation to the possibilities provided for under the Act for the determination of its procedure by the Lord Chancellor.[130]

In criminal proceedings on the new application of the special terrorist offences the courts will have the opportunity of interpreting them, under s3 of the HRA, compatibly with the Convention rights. They must also discharge their duty under s6 of the HRA. The approach of the courts towards the new legislation will clearly be crucial. Traditionally, since terrorism has been viewed as threatening national security, the courts have adopted a deferential stance.[131] While a far wider range of persons and activities will be designated 'terrorist' under the new Act, it is apparent that the actions of many such persons and groups do not genuinely threaten national security, not least because the scale of their operations is likely to be small. The approach taken by the House of Lords in *ex p Kebilene*[132] to counter-terrorist provisions, particularly the findings of Lord Hope of Craighead, suggests that where national security *is* in issue the judges will refuse (overtly) to apply the margin of appreciation doctrine

[128] See *Rowe and Davis* v *UK* No 28901/95; judgment of the Court of 16 February (2000) 30 EHRR 1.

[129] See *Campbell and Fell* v *UK* A 80 (1984).

[130] *Sramek* v *Austria* A 84 (1984). One of the central questions, which cannot yet be answered, will be the practice adopted: *Campbell and Fell* v *UK* A 80 (1984). See also the findings on impartiality in the context of military discipline – *Findlay* v *UK* (1997) 24 EHRR 221; *Hood* v *UK* judgment of 25 February 1997.

[131] In *CCSU* v *Minister for the Civil Service* [1985] AC 374 the House of Lords accepted the government's claim that national security was at risk, without demanding that evidence should be put forward to support it. In the case of *Shafir ur Rehman* (judgment of 24 May 2000) the Court of Appeal accepted that it was for the government alone to determine whether a threat to national security, broadly defined, existed. Thus, the judiciary tends to accept government claims that such a threat is self-evident or must be taken on trust.

[132] Below. Divisional Court [1999] 3 WLR 175.

in adjudicating on the new provisions, and yet may adopt a restrained approach. It was said in *ex p Kebilene* in the context of the case, which concerned the compatibility of terrorist legislation with Article 6, that a deferential approach could be justified. The approach of the courts is likely to continue to depend on the extent to which national security can be said to be at stake. Under the previous legislation, in the context of Irish terrorism, the courts tended to take an absolutist approach, readily making the assumption that considerations of national security outweighed the individual rights at stake. The courts are less likely to be deferential where national security is not an issue and therefore may show a greater willingness to take a robust approach to the new Act than they would if adjudicating on the activities of IRA terrorists. Under the current legislation, bearing in mind its width and the influence of the HRA, the approach might be more nuanced, and might depend more on the particular circumstances of each case, since the groups or the activities in question may be far more divergent from each other, and many persons who are not part of any such group may fall within the new provisions.

The notion of increasing the number of groups to be proscribed lies at the heart of the new legislation. A key issue will therefore be the compatibility of the proscription of new groups with Articles 10 and 11 since, as the Introduction to this chapter indicated, the complete outlawing of a group constitutes *prima facie* a breach of those Articles. In findings as to proscription, therefore, paragraph 2 of those articles will be of most relevance. As Chapter 2 indicates, state interference with the Article 10 and 11 guarantees must be prescribed by law, have a legitimate aim, be necessary in a democratic society and be applied in a non-discriminatory fashion if it is to be justified. It can probably be assumed that the exercise of the proscription power would be viewed domestically as prescribed by law since it is enshrined in primary legislation, although the 'quality' of that legislation should also be questioned.[133] In freedom of expression cases Strasbourg's main concern has been with the 'necessary in a democratic society' requirement. In *Sidiropoulos* v *Greece*[134] the Court considered the outlawing in Greece of an association called *the Home of Macedonian Civilisation* which had been formed in Macedonia. The authorities refused to register it, on the basis that it was viewed as intended to undermine Greece's national integrity, contrary to Greek law, since it intended to publicise the idea that there is a Macedonian minority in Greece. The Court indicated the stance it would take towards the aims of the state authorities – the preservation of national security and the prevention of disorder – in this context. They were found to be legitimate but the means used to further them – disallowing the registration of the group and therefore outlawing it – was found to be

[133] See Chapter 2 p25.
[134] (1998) Available from the Court's web-site, see note 30, above.

disproportionate to them and therefore unnecessary in a democratic society. Thus, proscription of a particular group, depending on the extent to which there was evidence that it threatens national security and public order, might be found domestically to violate these two Articles. Where, for example, an environmental activist group had been proscribed on the basis that it was encouraging another group to damage a public utility, it might be found that proscription was disproportionate to the aims in view.

Certain of the proscription-linked offences strike directly at freedom of political expression, which, as indicated above, is viewed as one of 'the essential foundations of a democratic society', so that exceptions to it 'must be narrowly interpreted and the necessity for any restrictions . . . convincingly established'.[135] Such offences include those of wearing any item which arouses a reasonable apprehension that a person is a member or supporter of a proscribed organisation, that of organising a meeting at which a member of a proscribed organisation is speaking, and that of soliciting support for such an organisation. The use of these offences is *prima facie* an interference with the guarantee under Article 10 since all, including the wearing of an item, involve exercises of expression. Obviously the view taken of the necessity of the interference would depend on the particular circumstances behind the charging of the offence in the instance before the court. But to take the example used above of a person meeting privately with two others and hearing a member of a proscribed group speaking: it might be problematic to find that the necessity for the interference with freedom of expression in a democratic society had been convincingly established.

The offence under section 56 of the new Act to direct 'at any level' a terrorist organisation is not confined to proscribed groups. If a minor figure in an organisation which fell within the wide definition of terrorism under s1, but within its less serious aspects, was charged with this offence, a court which found that this interference with Article 11 was disproportionate to the aims pursued could interpret the terms used in s56, especially 'directing' and 'at any level' under s3 HRA so as to exclude such figures from the ambit of the section. For example, taking the terms together it could be argued that the term 'directing' qualifies 'at any level' so that only figures at some level within the *leadership* sector of the organisation are covered. The incitement offence under ss59, 60 and 61 is similarly unconfined to members of proscribed groups. Taking the example used above of charging the offence in respect of persons at a public meeting denouncing a terrorist dictator, a court which viewed the interference with freedom of expression as, in the circumstances, disproportionate to the aims in view, could take the opportunity of construing

[135] *Observer and Guardian* v *the United Kingdom* judgment of 26 November 1991, Series A No 216 pp29–30 para 59.

the wording of the provisions very strictly. In particular, where there was leeway to do so, on a very strict interpretation of the application of certain of the offences listed in s59(2), it might be found that incitement merely of lesser, similar, but unlisted offences had occurred.

As noted above, the offences of failing to report information to the police which might be of material assistance in preventing an act of terrorism, or of possessing information potentially useful in preventing someone carrying out such an act, curb journalistic investigation into the activities of a very wide range of groups, unless journalists are prepared to incur the risk of a lengthy prison sentence. These provisions afford very little recognition to the role of the media in investigating matters of public interest and informing the public. Strasbourg, as indicated in the Introduction to this chapter, gives pre-eminence to the role of the press in a democracy.[136] Restrictions placed on the press in performing this vital role have been subjected to the strictest scrutiny.[137] Charging a journalist with these offences would clearly, therefore, amount to an interference with the Article 10 guarantee. The domestic court would be expected to observe the same or higher standards than Strasbourg in scrutinising the need for the interference, bearing in mind the narrow margin of appreciation afforded to states in respect of interference with political speech, especially where it concerns criticism directed at the government itself.[138] The Divisional Court in *ex p Kebilene*[139] (discussed below) indicated the strictness of the standards which domestic courts are capable of applying, albeit in relation to Article 6(2) rather than Article 10. The defence of 'reasonable excuse' under ss19 and 58 could be afforded a very wide interpretation in order to protect investigative journalism.

If a domestic court found an incompatibility in the particular circumstances of a case between one of the provisions considered and the Convention rights, it would merely have to apply the primary legislation. But where the group in question had an interest in obtaining a declaration of incompatibility, despite the fact that any convictions obtained would stand, the defendants might be prepared to appeal the case up to the level of a court which could issue such a declaration, in the general interests of the group. If a court found in judicial review proceedings that a decision taken under one of the provisions of the new Act could not be justified under the relevant Article, it could arguably quash the decision on the basis, as argued in Chapter 2, that it can never be said to be impossible for a person who has a discretion conferred by primary legislation, such as that to proscribe an organisation, to act otherwise.[140]

[136] *Castells* v *Spain* judgment of 23 April 1992, Series A No 236 p23 para 43.
[137] *Goodwin* v *UK* (1996) 22 EHRR 123.
[138] *Incal* v *Turkey* (2000) 29 EHRR 449 (above, p62).
[139] [1999] 4 All ER 801.
[140] See pp49–50.

Aspects of criminal procedure

Under the PTA and EPA criminal procedure in respect of suspected terrorists differed at significant points from that applicable to 'ordinary' suspects. The provisions regarding stop and search, arrest, detention, police interviewing, coerced statements, which are dealt with in Chapters 6 and 7, created a pre-trial scheme which was of a significantly lower standard in terms of safeguards for suspects than the ordinary scheme. This was also true of the trial process itself. In effect, a twin-track scheme was created in which lesser standards of criminal justice were maintained in respect of persons suspected of the special terrorist offences. This system is continued under the Terrorism Act 2000 and clearly it is likely to apply, potentially, to a far wider range of defendants.

Procedural aspects of terrorist offences

A number of provisions under the Terrorism Act 2000 may be regarded as infringing the presumption of innocence at trial. This may be due to the use of presumptions against the defendant, to the need to show reasonable suspicion only, regarding the main or only ingredient of the offence, and/or to the lack of a need to prove *mens rea.* A number of the special offences contain, as indicated above, a 'reversed' *mens rea*: the defendant has the burden of disproving knowledge or intent. Strictly speaking, the burden of proof is unchanged but, clearly, where the prosecution has merely to prove a minimal *actus reus* beyond reasonable doubt, its burden is significantly lowered, while the presumption of innocence is undermined. Under s57 an accused who chooses not to give or call evidence may be convicted by virtue of presumptions against him or her and on reasonable suspicion falling short of proof. S58 allows an accused who chooses not to give or call evidence to be convicted without any *mens rea* being proved. A number of the other offences under the 2000 Act, including those contained in ss11, 12, 13, 18, 19, 56, have similar features: there is no need for the prosecution to show *mens rea* and the *actus reus* of these offences tends to be minimal. For example, under s13 the *actus reus* can consist of doing something which gives rise to reasonable suspicion that support is being expressed for a proscribed organisation; under s19 the prosecution merely has to prove that the defendant failed to report information. Clearly, the interpretation of these provisions in practice will depend on the attitude of the domestic judiciary. A means of narrowing down the use of presumptions was established in *R v Killen*[141] which held that, under the existing law, although the fact of possession

[141] [1974] NI 220.

constituted a *prima facie* case, the guilt of the accused still had to be proved beyond all reasonable doubt.

Opinion of a police officer

S1 of the 1998 Act inserted ss2A and 2B into the PTA. S2A deals with two matters: the admissibility in evidence of a police officer's opinion that a person belongs to a proscribed organisation, and the drawing of inferences from the suspect's silence.[142] S2A(3)(a) of the PTA makes admissible in court the oral evidence of a police officer of or above the rank of superintendent who claims that an individual belongs to a proscribed organisation. It may be noted that s2A applies only in respect of the offence of membership of such an organisation under s2(1)(a) of the PTA and not to any other related offence under s2 PTA or indeed to any terrorist offence where an opinion as to membership of a proscribed organisation, while clearly not conclusive of guilt, might be viewed as relevant. Under s2A the officer need not substantiate his or her belief, on the ground that to reveal the source(s) would damage national security. However, under s2A(3)(b) the accused may not be committed for trial or convicted solely on the basis of the statement. This provision is reproduced in s108 of the 2000 Act but, as noted above, applied only to Northern Ireland.

This provision changes the role of the officer from that of the ordinary witness, who may only give evidence as to facts he or she has witnessed at first hand, to that of an expert who may give evidence based on an evaluation of facts. The evidence is likely to be based, not on an expert evaluation of facts observed at first hand (clearly any such first hand evidence would be admissible in any event), but on *inter alia* intercepted telephone conversations, information gathering via stops, searches, arrests and detentions under the PTA or EPA, prior convictions or acquittals, hearsay evidence from other officers or security agencies, information derived from forms of surveillance or from informants. Much of this evidence would be inadmissible. The evidence of expert witnesses can, of course, be challenged in cross-examination but the police officer would be able to claim that due to its sensitivity the sources of the evidence may not be revealed. Public interest immunity would probably be claimed regarding many of the sources and certain of the investigative techniques. Lord Lloyd criticised this provision in the following terms: 'A police officer's opinion is worth only what his sources will support. If he simply says "this is my opinion" that is worth nothing in a court of law'.[143] In other words, reliance should not be placed upon the opinion unless the court can make enquiry into its sources. The provision places courts in the position either

[142] Discussed in Chapter 7 pp266–7.
[143] Hansard House of Lords 3 September 1998 col 37.

of rendering the legislation virtually nugatory by refusing to place weight on an unsubstantiated opinion, or of accepting a subversion of the criminal process by coming close to rubber-stamping the decision of the executive as to guilt. The controversial nature of the provision and, perhaps, indications that the courts are refusing to use it in Northern Ireland,[144] did persuade the government to include it, under the Act of 2000, only in relation to Northern Ireland and only as a temporary measure.

Further changes floated in the Consultation Paper

In the Consultation Paper the government gave serious consideration to some further dramatic departures from current standards of criminal justice. The most controversial was the proposal that in certain categories of terrorist offence, the offence should be triable only on the civil, as opposed to the criminal, standard. This possibility was not pursued, presumably because it was viewed as incompatible with Article 6. But it finds a limited expression in s28 which provides for civil forfeiture proceedings in relation to seized cash. Evidence that the cash is terrorist property is required only to the civil standard of proof. Proceedings for a criminal offence are not needed. The provisions do not therefore allow for a *conviction* on the civil standard, but, as discussed below, it is not clear that they are compatible with Article 6.[145]

The possibility of *requiring* a court to accept presumptions of guilt was also raised. This would have meant, as regards s57 of the 2000 Act, reversing the burden of proof by requiring the court to accept the fact proved – that the item and the accused were both present in any premises at the relevant time, or that the item was in premises of which the accused was the occupier – as sufficient evidence of possession, unless the accused could prove that he or she had no knowledge or control of the item. The government did not consider it right to require the defendant to prove his or her innocence, but clearly this proposal would have severely undermined the presumption of innocence.

The government also considered the possibility that previous terrorist convictions should be admissible as evidence in respect of serious scheduled offences, so that they could be taken into account by the court. It stated that to do so would mirror the practice in France, without considering the implications which such a proposal would have under an adversarial as opposed to an inquisitorial system. This possibility, like the others considered, was not included in the new Terrorism Bill, although

[144] In debate on the Terrorism Bill Mr McNamara MP said: 'the courts in the Republic are now very reluctant to use that particular legislation and are not accepting the word merely of a senior police officer . . . They are looking for . . . more corroboration.' HC Debs 15 March 2000 col 354.

[145] It may be noted that these provisions reverse the principle put forward recently in *Webb* v *Chief Constable of Merseyside Police* [2000] 1 All ER 209 to the effect that the seizure of cash linked, on the civil standard of proof, to drug dealing, was unlawful.

such proposals may indicate future possibilities which the government would contemplate adopting, especially if the judges do interpret the new legislation restrictively.[146] Thus the Convention appears to have had an impact in persuading the government not to include these further provisions in the new Act, but it cannot be concluded that they have been ruled out entirely.[147]

Requirements of the Convention under the HRA

The most obvious and useful means of challenging the application of the new provisions will be during the criminal process itself. Convention arguments could be raised *inter alia* in relation to exclusion of evidence or in respect of abuse of process. Article 6, which provides a right to a fair and public hearing, will provide the means whereby aspects of the criminal procedure under the Terrorism Act 2000 will have to be examined. Article 6 provides guarantees that may come into conflict with a number of provisions of the new Act. If it appeared that a certain provision of the Act was incompatible with Article 6 the court would have three main and contrasting courses of action available to it. First it could seek to water down the Article 6 guarantee in the manner suggested by Lord Hope in *ex p Kebilene* (below) by balancing the individual right to a fair trial against the purposes of the terrorist legislation. In so doing it might be found that the provision of the 2000 Act could be fully or largely applied. Second, it could give full weight to the Article 6 guarantee in the manner suggested by the Lord Chief Justice in the Divisional Court in *ex p Kebilene,* and could go on to find that applying the statutory provision in question would lead to unfairness at trial, based on the standards of Article 6. It could then declare that to do so would be an abuse of process. Third, a court of sufficient authority could, on appeal, make a declaration of incompatibility.

(i) The presumption of innocence

The right to a fair trial arises under Article 6(1) and the presumption of innocence is guaranteed in Article 6(2). That presumption is an aspect of the right to a fair trial. Article 6(2) provides: 'Everyone charged with a criminal offence shall be presumed innocent until proved guilty according to law.' As indicated, presumptions against the accused and the lack of need to show *mens rea* are features of a number of provisions of the 2000 Act; they may therefore undermine the guarantee under Article 6(2).

[146] The proposal as regards presumptions was made, the government stated in Chap 14 of the 1998 Consultation Paper, as a result of the Appeal Court judgment in *R* v *Killen* [1974] NI 220 which narrowed down the provision under the EPA which became s16A of the PTA and then s56 of the 2000 Act.

[147] A statement to this effect was made in the Consultation Paper in relation to these further measures (in the Introduction to Chapter 14).

The decisions in the Divisional Court on appeal and in the House of Lords in *R* v *DPP ex p Kebilene and Others*[148] provide highly significant indications as to the stance which may be taken regarding the compatibility of Article 6 with such provisions, since they concerned provisions which have now been reproduced in that Act.

A robust interpretation of Article 6(2) was adopted in the Divisional Court. The first three defendants had been arrested and charged under section 16A of the Prevention of Terrorism Act 1989, as inserted. At trial the judge ruled that s16A is incompatible with Article 6(2). The DPP, when asked to reconsider his consent to the prosecution, appeared before the judge to argue that the ruling was wrong since in his opinion, based on legal advice, the two were compatible. The fourth defendant, Rechachi, was arrested and charged under ss16A and 16B of the 1989 Act, as inserted. Following the DPP's consent to the institution of proceedings, he was arraigned and pleaded not guilty. The defendants sought judicial review of the DPP's decisions. The Lord Chief Justice found that the crucial question concerned the impact, if any, of the HRA on the exercise of the DPP's decision to give his consent to prosecute, between its enactment and the bringing into force of its main sections. The decision to give consent was reviewed, taking into account the ruling of the judge as to the incompatibility of s16A and Article 6(2). The public interest in prosecution was taken into account. One relevant aspect of that interest was whether, if the applicants were convicted, their convictions would be upheld on appeal. If at the time of any appeal the main provisions of the HRA were in force, the applicants would be entitled to rely on ss7(1)(b) and 22(4) of the Act (affording the Act a measure of retrospectivity when used as a 'shield' against a public authority).[149] The DPP had relied on legal advice to the effect that the provisions in question were not incompatible with Article 6(2). The Court could therefore, properly, consider the soundness of that advice despite the provision of s29(3) of the Supreme Court Act 1981, which impliedly precludes such review.

The applicants submitted that the presumption of innocence under Article 6(2) was infringed if a legal burden was placed on a defendant to disprove any substantial ingredient of the offence with which the defendant was charged. They argued that ss16A and B placed such a burden on defendants. The Lord Chief Justice, Lord Bingham, found that both sections undermined the presumption of innocence under Article 6(2) 'in a blatant and obvious way' due to the use of presumptions and the possibility of conviction on reasonable suspicion falling short of proof under s16A, and the lack of a need to prove *mens rea* under s16B. Lord Bingham observed: 'Under section 16A a defendant could be convicted even if the jury entertained a reasonable doubt whether he knew that the

[148] [1999] 4 All ER 801.
[149] See Chapter 2 p53.

items were in his premises and whether he had the items for a terrorist purpose'.[150] He pointed out that this conclusion was influenced by the absolute nature of the guarantees under Article 6. Therefore the DPP's continuing decision to proceed with the prosecution of the defendants under ss16A and 16B was declared to be unlawful. This decision was intended to mean, in effect, that ss16A and 16B of the 1989 Act should be rendered nugatory owing to the incompatibility found. It was especially of interest for its robust interpretation of the requirements of the presumption of innocence under Article 6(2).

The House of Lords, in a cautious judgment, unanimously overturned the Divisional Court decision, on the narrow ground that under s29(3) of the Supreme Court Act the DPP's consent to a prosecution is not reviewable, or reviewable only in exceptional cases. The appeals before the House were only by Mr Kebeline and two others; the case against Rechachi had been discontinued. The focus was therefore only on section 16A. On the issue of judicial review Lord Steyn noted that the Divisional Court had accepted that once the HRA was fully in force it would not be possible to apply for judicial review on the ground that a decision to prosecute is in breach of a Convention right. The only available remedies would be in the trial process or on appeal. He found that it would be strange if in the interim period between the enactment of the HRA and the coming into force of its central provisions, defendants in criminal trials were entitled to an additional remedy by way of judicial review. He also found that since reverse legal burden provisions appear in other legislation,[151] the entertaining of such challenges outside the trial and appeal process might seriously disrupt the criminal justice system. In support of this point he also noted that if the Divisional Court's present ruling was correct, it would be possible in other cases, which did not involve reverse legal burden provisions, to challenge decisions to prosecute in judicial review proceedings.

Lord Hope agreed with Lord Steyn as regards the non-availability of judicial review. He went on to consider the view that might be taken of the compatibility of s16A with Article 6(2). He said: 'I see great force in the Divisional Court's view that on the natural and ordinary interpretation there is repugnancy [in s16A]. To introduce concepts of reasonable limits, balance or flexibility, as to none of which article 6.2 says anything, may

[150] At 190H.

[151] The Prevention of Corruption Act 1916, section 2; the Sexual Offences Act 1956, section 30(2); the Obscene Publications Act 1959, section 2(5); the Obscene Publications Act 1964, section 1(3); the Misuse of Drugs Act 1971, section 28; the Public Order Act 1986, sections 18(4), 19(2), 20(2), 21(3), 22(3)–(5) and 23(3); the Criminal Justice Act 1988, section 93D(6); the Prevention of Terrorism (Temporary Provisions) Act 1989, sections 10(2)–(3), 11(2), 16A(3), 16B(1) and 17(3)(a) and (3A)(a); the Official Secrets Act 1989, sections 1(5), 2(3), 3(4) and 4(4)–(5); and the Drug Trafficking Act 1994, sections 53(6) and 58(2)(a). To this list there may be added the Explosive Substances Act 1883, section 4(1): see *Reg.* v *Fegan* [1972] NI 80; *Reg.* v *Berry* [1985] AC 246.

be seen as undermining or marginalising the philosophy embodied in the straightforward provision that everyone charged with a criminal offence shall be presumed innocent until proved guilty according to law'. But he went on to find that s16A might be compatible with Article 6(2) bearing in mind the 'strong adjuration' of s3 HRA. He considered that s3 might require s16A to be interpreted as imposing on the defendant an evidential, but not a persuasive (or ultimate), burden of proof, although he found that this was 'not the natural and ordinary meaning of section 16A'. It was, however, he found, a *possible* meaning. In so finding he cited Professor Glanville Williams in 'The Logic of "Exceptions"'[152] to the effect that: 'unless the contrary is proved' can be taken, in relation to a defence, to mean 'unless sufficient evidence is given to the contrary'; and that the statute may then be satisfied by 'evidence that, if believed and on the most favourable view, could be taken by a reasonable jury to support the defence'. Lord Hope took *R* v *Killen*[153] into account in support of the possibility of such an interpretation. It was held in *Killen* that an identical provision in section 7(1) of the Northern Ireland (Emergency Provisions) Act 1973, placing an onus on the accused to disprove his or her knowledge of possession, should not be used unless, having done so, the court would be left satisfied beyond reasonable doubt of the guilt of the accused.

In other words, Lord Hope considered that the meaning of s16A could be affected by reading into it an implied meaning under s3 HRA. But in arriving at the meaning of s16A he thought that Article 6(2) could be viewed as qualified to an extent despite the fact that the guarantee it enshrines is expressed in absolute terms.[154] He said: 'In this area difficult choices may have to be made by the executive or the legislature between the rights of the individual and the needs of society'. He considered that in interpreting s16A in the light of Article 6(2) the interests of the individual could be balanced against those of society and that in striking that balance the Convention jurisprudence and that which is to be found from cases decided in other jurisdictions suggest that account might legitimately be taken of the problems which the legislation is designed to address. He looked at the example of *Salabiaku* v *France*[155] in which it was found that

[152] [1988] CLJ 261, 265.

[153] [1974] NI 220.

[154] He recognised the difficulty that Article 6(2) is expressed in unqualified terms: 'It will be easier for such an area of judgement to be recognised where the Convention itself requires a balance to be struck, much less so where the right is stated in terms which are unqualified. It will be easier for it to be recognised where the issues involve questions of social or economic policy, much less so where the rights are of high constitutional importance or are of a kind where the courts are especially well placed to assess the need for protection. But even where the right is stated in terms which are unqualified the courts will need to bear in mind the jurisprudence of the European Court which recognises that due account should be taken of the special nature of terrorist crime and the threat which it poses to a democratic society'. He gave the example of the ruling of the Court in *Murray* v *United Kingdom* (1994) 19 EHRR 193, 222, para 47.

[155] (1988) 13 EHRR 379.

while Article 6(2) 'does not . . . regard presumptions of fact or of law provided for in the criminal law with indifference', it permits the operation of such presumptions against the accused so long as the law in question confines such presumptions 'within reasonable limits which take into account the importance of what is at stake and maintain the rights of the defence'.[156] The Court was concerned with an article in the Customs Code dealing with the smuggling of prohibited goods. Where possession of prohibited goods was established, the person was deemed liable for the offence of smuggling. The provision appeared to lay down an irrebuttable presumption; the Code did not provide expressly for any defence. But the Court held that there was no failure to comply with Article 6(2), because in practice the courts were careful not to resort automatically to the presumption but exercised their power of assessment in the light of all the evidence. Lord Hope noted that the guidance which was given in *Salabiaku* was applied by the Commission in *H.* v *United Kingdom*,[157] in which the complaint was that the burden on the accused in criminal proceedings to prove insanity on the balance of probabilities was contrary to the presumption of innocence and therefore in violation of Article 6(2). He also considered *Bates* v *United Kingdom*,[158] in which the complaint was that Article 6(2) had been violated by the presumption of fact in section 5(5) of the Dangerous Dogs Act 1991 by which it is to be presumed that the dog is one to which section 1 of that Act applies unless the contrary is shown by the accused. In the *Bates* case the Commission held that section 5(5) fell within reasonable limits, even in the light of what was at stake for the applicant, given the opportunity expressly provided to the defence to rebut the presumption of fact, and that section 5(5) was applied in a manner compatible with the presumption of innocence.

Lord Hope concluded that although Article 6(2) is expressed in absolute terms, it is not regarded as imposing an absolute prohibition on reverse onus clauses, whether they be evidential (presumptions of fact) or persuasive (presumptions of law). Applying an approach which balanced the interests of the individual and society[159] he found: 'It is not immediately obvious that it would be imposing an unreasonable burden on an accused who was in possession of articles from which an inference of involvement in terrorism could be drawn to provide an explanation for his possession of them which would displace that inference'. He left open the question whether s16A did in fact strike the right balance, but he clearly reached a conclusion which differed sharply from that of Lord Bingham in the Divisional Court in finding that Article 6(2) could be

[156] At p388 para 28.
[157] Application No 15023/89.
[158] Application No 26280/95.
[159] With reference to Lord Woolf's findings in *Attorney-General of Hong Kong* v *Lee Kwong-kut* [1993] AC 951 at pp970–971.

interpreted in such a way as to permit the use of presumptions against the accused.

Lord Hope's approach is open to criticism in two respects. He rejected the use of the doctrine of the margin of appreciation as inapplicable in national courts. But he proceeded to take the outcomes of applications at Strasbourg into account without adverting to the influence the doctrine had had on them. He also took account of s1 of the Canadian Charter which states that the rights and freedoms it guarantees are 'subject only to such reasonable limits prescribed by law as can be demonstrably justified in a free and democratic society' without adverting to the deliberate omission of such wording from certain Articles of the Convention, including Article 6. In contrast, such wording is clearly reflected in the exceptions of paragraphs 2 of Articles 8–11 which allow interferences with the primary rights if *inter alia* 'necessary in a democratic society'. The clear implication is that certain of the Articles, including Article 6, do not admit of an interpretation similar to that of s1 of the Charter. Although the Court in *Salabiaku* accepted that some presumptions against the accused might not infringe Article 6(2), such acceptance appeared to rest partly on the application of the margin of appreciation doctrine, and partly on the finding that in practice the courts were careful not to resort automatically to the presumption, but exercised their power of assessment in the light of all the evidence. Lord Hope's approach would tend to water down the rights enshrined in the Convention, even where they were unqualified. The Lord Chief Justice's approach was more robust than that of Lord Hope and would tend to give the rights full weight and efficacy.

Ex p Kebilene therefore provides some guidance as to the approach which might be taken when the substantive issue as to the compatibility of s57 of the 2000 Act (reproducing s16A) with Article 6 arises.[160] It is also relevant to all those offences under the new Act which have similar features. Findings that those features are incompatible with Article 6(2) would have to be made during the trial or on appeal, rather than in judicial review proceedings. Lord Steyn's judgment suggests that a finding of an abuse of process might be made at trial even where the primary legislation allowed, in effect, such an abuse and that if this occurred Parliamentary sovereignty would not be undermined even if, effectively, certain provisions of the 2000 Act were thereby rendered virtually nugatory. A number of the new terrorism provisions might thereby become unusable in practice. But the applicability and interpretation of s6(2)(b) HRA would have to be addressed, since on its face it contemplates the

[160] *Ex p Kebilene* itself will not provide such guidance. When it came to trial, in February 2000, the prosecution offered no evidence and it was therefore found that there was no case to answer. The prosecution took that course, it appeared, in order to avoid the possibility of having to reveal their sources of information.

possibility of a prosecution under a provision incompatible with the Convention.[161]

(ii) Equality of arms: examination of witnesses

The question of the compatibility between Article 6 and s108 of the 2000 Act clearly arises. As Chapter 5 indicates, the term 'a fair hearing' under Article 6(1) has been found to connote equality between the parties.[162] The right to cross-examine witnesses under Article 6(3)(d) may be subject to conditions and restrictions so long as they apply equally to both sides.[163] The 'equality of arms' principle would, it is suggested, appear to be violated where the opinion of a police officer under s108 was based on evidence which could not be disclosed, such as the identity of a source or intercepted telephone conversations. If an intercept was used as the basis of an officer's opinion for the purposes of s108, the defence would not be able, owing to the provision under s9 of the Interceptions of Communications Act 1985,[164] to adduce any evidence derived from the intercepted conversations, with a view to undermining the opinion. In an ordinary criminal trial s9 appears to cause offence to the equality of arms principle since the prosecution may obtain an advantage, in terms of aiding the investigation, which may be denied to the defence. But neither side can rely directly on the intercepted conversations. S108 of the 2000 Act, in conjunction with s9, therefore creates greater unfairness since the opinion of the police officer may be based solely upon the use of an intercept. A domestic court might therefore determine that admitting an opinion probably or apparently based on intercepted telephone conversations would offend against the second limb of Article 6(3)(d).

A domestic court might also take the stance that admitting an opinion given under s108 which appeared to be based on hearsay evidence would offend against the first limb of Article 6(3)(d) since the hearsay evidence itself would not be admissible. Similar considerations would apply to admitting an opinion based on evidence protected by public interest immunity; it could be regarded as offending against Article 6(1) and against the second limb of Article 6(3)(d). In such circumstances a large part of the prosecution case would not be able to be disclosed or tested

[161] See Chapter 2 p49.
[162] Judgment of 27 June 1968, *Neumeister*, A.8 (1968) p43. See pp184–5.
[163] See further Chapter 10 p393.
[164] S9 of the Interceptions of Communications Act 1985 provides that in tribunal or court proceedings no questions may be asked and no evidence adduced which suggests that an intercept warrant has been issued or that an unauthorised intercept has occurred. This means that if an intercept is used, whether unauthorised or not, the information gained will be inadmissible in evidence: *Preston* [1993] 4 All ER 638; (1994) 98 Cr App R 405, HL. See also *Preston* v *UK* Chapter 9 p360. The position will be broadly the same under the Regulation of Investigatory Powers Act 2000, which has repealed almost all of the 1985 Act; see further Chapter 9 pp358–9.

in open court. The right to a fair trial under Article 6(1) has been found in the Commission and Court to require the prosecution to disclose all relevant material to the defence, as an aspect of the 'equality of arms' principle. It is also recognised within Article 6(3)(b). The Court has found that the assessment of evidence is for the domestic courts (*Edwards* v *UK*)[165] and that Article 6 does not require any particular rules of evidence. Thus a tendency to allow the national authorities a wide margin of appreciation in this respect was evident. However, in a number of very recent decisions the Court has retreated from this stance, and adopted a much more interventionist approach.[166] In one such decision, *Rowe and Davis* v *UK*,[167] a lesser margin was conceded. In *Rowe and Davis* the Commission said: 'national authorities are not free from effective control by the domestic courts whenever they choose to assert that national security and terrorism are involved.[168] The handicaps under which the defence laboured in not having access to relevant material were insufficiently counter-balanced by the procedure followed by the judicial authorities'.[169] A more activist-minded domestic judge who took into account the findings in *Rowe and Davis* would probably come to the conclusion that a conviction based on undisclosed evidence was not satisfactory and would amount to a breach of Article 6. Absent the margin of appreciation doctrine, the Court would probably have come to that conclusion in *Edwards.*

A strict approach to s108, especially where public interest immunity is claimed in respect of sources or where it appears that the opinion is based on evidence derived from a telephone tap, is therefore likely. Although the opinion is admissible in evidence under s108, it will clearly remain subject to the judge's discretion to exclude it under s78 PACE (Police and Criminal Evidence Act 1984). If the opinion was excluded from evidence and no evidence other than inferences drawn from the defendant's silence was available, the judge would then presumably discontinue the trial since s109 provides that the conviction cannot be based on inferences alone. Alternatively, a first instance judge might admit the evidence but direct the jury to place little or no weight upon it owing to its untested nature. Eventually, on appeal a higher court might make a declaration of incompatibility between s108 and Article 6, depending on the view taken of the meaning of s6(2)(b) HRA.[170]

165 A 247-B (1992) 15 EHRR 417. But see the strong dissenting judgment of Judge Pettiti.
166 See Chapter 5 pp200–201.
167 A/28901/95. Judgment of the Court 16 February 2000, available from the Court's web-site. See in contrast *Jasper* v *UK* A/27052/95, *Fitt* v *UK* A/29777/96 in which the evidence was disclosed to the judge who was therefore able to balance the interests of the prosecution and defence. See also *Kostovski* v *Netherlands* (1990) 12 EHRR 434. See further on disclosure, Chapter 10 pp393–4.
168 Para 75.
169 Para 80.
170 See Chapter 2 pp49–50.

(iii) Fair hearing and burden of proof

The forfeiture provisions under s28 may not satisfy the requirements of a fair hearing under Article 6. Rules are to be made, under s31, governing the procedure to be followed and therefore a judgment cannot be made yet on their fairness.[171] But it is arguable that the proceedings should be viewed as criminal rather than civil. In *Benham* v *UK*,[172] the leading case on 'criminal charge', the Court found that although s41 of the Community Charge (Administration and Enforcement) Regulations, the legislation in question, clearly did not create a criminal offence in UK law, it should be accounted criminal for Article 6(1) purposes. The proceedings against the applicant (in respect of default on payment of the community charge or poll tax) were brought by the public authorities; the proceedings had some punitive elements and the bringing of them implied fault on the part of the applicant: the magistrates could only exercise their power of committal on a finding of wilful refusal to pay or culpable neglect.[173] Further, the penalty was severe (committal to prison for up to three months). S28 has certain features which are comparable with those of s41; if forfeiture is ordered the implication is that the defendant is concerned in terrorism although the possibility of imprisonment does not arise. Article 6(1) and (2) do not require proof beyond reasonable doubt: a wide margin of appreciation has been conceded to national courts in respect of the burden of proof.[174] But as a matter of domestic law proceedings viewed as criminal in character would require proof beyond reasonable doubt.

Conclusions

This chapter has charted a dramatic change from the old model for counter-terrorist laws to the new, introduced under the New Labour government. The Terrorism Act 2000 represents one of the most significant extensions of 'emergency' legislation over the last 30 years. Its introduction in the absence of any 'clear and present' danger may be said to provide a signal example of a failure of democracy to protect civil liberties. The legislation is remarkable in its abandonment of all the features which sought to make the original legislation appear tolerable: its limited application, its temporary nature, annual review and scrutiny of the continuing threat. Paradoxically, it affords the legislation all the hallmarks of ordinary

[171] *Raimondo* v *Italy* A 21-4 (1994), a decision on similar provisions, suggested that they may be compatible with the Convention on the basis that the aim of such provisions is in the general interest.
[172] (1996) 22 EHRR 293.
[173] Para 56 of the judgment.
[174] See *Austria* v *Italy* 6 YB 740 at 784 (1963) Com Rep; CM Res DH (63) 3.

criminal law while continuing to justify its draconian nature on the basis of the special need to combat terrorism. In this sense it is contradictory and possibly counter-productive: the more that terrorism becomes indistinguishable from ordinary criminal activity the less the term 'terrorist' is likely to appear to justify special measures. The failure to include safeguards, such as renewal, in the legislation comes to seem even more indefensible. Such safeguards may have been weak and hypocritical, but they showed some symbolic attachment to a notion of respect for the rule of law.

The old model relied on actual terrorist activity to justify the adoption of draconian laws, on incremental development and a nuanced approach. In other words, particular temporary measures were adopted for periods of time and on a localised basis, to answer to particular threats. Graduation was, in a sense, achieved since where the threat was perceived to be most severe, more severe measures were adopted to meet it. Had the new model introduced greater graduation, depending on different offences and levels of threat, together with a more specific and limited definition of terrorism, its permanent nature might have been less objectionable. But the new model adheres to an absolutist approach in failing to introduce graduation while abandoning each of the features of the old. It is more coherent and bold than the previous legislation; it has spurned the hypocrisy of the past which pretended that these measures were temporary. But, it is argued, its adoption shows an even greater degree of cynical opportunism than that which has such a marked pedigree in the long history of counter-terrorist measures. The government seems to fail to understand that the reluctance to take each step reflected some adherence to democratic principle and explained *why* the previous legislation was piecemeal, anomalous, incremental and localised. In so far as the new Act allows for greater breadth and unpredictability in the application of the terrorist offences, the HRA must be looked to, to seek to prevent the departures from the rule of law it threatens, and which Parliament was unable or unwilling to prevent.[175]

[175] At a number of points in the debate on the Second Reading of the Bill in the Commons MPs noted that it did not appear to be compatible with the Convention: 'we are continuously finding as we go through the Bill provisions that seem contrary to the spirit and precise provisions of the Convention and of the decisions of the Court' (HC Debs 15 March 2000 col 432). Nevertheless, all amendments which might have removed incompatibilities were overwhelmingly defeated owing to the government's very large majority and the determination of the Conservative Opposition to appear to be 'tougher on terrorism' than the Labour Party.

Chapter 4

New Rights of Public Protest and Assembly

Introduction: the legal and political context

Historically, the UK has had no formal Constitutional or statutory provision providing rights to protest and assemble. Instead, it has seen a series of often ill-considered and needlessly broad statutory responses to disorder. Thus, the activities of the followers of Mosley underpinned the Public Order Act 1936,[1] while in the period leading up to the inception of the Public Order Act 1986 there were a series of disturbances beginning with the Brixton riots in 1981[2] and continuing with the disorder associated with the miners' strike 1984–1985, probably the most significant event in UK public order history. The strike largely provided the justification for the introduction of the Public Order Act 1986, although it does not appear that further police powers to control disorder were needed. The police did not seem to have lacked powers to deal with the disturbances; on the contrary, a number of different common law and statutory powers were invoked, including powers to prevent a breach of the peace, s3 of the Public Order Act 1936, offences of unlawful assembly, of obstruction of a constable and of watching and besetting under s7 of the Conspiracy and Protection of Property Act 1875.[3] However, the government took the view that the available powers were confused and fragmented and that there was scope for affording the police additional powers to prevent disorder before it occurred.[4] It therefore introduced a number of low level public

[1] For an excellent account of this period see Ewing and Gearty *The Struggle for Civil Liberties: Political Freedom and the Rules of Law in Britain 1914–1945* (1999).

[2] See the inquiry by Lord Scarman *The Brixton Disorders* (1981) Cmnd 8427.

[3] See S McCabe and P Wallington *The Police, Public Order and Civil Liberties: Legacies of the Miners' Strike* (1988) London: Routledge, esp Appendix 1; P Wallington 'Policing the Miners' Strike' (1985) 14 ILJ 145. During the miners' strike over 10,000 offences were charged; see P Wallington ibid.

[4] See House of Commons, Fifth Report from the Home Affairs Committee, Session 1979–80, *The Law Relating to Public Order* HC 756–1; Lord Scarman *The Brixton Disorders* Part VI

order offences and created a cumbersome, unwieldy framework for the policing of processions and assemblies under the 1986 Act.

The late 1980s and the early 1990s witnessed some similar protests, notably the anti-poll-tax demonstrations, protest against *The Satanic Verses* and against the Criminal Justice and Public Order Act 1994 itself ('Kill the Bill' protests). Mass protest was not a hallmark of the 1990s, but the period did see an enormous growth in the use of direct action by a variety of groups, usually protesting about environmental and animal rights issues. These included hunt saboteurs, fishing saboteurs, motorway and bypass protesters, and veal calf protesters. The protests at Newbury, Twyford Down and Oxleas Wood against bypasses[5] and at Brightlingsea and Shoreham Ferry Port against the export of veal calves were particularly notable. The growth in the use of direct action was arguably traceable to the perception of animal rights and environmental groups that the government's pursuit of free-market policies meant that it had little concern with environmental as opposed to commercial values.[6] Therefore during its lengthy period in office it was assumed that it would be unresponsive to a minority view, and peaceful protest as part of the democratic process would be ineffective. The rise in direct action suggested that the traditional aim of protest – to persuade – was being abandoned. The response of the Major government was to introduce more draconian measures under the Criminal Justice and Public Order Act 1994 aimed largely at direct action in order to suppress it.

The coming into power of the Labour Party in 1997 did not herald any diminution of the direct action form of protest, on the government's own analysis of its predicted prevalence.[7] The concerns of protesters against motorway development, abuse of human rights and on environmental matters, including the introduction of genetically modified crops, continued to be expressed in this form.[8] Diverse groups continued to view protest as a valuable means of drawing attention to viewpoints which tended to be excluded from what may be termed the mainstream communications market place, particularly the tabloid press. Demonstrations against the impact of trading globalisation took place in London in 1999 and 2000, and human rights groups, including Amnesty, attempted to protest against the abuse of human rights in China on the occasion of

(1981) Cmnd 8427; A T H Smith 'Public Order Law 1974–1983: Developments and Proposals' [1984] Crim LR 643; White Paper *Review of Public Order Law* Cmnd 9510 London: HMSO.

5 See B Bryant *Twyford Down: roads, campaigning and environmental law* (1996) London: E & FN Spon; 'Roads to Nowhere' *Green Party Election Manifesto 1997* Transport Section.

6 See G Monbiot 'The End of Polite Resistance' TLS 8 March 1997; B Bryant *Twyford Down: roads, campaigning and environmental law* (1996) London: E & FN Spon.

7 *Legislation Against Terrorism: A Consultation Paper* (1998) Cm 4178.

8 See the Newbury Bypass web-site – geocities.com/newburybypass/index.html; Reports of Protests at Newbury *Daily Telegraph* 11 January 1999 and 30 April 1999; the Greenpeace web-site: greenpeace.org.uk/.

the visit of the Chinese President in October 1999[9] but were met by heavy-handed policing. Flags and banners were forced from the hands of protesters and removed from the windows of private houses. In March 2000 demonstrations at the new Oakington detention centre against the 'internment' of asylum-seekers were notable. The availability by 2000 of a range of other means of communication, particularly via the Internet, did not appear to lead to the marginalisation of protest as a means of communicating and of participating in the democratic process. Indeed, the Internet, far from providing an alternative means of communication, facilitates protest and publicises it.[10] The movement away from socialist policies under New Labour and the similarities between the criminal justice policies of the two main parties appeared to give rise to a continued perception that radical views could find no place within mainstream politics.

The response of the New Labour government to the likelihood that the direct action form of protest would continue in evidence during its period of office mirrored that of the Major government. It passed the Terrorism Act 2000, largely aimed, like the 1994 Act, at this form of protest, but it used the technique, as Chapter 3 explains, not of introducing new, draconian offences, but of applying the established terrorism offences to the new targets. By using the rubric 'terrorist' to denote the groups to be targeted, it sought to deflect the opposition which would have arisen had the terrorism offences merely been used overtly as a means of curbing the activities of environmental activists and the like, under a new Public Order Act. However, the constantly reiterated plea of government ministers to the effect that the Act of 2000 is aimed only at those who are likely to undermine democracy, has not prevented the perception from arising among many protest groups that they are the target of its provisions, for the very straightforward reason that the new definition of terrorism in s1 is not remotely confined to combating a threat to democracy, but rather connotes, quite clearly, the notion of stifling dissent.[11] The introduction of a new Terrorism Act, as the government's Consultation Paper preceding the Act explains,[12] can only be justified in relation to non-Irish domestic groups, including groups motivated by ideological as well as political concerns; two of the key target groups expressly mentioned are animal rights or environmental activists.

[9] The Home Office stated that it had not placed pressure on the Metropolitan Police to prevent demonstrators disrupting the visit of the Chinese President (National News Reports 25 October 1999). A routine internal review was carried out which exonerated the police; Report published on 17 March 2000. Eventually, in judicial review proceedings brought by lawyers for the Free Tibet campaign, the Metropolitan Police admitted that the treatment of the demonstrators had been unlawful: News Reports 4 May 2000.

[10] The Newbury Bypass web-site – geocities.com/newburybypass/index.html – for example, runs to 23 pages and has links to a mass of connected pages.

[11] See Chapter 3 pp76–79.

[12] *Legislation Against Terrorism: A Consultation Paper* (1998) Cm 4178 Chap 2.

Although the method adopted by the Terrorism Act 2000 differs, as indicated, from that of its predecessors, the effect is the same: it follows the tradition they established, whereby provisions likely to affect public protest and assembly are simply added to the existing and extensive ones. A number of trends inimical to public protest are discernible, carried through from the Public Order Act 1986, to the Criminal Justice and Public Order Act 1994, the Protection from Harassment Act 1997, ss1 and 25 of the Crime and Disorder Act 1998, and culminating in the Terrorism Act 2000. Certain features of these statutes exhibit the traditional hallmarks of UK public order law, but in the more recent legislation their illiberal tendency is more greatly marked. These statutes are littered with imprecise terms such as 'disorderly' or 'insulting' or 'disruptive', all objectionable under rule of law notions since protesters cannot predict when a protest may lead to criminal liability. Reliance on the likelihood that police, magistrates or the CPS will under-enforce the law is unsatisfactory owing to the likelihood that their decisions, in any particular instance, will not be subjected to independent scrutiny. Such reliance hardly provides the firm basis for the exercise of rights to assemble and to protest which one would expect to find in a mature democracy.

The more recent statutory offences tend to have the ingredients of a minimal *actus reus* and an absent, minimal or reversed *mens rea.*[13] This tendency contributes to the conflation of substantive offences with police powers, evident in the 1986 Act, which has recently become more marked. The Criminal Justice and Public Order Act 1994 continued the trend begun by the 1986 Act of introducing a number of offences which depended on taking orders from the police and which were based on the reasonable suspicion of a police officer.[14] For example, s60 of the 1994 Act was amended by s25 of the Crime and Disorder Act 1998 to provide a power under s60(4A)(a) to demand the removal of a face covering 'if the constable reasonably believes that person is wearing [it] wholly or mainly for the purpose of concealing his identity' and to create an offence punishable by one month's imprisonment of failing to remove the covering. A reasonable, if erroneous, belief is sufficient and no *mens rea* need be established, so that the wearing of a covering for religious reasons could be irrelevant. No defence of reasonable excuse is provided, so that, for example, it would be unavailing for a farm worker protesting against hunting to claim to wish to conceal his or her identity, not from the police but from his or her employer. This trend was strongly continued under the Terrorism Act 2000, as Chapter 3 indicates.[15]

[13] See discussion of ss14A, 14C of the Public Order Act 1986; s69 of the Criminal Justice and Public Order Act 1994 and s1 of the Crime and Disorder Act 1998, below.

[14] See ss12 and 14 of the 1986 Act. Ss14A and C, introduced under s70 of the 1994 Act, are discussed below, as are ss68 and 69 of the 1994 Act.

[15] See pp82–86 for discussion of the relevant counter-terrorist offences.

The more recent provisions affecting public protest also exhibit a tendency not only to create restrictions at the outer limits of what might be tolerated in a democratic society, but to impose criminal penalties while marginalising the criminal process in dealing with disorder. Thus s69 of the 1994 Act allows for the conviction of the defendant due to disobedience to a ban on entering land imposed by a police officer, even if the original order was based on an error.[16] S3 of the Protection from Harassment Act 1997 and s1 of the Crime and Disorder Act 1998 provide criminal penalties for disobedience to civil orders. S1 of the 1998 Act provides a penalty of a maximum of five years' imprisonment for failing to obey an order obtained on the civil standard of proof,[17] forbidding any form of 'anti-social' behaviour.[18] As Chapter 3 explains, the Terrorism Act 2000 s3(4) empowers the Home Secretary to add a group to the list of those proscribed 'if he believes that it is concerned in terrorism'. There is no express requirement of reasonable belief; nor is it necessary for the group to fall within the definition of terrorism under s1.[19] No criminal or other proceedings are necessary and there is no right of appeal to a court.[20] Not only do the proscription provisions have immense implications for the rights of the groups proscribed to association, expression and assembly, they also provide the basis for criminalising a wide range of persons who are in some way associated with such groups, including those who merely organise informal meetings at which a member of a proscribed group is speaking, regardless of the purpose of the meeting as a whole.[21]

These recently introduced statutes tend to provide a minimal recognition of a need to protect freedom of expression and assembly by including certain defences of 'reasonableness' without attempting to define the meaning of the term[22] and without making any reference to expression. Such defences stand in contrast to those provided in statutes affecting *media* freedom of expression, such as the Contempt of Court Act 1981 s5, the Obscene Publications Act 1959 s4, and s12 of the HRA, all of which provide explicit and detailed defences, allowing, in effect, for a balancing act between protecting expression and the societal interest at stake.

The domestic focus of attention has therefore been on the many areas of law which delimit the residual freedom to make public protest. Clearly, it is understandable that public protest suffers greater circumscription than political expression generally since it conflicts with a large number

[16] See *Capon* v *DPP* Case CO/3496/97 judgment 4 March 1998, LEXIS transcript, discussed Mead [1998] Crim LR 870; discussed below.

[17] According to the 1998 Magistrates Courts Rules applicable to these orders.

[18] S1(10)(b).

[19] See s3(5) of the Act of 2000 and Chapter 3 p83.

[20] See Chapter 3 pp86–87.

[21] See further Chapter 3 p85.

[22] For example, ss5(3)(c) and 4A(3)(c) of the Public Order Act 1986, s1 of the Protection from Harassment Act 1997, s3(1)(c) and s1(10) of the Crime and Disorder Act 1998.

of societal interests and may create invasions of individual autonomy,[23] damage to property and even personal injury. But the traditional marked judicial reluctance to consider the free expression claims of public protest in a democracy provides, it will be argued, too great a contrast not only with the stance taken in Strasbourg, but with that taken by the domestic judiciary, and the House of Lords in particular, in relation to the political expression of the media.[24]

In considering public protest Strasbourg has viewed it as a form of political expression and has therefore relied on case law in other areas of expression.[25] In contrast, in the domestic courts, 'rights' to the freedoms of protest and assembly are occasionally mentioned[26] but their content is hardly considered; far more typically the interest of the judgment centres on the legal content of proprietorial rights. Perhaps even more significantly, the status of Articles 10 and 11 as providing claim rights subject to exceptions which are 'necessary in a democratic society' has provided Strasbourg, as *Handyside* v *UK*[27] makes clear, with the opportunity of considering the hallmarks of such a society. Strasbourg is therefore able to consider what is required in terms of the necessity of an interference with public protest, both in terms of the maintenance of the democracy and of effective participation in it. In contrast, the domestic judiciary have been confined to applying the law, whether or not its restrictions go beyond those nationally and internationally deemed necessary in democracies. The UK courts have hardly participated in the ongoing debate in democracies regarding the permissible extent of such restrictions, and to an extent this is due to their inevitable preoccupation, under a constitution based on negative liberties, with the legal content of the restriction in question.

Clearly, the nature of the statutory provisions is only one factor contributing to the real extent of rights to protest and assemble. The common law power to prevent a breach of the peace or to be of good behaviour arguably outdoes such provisions in terms of exhibiting many of the features just criticised, and, as indicated, judicial influence in developing and interpreting public order law has been significant. The key factor, however, continues to be the working practice of the police.[28] The police may already have developed a practice which renders a statutory power irrelevant, or they may consider that the use of the power would exacerbate a public order situation, rather than defusing it. The police may therefore tend to pick and choose among the available powers,

[23] In the sense that the protest must be experienced by those who may not wish to experience it. It may also interfere with individual choices as to activities and movement.

[24] See *Derbyshire CC* v *Times Newspapers* [1993] AC 534 and *Reynolds* v *Times Newspapers* [1999] 4 All ER 609.

[25] See, for example, *Steel and Others* v *UK* (1998) 28 EHRR 603, para 101.

[26] See, for example, Lord Denning's comments in *Hubbard* v *Pitt* [1975] 3 All ER 1.

[27] (1976) 1 EHRR 737.

[28] See P A J Waddington *Liberty and Order* (1994).

tending to prefer familiar or very broad ones, particularly the power to prevent a breach of the peace. These factors appear to explain why certain of the far-reaching provisions of the Public Order Act 1986, including the obligation to notify the police of a march,[29] the powers to impose conditions on marches[30] and assemblies,[31] and to ban assemblies on the basis of a reasonable belief in the risk of serious public disorder,[32] have hardly been used.[33] In contrast, there is emerging evidence that the broader, less cumbersome provisions discussed below, including the recently introduced statutory powers, are being utilised against protesters. The accountability of the police has lain in this context largely in the hands of magistrates owing to the dominance of summary offences and the use of binding over powers; therefore the reality of freedom of protest has frequently been determined at that level. As Palmer puts it, 'prosecutions before magistrates' courts [which] may give rise to [frequently unreported] decisions of the Divisional Court of the Queen's Bench . . . are the gauge by which the health of civil liberties in this country can be measured'.[34]

Protesters are therefore currently in an especially precarious legal position since such a maze of overlapping and imprecise public order provisions exists, but for the first time they can rely on an express recognition in domestic law of rights to protest and assemble within Articles 10 and 11 of the European Convention on Human Rights as received into UK law under the HRA 1998. It is perhaps worth pausing for a moment to remember that the same government which introduced the Terrorism Act 2000 is responsible for this climactic break with the traditional UK Constitutional position. That position was that citizens might do anything which the law did not forbid, whereas under the HRA they are able to exercise rights to protest and assembly, circumscribed, as Chapter 2 explains, only in a manner compatible with specified Convention exceptions or, exceptionally, by incompatible domestic legislation.[35] As Sedley LJ put it in *Redmond-Bate* v *DPP*,[36] 'A liberty, as AP Herbert repeatedly pointed out, is only as real as the laws and bylaws which negate or limit it. A right, by contrast, may be asserted in the face of such restrictions and must be respected, subject to lawful and proper reservations, by the courts'.[37] Since, as indicated, the extent of such reservations, which may undermine the right, will largely be determined by police officers and magistrates, it is important to bear in mind their obligations to abide by the Convention rights under s6 HRA. Most significantly, this

[29] S11.
[30] S12.
[31] S14.
[32] S13.
[33] See P A J Waddington ibid.
[34] S Palmer 'Wilfully Obstructing the Freedom to Protest?' [1987] PL 495.
[35] S3(2) HRA.
[36] *The Times* 23 July 1999; see below for discussion.
[37] Transcript para 15.

means that for the first time the Constitutional duty placed personally on individual police officers[38] and magistrates to keep the Queen's peace will be coupled with a corresponding duty to uphold public freedom of expression.

The focus of this chapter is on selected recent developments in public order law in the light of the new rights to protest and to assemble. Having considered the justifications underpinning such rights, the chapter will evaluate possible responses of the judiciary to the acceptance of the substantive values underlying public expression under Articles 10 and 11 in UK public order law. Its central theme will concern the potential, depending on such responses, for creating 'empty' rights in the established context of the mass of statutory and common law restrictions.

The value of public protest and assembly

It is often said that toleration of public protest is a hallmark of a democratic, free society. The logic of such a society is that it is prepared to take at least some account of the wishes of its citizens and will not wish to stray too far from the path of majority acceptance in decision-making. Further, it does not impose one vision of the good life on its citizens; therefore it tolerates and even encourages the public expression of various political visions. Public protest as a form of expression is therefore tolerated in free societies.[39] Those jurisdictions which provide Constitutional protection for free expression have generally accepted that the protection will extend to some but not all forms of public protest. The distinction is based on the classification – in the USA – of some forms of protest as outside the meaning of 'speech'[40] or arises because the threat posed by the conduct element outweighs the significance of the speech. These distinctions may reflect perceptions that the well-known free speech justifications[41] are not all equally applicable to public protest and that not all forms of protest participate equally in those which are applicable. The justification based on the argument from truth[42] is present in the sense that citizens must be able to communicate with each other if debate which may reach the truth is to occur: public protest provides one means of ensuring that speech reaches a wider audience.

38 See *Humphries* v *Connor* (1864) 17 ICLR 1.

39 See, for example, M B Nimmer 'The Meaning of Symbolic Speech Under the First Amendment' (1973) 21 UCLA LR 29, 61–62; H Kalven 'The Concept of the Public Forum' (1965) Sup Ct Rev 1, 23.

40 In *United States* v *O'Brien* 391 US 367 (1968) it was found that conduct should not be classified as 'speech' simply because it was intended to communicate opposition to the war in Vietnam.

41 See E Barendt *Freedom of Speech* (1985) Oxford: Clarendon Press, Part I Chap 2.

42 J S Mill *On Liberty* (1972) Everyman edn.

Political speech is justified instrumentally on the basis that it allows participation in the democracy;[43] public protest is one particular and direct means of allowing such participation to occur outside election periods. A clear example was provided by the anti-poll-tax marches in the 1990s. As Chapter 3 indicates, this justification for expression is the one most favoured by the European Court of Human Rights,[44] which has also given a very wide meaning to the concept of political expression. A further justification for speech based on moral autonomy[45] counters public protest in one respect, since the right of a citizen to choose what he or she will see or hear would seem to include a right not to be forced to encounter protest which he or she finds offensive.[46] Article 10 of the European Convention on Human Rights protects the 'freedom of expression and the freedom . . . to receive . . . information and ideas'. This includes a right not to speak, according to the Commission in *K* v *Austria*,[47] and may therefore include a right not to be forced to encounter speech. In the context of public protest this would probably depend on the duration of the protest and its probable impact on passers-by and others. It might also depend on the extent to which the protesters could be viewed as exercising, through the protest, a choice as to their mode of participation in political activity, a choice, which in the case of some minority groups, may not be a real one, in the sense that they may be, in effect, excluded from mainstream politics. Its exercise may also be bolstered therefore by arguments in favour of equality of democratic participation, in addition to those reliant on the values most readily viewed as underlying expressive rights. As Barendt points out, in relation to the German *Brokdorf* case,[48] freedom of assembly (protected, in Germany, by Article 8 of the Basic Law) 'enables people, especially minorities, to participate in the political process. Participation rights are not exhausted by membership of political parties . . . the exercise of the right enables protesters to express their personalities by their physical presence'.[49]

One of the most significant justifications underpinning public protest is that it provides a means whereby the free speech rights of certain groups can be substantively rather than formally exercised. Disadvantaged and marginalised groups, including racial or sexual minorities and groups following 'alternative' life-styles, may be unable to exercise such rights in any meaningful sense since they cannot obtain sufficient access to the media. At the same time the media, particularly the tabloid press, may

[43] See Meiklejohn 'The First Amendment is an Absolute' (1961) Sup Ct Rev 245.
[44] See *Castells* v *Spain* A 236 paras 42, 46 (1992); *Goodwin* v *UK* 22 EHRR 123 (1996).
[45] See T Scanlon 'A Theory of Freedom of Expression' (1972) 1 Phil and Public Affairs 204; H Fenwick *Civil Liberties* (1998) London: Cavendish 2nd edn pp137–138.
[46] Cf Dworkin's distinction between display and distribution: 'Do we have a right to pornography?' in *A Matter of Principle* (1985) Oxford: Clarendon Press at pp355–358.
[47] A 255-B (1993) Comm Rep paras 45, 49.
[48] 69 BVerfGE 315 (1985).
[49] Paper given February 2000 at the Cambridge Public Law conference.

tend to misrepresent them. However impoverished members of such groups may be, they are able to band together to chant slogans, display placards and banners and demonstrate by means of direct action. By these means they may be able both to gain access to methods of communication through publicity and to persuade members of their immediate audience to sympathise with their stance. As Barnum puts it, 'the *public* forum may be the *only* forum available to many groups or points of view'.[50] Thus public protest can act both as a means of access to the media and as a substitute for fair media exposure.[51] The truism that speech in general generates speech is especially applicable to speech or expression as protest. These methods may provide the only avenue available to such groups if they wish to participate in the democracy and it is of crucial importance that they should be able to take it since by its very nature the democratic process tends to exclude minorities with whom the majority may be out of sympathy. Minority interests may be safeguarded only indirectly within that process, by persuading sufficient numbers of people to sympathise with causes which do not directly affect them. There is a reasonable degree of academic consensus regarding the need to protect public protest in order to safeguard minority interests:[52] while it has frequently been suggested that state regulation of the media, far from inhibiting free expression, tends to safeguard it,[53] that argument has been applied to public protest only in respect of the regulation of counter-protest. Unsurprisingly, the intense debate on these issues derives from the First Amendment jurisprudence; within the American academic community there appears to be agreement not only that the state cannot deny a forum to those whose ideas it finds acceptable while denying it to those expressing unpopular views,[54] but also that 'equality of status in the field of ideas' or equality in the exercise of speech rights[55] requires substantive protection. Denial of a public forum for the exercise of expressive rights bears unequally on different groups: it may amount in effect to a denial of the free speech rights of certain minority groups since equal access to other means of exercising those rights will tend to be unavailable. This has also been recognised in the UK context; as Bevan has put it: '[public protest]

[50] D G Barnum 'The Constitutional Status of Public Protest Activity in Britain and the US' (1977) PL 310, 327. See also D Williams *Keeping the Peace* (1967) p10.

[51] As indicated above (see note 8), public protest web-sites may act as one such substitute.

[52] See, for example, M J Allen and S Cooper 'Howard's Way: A Farewell to Freedom?' 58(3) MLR 364, 378; D G Barnum 'The Constitutional Status of Public Protest Activity in Britain and the US' (1977) PL 310.

[53] See, for example, R Abel *Speech and Respect* (1994) London: Sweet and Maxwell pp48–58. Abel argues, using examples of media regulation by the market, that: 'state withdrawal exposes speech to powerful market forces'. See also M Feintuck *Media Regulation, Public Interest and the Law* (1999) Edinburgh University Press.

[54] See *Police Dept of the City of Chicago* v *Mosley* 408 US 92, 95–96 (1972). The case concerned an anti-racist protest by a single black protester.

[55] See Karst 'Equality as a Central Principle in the First Amendment' 43 University of Chicago Law Review 20.

assists the "unknowns", those who do not have the capability or resources to exercise expression through the conventional media'.[56]

Public protest occurs in various forms,[57] admittedly overlapping, ranging from the peaceful expression of views to rioting and extreme violence; it can be categorised as: peaceful persuasion,[58] offensive or insulting persuasion,[59] intimidation,[60] symbolic or persuasive physical obstruction or interference,[61] actual physical obstruction or interference,[62] forceful physical obstruction[63] and violence.[64] The first three forms, which may occur by means of both speech and conduct, may be supported by the arguments from truth and democracy so long as they are not outweighed by the threat posed by the action. Since these justifications are goal – as opposed to rights – based they would support only public protest which did not run counter to the goals in question (such as an anti-democratic protest).[65] Further, since they set out goals for society as a whole they would seem to allow interference with speech in the interests of other public concerns which may be immediately and directly damaged by the exercise of speech. As Barendt puts it, in discussing the argument from truth, 'a government worried that inflammatory speech may provoke disorder is surely entitled to elevate immediate public order considerations over the long term intellectual development of the man on the Clapham omnibus'.[66]

The last four forms, often loosely referred to as 'direct action', cannot be termed 'speech' but may be viewed as forms of expression and as having, to varying extents, the same role as political speech. If, as in the last three, a group seeks not to persuade others but by its actions to bring about the object in question, the democratic process may be said to have been circumvented rather than underpinned. Such action is also likely to create an invasion of personal autonomy. For example, a person engaging in a lawful sport may expect to be able to pursue it free from interference. Suppose that a racist group wished to prevent Asians playing cricket on the ground that it is 'a white man's sport'. Without using any violence they came onto a pitch where Asians were engaged in playing cricket and sat down in the batting area, preventing the game from occurring. A clear invasion of autonomy has occurred. This argument may be countered where strong justification for the direct action is put

[56] V T Bevan 'Protest and Public Disorder' (1979) PL 163, 187.
[57] I am indebted to Gavin Phillipson, University of Durham, for suggestions as to their categorisations.
[58] For example, offering innocuous leaflets or chanting inoffensive slogans.
[59] For example, carrying racist banners, displaying pictures of dead foetuses.
[60] For example, shouting and gesturing at individuals crossing picket lines.
[61] For example, lying passively in front of earth-moving machinery, conducting a vigil.
[62] For example, blowing horns during a hunt or chaining oneself to a tree.
[63] For example, resisting official attempts to remove members of a sit-in.
[64] For example, attacking counter-demonstrators or police officers.
[65] See *Kuhnen* v *FRG* No 12194/86, 56 DR 205 (1988).
[66] *Freedom of Speech* (1987) Oxford: Clarendon Press p10.

forward. An obvious example is its use by the suffragettes in order to persuade and to draw attention to a cause of immense importance in a democracy. It is clearly questionable whether, short of violence, such protest should be placed, in the eyes of the law, in the same category as late night high street rowdiness. The same cannot be said so readily of direct action which seeks to prevent an outcome of lesser significance – such as the building of a bypass – which has been determined upon by an application of the democratic process.[67]

The fourth form of protest, persuasive physical obstruction or interference, is in a rather different position, although the line between the fourth and fifth tiers will often be hard to draw. Such action is not intended to bring about the object in question directly but to draw attention to a cause. Of course, some direct action may exemplify both purposes. This may be said of the actions of hunt or fishing saboteurs and motorway protesters.[68]

Political riots do not present states with the dilemmas normally associated with public protest. The difficulty usually lies in determining whether a protest, which is justified by reference to the arguments above, has the potential to threaten public order. This possibility clearly raises issues as to the scope of state duties to keep the peace and to safeguard the interests of citizens upon whom protests may impinge. Forms of direct action may infringe privacy rights and the freedom from physical attack or threats. The substance of the protest may be offensive and hurtful to others. The manner of the protest may involve intimidation, thereby potentially infringing the rights of persons to security of the person, freedom of movement and possibly to freedom of assembly. Non-violent or more vulnerable groups may require a calm public order situation in order to be enabled to make an effective protest. Protecting the freedom to protest can mean protecting powerful and well-organised groups at the expense of the weak.

In a mature democracy it would be expected that the extent to which a protest was persuasive rather than simply obstructive would tend to determine the extent of its Constitutional protection, although even obstructive protest may be viewed as falling within the range of expressive rights,[69] as raising issues of association and, arguably, of participation in

[67] In the case of road-building the extent to which the outcome may be said to represent an application of the democratic process is debatable, especially where the road is within the remit of the Department of Transport rather than a local council. In both instances, under s258 of the Highways Act 1980, objections may be made by those directly and indirectly affected and usually a Public Inquiry will be arranged and conducted by an 'independent' inspector – a civil servant in the Department of Transport – who then makes a recommendation to the Secretary of State.

[68] A good example is the protest at Newbury against the A34 bypass. Between 1994 and 1998 every form of protest was used, from non-violent direct action to criminal damage; see the Newbury Bypass web-site, note 8 above.

[69] Such protest will be viewed as an expression of opinion according to the findings of the European Court of Human Rights in *Steel* v *UK* and *Hashman and Harrup* v *UK*, both

the democracy. The direct action forms of protest might be justified, particularly when exercised by minority groups, on the grounds that they provide a substantive means of engaging in the more *effective* means of communicating with others (since such forms are most likely to attract media attention) and of participating freely in political activity.[70] The same arguments could be applied to persuasive protest requiring a particular forum and time for its exercise. In other words, the equality principle in terms of free expression and rights to engage in political activity might be taken to demand that minorities should be allowed access to forms and places of protest going beyond the relatively innocuous or convenient. Such an argument might allow interference with forms of direct action exercised by minority groups to be considered as interferences with the freedoms of expression, assembly and association though subject to justification, although this raises the difficult issue of the relationship between equality and freedom.[71] Constitutional protection for such freedoms might be expected to override societal interests in preventing mere inconvenience or preserving decorum but, depending on considerations of proportionality, might give way to justifications based on moral autonomy, the risk of personal harm and, perhaps, economic loss. If the value of minority political participation is at stake, a protest expressing a minority viewpoint tending to marginalise a further minority might undermine any special claim it might otherwise have had to access to a particular place.[72] These are the issues with which, on the whole, the domestic courts have not had to grapple in determining public order questions[73] but with which they are now confronted under the HRA 1998.

Rights to make public protest within Articles 10 and 11

Article 11 is specifically aimed at freedom of assembly, although it may be, in accordance with the arguments above, that protection for public protest will most frequently flow from the provisions of Article 10. The

discussed below. The protests at issue in those decisions might be viewed as having both persuasive and destructive elements, but it might be argued that a protest intended by the protesters to be purely obstructive could also be viewed as the expression of an opinion; it could also lead incidentally to publicity for the cause and on that basis also could be viewed as a form of expression.

70 See Barendt's argument, note 49, above and associated text.

71 See Karst 'Equality as a Central Principle in the First Amendment' 43 University of Chicago Law Review 20, 43.

72 For example, racist groups were diverted from marching through Asian communities in Leicester in 1974 and 1979, by the imposition of conditions under s3(1) of the Public Order Act 1936. Such conditions could now be imposed under s12 of the 1986 Act.

73 As D Feldman puts it: 'the central value [in UK public protest cases] is public order', *Civil Liberties and Human Rights in England and Wales* (1993) Oxford: Clarendon Press p785.

value of freedom of choice as to the *manner* of participation in political activity may, however, fall most readily within Article 11 which in this instance should not therefore be viewed simply as providing assembly rights interchangeable with expression rights under Article 10. Article 11 protects both association and assembly, and in its judgment in *Socialist Party and Others* v *Turkey*[74] the Court linked the three guarantees together. It found that the dissolution of the Socialist Party of Turkey had breached Article 11 since: 'there can be no democracy without pluralism . . . It is of the essence of democracy to allow diverse political programmes to be proposed and debated, even those that call into question the way a state is currently organised'. In other words, the individuals affected by the interference in question could be viewed as exercising rights to participate in political activity, of a central nature in a democracy. As indicated above, such participation can occur by various means, including direct action, and is clearly not confined to activity associated only with general elections. The persons participating may be viewed as exercising a choice as to the particular manner of their participation. The close connection which the Court perceived between the freedoms of association and expression echoes in the findings of Judge Harlan in the US Supreme Court in 1958: 'Effective advocacy of both public and private points of view, particularly controversial ones, is undeniably enhanced by group association, as this Court has more than once recognised in remarking upon the close nexus between the freedoms of speech and assembly'.[75] If the argument in favour of rights of association and participation in political activity is applied to public protest, it may in certain circumstances provide a foundation for the claims of protesters which might not readily arise if Article 10 alone was relied on. As Barendt has pointed out,[76] the US Supreme Court has shown itself willing to protect rights of access to particular public places in order to hold meetings or demonstrations, in contrast to its stance in respect of the exercise of speech rights. Although this stance appears to flow from the wording of the First Amendment which, in contrast to Article 10, refers to speech rather than expression, the argument may be of relevance in relation to 'manner' issues and have value in carving out a distinctive, or any, role for Article 11 which is not at present apparent in the recent Strasbourg public protest jurisprudence.

Article 11 leaves a great deal of discretion to the judiciary. It is not a far-reaching provision since it protects only freedom of peaceful assembly and since, in common with Articles 8–10, it contains a long list of exceptions in paragraph 2. In interpreting it the UK judiciary is obliged, under

[74] Judgment of 25 May 1998 (1999) 27 EHRR 51, paras 41, 47, 50.
[75] *NAACP* v *Alabama* 357 US 449 (1958) at p460.
[76] In a paper given at the Cambridge University Centre for Public Law Conference, February 2000.

s2 HRA, to take the relevant Strasbourg jurisprudence into account. That jurisprudence is not, on the whole, of a radical nature, although the Court has found that the right to organise public meetings is 'fundamental'[77] and includes the right to organise marches, demonstrations and other forms of public protest. Article 11 may impose limited positive duties on the state to ensure that an assembly or a protest can occur even though it is likely to provoke others to violence; the responsibility for any harm caused appears to remain with the counter-demonstrators.[78] The acceptance of further positive duties, including a duty to require owners of private land to allow some peaceful assemblies on their property, has not yet been accepted under the Convention but remains a possibility,[79] especially, as Harris, O'Boyle and Warbrick point out,[80] in view of the growth of quasi-public places such as large, enclosed shopping centres and the privatisation of previously public places.

'Direct action' used in a symbolical sense – the fourth form of protest referred to above – has been found to fall within Article 11.[81] The key factor in determining whether a protest counts as a peaceful assembly appears to be whether it is violent in itself or whether any violence arises incidentally.[82] The Court has only found an infringement of freedom of assembly in one judgment, *Ezelin* v *France*,[83] and it has been a feature of the practice that applications do not reach the Court since the Commission has readily found them to be manifestly ill-founded.[84] This cautious stance largely arises from the wide margin of appreciation which has been afforded to national authorities in determining what is needed to preserve public order at local level.

The Article 10 jurisprudence relating specifically to public protest is meagre, as this chapter will indicate. However, the extensive jurisprudence on expression generally, especially political expression, is clearly applicable

77 *Rassemblement Jurassien Unite Jurassienne* v *Switzerland* No 819/78, 17 DR 93, 119 (1979).

78 *Platform 'Artze fur das Leben'* v *Austria* Series A No 139 para 32 (1988); judgment of 21 June 1988; 13 EHRR 204.

79 See *De Geillustreede Pers* v *Netherlands* No 5178/71, 8 DR 5 (1976) Com Rep; the Commission accepted that states may have positive obligations to uphold freedom of expression in the context of media ownership. In the USA the 'access' issue was initially resolved in favour of the property right but now seems to be moving towards acceptance of exceptions favouring expressive rights; see Nardell 'The Quantock Hounds and the Trojan Horse' [1995] Public Law 27 on *R* v *Somerset CCV ex p Fewings*, for discussion of the shopping mall/'constitutional fora' cases. See further below, pp158–9.

80 *Law of the European Convention on Human Rights* (1995) London: Butterworths at p419.

81 *G* v *Federal Republic of Germany* No 13079/87, 60 DR 256, 263 (1989). Currently the Court views such protest as falling most readily within Article 10; see below.

82 *Christians against Racism and Fascism* v *UK* No 8440/78, 21 DR 138, 148 (1980).

83 A 202-A (1991). In *Steel and Others* v *UK* (1998) 28 EHRR 603, judgment of the Court 23 September 1998 a violation of Article 10 was found in respect of interferences with public protest. Both judgments are discussed below.

84 *Friedl* v *Austria* No 15225/89 (1992) unreported; *Christians Against Racism and Fascism* v *UK* No 8440/78, 21 DR 138 (1980).

to public protest.[85] The *content* of speech will rarely exclude it from Article 10 protection: thus, speech as part of a protest likely to cause such low level harm as alarm or distress may be protected according to the *dicta* of the Court in *Muller* v *Switzerland*[86] to the effect that the protection of free speech extends equally to ideas which 'offend, shock or disturb'. The Court has repeatedly asserted that freedom of expression 'constitutes one of the essential foundations of a democratic society', that exceptions to it 'must be narrowly interpreted and the necessity for any restrictions . . . convincingly established'.[87] As Chapter 3 indicates, it is a marked feature of the Strasbourg jurisprudence that political expression receives a high degree of protection. One of the leading works on the Convention concludes: 'It is clear that the Court ascribes a hierarchy of value' to different classes of speech, attaching 'the highest importance to the protection of political expression . . . widely understood'.[88]

The emphasis is therefore on the paragraph 2 exceptions which include 'in the interests of national security . . . public safety . . . for the prevention of disorder or crime . . . for the protection of the . . . rights of others'. The Court tends to afford a wide margin of appreciation when reviewing interferences with expression on these grounds, viewing measures taken on those bases as peculiarly within the purview of the domestic authorities, in contrast to its stance in respect of 'pure' speech. Therefore speech as part of protest tends to be in a precarious position. Owing to the existence of Article 11 it is fair to say that until recently Strasbourg had not developed a distinct Article 10 jurisprudence on expression as public protest. However, recent decisions, discussed below, suggest that such a jurisprudence may be developing and that Strasbourg currently views freedom of assembly simply as an aspect of freedom of expression.[89] This stance is appropriate given the deliberate adoption of the wider term 'expression' rather than 'speech' in Article 10; it also avoids the problems experienced in the USA, in distinguishing between message-bearing

85 *Steel and Others* v *UK* Application No 24838/94; see note 83, above; available from the Court's web-site: www.dhcour.coe.fr.

86 (1991) 13 EHRR 212.

87 *Observer and Guardian* v *the United Kingdom* judgment of 26 November 1991, Series A No 216 pp29–30 para 59; 14 EHRR 153.

88 Harris, O'Boyle and Warbrick *Law of the European Convention on Human Rights* (1995) London: Butterworths pp397 and 414. The second rank is artistic speech, the third commercial speech, for example, advertising. They acknowledge that these terms may be too narrow (p397 fn 14 and associated text). In particular, the term 'artistic' is too restrictive since it does not cover all speech, including some forms of protest, which may be said to be supported by the free speech arguments.

89 *Ezelin* v *France* A 202-A (1991). However, it may be noted that in his partly dissenting Opinion Judge de Meyer took the view that the two Articles were inextricably linked in their bearing on the instant situation and that there had been a violation of both (at p31).

conduct and conduct *simpliciter*. The conduct element of assemblies and protests may exclude it from Article 11 protection owing to the requirement that they should be 'peaceful' and possibly this restriction should also be read into Article 10, at least in respect of *group* protest, in order to ensure the consistency and coherence of the two Articles. This does not imply that the 'assembly' element within the exercise of Article 11 rights is necessarily subordinate to the 'expression' element or that it is unnecessary to distinguish between the two elements. In *Chorherr v Austria*[90] the expression of protesters appeared likely to offend some spectators, leading to an interference with their peaceful enjoyment of a parade. The interference of the state with the Article 10 rights of the protesters was justified since it had the aim of upholding freedom of assembly.

Once domestic courts begin to develop a distinctive Convention jurisprudence on public protest it is suggested that, as indicated above, they should question the treatment of protest as simply a form of political expression. Although protest is thereby bolstered by the arguments outlined supporting the special position of such expression, there may be instances in which other arguments based on the exercise of autonomy in relation to political activity, deriving solely or mainly from Article 11, should be utilised. If protesters rely on both Articles 10 and 11 the argument that other means of communication, such as the Internet, are available or that free expression arguments may not fully support rights to determine the place, manner and time of the protest, will carry less weight since each protester may be viewed as exercising rights to self-determination in choosing both to associate with a particular group and to participate in the political process in a particular manner, time and place.

It would appear that certain forms of protest – peaceful persuasion, offensive persuasion and symbolic obstruction – are protected under Articles 10 and 11 as forms of expression and as providing methods of participating in political activity under the HRA. Intimidation and actual obstruction as forms of protest are in a much more doubtful position, while forceful obstruction and violent protest will not be protected since they clearly cannot be termed 'peaceful'. Once protection is available for public protests falling within Articles 10 and 11, the state will have to provide some evidence justifying interferences with them. Thus, broadly speaking, the form of the protest rather than its content will determine whether it receives any protection at all.

Under the familiar formula discussed in Chapter 2, in order to be justified state interference with Article 10 and 11 guarantees must be prescribed by law, have a legitimate aim, be necessary in a democratic society and be applied in a non-discriminatory fashion. In freedom of

[90] A 266-B (1993).

expression cases Strasbourg's main concern has been with the 'necessary in a democratic society' requirement; the notion of 'prescribed by law' has been focused upon to some extent but almost always with the result that it has been found to be satisfied. The 'legitimate aim' requirement will normally be readily satisfied; as Harris, O'Boyle and Warbrick point out, the grounds for interference are so wide that 'the state can usually make a plausible case that it did have a good reason for interfering with the right'.[91] The provision against non-discrimination that arises under Article 14 is potentially very significant, especially in relation to minority public protests, but so far it has not been a significant issue in the relevant freedom of expression jurisprudence.

The requirements of precision and foreseeability connoted by the term 'prescribed by law'[92] have been flexibly applied in this context; for example, in *Rai, Allmond and 'Negotiate Now'* v *UK*[93] the Commission had to consider the ban on public demonstrations or meetings concerning Northern Ireland in Trafalgar Square. The ban was the subject of a statement in the House of Commons and many refusals of demonstrations had been made subsequent to it. The Commission found that the ban was sufficiently prescribed by law: 'It is compatible with the requirements of foreseeability that terms which are on their face general and unlimited are explained by executive or administrative statements, since it is the provision of sufficiently precise guidance to individuals . . . rather than the source of that guidance which is of relevance'.[94] In *Steel and Others* v *UK*[95] the Commission introduced a very significant qualification to the requirement: 'The level of precision required depends to a considerable degree on the content of the instrument, the field it is designed to cover, and the number and status of those to whom it is addressed'.[96] Although the term 'margin of appreciation' was not used, this finding appears to allow the member state a certain leeway in public protest cases in relation to the 'prescribed by law' requirement. As indicated below, that leeway was overstepped by the *contra bono mores*, 'contrary to a good way of life', power arising under the Justices of the Peace Act 1361, due to its imprecision.[97]

[91] *Law of the European Convention on Human Rights* (1995) London: Butterworths p290.

[92] *Sunday Times* v *UK* A30 para 49 (1979).

[93] 81-A D&R 146 (1995).

[94] Ibid at p152. The power in question arose from the Trafalgar Square Regulations 1952 (1952 SI 776) para 3 made under The Parks Regulation (Amendment) Act 1926. The Act allowed the Secretary of State to 'make any regulations considered necessary . . . for the preservation of order' in the parks.

[95] Application No 24838/94; (1998) 28 EHRR 603; (1998) Crim LR 893.

[96] At para 145. The Commission based these findings on the judgments of the Court in *Chorherr* v *Austria* Series A 266-B para 23 (1993) and in *Cantoni* v *France* para 35 (1996) (not yet published).

[97] See *Hashman and Harrup* v *UK* Application No 25594/94 (1999) European Court of Human Rights 25 November 1999.

The notion of a margin of appreciation conceded to states permeates the Article 10(2) and 11(2) jurisprudence, although it has not influenced the interpretation of the substantive rights. In finding that applications are manifestly ill-founded, the Commission has been readily satisfied that decisions of the national authorities to adopt quite far-reaching measures, including complete bans, in order to prevent disorder are within their margin of appreciation.[98] The Court has also found 'the margin of appreciation extends in particular to the choice of the reasonable and appropriate mean to be used by the authority to ensure that lawful manifestations can take place peacefully'.[99]

As explained in Chapter 2, if a common standard cannot be discerned among the member states, Strasbourg will afford a wide margin of appreciation. But where a principle has received general acceptance in the member states and in particular where it is closely linked to the notion of democracy, the Court will afford a narrow margin of appreciation only. In *Socialist Party and Others* v *Turkey*[100] the Court found that the dissolution of the Socialist Party of Turkey had breached Article 11, taking into account 'the essential role of political parties in the proper functioning of democracy . . . In determining whether a necessity within the meaning of Article 11 exists, the Contracting states possess only a limited margin of appreciation'. This stance is in accordance with the Convention jurisprudence which has quite consistently recognised the need to protect the interests of minority and excluded groups.[101] Its failures to do so in practice have on occasion attracted strong dissenting opinions within the Court itself. For example, in *Cossey* v *UK*[102] Judge Martens said, in his dissenting Opinion: 'this caution [in allowing a wide margin of appreciation based on a strict application of the common standards doctrine] is in principle not consistent with the Court's mission to protect the individual against the collectivity'.[103] This stance would suggest that where a protest provided the only practical or effective means available to a minority group to communicate its views to others, a narrow margin of appreciation only might be allowed.

[98] See *Christians against Racism and Fascism* v *UK* No 8440/78, 21 DR 138, and *Friedl* v *Austria* No 15225/89 (1992) unreported.
[99] *Chorherr* v *Austria* Series A 266-B para 31 (1993).
[100] Judgment of 25 May 1998 (1999) 27 EHRR 51, paras 41, 47, 50.
[101] Such groups have included criminals: *Soering* v *UK* A 161 (1989); prisoners: *Ireland* v *UK* A 25 (1978), *Golder* v *UK* A 18 (1975); racial minorities: *East African Asians* cases 3 EHRR 76 (1973), *Hilton* v *UK* No 5613/72, 4 DR 177 (1976) (no breach found on facts); sexual minorities: *Dudgeon* v *UK* A 45 (1981), *B* v *France* A 232-C (1992); political minorities: *Arrowsmith* v *UK* No 7050/75, 19 DR 5 (1978); religious minorities: *Kokkinakis* v *Greece* A 260-A (1993).
[102] A 184 (1990).
[103] At para 5.6.3.

The domestic application of Articles 10 and 11

This is a context in which the possible stances which the domestic judiciary might adopt when confronted with public order cases raising Articles 10 and 11 issues are quite clearly opposed. A minimalist or 'review' approach might be, in this context, almost indistinguishable from a 'traditionalist' one and might yield similar results, since this is a field in which the judiciary has, since *Beatty* v *Gillbanks*,[104] almost invariably eschewed an activist approach. The 'review' or minimalist approach could be justified on the basis that a balance has always been struck in UK law between freedom of assembly and public order by reference either to common law principle or Parliamentary restraint; with only two exceptions[105] that balance has been found to accord with Articles 10 and 11 at Strasbourg[106] and therefore there is no reason to disturb it now.

The traditionalist judge would tend to take the view that common law principle has long recognised values which are coterminous with the factors taken into account at Strasbourg in evaluating the balance in question, and that, in most instances, the outcome of cases would not differ whether freedom of expression was viewed as a common law principle or as protected under the Convention. Occasional judicial pronouncements suggest that the common law recognises legal rights to assemble and protest. In *Hubbard* v *Pitt*,[107] in a well-known minority judgment, Lord Denning referred to 'the right to demonstrate and the right to protest on matters of public concern'.[108] Recently, Mr Justice Eady found, in a decision concerning animal rights activists, that the Protection from Harassment Act 1997 'was . . . not intended by Parliament to be used to clamp down on . . . the rights of political protest and public demonstration which are so much a part of our democratic tradition'.[109] The traditionalist judge might note, however, that the two decisions at Strasbourg which have found that the UK had breached Article 10 in interfering with public protest, both concerned common law doctrines. Such a judge might perhaps also acknowledge that there has been more reluctance to accept that the freedoms of protest and assembly, as opposed to media freedom

[104] [1882] 9 QBD 308, discussed below.

[105] See the findings of the Court under Article 10 regarding the third, fourth and fifth applicants in *Steel, Lush, Needham, Polden and Cole* v *UK* Application No 24838/94 (1998) 28 EHRR 603, available from the Court's web-site: www.dhcour.coe.fr and *Hashman and Harrup* v *UK* Application No 25594/94 (1999) European Court of Human Rights 25 November 1999.

[106] See, for example, *Chappell* v *UK* (1988) 10 EHRR 510; *Christians Against Racism and Fascism* v *UK* No 8440/78 21 DR 138 (1980); the findings as regards Steel and Lush in *Steel, Lush, Needham, Polden and Cole* v *UK* Application No 24838/94 (1998), see note 105, above.

[107] [1975] 3 All ER 1.

[108] At 10D and 11B.

[109] *Huntingdon Life Sciences Ltd and Another* v *Curtin and Others* (1998) 3(1) J Civ Lib 37.

of speech, are recognised as reflecting common law values[110] coterminous with Convention ones.[111]

Since under the HRA the courts must take account of rights to protest as opposed to negative liberties[112] these approaches will have to be modified in order to provide a little more protection for such rights than was provided previously. Under judicial review principles the domestic courts must consider proportionality: a restriction will be disproportionate where there is insufficient need for it or where no evidence of such need is advanced by the state. Where different views might be taken of the need for a particular interference, such as a ban imposed on a march under s13 Public Order Act 1986, a domestic court fully applying the Strasbourg jurisprudence, including its margin of appreciation aspects, would tend to defer to the judgment of the executive. Clearly, this approach is distinguishable from that of heightened *Wednesbury* unreasonableness[113] but it would often lead to the same outcome.

The likelihood that a domestic doctrine of judicial restraint will be developed in relation to aspects of executive decision-making, including the policing of public protest, derives support from the decision of the House of Lords in *R* v *Chief Constable of Sussex ex parte International Ferry Traders Ltd.*[114] International Ferry Traders Ltd, who were engaged in exporting live cattle, had sought judicial review of the decision of the Chief Constable of Sussex to limit the policing of animal rights protesters

[110] Compare the following pronouncement of Lord Hewart CJ in finding that where a public meeting might lead others to breach the peace the speaker could be arrested: 'There have been moments during the argument in this case where it appeared to be suggested that the court had to do with a grave case involving what is called the right of public meeting. I say "called" because English law does not recognise any right of public meeting for political . . . purposes' (*Duncan* v *Jones* [1936] 1 KB 218 at p221), with these pronouncements from *Derbyshire CC* v *Times Newspapers* in which it was found that local (or central) government cannot sue for libel: Lord Keith said: 'I find it satisfactory to be able to conclude that the common law of England is consistent with the [freedom of expression] obligations assumed under [the Convention]' [1993] AC 534 at 551 HL. Butler-Sloss LJ said: 'I can see no inconsistency between English law upon this subject and Article 10 . . . This is scarcely surprising, since we may pride ourselves on the fact that freedom of speech has existed in this country perhaps as long, if not longer than . . . in any other country in the world' ([1992] 3 WLR 28 at 60 CA). Admittedly, in view of the dates of these findings, this comparison might be viewed as mischievous and unfair, since the later decisions might be said to have been reached in the 'shadow' of the Convention. But the decision of the House of Lords in *DPP* v *Jones and Lloyd* [1999] 2 All ER 257, discussed below, could hardly be viewed as upholding the right to protest and assemble as strongly as *Derbyshire* upheld media freedom of speech.

[111] The Divisional Court decision in *Jones and Lloyd* v *DPP* [1997] 2 All ER 119, discussed below, found that there is no right to assemble on the highway, merely a voluntary toleration of such assemblies. No reference was made to an acceptance of Convention values within the common law except to say that Article 11 need not be referred to since the law was not ambiguous.

[112] The Convention rights will be claim rights in the sense that they are binding on public authorities under s6 HRA.

[113] See *R* v *Secretary of State for Defence ex parte Lustig-Prean, Smith and Others* [1996] 1 All ER 257, 263.

[114] [1999] 1 All ER 129.

at Shoreham ferry port. The Lords had to consider the discretion of a Chief Constable to deploy powers to prevent a breach of the peace against protesters and the relevance of the margin of appreciation allowed to member states in respect of satisfying their Community obligations under the free movement of goods provisions of Article 34 of the Treaty of Rome. Lord Slynn, in a speech with which the other Law Lords agreed, found: 'the courts have long made it clear that . . . they will respect the margin of appreciation or discretion which a Chief Constable has', and in this instance that margin had not been exceeded. As to the European aspects of the case, Lord Hoffman found: 'on the particular facts of this case the European concepts of proportionality and margin of appreciation produce the same result as what are commonly called *Wednesbury* principles . . . in this case I think that the Chief Constable must enjoy a margin of discretion that cannot differ according to whether its source be found in purely domestic principles or superimposed European principles'. The decision illustrates the attachment of the judiciary to the doctrine of deference to policing decisions, even where the application of European law might have led to a different result. Lord Hoffman's judgment above suggests that in the post-HRA era the application of the Strasbourg public protest jurisprudence in order to determine questions of proportionality might lead to the same results as the application of the *Wednesbury* doctrine, since decisions of Chief Constables as to the needs of public order would tend to be as readily deferred to within the 'review' model as those in respect of the allocation of resources.

In this context an 'activist' approach would lead to much greater interference with executive decision-making. It would be in accordance with this approach to have regard to the balance struck in public protest matters in other European courts within the margin of appreciation, and perhaps also to that struck by the International Covenant on Civil and Political Rights and in the USA or Canada.[115] In support of this approach it might also be pointed out that the Strasbourg public protest jurisprudence is very heavily influenced by decisions of the Commission, which is not a fully judicial body[116] and therefore has less authority than the Court. As Chapter 2 indicates, within the Court there is disagreement as to the interferences which fall within a state's margin of appreciation,[117] and this is

[115] See, for example, *Brandenburg* v *Ohio* 395 US 444 (1969) in which it was found that an interference with public protest was acceptable only where incitement to unlawful action occurred. This may be compared with the decision on breach of the peace in *Nicol* v *DPP* [1996] 1 J.Civ.Lib 75 (discussed below) in which such interference was permitted on the ground that it would not be unreasonable for others to react violently; no element of incitement was necessary.

[116] See Chapter 2 pp20–21.

[117] For example, in *Cossey* v *UK* A 184 para 3.6.5 (1990) Judge Martens in his dissenting opinion differed sharply from the majority in the Court in finding: 'I think that the Court should **not** have built its reasoning on the assumption that "this is an area in which the Contracting Parties enjoy a wide margin of appreciation" . . . In this context there simply is no room for a margin of appreciation.'

particularly so in the only decision of the Court finding a violation of the freedom of assembly guarantee of Article 11, *Ezelin* v *France*.[118] Two of the partly dissenting judges considered that the interference in question fell within that margin,[119] although the majority found that the state had exceeded it. Nevertheless, the domestic judiciary may find the 'activist' approach problematic, especially in determining whether a restriction is necessary in a democratic society in an instance covered by an adverse Commission decision on admissibility. It is inevitable, at least in the early decisions under the HRA, that in such circumstances some practitioners, magistrates or judges, lacking familiarity with the Strasbourg system, will view the finding of manifest ill-foundedness in a number of Strasbourg public protest cases as virtually conclusive of the issue since on its face it appears to mean that the case was almost unarguable.[120] This problem will be exacerbated since public protest issues are usually adjudicated on in low level courts.

Judicial uncertainty in applying the Convention will arise in a number of contexts but public protest cases will present them with an especially stark choice since the HRA provides that public authorities must not infringe Articles 10 and 11; on its face this requirement demands a break not only with the traditional acceptance that there is no legal right to assemble or engage in public protest in the UK, but with the failure to prevent encroachment on the negative liberty. Wills J said in *Ex parte Lewis*:[121] 'Things are done every day in . . . the kingdom . . . without let or hindrance, which there is not and cannot be a legal right to do, and not infrequently are submitted to with a good grace', and this statement was recently approved of by the Divisional Court in *Jones and Lloyd* v *DPP*.[122] As indicated above, references to 'rights' are occasionally made, but they appear to be, loosely, to negative liberties.[123] The HRA requires more of public authorities than a mere voluntary tolerance of public protest, and, moreover, if the judiciary, while paying lip-service to rights to freedom of

[118] A 202-A (1991).

[119] Judges Ryssdal and Pettiti, at pp26 and 28–30.

[120] Under Article 27(2) of the Convention the Commission shall consider inadmissible any petition submitted under Article 25 which it considers manifestly ill-founded. The Court has said: 'rejection of a complaint as "manifestly ill-founded" amounts to a decision that there is not even a prima facie case against the respondent state . . .': *Boyle and Rice* v *UK* A 131 paras 53–54 (1988). However, Harris, O'Boyle and Warbrick in *Law of the European Convention on Human Rights* (1995) London: Butterworths p627 observe '[the manifestly ill-founded provision] is possibly the only provision in the Convention where the Commission, in its practice, has departed from the literal and ordinary meaning of the words employed'.

[121] (1888) 21 QBD 191, 197.

[122] [1997] 2 All ER 119.

[123] It may be noted that when approval has been expressed of Lord Denning's defence of 'rights to protest' the 'right' has become a freedom: per Otton J in *Hirst and Agu* v *Chief Constable of West Yorkshire* (1986) 85 Cr App Rep143: having quoted Lord Denning's findings with approval, he went on to say: 'the freedom of protest on matters of public concern would be given the recognition it deserves'.

protest, maintains something close to the present balance between public order and freedom of assembly, in the new era, it will fail to give it full effect. This appears to be the case even though voluntary tolerance of assemblies has so far been sufficient to meet the standards maintained at Strasbourg. Under the 'activist' model, then, it appears to be unlikely that justifications for judicial restraint in public protest decisions, if any, will be fully coterminous with Strasbourg restraint.

A key factor affecting the reception of Articles 10 and 11 into UK law will be, as indicated, the model favoured by the senior UK judiciary. But there may also be procedural difficulties in bringing about statutory change. Relying on Articles 10 and 11, protesters will be able to challenge public order provisions in criminal proceedings or seek judicial review of public order decisions made by police or local authorities. However, as Chapter 2 explains, s6 HRA provides that it is lawful for a public authority to act in a way which is incompatible with Convention rights if it is authorised to do so by primary legislation. If the legislation is thought to be incompatible the court must nevertheless apply it; the higher courts can make a declaration of incompatibility which will have no impact on the instant decision but which will probably trigger off a legislative change by ministerial amendment.[124] Public order questions are rarely adjudicated on in those courts which are able to make a declaration,[125] and some defendants would have little interest in appealing to a higher court in order to obtain the declaration since it would be of no personal benefit. However, members of some protest groups may be likely to appeal test cases to the higher courts in order to obtain changes in the law. But unless they do so as defendants in criminal proceedings, this will be possible under the HRA only if they themselves have been 'victims' or are likely to become victims in future, within the meaning of s7(7) of the HRA.[126] Owing to the effect of s11 they could, however, raise Convention points in judicial review proceedings based on the old standing rules. But this course might be unavailing since the scrutiny would be less intensive, especially in this context.[127] In contrast, reform of common law powers under s6 may occur more readily. As Sedley LJ said in *Redmond-Bate* v *DPP*,[128] before the HRA was fully in force, 'it is now accepted that the common law should seek compatibility with the values of the Convention'. If incompatibility is found the Convention guarantee should prevail since no provision was included in the Act allowing the common law to override the Convention or creating restrictions as to those courts which can find incompatibility between the two.

[124] S10(2) of the HRA provides: 'If a Minister of the Crown considers that there are compelling reasons for proceeding under this section, he may by order make such amendments to the legislation as he considers necessary to remove the incompatibility'.

[125] See ss4(4) and (5) of the Act which provide that no court lower than the High Court or Court of Appeal may make a declaration of incompatibility.

[126] See Chapter 2 p50.

[127] See Chapter 2 p51.

[128] (1999) *The Times* 28 July; [1999] All ER (D) 864.

Common law powers

Breach of the peace

Ancient powers to arrest without warrant and to bind over to keep the peace still play a crucial part in public order policing owing to the wide discretion they hand to police and magistrates. Academic writers agree that the notion of maintaining the Queen's peace continues to be the central one in public order law.[129] It has been said to express the idea that 'people should be free to act as they choose so long as they do not cause violence'.[130] This simple concept appears to be unobjectionable in civil liberties terms since it would not sanction interference with the freedom to protest peacefully. However, as will be indicated below, this concept no longer expresses the central value underlying the doctrine of breach of the peace. In many respects it has been replaced by a notion of freedom of action so long as serious inconvenience is not caused. The concept itself has also changed and grown in a way that has taken it some distance from the values it may originally have expressed. Since the breach of the peace doctrine may curb all forms of protest – not excluding peaceful persuasion – it may be likely to come into domestic conflict with Articles 10 and 11 of the Convention.

The definition of breach of the peace from *R* v *Howell*[131] is usually taken as definitive. The Court said that a breach of the peace will arise if a positive act is done or threatened to be done which either: 'harms a person or in his presence his property, or is likely to cause such harm, or which puts a person in fear of such harm'. This definition excludes some disturbances in public, including causing damage to public property, which are unlikely to lead to violence. Nevertheless, the definition is broad since it does not confine itself to actual harm. Nor does it require that the behaviour in question should be unlawful under civil or criminal law. Most significantly, the courts have accepted for some time that a person may be bound over for conduct likely to cause a breach of the peace, not merely for conduct actually amounting to a breach.[132] Since breaching the peace is not in itself a criminal offence[133] and can lead only, in the first instance, to a binding over order to keep the peace or to be of good

[129] See, for example, D Feldman *Civil Liberties and Human Rights in England and Wales* (1993) Oxford: Clarendon Press p786; 'Breaching the Peace and Disturbing the Quiet' (1982) PL 212; D G T Williams *Keeping the Peace* (1967).

[130] D Feldman, note 129 above, at p787.

[131] [1981] 3 All ER 383.

[132] See *Wise* v *Dunning* [1902] 1 KB 167.

[133] This is the current UK position. The European Court of Human Rights considered that breach of the peace amounts to a 'criminal charge' under the autonomous Convention meaning of that term: *Steel and Others* v *UK* (1998) Application No 24838/94 (1998) 28 EHRR 603, available from the Court's web-site: www.dhcour.coe.fr; *McLeod* v *UK* (1998) judgment of the Court 23 September 1998, available from the Court's web-site, ibid; see Davenport 4 JCIVLIBS 140.

behaviour,[134] it is indistinguishable, for practical purposes, from conduct which leads to apprehension of a breach of the peace. Thus, the doctrine with its bind over and imprisonment possibilities[135] reaches beyond positive acts and includes words, since words may signal that the harm in question is likely to arise.

It has also been recognised for some time that a person may be bound over for conduct which is not itself a breach of the peace and which does not suggest that the individual concerned is about to breach the peace, but which may cause *another* to breach the peace.[136] This possibility is implicit in the *Howell* definition itself and is insufficiently distinguished, within that definition, from conduct which in itself amounts to a breach of the peace. This additional possibility is of great significance in the context of public protest since it means that if peaceful, lawful protest may provoke others, it can lead to the arrest and binding over of the protesters. In other words, although the doctrine may be confined to situations in which there is an 'element of violence' or the threat of violence,[137] that inhibiting requirement is diluted since it may arise owing merely to its apprehended possibility emanating from persons other than the arrestee.[138] Of particular significance is the possibility that protest reflecting minority views may most readily be regarded as provocative.

The very significant, 'activist' decision for public protest and freedom of assembly in *Beatty* v *Gillbanks*[139] had established prior to *Howell* the important principle that persons acting lawfully cannot be held responsible for the actions of those who are thereby induced to act unlawfully. However, subsequent decisions, including *Howell*, undermined that principle. In the most notorious decision, *Duncan* v *Jones*,[140] a speaker wishing to address a public meeting opposite a training centre for the unemployed was told to move away to a different street because the police apprehended that her speech might cause a breach of the peace. A year previously there had been some restlessness among the unemployed following a speech

[134] The powers to bind over to keep the peace under the Justices of the Peace Act 1968 s1(7); to be of good behaviour under the Justices of the Peace Act 1361.

[135] A binding over order cannot be made if a person does not consent to it and if he or she refuses to recognise his or her indebtedness to the Queen; by that acknowledgement the person becomes liable to pay the sum fixed by the court if he or she fails to keep the peace or to be of good behaviour (Justices of the Peace Act 1361). If a person refuses he or she can be committed to prison for up to six months or until he or she complies: Magistrates' Courts Act 1980 s115(3).

[136] *O'Kelly* v *Harvey* (1883) 15 Cox CC 453; *Wise* v *Dunning* [1902] 1 KB 167; *Lansbury* v *Riley* [1914] 3 KB 229.

[137] This element is frequently referred to as a means of limiting the reach of the doctrine. See, for example, P Thornton *Public Order Law* (1987) p74.

[138] The notion that an element of violence is required, in this sense, by *Howell* was emphasised by Sedley LJ in *Redmond-Bate* v *DPP The Times* 23 July 1999, Transcript para 9.

[139] [1882] 9 QBD 308.

[140] [1936] 1 KB 218; for comment see Daintith [1966] PL 248. For detailed discussion of the policing background see Ewing and Gearty *The Struggle for Civil Liberties: Political Freedom and the Rule of Law in Britain 1914–1945* (1999) OUP.

by the same speaker. She refused to move away from the centre and was arrested for obstructing a police officer in the course of his duty. On appeal it was found that the police had been acting in the course of their duty because they had reasonably apprehended a breach of the peace. The case therefore clearly undermined the *Beatty* v *Gillbanks* principle in that the freedom of the speaker was infringed, not because of her conduct, but because of police fears about the possible response of the audience.

In *Wise* v *Dunning*[141] it was found that a breach of the peace would arise if there is an act of the defendant 'the natural consequence of which, if the act be not unlawful in itself would be to produce an unlawful act by other persons'. An extremely wide interpretation of this possibility was accepted in *Holmes* v *Bournemouth Crown Court*;[142] an anti-smoking campaigner who held up a placard and shouted anti-smoking slogans, but in no way threatened violence, was arrested on the ground that if he stayed in his position – outside the designated lobbying area at a Conservative Party Conference – a breach of the peace might arise. The finding that in arresting him the officer had acted in the execution of his duty, was upheld on appeal. A similar stance was taken in *Kelly* v *Chief Constable of Hampshire*[143] which concerned an altercation between a hunt saboteur and a huntsman, resulting in the arrest of the saboteur. According to the Court of Appeal, if a constable reasonably believes that a breach of the peace is about to occur owing to a dispute he may arrest one of the participants: he has complete discretion as to which participant to arrest, and this may even be the case where the evidence suggests that the one not arrested has committed an assault on the other.[144] In other words, the victim of the assault may be arrested to prevent a fight between the two from breaking out. A similar situation arose in *Morpeth Ward Justices ex parte Ward*,[145] which concerned the behaviour of protesters against pheasant shooting. Brooke J stated: 'provocative disorderly behaviour which is likely to have the natural consequence of causing violence, even if only to the persons of the provokers, is capable of being conduct likely to cause a breach of the peace'.[146] The reasonableness of the shooters' behaviour or potential behaviour (one of the shooting party had threatened to kill a protester) was not called into question. The response of the shooters was viewed as the natural and probable consequence of the protest; the attribution of responsibility for the apprehended breach of the peace on the basis of proportionality between the provocation and the reaction was avoided.

[141] [1902] 1 KB 167. See also *Duncan* v *Jones* [1936] 1 KB 218.

[142] 6 October 1993, unreported, DC; cited in Bailey, Harris and Jones *Civil Liberties: Cases and Materials* (1995) London: Butterworths p256.

[143] (1993) *Independent* 25 March.

[144] *Obiter* comment from Lloyd LJ. The huntsman had assaulted Kelly with his whip.

[145] [1992] 95 Cr App R 215.

[146] Ibid at p221.

This question, however, received some attention in *Nicol* v *DPP*[147] which concerned the behaviour of fishing protesters in blowing horns, throwing twigs into the water and attempting to dissuade the anglers from fishing. It was found that the protesters were guilty of conduct whereby a breach of the peace was likely to be caused, since their conduct, although lawful, was unreasonable and was likely to provoke the anglers to violence. This was clarified by Simon Brown LJ who found that a natural consequence of lawful conduct could be violence in another only where the defendant rather than the other person could be said to be acting unreasonably, and, further, that unless the anglers' rights had been infringed, it would not be reasonable for them to react violently. It was assumed that their rights had been infringed,[148] and that as between the two groups the behaviour of the fishing protesters was clearly unreasonable. The need to show an infringement of 'rights' and the findings as to reasonableness place a limitation on the 'natural consequence' test which was not present in *Wise* v *Dunning*. But of course this restriction depends upon a wide and uncertain test of reasonableness; the judiciary may well be disinclined to find that the behaviour of groups espousing minority, 'alternative' viewpoints, such as hunt saboteurs or tree protesters, while lawful, was also reasonable. This decision may well be interpreted to mean that any activities as part of peaceful protest, which may provoke those whose behaviour is the subject of the protest to use force, should be accounted behaviour likely to give rise to a breach of the peace, so long as the protesters can be said to have infringed 'rights'.

Once it is accepted that an arrest may be made in respect of an apprehended breach of the peace, the question of the necessary degree of immediacy arises. There is UK authority to the effect that an arrest can occur well before the point is reached at which a breach of the peace is apprehended. In *Moss* v *McLachlan*[149] a group of striking miners was stopped by the police a few miles away from a number of collieries; the police told them that they feared a breach of the peace if the miners reached the pits and that they would arrest the miners for obstruction if they tried to continue. After some time, a group of miners tried to push past the police, was arrested and convicted of obstruction of a police officer in the course of his duty. The miners' appeal on the ground that the officers had not been acting in the course of their duty was dismissed. It was said that there was no need to show that individual miners would cause a breach of the peace, nor even to specify at which pit disorder was expected. A reasonable belief that there was a real risk that a breach would

[147] [1996] 1 J.Civ.Lib 75.

[148] The rights referred to were left unclear. There is, of course, in general no right to fish, merely a freedom to do so; fishing rights may be obtained under a contract with the landowner, but this does not appear to have been the case in this instance since the anglers were fishing in a public park.

[149] [1985] IRLR 76.

occur in close proximity to the point of arrest (the pits were between two and four miles away) was all that was necessary.

The decision in *Peterkin* v *Chief Constable of Cheshire*,[150] taken one year before the HRA came fully into force, takes a strongly differing stance. Peterkin, a hunt protester, had access to intelligence that told him when and where the Cheshire Hunt was to meet. He was making his way to the hunt in a convoy of vehicles carrying other protesters when he was arrested for conduct likely to cause a breach of the peace. The arresting officer said that he anticipated that Peterkin and the other protesters would enter private land, causing a serious breach of the peace. Peterkin argued that he was arrested merely for walking on a country lane, half a mile from where the hunt was taking place, and was not in sight of it at the time. He claimed unlawful arrest, false imprisonment and assault and battery against the Cheshire police on the basis that they had no legal grounds for the arrest and therefore any actions used to effect it were unlawful. In awarding damages, Manchester County Court found that there were no such grounds since there was no apprehension or imminent threat of any breach of the peace. In requiring a clear element of immediacy, this decision, if followed, will create a strong inhibitory rule, not as to the nature of the doctrine, but as to the point at which it can be invoked. It is in accordance with the stance taken in *McLeod* v *UK*[151] in which it was found that it is insufficient to find that a breach may occur at some future point but is not immediately probable.

On the basis of the decisions discussed the breach of the peace doctrine not only fails to distinguish fully between the forms of protest referred to above, but also makes no attempt to enquire into their significance in terms of free expression. The doctrine provides no means of distinguishing between rowdy football supporters and protesters. There is no recognition of the particular need to protect the communicative rights of minority groups, on the basis that their views may find little expression within mainstream speech, or of the likelihood that the provision of such broad police powers, while neutral on their face as between collective and minority standpoints, will tend to bear disproportionately on the latter. The recent decisions discussed here exhibit an arbitrariness which fuels the general argument that these powers provide the police with an unacceptably wide discretion which is not fully held in check by the courts. Even where cases do not come to court, or where decisions to bind over are overturned on appeal, as in *Percy* v *DPP*,[152] the detention of the defendant

[150] (1999) *The Times* 16 November 1999.

[151] (1998) Judgment of the Court 23 September 1998, available from the Court's web-site: www.dhcour.coe.fr.

[152] [1995] 3 All ER 124. The case concerned a solitary protester who trespassed at a US military base; it was found that her conduct was likely to give rise to a breach of the peace and when she refused to be bound over she was imprisoned. However, on appeal the Divisional Court found that trained military personnel were unlikely to be provoked into responding to her trespass with violence.

will have occurred on what is often a flimsy and imprecise legal basis. Within the models indicated above, what effect will Articles 10 and 11 have on the development of the doctrine of breach of the peace?

As noted above, any interference with freedom of peaceful assembly must be 'prescribed by law' according to Articles 10(2) and 11(2). These words import requirements of certainty and fair warning and therefore under the HRA the arrest and bind over powers are likely to be reviewed by the judiciary in order to determine whether they meet these standards. The view of the Law Commission is that 'binding over falls short of what ought to be two elementary principles of criminal or quasi-criminal law. These require the law to be both certain and readily ascertainable.'[153] However, as indicated above, the actual standards connoted by the words 'prescribed by law' may not be very high, particularly where public order matters are in issue. In *Steel and Others* v *UK*,[154] which concerned the arrest and detention of applicants engaged in various forms of public protest, the European Commission on Human Rights took note of the findings of the Law Commission regarding certainty, but, taking account of the notion of varying levels of precision referred to above, it found that 'the concept of "breach of the peace" is sufficiently certain to comply with the notion of "prescribed by law" under Article 10 para 2'.[155] The Court found that the breach of the peace doctrine provided sufficient guidance and was formulated with sufficient precision to satisfy the requirement of Article 5(1)(c) that arrest and detention should be in accordance with a procedure prescribed by law, and that the prescribed by law requirement of Article 10 was also satisfied.[156] In *McLeod* v *UK*[157] the Court found that the breach of the peace doctrine was 'in accordance with the law' under Article 8. Thus, in respect of the key elements of 'prescribed by law' – legal basis, certainty and accessibility – the breach of the peace doctrine meets Strasbourg standards. Within the 'review' model it is therefore almost inconceivable that domestic courts would wish to import higher standards under the 'prescribed by law' rubric. Within the 'activist' model, however, this would be possible on the argument that the findings

[153] Law Commission Report No 222 para 4.16. The Law Commission relied in part on the failure of these powers to meet the standards laid down by the European Convention on Human Rights.

[154] (1998) Application No 24838/94; judgment of the Court 23 September 1998 (1998) 28 EHRR 603.

[155] Para 148. Usually, Strasbourg will find a violation of the 'prescribed by law' requirement only where the interference has *no* legal basis: *Malone* v *UK* A 82 (1985); 7 EHRR 14; *Halford* v *UK* [1997] IRLR 471. But, exceptionally, in *Hashman and Harrup* v *UK* Application No 25594/94 (1999) European Court of Human Rights judgment of 25 November 1999 a basis in law was present but did not satisfy the requirements of this test; discussed below.

[156] *Steel and Others* v *UK* (1998), see note 154, above.

[157] (1998) Judgment of the Court 23 September 1998, available from the Court's web-site: www.dhcour.coe.fr.

in question depended on the application of relatively low standards of precision and accessibility.

Reappraisal and reform of the doctrine of breach of the peace is more likely to occur by reference to the notion of what is 'necessary in a democratic society' within Articles 10 and 11 para 2. This issue was extensively considered by the Court in *Steel* but the findings were quite strongly influenced by the doctrine of the margin of appreciation.[158] The first applicant had taken part in a protest against a grouse shoot and had stood in the way of participants to prevent them taking shots. Since this behaviour was likely to be provocative, the Court found that her arrest and detention, although constituting serious interferences with her freedom of expression, could be viewed as proportionate to the aim of preventing disorder and of maintaining the authority of the judiciary[159] and this could also be said of her subsequent detention in the police station for 44 hours,[160] bearing in mind the findings of the police or magistrates that disorder might have occurred. The Court made little attempt to evaluate the real risk of disorder, taking into account the margin of appreciation afforded to domestic authorities in determining what is necessary to avoid disorder in the particular domestic situation.[161] It may be noted that this conclusion was reached only by a five to four majority; the partly dissenting Opinions of Judges Valticos and Makarczyk termed the measures taken against the first applicant, Helen Steel, 'so manifestly extreme' in proportion to her actions during the protest that a violation of Article 10 had occurred. The second applicant had taken part in a protest against the building of a motorway, placing herself in front of the earth-moving machinery in order to impede it. The Court found unanimously that her arrest also could be viewed as proportionate to the aim of preventing disorder, even though it accepted that the risk of immediate disorder was not so high as in the case of the first applicant.[162] The Court accepted the finding of the Magistrates Court that there had been such a risk.

The third, fourth and fifth applicants were peacefully holding banners and handing out leaflets outside a fighter helicopter conference when they were arrested for breach of the peace. The Court found that there was no justification for their arrests at all since there was no suggestion of any threat of disorder.[163] A violation of Article 10 was therefore found in respect of those applicants. These findings draw a distinction between the first category of protest and the fourth and fifth forms – symbolic

[158] This was acknowledged by the Court, para 101.

[159] Paras 104 and 107.

[160] Para 105. The Commission acknowledged (at para 156) 'some disquiet as to the proportionality of a detention of this length' which continued long after the grouse shoot was over.

[161] Para 101.

[162] Para 109.

[163] Para 110.

physical action and obstructive action – suggesting that interferences with protest as direct action may frequently fall within the national authorities' margin of appreciation. But, significantly, the findings also make it clear that the fourth and fifth forms constitute expressions of opinion and therefore fall within Articles 10 and 11. This was reaffirmed in *Hashman and Harrup* v *UK*,[164] which is discussed below.

The stance of the Court in *Steel* in fact implies less tolerance of peaceful direct action than the stance taken in *Nicol* since the Court required only an interference with the rights of others and the possibility of disorder in order to be satisfied regarding proportionality; no added requirement to show that the defendant rather than the other party was acting unreasonably was imposed. The dissenting minority judgments in *Steel* made an oblique reference to such a comparison in noting that the behaviour of the first applicant, albeit 'extreme', was aimed at preserving the life of an animal.[165] The findings of the Court provide little basis for curbing interference under the breach of the peace doctrine with certain forms of public protest of the direct action type, although they do require a restructuring of the domestic scrutiny of such interference, which takes the primary right as the starting point. *Steel* clearly affords the domestic judiciary a wide discretion in interpreting the requirements of the Convention in an analogous case. In evaluating the risks posed by a protest the courts might tend to adopt notions of deference to decisions of the executive in respect of the possibility of disorder in accordance with the tradition in such cases, and take the view that the courts should be reluctant to interfere with the decision of the police officer or magistrate (as the tribunal of fact) in question. A minimalist approach to Articles 10 and 11 would lead to a similar result. If *Steel* was simply applied regardless of the influence of the margin of appreciation, little protection would be available for most direct action forms of protest. But, following an activist approach, the domestic judiciary, faced with similar facts, but disapplying the margin of appreciation aspects of *Steel*, would find that the interference was unjustified since its review of the decisions of the police or of magistrates would be less restrained. Within this model some interferences with freedom of expression would be allowed, where direct action was likely to provoke immediate disorder due to the degree of provocation offered, but the measures taken in response, such as the length of detention, would be much more strictly scrutinised for their proportionality with the aims pursued.

The decision in *Steel* is of most value in placing the form of protest most deserving of protection, peaceful persuasion, in a specially protected position. Therefore it will be problematic, even within the 'review' or

[164] Application No 25594/94 (1999) European Court of Human Rights judgment of 25 November 1999.

[165] Partly dissenting Opinions of Judges Valticos and Makarczyk.

minimalist model, to uphold arrest or binding over decisions in such instances or in cases of the *Holmes* v *Bournemouth*[166] type. This would be a welcome restriction and clarification of the breach of the peace doctrine but, in terms of protecting public protest, it would achieve no more than *Nicol* has already done. Both *Steel* and *Nicol* leave open leeway for deciding when it should be found that protest, which has some provocative effect, should nevertheless be termed peaceful. In other words, in terms of the categories of protest indicated, their application to the second form of protest – insulting or offensive persuasion – is dependent on the degree of provocation. The findings in *Steel* impliedly drew a distinction in terms of reasonableness between action which is directly and physically provocative and speech which might have some provocative effect but which could nevertheless be viewed as part of a peaceful protest. It is not clear that they simply drew a distinction between physical and verbal protest. Such a distinction would fail to take account of forms of hate speech which may be far more provocative to hearers than forms of physical obstruction such as the ones at issue in *Steel*. Thus, a minimalist approach to *Steel* would be to confine it to speech which had little provocative effect. In *Steel* itself, in respect of the successful applicants, there was no evidence that the audience in question – those participating in the fighter helicopter conference – were provoked. A traditionalist approach would be to defer to the opinion of the officer on the ground as to the likelihood that disorder would follow the provocation.

But a more activist approach would be to afford protection to the second and fourth forms of protest on a broad interpretation of *Steel*, and this approach would also receive some endorsement from *Platform 'Artze fur das Leben'* v *Austria*[167] which adopted a version of the *Beatty* v *Gillbanks*[168] approach. Such an approach to the decision in *Steel* was, in some respects, taken by Lord Justice Sedley in *Redmond-Bate* v *DPP*[169] in the period before the HRA was fully in force. Ms Redmond-Bate and other women, a group of fundamentalist Christians, were preaching forcefully on the steps of Westminster Cathedral. A large crowd gathered who were angered by their preaching. Fearing a breach of the peace, a police officer asked the women to desist; when they refused he arrested them. The Divisional Court found that in the circumstances two questions should be asked of the action of the police officer. First, was it reasonable to believe that a breach of the peace was about to be caused? Second, where was the threat coming from? These questions could have been answered by distinguishing the facts from those relating to the successful applications in *Steel* and bringing them, at the same time, within the rule from *Nicol*, on the basis that the women did in fact provoke their audience and

[166] 6 October 1993, unreported, DC.
[167] Series A No 139 para 32 (1988); judgment of 21 June 1988; 13 EHRR 204.
[168] [1882] 9 QBD 308, discussed below.
[169] (1999) *The Times* 28 July; [1999] All ER (D) 864.

could have been viewed as acting unreasonably since they continued to preach despite the growing restlessness of the crowd. It could have been said that the natural consequence of the lawful but arguably unreasonable conduct of the women was the provocation of others. Applying *Steel,* however, the Divisional Court found, in answer to both the questions posed, that there were no sufficient grounds on which to determine that a breach of the peace was about to be caused or, moreover, on which to determine that the threat was coming from Ms Redmond-Bate, bearing in mind the tolerance one would expect to be extended to offensive speech. Sedley LJ said: 'Free speech includes not only the inoffensive, but the irritating, the contentious, the eccentric, the heretical, the unwelcome and the provocative providing it does not tend to provoke violence. Freedom only to speak inoffensively is not worth having.'[170] He went on to find that the Crown Court had correctly directed itself that 'violence is not a natural consequence of what a person does unless it clearly interferes with the rights or liberties of others so as to make a violent reaction not wholly unreasonable'[171] and he emphasised that the Court should make its own independent judgment of the reasonableness of the police officer's belief.

This decision simplified the tests from *Nicol* of determining which party was acting reasonably where one was provoked to violence and as to which was exercising rights. The key test put forward was one of reasonableness: a breach of the peace will occur where violence was threatened or provoked, in the sense of infringing rights or liberties, unless the provoked party acts wholly – not partly – unreasonably. Lord Justice Sedley then categorised certain of the decisions mentioned above into those where the provoked party was reasonable or unreasonable, in order to offer some guidance on this matter. He placed *Beatty* v *Gillbanks* and *Percy* v *DPP* in the first category, but, strangely, put *Wise* v *Dunning* and *Duncan* v *Jones* in the second. In *Duncan,* there was little evidence on which to base an apprehension of a breach of the peace and it was unclear that persons provoked by the speech in question could be said to have acted reasonably. Thus, although *Redmond-Bate* applies *Steel* quite broadly, it still leaves some uncertainty as to the status of provocative speech; the test of reasonableness will be, it is suggested, no more certain in its application than the tests from *Nicol* and will therefore have some chilling effect on protest.

In the post-HRA era a more activist approach to *Steel* would afford the substantive rights under Articles 10 and 11 greater weight in cases of persuasive or provocative speech by disallowing interferences with these forms of protest unless *incitement* to violence or to hatred of racial, religious or sexual groups had occurred. A presumption that it is normally unreasonable to be provoked to violence or the threat of it by speech

[170] Transcript para 12.
[171] Transcript para 16.

could be imported into the doctrine, a stronger test than the one put forward by Lord Justice Sedley. In response to the finding in *Steel* that breaching the peace is a criminal offence it would appear that the courts will have to create a clearer distinction between conduct likely to cause a breach, allowing for a preventive arrest, and conduct actually amounting to a breach. The former could not, it seems, if *Steel* is followed on this point, lead to binding over since no offence has been committed which would allow for this punishment. Since such preventive powers are frequently, although not exclusively, used where the arrestee may cause another to breach the peace, *Steel* might therefore herald a return to the more minimal interpretation in *Howell*, leaving the possibility of causing another to breach the peace to the statutory provisions discussed below, in particular ss5 and 4A of the Public Order Act 1986 which cover much of the same area. Admittedly, ss5 and 4A, unlike the breach of the peace doctrine, criminalise offensive speech *per se* without requiring a public order rationale. The 'victim' need only be distressed rather than likely to react violently. However, the nature of the language required for both provisions curtails their ambit, in contrast to the breach of the peace doctrine. Almost all the cases concerning peaceful persuasion discussed above, in which the doctrine was successfully invoked, would fall outside ss5 and 4A, apart, probably, from *Wise* v *Dunning* in which abusive or insulting words or behaviour were used. The peaceful direct action cases of *Nicol* and *Percy* probably would not be covered, although they would fall within s68 CJPOA, discussed below. In other words, if the use of provocative speech requires a legal response at all, such a response should be left to those provisions which lay down a more precise test for liability than the breach of the peace doctrine.

But such determinations, which would have the effect of greatly narrowing down the doctrine, would not be fully rooted in the application of *Steel* or other analogous decisions at Strasbourg: they would have to be based largely on an appeal to a notional 'higher' standard of human rights, articulated by the general principles informing the Strasbourg jurisprudence, which might have been adhered to but for the margin of appreciation doctrine.[172] If one of the key principles at stake is the need to protect the communicative rights of minority groups, such as pacifists, animal rights or environmental activists, reliance might be placed, by analogy, on strong pronouncements of the need to protect minority rights and plurality within democracies which, as indicated above, are scattered across the Convention jurisprudence.[173]

[172] For example, the Court in *Handyside* v *UK* 1 EHRR 737 para 49 (1976) found, in a famous passage, that Article 10 is applicable 'not only to ideas that are . . . regarded as inoffensive, but also to those which offend, shock or disturb', although in the particular instance, owing to the operation of the margin of appreciation doctrine, the application failed.

[173] Note 101, above.

Behaviour contra bono mores

The criticism that powers to prevent a breach of the peace are unacceptably broad and uncertain may be levelled with even greater strength at the *contra bono mores*, 'contrary to a good way of life', power. This power allows the binding over of persons, under the Justices of the Peace Act 1361, whose behaviour is deemed by a bench of magistrates to be anti-social although not necessarily unlawful. This vague and broad power hands an unacceptably wide discretion to police and magistrates to determine the standards of good behaviour; it has been severely criticised as a grave breach of rule of law standards.[174] It has been used in this century against those engaging in political public protest and against groups such as animal rights activists. In *Hughes* v *Holley*[175] the Court of Appeal confirmed its existence and its availability regardless of the lawfulness of the behaviour in question.

This power was considered in *Hashman and Harrup* v *UK*.[176] The applicant, a hunt saboteur, had blown a horn with the intention of disrupting a hunt. There was no threat of violence and, in the particular circumstances, no breach of the peace. Blowing a horn is not unlawful. However, it was probable that the defendant would have repeated the behaviour in question which was found to be anti-social by the magistrates. He was therefore bound over to be of good behaviour and the binding over order was upheld on appeal. The European Commission on Human Rights considered the application under Articles 10, 11 and 5 and declared it admissible under Articles 10 and 11.[177] Before the Court, the applicants contended that the concept of behaviour *contra bonos mores* was so broadly defined that it did not comply with the requirement, in Article 10(2), that any interference with freedom of expression must be 'prescribed by law'. They also claimed that even if the interference was 'prescribed by law', the binding over in this case was a disproportionate interference with their freedom of expression.

The Court found that whilst the applicants' protest had taken the form of impeding the activities of which they disapproved, it nonetheless constituted an expression of opinion within the meaning of Article 10, following *Steel and Others* v *United Kingdom*.[178] The measures taken against the applicants therefore constituted an interference with their right to freedom of expression. To be justified, an interference with that right must first be prescribed by law under Article 10(2) and as Chapter 2 indicated, one of the requirements connoted by that expression is

[174] See Glanville Williams (1953) 16 MLR 417; P Hewitt *The Abuse of Power* (1982) at p125.
[175] [1988] 86 Cr App R 130.
[176] Application No 25594/94 (1999) European Court of Human Rights judgment of 25 November 1999.
[177] *Hashman and Harrup* v *UK* (1996) 22 EHRR CD 185.
[178] Application No 24838/94; (1998) 28 EHRR 603; (1998) Crim LR 893.

foreseeability. Conduct *contra bonos mores* was defined in English law as behaviour which was 'wrong rather than right in the judgement of the majority of contemporary fellow citizens'. This definition failed to give the applicants sufficiently clear guidance as to how they should behave in future. The interference with the applicants' freedom of expression was therefore too imprecise and unpredictable in its operation to satisfy the 'prescribed by law' requirement and there had therefore been a violation of Article 10. The Court found that it was not necessary to consider the remainder of the complaints.[179] This decision reaffirms the application of Article 10 to public protest taking the form of direct action. It also provides a clear illustration of the difference between the Strasbourg and the common law approaches to public protest. It reveals the failure of the common law to recognise the value of public protest as a form of expression. Had such value received recognition, the need for stricter adherence to rule of law standards might have been accepted domestically and this embarrassing decision avoided.

Criminalising trespass

In order to assemble or demonstrate, protesters require access to land. But the tendency for public spaces to be privatised has been reinforced by the direction of UK law. Not only are there virtually no positive rights of access to forums for the holding of meetings,[180] but under the provisions discussed below a 'creeping criminalisation of trespass'[181] has occurred, denying protesters access to private or quasi-public land on pain of the risk of arrest and conviction, not merely of incurring tortious liability. There are now a number of circumstances in which a person who merely walks onto land may incur criminal liability. A central issue, therefore, is the impact of the HRA on the creation of such liability.

Banning orders

Section 14A of the Public Order Act 1986 (inserted into the Act by s70 of the Criminal Justice and Public Order Act 1994), which criminalises certain forms of trespass, overlaps with common law powers and, like them, is potentially applicable to all forms of public protest. Once a ban is in

[179] Under Article 41 the applicants were awarded £6,000 for legal costs and expenses.

[180] See ss95 and 96 of the Representation of the People Act 1983 (providing a right for Parliamentary candidates to hold meetings at election times) and s43 of the Education (No 2) Act 1986 (providing that university and college authorities must secure freedom of speech for persons, including visiting speakers, within their establishments).

[181] See Wasik and Taylor *The Criminal Justice and Public Order Act 1994* (1995) London: Blackstones at p81.

place it will *prima facie* catch any assembly, however peaceful, on land in the open air, if section 14A(5) applies. Section 14A provides that a Chief Officer of Police may apply for a banning order[182] if that officer reasonably believes that an assembly is likely to be trespassory[183] and may result in serious disruption to the life of the community or damage to certain types of buildings and structures. Section 14A(5) of the 1994 Act provides that once an order is in being it operates to prohibit any trespassory assembly on 'land in the open air'[184] where there is no or a limited right of access to the land and the assembly 'takes place in the prohibited circumstances, that is, without the permission of the occupier . . . or so as to exceed the limits of any permission of his or the limits of the public's right of access'. Objection to section 14A has focused on its use of the broad and imprecise concept of 'serious disruption to the life of the community' as the basis for imposing the most draconian form of prior restraint – a complete ban, albeit in restricted circumstances.[185] Further, the term 'the life of the community' connotes, it is argued, the life-style of the majority and therefore renders section 14A especially apt to interfere with the expression of minority, 'alternative' viewpoints.

The meaning and ambit of section 14A were considered in *DPP* v *Jones and Lloyd*[186] which concerned an assembly on the road leading to Stonehenge, at a time when a section 14A order was in force. The purpose behind the ban was to protect Stonehenge from possible damage by 'New Age' and other groups gathering there for the summer solstice. This assembly was not held as part of a semi-religious ceremony but to protest against the imposition of the ban. Its members were arrested and charged with the offence under s14B(2) of taking part in an assembly, knowing of the ban. In the Divisional Court the prosecution argued that this peaceful assembly, which was simply present on the highway but inside the radius of the ban, was subject to the section 14A order as a 'trespassory' assembly

[182] If an order is made it will subsist for four days and operate within a radius of five miles around the area in question.

[183] The element of trespass will be satisfied where the Chief Constable reasonably believes that an assembly is intended to be held in any district at a place on land to which the public has no right of access or only a limited right of access and that the assembly is likely to be held without the permission of the occupier of the land or to conduct itself in such a way as to exceed the limits of any permission of the occupier's or the limits of the public's rights of access.

[184] The definition of 'land' as 'land in the open air' under s61(9) includes common land and non-metalled roads; it does not include metalled highway or buildings apart from certain agricultural buildings and scheduled monuments. The definition thus covers a number of private and semi-public places; it may include semi-enclosed shopping malls, railway stations, airports, parks.

[185] See, for example, M J Allen and S Cooper 'Howard's Way – A Farewell to Freedom?' 58 MLR 364, 384. It may be noted that this term is also used to justify the imposition of conditions on assemblies under s14 and on marches under s12 of the Public Order Act 1986.

[186] [1999] 2 All ER 257 House of Lords; judgment of the Divisional Court [1997] 2 All ER 119. For comment see 63(2) MLR 252

under s14A(5). The key question was whether the category of legitimate purposes for which the highway might be used included use of it by peaceful assemblies. On behalf of the respondents it was argued that any assembly on the highway is lawful so long as it is peaceful and non-obstructive, since such an assembly is making a reasonable use of the highway. Relying on *Hickman* v *Maisey*,[187] an authority concerned solely with the extent of proprietorial rights, the Divisional Court found that the highway was to be used for passing and repassing only and that assembling on it was outside the purpose for which the implied licence to use it was granted. The holding of meetings or demonstrations on it might be tolerated, it was found, but there could be no legal right to engage in them. S14A(5) was found to operate to prevent assemblies which would probably otherwise be permitted on a voluntary basis. The Court was content to find impliedly that since there is no legal right to assemble on the highway, and since the common law suggests that any assembly on the highway is trespassory, any provision which criminalises the holding of 'trespassory' assemblies on the highway in fact prohibits the holding on it of all assemblies of any significant size.[188] It was also argued on behalf of the respondents that unless there was a right to hold an assembly as opposed merely to a toleration, Article 11 of the European Convention on Human Rights would be breached. The Court found, however, that recourse to the Convention was unnecessary since the law in question was not ambiguous, and, further, that since peaceful assemblies are normally permitted, the law was in any event in conformity with the Convention.

The Court concluded that, since the assembly had exceeded the limited rights of access to the highway it fell within section 14A(5); the fact that, but for the section 14A order, it would probably have been tolerated, was found to be irrelevant. The Divisional Court's judgment was overturned by the House of Lords by a three to two majority. The very narrow basis of the decision was that under the common law a peaceful, non-obstructive assembly on the public highway is not inevitably tortious. The assembly in question had been found by the tribunal of fact to be a reasonable user, but the Lords found that the fact that an assembly is peaceful and non-obstructive will not mean that it will necessarily amount to a reasonable – and therefore non-trespassory – use of the

[187] [1900] 1 QB 752 CA. The decision concerned the defendant's use of the highway in order to gain information by looking over the plaintiff's land. The defendant was on the highway watching the plaintiff's land. It was found that the plaintiff owned the land under the highway and that the defendant was entitled to make ordinary and reasonable use of it. Such watching was held not to be reasonable; the defendant had gone outside the accepted use of the highway and therefore had trespassed.

[188] S16 of the Public Order Act 1986 defines an assembly as 20 or more people in a public place. As far as the common law is concerned an assembly would have to be of a size and duration such that it could not be said to be merely incidental to passage on the highway.

highway. The Lords differed from the view of the Divisional Court only on the question of the meaning of a reasonable user of the highway, finding that use of it for the purpose of peaceful assembly would not inevitably be unreasonable. In that narrow sense a liberty to assemble on the highway was affirmed. In future, the fact that an s14A order is in force will no longer mean that any assembly present on the highway within the area covered will automatically fall within the prohibition under s14A(5). The case was not decided on Article 10 or 11 grounds, since despite the divergence between the majority and minority interpretations of the common law, it was not viewed as ambiguous or unclear. The Lords in fact failed to recognise Article 10 as having any bearing at all on the matter. No recognition was given to the significance of the particular expression in question – that it was political in that it was protesting against an illiberal law which curbed freedom of protest and therefore potentially infringed Articles 10 and 11. The case was remitted to the Crown Court for a rehearing. The Lords' decision anticipated an inevitable departure, in an analogous case, from the Divisional Court's stance once the HRA was fully in force. Courts would have been likely to find that s14A, as interpreted by the Divisional Court, represents an interference with the substantive rights under Articles 10 and 11 since it allows interferences with peaceful assemblies. Under both the 'review' and 'activist' models, it would almost certainly have been concluded that public authorities are under an obligation to allow peaceful assemblies on the highway.

The findings of the Divisional Court and, to an extent, of the Lords are, it is contended, in keeping with the traditional illiberal stance of the judiciary towards public protest. No account was taken of the value of the political expression dimension of public protest; the decision turned solely on the extent of proprietorial rights. The decision of the Divisional Court revealed both the precarious nature of the liberty to assemble and the narrow, technical approach often taken to it.[189] Although the Law Lords achieved the outcome which afforded some protection to public protest, they did so on the narrowest possible basis. They recognised a liberty to assemble on the highway which is almost without content since the circumstances in which a peaceful non-obstructive assembly might still be seen as unreasonable and therefore criminal are left unclear. No infusion of Strasbourg concepts into the relevant domestic jurisprudence occurred, although it might have been expected that the imminence of the HRA would have encouraged the Lords to move beyond the traditional limited perspective adopted towards public protest and to consider instead its political expression dimension. Since the Act will represent a complete break with the previous Constitutional order one might have

[189] John Wadham of *Liberty* said of it: 'A peaceful, non-obstructive gathering is a reasonable use of a public highway. To say that it is a form of trespass seems extraordinary': *The Times* 24 January 1997.

expected this decision to foreshadow that upheaval and to exhibit an acceptance of the Strasbourg conception of the significance of such expression in a democracy. The response of the Lords does not suggest that they are prepared to adopt a robust approach to curbing interference with Article 10 and 11 rights and provides little cause for optimism regarding the judicial response to their reception into domestic law.

Following the Lords' findings, organisers of assemblies are still in a difficult position due to uncertainty as to when the tribunal of fact – the Magistrates' Court – will be likely to deem an assembly reasonable. Merely ensuring its peacefulness may be insufficient. The ruling in the Lords may, therefore, lessen only slightly the chilling effect flowing from the previous position. It is possible that in a future case analogous to *Jones*, it might be argued that s14A as interpreted by the House of Lords is incompatible with Articles 10 and 11. In *Steel* v *UK* the Court found that the interference with an entirely peaceful protest which had occurred was disproportionate to the aim of the exception – the prevention of disorder. The criminalisation of such a protest under s14A would equally appear to amount to such a disproportionate interference. That aspect of the ruling in the House of Lords could be overruled or departed from[190] in a lower court since that is what the interpretative obligation under s3 HRA demands, where necessary. A lower court could find that if an assembly on the highway is peaceful and non-obstructive it must inevitably be termed reasonable. In other words, it could determine that there was no room in the post-HRA era for finding such an assembly unreasonable and therefore trespassory. If it was prepared to adopt that stance the right to make public protest would be given a somewhat wider scope. It would not be obliged to adopt it, however, since it is not *bound* by the Strasbourg case-law under s2 HRA. A lower court would be bound under s3 to render s14A of the 1986 Act compatible with the Convention if at all possible, but the question of what was required in order to render the two compatible would be open to interpretation since the court need only take the relevant jurisprudence, including *Steel*, into account under s2. S14A might well be viewed as compatible with Articles 10 and 11 since *Jones* made it clear that a liberty, albeit a narrow one, to assemble on the highway is recognised in UK law. If a lower court was reluctant to depart from the findings of the Lords in *Jones* it could therefore merely confine its ruling to the particular assembly in question, finding that it was 'reasonable'. This would be compatible with both *Jones* and *Steel* but the chilling effect of s14A would be maintained.

The ruling of the Lords did not address, and for the purposes of the decision did not need to address, the question whether the ban initially imposed was compatible with the Convention. But under the HRA, in a

[190] In fact that aspect of the ruling was technically *obiter* since it was not essential to the decision.

case analogous to *Jones,* collateral challenges to such bans could be used by way of defence under s7(1)(b) HRA by a person prosecuted for infringing a ban, on the basis of its non-compatibility with Articles 10 and 11. A group which had been affected by the ban in that it had had to cancel a meeting at the place in question could seek judicial review of the decision to impose it. The ban might be in existence, under s14A(6) for four days only, in which case, unless it was renewed, it would not be in place once the case came to court. The question of a remedy, if the application was successful, would therefore arise. A declaration under s8(1) HRA that the ban was unlawful would be of some value where, for example, the same circumstances were likely to arise. This point would be relevant in a case such as *Jones* itself, involving a summer solstice gathering at an ancient monument. As Chapter 2 indicates, it is probable that an action for breach of statutory duty could not be mounted in such circumstances as an alternative to judicial review.[191]

In the judicial review proceedings the applicant could raise Convention points regarding the compatibility of an s14A order with Articles 10 and 11 on various grounds. It could be argued that the banning of a peaceful assembly which had not itself caused or threatened serious disruption to the life of the community was disproportionate to the aims of paragraph 2 of Articles 10 and 11. Under the minimalist or review model the decision of the Commission in *Christians Against Racism and Fascism* v *UK*[192] could be relied on in finding that an s14A order constituted a proportionate interference with Article 10 and 11 rights. A wide margin of appreciation was allowed in finding that a ban aimed at violent racist groups was necessary and proportionate despite its effect on a peaceful group – CND. But under a more rigorous scrutiny, distinctions could be found between the ban at issue and s14A orders. The CND marches were banned because of the effect of s3 of the 1936 Public Order Act (the predecessor of the current s13 of the 1986 Act) which was based on one ground only – serious disorder – and required the police to consider whether the power to impose conditions under s3(1) provided another means of preventing it. Under s14A the police are not required to consider other possibilities and the test to be satisfied in order to apply for the banning order denotes a much lower level of harm.[193] The stance

[191] See p52.

[192] No 8440/78, 21 DR 138 (1980).

[193] It may be noted that challenges by way of judicial review could also be mounted to s13 bans, arguing that had *Christians Against Racism and Fascism* No 8440/78, 21 DR 138 (1980) been less heavily influenced by the doctrine of the margin of appreciation, a different outcome might have been achieved. On that basis a very strict scrutiny of the use of s13 to interfere with the assembly and expression of a peaceful group would be required, and in particular it might be argued that the imposition of a condition under s12 of the 1986 Act would have represented, as a ban does not, a proportionate interference. S13 expressly requires the Chief Officer of Police to consider this matter before applying for a ban.

taken to prior restraints under Article 10 in contexts other than that of protest could be taken into account,[194] bearing in mind the special propensity of Strasbourg to concede a wide margin of appreciation in protest cases.

Aggravated trespass

The Criminal Justice and Public Order Act 1994 also introduced the similar and overlapping offence of aggravated trespass under s68, also aimed at groups such as hunt saboteurs or motorway protesters.[195] S68 creates a two-stage test: first it must be shown that the defendant trespassed on land in the open air, and second, in relation to lawful activity which persons are engaging in or are about to engage in, that the defendent did there anything intended by him or her to have the effect of either intimidating those persons so as to deter them from the activity or of obstructing or disrupting that activity. No defence is provided and it is not necessary to show that the activity was actually affected. This is a very broadly drawn provision: its impact in practice will depend on the meaning attached to the vague terms 'disrupt' and 'obstruct'. A great many peaceful but vociferous demonstrations may have some impact of an obstructive nature on lawful activities. It is, however, limited in its application: it does not apply to assemblies on a metalled highway, or in most but not all buildings,[196] although it does include public paths such as bridleways. The offence of obstruction of the highway under s137 of the Highways Act 1980 can be used against assemblies on the highway; the function of this provision is to extend liability for forms of obstruction beyond the highway. It was arguably unnecessary to enact this offence given the availability of civil remedies and the possibility of using powers to prevent a breach of the peace against mass trespassers or of charging them with low level public order offences.[197]

S68 has been used against hunt saboteurs and others on a number of occasions, and some of the decisions on the section have had the effect of widening the area of liability created still further. In *Winder and Others* v *Director of Public Prosecutions*[198] the appellants had been running after the hunt. It was accepted that they did not intend at that point to disrupt it, but it was found that running after it was a more than preparatory act, and that it was close enough to the contemplated action to incur liability. It was found that the offence under s68 was established on the basis that

[194] *Observer and Guardian* v *UK* (1991) 14 EHRR 153; see p168, below.
[195] See *Hansard* Commons 11 January 1994 col 29.
[196] See s61(9) of the 1994 Act.
[197] See A T H Smith *Offences Against Public Order* (1987) paras 14–18, in relation to criminalisation of trespass under s39 of the Public Order Act 1986 (now replaced by s61 of the 1994 Act).
[198] *The Times* 14 August 1996.

the appellants were trespassing on land in the open air with the general intention of disrupting the hunt and were intending when in range to commit the acts in question with the required intention. This decision came very close to punishing persons for their thoughts rather than for their actions.

The decision in *Director of Public Prosecutions* v *Barnard and Others*[199] also failed to afford a restrictive interpretation to s68. The decision concerned protesters against open cast mining who came onto land at an open cast site. The information against them alleged that having trespassed on land in the open air, they then, in relation to a lawful activity of open cast mining which persons were about to be engaged in on that land, did an act of unlawfully entering on that land, intended by them to have the effect of intimidating those persons so as to deter them from engaging in that activity, or obstructing or disrupting that activity, contrary to s68(1). The magistrate, relying on *Winder*, found that three elements were required to establish the offence of aggravated trespass: namely, trespass, an intention to disrupt a lawful activity and an act done towards that end. The magistrate found that the allegation in the informations that the respondents 'unlawfully entered on land' alleged no more than that they had trespassed, and therefore was not capable of amounting to the second aggravating act required by the words in s68(1) 'does there anything which is intended by him to have the effect'. The magistrate refused an application by the prosecution to amend the informations to allege the act of 'unlawfully occupying the site in company with numerous other people' on the ground that it still would not have disclosed an offence, as occupation of the site was the act of trespass, and not an additional act aggravating that trespass. Reference to the number of people was no more than an indication that some were trespassing.

Lord Justice Laws found that the magistrate was clearly correct in finding the original information to be defective. Proof was required of trespassing on land in the open air and of doing a distinct and overt act other than the act of trespassing which was intended to have the effects specified under subsections (a) to (c) of s68(1). Unlawful occupation could equate to no more than the original trespass, but there might, he found, be circumstances where it could constitute the second act, other than trespass, required under the offence. However, a bare allegation of occupation was insufficient. It had to be supported by particulars of what the defendant was actually doing, and the occupation had to be distinct and overt from the original trespass. The proposed amendment would, he found, have disclosed an offence under s68(1) of the 1994 Act, but it would not have been appropriate to allow the amendments; accordingly, the appeal was dismissed.

[199] (1999) before Lord Justice Laws and Mr Justice Potts (Judgment 15 October 1999) *The Times* 9 November 1999.

This decision suggests at first sight that when a group of protesters merely come onto land to protest about something taking place there, they do not thereby commit a criminal offence. It reiterates that the offence under s68 consists of distinct elements all of which must be shown to be present. But the potential blurring of the distinction between the first two to the effect that for the purposes of the offence of aggravated trespass, the occupation of land *could* constitute an act intended to intimidate, obstruct or disrupt, if it was distinct from a mere act of trespass, might lead to confusion as to the difference between simple and aggravated trespass. The circumstances in which an occupation of land will be viewed as distinct from a trespass on it are left unclear. The mere fact that the defendants unlawfully (i.e. committing the tort of trespass) occupied the site in company with numerous other people does not necessarily mean that the offence under s68 is made out unless the group do there anything which, in relation to others engaging in a lawful activity, is intended to have the effects mentioned in subsections (a) to (c) of s68(1). If, for example, a large group walked onto land and engaged in a peaceful sit-in without making any effort to approach the persons the protest was aimed at, it is unclear that any of the effects mentioned above could be said to have occurred. The terms are ambiguous, but bearing Articles 10 and 11 in mind, they should now be interpreted more strictly under s3 HRA. On the facts, the protesters' behaviour was quite closely analogous to that of the successful applicants in *Steel* in that the protest clearly constituted an expression of opinion, albeit occurring by means of action rather than speech, which was peaceful and unlikely to lead to disorder.

If a case analogous to *Winder* recurs in the post-HRA era, it might be argued that the activity in question could be viewed as provocative and therefore as falling within the findings as to the first two applicants in *Steel*. But under the activist approach the findings as to those two applicants should be applied without reliance on the margin of appreciation aspects of the judgment. In other words, depending on the specific circumstances, the use of s68 in such an instance could be viewed as disproportionate to the aim in view, the prevention of disorder (under Articles 10(2) and 11(2)), applying *Steel* but disapplying the margin of appreciation doctrine when arriving at the determination regarding proportionality. The path to domestic departure from *Steel* in favour of public protest would be open.

S69, which greatly extends the impact of s68, may also require a restrictive interpretation in order to achieve compatibility with Articles 10 and 11, taking the findings in *Steel* into account. S69 provides *inter alia* that if the senior police officer present at the scene reasonably believes that a person is committing, has committed or intends to commit the offence under s68 the officer can direct the person to leave the land. Under s69(3) if the person in question, knowing that the s69 direction has been given, fails to leave the land or re-enters it within three months that person commits an imprisonable offence. In other words, s69 allows police officers, without reference to any independent authority, to impose bans on entry to land, lasting for three months, on certain persons. It is a defence for the person to show that he or she had a reasonable excuse for failing to leave the land or for returning as a trespasser.[200] It may be noted that s69 has an equivalent under s14C Public Order Act 1986, which allows a constable to stop a person whom he or she reasonably believes is on his or her way to an assembly in an area to which an s14A order applies, and to direct the person not to proceed in that direction. The power can only be used within the area to which the order applies. Failure to comply is an offence and renders the person liable to arrest. The similarities between s14C and s69 mean that much of the discussion below would apply also to s14C.

Although s68 under the strict interpretation indicated above is not apt to lead to the criminalisation of persons who simply walk onto land as trespassers, s69 appears to have the potential to do so, depending on the interpretation given by the courts to the 'reasonable excuse' defence. For example, where a person is in receipt of the direction under s69, given erroneously but on reasonable grounds, that person might commit an offence if thereafter he or she re-entered the land in question during the specified time. The fact that on the second occasion the person was merely walking peacefully on to land in order to engage in a non-obstructive public protest would be irrelevant unless he or she could also produce an excuse which could be termed reasonable. In such circumstances, since the term 'reasonable' is ambiguous, interpretation of s69 by reference to Articles 10 and 11 might lead to a finding that the erroneousness of the senior police officer's original 'reasonable belief' should amount to a reasonable excuse. It is also possible, depending on the particular circumstances, that certain s69 'bans' may be unjustifiable under paragraph 2 of Articles 10 and 11, bearing in mind the extent of the discretion to interfere with peaceful protest which this section vests in the police without any independent check, and the extent of the interference – in effect, a complete ban on entering the land in question, potentially lasting for three months. Since s69 can operate as a prior restraint, Article 10 would demand that any direction given should be strictly scrutinised.[201]

Capon v *DPP*[202] made it clear that the offence under s69 could be committed even though the offence under s68 was not established. The defendants were videoing the digging out of a fox when they were threatened with arrest under s68 by a police officer if they did not leave and asked whether they were leaving the land. This exchange and question was found

[200] S69(4).
[201] See p168, below.
[202] Case CO/3496/97 judgment 4 March 1998 LEXIS; considered: Mead [1998] Crim LR 870.

to be sufficient, in the circumstances, to constitute the direction necessary under s69. Their intention in undertaking the videoing was not found to be to disrupt, intimidate or interfere with the activity in question. This decision raises the possibility that a direction under s69, if it can be given in such an imprecise form, might be found in future to fail to satisfy the test denoted by the term 'prescribed by law' under Articles 10 and 11, assuming that the activity in question could be viewed as constituting the expression of an opinion so as to engage those Articles. It might well be argued that a direction given in the form of a question as in *Capon* would be too imprecise to satisfy that test. But, equally, the domestic court would be free to apply a doctrine of deference to the executive, whereby the nature of the direction should not be scrutinised too closely since the circumstances could be best assessed by the police officer on the ground. In the words of Lord Slynn, in the *International Ferry Traders* case,[203] the courts might show respect to 'the margin of appreciation or discretion' of the police officers in question in refusing to undertake a rigorous review of the wording of a direction.

Under this approach, the outcome in instances similar to *Winder* or *Capon* might not differ in the post-HRA era, although the reasoning process by which it was reached would, since the value of political expression – taking that term to encompass an animal rights protest – would receive some consideration.

Rights of access to land

The discussion so far has not centred on the question of rights of access to land, except in relation to the highway, under s14A. It is now established that the right of access to the highway may include holding an assembly on it. But *prima facie* assemblies on other quasi-public or private land will virtually always be trespassory, unless in the circumstances it is found that permission to hold some peaceful protests was given. As indicated above, the Convention has not yet accepted that there is a positive obligation on the public authorities to require private individuals to allow the exercise of protest and assembly rights on their land. But an activist domestic court might be prepared to uphold such a claim, thereby anticipating the stance on this matter which some commentators view Strasbourg as not unlikely to adopt.[204] When the issue of exclusion of persons from a quasi-public place, a shopping mall, was raised before the Commission, it declared the application inadmissible, on the basis that Article 11 was not applicable, since the applicants were gathering there for

[203] [1999] 1 All ER 129; see note 114, and associated text, above.

[204] Harris, O'Boyle and Warbrick *Law of the European Convention on Human Rights* (1995) London: Butterworths at p419.

a purely social purpose.[205] Clearly, had Article 11 been engaged, a different outcome might have been achieved. In the USA the courts are moving away from a position of upholding proprietorial rights and towards providing protection for expressive activity in quasi-public forums.[206] This can also be said of the Canadian and Australian courts.[207] In contrast, the traditional stance of the UK judiciary is to favour the property right when it conflicts with rights of protest. In general, the judiciary tend to uphold proprietorial rights in an abstract fashion, regardless of any real harm which may occur owing to their infringement.[208] But Article 11 arguments might persuade the judiciary in future to consider the possibility of recognising broader access rights to quasi-public land. *DPP* v *Jones* has already found that this is the case as far as the highway is concerned, but a large number of quasi-public places exist to which the public has limited rights of access, such as unenclosed shopping malls, parks, the grounds and forecourts of town halls or civic centres, monuments and their surrounding land or rights of way across private land. At present such rights of access would not include assemblies for the purpose of protests and demonstrations.

The issue might arise in two ways. A group seeking access to a forum for the holding of an assembly or demonstration might seek to bring an action against the relevant landowning body under s6 HRA, claiming that a refusal to allow an assembly in a particular place had constituted an interference with its Article 10 and 11 rights. For example, it might seek judicial review of the decision of a local authority refusing it access to a park in order to hold a meeting. Where a group was charged with infringing a ban imposed under s14A of the Public Order Act 1986 in respect of private or quasi-public land, its main recourse (apart from a challenge to the ban itself, discussed above), since *prima facie* it would appear to be tresspassory, would be to argue that in the circumstances it had an implied licence to enter the land on the basis of the demands of the guarantees under Articles 10 and 11. A failure to accept such an argument could lead, potentially, to a serious interference with those guarantees.[209] A successful claim of such access rights would mean reinterpreting s14A(5) in order to find that rights of access to certain areas,

[205] *Anderson* v *UK* [1998] EHRLR 218. As the Commission implied, the outcome would probably have been different had the UK ratified Protocol 4, Article 2, which guarantees freedom of movement.

[206] See *Shad Alliance* v *Smith Haven Mall* 484 NYS 2d 849 esp at p857.

[207] See *Harrison* v *Carswell* (1975) 62 DLR (3d) 68 Supreme Court of Canada; *Gerhardy* v *Brown* (1985) 159 CLR 70.

[208] See on this point Gray and Gray 'Civil Rights, Civil Wrongs and Quasi-Public Places' [1999] EHRLR 46.

[209] The members of the assembly would be convicted of various offences arising under s14B, however peaceful or non-obstructive the assembly was. Its organiser could be imprisoned (s14B(5)), as could anyone who could be proved to have incited a member of the assembly to come onto the land (s14B (7)).

going beyond the highway, exist for the purpose of holding peaceful assemblies. If such a claim was upheld it would also preclude the imposition of tortious liability.

Similar arguments could be raised under ss68 or 69 CJPOA; a group charged with aggravated trespass could argue, as a preliminary issue, that they had not trespassed since they were within the limited rights of access to the land. Upholding such a claim would mean, in effect, deeming under s68 that an implied licence to enter the land existed, imposed by the HRA. Any such implied licence would no doubt be highly circumscribed. For example, it would have to avoid allowing any infringement of Article 8 rights, including respect for the home. It would probably apply for a limited period and possibly only to peaceful protests such as a sit-in.

The status of the landowning body under s6 HRA would be relevant. Further, since the offences in question are statutory the court would have to satisfy its obligation under s3. If the landowning body was itself a public authority, it would clearly be bound by the Convention rights. If it was a 'hybrid' body[210] it would depend whether its public function could be said to be engaged by the claims of the protesters. As Chapter 2 indicated, s6 HRA will bring a number of bodies which manage or own land within its ambit, including bodies such as Railtrack which are classic hybrid bodies. If, for example, Railtrack bought land, perhaps by means of a CPO (Compulsory Purchase Order), in order to place railway lines across it, it would then own the land for the purpose of satisfying its public function as the manager of rail infrastucture, but such ownership would nevertheless probably be part of its private function.[211] But if it acted in order to secure the lines by, for example, placing fences round them, it would be doing so in pursuance of its statutory duty in respect of rail safety and therefore might be viewed as acting in that respect as a public authority.[212] A body exercising a private function, or a fully private body, would not be bound by s6 but would still be affected by s3 HRA. If, for example, an assembly took place, in the period to which an s14A ban applied, on land owned by a privatised body which could not be viewed as related to the public function of that body, a court would still have to interpret s14A(5) in order to ensure compatibility with Articles 10 and 11. If, alternatively, a person was charged with an offence under ss68 or 69 in respect of such an assembly, the court would have to ensure compatibility in respect of the term 'trespass' in ss68(1) or 69(1).

[210] See Chapter 2 p49.

[211] There was a *Pepper* v *Hart* statement in Parliament to this effect: 583 HL 796, 811 (24 November 1997).

[212] Clearly it does not necessarily follow in any particular circumstance that Articles 10 and 11 would require that access to the land should be allowed for protesters. Both Articles contain exceptions in the interests of public safety.

Conflicting rights

Where, as is frequently the case, ss68, 69 CJPOA, and ss14A and 14C of the Public Order Act (PO) 1986 are used in respect of a conflict between two groups, such as hunters and hunt saboteurs, the argument might be raised in court that those provisions should be interpreted in such a way as to protect freedom of assembly in the sense of allowing persons to engage in group activities, such as hunting, shooting or fishing, free from interference by others.[213] The provisions might appear to allow the state to discharge a positive obligation to ensure that such groups are able to assemble. This argument finds some support from the ruling in *Chorherr* v *Austria*.[214] The expression of protesters appeared likely to offend some spectators, leading to an interference with their peaceful enjoyment of a parade. The interference of the state with the Article 10 rights of the protesters was justified since it had the aim of upholding freedom of assembly. This argument would place the law in the position of choosing between the Article 11 rights of opposing groups or between the Article 10 rights of one group and the Article 11 rights of another. This would be the case, of course, only if the activities of hunters, fishers and the like were able to take advantage of the Article 11 guarantee. As noted above, the Commission has found that Article 11 does not cover peaceful assembly for purely social purposes[215] and it is therefore probable that it does not cover the activities in question. However, this decision is not directly in point and, in any event, the domestic courts would not be bound by it.

The group activities in question might also, or alternatively, find protection under Article 8 since, depending on the circumstances, the activities of the protesters in coming onto private land in order to protest against activities taking place there could be viewed as interfering with the right to respect for private life, the home and the family.[216] The interference with the Article 10 and 11 rights of protesters under ss68, 69 or s14A could then be justified on the basis that it allowed discharge of the state obligation under Article 8 to ensure that the exercise of the rights it guarantees is not threatened by the interference of private

[213] See *Platform 'Artze fur das Leben'* v *Austria* Series A No 139 para 32 (1988); 13 EHRR 204.

[214] A 266-B (1993).

[215] *Anderson* v *UK* Case No 33689/96, 25 EHRR (1998) CD 172. This application arose from *CIN Properties Ltd* v *Rawlins* [1995] 2 EGLR 130.

[216] See *Earl Spencer* v *United Kingdom* 25 EHRR CD 105 (1998). The applicants complained that English law provided no remedy for the invasion of their privacy through the publication in the press of various (truthful) stories relating to the bulimia and mental health problems of Countess Spencer, including photographs taken of her walking in the grounds of the clinic. The Commission dismissed the claim as manifestly ill-founded, not on the basis that the Convention did not require a remedy in such circumstances, but on the basis that such a remedy – breach of confidence – did exist in UK law, but had not been exhausted.

persons.[217] The court itself would have to ensure that it did not fail to protect the Article 11 or 8 rights of the hunters or shooters,[218] if it was prepared to countenance the argument that those rights were at stake. It would then have to perform a balancing act between the exercise of two conflicting rights with very little guidance from Strasbourg, since where such a conflict arises Strasbourg allows a very wide margin of appreciation.[219]

Anti-social behaviour

The criminalisation of low level forms of anti-social behaviour, begun under s5 of the Public Order Act 1986, continued under the Criminal Justice and s154 Public Order Act 1994,[220] and taken further under the Protection from Harassment Act 1997, culminated in s1 of the Crime and Disorder Act 1998. These provisions target similar forms of anti-social behaviour which had previously been viewed as too trivial or too imprecise to attract criminal or, in most instances, civil liability. All are aimed at behaviour causing harassment, alarm or distress or, under the 1997 Act, amounting to harassment, and all are targeted at particular social problems, largely unrelated to public protest. S5 of the 1986 Act was aimed at the perceived problem of disturbance from football hooligans or late night rowdies; the 1997 Act at the problem of so-called 'stalkers'; s1 of the 1998 Act at anti-social neighbours. But all, owing to their breadth, have a potential application to protest within all the categories indicated above, probably not in all circumstances excluding the first.

The offences created require establishment of a minimal and imprecise *actus reus*. Ss5 and 4A of the 1986 Act criminalise threatening, abusive, insulting words or behaviour or disorderly behaviour which, under s5, takes place in the 'hearing or sight of a person likely to be caused harassment, alarm or distress thereby' or, under s4A, which subjectively causes those effects. In *Swanston* v *DPP*[221] it was found, in respect of s5, that if a bystander gives evidence to the effect that the 'victim' perceived the threatening, abusive or insulting words then the court can draw the

[217] In *X and Y* v *Netherlands* (1985) 8 EHRR 235 the Court stated: 'these [Article 8] obligations may require the adoption of measures even in the sphere of relations between individuals'. In other words, the term 'interference by a public authority' used in Article 8 can mean 'unjustified failure to prevent interference by others'.

[218] Since, as Chapter 2 points out, the court is itself a public authority under s6 HRA and is itself bound to respect the Convention rights.

[219] See *Otto-Preminger Institut* v *Austria* (1994) 19 EHRR 34. The conflict in the case between Articles 10 and 9 played a part in the concession of a very wide margin of appreciation to the state.

[220] Which inserted s4A into the 1986 Act.

[221] (1997) *The Times* 23 January 1997.

inference that they were so perceived. It was determined in *DPP* v *Orum*[222] that a police officer may be the person mentioned who was caused harassment, alarm or distress. These two decisions enhance the ease with which this offence may be deployed, as does *DPP* v *Fidler*[223] in which it was found that a person whose own behaviour would not satisfy the requirements of s5 may be guilty of aiding and abetting this offence if he or she is part of a crowd who are committing it. S1 of the 1997 Act defines harassment as a course of conduct which a reasonable person would consider amounted to harassment of another where the harasser knows or ought to know that this will be its effect; s2 makes harassment an offence. An interim injunction, breach of which is an offence (s3(6)) punishable by up to five years' imprisonment (s3(9)), can be obtained under s3 in civil proceedings. No definition of a course of conduct which might amount to harassment is offered. S1 of the 1998 Act provides a penalty of a maximum of five years' imprisonment for failing to obey an order obtained on the civil standard of proof,[224] forbidding any form of 'anti-social' behaviour,[225] defined under s1(1)(a) as behaving: 'in an anti-social manner, that is to say in a manner that caused or was likely to cause harassment, alarm and distress to one or more persons' other than those of the same household as the defendant.

These statutory provisions all provide defences of reasonableness, none of which are defined or specifically aimed at protecting expression.[226] It was determined in *DPP* v *Clarke*,[227] in respect of charges under s5 of the 1986 Act in relation to an anti-abortion protest, that the defence under s5 is to be judged objectively and it will therefore depend on what a bench of magistrates considers reasonable. In that case the behaviour of the protesters outside an abortion clinic was not found to be reasonable. The use of pictures and models appeared to contribute to this conclusion. This decision, which would clearly also apply to charges under s4A, and, where appropriate, to s12(3) of the 1997 Act and s1(5) of the 1998 Act as well, obviously does not give much guidance to protesters seeking to determine beforehand the limits or meaning of 'reasonable' protest. As a deliberately ambiguous term it obviously leaves enormous discretion to the judiciary to adopt approaches to its interpretation in accordance with Articles 10 and 11 as interpreted in *Steel*, ranging from the minimalist to the activist. Under the former approach, it might be found that only

[222] [1988] 3 All ER 449.

[223] [1992] 1 WLR 91.

[224] According to the 1998 Magistrates Courts Rules applicable to these orders.

[225] S1(10)(b).

[226] Under s5(3)(c) and s4A(3)(b) of the 1986 Act, s1(3) of the 1997 Act and s1(5) of the 1998 Act. It may be noted that under the 1997 and 1998 provisions the 'defence' operates as partially reversed *actus reus*, in the sense that if the defence is proved (the burden of so doing is on the defendant), then harassment or anti-social behaviour is not established.

[227] (1992) Crim LR 60.

innocuous, peaceful persuasion could be termed reasonable. Such a finding might be of value where, for example, a large number of groups were served with injunctions under s3 of the 1997 Act since it might serve to allow differentiation between those whose peaceful persuasion had nevertheless been viewed by its target as 'harassment' and those groups which had adopted more forceful means. But a more 'activist' interpretation of this defence would have to find a basis in the general principles articulated above,[228] especially applicable in relation to protest expressing minority viewpoints. This would be a matter of significance, since such viewpoints may be unlikely to be favourably received by others.

The defence of reasonableness assumes especial significance in relation to the 1997 and 1998 provisions, since in contrast to the earlier ones, either there is no need to establish *mens rea* or its establishment is likely to have little inhibitory effect. The *mens rea* requirements of ss5 and 4A of the 1986 Act may in contrast create such an effect. Under s6(4) it must be established that the defendant intended that others would be caused – or (under s5 only) was aware that they might experience – harassment, alarm or distress due to the forbidden behaviour. In *DPP* v *Clarke*[229] it was further found that to establish liability it is insufficient to show only that the defendant intended or was aware that he or she might cause the forbidden harm; it must also be shown that the defendent intended his or her conduct to be threatening, abusive or insulting, or was aware that it might be. Both mental states have to be established independently. Using this test, it was found that anti-abortion protesters had not realised that their behaviour in shouting anti-abortion slogans, displaying plastic models of foetuses and pictures of dead foetuses would be threatening, abusive or insulting. This decision allows those who believe fervently in their cause, and therefore fail to appreciate that their protest may insult or offend others, to escape liability. It therefore places a significant curb on the ability of ss5 and 4A to interfere with Article 10 and 11 rights. Once a particular group of protesters has been prosecuted, however, and it has been found, as in *Clarke*, that others found their protest threatening, abusive or insulting, the subjective element of the *mens rea* will be in future readily made out even if the instant prosecution fails.

Clarke will not have a ready application under the 1997 and 1998 Acts. Ss1 and 2 of the 1997 Act make it a requirement of establishing the offence that the harasser knows or ought to know that the course of conduct amounts to harassment. However, since an interim injunction can be obtained under s3 of the Act, in *ex parte* proceedings, the establishment of that state of mind would be aided in proceedings for its breach once it had been served on the defendant. Breach of such an injunction is punishable by five years' imprisonment. Therefore, although *prima facie*

[228] See pp119–127, above.
[229] (1992) Crim LR 60.

the 1997 Act imports a *mens rea* requirement, the existence of punishment on the civil standard of proof allows for its circumvention. Criminal proceedings relating to the same course of conduct but under s2 may also be affected, as explained below, once an injunction has been obtained. S1 of the 1998 Act requires no circumvention of *mens rea* requirements since it merely abandons them. They could be reintroduced only in the form of a 'reversed' *mens rea*, under the defence of reasonableness, unless, in a public protest case, with a view to narrowing down the potential of this section to interfere with Article 6, 10 or 11 rights, a judge was prepared to import the additional *mens rea* element identified in *Clarke*.

These matters are linked to the key difference between these two recent provisions and the previous ones – their hybrid nature in allowing for criminal sanctions, including imprisonment, on the civil standard of proof for breach of an injunction or order. The 1997 Act allows for an injunction to be obtained at the instigation of the 'victim' in *ex parte* proceedings, merely on his or her affidavit. This probably explains why the 1997 Act is proving to offer a primary means of curbing various forms of protest. It provides a contrast to ss5 and 4A of the 1986 Act, which are widely used, but not, research suggests, frequently in the context of political protest.[230] Unlike the 1997 Act, they appear, on the whole, to have been used to target those at whom they were originally aimed.

The features of the 1997 Act which have made it attractive as a measure to be used against protesters are, it should be noted, also present in the 1998 Act in the sense that the subject of the protest can (indirectly) instigate proceedings[231] and criminal sanctions, including imprisonment, may be imposed on the civil standard. These features are likely to raise questions about the compatibility of these provisions with Article 6. At Strasbourg, the fact that national law classifies an act as non-criminal is relevant but not conclusive. In *Benham* v *UK*,[232] the leading case on 'criminal charge', the Court found that although the legislation in question[233] clearly did not create a criminal offence in UK law, it should be accounted criminal for Article 6(1) purposes. The proceedings against the applicant[234] had been brought by the public authorities; the proceedings had

[230] Waddington explains the reluctance to arrest in this context on the basis that it risks sparking off hostility among other protesters and can create trouble later since the arrest may be scrutinised in court: see *Liberty and Order* (1994) at pp54–55. Independent records of arrests may be available since supporters of the protest may photograph them and reporters may well also be present. Records and reports of arrests may help to lead to acquittals and may fuel public criticism of the police. This would be unlikely to be the case in relation to the arrest of, for example, drunken football supporters.

[231] The application for the order is made by the 'relevant authority' under s1(1) but it may be triggered off by allegations made to the police or housing authority.

[232] (1996) 22 EHRR 293. See also *Lauko* v *Slovakia* (1999) 1 EHRLR 105 in which it was found that a penalty for anti-social behaviour was inherently criminal in nature.

[233] S41 of the Community Charge (Administration and Enforcement) Regulations.

[234] In respect of default on payment of the community charge or poll tax.

some punitive elements and the bringing of them implied fault on the part of the applicant. Further, the penalty was severe (committal to prison for up to three months).[235]

Under the HRA the national court, however, may be placed in a difficulty where s3 of the 1997 or s1 of the 1998 Act classifies an act as non-criminal, but Article 6 suggests that it is criminal. Anti-social behaviour orders, according to the applicable 1998 Magistrates Courts Rules, will be made on the civil standard of proof, no legal aid is available, and under s1(10)(b) of the 1998 Act, there is the possibility of five years' imprisonment if the order is breached. If, for example, a defendant in a magistrate's court raises the issue of the compatibility of an order under s1 of the 1998 Act with Article 6, it might be necessary to stay the proceedings while the issue is dealt with on an appeal by way of case stated. Owing to the provision of s3 of the HRA, it would appear that a national court could not merely redefine ss1 and 2 as creating criminal offences if that involved finding that Article 6 and ss1 and 2 were incompatible.

The extent to which the hybrid nature of s3 of the 1997 Act has the potential to allow interferences with the Article 6, 10 and 11 guarantees was illustrated in two recent, significant decisions. In *Huntingdon Life Sciences Ltd and Another* v *Curtin and Others*[236] the company (HLS) obtained an *ex parte* injunction against six groups under s3 of the Act, which prohibited conduct amounting to harassment within the terms of the Act, or entering HLS research sites. HLS was engaged in animal experimentation and was the subject of a campaign by a number of animal rights organisations. One of the defendants, the British Union of Anti-Vivisectionists (BUAV), a peaceful campaigning group, applied to have the injunction varied so that it was not covered. Mr Justice Eady found, in the *inter partes* proceedings, that the plaintiff had not provided sufficient evidence to support the claim that the defendants should be covered by the injunction. He also considered it unfortunate that the provisions of the Act were couched in such wide terms that they could appear to cover 'the rights of political protest and public demonstration which are so much a part of our democratic tradition'. This judgment clearly recognised, as the legislators did not, the general need to seek to delineate forms of anti-social behaviour sufficiently clearly so as to avoid infringing the rights in question.

The BUAV was exempted from the injunction, but the case illustrates the ease of obtaining interim injunctions against a wide range of persons and groups in these circumstances. In practice, once such an injunction is obtained, the police are likely to enforce it against a number of persons who are not covered or are only doubtfully covered by it, on the basis

[235] The magistrates could only exercise their power of committal on a finding of wilful refusal to pay or culpable neglect (para 56 of the judgment).

[236] (1998) 3(1) J.Civ.Lib 37.

that they appear to be acting under the authority of, or in concert with, one of the groups which are enjoined. This will commonly occur in such situations.

A rather similar situation arose in *DPP* v *Moseley, Woodling and Selvanayagam.*[237] One of the defendants, Ms Selvanayagam, had been served with an *ex parte* interim injunction under s3 of the 1997 Act, which she was seeking to challenge. After she had been served with the injunction, she and the other two defendants continued to demonstrate peacefully against the fur trade, at a fur farm. They were arrested and charged with the offence under s2 of the 1997 Act. All of them relied on the defence that the conduct was reasonable in the circumstances under s1(3)(c), and this defence was accepted by the magistrate. He further found that the injunction was obtained only on the basis of affidavit evidence and could not as a matter of law preclude the finding of reasonableness. Therefore he acquitted all three. On appeal, the High Court found that pursuit of a course of harassment in breach of an injunction would preclude establishing the defence of reasonableness and that the magistrate had not been entitled to go behind the terms of the injunction. The other two respondents were not named in the injunction and there was no basis for considering that they were acting in concert with Ms Selvanayagam. Therefore, they were not precluded from putting forward the defence of reasonableness. Accordingly, Ms Selvanayagam was convicted under s2.

The most striking feature of this case is the acceptance that a central issue in a criminal trial can be predetermined in civil proceedings, particularly uncontested *ex parte* proceedings, in which the only evidence is 'on the papers'. The Act, as indicated, provides a remedy of imprisonment for breach of an injunction; there is therefore no reason why its breach should also be determinative of separate criminal proceedings. This matter clearly raises Article 6 issues; it comes close to obtaining a conviction 'on the papers' since if an injunction has been previously obtained the burden on the prosecution will be considerably eased. Although Strasbourg has not dealt with the precise point regarding the usurpation of the function of the criminal court by previous civil proceedings, it has made it clear in a series of cases that the use of written statements from witnesses who are not present at the trial will contravene Article 6(3)(d) except in limited, exceptional circumstances.[238] It may be said that an injunction obtained at an uncontested hearing is analogous to such statements. The use of such an injunction to predetermine a key issue in the criminal trial might also be viewed as infringing the presumption of innocence under Article 6(2) since the defendant may be confronted with an irrebuttable presumption against him or her. In *Salabiaku*

[237] Judgment of 9 June 1999; reported [1999] J.Civ.Lib 390.

[238] *Unterpinger* v *Austria* (1991) 13 EHRR 175; *Van Mechelen* v *Netherlands* (1998) 25 EHRR 647; *Kostovski* v *Netherlands* (1990) 12 EHRR 434; *Delta* v *France* (1993) 16 EHRR 574; *Doorson* v *Netherlands* (1996) 22 EHRR 330.

v *France*[239] it was found that while Article 6(2) 'does not . . . regard presumptions of fact or of law provided for in the criminal law with indifference' it permits the operation of such presumptions against the accused so long as the law in question confines such presumptions 'within reasonable limits which take into account the importance of what is at stake and maintain the rights of the defence'.[240] It is debatable whether the rights of the defence can be said to be preserved where no means at all of going behind an injunction are available.

Clearly, the use of injunctions as in *Huntingdon Life Sciences* and *Moseley* represents an interference with the Article 10 and 11 rights of the protesters, which must be justified under the para 2 exceptions. The fact that the injunction operates as a prior restraint is not conclusive of the issue since, as indicated above, Strasbourg has accepted that the use of such restraint may be justified in certain circumstances in public protest cases.[241] The leading case on prior restraints is *Observer and Guardian* v *UK*,[242] in which the Court considered the compatibility with Article 10 of interim injunctions preventing those newspapers from publishing *Spycatcher* material. The Court laid down the basic principle that 'while Article 10 does not in terms prohibit the imposition of prior restraints on publication . . . the dangers inherent in [them] are such that they call for the most careful scrutiny on the part of the Court'.[243] These findings were based on the perishable nature of news, a relevant consideration on the facts. But there is no reason to view the stance of the Court as precluding consideration of other values which are threatened by the use of injunctions as a prior restraint on expression, bearing in mind the arguments set out at the beginning of this chapter as to the value of public protest. Injunctions may not prevent the protest completely, but they may prevent it from being effective by excluding it from the place where it will have most impact. Moreover, arguments opposed to prior restraint need not rest only on values associated with expression, but may take into account the value of rights of participation in the political process, and such arguments may be raised under Article 11. In other words, while it might be argued that the terms of an injunction under s3 of the 1997 Act preventing protesters from demonstrating, say, outside the new detention centre for asylum-seekers at Oakington, Cambridge, on the anniversary of its opening, would not prevent them from distributing leaflets or holding a peaceful protest elsewhere, it would undermine the exercise of rights of effective expression and of participation in the political process.

239 (1988) 13 EHRR 379.
240 At p388 para 28.
241 See, for example, the decision of the Commission in *Christians Against Racism and Fascism* v *UK* No 8440/78, 21 DR 138 (1980).
242 (1991) 14 EHRR 153; for comment see I Leigh [1992] PL 200.
243 Ibid para 60.

Such arguments, where linked to Article 10, could be given added impact by invoking s12 HRA in relation to the use of *ex parte* injunctions in cases analogous to *Moseley*.[244] S12(1) provides: 'this section applies if a court is considering whether to grant any relief which, if granted, might affect the exercise of the Convention right to freedom of expression . . . (2) if the person against whom the application for relief is made (the respondent) is neither present nor represented no such relief is to be granted unless the court is satisfied . . . that the applicant has taken all practical steps to notify the respondent or that there are compelling reasons why the respondent should not be notified'. Under s12(4), 'the court must have particular regard to the importance of the Convention right to freedom of expression'. S12(2) provides a strong adjuration against the use of *ex parte* injunctions which, it is suggested, is as applicable in public protest cases as it is in those for which it was intended – injunctions against publications by the media. It may be noted that Article 10 only is referred to and therefore, as far as s12 is concerned, the Article 11 argument would be irrelevant, an unfortunate effect of seeking to afford added weight to the Article 10 rights of one group – the media – while disregarding those of another – protesters. S12 may have been limited in its application to civil proceedings[245] with the intention *inter alia* of excluding public protest from its ambit. If so, the failure to take account of the use of injunctions and orders obtained in civil proceedings in protest cases may have led to this unintended result.

S12 may apply to orders made under s1 of the 1998 Act, which potentially could also operate as prior restraints. The procedure to be followed appears to allow the grant of *ex parte* orders, but the defendant should be informed before the hearing that an application for an order has been made.[246] In a public protest case the defendant would be likely to attend the hearing in order to raise the question of the interference with Article 10 and 11 rights which would occur if the order was made. S12(2) would not therefore normally be of relevance, but s12(4) would be, and might tip the scales against the grant of an order in a protest case.

The arguments which will be raised under the HRA in relation to injunctions or anti-social behaviour orders when used in protest cases will seek to create a clear distinction, which the architects of the 1997 Act and s1 of the 1998 Act failed to create, between their operation in relation to those at whom they were targeted, and protesters. Under the activist model, such orders or injunctions would be subject to strict scrutiny under Articles 6, 10 and 11. The Article 8 rights, if in question, of those subject to the protest would also be relevant. Where an order or

[244] See also the discussion of injunctions more generally in Leigh and Lustgarten 'Making Rights Real: the Courts, Remedies and the Human Rights Act' [1999] 58 (3) CLJ 509.

[245] Under s12(5).

[246] The Magistrates Courts (Sex Offender and Anti-Social Behaviour Orders) Rules 1998.

injunction was issued, the result might be that it would be carefully limited in order to answer to the strict requirements of proportionality.

Conclusions

Before the HRA came into force the true boundaries of public protest were drawn, not by reference to the Constitutional significance in a democracy of rights of political participation or of affording expression, through the medium of forms of protest, to a variety of viewpoints, but often arbitrarily owing to the imprecision of the law and the approach frequently taken to it in low level courts or by the police. It is tempting to look forward to the use of Articles 10 and 11 in the post-HRA era in the expectation not only that the boundaries will eventually be redrawn more precisely, but also that legal discourse in this area will no longer focus simply on disorder, but rather will seek to engage in the ongoing debate, at Strasbourg and in other jurisdictions, as to the values underlying the Constitutional significance of protest and the weight they should be afforded. Whether that expectation will be fulfilled appears to depend, somewhat ironically, on the readiness of the domestic judiciary to disregard much of the Strasbourg public protest jurisprudence.

Judges within the 'activist' model may find, however, that their decision-making can be rooted in the general principles upheld at Strasbourg as underpinning the Convention rather than in its particular application. The justification for affording greater weight to communicative rights than that afforded at Strasbourg in findings under Articles 10 and 11 can be found in the need to ensure the genuine efficacy of the rights, with a view to realising the free expression and assembly objectives referred to above, especially in the case of minority groups or viewpoints. As argued, the Convention jurisprudence clearly recognises the need to protect a plurality of views in a democracy even in the face of offence caused to the majority.[247] It would be in accordance with the Convention concept of a democratic society to refuse to place those seeking to exercise communicative rights in the same position as football hooligans and to reject a legal tradition of valuing the general societal interest in public order over the exercise of such rights. In accordance with the values of the Convention, safeguarding the interests of minorities in a democracy is not to circumvent the democratic process but to uphold it by obviating the danger that those interests will be marginalised.

[247] Above, note 101 and see Chapter 3, p60.

Chapter 5

Criminal Procedure I

POLICE DISCRETION AND ACCOUNTABILITY

Introduction

Theoretical background

Current analysis of aspects of the criminal justice system continues to rely heavily on the two familiar models of crime control and due process,[1] although the taxonomy for criminal justice has increasingly been viewed as including further models,[2] and alternative models of crime control unopposed to due process have proliferated during the 1980s and 1990s.[3] Despite such proliferation, the dominant model of crime control has remained the classic 'situational' one, that is one based on responses to specific crime events or targets.[4] But while a rhetorical commitment to due process is still evident,[5] there is a clear perception that the law does not currently reflect this model. As Sanders and Young put it, 'Police and Court officials need not abuse the law to subvert the principles of justice; they need only use it'.[6] Together with the failure of the due process model to influence policy-making during the 1990s and post-2000, it is evident that the perception of antimony between the two models has become more apparent, especially in Parliamentary debate. Although it may quite readily be argued that the 'implied dichotomy between

[1] H Packer *The Limits of the Criminal Sanction* (1968). For example, the two models are extensively relied on in *Miscarriages of Justice* (1999) C Walker and K Starmer (eds).

[2] See M King *The Framework of Criminal Justice* (1981) (London: Croom Helm); 'Beyond Managerialism in Criminal Justice' (1997) 36 Howard Journal 80.

[3] There have been attempts to move from 'situational crime prevention' (Clarke *Situational Crime Prevention* (1992) New York) to 'social' crime prevention (see Clarke (1981) RVG Research Bulletin No 12 London: Home Office), including a corporate approach and 'active' citizenship.

[4] Clarke *Situational Crime Prevention* (1992) New York.

[5] See, for example, *Legislation Against Terrorism: A Consultation Paper* (1998) Cm 4178 esp para 8 of the Introduction.

[6] A Sanders and R Young *Criminal Justice* (1994) p20.

"individual rights" and ["crime control"] is untenable',[7] the argument has not so far been influential. The perception of the two main political parties that attachment to crime control values inevitably involves departure from due process appears to have increased markedly during the last 10 years.

This chapter will chart the increasing dominance, as providing an underpinning for policy-making in the 1990s and at the present time, of the crime control model which values a 'quick, accurate and efficient administrative fact-finding role . . . over slow, inefficient, and less accurate judicial trials' in order to achieve 'the dominant goal of repressing crime'.[8] Conversely, within the rights-based due process model which seeks to recognise the 'primacy of the individual and the complementary concept of limitation of official power',[9] many aspects of current police powers, particularly detention and interviewing powers applicable under counter-terrorist provisions, have become suspect since, together with conflation of police powers with substantive criminal law,[10] they are viewed, increasingly, both as undermining the full trial and as unacceptably enhancing police discretion. Antimony between these two models has tended to obscure a distinctive victims' viewpoint and has allowed victims' interests to be too readily equated with those of crime control. However, emergent recognition of victims' interests[11] is likely to gain momentum in the post-HRA era[12] and there is acknowledgement that due process norms and victims' interests are not necessarily opposed.[13]

The dominant theme running through the legislative grant of police powers in the 1990s was, it is suggested, the desirability of an increase in police discretion underpinned by a perception of its link with crime control. As this chapter will point out, an appreciation of the possibility of conflict between victims' interests and such discretion is currently

[7] R Reiner 'The Politics of the Act' [1985] PL 394 at p395.

[8] H Packer *The Limits of the Criminal Sanction* (1968). Proposals to curb the right to jury trial made in February 2000 reflect this model.

[9] Packer, ibid. As Walker puts it: 'The primacy of individual autonomy and rights is central to the due process model', *Miscarriages of Justice* (1999) p39.

[10] See below, p221. This is markedly the case, it is suggested, in respect of a number of offences under the Terrorism Act 2000.

[11] See H Fenwick 'Procedural "Rights" of Victims of Crime: Public or Private Ordering of the Criminal Justice Process?' [1997] 60 MLR 317. The *McPherson Report* (1999) Cm 4262-I Proposals 40–41 recommended that consideration should be given to allowing victims or victims' families to become civil parties to criminal proceedings. This possibility has not yet been acted on, but since February 2000 has been under discussion.

[12] The Convention provides a growing recognition of victims' rights. See *X and Y* v *Netherlands* (1985) 8 EHRR 235, and, in a different context, the significant strand of jurisprudence recognising rights of victims and victims' families within the criminal justice system where the state is the 'attacker': *Kaya* v *Turkey* (1998-I) EctHR 297; *Akdivar* v *Turkey* (1996) 23 EHRR 143; *Mentes* v *Turkey* (1997) 27 EHRR 595; *Gulec* v *Turkey* (1998) 28 EHRR 121; *Cetin* v *Turkey* (unrep); *Tekin* v *Turkey* (not yet reported).

[13] See A Sanders and R Young *Criminal Justice* (1994) pp23–25. H Fenwick 'Procedural "Rights" of Victims of Crime: Public or Private Ordering of the Criminal Justice Process?' [1997] 60 MLR 317 at pp320 and 322.

evident,[14] but at the same time the dangers of enhanced discretion in due process terms have gone largely unrecognised. Packer viewed the criminal justice process as, in theory, an obstacle course in which as the degree of coercion, flowing initially from the police in the interests of crime control, increased, so the due process requirements became greater. Thus, arrest requires reasonable suspicion only, whereas a conviction requires proof beyond reasonable doubt. Where there is no coercion, as in questioning a person not yet a suspect on the street, equally the due process safeguards are not in place or are minimal. As the discussion will indicate, the image of an obstacle course should not be taken too far since it may fail to take account of the divergence between appearance and reality inherent in such questioning: while formally speaking no coercion is present, in reality such encounters may structure and influence later formal ones undertaken under coercion.

As Dworkin has argued, the very concept of a right precludes the idea of an open-ended discretion to infringe or override it in the pursuit of competing interests.[15] Rights worth the name must be protected by rules which are precise in terms, non-discretionary and binding – in other words, by clear rules of law. From a due process perspective a compelling case can be made out in favour of two principles of the traditionalist conception of the rule of law – clear legal rules and a minimum of discretion. If these two principles are accepted the elements of review by an independent court and the existence of clear remedies for infringement of rights follow fairly readily. The fundamental nature of the rights concerned seems to make this an area where breach of the relevant rules should be addressed within an independent legal process with the possibility of compulsory remedies. This perspective is generally viewed as liberal but given its hostility to any expansion of police powers, the left is seen to yield no distinctive response to such issues; as Reiner observes, the leftist response to a concrete issue to respond to, such as the 1981 Report of the Royal Commission on Criminal Procedure,[16] amounted to a straightforward condemnation of it on traditional civil liberties grounds:[17] leftists lined up with the most critical liberal commentators in calling for the police to be subject to tightly defined and rigorous control and for clear, legally guaranteed safeguards for suspects, with clear remedies for abuse through the courts.[18] In other words, in practice, the left called for an application

[14] Partly due to the *Stephen Lawrence* case which was the trigger for the *McPherson Report* (1999) Cm 4262-I; see below at pp188–9. See also *the Review of the Criminal Courts* (2000).

[15] Dworkin argues that it only makes sense to denote an interest as a right if it will generally win any battle with competing societal considerations; hence his well-known conceptualisation of 'rights as trumps' (see *Taking Rights Seriously* (1977) p191).

[16] Cmnd 8092.

[17] 'The Politics of Police Justice' in *Politics and Power* (1981) Vol 4 p26.

[18] The argument of the left, as Reiner summarises it, 'impl[ied] that any extension of police power [was] necessarily disruptive of the communal interest . . . the Report [was] interpreted as increasing police power, and objected to accordingly' (op cit). For examples

of the traditional rule of law model when due process rights were in issue with a view to restoring or creating a balance between such rights and crime control interests, while accepting that ultimately, as Sanders and Young have argued, the 'balance' between the two rests on a value judgement.

A number of the rules, including the arrest and stop ones more recently introduced, are discretionary on their face. But a number of the key safeguards for suspects contained in the Police and Criminal Evidence Act 1984 (PACE), the Terrorism Act 2000 (and in Articles 5 and 6 of the European Convention on Human Rights) are not; indeed, they are in general phrased in the imperative and precise terms of mandatory instructions. But it will be contended that since in the pre-HRA era in most instances no formal sanction could or would follow breach of the PACE rules, police officers were in effect given at least a partial *de facto* discretion as to whether to follow the rules and thus whether to respect the rights they enshrine.[19] This is not the formal discretion the police would be able to exercise if PACE in terms stated that they could enforce such of the rules as they thought fit; it therefore provides an instance in which the law on its face observed a rhetorical attachment to due process principles, which was revealed to be hollow in its failure to adhere to rule of law requirements.

The normative contention of this chapter, and the two following ones, will be that the granting of such discretion in relation to suspects' rights violated widely accepted rule of law norms. The key argument will be that unless rigorous, independent review of rule-compliance and a clear remedy for breach is available, the rules will remain, in effect, largely discretionary, and the rights protected by them illusory. During the 1980s and 1990s the extent to which the rules were complied with depended largely on internal police governance together with the possibility of exclusion of evidence and, conceivably, of disciplinary action. But, as suggested by the large number of decisions on breaches of the PACE Codes,

of this tendency, see Baldwin 'Taking Rules to Excess: Police Powers and the Police and Criminal Evidence Bill 1984' in M Brenton and C Jones (eds) *The Year Book of Social Policy in Britain 1984–5* (1985) pp9–29; Phil Jones 'Police Powers and Political Accountability: the Royal Commission on Criminal Procedure'; P Hillyard 'From Belfast to Britain: Some critical comments on the Royal Commission on Criminal Procedure' both in *Politics and Power* Vol 4 (1981); T Jefferson 'Policing the Miners: Law, Politics and Accountability' in Brenton and Ungerson (eds) *The Year Book of Social Policy in Britain 1985–6* (1986) pp265–286.

[19] Ronald Dworkin has argued that if an official's decision whether to comply with a given rule is final and unreviewable, he or she is endowed with a form of discretion (*Taking Rights Seriously* (1977) p69). K C Davis has argued along similar lines, pointing out that the US police are directed by certain state statutes to enforce the laws, such as those forbidding social gambling or jay-walking, in terms which appear to give them no discretion to enforce the rules selectively, but that since a police decision not to enforce certain laws is unreviewable by any other body, they have an effective discretion in relation to law enforcement (*Discretionary Justice,* (1980) pp84–88 Greenwood Press).

together with the evidence from research into police working practices discussed in these chapters, this system did not deliver sufficient adherence to the rules. Moreover, it offered no remedy in the normal sense of the word for the aggrieved citizen. It follows, it will be contended, that the rights require court enforcement, although the influence of such enforcement is likely to be far from straightforward in this particular institutional context.

As many scholars have argued, the impact of externally imposed rules on actual police practice is limited and uncertain;[20] in particular, researchers have highlighted the problems of rule-evasion – the avoidance of apparent safeguards through the use of informal practices[21] – and of deterrence.[22] There is general agreement that internal police governance and culture will be highly significant in determining the extent to which suspects' rights are delivered, but it should also be emphasised that that culture is itself likely to be influenced by enhanced possibilities of external review of internal police decisions.

There appears to be academic agreement that the relationship between external rules and police culture is a complex one and that rather than tending merely towards straightforward evasion of the legal rules, the institutional culture may encourage the development of strategies intended to adapt and accommodate the rules within the practices it has already fostered,[23] thereby allowing for subversion of the rules by a more subtle route. But it is also contended that enhanced external review of such accommodation under the HRA may decrease the *de facto* discretionary element within the rules discussed in Chapters 6 and 7, thereby encouraging a shift from the working rules informally formulated by the police towards an infusion of the legal rules into their informal counterparts. Under the influence of such review police institutional culture

[20] See the PSI Report's distinction between Presentational, Inhibitory and Working Rules; D Dixon *Law and Policing: Legal Regulation and Police Practices* (1997) Oxford: Clarendon Press.

[21] See, for example, A Goldsmith 'Taking Police Culture Seriously: Police Discretion and the Limits of the Law' *Policing and Society* (1990) Vol 1 pp91–114.

[22] There is some evidence that use of exclusion of evidence may encourage police officers to observe suspects' rights. See Myron W Oldfield Jr 'The Exclusionary rule and deterrence: an empirical study of Chicago Narcotics Officers'; (1987) 54 *U. Chicago L. Rev.* 1016–1069. In the context of PACE this finding receives some support from research by A Sanders, L Bridges, A Mulvaney and G Crozier entitled 'Advice and Assistance at Police Stations' (November 1989); it was thought that unlawful denials of legal advice had been discouraged by the ruling in *R* v *Samuel* (1988) 2 All ER 135. The research found that in 1987, before the ruling, delay was authorised in around 50% of applicable cases; in 1990–1991, in only one case out of 10,000. Such evidence cannot, however, be treated as conclusive of the issue; apart from other factors, police officers will be aware that the question of exclusion of evidence is unlikely to arise since the case is unlikely to come to a full trial; even if it does arise a conviction may still be obtained. Any deterrent effect is therefore likely to be undermined.

[23] See D J Smith 'Case Construction and the Goals of the Criminal Process' [1997] 37 Br Journal of Criminology 319; R V Ericson *Making Crime: A Study of Detective Work* (1981) London: Butterworths.

may be likely to seek a greater assimilation of the legal rules within the working rules, as opposed to simply avoiding the former, since the police practice of utilising the legal rules and assimilating them into informal practice is itself institutionalised. As Dixon puts it: '[Rule] compliance has to be sought by skillfully blending negotiation and imposition'.[24] Thus, the balance might shift in favour of the legal rules and therefore towards a more than rhetorical attachment to due process. This chapter will adopt a largely liberal perspective in making the normative contention that an ideological commitment to due process, which continues to be evident, should be realised within the law itself through the curtailment of police discretion in the post-HRA era.

The legal and political context

Post-PACE, during the Thatcher and Major years, and now under the Blair government, the powers of the police were added to at regular intervals, largely in an apparent response to Irish terrorist activity. As Chapter 3 documents, in 2000 they were extended to a far wider range of new 'terrorist' groups.[25] A high level of 'ordinary' crime was also recorded throughout these years with intermittent rises in certain forms of crime.[26] The Thatcher, Major and Blair governments sought to make political capital out of appearing 'tough on crime'; this meant *inter alia* providing the police with further powers or curbing due process rights, even where the crime control value of so doing was not apparent.[27] The post-PACE powers have been characterised by their greater emphasis on the enhancement of police discretion, which has not been matched by the introduction of further due process rights.

The dual themes of the need for enhanced police powers but also for the introduction of rules to protect due process are only clearly evident in the piece of legislation which is still central to police powers – the Police and Criminal Evidence Act 1984. The notion of achieving in PACE what Reiner has called 'a fundamental balance'[28] has some foundation, especially, it will be contended, when PACE is compared with similarly significant later statutes – the Criminal Justice and Public Order Act 1994 (CJPOA) and the Terrorism Act 2000 (TA). One of the triggers for PACE was the need to ensure that miscarriages of justice such as that which

[24] In C Walker and K Starmer (eds) *Miscarriages of Justice* (1999) at p67.

[25] See p79.

[26] In 2000 violent crime was reported via Home Office statistics to have risen for the first time in six years. A 19% increase in robberies was recorded compared with a 6% decline in 1998.

[27] For example, the curtailment of the right to silence was never expected to make any significant impact on crime figures; see *Royal Commission on Criminal Justice Report* (1993) Cm 2263 esp para 4.

[28] R Reiner 'The Politics of the Act' [1985] PL 394 at p395.

occurred in the *Confait* case,[29] would not recur.[30] The Phillips Royal Commission on Criminal Procedure,[31] whose report influenced PACE, was set up largely in response to the inadequacies of safeguards for suspects which were exposed in the Confait report.[32] The Commission also took into account the claim that general police powers of arrest, stop and search, detention and entry to premises should be put on a statutory basis. Although when the PACE Bill was first introduced into Parliament it clearly differed in some respects from the Phillips recommendations, it derived some benefit from the considered and detailed deliberations conducted over three years by the Commission. The Labour Party consistently opposed the Bill and it took two years, interrupted by the general election, to pass through the Parliamentary process. Zander finds: 'there can be no denying that the whole exercise was an example of the democratic system working'.[33]

The result was a scheme in which the broad discretionary powers granted were to be balanced by two central structuring constraints. First, there were general precedent conditions for the exercise of such powers, the most common and significant being the requirement of reasonable suspicion or belief. Second, there was the provision of specific countervailing due process rights, in particular a general right of custodial access to legal advice, in most cases laid down in, or underpinned by, quasi- and non-legal rules – the Codes of Practice and Notes for Guidance made under PACE.[34] Redress for breaches of the due process safeguards was largely to be within the disciplinary rather than judicial sphere: breach of the Codes constituted automatically a breach of the police disciplinary Code.[35] The driving force behind PACE may have been, despite concerns raised by the *Confait* case, much more to do with crime control than with due process, but it did not lose sight entirely of the reasons for adopting it.

Post-PACE, the discovery of a number of miscarriages of justice – the cases of the Birmingham Six,[36] the *Guildford Four,*[37] *Judith Ward,*[38] *Stefan Kiszko,*[39] the *Tottenham Three,*[40] the *Maguire Seven*[41] – raised due process

[29] See *Report of the Inquiry* by the Hon Sir Henry Fisher HC 90 of 1977–1978.
[30] See *the Confait Confessions* Christopher Price (1976).
[31] *Royal Commission on Criminal Procedure Report* (Cmnd 8092, 1981) (RCCP Report).
[32] *Report of an Inquiry* by Sir Henry Fisher, ibid.
[33] M Zander *The Police and Criminal Evidence Act* 1984 (1995) pxi.
[34] Police and Criminal Evidence Act 1984 (s66) Codes of Practice.
[35] PACE s67(8).
[36] See *R* v *McIlkenny and Others* [1992] 2 All ER 417.
[37] See Sir John May *Report of the Inquiry into the circumstances surrounding the convictions arising out of the bomb attacks at Guildford and Woolwich in 1974, Final Report* (1993–94 HC 449) ch 17.
[38] *R* v *Ward* [1992] 96 Cr App R 1.
[39] *The Times* 18 February 1992.
[40] *The Times* 9 December 1991.
[41] See *R* v *Maguire* [1992] 2 All ER 433.

concerns again, although in only one of these instances was PACE applicable.[42] After the Birmingham Six were freed in 1992 the Home Secretary announced the setting up of another Royal Commission under Lord Runciman[43] in order to consider further measures which could be introduced, but although there appeared to be a link between the announcement of the Royal Commission and the Birmingham Six case due to proximity in time, the Commission interpreted its remit as not requiring an analysis of the miscarriage of justice in that case. The remit was to examine the efficacy of the criminal justice system in terms of securing the conviction of the guilty and the acquittal of the innocent.[44] Once again a Royal Commission was seeking to reconcile potentially conflicting aims – concern to protect due process but also to further crime control. As a number of commentators have observed, however, not only was the former part of this remit largely swallowed up in the latter,[45] it failed to articulate a principled account of investigative procedures. The Commission came to seem mainly concerned with the efficient processing of persons through the system and the rapid attainment of a conviction. 'It allowed miscarriages . . . to slip from its central focus, as it became obsessed with a narrowly defined 'efficiency' in crime control . . . its account of . . . procedure was threadbare: there was no sense of the significance of the structural and cultural contexts in which investigative procedures were deployed'.[46] Where it did make proposals which reflected due process concerns but conflicted with government perceptions of measures of apparent crime control value, the government on the whole refused to act on them.[47]

At about the time the Royal Commission reported, in 1993, a sea-change in the political climate became evident which in the view of a number of commentators explains the political reception given to the Report, and the subsequent criminal justice developments. As Dixon puts it, 'The

42 The case of the *Tottenham Three* revealed flaws in the PACE scheme. It predated the introduction of PACE but PACE was being used on a dry-run basis by the Metropolitan Police at the time. In the case of Winston Silcott, one of the Three, case notes of his confession, supposedly contemporaneous, were found under ESDA to have been tampered with, and his conviction was quashed in 1991; see *The Times* 9 December 1991.

43 Runciman Report (1993) Cm 2263 Chap 1 para 5; *The Royal Commission on Criminal Procedure* chaired by Lord Runciman; it was announced by the Home Secretary on 14 March 1991, HC Deb Vol 187 col 1109. It reported on 6 July 1993; see 143 NLJ 933–996 for a summary of its recommendations in respect of Police Investigations, Safeguards for Suspects, the Right to Silence and Confession Evidence.

44 Effectiveness in securing 'the conviction of those guilty of criminal offences and the acquittal of those who are innocent' *Runciman Report* ibid Chap 1 para 5.

45 See A Sanders and R Young 'The RCCJ' [1994] 14 OJLS 435; C Walker and K Starmer (eds) *Miscarriages of Justice* (1999) esp at p57.

46 D Dixon in C Walker and K Starmer (eds) *Miscarriages of Justice* (1999) at p71.

47 The Commission recommended by a majority of nine to two (RCCJ Report ibid Chap 4 para 22) that the right to silence should be retained but this was rejected by Michael Howard; speaking at the Conservative Party Conference in Autumn 1993 he stated that he intended to adopt the recommendation of the minority.

political and professional consensus about the need for criminal justice reform had broken down . . . the new Home Secretary encouraged renewed populist obsession with law and order'.[48] A steady movement to the right was occurring in the Conservative Party, and the Major government was placed at the mercy of its right wing owing to its tiny Parliamentary majority which by Spring 1996 was reduced to one. It had a new Home Secretary in Michael Howard, who was perceived in many quarters as long on right wing law and order rhetoric and tabloid appeal but short on balanced criminal justice policies.[49] The aims of crime control were furthered, so Howard claimed, by ensuring an enormous increase in the prison population, by increasing, on pain of penal sanctions, the number of instances in which the citizen must take orders from the police,[50] and by abolishing or undermining the rights of suspects, in particular the right to silence.[51] The stance taken was well summed up in Howard's own words as seeking to redress 'the balance in our criminal justice system which has tilted much too far in favour of the criminal and away from the protection of the public'.[52]

Whether any of the extensions of police powers adopted under the post-PACE legislation are causally linked to the prevention of crime or of terrorism and whether, if they are, they are in proportion to their impact on civil liberties, were issues which hardly received an airing from Cabinet and Shadow Cabinet Members of Parliament. From the mid-1990s, once Tony Blair became Shadow Prime Minister and Jack Straw Shadow Home Secretary, the Labour Party in Opposition adopted a very similar crime control stance to that of the Conservative Party. The Parliamentary climate, ironically, become less conducive to real debate as to criminal justice issues after the point at which the Labour Opposition ceased to be faced with a large Commons Conservative majority. Thus, debate on the Police and Criminal Evidence Act 1984, which was passed under the Thatcher government, was far more far reaching and considered than debate on the Criminal Justice and Public Order Act 1994 or the Prevention of Terrorism (Additional Powers) Act 1996 passed under the Major government. Since New Labour took office in 1997 there have been, apart from the passing of the HRA, no indications of attempts to break with the criminal justice legislative policies of the Conservative Party. In 2000 both major parties were seeking to outdo each other in encouraging and pandering to populist notions of crime control.

The CJPOA, extensions of the PTA and the Terrorism Act 2000 have effected continued extensions of police powers and have, this chapter,

[48] In C Walker and K Starmer (eds) ibid p73.

[49] M Maguir 'The wrong message at the wrong time?' in D Morgan and G Stephenson (eds) *Suspicion and Silence* (1994) at p48.

[50] In the Criminal Justice and Public Order Act 1994, esp ss71 and 68.

[51] In the Criminal Justice and Public Order Act 1994, ss34, 36, 37; see Chapter 7 at pp261–4.

[52] HC Debs 2 April 1996 col 211.

and the two following, will contend, eroded the balance PACE was supposed to create. One especially evident tendency has been the movement away from the need to show reasonable suspicion as a condition precedent for the exercise for police powers. Despite the fact that this condition appeared to offer little restraint in practice to police officers[53] it may be said that its abandonment in the introduction of new arrest and detention powers is indicative of a formal acceptance of a less fettered police discretion, as opposed to the discretion developed *de facto* in police practice. This chapter, together with Chapters 6 and 7, will not consider the main provisions of PACE in detail; they have been discussed in an extensive literature.[54] They will seek to ground selected recent legal developments in policing and their relationship with the HRA within the theoretical framework outlined.

The HRA and police accountability

As Chapter 2 argues, the Convention should not be viewed uncritically as a panacea for all that is amiss with criminal justice. Convention standards may reflect practice from countries aspects of whose criminal justice systems might appear alien to a domestic criminal practitioner. Practices developed under non-adversarial systems and reflected in both the Convention guarantees and their jurisprudential accretions may be irrelevant to domestic ones[55] or may even lead to a lowering of standards,[56] although

[53] A wealth of academic research and analysis has established that the need for reasonable suspicion provides little protection against wrongful arrest. Very doubtful grounds often appear to be sufficient to provide reasonable grounds to justify deprivation of liberty. Further, only in exceptional instances will an officer's use of this power be found to have been wrongful; the courts are quite ready to find that these somewhat hazy tests have been satisfied. See M McConville, A Sanders and R Leng *The Case for the Prosecution* (1991) London: Routledge; Sanders and Young (1994) op cit pp92–98; C Ryan and K Williams 'Police Discretion' [1986] *Public Law* 285, and Clayton and Tomlinson 'Arrest and reasonable suspicion' (1988) 85 LS Gaz. 7 September p22.

[54] For early comment on PACE see: Leigh *Police Powers* 2nd ed (1985); *Police Powers and the Individual* J Robilliard and J McEwan (1986); Benyon and Bourn, *The Police: Powers, Procedures and Proprieties* (1986); Levenson and Fairweather *Police Powers* (1990); For current comment on PACE and the relevant provisions under the CJPOA see: Bailey Harris & Jones 4th ed (1995) Chap 2; Zander, *The Police and Criminal Evidence Act 1984* 3rd ed (1995); Lidstone & Bevan, *The Investigation of Crime* 2nd ed (1996); D Feldman *Civil Liberties and Human Rights in England and Wales* (1993) Chaps 5 and 9 (2nd ed 2001); H Fenwick *Civil Liberties* 2nd ed (1998) Chap 9; Sanders and Young *Criminal Justice* (1994); A Ashworth *The Criminal Process: an Evaluative Study* (1998); *Miscarriages of Justice* C Walker and K Starmer (eds) (1999); N Padfield *The Criminal Justice Process: Text and Materials* 2nd ed (2000) Chap 2.

[55] For example, practices associated with using a *juge d'instruction.* The inquisitorial system used in Western European countries explains why there is no right to jury trial under the Convention.

[56] Compare the pronouncements of Lord Bingham in *ex parte Kebilene* [1999] 2 WLR 972 to the effect that legal presumptions against the defendant which effectively reverse the

where there is a clear distinction between Strasbourg and domestic practice to the detriment of the complainant (such as the availability of exemplary damages domestically but not at Strasbourg) s11 HRA would apply. There will remain fundamental rights, such as the right to jury trial, which will continue to require protection, so far as the legislation currently proposed allows,[57] largely as a matter of common law principle.[58]

However, the UK now has a benchmark by which to measure standards of procedural justice. Given the current trend away from due process which this chapter has outlined, the concomitant tendency to render police powers susceptible to subjective exercise, and the *de facto* discretion in respect of the delivery of due process rights which has developed, owing at least in part to a largely unmet need for their enforcement, the HRA may be perceived as providing opportunities to reinfuse due process into criminal procedure. With this end in mind, the discussion below will seek, in particular, to identify methods of providing redress under the HRA for breach of suspects' due process rights. There will not be many instances in which it can readily be said that a criminal justice provision is irretrievably incompatible with a Convention guarantee; compatibility will frequently be a matter of domestic interpretation and will be influenced by the judicial approach adopted. In accordance with a minimalist or review approach, the view may be taken that the system is already broadly in accordance with the Convention as interpreted at Strasbourg, regardless of the often strong influence of the margin of appreciation in this area, in which case change is likely to be marginal.[59] From a traditionalist standpoint, the concepts encapsulated under the Convention, especially Article 6, have long formed fundamental principles of English criminal justice, and therefore an application either of the Convention jurisprudence or of such principles would yield the same result. As Auld LJ puts it: 'I do not know how much assistance on the broad notion of fairness the United Kingdom courts can hope to obtain from the very general terms of Article 6 that they do not already derive from the same notion in common law or s78 [of PACE], still less from the somewhat diffident jurisprudence of the ECHR'.[60] But from an activist stance, the

burden of proof on a particular issue infringe Article 6(2), with the judgment of the Strasbourg Court in *Salabiaku* v *France* (1988) 13 EHRR 379 in which the Court held that such presumptions are not necessarily prohibited under Article 6(2); see further Chapter 3 pp103–4.

57 In April 2000, a new Bill which would further the process of curtailment of the right to jury trial, the Criminal Justice (mode of trial) Bill 2000, was reintroduced to the Lords, after its second reading in the Commons, having been rejected once in the Lords.

58 See *R* v *Lord Chancellor's Dept ex p Witham* [1997] 2 All ER 779. The term 'largely' is used since it could also be argued that within an adversarial context, a right to jury trial might be viewed as an aspect of the fair trial guarantee of Article 6(1).

59 See, for example, *R* v *Khan* [1996] 3 All ER 289 discussed below, p202.

60 Paper given at a conference held by the Centre for Public Law at Cambridge *The Human Rights Act and the Criminal Justice and Regulatory Process* January 1999.

source of the discretion to control the trial process in the interests of fairness is relevant to the standards controlling its exercise where they derive from a normative document such as the Convention. As the judgment of the Divisional Court in *ex p Kebilene*[61] indicated, adoption of the interpretation which affords the greatest weight to the guarantees would raise criminal justice standards by affording further protection to due process.

The doctrine of the margin of appreciation has been influential in most decisions regarding custodial treatment at Strasbourg; in certain contexts, such as that of exclusion of improperly obtained evidence, a very wide margin has been conceded on the basis that each state must, in principle, determine its own particular rules of evidence.[62] Recently the Court has, however, adopted a less deferential stance where it can be said that the trial was unfair on the facts.[63] The doctrine is influenced by the notion of common European standards which, as Professor Ashworth has observed, have had an influence in diluting Convention standards[64] due to the effect of the common standards doctrine, and as states with less well developed criminal justice systems become parties to the Convention[65] further dilution may occur. As Chapter 2 argues, a minimalist approach would mean relying fully on the margin of appreciation doctrine as developed at Strasbourg (without necessarily acknowledging such reliance), or maintaining and developing an equivalent domestic doctrine based on traditional notions of deference to the legislature or to police operational discretion.[66]

Realisation of the potential of the Convention as a means of enhancing the protection of suspects' rights will partly depend, it is contended, not only on the readiness of the courts to reject the notion of sustaining and developing such a domestic doctrine, but also on their ability to disregard so far as is possible the margin of appreciation aspects of the Strasbourg criminal justice jurisprudence. But in infusing Convention standards of criminal justice into domestic criminal practice, the judiciary will be confronted with the difficulty that the HRA may provide remedies within UK law which were not in certain respects previously available, but which are dependent on the interpretation of often elusive

[61] [1999] 4 All ER 801.

[62] *Schenk* v *Switzerland* A 140 para 46 (1988); see below at p200.

[63] See *Teixiera* v *Portugal* (1999) 28 EHRR 101; (1998) Crim LR 751; *Van Mechelen* v *Netherlands* (1998) 25 EHRR 647 and *Rowe and Davis* App No 28901/95; judgment of the Court 16 February 2000, (2000) 30 EHRR 1.

[64] 'Introduction to Professor Ashworth's The European Convention on Human Rights and English Criminal Justice: Ships Which Pass in the Night?' chapter in *The Public Law of Europe and the Common Law of the UK* 215 Dr M Andenas (ed) (1998) Keyhaven Publications.

[65] For example, Romania, Slovenia, Turkey and the Ukraine have recently ratified the Convention.

[66] See Chap 2, pp31–35. Lord Hoffman advocates this approach: see 'Human Rights and the House of Lords' [1999] 62(2) MLR 159, 161. See also Lord Hope's judgment in *ex p Kebilene* [1999] 3 WLR 973.

guarantees.[67] As Warbrick observes, 'judges need to know what it is that [the Convention] requires of them. In the present context [of the privilege against self-incrimination] this is not easy to find out'.[68] This difficulty forms a central theme in the following discussion.

Under the HRA the police, the DPP, the Crown Prosecution Service (CPS) and the courts, as public authorities under s6, will be bound by the Convention rights. Under s3 the courts will also come under an obligation to interpret PACE, the Criminal Justice and Public Order Act 1994, the Police Act 1996, the Terrorism Act 2000, and other relevant legislation as primary legislation, and the relevant Codes of Practice as subordinate legislation[69] compatibly with the Convention Articles 'so far as it is possible to do so'. The statutory and Code-based rules[70] which may be found to answer to the provision of suspects' rights within the Convention could be protected by the provision of tortious liability for their breach. This is an extremely significant matter since tortious liability for breach of the PACE and TA Codes is statute barred and existing tortious liability arising in respect of the conditions of detention is limited.[71] Judicial review of decisions within the police complaints process, or of CPS decisions not to prosecute police officers, or in respect of judicial or other authorisations within the PACE, CJPOA or TA schemes, would also be available, and would be based on the Convention provisions.

But by far the most significant means of adhering to the Convention guarantees as regards custodial and investigative procedures will be by the regulation of the trial process with a view to addressing flaws in those procedures.[72] Such regulation will occur most commonly by means of

[67] For example, the precise relationship between the presumption of innocence in Article 6(2) and the right to silence in police interviewing is unclear.

[68] *Pressing Problems in the Law* Vol 1 'Self-incrimination and the ECHR' (1995) OUP. This was written before *Saunders* v *UK* (1997) 23 EHRR 313 (see Chap 7 pp281–2 was decided, but it illustrates the difficulty at any particular point in the necessarily erratic development of the Convention jurisprudence, of determining the interpretation of a particular guarantee.

[69] The Codes are 'subordinate legislation' within the meaning of s21(1)(f) HRA.

[70] These include those arising under PACE, including the PACE Codes of Practice, those arising under the Terrorism Act 2000, with its accompanying Codes and other relevant legislation. They may also include Notes for Guidance which could be deemed to be – in effect – part of the PACE or TA Codes: see Cox (1993) 96 Cr App R 464, 470.

[71] See *Weldon* v *Home Office* [1990] 3 All ER 672; the action for false imprisonment is not available in respect of further confinement *within* detention, such as being transferred to solitary confinement inside a prison.

[72] Evidence from other jurisdictions which have introduced Charters or Bills of Rights suggests that the vast majority of Convention cases in the post-HRA era will concern criminal procedure. As M Taggart has put it in relation to the New Zealand experience: 'The abiding impression of the first seven years of [Bill of Rights] jurisprudence is the utter domination of criminal cases. From the literally thousands of cases in which the Bill has been invoked on behalf of an accused, a . . . disproportionately large number have gone up to the Court of Appeal . . . All of this is consistent with the Canadian experience.' 'Tugging on Superman's Cape: lessons from experience with the New Zealand Bill of Rights Act 1990' in C Forsyth and I Hare (eds) *Constitutional Reform in the UK* (1998).

exclusion of evidence, especially under the exclusionary discretion provided by s78 PACE, acquittals on appeal and findings that evidence should have been excluded,[73] but other possibilities, including staying or otherwise controlling proceedings for abuse of process, may be resorted to.[74] Whether there will be an increase in the use of such regulation in the post-HRA era will depend on the view taken by the judiciary of the opportunity offered by the reception of the Convention into UK law.

Convention rights

The most relevant Articles are Articles 2, 3, 5, 6, 8, 13 and 14. Article 6, seen as a central Convention Article, will be of greatest significance. It holds a pre-eminent position in the Convention jurisprudence since the right it protects is so fundamentally important in a democratic society; it expresses a 'fundamental principle of the rule of law'[75] and is to be interpreted broadly.[76] Recently the Court has tended to take an increasingly interventionist stance towards the right to a fair trial. Such a stance was evident in *Teixiera* v *Portugal*,[77] *Van Mechelen* v *Netherlands*,[78] *Saidi* v *France*[79] and *Rowe and Davis* v *UK*[80] and in a number of decisions affecting certain Western European countries which adhere most closely to the French model[81] in adopting the practice (*procès verbaux*) of admitting official written records of the pre-trial questioning of witnesses even where the witness is not present at trial for examination.[82] Apart from access to legal advice and the other minimal guarantees of Article 6(3),[83] the Court has found that a number of rights are implicit in the term a 'fair hearing'.[84] For example, in an early decision, *Austria* v *Italy*,[85] the Court found that maltreatment with the aim of extracting a confession was a breach of the right to a fair hearing. The principle of 'equality of arms' – equality between defence and prosecution – arising from Article 6(1) affects all

[73] The single ground for appeal from the Crown Court is that the conviction is unsafe: Criminal Appeal Act 1968 s2, as amended by the Criminal Appeal Act 1995.
[74] See *R* v *Chalkley and Jeffries* [1988] QB 848 at 874D–876C.
[75] *Salabiaku* v *France* 13 EHRR 379.
[76] *Delcourt* v *Belgium* 1 EHRR 355.
[77] (1998) 28 EHHR 101; (1998) Crim LR 751.
[78] (1998) 25 EHRR 657.
[79] (1994) 17 EHRR 251.
[80] No 28901/95, judgment of the Court 16 February 2000, (2000) 30 EHRR 1.
[81] Based on the *Code d'instruction criminelle* 1808.
[82] In a series of cases the Court has made it clear that the use of written statements from witnesses who are not present at the trial will contravene Article 6(3)(d) except in limited, exceptional circumstances: *Unterpinger* v *Austria* (1991) 13 EHRR 175; *Van Mechelen* v *Netherlands* (1998) 25 EHRR 647; *Kostovski* v *Netherlands* (1990) 12 EHRR 434; *Delta* v *France* (1993) 16 EHRR 574; *Doorson* v *Netherlands* (1996) 22 EHRR 330.
[83] See Chapter 2 p22; Chapter 3 pp108–9.
[84] For general discussion see J Harris, M O'Boyle and C Warbrick *Law of The European Convention on Human Rights* (1995) Chap 6; C Ovey 'The ECHR and the Criminal Lawyer: An Introduction' (1998) Crim LR 4.
[85] No 788/60 4 YB 112 (1961).

aspects of a hearing, therefore overlapping with its expression under Article 6(3).[86] Certain due process rights covered by the PACE and TA provisions, including some of those arising within their accompanying Codes, may also be viewed as impliedly covered by Article 6 in so far as they have a bearing on the fairness of the hearing.[87]

Under Article 5(1) deprivation of liberty can occur only in certain specified circumstances. Article 5 therefore provides a free-standing right which can be invoked outside the trial process. An Article 5 argument could also be raised within it on the basis, for example, that evidence obtained owing to an unlawful arrest should be excluded. This could, clearly, occur at present under the exclusionary discretion of s78 PACE. But the Article 5 requirements discussed in Chapter 6 may go further than those of current domestic law, and therefore may more frequently raise arguments regarding the fairness of the trial.

The guarantee under Article 3 is clearly coterminous with some substantive domestic criminal law and may overlap with certain provisions of Code C under PACE. It has an application in the context of police arrest and detention and provides a substantive guarantee against certain types of custodial maltreatment, which arises independently of the question of fairness at trial. But, broadly speaking, only the grossest instances of ill-treatment are covered. Article 8 is of relevance in the context of intrusive questioning and in respect of humiliating custodial treatment. It is notable that the Convention contains no provision equivalent to that under Article 10 of the International Covenant on Civil and Political Rights, which provides: 'persons deprived of their liberty shall be treated with humanity and with respect for the inherent dignity of the human person'. Similarly, the South African Bill of Rights contains a general provision guaranteeing the right to respect for dignity, in Article 10.

Means of redress

(i) Police complaints, discipline and prosecutions

The police complaints mechanism potentially provides a means of creating police accountability, both in terms of underpinning the balance apparently struck by PACE and in ensuring compliance with the Convention under the HRA. The bodies administering the mechanism, the Police Complaints Authority (PCA), Chief Police Officers, and police disciplinary tribunals are all bound by the Convention as public authorities under s6 HRA. They are also in the position of hearing complaints

[86] The principle is fully established and long standing in the Article 6 jurisprudence: see *X* v *FRG* 6 YB 520 at 574 (1963). See further pp22 and 108–9.

[87] See, for example, *Murray (John)* v *UK* (1996) 22 EHRR 29; *Barbera, Messegue and Jabardo* v *Spain* A 146 (1988); *Teixeira* v *Portugal* (1999) 28 EHRR 101; (1998) Crim LR 751. These decisions are discussed below.

regarding police officers who are themselves so bound. Both aspects should inform their work and could be raised as issues by way of judicial review. Further, the statutory provisions governing police complaints should be interpreted compatibly with the Convention under s3 HRA.

It is argued that the issue of independence arises at every stage in the process and that this is also true of decisions taken by the CPS whether to prosecute police officers where complaints appear to disclose criminal offences. The CPS is, of course, independent of the police but 'the issue is whether it exercises this independence properly'.[88] Evidence submitted in 1997 to the Home Affairs Committee regarding the matter indicated a 'lack of willingness' on the part of the CPS and DPP to prosecute: 'There is clearly bias which pervades both the police and the CPS preventing viable prosecutions through nonsensical analysis of evidence'.[89] The issue of the quality of CPS decision-making in this context is indicated at a number of points below. It clearly raises a number of Convention-based arguments.

Under s67(2) of the Police Act 1996 a complaint will go in the first instance to the Chief Officer of Police of the force in question who must determine by reference to the section whether or not he or she is the appropriate person to deal with it and whether it, in fact, constitutes a complaint about 'the conduct of an officer' and not about 'the direction or control' of a police force.[90] The decision as to the side of the dividing line on which a particular complaint falls is made by the police force complained about. Therefore, at the very outset, 'an issue of independence arises'.[91] A complaint must be referred to the PCA if it concerns serious misconduct.[92] Under s75(3) of the 1996 Act, if the Chief Officer determines that the report on the complaints investigation indicates that a criminal offence may have been committed, he or she must send a copy of it to the DPP. In addition there is a discretionary power to refer complaints to the PCA. It does not carry out the investigation itself in such cases but supervises it and receives a report at the end of it under s72. Thus its role in relation to complaints is very limited. The overwhelming majority of complaints do not result in disciplinary proceedings: as many as 30% of complaints are dealt with by informal resolution[93] and 50% of complaints are withdrawn.[94] Clayton and Tomlinson noted that the 16,712 complaints dealt with in 1990 led to 305 criminal or disciplinary charges and advice or admonishment in 573 cases; thus less than 2% of complaints

[88] See Home Affairs Committee First Report 1997–8 at para 88.
[89] Ibid para 90.
[90] PACE ss84(4) and 84(5). The requirement regarding 'the conduct of a police officer' now arises under s65 of the 1996 Act.
[91] Ibid para 47.
[92] Section 70 of the Police Act 1996, formerly s87(4) of PACE.
[93] PCA Triennial Review 1985–1988 HC 466 para 1.14 p8.
[94] See Triennial Review of the PCA 1991–94 HC 396 (1994–5); Clayton and Tomlinson *Civil Actions Against the Police* (1992) p13.

led to any disciplinary action.[95] The PCA Report of 1995 reported that out of 245 complaints of serious assault by police officers eight led to disciplinary charges; none led to dismissal of an officer from the service. Out of 6,318 complaints of assaults disciplinary charges were preferred in 64 cases; none led to dismissal of the officer.[96] The 1998 Report stated that 141 complaints concerned serious assaults; 8% of those fully investigated led to disciplinary action. A total of 16,550 complaints were received in 1998–1999; 317 were fully investigated, a figure of approximately 2%.[97] In 1997 the Home Affairs Committee considered the figures for the outcome of complaints and found that over the previous two years 2% of all recorded complaints were substantiated following a formal investigation and less than one-half of 1% of complaints led to disciplinary or criminal charges.[98] The records for 1998–1999 suggest that the figures would be approximately the same. While the figures may be, to an extent, misleading,[99] they strongly suggest that the system is not operating fairly and effectively.

The Committee found 'perhaps the most telling evidence that all is not well . . . comes from the opinion of almost all the parties involved';[100] they concluded: 'there is a great deal of justified dissatisfaction with elements of the disciplinary and complaints system'.[101] These criticisms echo those which have for a number of years been directed against the whole police disciplinary process, including the hearings, and it is generally agreed that the present system is defective as a means of redress.[102] Maguire and Corbett conducted a review of the operation of the complaints system from 1968 to 1988[103] which found that the majority of complainants were dissatisfied and that the public did not have confidence in the system. The Runciman Commission considered that the existing arrangements probably do not command public confidence.[104]

95 Clayton and Tomlinson *Civil Actions Against the Police* (1992) p13.
96 See Triennial Review of the PCA 1991–94 HC 396 (1994–5).
97 *The 1998–99 Annual Report of the PCA, Table 5.* 2,415 complaints concerned assaults; 81 disciplinary charges were preferred. 203 complaints concerned racially discriminatory behaviour; 3 charges were preferred. The Report does not give the figure for disciplinary action as a percentage of fully investigated complaints.
98 Home Affairs First Report 1997–8, *Police Disciplinary and Complaints Procedures* printed 16 December 1997 para 27.
99 See K Lersch and T Mieczkowski [2000] 23(1) Policing. They considered arguments that the numbers of complaints may not be indicative since citizens may undercomplain for various reasons, including lack of confidence in the process. They also looked at the possibility of overcomplaint.
100 Para 35.
101 Para 40.
102 See A Greaves (1985) Crim LR; A Khan 129 SJ 455; Williams (1985) Crim LR 115; Lustgarten *The Governance of Police* (1986) pp139–140; J Harrison *Police Misconduct: Legal Remedies* LAG (1987); J Harrison and S Cragg (1993) 143 *NLJ* 591; M Maguire 'Complaints Against the Police: the British Experience' in *Complaints Against the Police: A Comparative Study* ed A Goldsmith (1990) OVP; the RCCJ Report Cm 2263 p46; Helena Kennedy in *Miscarriages of Justice* (1999) C Walker and K Starmer (eds) p374.
103 *A study of the Police Complaints System* (1991) HMSO.
104 RCCJ Report Cm 2263 p46.

A number of high profile cases have failed to lead, ultimately, to successful disciplinary proceedings or prosecutions. The Home Affairs Committee noted that no convictions of police officers had arisen from the recent miscarriage of justice cases despite strong evidence of fraud or perjury on the part of some of the officers involved.[105] After the *McPherson Report*[106] into the *Steven Lawrence* case disciplinary charges were recommended against five officers involved. All, however, retired and therefore could not face charges. The Home Office is currently considering the possibility of disciplinary action up to five years after retirement.[107] In the wake of the *McPherson Report* racist police behaviour may begin to lead more frequently to disciplinary charges,[108] although such a trend cannot yet be discerned.[109] The number of deaths annually in police custody remains high; between January 1990 and December 1996 380 such deaths were reported to the Home Office,[110] and the failure of disciplinary charges or prosecutions in relation to complaints arising from such deaths has attracted quite severe criticism.[111] In 1997 the Home Affairs Committee considered evidence from the organisation *Inquest* which submitted 11 case studies, in certain of which no prosecution or disciplinary action had been taken against officers, despite apparently substantial evidence against them.[112] There is also a disparity between successful civil actions against the police and disciplinary action or prosecution.[113] For example, in the *Hsu* case,[114] it was found that Mr Hsu was assaulted, racially abused and falsely arrested. It was accepted that the police officers in question had lied on oath and fabricated notebook entries. Mr Hsu was awarded

[105] Ibid para 24.

[106] (1999) Cm 4262-I.

[107] McPherson Report Recommendations 55–57.

[108] For example, in February 2000 a police officer, PC Hutt, was disciplined and dismissed from the force for oppressive, racist behaviour (News Report 22 February 2000).

[109] See note 97 above.

[110] Leigh, Johnson and Ingram, *Deaths in Police Custody* Police Research Series Paper 26 (1998).

[111] See *The Butler Report* (1998); Helena Kennedy in *Miscarriages of Justice* (1999) C Walker and K Starmer (eds) p374. Note the report in June (1999) LAG 21 regarding the inquest into the death of N Delahunty due to cocaine intoxication aggravated by police restraint. See also November (1999) LAG 6 regarding the acquittal of police officers for the death of a Mr O'Brien in custody after a restraint by a number of police officers. His death was considered in *The Butler Report* section 6. In section 8 the Report crticised the CPS system for considering prosecutions in respect of deaths in custody (including that of O'Brien) as 'inefficient and fundamentally unsound'.

[112] Ibid para 25.

[113] *The Butler Report* (1998) criticised the CPS for its decision-making in the *Treadaway* case; Derek Treadaway was awarded £50,000 in damages in respect of a serious assault by police officers while he was in custody: *R* v *DPP ex p Treadaway The Times* 18 November 1997. The CPS decided not to prosecute the officers. Treadaway successfully sought judicial review of this decision and the case was remitted for reconsideration by the CPS.

[114] *Thompson* v *Commissioner of Police for the Metropolis, Hsu* v *Commissioner of Police for the Metropolis* [1997] 2 All ER 762.

£200,000 damages (reduced on appeal to £35,000), but no officer was disciplined.[115]

There appears to be a strong consensus that the independent element in the complaints and disciplinary process is too weak and is the key factor in the inefficacy of the system.[116] Maguire and Corbett commented in their 1991 review that an independent system might lead to an improvement in public confidence in the system, although they expressed doubts about its efficacy in other respects.[117] The *McPherson Report* recommended that there should be an independent tribunal for serious complaints.[118] Morgan and Newburn find: 'The fact that most complaints . . . continue to be investigated exclusively by the police themselves is almost certainly an important factor in explaining why so few complaints are made compared with the proportion of members of the public who report having felt like making a complaint'.[119] The *Police Action Lawyers Group* has stated: 'the fundamental problem . . . is the lack of independence in the system'.[120] The House of Commons Home Affairs Committee found that the introduction of an independent element is desirable in principle.[121] Doubts have been expressed, however, taking into account experience from other jurisdictions, about the efficacy of a completely independent investigatory body,[122] but there appears to be a degree of consensus regarding the need for a stronger element of independence which might be achieved through the cooperation of police and expert civilian investigators, drawn from the ranks of bodies such as lawyers and customs officials.

The changes to the complaints procedure which occurred in the mid-1990s, partly in response to the Runciman Royal Commission Report, did not involve any radical reform. In particular, they did not include the

[115] See further the Home Affairs Committee First Report (1998) Section B 'the Evidence from Civil Actions'. A further example, in which the disciplinary sanction was, in effect, rescinded, is provided by *Goswell* v *Commissioner of Metropolitan Police* (*Guardian* Report 27 April 1996). The officer who was found in that case to have perpetrated a serious assault, PC Trigg, was dismissed as a result of a complaint from Goswell. In the civil action Goswell had been awarded £120,000 for assault, £12,000 for false imprisonment and £170,000 for arbitrary and oppressive behaviour. Trigg appealed against his dismissal and was reinstated by the Home Secretary, Michael Howard. On the face of it, his reinstatement after it had been proved beyond reasonable doubt (in the disciplinary proceedings) that Trigg had perpetrated the assault in question appeared highly questionable.

[116] Sanders and Young (1994) p404; Helena Kennedy in *Miscarriages of Justice* (1999) C Walker and K Starmer (eds) p374.

[117] *A study of the Police Complaints System* (1991) HMSO.

[118] (1999) Cm 4262-I Recommendation 58.

[119] *The Future of Policing* (1997) p53; finding based on W Skogan (1994) *Contacts between police and public: findings from the 1992 British Crime Survey* HO Research Study No 134 London: HMSO.

[120] Home Affairs Committee Report para 43.

[121] Home Affairs Committee (1997–8) HC 258-I, Recommendation 11.

[122] See A Goldsmith *External Review and Self Regulation: Complaints Against the Police: The trend to External review* (1988) OUP; B Loveday 'Police Complaints in the USA' (1988) 4 Policing 172.

introduction of a new, independent element into the process. The Police and Magistrates Courts Act 1994, which was then consolidated in the Police Act 1996, made only limited changes to the functions and powers of the PCA. Under the 1994 Act s37(a) a breach of the PACE Codes became no longer automatically a breach of the Police Discipline Code.[123] This change could be seen merely as legitimising police working practices since it appeared that very few complaints in respect of breaches of the Codes were made; those that were rarely led to disciplinary proceedings. Unsurprisingly, this trend continued after the 1994 Act came into force.[124] Part IV of the Police Act 1996, which now governs complaints and discipline, was merely a consolidating, not a reforming, measure. The 1997 Report of the Select Committee on Home Affairs[125] made a number of recommendations, reflecting certain of the criticisms noted above, and the Home Secretary, Jack Straw, said that he had accepted the case for speedy reform. But the initial proposals for reform[126] mirrored the moderate changes proposed by the Conservative government in 1993.[127] New procedures were introduced in April 1999[128] which reflected certain of those proposals, including in particular abolition of the criminal standard of proof in disciplinary proceedings.[129] Under the new procedure the hearing will be private but the complainant can attend the proceedings although not before his or her evidence is given;[130] the complainant may be allowed to cross-examine witnesses.[131] A number of provisions, however, allow for the exclusion of the complainant.[132] Racist language and behaviour is now a breach of the police code of conduct, but it is not yet possible to determine how far reaching such change might be. The PCA in its 1998–99 Report noted that further, more radical changes, in particular the 'use of non-police investigators in exceptional cases', although accepted by the Home Secretary in principle, had been relegated to

[123] S37(a) repealed PACE s67(8).

[124] For example, the PCA Report for 1998–9 showed that there were 107 complaints relating to breach of Code A, governing stop and search in the period 1 led to disciplinary charges (Table 5 p13).

[125] HC 258/I 1997–98.

[126] HC 683 1997–98.

[127] The government issued a Consultation Paper in April 1993 which included various proposals, including abolition of the criminal standard of proof in discipline cases and the double jeopardy rule, which means that criminal proceedings against officers are not followed by disciplinary proceedings. See 143 NLJ 591; in its Triennial Review 1988–91, HC 352, 1991 the PCA also made this proposal. The Labour proposals also address the tendency of police officers who are facing disciplinary charges to take extended sick leave and/or early retirement, thereby evading the disciplinary process.

[128] *The Police (Conduct) Regulations 1999.* The new procedures operated alongside the 1995 ones until March 2000, when the transitional arrangements ended; all cases are now being dealt with under the new procedures.

[129] Under Regulation 23(3).

[130] Reg 25(3).

[131] Reg 25(4).

[132] Under Reg 25(5) the complainant can be removed if he or she interrupts. Under Reg 27 the complainant can be excluded if matters arise which it would not be in the public interest to disclose to him or her.

future legislation. The PCA concluded that there was no prospect of early legislation and mentioned its unsuccessful attempts to make the more non-controversial changes by means of Private Members Bills.[133] In 2000 the government commissioned a feasibility study into the practicality of using independent investigators in exceptional cases,[134] and put proposals to use such investigators to the annual Police Federation Conference in May 2000.[135]

The Butler Report (1998) made a number of recommendations designed to improve the quality of CPS decisions as to prosecution. They included sending every death in custody case for a decision as to whether or not to prosecute to the Assistant Chief Prosecutor and instituting a compulsory training programme for all those employed in central casework at the CPS.[136] The Report also expressed unease with the system whereby the police themselves investigate and report to the CPS on a death in custody. It also suggested that where such a death had occurred and an inquest jury returned a verdict of unlawful killing, the reason for the decision not to prosecute should be given.[137]

Thus despite evidence of police malpractice from miscarriage of justice cases such as that of the *Birmingham Six*[138] and the subsequent indications discussed above of poor practice and deliberate wrong-doing within the police service, the system for accountability has remained, in essentials, the same. As it stands, the system raises various serious issues under the HRA. It does not generate confidence that it will play a significant part in ensuring that police officers and forces act in compliance with the Convention. In so far as the due process rights reflected in the Convention are contained in PACE, the TA and their associated Codes, it is not apparent that it is likely to ensure adherence to them.

It is arguable that disciplinary proceedings and the occasional disciplinary hearings ordered by the PCA fail to comply with Article 6 since the complainant is in such a weak position in them. Under Article 6 the hearing might be viewed, first and foremost, as forming the determination of a 'criminal charge' against the officer concerned, although this is uncertain.[139] Disciplinary proceedings and hearings might also be viewed

[133] Ibid p53.

[134] The study was conducted by the consultants KPMG. It reported on 17 May 2000; its report was accompanied by an independent report by *Liberty*, recommending the setting up of an independent body to hear police complaints.

[135] On 17 May 2000.

[136] Ibid pp53–54.

[137] Ibid p55.

[138] See *R* v *McIlkenny and Others* [1992] 2 All ER 417.

[139] Military and prison disciplinary proceedings fall within the term, owing to the severity of the possible penalty which includes the possibility of imprisonment. The position regarding disciplinary proceedings carrying the possibility of lesser, albeit quite severe, penalties, such as dismissal or the loss of pension rights, is not yet clearly settled, although there are indications that the Court would view proceedings carrying the possibility of lesser penalties as falling outside the meaning of criminal charge: *Demicoli* v *Malta A 210* (1991) and *Ravnsborg* v *Sweden A 283-B* (1994).

as the determination of the 'civil rights and obligations' of the complainant under Article 6(1), since they may frequently involve inquiry into breaches of such rights, including breaches of the Convention itself. The term 'civil' has, however, been taken to mean that these are rights in private rather than public law,[140] although a clear distinction between rights in private as opposed to public law is not apparent in recent Strasbourg jurisprudence. Possibly complaints proceedings might be found to fall within this term at Strasbourg or domestically in future. This view might be encouraged since, as indicated above, the proceedings became more court-like after the 1999 reforms.

On the basis that the proceedings and hearings in question might be found in future to fall within Article 6, it is argued that they fail to provide a fair hearing for the complainant, bearing in mind the procedure they follow. In investigating a fair hearing the domestic authorities may take into account the Article 6(3) guarantees even in respect of civil determinations, since they are viewed as minimum guarantees which are covered by the wider paragraph 1 protection of a fair hearing. If consideration is given to the procedures in question it is apparent that, apart from any of the other requirements of fairness, the minimal safeguards of Article 6(3) may not be present, depending on the application of the new Regulations in any particular case.[141] The system does not allow for the complainant or his or her legal representative to attend the full disciplinary proceedings or hearings. The independence and impartiality of the hearing may also be questioned, particularly as the vast majority of hearings are not ordered or supervised by the PCA. No compensation can be awarded to the complainant.

There would also be the possibility of considering whether the disciplinary system affords the complainant an effective remedy for breach of his or her Convention rights. This argument could be raised under Article 13 which, while omitted from the rights given further effect under the HRA, has some effect in domestic law.[142] It is debatable whether the police complaints and discipline process should be seen as being the forum for s7(1)(a) HRA purposes since breach of Convention rights by police officers could be raised in the ordinary courts under s6. But, in any event, the Article 13 issue could be raised in, for example, a challenge to a breach of a Convention right in judicial review proceedings, if the applicant had made an unsuccessful complaint. In *Govell* v *UK*,[143] the Commission found that the police investigative system did not meet the requisite standards of independence under Article 13 since the Chief Constable can appoint a member of the same force to investigate; the Home Secretary appoints and remunerates members of the PCA and has

[140] *Ringeisen* v *Austria* A 13 para 94 (1971).
[141] See further Chapter 3 pp108–9.
[142] See Chapter 2 p22.
[143] (1997) 4 EHRLR 438. See also *Kahn* v *UK* Judgment of 12.5.00, paras 45–47.

a guiding role in determining the withdrawal of charges. The rules considered in *Govell* were the PACE rules, but the new rules maintain the same system. The remuneration system is still under the control of the Home Secretary[144] and under s83 of the Police Act 1996[145] his guiding role is retained. Under s69(5)[146] a member of the force which is the subject of the complaint can conduct the investigation.

A further issue may arise in respect of public interest immunity attaching to documents coming into existence during a police complaints investigation. The position of the parties to court actions in relation to disclosure of material relating to a complaint was placed on a more equal basis as a result of *Chief Constable of West Midlands Police, ex parte Wiley, Chief Constable of Nottinghamshire Police, ex parte Sunderland.*[147] All the parties concerned argued that public interest immunity did not attach, on a class basis, to documents coming into existence during a police complaints investigation. The House of Lords had to consider whether *Neilson* v *Laugharne*[148] and the decisions following it were wrongly decided. In *Neilson* Lord Oliver had determined that a class immunity should attach to police complaints documents on the basis that the police complaints procedure would be placed in jeopardy if that was not the case. However, the House of Lords considered that there was insufficient evidence to support Lord Oliver's conclusion as to the need for a new class claim to public interest immunity. Thus it was found that *Neilson* must be regarded as wrongly decided, but that did not mean that public interest immunity would not attach to police complaints documents: whether it did or not would depend on the nature of the particular document or documents in question. This decision emphasises that a clear case must be made out for use of a broad class claim to public interest immunity. It is in the interests of a fair hearing under Articles 6(1) and 6(3)(d) since it goes some way towards ensuring that, in actions against the police, or in prosecutions where previous disciplinary findings may be relevant, both parties have access to the same information. However, it leaves open the possibility of a contents claim or of a class claim in relation to specific groups of documents, although a strong justification would be required to establish such a claim. In *Taylor* v *Anderton*[149] the Court of Appeal found that the reports prepared by investigating officers were entitled to class immunity, but that a litigant might nevertheless obtain disclosure of part or all of a report if the judge could be persuaded that the public interest in disclosure outweighed the interest in immunity.

[144] See PCA Report 1998–9 Appendix C para 5.
[145] Which came into force on 1 April 1999, replacing Part IX of PACE.
[146] Which has replaced s105(4) PACE.
[147] [1995] AC 274; [1994] 3 All ER 420; (1995) 1 Cr App R 342 HL.
[148] [1981] QB 736.
[149] [1995] All ER 420 CA. See also *Kelly* v *Commissioner of Police of the Metropolis* (1997) *The Times* 20 August in which it was found that Public Interest Immunity (PII) attaches to certain of the new forms which are sent to the CPS by police forces.

It is debatable whether the current position would satisfy the findings as to the duty of disclosure to the defence in *Rowe and Davis* v *UK*[150] or in *Tinelly and McElduff* v *UK*,[151] depending on the particular circumstances of a case. In *Tinelly* the Court found that the use of a conclusive certificate preventing disclosure of the reasons for a decision[152] breached Article 6 since it prevented the tribunal from effectively reviewing the facts. Any judge determining the imposition of a contents immunity, whether in a civil action against the police or in a prosecution, would have to take into account the jurisprudence regarding the equality of arms provision arising under both Articles 6(1) and 6(3), as well as the general requirements of a fair trial. The latter requirement is ultimately the overriding one since merely placing both parties in an equally disadvantageous position would not necessarily satisfy it.

Decisions as to prosecutions of the police raise a number of Convention issues.[153] The burden of proof would be affected where it was alleged that Article 3 had been breached by custodial maltreatment, or, under Article 2, where a death had occurred in custody. Once it was shown that the detainee was free of the injury in question[154] or was not already in a life-threatening condition, before arrest, the state would bear the burden of exculpating the officers involved. This test appears to differ from that currently used by the CPS which was criticised in the Butler Report.[155] The Butler recommendations, which were largely concerned with procedural matters, including clarification of the system of decision-making in the CPS, did not, it is argued, fully address these Convention matters. It will be likely to become apparent that reforms based on a greater awareness of the demands of the Convention in this context are necessary, now that the HRA is fully in force.

(ii) Tortious remedies

The HRA s6 requires the courts to offer a remedy where a public authority violates the Convention rights[156] unless in so doing it is acting in accordance with incompatible legislation.[157] As indicated, Articles 3, 5, 8 and 14 potentially cover certain pre-trial rights of suspects, regardless of the trial context. Arguably, tortious liability could arise and damages could

[150] (1998) 25 EHRR CD 118 (admissibility decision); judgment of the Court of 16 February 2000, (2000) 30 EHRR 1.

[151] (1999) 27 EHRR 249; judgment of the Court 10 July 1998.

[152] This was not a PII certificate, which would not be conclusive, but a certificate provided for under the Fair Employment Act 1976 in Northern Ireland.

[153] No criminal liability is created under the HRA, so that a breach of e.g. Article 3 or 8, non-coterminous with existing offences, could not found a prosecution. See also note 12, above.

[154] *Tomasi* v *France* A 241-A (1992). See also Chapter 6 p254.

[155] Ibid.

[156] Sections 6(1), 7 and 8. For discussion see Chapter 2 p52 et seq.

[157] S6(2). S3 requires that the legislation should be rendered compatible with the Convention rights 'so far as it is possible to do so'.

be awarded under s8 of the Act if one or more of these Articles were found to have been breached in respect of police treatment of suspects. Some custodial treatment in breach of these Articles is already tortious under domestic law, and civil actions against the police have provided an increasingly significant means of creating some police accountability,[158] but this possibility would clearly be of particular significance where domestic law currently fails to provide a tortious remedy in respect of maltreatment of detainees. Following *Barbéra, Messegué and Jabardo*[159] the domestic courts might reconsider their current approach to conditions of detention in terms of tortious liability.

At present, so long as existing torts or offences, such as assault, are not committed in detention, it follows from the findings in *Weldon* v *Home Office*[160] that no means of redress in respect of adverse conditions, other than a complaint, are available. The possible creation of liability[161] under the Convention by means of a creative interpretation of its guarantees would not only fill a gap in domestic law, it would fill the gap in the Convention which, as noted above, does not on its face cover most conditions of detention. Such a course would not necessarily involve departing from the findings in *Weldon* v *Home Office* since the liability would be for breach of a Convention right under ss6 and 7 HRA, not for false imprisonment. In any event, departure from case-law is clearly possible under the HRA. At present it is very doubtful whether Article 6 itself could be viewed as providing free-standing rights. Breaches of Article 6 are clearly most likely to be addressed within the criminal process itself. The jurisprudence does not cover instances in which the pre-trial procedure is flawed in a manner which might be viewed, potentially, as infringing the Article 6(1) guarantee of a fair trial, but where no court action in fact occurs. The possibility that breach of Article 6 might lead to tortious liability under s8 HRA is pursued in Chapter 6.

It appears probable that a breach of the Code-based safeguards applying to the exercise of a *prima facie* tortious power will not deprive it of lawful authority due to the provision against civil liability for such a breach under s67(10) PACE and schedule 12 para 6 TA. This will also be the case, *a fortiori*, where a police action which does not require lawful authority in order to avoid such liability breaches a Code provision. But

[158] See generally Clayton and Tomlinson *Civil Actions Against the Police* 2nd edn (1992); for a list of examples of recent damages awards see pp411–431. See Fenwick *Civil Liberties* 2nd edn (1999) p502 for further recent examples. The Home Affairs Committee First Report 1997–8, *Police Disciplinary and Complaints Procedures* printed 16 December 1997, noted at para 32 the 'striking' rise in the cost of civil settlements for the Metropolitan Police, from £0.47 million in 1991 to £2.69 million in 1996. (This figure may decline due to the decision in *Thompson* note 166 below.) The Police Action Lawyers Group and the Commission For Racial Equality attributed the rise to disillusionment with the complaints process.

[159] A.14 6(2) (1989) 33.

[160] [1990] 3 All ER 672.

[161] Under ss6 and 7 HRA. The HRA does not allow for the creation of new criminal liability.

where provisions of Articles 3, 8, 5 or 14 are coterminous with Code safeguards, liability to pay damages under the HRA for breach of the Convention guarantees might provide the Code provisions with a form of indirect protection, as the more detailed embodiment of the Convention requirements. Chapters 6 and 7 identify, at the relevant points, Convention guarantees which have no domestic statutory basis, but are recognised only in certain Code provisions. The creation of new tortious liability indirectly protective of such provisions under the HRA would be a very significant matter since it might lead to a regulation of police interviewing practices and techniques which has been largely absent from UK law.

The quantum of damages would be determined in accordance with the provisions of s8 which include the requirement, under s8(4) of the HRA, that the court should take into account the principles applied by the European Court of Human Rights in relation to the award of compensation.[162] As indicated in Chapter 2, reliance on such principles means that the level of damages awarded may be fairly low;[163] in particular the Court has not, formally, awarded exemplary or aggravated damages.[164] But where the applicant has a coterminous tort action, such as false imprisonment, s8 should not be used to detract from the level of damages which would have been awarded prior to enactment of the HRA.[165]

It may be noted that Article 5(5) provides an independent right to compensation if Article 5 is breached. The domestic courts will have to determine whether this guarantee is satisfied by the right to the award of damages for false imprisonment. The question of the appropriate level of damages was addressed by the Court of Appeal in *Thompson* v *Commissioner of Police for the Metropolis*.[166] The court laid down guidelines for the award of damages which took as a starting point a basic award of £500 for the first hour of unlawful detention, with decreasing amounts for subsequent hours. Aggravated damages could be awarded where there were special features of the case such as oppressive or humiliating conduct at the time of arrest. Such damages would start at around £1,000 but would not normally be more than twice the level of the basis damages. Exemplary damages should only be awarded where aggravated and basic damages together would not appear to provide a sufficient punishment. Exemplary damages would be not less than £5,000, but the total figure awarded as exemplary damages would not be expected to amount to more than the basic damages multiplied by three. The overall award should

[162] See further I Leigh and L Lustgarten 'Making Rights Real: the Courts, Remedies and the Human Rights Act' [1999] CLJ 509; D Feldman 'Remedies for Violations of Human Rights under the Human Rights Act' [1998] EHRLR; M Amos 'Damages for Breach of the Human Rights Act' [1999] EHRLR 178.

[163] Non-pecuniary damages are likely to be in the range of £10,000–15,000: see *Johnson* v *UK* (119/1996/738/937) (1997).

[164] *B* v *UK* A 136-D paras 7–12 (1988).

[165] This follows from s11 HRA.

[166] [1997] 2 All ER 762.

not exceed £50,000. Although these levels of damages are significantly lower than those which could previously be awarded, Strasbourg would be likely to view them as satisfying Article 5(5), given the wide margin of appreciation probably allowable to member states in respect of the national level of compensation available. It is probable that this will also be the view of the national courts under the HRA.

(iii) Redress within the criminal process

Article 6 issues are likely to be raised very frequently at all levels of criminal courts and at plea and directions hearings. As Chapter 2 indicates, the domestic courts will, save for the s6(2) proviso concerning incompatible legislation, fail to satisfy s6 HRA if they act incompatibly with the Convention rights, since they are themselves public authorities. The position appears to be that wherever a court has a discretion in the course of criminal procedure, a decision regarding its use of that discretion will amount to an 'act' within the meaning of s6 HRA.[167] If a court does violate the rights in taking decisions as to *inter alia* exclusion of evidence or abuse of process, ss7 and 8 HRA will be relevant. As Chapter 2 explains, s7 allows a victim of an alleged violation, or proposed violation, of a Convention guarantee to rely on the right in litigation, and to argue in particular that he or she would be a victim of an unlawful act if the act proposed is undertaken. S8 allows courts to grant such remedies as seem to them just and convenient for such violations. The view might be taken that breaches of Convention rights by courts should be remedied through the appeal process and that s6 alone, rather than ss7 and 8, is therefore relevant during the trial process. This view would not accord, however, with the stance of the House of Lords in the leading pre-HRA decision, *R* v *DPP, ex p Kebilene and Others.*[168] In considering Article 6, the House of Lords pointed out, the domestic court is not, of necessity, in the same position as the Strasbourg court: 'it was inevitable that the European Court would conduct a retrospective review of [whether a trial was fair or unfair in Article 6(1) terms] in the national court', but that in the domestic court, this matter could be considered before completion of a trial. In other words, the Strasbourg Court could consider the whole pre-trial and trial process and come to a determination as to its fairness under Article 6(1). The domestic court would have to consider, during pre-trial hearings, the trial process, or on appeal, not only whether an actual or potential breach had occurred, but also whether Article 6 would be breached owing to its own regulation of the process. *Ex parte Kebilene* suggests that appeals will not provide the only means of enforcing the Convention

[167] This is the stance of the Strasbourg Court: see *Z* v *Finland* (1998) 25 EHRR 371.
[168] [1999] 3 WLR 972.

against courts. The better view therefore is that all three sections may be relied upon during the trial as well as on appeal.

The defendant might, for example, raise the argument that if the court failed to exclude evidence Article 6(1) would be breached and that therefore ss7 and 8 require that the evidence should be excluded in order to avoid the breach. S8, as indicated, appears to afford some discretion to a court as to awarding the remedy, but it is almost inconceivable that a court during a trial would accept the argument that it was about to act unlawfully, within s6, but then, although it found leeway to do so under s3, fail to provide a remedy by resiling from the threatened unlawfulness. A court might, of course, find, erroneously, that its particular decision during the criminal procedure would not breach Article 6, in which case the issue would have to be raised on appeal. A court adjudicating on the current grounds for allowing an appeal would itself be bound by s6 but would theoretically also retain a discretion under s8 as to the award of a remedy.

It might be established at trial that a breach of one or more of Articles 3, 8, 5 or 6, perhaps combined with Article 14, had occurred during the pre-trial procedures and that the breach would lead to a further breach of Article 6(1) if evidence was not excluded or the prosecution was not stayed for abuse of process. Obviously the argument would be that the police as a public authority had perpetrated the violation in question, acting unlawfully under s6, and that the court should use the means available to it within the criminal procedure to (i), under s7, remedy the breach by the police and (ii), under ss6 and 7, ensure that it did not itself breach Article 6 in allowing the former breach by the police to affect the fairness of the trial. Depending on the circumstances, the argument under (i) would not normally run independently of the argument under (ii) since if the unlawfulness of the police could not be said to affect the trial,[169] the court would not have a remedy available to award (unless, in the circumstances, it was found that an abuse of process should be declared), in which case a separate action would have to be mounted. Or it might be found that flaws in the custodial and investigative procedures, including breaches of the PACE or TA Codes of Practice, not amounting in themselves to breaches of Convention rights, should be addressed, under ss6 and 7, by means of exclusion of evidence or a stay for abuse of process, in order to avoid breaching Article 6(1).

The House of Lords found in *Latif*[170] that in considering whether to stay the proceedings for abuse of process, the judge should weigh the public interest in ensuring that those accused of serious crimes are brought to trial, against the public interest in avoiding giving the impression, based on classic crime control norms, that courts are prepared to find that the end justifies the means. This balancing of interests may be termed 'the

[169] For example, if the police had breached Article 8 by unlawfully entering the defendant's home (see *McLeod* v *UK* (1998) unrep) but had not discovered any evidence.

[170] [1996] 1 All ER 353.

Latif test'. In *Chalkley*[171] Auld LJ stated that the issue of exclusion of evidence is distinct from the question whether the prosecution should be stayed for abuse of process. This is clearly the case in the sense that an abuse of process might be found even where the court finds no unfairness in or affecting the instant proceedings. It might be said that such unfairness is not necessary but may be sufficient to warrant a finding of abuse of process, whereas it may be both necessary and sufficient to warrant exclusion of evidence under s78 PACE (the exclusionary discretion). Both mechanisms may be used in order to 'set the limits of fairness in the system as a whole',[172] although the courts have consistently found that the abuse of process doctrine should be used only exceptionally. It may be argued, therefore, that if, applying 'the *Latif* test', a prosecution was allowed to proceed although there was quite a strong abuse of process argument due, for example, to the illegal obtaining of evidence, the judge at trial could seek to cure the abuse by *inter alia* excluding the illegally obtained evidence, again applying that test. Nothing in s78 PACE precludes applying it since s78 requires 'all the circumstances *including the circumstances in which the evidence was obtained* to be taken into account' (emphasis added). The test could fall within the former rubric.

In accordance with the Strasbourg jurisprudence and s6 HRA, the Appeal Court is itself bound by Article 6.[173] The test for criminal appeals from the Crown Court is simply whether the conviction is 'unsafe'.[174] In *R* v *Mullen*[175] the Court of Appeal said that an abuse of process, or, equally, material irregularities at the trial would empower the Court to find that a conviction was unsafe. If the Court of Appeal considered that despite a pre-trial breach of the Convention, a conviction was safe, this view could be challenged as itself – in the particular circumstances – contrary to Article 6. If Article 6 was itself breached owing to pre-trial improprieties, which were not cured at trial, it is hard to see that the conviction could be regarded as 'safe'. This is the stance, with a narrow caveat, currently taken by the Court of Appeal. In *R* v *Pearson*[176] the Court of Appeal said: 'where this court takes the view that an appellant did not receive a fair trial this court would not, save in the most exceptional circumstances, reach the view that the conviction was nevertheless safe'. Now that Article 6 is binding on the Court of Appeal the exception mentioned would cease to apply since otherwise that Court would be declaring, in effect, its intention to breach its guarantee of a fair trial, contrary to s6 HRA.

[171] [1998] 2 Cr App R 79.

[172] The Justice Report recommendation 14 p76.

[173] *Delcourt* v *Belgium* A 11 (1970).

[174] S2(1) of the Criminal Appeals Act 1968, as amended by the Criminal Appeal Act 1995. This provision, which allows the conviction to stand despite, for example, a misdirection of the judge, may require modification due to the findings of the European Court in *Condron* v *UK* No 35718/97 judgment of 2 May 2000, see JCIVLIB (2000) at p253.

[175] [1999] 2 Cr App R 143.

[176] *The Times* 20 February 1998.

However, while Article 6 applies to appellate proceedings, appeals may not need to adhere fully, according to Strasbourg, to all the requirements of Article 6, depending on the nature and function of the appeal court.[177] This is an instance in which common law traditions regarding standards of fairness in appeals would be expected to prevail over the Strasbourg stance, in so far as they differ.

Theoretically, a defendant could be convicted after a trial which failed to meet Article 6 standards, where the unfairness was due to incompatible domestic legislation. This is allowed for under s6(2)(b), as Chapter 2 points out.[178] If so, the conviction would have to stand and therefore in general there would appear to be no benefit in appealing to a higher court which could issue a declaration of incompatibility. But there would be an incentive to appeal where there was leeway for the higher court to take a different view on incompatibility by finding a way of reconciling the domestic legislation with Article 6 or if there were grounds for expecting the higher court, once it had made the declaration, to award a lower sentence. In practice, however, it is likely that the domestic courts will be determined to avoid convicting and perhaps imprisoning a defendant under legislation which breaches the Convention, by declaring an abuse of process.[179]

Article 6(1) is silent as to the admissibility of improperly obtained evidence. The Strasbourg Court has emphasised that the assessment of evidence is for the domestic courts[180] and that Article 6 does not require any particular rules of evidence. Thus it has allowed the national authorities a wide margin of appreciation in this respect. In *Schenk* v *Switzerland*[181] the Court found no breach of Article 6(1) when an illegally obtained incriminating tape recording was admitted in evidence, and made it clear that unlawfully obtained evidence is not necessarily inadmissible. The Court found: 'While Article 6 guarantees the right to a fair trial it does not lay down any rules as to admissibility of evidence as such, which is therefore primarily a matter of regulation under national law'. The test is to ask whether the trial as a whole would be rendered unfair if the 'tainted' evidence was admitted.[182]

In the late 1990s a change in the Court's stance occurred although the *principle* deriving from *Schenk* remained unaffected. A much more interventionist approach was adopted in a number of judgments, including that in *Teixeira de Castro* v *Portugal*.[183] The applicant, who had no criminal

[177] *Jan-Ake Anderson* v *Sweden* A 212-B (1993).
[178] At p49.
[179] See the judgment of Lord Steyn in *ex p Kebeline*, note 168, above.
[180] *Edwards* v *UK* A 247-B (1992).
[181] (1988) 13 EHRR 242.
[182] A 140 (1988) at para 46. This test was also used in *Khan* v *UK*: note 205 below.
[183] (1999) 28 EHHR 101; (1998) Crim LR 751. See also *Van Mechelen* v *Netherlands* (1998) 25 EHRR 647; the findings of the Commission and Court in *Rowe and Davis* App No 28901/95 (1998), (2000) 30 EHRR 1; *Condron* v *UK*, note 174, above.

record and was previously unknown to the police, was introduced by a third party to two undercover police officers who told him that they wished to buy 20 grams of heroin. He bought the drugs on their behalf at a price allowing him to take a profit. He was then tried and convicted on the evidence of the officers of drug dealing and sentenced to six years' imprisonment. The Court found, by eight votes to one, that the entrapment by the police officers in order to secure evidence had made a fair trial impossible: 'right from the outset the applicant was definitively deprived of a fair trial'.[184] The case could be distinguished from *Ludi* v *Switzerland*[185] in which no breach of Article 6 was found where a police officer had posed as a buyer in a drug deal which was already under way. The Court therefore did not find that undercover work of this type would inevitably affect the fairness of the trial. The test was whether the defendant could be said to be 'predisposed' to commit the offence in question. If so, unfairness would not be established. This test arguably differs slightly from the current one under UK law.[186] In *Teixeira de Castro* the Court implied that since a fair trial was impossible from the outset, the prosecution should not have been brought at all. In so far as the unfairness might have been cured by exclusion of the evidence, the Court implied that there would be virtually no judicial discretion left to exercise to admit it. Exercising a discretion to exclude the evidence obtained under s78 would not appear to be an adequate response to a notion of such fundamental unfairness.

In response to this more robust approach, the domestic courts would be expected to develop clearer guiding principles for the application of s78, based on presumptions that certain types of impropriety would almost always demand the exclusion of the evidence affected by them. In a departure from current domestic practice, where such an impropriety was in question, there would be little discretion left to exercise. Where certain improprieties were concerned, such as the one at issue in *Teixiera*,[187] a court dealing with the matter as a question of exclusion of evidence, as opposed to staying the proceedings as an abuse of process, might itself

[184] Ibid at para 39.

[185] (1993) 15 EHRR 173.

[186] If undercover officers give D an *opportunity* to commit the offence where it appears that he would have committed it had the opportunity been offered by someone else that is not entrapment; but it will amount to entrapment if they impliedly persuade him into it or otherwise can be said to instigate it; see *Smurthwaite* [1994] 1 All ER 898. In *Williams and O'Hare* v *DPP* [1993] Crim LR 775 police officers set up a 'virtue-testing' operation in order to see who might succumb to temptation. An insecure vehicle apparently loaded with cigarettes was left in a high crime area in order to catch would-be thieves. The resultant evidence was not excluded since it was not found that it had been obtained as a result of entrapment. It is suggested that while *Smurthwaite* is probably in harmony with the test as laid down by the Court in *Teixiera, Williams and O'Hare* v *DPP* is not. In general, determinations on this matter will turn on the meaning of 'predisposed' as interpreted domestically. See also *Nottingham CC* v *Amin* (1999) *The Times* 2 December, note 207, below.

[187] (1999) 28 EHHR 101.

breach Article 6. But even in less clear-cut cases exclusion of evidence might be used in order to ensure adherence to Article 6. A robust interpretation of its guarantee of fairness, bearing *Teixiera* in mind, would support a requirement that an impropriety or illegality in the custodial or investigative procedures would tend to tip the scales towards exclusion of the evidence obtained as a result.[188] The very significant difference between the positions of the Strasbourg and the national court would support such an interpretation. Article 6 may require exclusion of evidence or, depending on the circumstances, a stay for abuse of process in three instances. First, where a breach of another Article has occurred which is causally linked to obtaining the evidence.[189] Where it is not so linked, it might nevertheless be found that the trial should be stayed for abuse of process, if the breach is due to grave impropriety and the position of the defendant may have been prejudiced.[190] Second, where an impropriety has occurred in the pre-trial procedure which does not in itself amount to a breach of any other Convention Article but where a breach of Article 6 could be found to occur if the evidence is admitted. The third possibility is more debatable. It arises where a breach of Article 6 could – at least potentially – be said to have occurred already owing to impropriety in the pre-trial procedure, but where the breach could be 'cured' by excluding evidence in some way 'tainted' or affected by the breach or causally linked to it.

Domestic law and practice regarding exclusion of evidence must be considered in relation to the new and still-evolving Strasbourg stance. The general rule, originally deriving from the common law,[191] still prevails following the judgment of the House of Lords in *R* v *Kahn*,[192] that improperly obtained evidence (other than involuntary confessions)[193] is admissible subject to a discretion to exclude it, but in respect of evidence other than admissions or identification it has rarely been exercised in

[188] In this context the decision of the Court of Appeal in *R* v *Radak and Others* [1999] 1 Cr App R 187, *The Times* 7 October 1999, should be noted. The decision related to admission of a written witness statement pursuant to ss23, 25 and 26 of the Criminal Justice Act 1988 and was concerned with prosecution rather than police impropriety. But the decision is of interest since the Court relied heavily on Articles 6(1) and 6(3)(d) in finding that the judge's discretion under s26 had been wrongly exercised since he had failed to safeguard the defendants' rights in accordance with the Article 6 requirements.

[189] An example would be a stop and search in breach of Article 5 which had produced evidence. A very clear example, which is catered for under domestic law – s76(2)(a) PACE – would be where a breach of Article 3 had led to a confession.

[190] This might be found where, for example, a refusal of bail had occurred in breach of Article 5 which would be likely to affect the trial. See the findings of the House of Lords on impropriety in *Latif* [1996] 1 All ER 353 which would appear to have an application to the circumstances envisaged.

[191] *R* v *Sang* [1980] AC 402.

[192] [1996] 3 All ER 289.

[193] S76 was intended to encapsulate the common law principle as stated in *R* v *Sang* [1980] AC 402 that involuntary confessions were inadmissible in evidence.

the absence of deliberate illegality.[194] The discretion arises under s78 PACE which provides: 'In any proceedings the court may refuse to allow evidence on which the prosecution proposes to rely to be given if it appears to the court that, having regard to all the circumstances, including the circumstances in which the evidence was obtained, the admission of the evidence would have such an adverse effect on the fairness of the proceedings that the court ought not to admit it.' The section, which provides by far the most significant exclusionary rule in domestic law, has not been interpreted as taking an absolutist due process stance since it does not demand automatic exclusion of evidence after certain forms of impropriety have occurred. But equally it has not been found to follow a crime control approach since it has been invoked to exclude confessions despite their probative value. The section epitomises an uneasy compromise between due process and crime control which may have contributed to the uncertainty which has surrounded its operation. In so far as s78 does play some part in ensuring due process, this has been due to judicial interpretation and does not appear to have been the intention of the government in including it.[195]

Confessions obtained due to serious police impropriety, including behaviour which would fall within Article 3, are subject to an absolute exclusionary rule. S76(2)(a) provides that where 'it is represented to the court that the confession was or may have been obtained by oppression of the person who made it . . . the court shall not allow the confession to be given in evidence against him except in so far as the prosecution proves to the court beyond reasonable doubt that the confession (notwithstanding that it may be true) was not obtained as aforesaid'. Oppression is non-exhaustively defined in s76(8): 'In this section "oppression" includes torture, inhuman or degrading treatment, and the use or threat of violence (whether or not amounting to torture)'. The Court of Appeal in *Fulling*

194 There have been a number of cases (e.g. *R* v *Gall* (1990) 90 Cr App R 64, *Conway* (1990) 91 Cr App R 143) in which the courts have rejected identification evidence under s78 because the Codes have been breached and many more cases in which admissions have been rejected on this basis. The factor which may persuade courts to reject other evidence, including physical evidence, may be deliberate illegality (*Thomas* [1990] Crim LR 269) but this cannot be said to be the only factor (*Sharpe* v *DPP* [1993] 158 JP 595; *R* v *Cooke* [1995] Crim LR 497); the House of Lords in *Kahn* did not require that there should be *mala fides* before evidence could be excluded, while suggesting that the exclusionary discretion is very narrow. This was also the stance taken in *R* v *Chalkley* [1998] QB 852 at pp873–874.

195 The clause which became s78 was adopted as a compromise after Lord Hailsham had accepted at the Committee stage in the Lords that there should be a form of discretion to exclude evidence which it would be unfair to the accused to admit. He accepted this in order to head off an amendment, which might have been more far reaching, put forward by Lord Scarman at the Report stage in the Lords: House of Lords, Hansard 31 July 1984 cols 635–675. Lord Scarman's amendment was approved but the government did not accept it and put forward an amendment, which became s78, based on Lord Hailsham's.

offered a wider definition of oppression: 'the exercise of authority or power in a burdensome, harsh or wrongful manner; unjust or cruel treatment of subjects, inferiors, etc; the imposition of unreasonable or unjust burdens'.[196] But it is now clear that the impropriety must be of a high level of seriousness[197] and must be perpetrated deliberately.[198] S76(2)(a) recognises the acceptable limits of the crime control principle. It accepts that even though the defendant appears to be guilty, and the police officers who have behaved oppressively can be punished by other methods, the criminal justice system cannot be seen to accept evidence obtained by these means. Threats of violence or other oppressive behaviour are so abhorrent in a civilised society that no further question as to the reliability of a confession obtained by such methods should be asked. Thus, the rule takes a due process stance since it allows for the rejection of reliable evidence, whereas some advocates of crime control would demand that reliable evidence should be included even if obtained by oppressive behaviour, including – it logically follows – torture or inhuman and degrading treatment, assuming that it could be shown, objectively, to be reliable. Within the crime control model miscarriages of justice due to unreliable confessions are unwelcome since they waste resources and, where the person convicted was not factually guilty, allow the real offender to remain free to commit further offences.

The extent to which the rule under s76(2)(a) really does uphold due process remains highly debatable. This is partly because it shares the limitations of all exclusionary rules,[199] but it is also because the interpretation given to oppression by the Court of Appeal appears to exclude much improper behaviour from its ambit. It will not operate simply because the detainee, for whatever reason, experienced the police questioning as oppressive; it probably has not helped to uphold the Code C or PACE rules. It may not deter the police even from clearly oppressive questioning, partly because it is unlikely to be invoked and partly because the questioning may lead to the uncovering of non-confession evidence even if the confession itself is excluded. Over the 14 years since the inception of PACE it has only, so far as commentators are aware, been successfully invoked twice.[200]

Some improper police behaviour affecting admissions which falls outside s76(2)(a) may be caught by s76(2)(b) which provides that where a confession was or may have been obtained 'in consequence of anything

[196] [1987] 2 All ER 65.

[197] *Mason* [1987] 3 All ER 481; *R* v *Paris, Abdullah and Miller* (1993) 97 Cr App R 99 (the case of the 'Cardiff Three').

[198] Hughes [1998] Crim LR 519.

[199] The key limitation is that they can have an impact only where the defendant pleads not guilty.

[200] In *Paris, Abdullah and Miller* (1993) 97 Cr App R 99 and *Heron* (1993) unreported. It is of course possible that some decisions to discontinue cases may have been based on the expectation that this rule would be successfully invoked.

said or done which was likely in the circumstances existing at the time, to render unreliable any confession which might be made by him in consequence thereof, the court shall not allow the confession to be given in evidence against him except in so far as the prosecution proves to the court beyond reasonable doubt that the confession (notwithstanding that it may be true) was not obtained as aforesaid'. The 'something said or done' will often consist of some impropriety on the part of the police, and in such instances a court will go on to consider whether in the circumstances existing at the point at which the impropriety occurred it would be likely to render the confession unreliable. The 'circumstances' can include the particularly vulnerable state of the detainee which may relate to a physical or mental state.[201] S76(2)(b) seeks to uphold due process in the sense that it deters the police from some forms of improper behaviour, such as misrepresenting the evidence against a detainee, which do not amount to oppression, but which might render a confession unreliable. It may have had the effect of encouraging the police to abide by the Code C rules when interviewing particularly vulnerable suspects, including those who are mentally disordered. It has therefore had a relatively limited effect. In common with s76(2)(a), it creates the anomaly that true or apparently true confessions may be excluded from evidence, if its terms are fulfilled, but other evidence obtained as a result can be included, under s76(4).

This survey of the exclusionary rules under domestic law reveals that they may not be fully in accordance with the emergent exclusionary rule under Article 6(1), bearing in mind the approach to rules of evidence which, under the HRA, should be more activist than taken at Strasbourg. S76 covers confession evidence only and demands either oppression or circumstances leading to the objective unreliability of the confession, while s78 confers a discretion only. The PACE scheme has therefore not allowed for the near-absolute exclusionary rule from *Teixiera*,[202] requiring exclusion of non-confession evidence deriving from unlawfulness or impropriety (including entrapment).

In practice, bearing in mind their previous tendency to exclude such evidence where impropriety or unlawfulness has occurred in the investigative or custodial process, domestic courts will probably exercise discretion in such a way as to ensure that admissions and, probably, silences are excluded under s78 in compliance with Article 6(1). The domestic jurisprudence is far more extensive on this matter than that regarding confessions under Article 6, and, despite the reluctance of the judiciary to lay down guiding principles for the application of s78, academics in an extensive literature have identified some indications of adherence to such

[201] See *Delaney* 88 Cr App R 338.
[202] (1998) 28 EHHR 101.

principles.[203] The effect of Article 6 may be to encourage some clearer statements of principle.

But the stance currently taken towards *non-confession* evidence, including evidence obtained from informers and from other forms of surveillance, may not satisfy Article 6(1). As indicated, under domestic practice evidence gained owing to a very serious impropriety, including a breach of a Convention right, is admissible, as is, under s76(4), physical evidence uncovered owing to an inadmissible confession gained as a result of impropriety, including Article 3 treatment. The discretion to exclude non-confession evidence is very narrow and the impact which s78 has had in encouraging adherence to due process may be diminishing at the present time. As L T Choo observes: 'recent decisions of the Court of Appeal signal a movement away from focusing on the nature of the breach [of PACE or the Codes] and towards an approach which takes the nature of the evidence as its central consideration'.[204] In other words, the movement is away from due process values and towards acceptance of the crime control norm that the end – a conviction – justifies the means. Such movement may, however, be reversed under Article 6 if the *Teixiera* approach is adopted, and it may be found *domestically* that *Kahn* will require reconsideration.[205] A near-absolute exclusionary rule in respect of improperly or illegally obtained non-confession evidence could be adopted within s78 PACE[206] or arise simply as a free-standing application of Article 6(1). Although the first domestic decision to apply *Teixiera*[207] gave it a restrictive interpretation in distinguishing it on somewhat narrow grounds,[208]

[203] For discussion of the operation of s78 see C J W Allen (1990) CLJ 80; M Gelowitz 106 LQR 327; R May [1988] Crim LR 722.

[204] 'What's the matter with s78?' Andrew L T Choo and S Nash (1999) Dec. Crim LR 929–940.

[205] A Chamber of the Court found no breach of Article 6 in *Kahn* v *UK*, despite the breach of Article 8: (1999) 27 EHRR CD 58; judgment of the Court of 12.5.00. But since the decision rests on the different positions of the Strasbourg and domestic courts, in relation to the assessment of evidence, it should be treated with caution domestically in order to avoid a minimalist approach. See further Chapter 10 pp390–391.

[206] Although s78, on its face, clearly provides a discretion, there are already circumstances in which confessions could be viewed as absolutely inadmissible under s78. If a confession was obtained by oppression s76(2)(a) should be used to exclude it, but if a judge were to consider its exclusion under s78 as well, there would be, it is argued, no discretion left to admit it. S78 would operate, *de facto*, as an absolute exclusionary rule. By analogy, since Article 6 now contemplates the existence of a near-absolute exclusionary rule in respect of non-confession evidence, that possibility should also be apparent within s78.

[207] *Nottingham City Council* v *Mohammed Amin* (1999) judgment of 15 November 1999.

[208] The respondent, who was driving an unlicensed motor vehicle, responded to a flagging down by two constables posing as members of the public; he took them to their destination where the fare was paid over. He contended that the constables had not confined themselves to passive investigation but had incited him to commit the offence, thereby rendering the proceedings as a whole unfair. Lord Bingham found that he had not been pressured or incited into committing an offence. Leave to appeal to the House of Lords was granted. The basis on which it was found that flagging him down – a positive action – was not incitement to commit the offence is, it is suggested, unclear. The respondent had turned off his light, thereby indicating that he was not for hire.

the findings did not affect the argument that some forms of pre-trial impropriety, especially breaches of rights, demand exclusion of evidence deriving from them.[209] This argument would be very strong where the illegality consisted of a fundamental breach of another Convention right.[210] Such an argument has been accepted in New Zealand,[211] and receives explicit recognition under the Canadian Charter.[212] The findings of the Privy Council in *Allie Mohammed* v *State*[213] in respect of a denial of custodial access to legal advice lend support to such a possibility although, admittedly, they were made in the context of confession evidence: 'The stamp of constitutionality on a citizen's rights is not meaningless: it is clear testimony that added value is attached to the protection of the right . . . Not every breach will result in a confession being excluded. But their Lordships make clear that the fact that there has been a breach of a constitutional right is a cogent factor militating in favour of the exclusion of the confession. In this way the constitutional character of the infringed right is respected and accorded a high value'. These findings reflect a normative approach: if courts were to take such an approach to the Convention rights, which may clearly be termed 'constitutional rights', the traditional, amoral stance of the common law regarding exclusion of evidence might become a more robust, activist one.

A similarly strong argument for exclusion of evidence under Article 6(1) could be raised where the evidence of informers, although not illegally obtained, might affect the fairness of the trial,[214] particularly where part of the evidence and/or the identity of the informer is not disclosed to the defence.[215] As Chapter 10 points out, the rules on disclosure under

[209] This argument has been put forward by, for example, Cross *Evidence* 5th edn (1979); see also Ashworth 'Excluding Evidence as Protecting Rights' [1977] Crim LR 723 and A Sanders and R Young *Criminal Justice* (1994) at p416.

[210] This argument failed in *Khan* v *UK*, note 205 above: a fundamental breach of Article 8 occurred in obtaining the only evidence against the defendant but, following *Schenk* [1988] 13 EHRR 242 no breach of Article 6 was found due to the admission of the evidence. The Court said that it was not its role to determine whether unlawfully obtained evidence should be admissible. That *is* the role of the national court which could therefore take a different stance on this matter, under the HRA.

[211] *R* v *Butcher* [1992] 2 NZLR 257; *R* v *Te Kira* [1993] 3 NZLR 257; *Simpson* v *Attorney-General* [1994] 3 NZLR 703.

[212] Section 24(2). In *R* v *Feeney* [1997] 2 SCR 13 the Canadian Supreme Court said that admission of evidence obtained owing to a serious breach of the appellant's Charter rights would be more damaging to the reputation of the criminal justice system than would its exclusion. (See also *R* v *Burlingham* [1995] 2 SCR 206.) A more technical breach has not been found, however, to demand exclusion since to do so would cause greater affront to the system than its inclusion: *R* v *Belnavis* [1997] 3 SCR 341.

[213] Judgment delivered by Lord Steyn on 8 December 1998, unreported.

[214] For detailed discussion see *Under Surveillance: Covert Policing and Human Rights Standards* Justice (1998) Chapter 2 esp pp37–51 and Chapter 3 esp pp70–74.

[215] For example, the evidence might be tainted owing to the motivation of the informer. In *Windisch* v *Austria* [1991] 13 EHRR 281 the Court said: 'the Convention does not preclude reliance, at the investigation stage, on sources such as anonymous informants. However, the subsequent use of their statements by the trial court to found a conviction is another matter.' But see *Edwards* v *UK* (1992) 15 EHRR 417 (it was found that the

the Criminal Procedure and Investigations Act create a regime which allows sensitive material to be withheld by the prosecution so that neither the court nor the defence are aware of its existence.[216] Where this occurred, argument for exclusion of evidence could be raised under Article 6 at first instance or on appeal, based on the general requirements of fairness and on the equality of arms principle.[217] The domestic courts would be expected to test issues of admissibility of evidence and of disclosure much more directly against the requirements of Article 6 than has generally occurred at Strasbourg.

The rule from *Teixeira* could also be applied where 'compelled' admissions, including those obtained by treatment falling within s76, and those obtained on pain of a penalty under the TA,[218] while not themselves used in evidence had led to the uncovering of other evidence. It could be argued, in furtherance of a fair procedure under Article 6, that that other evidence should be excluded under s78. The question of pressure on the applicant in the interview was taken into account by the Court in reaching its conclusion that Article 6 had been breached in *Saunders* v *UK*[219] by the admission in evidence of the coerced admissions, and the argument could be extended to encompass other evidence uncovered as a result of such admissions.

The courts may also find that certain of the due process rights enshrined in PACE, the TA and their associated Codes reflect certain of the principles enshrined in Articles 3, 5, 8 or 6, and that their breach would therefore make it virtually inevitable that the trial would be rendered unfair if evidence deriving from the breach were not excluded. One particular effect would be that the PACE or TA Code provisions in question, as the detailed domestic embodiment of those rights, would be accorded *de facto* a higher value than their legal status would appear to warrant.

Clearly, the notion of an increase in the use of exclusion of evidence as a means of upholding suspects' Convention rights would create polarisation between adherents of crime control and of due process. From a crime control perspective it would be argued[220] that any such increase would be undesirable since evidence should be excluded only if it appears to be unreliable. The function of a criminal court is to determine the truth of the charges against the accused, not to enquire into alleged improprieties on the part of the police. Impropriety in the investigation is not linked to the guilt of the defendant and therefore should not be instru-

hearing in the CA remedied the failure of disclosure). These issues were, however, raised successfully under Article 6 in *Rowe and Davis* v *UK* (note 183, above).

216 See p390.

217 In *Jespers* v *Belgium* the Commission found that under Article 6(3) the accused has the right 'to have at his disposal . . . all relevant elements that have been or could have been collected by the relevant authorities' App No 8403/78, 27 DR 61.

218 See Chapter 7 at pp267–269.

219 (1997) 23 EHRR 313. *Saunders* is discussed in Chapter 7 at p281.

220 By Wigmore: see *Treatise on Evidence* 3rd edn (1940) and Andrews (1963) Crim LR 15, 77.

mental in allowing him or her to walk freely from the court. On this argument, the court is not condoning improper methods by admitting evidence thereby obtained: it is merely acknowledging that it is not within its function to enquire into them. This argument may also be supported from a victim-oriented perspective. The victim of a serious violent or sexual offence may be said to suffer a violation of his or her right to security of the person and possibly to privacy and freedom of movement if an offender is acquitted, not on the basis of doubts about his or her guilt, but as a result of police impropriety. The victim of a rapist is likely to be profoundly affected in the free ordering of her life by the knowledge that the rapist has walked free from the court. The victim of a racial attack, or the family of the victim, may experience a similar restriction. Thus, arguably, the interests of the victim, which may be coterminous with Convention rights should be taken into account under s78, although, clearly, the court has a public duty to uphold standards of criminal justice which goes beyond those interests.[221]

From a due process perspective an activist interpretation of Article 6 would be urged, and some commentators currently argue for a near-absolute rule requiring exclusion of evidence where it has been obtained in breach of a fundamental Constitutional right or where its admission would breach the right to a fair trial.[222] It can be argued that Article 6 requires that a court should not merely enquire into the truth of the charges against a defendant: it should also play a part in maintaining standards in criminal investigations and in discouraging police abuse of power. From this standpoint the judiciary should use exclusion of evidence as a means of protecting the due process elements within the investigative process which correspond to the rights of the detainee.

Article 6, as interpreted in *Teixiera*, and in certain decisions discussed in Chapter 7,[223] clearly adheres more closely to a due process rather than a crime control position. As this chapter has argued, adoption of a due process approach to exclusion of evidence under the HRA, which would involve departure from *Kahn*, may be viewed *domestically* as a requirement of Article 6, and would provide a means of protecting both the Convention guarantees and suspects' rights under PACE and the TA. But while due process demands that improperly obtained evidence should be excluded, that the police officers involved should be disciplined, or prosecuted, and, where appropriate, that compensation should be available, it is unclear that it demands, in principle, that a person who is factually guilty of an offence should be acquitted. If evidence is excluded and, as a result, the burden of proof cannot be discharged, acquittal must clearly follow. But methods of escaping from the conflicts of interest inherent in

[221] See H Fenwick 'Procedural Rights of Victims of Crime: Public or Private Ordering of the Criminal Justice Process?' [1997] 60 MLR 317–333.

[222] See, for example, Ashworth 'The Human Rights Act 1998' [1999] Crim LR 263 at p271.

[223] In particular, *Murray (John)* v *UK* (1996) 22 EHRR 29, discussed at p282.

such exclusion should be sought. Such acquittals uphold the integrity of the criminal justice system since they demonstrate a refusal of the courts to associate themselves with a fundamental breach of rights, but they profoundly fail to address the interests of victims (also recognised at Strasbourg),[224] their relatives, and the general societal interest in the prevention of crime.

These arguments strengthen the case for further, more radical reform of the police complaints and disciplinary system and of CPS decision-making since so doing would tend to discourage illegality and impropriety and enhance levels of adherence to the PACE rules, including the Code provisions. Arguments for exclusion of evidence on the basis of police impropriety might be raised less frequently. But if in fact there is an increased tendency to exclude evidence on this basis in the post-HRA era, there are strong arguments for developing much clearer guiding principles for so doing, especially under s78, which are based on both due process *and* crime control norms. Such principles would be based on Article 6 and would be intended to allow the police and prosecution to predict more clearly and at an early stage when evidence would be excluded. In some instances, this would mean the redirection of energy towards the uncovering of other evidence, with the result that attention turned to the real perpetrator.[225] In others it would mean that the conviction of the true perpetrator could be obtained despite the exclusion of some evidence. As this chapter has indicated, Parliament has almost entirely abrogated its responsibility for such development, despite the extremely significant matters at stake, in societal terms, leaving it largely in the hands of the judiciary. Assuming that, under the HRA, the judiciary accepts a greater responsibility for clearer development[226] this would

[224] In *UK* v *Ireland* App No 9825/82 8 EHRR 49 it was argued under Article 2 that the government had taken insufficient steps to prevent the murder of the applicant's husband. The Commission found that it was not its task to scrutinise the measures taken in detail but noted that a number of positive measures had in fact been taken (p515 para 16). Thus, the possibility that positive measures might be required was accepted. To take an extreme example, if, in the case of a trial for murder, a court excluded, owing to a serious breach of Article 8, a tape recording, the only evidence linking a defendant to the killing of an accomplice–informer, in circumstances which suggested that a further informer was also under threat, the defendent's subsequent killing on acquittal of that person might be viewed as raising Article 2 issues. See also the developing jurisprudence from certain Turkish cases under Articles 2, 3 and 13 on the right, of victims and victims' families: note 12, above. The rights of victims of crime might also be raised under Article 8, particularly under the guarantee of respect for family life.

[225] In the *Confait* case the confessions of the accused almost mesmerised the police into pursuing their prosecution. The other evidence pointing to the real perpetrator was ignored or explained away owing to the tunnel vision developed by the police as a result of the confessions (see *Report of the Inquiry* by the Hon Sir Henry Fisher HC of 1977–1978). A similar phenomenon occurred in the *Kiszko* case (*The Times* 18 February 1992).

[226] This would involve a departure from the position still maintained by the judiciary, that it is preferable not to lay down any general rules in order to structure the discretion under s78. In *Samuel* [1988] QB 615 at p630, for example, Hodgson J said: 'It is undesirable to attempt any general guidance as to the way in which a judge's discretion under s78 or his inherent powers should be exercised'.

mean that once the principles reached a certain level of clarity the investigation and prosecution case could be planned on the basis, for example, that a secretly recorded conversation, or the evidence of an informer, would not be admissible.[227] Such development would provide a means, currently largely lacking in criminal procedure, of adhering to Article 6 while seeking to reconcile the conflicting demands discussed here. It might lead to recognition, largely absent in populist and political debate, that conflicts between crime control and due process may be resolvable.

[227] This might have been beneficial, for example, in the *Heron* case (judgment at Leeds Crown Court 1 November 1993), in which a 9-year-old girl was murdered. The police interviewed the suspect oppressively with the result that his confession was excluded from evidence and the prosecution collapsed. Judge Mitchell said: 'the means adopted to achieve that end [of breaking his resolve to make no admissions] meant in effect, that regardless of the fact that his eventual confession may very well have been true, the prosecution [could not prove that the confession was not obtained oppressively]'. The police were astonished by this finding; had it been clearly predictable during the investigation, the outcome might have been different. Possibly the point about predictability might also be made in relation to the private prosecution of certain of the suspects in the *Lawrence* case (see the *McPherson Report* (1999) Cm 4262-I).

Chapter 6

Criminal Procedure II

ASPECTS OF POLICE POWERS

Introduction

Chapter 5 set forth the theoretical framework within which the powers to be considered in this chapter – detention short of arrest, arrest, custodial detention – will be grounded. As Chapter 5 indicated, the dominant model affecting the grant of further police powers is the crime control one which views the enhancement of police discretion as linked to the prevention or detection of crime and terrorist activity. As this chapter will indicate, the grant of further powers has not been accompanied by a concomitant strengthening of the protection for the due process rights affecting arrest and detention. The two structuring constraints identified in Chapter 5 as intended to protect due process under the Police and Criminal Evidence Act 1984 (PACE) – the requirements of reasonable suspicion and the establishment of procedural safeguards – have been eroded in the post-PACE developments. The reasonable suspicion requirement has been dropped from the new powers while the safeguards are still largely protected by quasi-legislation only – Codes of Practice – and in some respects can now be regarded as virtually unenforceable guidance only. These weaknesses in the scheme continue to be exacerbated in respect of terrorist suspects under the Terrorism Act 2000. The central focus of this chapter is the effect which the HRA can have in reasserting the significance of due process in relation to the powers it considers, particularly in respect of such suspects, taking into account the methods of creating accountability considered in Chapter 5.

Detention short of arrest

Introduction

Under the due process model detention short of arrest – usually, although not invariably, exercised in the form of stop and search powers – should be based on reasonable suspicion relating to the specific actions of an individual. Under the crime control model such detention is viewed as an investigative tool which should be based on general police experience; inhibitory rules should be kept to a minimum in order to allow police officers to act on instinct; police discretion should be the guiding principle. Under this analysis it may be found that while PACE adhered, formally, to due process requirements, stop and search in practice was underpinned by crime control norms. Further, the additional powers introduced over the succeeding years failed to include the reasonable suspicion requirement and therefore appeared to give a formal imprimatur to the movement from a due process towards a crime control model which was occurring in practice.

The use of these powers remains a contentious matter which continues to attract public attention, especially as it has frequently been suggested that they may be used in a discriminatory fashion. While it now appears incontrovertible that racial discrimination affects their use, the extent to which this is the case remains controversial.[1] Their recorded use has more than trebled since PACE came into force in 1986[2] and, as indicated below, a large number of further powers have been introduced in the post-PACE period. One factor influencing the rise in their use may have been the introduction of the notion of 'zero tolerance' policies in the mid-1990s. This proliferation of usage and of powers was not accompanied by a full official review of their crime control value or adverse due process impact[3] until the issues were raised in relation to the *Lawrence* case, in the *McPherson Report* in 1999.[4] Owing to its remit they did not form a central focus of the Report; in so far as powers to detain short of arrest were considered, the concern centred on the question of institutionalised racism in relation to their use. The part which such powers might play in miscarriages of justice and their general links with other aspects of policing, especially the interview, has hardly had an airing in recent official reports. For example, the 1998 *Consultation Paper on Terrorism*[5] which recommended the retention of counter-terrorist stop and search powers,[6] failed to consider these matters, and made no reference

[1] See note 36 below.
[2] Home Office Statistical Bulletin 21/93; Statistical Bulletin 27/97.
[3] They were outside the remit of the Runciman Royal Commission.
[4] Cm 4262-I.
[5] Cm 4178.
[6] See below, pp220–224.

to research it might have been based on. As discussed below, the possibility that informal street contacts may influence and structure the formal interview are especially significant in the post-HRA era.

In crime control terms such powers are of debatable value. Their use may have a counter-productive effect in terms of alienating sections of the community. Feelings of grievance at an apparently arbitrary use of the powers can contribute to the alienation of the police from the community, leading to a breakdown in law and order expressed in its most extreme form in rioting[7] and otherwise in general lack of cooperation with the police. They are also of rather uncertain efficacy. Only around 10% to 14% of stops lead to an arrest and only around 3% to a charge.[8] These figures do not include stops which did not lead to a search, or voluntary stops, and therefore the percentage of stops leading to a charge must be lower than this. There are, of course, other methods of measuring the crime control value of stop and search powers; in particular they have some value in terms of information gathering. Such value is, however, hard to evaluate owing to the lack of transparency as to their impact in practice. However, debate as to the real crime control value of such powers has hardly occurred during the post-PACE years; the notion that more stop and search powers add up to more crime control has gained currency and the powers have therefore proliferated.

These powers pay lip-service to due process in the sense that they are apparently accompanied by some safeguards against abuse, partly contained in Code A of the Police and Criminal Evidence Act 1984 and the Code under Schedule 14 of the Terrorism Act 2000 (TA). But apart from the possibility, in restricted circumstances, of a civil action, no clear means of ensuring that these safeguards actually affect police practice is provided. By 2000, 14 years after PACE came into force, only a tiny handful of cases on breaches of the stop and search rules had been reported. This suggests either that on the whole the powers are not misused, or that the avenues available by which to seek redress are extremely limited and difficult to use. The recent reports on the use of stop and search powers, including the *McPherson Report*, suggest that the latter is the case. Clearly, some of those stopped may not wish to take the matter further, especially if the stop does not lead to an arrest. But those who are targeted on a number of occasions, or who consider that an improper stop and search influenced the subsequent investigation, may well wish to seek redress. The judiciary have adopted, it is suggested in Chapter 7, an activist stance in supervising the interview in the police station – the point at which the infusion of due process into custodial procedures is especially crucial – but, in contrast, judicial intervention in the exercise of arrest and stop and search has been minimal.

[7] See Lord Scarman *The Brixton Disorders* Cmnd 8427 (1981); McConville 'Search of Persons and Premises' (1983) Crim LR 604–614.

[8] Home Office Statistical Bulletin 21/93.

The most significant due process requirement – reasonable suspicion – is increasingly discarded in the post-PACE powers. If reasonable suspicion, in practice, has little influence on the working practices of the officer on the beat, it is nevertheless a formal assertion of a willingness 'to impose due process on street policing'.[9] The introduction of these broad powers may be part of a movement towards acceptance of policing with objects in view other than preventing or detecting specific offences. This may include their contribution to intelligence-led policing[10] and, more simply, to the assertion of authority against certain groups on the street who are regarded as socially undesirable. These powers may facilitate use of such authority rather than necessarily ensuring crime control. Their use may also tend to circumvent use of the s1 PACE power with its reasonable suspicion limitation.

The discussion below suggests that this stage is under a due process deficit in both formal and substantive terms. It is difficult to evaluate how far such a deficit is warranted and therefore proportionate to the benefit gained in crime control terms since such benefit is itself hard to evaluate. Nevertheless, there are grounds for concern as to the effect the most recent powers will have, and as to how they will be used in practice. In so far as the special powers introduced post-PACE may be used in such a way as to undermine the s1 PACE power, such 'balance' as it creates will not be maintained. There may be scope, however, as argued below, for the Convention guarantees to reduce the degree of untrammelled discretion which has become increasingly evident in the stop and search scheme post-PACE.

The prevalence of voluntary searches also continues to undermine the reasonable suspicion requirement, and while this problem has been recognised post-PACE, no serious attempt has been made to address it. The apparently voluntary basis of a large number of searches has continued to be questionable.[11] Inconsistency of practice between forces is readily apparent.[12] Persons may be intimidated by police authority and may submit to a search where no power to search in fact exists. Such searches may come to light only if the suspect later raises the argument that the police were not entitled to assume that he or she had consented or if, after initial compliance, the suspect resists and is charged with assaulting an officer in the course of his or her duty.[13] The only safeguards against

[9] Sanders and Young *Criminal Justice* (1994) p62.

[10] See Chapter 9 p341 and Chapter 10 p377, note 25.

[11] D Dixon, C Coleman and K Bottomley 'Consent and the Legal Regulation of Policing' (1990) 17 Journal of Law and Society 345.

[12] Certain forces such as Bedfordshire use a separate consent form for voluntary searches, but such practice is by no means universal. See 'Modernising the Tactic: Improving the Use of Stop and Search' *Policing and Reducing Crime: Briefing Note No 2* November 1999.

[13] See *Osman* v *Director of Public Prosecutions The Times* 29 September 1999, judgment 1 July 1999 in which Lord Justice Sedley indicated that an initial passive response to a search would not entitle officers to assume that the subject was consenting to it.

police pressure to submit to a 'voluntary' search are contained merely in Notes for Guidance. Note 1D of Code A provides for a warning that the person need not submit to the search. Note 1E prohibits the voluntary searching of persons belonging to vulnerable groups, including the mentally disordered. These provisions probably have no legal status at all and therefore may be viewed as objectionable in terms of rule of law and due process values since a stark mismatch is created between their potential due process value and the possibility of their enforcement by a court. Adherence to them by the police is also probably influenced by the signal their non-legal status provides as to their insignificance. The leeway these provisions create for 'consensual', 'invisible' contacts is significant, not only in terms of evidence which may be obtained due to a stop and search, but in terms of their influence on later stages in the investigative process, especially the interview. They also create latitude for 'invisible' racism in street policing.

PACE and post-PACE powers

The Thatcher government was responsible for the introduction for the first time of a general power to stop and search. There was no general power at common law to detain without the subject's consent in the absence of specific statutory authority.[14] Instead there were a miscellany of such powers, the majority of which were superseded by PACE. The Phillips Royal Commission, whose report influenced PACE,[15] recommended the introduction of a new general power, but accepted the need to maintain a balance between the interest of society as represented by the police in crime control, and the interest of the citizen in personal liberty and privacy. This balance was sought to be achieved partly by introducing a reasonable suspicion element into the PACE powers, a due process requirement intended to differentiate the new powers quite sharply from the random powers favoured by the adherents of crime control.

Consideration of the PACE and post-PACE powers below reveals an incremental departure from the balance the pre-PACE Phillips Royal Commission had in mind. First, the reasonable suspicion requirement was dropped when new powers were introduced; they were 'balanced' by the doubtful due process safeguards of authorisation by senior police officers or the Home Secretary. Second, failing to stop when requested to do so became a new offence under a number of post-PACE special stop and search powers. These changes were foreshadowed in the special powers introduced in Northern Ireland under the Northern Ireland (Emergency Provisions) Act 1996 (EPA), as amended.

[14] For a full list of the powers available at the time, arising from 16 statutes, see RCCP Report Cmnd 8092, 1981.

[15] Ibid.

(i) The reasonable suspicion requirement

Under s1 of PACE a general power to search persons[16] (s1(1)) or vehicles (s1(2)) and to detain them for that purpose was conferred on the police if there was reasonable suspicion that stolen goods, offensive weapons or other prohibited articles might be found.[17] The relationship between s1(2) of PACE and the power arising under s163 of the Road Traffic Act 1988 (RTA) remains unclear. S163 provides a constable in uniform with power to stop vehicles, which may be unqualified as to purpose[18] and does not depend upon reasonable suspicion. If s163 is of general application, s1(2) appears to provide a power to search a vehicle and to detain it for that purpose once it has been stopped under s163.[19] If s163 is concerned only with traffic offences, s1(2) must contain an implied power to stop a vehicle in order to detain it for a search.

Under s1(6) if an article is found which appears to be stolen or prohibited the officer can seize it. Further powers to stop and search pedestrians, vehicles and their occupants are contained in a number of statutes,[20] including s23 of the Misuse of Drugs Act 1971. S4 of PACE enables the police to use their RTA powers to set up road blocks and to stop and search any vehicle to see whether it contains a wanted person. The PACE powers and s23 of the 1971 Act are balanced by the reasonable suspicion requirement which theoretically places restrictions on their exercise. Reasonable suspicion arises where a police officer considers on reasonable grounds that particular articles may be found. It is a flexible, broad and uncertain concept, but para 1 of Code of Practice A made under PACE, and applying to all statutory search powers dependent on reasonable suspicion, sets out to explain what it means. Paras 1.6 and 1.7 of Code A explain the objective nature of reasonable suspicion and forbid stereotyping in arriving at such suspicion,[21] although the revision of Code

16 It should be noted that the police do not need to search the suspect once he or she has been stopped; they may decide not to. Nevertheless reasonable suspicion that stolen goods or articles are being carried must arise before the stop can be made.

17 Under s1(7) the articles are those '(i) made or adapted for use in the course of or in connection with an offence to which this sub-paragraph applies; or (ii) intended by the person having it with him for such use by him or by some other person'. Under s1(8) the offences to which s1(7)(b)(i) above applies are: (a) burglary; (b) theft; (c) offences under s12 of the Theft Act; (d) offences under s15 of that Act. S1(8A) applies to (any article which falls within) s139 of the Criminal Justice Act 1988.

18 See HC Standing Committee E, 13 December 1983 col 339.

19 This would confirm *Lodwick* v *Sanders* [1985] 1 All ER 577.

20 A non-exhaustive list of those to which Code A applies is given in Annex A to Code A (1999 version).

21 Under para 1.6 'Reasonable suspicion may exist, for example, where information has been received such as a description of an article being carried or of a suspected offender; a person is seen acting covertly or warily or attempting to hide something; or a person is carrying a certain type of article at an unusual time or in a place where a number of burglaries or thefts are known to have taken place recently'. Under para 1.7 'A person's colour, age, hairstyle or manner of dress, or the fact that he is known to have a previous conviction for possession of an unlawful article, cannot be used alone or in combination

A in 1997[22] effected some departure from this due process stance. Under the revision para 1.6A allows an officer to take into account information that members of a particular gang habitually carry knives, other weapons or have drugs in their possession, while para 1.7AA provides that if a person wears an item of clothing, or other insignia, suggesting that he or she belongs to such a gang, that person may be stopped and searched. No doubt these provisions merely legitimise police working practices, but they also signal formal permission to use coercive powers on the basis of a degree of stereotyping. Certain forms of stereotyping remain, formally, unpermitted: for example, stopping a black person with previous convictions simply on the basis of those two factors would obviously be unjustifiable and is therefore apparently forbidden.[23] The problem is that usually if the reasonable suspicion requirement, as interpreted in these provisions, is disregarded no clear consequences will follow[24] and therefore it may be regarded as largely unenforceable guidance, unless it receives further attention in the post-HRA era.

In practice, there is little evidence that reasonable suspicion acts as a constraint if police officers wish to stop and search without it. Research in the area suggests that there is a tendency to view reasonable suspicion as a flexible concept which may denote a low level of suspicion.[25] Sanders and Young conclude, having reviewed the relevant research, that 'the legal understanding of reasonable suspicion plays little part in officers' thought processes or decision-making',[26] although they also suggest that PACE may be bringing about some change in 'cop culture'; young officers may be taught to act 'according to the book' as opposed to acting instinctively. Zander concludes: 'the PACE rules seem to have had little impact on decision-making by officers on the beat'.[27] It is suggested that in this respect a contrast can be found between observance of the Code A and Code C (the Code governing police interviewing) rules which may be grounded, to an extent, within the rule of law values expounded in Chapter 5. While research and commentaries have consistently acknowledged the influence of police working practices on the observance of the Code C rules, the impact of the underpinning of judicial supervision has also been emphasised; the two have been viewed as engaged in a subtle interaction which has resulted in some respect for the due process force of the rules.[28] The

with each other as the sole basis on which to search that person. Nor may it be founded on the basis of stereotyped images of certain persons or groups as more likely to be committing offences.'

22 SI 1997/1159.

23 But note the provision of Code A para 1.16 in respect of stop and search authorisations under the TA; discussed below at pp223–4.

24 Theoretically an action for false imprisonment might lie. The lack of sanctions for breaches of the Codes is discussed below, at pp227–8.

25 See D Dixon (1989) 17 Int J Soc Law 185–206.

26 Op cit p43.

27 *The Police and Criminal Evidence Act* (1995) 3rd edn p18.

28 See D Dixon in *Miscarriages of Justice* (1999) C Walker and K Starmer (eds) at pp66–67.

Code A rules have failed to receive such an underpinning, partly because in practice they often operate 'invisibly', but partly, it is suggested, owing to the consistent refusal of the courts to exclude 'real' evidence.[29] In other words, while the courts have insisted on an infusion of due process into the working practices affecting interviewing, they have so far settled, in effect, for a crime control stance in harmony with such practices regarding stop and search.

It seems, then, that in practice the reasonable suspicion element fails to ensure that due process is observed. Police practice in this respect has to an extent been legitimised in the stop and search powers introduced mainly under the Major and Blair governments as additions to the general PACE power. The justification given for introducing stop and search powers untrammelled by the need to show reasonable suspicion, is that most of them are for use in circumstances in which an emergency or semi-emergency situation may be in being. The extent to which these powers genuinely relate to such situations is considered below.

S60 of the Criminal Justice and Public Order Act 1994, as amended by s8 of the Knives Act 1997, provides police officers with a further stop and search power which does not depend on showing reasonable suspicion of particular wrong-doing on the part of an individual. An officer of at least the rank of inspector can authorise the stop and search of any person or vehicle within a particular locality if he or she reasonably believes that incidents involving 'serious violence' may take place in that area and that authorisation is expedient in order to prevent their occurrence. The authorisation may apply to a period not exceeding 24 hours. If such an authorisation is in force an officer may stop anyone within the specified locality in order to look for offensive weapons or dangerous instruments. In contrast to s1 PACE, failure to stop is an offence under s60(8).

S60 was also amended by s25 of the Crime and Disorder Act 1998 to provide a power under s60(4A)(a) to demand the removal of a face covering 'if the constable reasonable believes that person is wearing [it] wholly or mainly for the purpose of concealing his identity'. S25 also amended s60 to provide a further, separate, power under s60(4A)(b) to 'seize any item which the constable reasonable believes any person intends to wear wholly or mainly for that purpose'. This is not, formally, a power to stop and search for face coverings. The constable must be

[29] The pre-PACE position was restated in the House of Lords' decision in *Kahn* [1996] 3 All ER 289: improperly obtained evidence, other than involuntary confessions, is admissible subject to a narrow discretion to exclude it. In practice this discretion is rarely exercised in respect of physical evidence. In the 14 years post-PACE in only two reported decisions has it been exercised to exclude the products of an unlawful search: *R* v *Fennelley* (1989) Crim LR 142 and *Samuels* v *Commissioner of Police for the Metropolis* (1999) 3 March 1999 CA unreported. In the latter instance no reasonable suspicion was found in respect of a stop and search which was therefore unlawful. The continued adherence of the courts to this traditional stance may have discouraged argument as to exclusion of evidence in this context.

acting under another power or the person must be carrying the covering (or item which could be used as a covering) openly. It is an arrestable[30] offence under new s60(8)(b) to fail to remove a face covering. These provisions have clear implications for public protest, which are discussed in Chapter 4.[31] While on their face they do not create a new power of stop and search, they may do so in practice since once an authorisation is in force under s60 a constable does not require reasonable suspicion that dangerous weapons or instruments will be found in order to stop and search.

The Prevention of Terrorism (Temporary Provisions) Act 1989 as amended (the PTA), and the Northern Ireland (Emergency Provisions) Act 1996, as amended, contained special powers providing for the detaining, questioning and searching of pedestrians and vehicles for articles of use in carrying out acts of terrorism and to prevent terrorist attacks. The powers under ss44–47 of the Terrorism Act 2000 (TA) are based on the PTA and EPA powers and, as Chapter 3 explains, they are applied to a far wider range of people under s1 TA owing to the new and broad definition of 'terrorism'. It may be noted that under s116(2) TA the powers conferred under the Act to stop persons are deemed to include powers to stop vehicles, and it is an offence to fail to stop a vehicle. Sections 15(3) and (4) of the PTA empowered a police officer to stop and search anyone who appeared to him or her to be liable for arrest under s14 of the Act and to search them for anything which might confirm the officer's suspicions as to their involvement in terrorism. Under s14(1)(b), in order to arrest, a constable had to have reasonable grounds for suspecting that a person was 'concerned in the preparation or instigation of acts of terrorism connected with the affairs of Northern Ireland or any other act' of non-domestic terrorism.[32] The s15 power was partially influenced by the reasonable suspicion requirement. It did not depend on the need to show reasonable suspicion that the suspect was carrying the items which might be searched for, but the officer had to have reasonable grounds for suspecting that the suspect was liable to arrest under s14. These stop and search powers are reproduced but broadened under s43 TA which provides: 'A constable may stop and search a person whom he reasonably suspects to be a terrorist to discover whether he has in his possession anything which may constitute evidence that he is a terrorist'. 'Being a terrorist' is not in itself an offence under the TA (unless the 'terrorist' group in question is also proscribed), although some but not all actions falling within the definition of terrorism in s1 TA are coterminous with existing offences; therefore this power is not dependent on suspicion of commission of an offence or of carrying prohibited articles.

[30] S27(1) of the 1998 Act amends s24 PACE for this purpose.
[31] At p115.
[32] See below at pp236–7.

There were also powers in s16 and paragraph 4(2) of Schedule 5 to the PTA which empowered the police and others to stop, question and search people, vehicles and unaccompanied freight, which were about to enter or leave Great Britain or Northern Ireland, to determine whether they had been concerned in the commission, preparation or instigation of acts of terrorism. These powers formed part of the 'ports and border controls' contained in the PTA. They are reproduced in Schedule 7 TA and, again, they are not dependent on showing reasonable suspicion.

Under the Major government additional stop and search powers were added to the PTA. These powers introduce a number of significant features. Not only do they arise independently of reasonable suspicion relating to objects suspected of being carried, but they make it an offence in itself to refuse to comply with the search. It is not an offence under PACE to refuse to comply with an s1 search, or to obstruct it, although to do so would probably amount to the offence of obstructing a constable under s89(2) of the Police Act 1996.[33] S81(1) of the Criminal Justice and Public Order Act 1994 amended the PTA by inserting into it a new s13A which provides that an officer of the rank of commander as regards the Metropolitan area or the City of London, or of the rank of assistant chief constable as regards any other police area, can authorise officers to stop and search vehicles and their occupants within a particular locality if he or she considers that it is expedient to do so to prevent acts of terrorism. The authorisation must stipulate both the area to which it applies and the period, not exceeding 28 days, for which it will remain in force. Authorisations may be renewed for a further period or periods of up to 28 days at a time. If such an authorisation is in force an officer may stop any vehicle within the specified locality in order to look for articles which could be used for the commission of acts of terrorism. Since the term 'expedient' is used, there is no requirement that the officer granting the authorisation should reasonably believe that it is necessary in order to prevent the commission of acts of terrorism. The term seems to connote a less rigorous requirement.

The PTA was further amended by the Prevention of Terrorism (Additional Powers) Act 1996 to include a number of new stop and search powers. The government considered that introduction of the new powers was necessary owing to the threat of IRA activity on the British mainland in Spring 1996. These include a power under s1, which inserts s13B into the PTA, to stop and search citizens in designated areas without reasonable suspicion.[34] The authorisation requirements are the same as those under s13A but for the added requirement that the authorisation must be confirmed by the Secretary of State within 48 hours. If it is not so confirmed

[33] Reproducing s51(3) of the Police Act 1964.

[34] The search only authorises a constable to require a person to remove headgear, footwear, outer coat, jacket or gloves (s4A).

it ceases to have effect (s13A(8)) but if it is confirmed it remains in force, and will subsist for up to 28 days. Refusing to comply with the search is an offence carrying a penalty higher than those which could be used, if necessary, under the general offence of obstructing a constable.

The powers under ss13A and B form the basis for the powers arising under ss44–46 of the Terrorism Act 2000, which will replace them. Authorisations apply to a specific area and are for a maximum of 28 days (although that period may be renewed). Reproducing ss13A(4) and 13B(3), the new provisions expressly confirm that reasonable suspicion remains irrelevant. S45(1)(a) provides that the powers under s44 'may be exercised only for the purpose of searching for articles of a kind which could be used in connection with terrorism' but in order to ensure that this is not interpreted as a limiting requirement, s45(1)(b) provides that the powers 'may be exercised whether or not the constable has grounds for suspecting the presence of articles of that kind'.

One difference between the TA and PTA powers is that vehicle stop and search authorisations, as well as pedestrian ones, will have to be confirmed by the Secretary of State within 48 hours of their being made, or they will cease to have effect. This appears to be a gesture in the direction of due process since it rectifies the anomaly of the difference between the exercise of the powers in respect of pedestrians and those in respect of vehicles, and provides, at least theoretically, a level of oversight in relation to both. The Secretary of State must confirm an authorisation if it is not to lapse within 48 hours. It can be renewed at the end of 28 days under s46(7) which provides: 'An authorisation may be renewed in writing by the person who gave it or by a person who could have given it; and subsections (1) to (6) shall apply as if a new authorisation were given on each occasion on which the authorisation is renewed'. Thus, theoretically, authorisations could be continually renewed, depending on the intervention of the Secretary of State. The tendency of this provision may be in practice to leave the authorisation power largely in police hands alone.

If a person fails to stop when asked by a constable acting under s44 TA to do so, or wilfully obstructs the constable in exercising these powers, he or she will be liable to a fine of £5,000 or a prison sentence of six months, or both, under s47. Thus, if someone who is not involved in terrorism resists a search in a designated area, and is, for example, found to be carrying a small amount of cannabis, they might in theory face a prison sentence, although the offence committed – possession of cannabis – would not usually lead to the imposition of such a sentence and might well be dealt with by way of caution.

It is notable that no judicial body is involved in the supervision of these powers. All of them are subject to executive supervision only, either by the police themselves or, in the case of s44 TA, by the Home Secretary. These powers discard a key due process safeguard and therefore might be justified only if they are likely to have real value in terms of curbing criminal or terrorist activity. In debate on the 1996 Bill Michael Howard was asked how many arrests and convictions had followed use of the existing s13A power to stop and search. In reply he said that there had been 1,746 stops and 1,695 searches of vehicles, 2,373 searches of persons as occupants of vehicles in the 5 Metropolitan police areas and 8,142 stops and 6,854 searches of vehicles and 40 searches of persons as occupants of vehicles within the Heathrow perimeter. These had together led to 2 arrests under the PTA and to 66 other arrests.[35] These figures are clearly telling. They suggest that stopping and searching without reasonable suspicion leads to an extremely low level of arrests and therefore may not be the most effective use of police resources. This very low level of arrests may be compared with the general level flowing from stop and search with reasonable suspicion, which is around 13%. This figure itself is low (and may not be reliable) but nevertheless suggests that stop and search with reasonable suspicion (even though that concept may be interpreted very flexibly) is more productive on the face of it in crime control terms than stop and search without it. Howard, however, also made the point, although unsupported by specific evidence, that this does not represent the whole picture since would-be terrorists may be diverted from their activities and weapons may be found.

The figures given above also suggest that in so far as these powers do have value it lies partly in their (albeit low) level of apprehension of persons engaged in non-terrorist offences. If one of the objects of introducing the powers under ss13A and 13B was in reality to curb drug trafficking, they should have been debated in Parliament on that basis. The 1999 revision of Code A introduced the requirement under para 1.16 that the ss13A and B powers should 'not be used for stop and search for reasons unconnected with terrorism'. However, as indicated below, this provision is virtually unenforceable.

Since these powers on their face allow for stop and search on subjective grounds they may tend to be used disproportionately against the black community. Post-PACE research has consistently suggested that stop and search powers are used in a discriminatory fashion[36] and in response a rather ambiguous anti-racism provision was introduced in the 1999 revision of Code A. Para 1.16 gives an appearance of seeking to address the problem of racist stops in stating: 'officers should take particular care not to discriminate against members of ethnic minorities in the exercise of these powers'. But the paragraph continues: 'There may be circumstances, however, where it is appropriate for officers to take account of a person's ethnic origin in selecting persons to be stopped in response

[35] HC Deb 2 April 1996 col 211.

[36] See W Skogan HO Research Study No 117 (1990) HMSO p34; *Entry into the Criminal Justice System* Home Office (August 1998) and *Statistics on Race and the Criminal Justice System* Home Office (December 1998); *McPherson Report* (1999) Cm 4262-I. According to the Report, in 1999 blacks were six times more likely than whites to be stopped; in 1998 blacks were five times more likely to be stopped than whites.

to a specific terrorist threat'. This hazily worded provision might be interpreted as legitimising racist stops and thereby negating its preceding words. In 1995 Note 1A of Code A was revised to add the requirement that 'the selection of those questioned or searched is based upon objective factors and not upon personal prejudice'. In the 1999 revision this requirement became part of Note 1AA and further requirements were added regarding the use of the power under s25 of the Crime and Disorder Act 1998 (introducing new ss60(4A) and (B) into the CJPOA) to provide a power to demand the removal of a face covering. Note 1AA provides that if asking a Muslim woman to remove a covering, the officer should permit this to be done out of public view. Thus, as far as s60 of the 1994 Act and s44 of the TA are concerned, these requirements contained in quasi- or non-legal provisions are the only 'safeguards' against a racially stereotyped or insensitive use of these powers. As discussed below, this problem may be addressed under the HRA, while the amendments made to the Race Relations Act 1976 in 2000 may have an impact on police practice.

This bundle of powers, which may allow near-random stopping once a designation is in force, may, as indicated, result not in arrests for terrorist offences or offences of serious violence, but for drug-related or other more minor offences. It has often been observed that arrests may well be entirely unrelated to the reason for the original encounter with the police. These powers are therefore objectionable in the sense that they have been adopted apparently in response to near-crisis situations, whereas they may be used in situations which would not alone have justified their adoption. Since the wide powers under s60 of the 1994 Act and s44 of the Act of 2000 are not subject to limitation flowing from the concept of reasonable suspicion, they represent a departure from the principle that only an individual who has given rise to such suspicion due to his or her actions should suffer the infringement of liberty represented by a stop and search.

(ii) Absence of authorisation requirements

The EPA provided stop, question and search powers under s25(1) in which the requirements of reasonable suspicion and of authorisation were both discarded. These powers are reproduced in s89(1) TA which provides: 'An officer may stop a person for so long as is necessary to question him to ascertain (a) his identity and movements; (b) what he knows about a recent explosion or another recent incident endangering life; (c) what he knows about a person killed or injured in a recent explosion or incident'. Under s89(2) it is an offence punishable by a fine not to stop; it is also an offence to refuse to answer a question asked during the stop or to answer it inadequately, failing to answer 'to the best of his knowledge and ability'. The power to search for and seize munitions and transmitters under section 20(6) EPA is reproduced in s84 and Schedule 10 TA.

There is no requirement of reasonable suspicion (except in private places) that such items will be found, or of authorisation.

These powers are contained in the transitional provisions for Northern Ireland under Part IV TA; therefore they are subject to annual review and may be repealed after five years.[37] But they represent a further clear departure from the notion of normalisation and harmonisation of the special terrorist powers.[38] The government considered but rejected the possibilities of repealing these powers or of retaining them but extending to them the authorisation requirements of the powers applicable in the rest of the UK. They are clearly based on crime control norms with virtually no balancing due process requirements. In particular, they show a departure from the due process ideal – that where, during the criminal justice process, coercion is at its greatest, so the due process requirements should be at their most stringent. The requirement, on pain of committing an offence, to answer questions, *inter alia*, regarding a person's 'movements', is clearly an abrogation of the right to silence and the privilege against self-incrimination under Article 6. The provision creates the anomaly that although the person in question is under detention (since it would be an offence to leave during the questioning) and under interrogation, no due process safeguards at all, including the caution, are applicable. If the same person was interviewed in detention in the police station such safeguards would be applicable, and the right to silence (albeit carrying with it, if exercised, the risk of adverse inference drawing) would also apply. Therefore s89 may undermine and influence the formal interview.

Information-giving and recording requirements

Under s2(1) PACE the procedural safeguards it sets out, together with those under s3, apply to the PACE power and to powers under any other statutory provisions. Statutory powers of search are also subject to the same procedural requirements under Code A as those relating to the powers under s1 PACE, apart – where relevant – from the Code A provisions relating to reasonable suspicion (Code A, para 1.5(b)). The special counter-terrorism powers have been subject to such requirements but in future will be covered by a new TA Code of Practice.[39] An element of due process is introduced into all these statutory stop and search powers by the information-giving and recording requirements under ss2 and 3 PACE

[37] See Chapter 3 p76.
[38] See further Chapter 3.
[39] PACE Code A was applied to the additional PTA powers introduced in 1996. Ss99 and 101 of the TA in respect of Northern Ireland and the new Code introduced under Schedule 14 para 6 in respect of the UK generally will apply the TA Codes to the TA powers. Under Schedule 14 para 5: 'An officer shall perform functions conferred on him by virtue of this Act in accordance with any relevant code of practice in operation under paragraph 6'. Para 6(1) provides: 'The Secretary of State shall issue codes of practice about the exercise by officers of functions conferred on them by virtue of this Act'.

and Code of Practice A, para 1.5(c) made under PACE[40] or, in respect of the TA powers, by the equivalent TA Code provisions. Such requirements give the impression of due process-based control since they mean that the citizen can make a complaint and the police station will have a record of the number of stops being carried out. These procedural requirements are supposed to inject some accountability into stopping and searching, but in so far as they rely on Code A they are effectively unenforceable, while they are entirely irrelevant to 'consensual' stops.

Under s2(3) PACE the constable must give the grounds for the search; under s3 he or she must make a record of the search either on the spot if that is practicable or as soon as it is practicable.[41] The subject of the search can obtain a copy of the search record later on from the police station. A failure to make a written record of the search will not render it unlawful: *Basher* v *DPP*,[42] whereas a failure to give the grounds for it will do so, following *Fennelley*[43] and *Samuel* v *Commissioner of Police for the Metropolis*,[44] as will a failure to comply with the duties to provide identification under s2(3), following *Osman* v *Director of Public Prosecutions*.[45] In *Osman* proper authorisation had been given for the police to search members of the public entering a park under ss60(4) and 60(5) of the Criminal Justice and Public Order Act 1994. When the defendant was searched, police officers failed to comply with s2; the search was resisted and the defendant charged with assaulting an officer in the execution of his duty. It was found on appeal that it was plain from the mandatory words of s2 that any search initiated without prior compliance with the duties set out in s2 would mean that no officer was actually assaulted in the execution of his or her duty since any search of a person might be a trespass requiring proper justification in law; the breach of s2(3) meant that the search was unlawful and therefore not in the execution of the officers' duty. The facts that the officers were clearly local and that numbers could have been obtained from their uniforms were found to be insufficient to avoid the finding of unlawfulness.[46] The strict interpretation of the information-

[40] Under ss2 and 3 PACE and Code A the constable in question must give the suspect certain information before the search begins including 'his name and the name of the police station to which he is attached; the object of the proposed search; the constable's grounds for proposing to make it'. Under s3 the constable must make a record of the search either on the spot if that is practicable or as soon as it is practicable.

[41] Code A para 4 (1999 version) fleshes out these requirements: *inter alia* the record must include the name, address, date of birth and ethnic origin of the person searched (unless he or she is not willing to disclose the name and address).

[42] 2 March 1993 (unreported).

[43] (1989) Crim LR 142.

[44] (1999) 3 March CA (unreported).

[45] *The Times* 29 September 1999 judgment 1 July 1999.

[46] The Crown Court had found that there had been a breach of s2(3)(a) of the 1984 Act, but given the fact that the officers were clearly local police officers policing a local event in broad daylight, as expeditiously as possible, and because numbers could readily be obtained from the officers' uniform, the breach was not so serious as to render the search unlawful. These findings would clearly have undermined s2(3).

giving duties evident in *Fenelley* and *Osnam* was equally apparent in *Lineham* v *DPP*[47] in the context of a search of premises.

Accountability under the HRA

The broad discretion to detain short of arrest, largely untrammelled by due process requirements, conferred on the police under counter-terrorist powers and *de facto* under PACE, has hardly been affected by judicial intervention, while the policy of recent Home Secretaries, including the present one, Jack Straw, has been to keep authorisations of stops firmly in executive hands. As indicated, a number of due process requirements are contained only in Codes[48] and therefore their breach cannot give rise to civil liability[49] although breach of the *statutory* procedural requirements will render searches unlawful, as will breach of the statutory powers. If such a breach occurs the citizen is, in theory, entitled to resist and to sue for assault. But if a search is conducted under one of the provisions which do not require reasonable suspicion, the citizen has no means of knowing that the search is unlawful. A citizen who believed that there could be no grounds for a search and therefore resisted it would be taking a risk. Resistance to an authorised TA or CJPOA search, or a search under s86 TA, would incur criminal liability, not only, in all probability, in respect of obstruction or assault of a constable,[50] but under the special TA or CJPOA search-related offences as well. The PACE and TA Codes are admissible in evidence.[51] However, an unlawful or improperly conducted stop and search is most likely to produce physical evidence, such as drugs or perhaps a weapon. As indicated in Chapter 5, following *Kahn*[52] and *Chalkley*,[53] the courts have been very reluctant to exclude physical evidence which has been obtained improperly or illegally[54] and therefore this

[47] (1999) Judgment of 8 October 1999 unreported. Laws LJ found that police officers who conducted a search under s18 Police and Criminal Evidence Act 1984 had not been acting in the execution of their duty because they had failed to inform the appellant so far as possible as to the reason why they intended to search the premises.

[48] Code A made under s66 PACE and the TA Code made under ss96 and 98 of the TA in respect of Northern Ireland and the new Code introduced under Schedule 14 in respect of the UK. See note 39, above.

[49] Under s67(10) PACE. The TA Codes will have the same status as the PACE Codes; under Sched. 14 para 6(2): 'The failure by an officer to observe a provision of a code shall not of itself make him liable to criminal or civil proceedings' but under sub-para (3): 'A code (a) shall be admissible in evidence in criminal and civil proceedings, and (b) shall be taken into account by a court or tribunal in any case in which it appears to the court or tribunal to be relevant'.

[50] Offences arising under ss89(1) and (2) Police Act 1996.

[51] S67(11) PACE. Schedule 14 para 6(3) TA. See note 49, above.

[52] [1996] 3 All ER 289.

[53] [1998] 2 Cr App R 79. A particularly strong statement disapproving of exclusion of improperly obtained evidence was made by Auld LJ in this case.

[54] See also the pre-PACE ruling of the House of Lords in *Fox* [1986] AC 281; *Thomas* (1990) Crim LR 269 and *Effick* 1992 142 NLJ 492; cf *Edward Fennelly* (1989) Crim LR 142.

method, uncertain as it is, of creating some police accountability has been largely irrelevant. In so far as it has been a possibility, it has not affected 'voluntary' searches because provisions relevant to such searches are contained in Notes for Guidance rather than Code A itself, and the Notes, which are not part of the Codes, are generally treated as having a very doubtful quasi-legal status.[55] There may have been a reluctance to raise breaches of the Notes in court and in any event such breaches are largely 'invisible'. But the status of the Note and Code provisions could be enhanced where they are expressly or impliedly coterminous with the Convention rights.

The lack of court-based accountability in enforcing the due process safeguards, especially in respect of consensual searches, encourages resort to the HRA, and arguments raised under the Act may lead to judicial intervention in this largely unregulated area. Article 6 could be relied upon where it was claimed at trial that a consensual search was in fact non-consensual or where breaches of Code A had occurred during the search, including breaches which might also amount to violations of Article 8.[56] Code A para 3.5 provides safeguards for a search of more than outer clothing which appear to be coterminous with the right to respect for privacy under Article 8. However, Note 3A provides that there is nothing to prevent officers from asking a suspect to remove more than outer clothing in public. This Note is therefore of doubtful compatibility with Article 8 since persons who complied with such a 'request', believing that they had to, would suffer an interference with their Article 8 rights which would not be in accordance with the law. The *Teixiera*[57] argument discussed in Chapter 5, to the effect that certain types of impropriety should lead almost automatically to exclusion of the evidence affected by them,[58] could be employed in an effort to escape from the constraints of *Kahn*[59] and *Chalkley*[60] in respect of evidence obtained in breach of Article 8 or the PACE or Code provisions. Further, where, in the circumstances, the contact during the stop could be said to have tainted the whole investigation, an argument for staying the prosecution or for excluding interviews subsequent to the stop could be raised under Article 6.

Article 6 arguments would also be available where a breach of Article 5 is alleged which might affect the fairness of the trial, and Article 5

[55] The Notes for Guidance are contained in the Codes but are not part of them. This is provided for in the first paragraph of each Code; see, for example, Code C para 1.3. They can sometimes be used as an aid to the interpretation of Code C as a whole: *DPP* v *Rouse* and *DPP* v *Davis* (1992) Cr App R 185.

[56] Regarding, for example, the requirements as to conduct of the search under Code A para 3, including requirements as to removal of only outer clothing in public.

[57] (1999) 28 EHHR 101.

[58] See Chapter 5 at pp200–207.

[59] See Chapter 5 pp202, 203 note 194, 206 and 207, note 210.

[60] [1998] 2 Cr App R 79.

arguments might be raised independently in a variety of contexts.[61] Article 5 provides a guarantee of 'liberty and security of person'. Deprivation of liberty can occur only on a basis of law[62] and in certain specified circumstances, including, under Article 5(1)(b), the detention of a person in order to secure the fulfilment of any obligation prescribed by law and, under Article 5(1)(c), the 'lawful detention of a person effected for the purpose of bringing him before the competent legal authority on reasonable suspicion of having committed an offence'. Both these provisions may cover temporary detention for the purposes of a search. The provision under Article 5(1)(b) raises difficulties of interpretation and is clearly not so straightforward as the form of detention permitted under Article 5(1)(c). On its face, its broad wording appears to allow arbitrary detention with none of the requirements of reasonable suspicion or authorisation which PACE and the TA (apart from the special Northern Ireland provisions) depend upon and without intervention by a court. It might even appear to allow preventive action before violation of a legal obligation. It gives the impression of representing a scheme which affords less weight to due process than the current domestic one.

However, para 5(1)(b) has received a restrictive interpretation at Strasbourg. In *Lawless*[63] it was found that a specific and concrete obligation must be identified; once it has been, detention can in principle be used to secure its fulfilment. The 'obligation' under the current statutory provisions would appear to be to submit to a search or, under s89 TA, to submit to questioning, and, apart from the power under s163 of the Road Traffic Act, to remain under police detention for the period of time necessary to satisfy those obligations.[64] Following this interpretation, the PACE, CJPOA and TA stop and search provisions may be compatible with Article 5(1)(b). However, the Convention rights are intended to provide a more than merely theoretical protection[65] and the requirement of a specific and concrete 'obligation' should be scrutinised carefully. In *McVeigh, O'Neill and Evans*[66] a requirement to submit to an examination on arrival in the UK was found not to violate Article 5(1)(b) since it was sufficiently specific and concrete, but the Commission emphasised that this was found on the basis that the obligation in question only arose in limited circumstances and had a limited purpose – to combat terrorism.

[61] Most frequently in the context of a civil action for false imprisonment or assault, or at trial in respect of failing to stop, either under one of the specific offences under the relevant statute or under s89(1) or (2) of the Police Act 1996.

[62] See discussion of this provision below at pp243–4.

[63] Report of 19 December 1959, B.1 (1960–61) p64; judgment of 1 July 1961, A.3 (1960–1961); (1961) 1 EHRR 15.

[64] See *McVeigh, O'Neill and Evans* (1983) 5 EHRR 71; the obligation imposed was a requirement to 'submit to examination'. In *Reyntjens* v *France* No 16810/90 unreported (1992) the obligation was to submit to an identity check.

[65] *Airey* v *Ireland* (1979) 2 EHRR 305, 314.

[66] (1983) 5 EHRR 71.

The PACE powers, the Misuse of Drugs Act 1971 power and, arguably, the power arising under s43 TA, which is a permanent power, not one adopted temporarily to meet an emergency as in *McVeigh*, could not readily be said to arise in limited circumstances. The CJPOA, and other TA powers, have more limited purposes in the sense that the place in which they can be exercised is circumscribed either by its nature (as in port or border controls) or by the authorisation given, which is based on the need for special powers. Whether any particular authorisation would be viewed as rendering the obligation in question sufficiently specific will be open to question, depending on the factual situation.

The PACE powers, the powers under the 1971 Act and under s43 TA are therefore fairly clearly of doubtful compatibility with Article 5(1)(b), while the compatibility of the other powers is uncertain. They may fall within Article 5(1)(c) which requires reasonable suspicion of the commission of an *offence.* This immediately calls into question s43 TA since no such suspicion is required. It also means that the exercise of the powers under PACE may, depending on the circumstances of a search, be of doubtful compatibility. S1 requires suspicion as to carriage of an article, not as to an offence; it is clearly aimed at gathering evidence of offences and its requirements are not fully coterminous with the relevant range of offences. Carrying certain of the articles which fall within s1 PACE is not an offence[67] even if the carrier can be said to 'possess' them, although the officer also requires suspicion as to *mens rea*, while carriage of prohibited articles without sufficient 'possession' will clearly not constitute an offence. Code A para 1.7A provides that where a police officer has reasonable grounds to suspect that a person is in innocent possession of a stolen or prohibited article, or other item for which he or she is empowered to search, the power of stop and search exists despite the absence of a power of arrest. That Code provision is clearly incompatible with Article 5(1)(c) and any stop undertaken in conformity with it would appear to be unlawful, unless in the circumstances it could be justified under Article 5(1)(b). It should also be noted that Article 5(1)(c) requires that the detention should be for 'the purpose of bringing him before the competent legal authority'. It may be said that the powers under s43 TA, the 1971 Act and PACE are exercised in order to determine whether sufficient evidence justifying an arrest is present or for general information-gathering purposes, and are therefore only indirectly aimed at the purpose Article 5 envisages. The exercise of the powers under s60 CJPOA, ss44 and 89 TA may also be of doubtful compatibility with Article 5(1)(c). The Strasbourg Court indicated in *Murray* v *UK*[68] that the essential matter is the identification of objective grounds for suspicion in the particular instance, even where the domestic legislation allows for detention on subjective grounds.

[67] Under s1(7)(b) such articles could include credit cards or keys.
[68] (1994) 19 EHRR 193.

In order for stops under these provisions to comply with that finding, police officers would have to satisfy a requirement which is not present in the domestic legislation.

The power under s163 of the Road Traffic Act appears to fall outside both Articles 5(1)(b) and (c) since it does not depend on reasonable suspicion of an offence and is not exercised in respect of a specific obligation, as explained in *McVeigh*. This is a matter of interpretation since the obligation might be viewed as confined to one inherent in the use of a vehicle on the roads. But if the obligation it depends upon is not sufficiently specific, its use can be justified only if it does not amount to a deprivation of liberty. The power probably carries with it, impliedly, the power to detain for a short period.[69] The offence under the RTA of failing to stop would probably be committed if the response to the stop was to brake and pause for an instant before driving on. The person stopped may also be given the impression that he or she is obliged to remain during questioning. Therefore, it is suggested that Article 5 may be engaged by the use of this power, in which case incompatibility almost certainly arises.

Article 5 also imposes further, general requirements. The detention must not be arbitrary; this is implicit in the requirement of lawfulness.[70] A detention with the real purpose of searching for drugs, which had been authorised under s44 TA in respect of terrorism, might be viewed as arbitrary in the sense that it was not proportionate to the purpose of ensuring the fulfilment of an obligation prescribed by the relevant law[71] – the TA. If such an argument was advanced at Strasbourg, involving, as it does, review of the proportionality of decisions taken by the state authorities, a certain margin of appreciation would be afforded to those authorities in respect of their assessment of the relevant circumstances.[72] But in the domestic courts, under the HRA, this approach would be inappropriate. Applying the notion of a discretionary area of judgement[73] would also arguably be inappropriate since a search under terrorism legislation, but for a non-terrorist purpose, does not call for deference.

In appropriate cases, bearing in mind the recent evidence noted above of a police tendency to show racial bias in decisions to stop and search,[74] violation of Article 5(1)(b) or (c) might be found when read with the Article 14 guarantee of freedom from discrimination in the enjoyment of the Convention rights. This possibility may be of less significance given the amendments made to the Race Relations Act 1976 in 2000, allowing claimants to bring actions against the police in respect of direct or indirect

[69] This may be suggested by the findings in *Lodwick* v *Sanders* [1985] 1 WLR 382.
[70] *Winterwerp* v *Netherlands* A 33 para 39 (1979).
[71] Ibid; *Bouamar* v *Belgium* A 129 para 50 (1988).
[72] Ibid para 40.
[73] See Chapter 2 p36.
[74] See note 36, above.

discrimination in policing decisions, including decisions to stop and search. However, a defendant would also have the option of raising an Article 5 and 14 argument during the criminal process. It could be argued, for example, under Article 6(1) that if Article 14, read with Article 5, had been breached owing to a discriminatory search (one which would otherwise be lawful as in conformity with, for example, s60 of the 1994 Act or s44 TA) any products of the search should be excluded from evidence under s78 PACE, and in so far as the contact had influenced the subsequent investigation, evidence deriving from it should also be excluded. Such an argument would of course require recognition to be given to possible racial stereotyping behind stop and search decisions as opposed to imposing neutral explanations on them.[75]

The use of force in order to carry out a stop and search is permitted under s117 PACE which provides: 'the officer may use reasonable force, if necessary, in the exercise of the [PACE] power'. The TA provides an equivalent provision in s114(2). But, under Article 3, the use of force must be strictly in proportion to the conduct of the detainee; this is discussed further in respect of forcible arrest.[76] Under these provisions the use of extreme force is permissible if necessitated by the conduct of the detainee, but if the use of such force causes death it would appear to breach Article 2 which permits the use of lethal force to 'effect an arrest', not to effect a detention short of arrest. However, if the detainee sought to escape *after* being detained for the purposes of a stop and search, this might fall within the second limb of Article 2(2)(b): 'to prevent the escape of a person lawfully detained'. The lawfulness of the initial detention would then have to be considered, bearing in mind the arguments above.

Arrest and detention

The due process and crime control views of arrest and detention are diametrically opposed. Under the due process model arrest should be based on strong suspicion that the individual has committed a specific offence, since arrest and subsequent detention represent a severe infringement of individual rights. Under the crime control model arrest and detention need not be sanctioned merely in relation to specific offences, but should be both an investigative tool and a means of asserting police authority over persons with a criminal record or doubtful characters, with a view to

[75] In the US context A C Thompson argues that the tendency of the judiciary is to impose such explanations (based on the notion of police expertise in spotting criminal possibilities in neutral behaviour) on stop and 'frisk' decisions and to ignore, if possible, any racial element. 'Race and the Fourth Amendment' (1999) 74(4) New York Univ. LR 956.

[76] At p253.

creating a general deterrent effect. Under this model reasonable suspicion is viewed as a needless irrelevancy, an inhibitory rule standing in the way of an important police function.

Taking this analysis into account, it may be said that powers of arrest and detention have followed a similar pattern to those covering detentions short of arrest, in the sense that police discretion as to their use has increased in a number of respects. Broad statutory arrest and detention powers introduced for the first time during the Thatcher years created a very significant extension of police powers, but they included the due process requirement of reasonable suspicion of a particular offence. If the PACE arrest power is compared with the main power arising under the TA, which, due to s1, is applicable to a new and wide range of suspects,[77] and does not include such a requirement, it can be said that movement from a due process towards a crime control model has occurred.

The body of research into the use of arrest and detention powers is to an extent conflicting, one school of analysis suggesting that the procedural due process elements which were supposed to create restraints on the powers largely fail to do so in practice in a number of respects.[78] A partially opposed view agrees as to 'the limited effectiveness of PACE's control mechanisms, including routinisation of supervisory controls', but suggests that 'the potential exists for [the PACE reforms] to be given more (or less) substance'.[79] It will be argued below that such potential may be realised under the impact of the HRA, but that its influence will be variable, especially as between the conventional and counter-terrorist schemes. While the conventional scheme shows a formal adherence to due process, which appears to have a subtle impact in practice, especially as regards controls on detention, the counter-terrorist scheme adheres, formally, to a lower standard, thereby providing greater leeway for departure from due process without necessarily breaching the rules.

Powers of arrest and procedural safeguards

The Police and Criminal Evidence Act 1984 introduced two separate powers of arrest without warrant, arising under ss24 and 25. In very broad terms s24 provides a power of arrest in respect of more serious offences, including those carrying a penalty of at least five years' imprisonment.[80]

[77] See further Chapter 3 pp78–79.

[78] See Sanders and Young (1994) Chap 3; McConville Sanders and Leng *The Case for the Prosecution* (1991) London: Routledge esp p189.

[79] D Dixon in *Miscarriages of Justice* (1999) C Walker and K Starmer (eds) p67.

[80] S24 applies: '(a) to offences for which the sentence is fixed by law; (b) to offences for which a person of 21 years of age or over (not previously convicted) may be sentenced to imprisonment for a term of five years (or might be so sentenced but for the restrictions imposed by section 33 of the Magistrates' Courts Act 1980); and (c) to the offences to which subsection (2) applies, and in this Act "arrestable offence" means any such offence'.

S24 therefore overlaps with the counter-terrorist arrest powers since a large number of the terrorist offences carry such a penalty and are therefore arrestable offences. There was also a power of arrest under s14(1)(a) of the PTA which empowered a constable to arrest for certain specified offences under the PTA. That power is reproduced in ss41 and 40(1)(a) TA which cover arrest in respect of certain TA offences.[81] S25 of PACE covers *all* offences, however trivial (including, for example, dropping litter), if certain conditions are satisfied and there is reasonable suspicion that the offence in question has been, is being or is about to be committed.[82]

Part II of the EPA contained powers of arrest which were supplementary to those in s14 of the PTA. They were applicable only in Northern Ireland and went further than those existing in the rest of the UK. Under s18 EPA a constable could arrest without warrant anyone whom he or she had reasonable grounds for suspecting of committing, having committed, or being about to commit a scheduled offence or an offence under the EPA which was not a scheduled offence. Under s19 EPA a member of the armed forces on duty could arrest and detain a person for up to four hours on suspicion that he or she had committed, was committing or was about to commit any offence. The soldier was not required to inform the arrested person of the grounds of the arrest; and to effect the arrest he or she could enter and search any premises without a warrant. These powers are reproduced in ss82 and 83 TA respectively. They continue to apply only in Northern Ireland, but are based on the much wider definition of terrorism introduced under the TA. The continued absence of the need to give the grounds for arrest clearly raises the possibility that incompatibility with Article 5 will be found; this is discussed below.

Ss24 and 25 PACE and the power under ss41 and 40(1)(a) TA depend on the concept of 'reasonable suspicion' as the main due process element in arrest. The idea behind it appeared to be, according to the Phillips

[81] The arrest under s41 is in respect of reasonable suspicion of being a terrorist; under s40(1)(a): 'In this Part "terrorist" means a person who has committed an offence under any of sections 11, 12, 15 to 18, 54, 56 to 63'. This definition is not exclusive; its other part, dependent upon s40(1)(b), which is discussed below, covers the former s14(1)(b) PTA arrest power.

[82] The general arrest conditions are: '(a) that the name of the relevant person is unknown to, and cannot be readily ascertained by, the constable; (b) that the constable has reasonable grounds for doubting whether a name furnished by the relevant person as his name is his real name; (c) that (i) the relevant person has failed to furnish a satisfactory address for service; or (ii) the constable has reasonable grounds for doubting whether an address furnished by the relevant person is a satisfactory address for service; (d) that the constable has reasonable grounds for believing that arrest is necessary to prevent the relevant person (i) causing physical injury to himself or any other person; (ii) suffering physical injury; (iii) causing loss of or damage to property; (iv) committing an offence against public decency; or (v) causing an unlawful obstruction of the highway; (e) that the constable has reasonable grounds for believing that arrest is necessary to protect a child or other vulnerable person from the relevant person'. The requirement for the officer to have reasonable suspicion relating to the offence in question *and* to the general arrest conditions was emphasised in *Edwards* v *DPP* (1993) 97 Cr App R 301; 1993 *The Times* 29 March.

Royal Commission,[83] that an arrest should take place at a reasonably late stage in the investigation; this would limit the number of arrests and make it less likely that a person could be wrongfully arrested. PACE may endorse a fairly high level of suspicion due to the distinction it maintains between belief and suspicion, belief probably being the lower standard. Also, in principle, the concept should be interpreted in accordance with the provisions as to reasonable suspicion under Code A, although the courts have not relied on Code A in ruling on the lawfulness of arrests. Annex B para 4 of original Code A stated that the level of suspicion for a stop would be 'no less' than that needed for arrest. Although this provision was omitted from Code A in the 1991 revision, it would seem that in principle the Code A provision should be viewed as relevant to arrests if the Codes and statute are to be treated as a harmonious whole. The objective nature of suspicion required under Code A is echoed in earlier decisions on the suspicion needed for an arrest.[84] In *Dallison* v *Caffrey*[85] Lord Diplock said that the test was whether 'a reasonable man assumed to know the law and possessed of the information which in fact was possessed by the defendant would believe there were [reasonable grounds]'. The notion of 'reasonable grounds', even without the Code A guidance, makes it clear that certain matters, such as an individual's racial group, could *never* be factors which could support a finding of reasonable suspicion.

However, research into the use of arrest suggests that in practice the concept of reasonable suspicion is interpreted very flexibly by the police, as it is in respect of stop and search powers. Sanders and Young speak of appearing 'suspicious' as 'a key working rule' in arrests and stops, and observe that association with other criminals is also often the basis for arrest even where the police are 'entirely without reasonable suspicion' since the object is to obtain statements against associates.[86] The courts appear to be reluctant to interfere with the police interpretation and use of the arrest power. Post-PACE decisions leave a great deal of leeway to officers to arrest where suspicion relating to the particular person is at a low level, but they want to further the investigation by gathering information.[87] These powers, especially the very broad power under s25, mean that, as a number of commentators have pointed out, arrest became under PACE avowedly no longer the culmination of the investigative process but an integral part of it.[88] The strong evidence founding the charge

[83] See RCCP Report Cmnd 8092 (1981).

[84] For example, *Dumbell* v *Roberts* [1944] 1 All ER 326; *Holgate-Mohammed* [1984] AC 437; *Nakkuda Ali* v *Jayaratne* [1951] AC 66 at p77; *Allen* v *Wright* [1835] 8 C&P 522.

[85] [1965] 1 QB 348 at p371.

[86] Sanders and Young *Criminal Justice* (1994) p92, based on research undertaken by R Leng (Royal Commission on Criminal Justice Research Study No 10) (1993) HMSO.

[87] See *Ward* v *Chief Constable of Somerset and Avon Constabulary* (1986) *The Times* 26 June; *Castorina* v *Chief Constable of Surrey* (1988) NLJ 180 Transcript from LEXIS.

[88] Sanders and Young (1994) p70; Ewing and Gearty *Freedom under Thatcher* (1989) at p24.

which used to be obtained, it has been suggested,[89] prior to arrest, thus ensuring that innocent persons were unlikely to be arrested and that the infringement of liberty of a person innocent in the eyes of the law was kept to a minimum, tended after PACE to be found in the form of a confession, after arrest. PACE also confirmed the movement away from judicial supervision of arrest, by means of the warrant procedure, which had already begun.

Judicial reluctance to interfere with street policing decisions is only one factor operating in favour of a very wide police discretion. Imprecision in the substantive law, particularly public order law, discussed in Chapter 4, also enhances and widens police discretion. There has also been a tendency evident particularly in the 1986 and 1994 Public Order Acts to conflate substantive offences with police powers.[90] Such a tendency is also readily evident in the Terrorism Act 2000. For example, the offence under s13 depends on showing reasonable suspicion that a person is a member or supporter of a proscribed organisation. Schedule 5 para 16 creates an offence of failing to provide police with an explanation regarding items seized.[91] Since a conviction may be obtained in these instances on the basis of evidence justifying arrest and since no independent evidence is necessary, the police will, in effect, take control not only over the arrest and detention, but over the obtaining of a conviction, thereby curtailing judicial supervision.[92]

Clearly, police discretion is wider still where no reasonable suspicion of any particular offence is necessary in order to arrest. Such a power is provided by s41 TA read with s40(1)(b) which largely reproduces s14(1)(b) PTA. The continuation of this power is controversial since it was adopted in the face of an emergency situation which is no longer in being and the arrest power will in future be applicable to a far wider range of groups under s1 TA. Under s14(1)(b) a constable had to have reasonable grounds for suspecting that a person was concerned in the preparation or instigation of acts of terrorism connected with the affairs of Northern Ireland or 'any other act of terrorism except those connected solely with the affairs of the UK or a part of the UK' in order to arrest. Under s41 TA and s40(1)(b) the qualifying words are omitted. S41 allows for arrest on suspicion of being a terrorist and s40(1)(b) defines a terrorist as 'a person who is or has been concerned in the preparation or instigation of acts of terrorism'. In other words, the arrest power can now be applied to non-Irish UK domestic groups, such as environmental activists. In practice, since s14(1)(b) did not require suspicion relating to an offence, it was used for investigation, questioning and general intelligence gathering which may be conducted, it has been said, for the

89 Ewing and Gearty ibid at p25.
90 See Chapter 4 at p115.
91 See Chapter 7 p269.
92 See Sanders and Young (1994) p87.

purpose of 'isolating and identifying the urban guerrillas and then detaching them from the supportive or ambivalent community'.[93]

The government, in its *Consultation Paper on Terrorism*,[94] acknowledged the criticisms which s14(1)(b) had attracted: 'if the police have proper cause to suspect that a person is actively engaged in terrorism, they must have sufficient information to justify an arrest under PACE . . . the absence of any requirement for reasonable suspicion of a specific offence effectively allows the police free rein to arrest whomsoever they wish without necessarily having good reason, including those who should not be arrested at all'.[95] However, the government took the view that although the ordinary powers of arrest are extensive, they are insufficient to deal with the sophisticated evasion techniques of terrorists.[96] This claim might have been applicable to the well-organised Irish groups which caused extensive and severe harm during 'the Troubles'. But in respect of the vast range of groups potentially covered by the new legislation, it is more doubtful, especially bearing in mind the wide range of TA offences, many based, as indicated in Chapter 3, on a minimal *actus reus* and requiring no proof of *mens rea*. The ordinary arrest powers under PACE or under the first power of s41 TA, read with s40(1)(a), would almost certainly cover arrests which could be undertaken under the second power covered by ss41 and 40(1)(b). This second power is clearly aimed at allowing arrest as a stage in the investigation, not as the culmination of it, and it may therefore be said to be firmly based on the crime control model which views the purpose of arrest as a means of furthering general investigative goals. It therefore represents a clear departure from the traditional due process view of arrest taken by Phillips in 1981 as justified only after the investigation has uncovered sufficient evidence. The power was severely criticised when used in the context of Irish terrorism; it is likely to attract further criticism when transplanted into a completely different context and afforded a far wider application.

Owing to its departure from due process principle in failing to require arrest for a particular offence, the reproduction of s14(1)(b) PTA in ss41 and 40(1)(b) TA renders the new power vulnerable to a challenge under Article 5 of the Convention, which in para 5(1)(c) encapsulates that principle. This possibility was recognised by Lord Lloyd, whose 1996 Report, prepared for Michael Howard, the then Conservative Home Secretary, underlies the new counter-terrorism Act.[97] He suggested that, in order to circumvent Article 5, a new offence of being concerned in the commission,

[93] D R Lowry (1976–77) 8–9 *Col Human Rights LR* 185, 210.
[94] *Legislation Against Terrorism: A Consultation Paper* (1998) Cm 4178.
[95] Ibid para 7.5.
[96] Since they are 'skilled in, and dedicated to, evading detection . . . terrorist crime is often quite different [from serious non-terrorist crime] both in terms of the sophistication of the techniques deployed and the (potential) harm caused'. Ibid para 7.8.
[97] Cm 3420.

preparation or instigation of acts of terrorism should be created. Having considered this suggestion, the government rejected it, coming to the view, which is evaluated below, that this arrest power is compatible with Article 5(1)(c).[98]

If an arrest has occurred a number of consequences follow, including an inherent loss of liberty and the right of the officer to use force in effecting it under s117 PACE or s114 TA, if necessary. If an arrest has not occurred the citizen is free to go wherever he or she will and any attempt to prevent him or her doing so will be unlawful.[99] It is therefore important to convey the fact of the arrest to the arrestee and to mark the point at which the arrest comes into being and general liberty ceases. Under s28 PACE both the fact of and the reason for the arrest must be made known at the time or as soon as practicable afterwards. Conveying the fact of the arrest does not involve using a particular form of words[100] and it is unfortunate that s28 did not make it clear that a reasonable degree of detail should be given. If such detail is given the arrestee will be in a position to give a convincing denial and therefore to be more speedily released from detention. It is consistent with the values encapsulated in Article 5 to seek to ensure that any infringement of liberty should be kept to a minimum consistent with the needs of the investigation. Interpretations of s28 which recognise those values may be viewed as holding the balance between due process and crime control.[101] A certain lack of rigour as to due process is also created by the provision as to practicability. In *D.P.P.* v *Hawkins*[102] the Court of Appeal found that an arrest becomes unlawful when the time comes at which it is practicable to inform the defendant of the reason but the defendent is not so informed. However, it will not become retrospectively unlawful and therefore will not affect acts done before its unlawfulness came into being, which will therefore remain acts done in the execution of duty. Some departure may therefore be said to have occurred from the principle that there should be a clear demarcation between the point at which the citizen is at liberty and the point at which his or her liberty is restrained.

[98] Ibid para 7.14. A further aspect of s40 may raise issues under Article 5. Between the First and Second Readings of the Bill s40 was subtly changed to include reference to persons concerned in terrorism 'whether before or after the passing of this Act'. Since the definition of terrorism in s1 is much wider than that previously used in s20 PTA, s40 allows arrest of a person for activity which would not have justified arrest (either under s14(1)(b) PTA or at all) at the time when it was undertaken. The coverage of pre-commencement activity is confirmed in s40(2).

[99] *Rice* v *Connolly* (1966) 2 QB 414; *Kenlin* v *Gardner* (1967) 2 QB 510.

[100] The Court of Appeal confirmed this in *Brosch* (1988) Crim LR 743. In *Abassey and Others* v *Newman and Others* (1989) *The Times* 18 August, it was found that there was no need for precise or technical language in conveying the reason for the arrest; the question whether the reason had been given was a matter for the jury. See also *Nicholas* v *Parsonage* (1987) RTR 199.

[101] See on this issue K W Lidstone (1978) Crim LR 332; D Clark and D Feldman (1979) Crim LR 702; M Zander (1977) NLJ 352; J C Smith (1977) Crim LR 293.

[102] DC [1988] 1 WLR 1166, 3 All ER 673; see also *R* v *Brosch* (1988) Crim LR 743 CA.

Detention in police custody

PACE formally acknowledged for the first time, in accordance with the Phillips recommendations,[103] that the purpose of the detention is to obtain a confession.[104] This was foreshadowed in the developing common law recognition that detention was for the purpose of questioning.[105] Phillips did not, however, envisage the decision to arrest becoming, in effect, the decision to detain. This is reflected in the role of the custody officer under s37 PACE. In theory he or she could refuse to accept the arrestee into detention. In practice this is extremely rare, if not unknown; the custody officer almost always simply rubber-stamps the arresting officer's decision that the suspect should be detained.[106] Thus, although s37(3) appears to protect due process since it provides that the custody officer must be satisfied that there are reasonable grounds for the detention,[107] in practice it does not appear to affect police working practices. Similarly, the requirement under s29 that volunteers at police stations – those who are not under arrest – should be able to leave at will unless placed under arrest, does not appear to have much impact on police practice since many people may not realise that they can leave. S29 is backed up by para 3.15 of Code C, which requires that if a volunteer is cautioned she must then be told that she may leave at will. However, this provision is less protective than it appears to be at first sight. A person need only be cautioned if there are grounds to suspect that person of an offence. But if there are such grounds the person could probably be arrested, depending on the nature of the offence. Thus, para 3.15 would only come into play at the point when arrest could occur. It would only protect due process (assuming that it was adhered to) if it demanded cautioning on arrival of a volunteer at a police station.

Under s41 PACE the detention can be for up to 24 hours, but in the case of a person in police custody for a serious arrestable offence (defined in s116) it can extend to 96 hours. Under s42(1) a police officer of the rank of superintendent or above can sanction detention initially up to 36 hours if three conditions apply: the officer has reasonable grounds for believing that either the detention is necessary to secure or preserve evidence relating to an offence for which the detainee is under arrest or to obtain such evidence by questioning him or her; an offence for which the detainee is under arrest is a serious arrestable offence; and the investigation is being conducted diligently and expeditiously. After 36 hours detention can no longer be authorised by the police alone. Under s43(1)

[103] See RCCP Report Cmnd 8092 (1981).

[104] Part IV s37(2).

[105] *Mohammed-Holgate* v *Duke* [1984] QB 209.

[106] See D Dixon *et al* 'Safeguarding the Rights of Suspects in Police Custody' 1 Policing and Society 115 at p130.

[107] Under s37(2) they are: 'To secure or preserve evidence relating to an offence for which he is under arrest or to obtain such evidence by questioning him'.

an application for an authorisation of further detention must be supported by information and brought before a magistrates court which can authorise detention under s44 for up to 96 hours if the conditions are met as set out above. Detention must be reviewed periodically, at 12 hourly intervals,[108] and the detainee *or* his or her solicitor (if available) has the right to make written or oral representations.[109] Research suggests, however, that these reviews are not treated as genuine investigations into the grounds for continuing the detention, but as routinised procedures requiring a merely formal adherence.[110] Perhaps in recognition of the need for rigour in relation to reviews, a proposal made in 1999 by the Chief Constable of Kent Police that detention review should be by video link in the majority of cases, was rejected in judicial review proceedings on the ground that it might undermine the protection for liberty they are intended to offer, taking Article 5 into account.[111]

The detention scheme adopted in respect of terrorist suspects allowed for the suspect to be detained for longer periods and for a lower level of due process safeguards to be applicable during detention.[112] If a person was arrested under s14 PTA as opposed to s24 PACE, whether the arrest was for an offence or on suspicion of being a terrorist, the detention provisions under PACE did not apply. The arrestee could be detained for up to 48 hours following arrest (s14(4) PTA), but this period could be extended by the Secretary of State by further periods not exceeding five days in all (s14(5) PTA). Thus the whole detention could be for seven days and, in contrast to the PACE provisions, the courts were not involved in the authorising process; it occurred at a low level of visibility as an administrative decision. The similar provision under the PTA 1984 was found to be in breach of Article 5(3) in *Brogan* v *UK*[113] on the ground that holding a person for longer than four days without judicial authorisation was a violation of the requirement that persons should be brought promptly before a judicial officer. The *Brogan* decision clearly presented the government with a difficulty in formulating the Terrorism Act 2000. Although the HRA continues the derogation entered in *Brogan*, under s14(1)(a), it was vulnerable to challenge at Strasbourg at some future point, in the light of the new settlement in Northern Ireland. The government put forward various justifications for producing new terrorist legislation in 2000, but it recognised that it might be in difficulties in

[108] Sched 8 para 21(3). The provisions for review are mandatory provisions; apart from para 22, there is no leeway to depart from them: *Roberts* v *Chief Constable of Cheshire Police* [1999] 1 WLR 662.

[109] Sched 8 para 26(1) and (2).

[110] D Dixon *et al* 'Safeguarding the Rights of Suspects in Police Custody' (1990) 1 Policing and Society 130–1.

[111] *Regina* v *Chief Constable of Kent Constabulary, Ex parte Kent Police Federation Joint Branch Board and Another The Times* 1 December 1999, judgment 18 November 1999. See further on this decision below, at pp244.

[112] See below pp274–5 for discussion of such safeguards.

[113] (1989) 11 EHRR 117.

arguing that a state of emergency sufficient to support the derogation could be said to exist post-2000.[114] Its solution, in the TA, was to make provision for judicial authorisation of detention, rather than to decrease the length of time during which terrorist suspects could be detained, harmonising it with the PACE period. In deciding on these arrangements, including the retention of the possibility of up to seven days' detention, the government rejected the suggestion of Lord Lloyd that once there is a lasting peace in Northern Ireland, it ought to be possible to reduce the maximum period for which a suspect could be detained under the new legislation to a total of four days – two days on the authority of the police and two days with judicial authorisation.

The maximum period of detention, applicable to a person arrested under s41 TA, continues to be seven days, but para 29 Schedule 8 provides that it must be under a warrant issued by a 'judicial authority'.[115] Under para 32 the warrant may be issued if there are reasonable grounds for believing that 'the detention of the person to whom the application relates is necessary to obtain relevant evidence whether by questioning him or otherwise or to preserve relevant evidence'. The detainee or his or her solicitor has the right to make written or oral representations under para 33(1). Thus, authorisation may not be merely 'on the papers'. Such a possibility might not have satisfied the aim of achieving compliance with Article 5(3), despite the involvement of a judicial figure.

The police can detain a person on their own authority for 48 hours under s41(3) which provides: '*Subject to* subsections (4) to (7), a person detained under this section shall (unless detained under any other power) be released not later than the end of the period of 48 hours beginning (a) with the time of his arrest under this section, or (b) if he was being detained under Schedule 7 when he was arrested under this section, with the time when his examination under that Schedule began' (emphasis added). These provisions differ quite significantly from those under the PTA. S14(4) PTA provided that the 48-hour period is subject *only* to subsection 5 which allowed for extension of detention by the Secretary of State. Ss41(4)–(7) TA provide three possibilities of continuing the detention beyond 48 hours, over and above the possibility of extension under judicial authorisation. These possibilities represent, depending on the interpretation they are afforded, quite notable departures from the previous scheme. S41(6) provides that if an application for an extension of detention is made, or under s41(5), it is intended that it will be made, detention can continue while it is pending. This impliedly means that

[114] See ibid para 8.2.

[115] Para 29(4) provides: 'In this Part "judicial authority" means (a) in England and Wales, the Senior District Judge (Chief Magistrate) or his deputy, or a District Judge (Magistrates' Courts) who is designated for the purpose of this Part by the Lord Chancellor, (b) in Scotland, the sheriff, and (c) in Northern Ireland, a county court judge, or a resident magistrate who is designated for the purpose of this Part by the Lord Chancellor'.

the police can continue to detain for more than 48 hours so long as an application is being made or is about to be made, even if it is subsequently refused. The application need not be made during the 48 hours; under Schedule 8 Part III para 30 it may be made within six hours of the end of that period.

The 48-hour period is also subject to s41(4) which provides: 'If on a review of a person's detention under Part II of Schedule 8 the review officer does not authorise continued detention, the person shall (unless detained in accordance with sub-sections (5) or (6) under any other power) be released'. The reviews have to occur every 12 hours. This appears to mean that the review officer (this must be an officer of at least the rank of superintendent after the first 12 hours) can continue the detention periodically, at 12-hour intervals, so long as the review conditions (which are the same as the warrant conditions) continue to apply. No express time limit is placed on the total period which the review officer can authorise. On their face the provisions suggest that there is a twin-track system of detention, one dependent on the judicial authority and one on the police themselves. Clearly s41(4) should be interpreted strictly to mean that *within* the 48-hour period there must be periodic reviews (subject to the provisions for delaying reviews); the possibility of providing the police with a new power to extend detention beyond 48 hours under s41(4) should be rejected since it seems to be due to ambiguous drafting. The words 'subject to' the decision of the review officer to continue detention could be interpreted either way. The stricter interpretation appears to accord with the government's intention as expressed in the Consultation Paper.[116] If in practice s41(4) was interpreted to allow some detentions on the authority of the review officer only, beyond 48 hours, such detentions would obviously be more likely than those under the previous provisions to create breaches of Article 5(3).

As part of the port and border controls regime, Schedule 5 of the PTA provided a further power of detention in allowing a person to be detained for 12 hours before examination at ports of entry into Britain or Northern Ireland. The period could be extended to 24 hours if the person was suspected of involvement in the commission, preparation or instigation of acts of terrorism. These provisions are partially reproduced in Schedule 7 TA; they are modified to take account of the abolition of the exclusion power.[117]

The PACE and TA detention schemes differ radically in due process terms, despite the fact that many of those who will be potentially subject to the new TA scheme are likely to represent a far more divergent group than the previous one which fell within the rubric of 'terrorist'. Even within that previous group, as a number of the most famous miscarriage of justice

[116] *Legislation Against Terrorism* (1998) Cm 4178.
[117] See Chapter 3 p81.

cases imply, those who were designated terrorist suspects, such as Judith Ward,[118] were often remarkably ill-suited to the draconian terrorist regime to which they were subject. The peace process presented an opportunity for the harmonisation of the PACE and counter-terrorist regimes that might have avoided the potential for future miscarriages which, it is suggested, is inherent in the TA scheme, bearing in mind the special propensity evidenced in the cases of the *Birmingham Six*,[119] *Guildford Four*,[120] *Maguire Seven*,[121] *Ward*[122] and *UDR Four*[123] of terrorist cases to miscarry.

Accountability under the HRA

As discussed above, Article 5(1) of the Convention provides a right to liberty subject to certain exceptions which must have a basis in law. Not only must an exception apply, the requirements under Articles 5(2), (3) and (4) must also be met. The current domestic arrest and detention scheme for non-terrorist suspects is, as one would expect, largely coterminous, formally speaking, with these provisions, and in some respects may afford a higher – or, at least, clearer – value to due process. But the use of Article 5 as an interpretative tool may lead to a rigorous judicial approach to the detention scheme. Breaches of Article 5 may be most likely to be established in respect of the special counter-terrorist arrest and detention powers available under the TA. Article 5 arguments could be raised within the trial process, by means of a civil action or under the police complaints provisions. Judicial review, on Article 5 principles, of decisions within the police complaints process, or in respect of judicial authorisations within the PACE or TA schemes, or of proposals relating to detention practice would also be available.

The first and most essential requirement of Article 5 is that a person's detention is in accordance with a procedure prescribed by law. This connotes the requirements that the procedure is in accordance with national law and with recognised Convention standards, including Convention principles and is not arbitrary.[124] Thus, where one of the Article 5(1) exceptions applies to a person's detention, this requirement will also have to be satisfied. The procedure covers the arrest provisions[125] and the procedure adopted by a court in authorisations of detention.[126] The requirement that the detention should be in accordance with the law was

[118] *R* v *Ward* [1992] 96 Cr App R 1.
[119] See *R* v *McIlkenny and Others* [1992] 2 All ER 417.
[120] See Sir John May *Report of the Inquiry into the circumstances surrounding the convictions arising out of the bomb attacks at Guildford and Woolwich in 1974, Final Report* (1993–94 HC 449) Chap 17.
[121] See *R* v *Maguire* [1992] 2 All ER 433.
[122] *R* v *Ward* [1992] 96 Cr App R 1.
[123] See [1988] 11 NIJB 1.
[124] *Winterwerp* v *Netherlands* A 33 para 39 (1979).
[125] *Fox, Campbell and Hartley* v *UK* (1990) A 182; 13 EHRR 157.
[126] *Weston* v *UK* 3 EHRR 402; *Van der Leer* v *Netherlands* A 170-A (1990).

given a robust interpretation based on due process norms in one of the first domestic decisions in the pre-HRA period to place a heavy reliance on Article 5. In *R* v *Chief Constable of Kent Constabulary, Ex parte Kent Police Federation Joint Branch Board and Another*[127] the court had to consider an application by Kent Police Federation Joint Branch Board, representing all ranks of the Kent Constabulary, for judicial review of the proposal by the Chief Constable of Kent that the conduct of reviews of police detention under s40(1)(b) of the 1984 Act should be, in the majority of cases, by video link. Lord Bingham referred to Article 5 and said that, although not yet part of domestic law, it embodied important and basic rights recognised and protected by English law. If citizens were to be deprived of their liberty such deprivation had to be in accordance with the law. He found that the court was dealing with an area of extreme sensitivity, namely the circumstances in which, and the conditions on which, a citizen not convicted or even charged with crime might be deprived of his or her liberty. The Act and the Codes giving it effect represented, he said, a complex and careful balance between the obviously important duty of the police to investigate crime and apprehend criminals on the one hand and the rights of the private citizen on the other. Under s37(5) a written record of the grounds of detention had to be made by the review officer 'in the presence of the person whose detention is under review'. He found that that condition was not met if the review officer was in one place and the person whose detention was under review was in another. S37(5) did not refer to physical presence, but 'presence' in ordinary parlance meant physical presence.

Lord Bingham concluded that Parliament had provided for a face-to-face confrontation between the review officer and the suspect, and if important rights enacted to protect the subject were to be modified, it was for Parliament after appropriate consultation so to rule and not for the courts. This decision indicates a determination to give real efficacy to Article 5, where a contrary interpretation, impliedly supported by a guiding note,[128] was readily available. Review by video link would have meant the intrusion of technology, controlled by the police, into the review process, leading arguably to a depersonalised confrontation and possibly to a further impression of tokenism.

In considering the following exceptional circumstances in which liberty can be taken away, the requirements connoted by the general provision that they must have a basis in law under Article 5(1) are also implied into the 'prescribed by law' rubric of each sub-paragraph.[129] Article 5(1)(c) of

[127] *The Times* 1 December 1999, judgment 18 November 1999.

[128] He found that the provisions of Code C do not provide conclusive support for either construction. Note for guidance 15C permits review by telephone so long as the requirements of s40 are met, but Lord Bingham had difficulty in seeing how a review conducted over the telephone could ever comply with those requirements, as that Note appeared to envisage.

[129] *Winterwerp* v *Netherlands* A 33 para 39 (1979).

the Convention sets out one of the circumstances in which an individual can be detained. It permits the lawful arrest or detention of a person effected for the purpose of bringing him or her before the competent legal authority on reasonable suspicion of having committed an offence, or where it is reasonably considered that an arrest is necessary to prevent the person in question from committing an offence or fleeing after having done so. In requiring arrest only for specific offences and not for general crime control purposes, Article 5(1)(c) adheres closely to the due process model of arrest indicated above. Ss24 and 25 of PACE and s41 TA (in so far as it relates to certain specific terrorist offences under s40(1)(a)) may *prima facie* comply with these provisions owing to their requirements of reasonable suspicion.

In what is usually regarded as the leading post-PACE case on the meaning of that requirement, *Castorina* v *Chief Constable of Surrey*,[130] the grounds for suspicion regarding a burglary of a firm were that the suspect was a former employee who appeared to have a grudge and the burglary appeared to be an 'inside job'. But the suspect was not considered by the victim to be likely to commit burglary and she had no criminal record. Nevertheless, the court found that reasonable suspicion had been established. Clayton and Tomlinson criticised the decision in these terms: 'if the police are justified in arresting a middle-aged woman of good character on such flimsy grounds without even questioning her as to her alibi or possible motives, then the law provides very scant protection for those suspected of crimes'.[131] *Castorina* may be compared with the findings of the Strasbourg Court in *Fox, Campbell and Hartley* v *UK*.[132] The applicants had been arrested in accordance with s11 of the Northern Ireland (Emergency Provisions) Act 1978 which required only suspicion, not reasonable suspicion. The only evidence put forward by the government for the presence of reasonable suspicion was that the applicants had convictions for terrorist offences and that when arrested they were asked about particular terrorist acts. The government said that further evidence could not be disclosed for fear of endangering life. The Court found that although allowance could be made for the difficulties of evidence gathering in an emergency situation, reasonable suspicion which 'arises from facts or information which would satisfy an objective observer that the person concerned may have committed the offence'[133] had not been established. Moreover, 'the exigencies of dealing with terrorist crime cannot justify stretching the notion of reasonableness to the point where the essence of the safeguard secured by Article 5(1)(c) is impaired'.[134] The arrests in question could not therefore be justified. In *Murray* v

[130] (1988) NLJ 180.
[131] (1988) LS Gaz 7 September 22 at p26.
[132] (1990) A 182; 13 EHRR 157.
[133] Ibid para 32.
[134] Ibid para 32.

UK,[135] this test was viewed as a lower standard for reasonable suspicion, applicable in terrorist cases, but it was again emphasised that an objective standard of reasonable suspicion was required,[136] although the information grounding the suspicion might acceptably remain confidential in the exigencies of a situation such as that pertaining at the time of the arrest in question, in Northern Ireland.[137] It is debatable whether the UK courts are in general applying a test of reasonable suspicion under PACE or the PTA which reaches the standards which the European Court had in mind, especially where terrorism is not in question. The departure which the HRA brings about is to encourage stricter judicial scrutiny of decisions to arrest.

The *purpose* of the arrest should also be in compliance with Article 5(1)(c), even where reasonable suspicion is established, in that it should be effected in order to 'bring [the suspect] before the competent legal authority', although this does not mean that every arrest must lead to a charge.[138] In the individual circumstances of a case a breach of Article 5(1)(c) might be found where, although reasonable suspicion was present on the facts, the arrest discretion was not exercised in accordance with Article 5(1)(c) since the purpose of the arrest was in reality for general information-gathering ends. This might occur where, although there were, objectively, reasonable grounds for suspicion, the police had no belief in the guilt of the suspect. In such an instance the arrest would be unlawful under s6 HRA, not merely *Wednesbury* unreasonable. A breach might also be established where the arrest was unnecessary in order to further the purpose in question. For example, if the suspect was cooperative, there would appear to be no need to arrest him or her since the purpose under Article 5(1)(c) could be served by interviewing the suspect in his or her own home. That purpose would not appear to cover an arrest undertaken merely for the purpose of interviewing such a suspect in the police station.[139] It was found, however, in *Chalkley* v *Jeffries*[140] that the existence of a collateral motive for an arrest would not necessarily render it unlawful. Under the HRA, a domestic court would have to consider whether Article 5 would be satisfied by an arrest with a 'mixed' purpose.

The test under Article 5(1)(c) relies on reasonable suspicion regarding an *offence* and therefore, as indicated above, calls into question s41 TA, in so far as it relates to suspicion that a person is a terrorist in the sense of (under s40(1)(b)) being concerned in the commission, preparation or instigation of an act of terrorism. S41 therefore allows for arrest without reasonable suspicion that a particular offence has been committed. The

135 (1994) EHRR 193.
136 Para 50.
137 Paras 58–59.
138 *K-F* v *Germany* (1997) 26 EHRR 390.
139 Cf *Holgate-Mohammed* v *Duke* [1984] AC 437.
140 [1998] 2 All ER 155.

compatibility of s41 and Article 5(1)(c) depends on the interpretation afforded to *Brogan and Others* v *UK*.[141] The case concerned the EPA provision which was largely reproduced in s41, read with s40(1)(b). The Court applied two tests to the basis for the arrests in finding that the power of arrest was justified within Article 5(1)(c). First, the definition of acts of terrorism was 'well in keeping with the idea of an offence'.[142] Second, after arrest, the applicants were asked about specific offences. Thus, 'the Court decided the point on the basis that involvement in "acts of terrorism" indirectly meant the commission of specific criminal offences under Northern Irish law, which would appear to be the better approach on the facts'.[143] On either test, arrests under s41 read with s40(1)(b) might be in a more doubtful position. The definition of terrorism relevant in *Brogan* was identical to the s20 PTA definition – the use of violence for political ends. The current definition under s1 TA is far wider: it covers the use or threat, 'for the purpose of advancing a political, religious or ideological cause', of action, designed to influence the government or intimidate the public, which involves serious violence against any person or serious damage to property, or is designed to seriously disrupt an electronic system, or endangers life, or creates a serious risk to health or safety. Unlike the previous one, this definition may cover matters, such as threatening to hack into a computer system, or to destroy genetically modified crops, which do not clearly correspond to existing offences and therefore might not be viewed so readily as 'in keeping with the idea of an offence'. The application of the second test would partly depend on practice in the particular instance which arose before a domestic court. If a person was arrested under s41 as part of an investigation and was not asked about specific offences on arrest, the connection with the basis of the arrest, bearing in mind the width of the s1 TA definition, might be viewed as too tenuous to be termed an arrest on reasonable suspicion of an offence. Moreover, the *purpose* of such an arrest would not appear to be in accordance with the Article 5 requirement since it would not be to 'bring [the suspect] before the competent legal authority'.

Article 5(1)(c) also calls into question the provision under s24 PACE allowing for arrest without reasonable suspicion so long as a 'hunch' turns out to be justified (s24(4)(a), (5)(a) and (7)(a)). Sanders and Young call this possibility a 'classic crime control norm since the ends are regarded as justifying the means'.[144] Such an arrest would appear to be unlawful under s6 HRA since no exception under Article 5 appears to allow for it.

Article 5(2), which provides that a person must be informed promptly of the reason for arrest, corresponds to s28 PACE. In *Fox, Campbell and*

[141] Judgment of 29 November 1988 (1989) Series A 145-B (1988) 11 EHHR 117.
[142] Para 51.
[143] *Law of The European Convention on Human Rights* (1995) Harris, O'Boyle and Warbrick (1995) p116.
[144] *Criminal Justice* (1994) p76.

Hartley v *UK*[145] the applicants, who were arrested on suspicion of terrorist offences, were not informed of the reason for the arrest at the time of it but were told that they were being arrested under a particular statutory provision. Clearly, this could not convey the reason to them at that time. At a later point, during interrogation, they were asked about specific criminal offences. The European Court of Human Rights found that Article 5(2) was not satisfied at the time of the arrest but that this breach was healed by the later indications made during interrogation of the offences for which they had been arrested. In *Murray* v *UK*[146] soldiers occupied a woman's house, thus clearly taking her into detention, but did not inform her of the fact of arrest for half an hour. The House of Lords had found that the delay in giving the requisite information was acceptable owing to the alarm which the fact of arrest, if known, might have aroused in the particular circumstances – the unsettled situation in Northern Ireland.[147] The European Court of Human Rights found no breach of Article 5(2); Mrs Murray was eventually informed during interrogation of the reason for the arrest and in the circumstances it was found acceptable to allow an interval of a few hours between the arrest and the point when she was informed of the reason for it. The claim also made, that Article 8 had been breached, was dismissed. The violation of privacy fell within the exception under Article 8(2) in respect of the prevention of crime and was found to be necessary and proportionate to the aims of that exception.

The decisions in both *Fox* and *Murray* were influenced by the terrorist context in which they occurred, and provide examples of the Court's tenderness to claims of a threat to national security made by governments of member states. In both a very wide margin of appreciation was allowed. Probably as a result, both were influenced by the crime control consideration of allowing leeway to the police to resort to doubtful practices in relation to terrorist suspects and both exhibit a lack of rigorousness in relation to due process. Such lack of rigour might be acceptable if there was a real connection between a failure to give information to suspects and an advantage to be gained in an emergency situation, since proportionality might be satisfied. However, in Mrs Murray's case, once she was in detention, and her house in effect sealed off from the outside world, it is unclear that telling her of the fact of the arrest could create or exacerbate an unsettled situation. Giving the requisite information would not have raised an alarm which had not already been raised when the soldiers entered the house. Following these judgments it seems that where special circumstances may be said to obtain, an arrest which does not comply with all the procedural requirements will still be an arrest, for a

145 (1990) A 182; 13 EHRR 157.

146 *Murray* v *UK* (1994) 19 EHRR 193.

147 *Murray* v *Ministry of Defence* [1988] All ER 521, HL; for comment see Williams (1991) 54 MLR 408.

period of time, as far as all the consequences arising from it are concerned, under Article 5(2).

Under s28 PACE the police also have a certain leeway as to informing the arrestee; the arrest will not be affected and nor will other acts arising from it, until the time when it would be practicable to inform of the reason for it has come and gone. However, if there is nothing in the behaviour of the arrestee or in the general situation to make informing him or her impracticable then the arrest will be unlawful from its inception. If the word 'practicable' in s28 is interpreted in accordance with the interpretation of Article 5(3) in both *Murray* and *Fox* it seems that, depending on the circumstances, a certain amount of leeway is created in respect of informing the arrestee. An arrest which fails to comply with the procedural requirements will be in a more precarious position than an arrest which from its inception complies with them, because it will cease to be an arrest at an uncertain point. On somewhat doubtful grounds, the Convention has allowed some departure from the principle that there should be a clear demarcation between the point at which the citizen is at liberty and the point at which his or her liberty is restrained. Sanders and Young observe, commenting on the House of Lords' decision in *Murray*, 'Even where the legislature, as in s28 of PACE, appears to be creating strong inhibitory rules, the judiciary still manages to draw their due process sting by rendering them largely presentational'.[148] This might also be said of the decision of the European Court. A domestic court in the post-HRA era might, however, be prepared to take a more activist approach to the application of Article 5(2), especially where an s41 TA arrest, accompanied by delay in informing of the reason due (apparently) to the terrorist context occurred, in circumstances which could not be compared, in terms of volatility, to the situation in Northern Ireland when *Murray* was decided.

As noted above, the temporary provision under s83 TA allowing members of the armed forces to effect arrests, applicable only to Northern Ireland, does not provide that the grounds must be given. S83(2) provides: 'A person making an arrest under this section complies with any rule of law requiring him to state the ground of arrest if he states that he is making the arrest as a member of Her Majesty's forces'. S83(6) then appears to accept that s83(2) will lead to findings that Article 5(3) has been breached in providing: 'The reference to a rule of law . . . does not include a rule of law which has effect only by virtue of the Human Rights Act'. If a judge is confronted with an arrest under s83 in which the arrestee merely stated that he or she was effecting it as a member of Her Majesty's forces, it would appear that the arrest would be likely to be found unlawful, unless in the circumstances, *Murray* could be applied. But the application of *Murray* might be viewed as inappropriate, given the influence of the margin of appreciation doctrine on the judgment.

[148] Sanders and Young *Criminal Justice* (1994) p103.

Article 5(3) confers a right to be brought promptly before the judicial authorities; in other words, not to be held for long periods without a hearing. It covers both arrest and detention. There will be some allowable delay in both situations; the question is therefore what is meant by 'promptly'. Its meaning was considered in *Brogan* v *UK*[149] in relation to the arrest and detention of the applicants considered above, arising by virtue of the special powers under s12 of the PTA. The UK had entered a derogation under Article 15 against the applicability of Article 5(3) to Northern Ireland, but withdrew that derogation in August 1984. Two months later the *Brogan* case was filed. The applicants complained *inter alia* of the length of time they were held in detention without coming before a judge, on the basis that it could not be termed prompt. The Court took into account the need for special measures to combat terrorism; such measures had to be balanced against individual rights. However, it found that detention for four days and six hours was too long. The Court did not specify how long was acceptable; previously the Commission had seen four days as the limit. The government made no move to comply with this decision; instead it entered a derogation under Article 15 to Article 5(3).

This derogation was challenged unsuccessfully in *Brannigan and McBride* v *UK*[150] as invalid. The European Court of Human Rights found that it was justified since the state of public emergency in Northern Ireland warranted exceptional measures. The Court found: 'a wide margin of appreciation [on the question] of the presence of an emergency . . . and on the nature and scope of derogations necessary to avert it [should be allowed]'.[151] Among the government contentions uncritically accepted by the Court was one to the effect that in the particular situation the judiciary should not be permitted a role in protecting the liberty of detainees. As Judge Walsh pointed out in his dissenting opinion, this was precisely a role which the public would expect a judge to have. As a result, at present, periods of up to six days' detention will not breach Article 5 in an emergency situation. *Brannigan* might appear a doubtful decision because the derogation was entered after the decision in *Brogan*, although it might also be said that states should not be encouraged to enter derogations too readily on 'insurance' grounds in order to pre-empt claims. Arguably, although there was a state of emergency in 1989, the UK had chosen not to enter a derogation even though one would have been warranted. Whatever the merits of this argument in the particular situation, it is questionable whether the exigencies of the situation did require detention of six days without recourse to independent review. Possibly it was assumed on insufficient grounds that such review would prejudice the legitimate purpose of the investigation.

[149] Judgment of 29 November 1988; (1989) 11 EHRR 117; A.145.
[150] Series A 258-B (1993); (1993) 17 EHRR 594.
[151] Para 207.

In requiring judicial authorisation for detention for up to seven days under s41 and Schedule 7 TA, the government has sought to ensure, as indicated above, that the new detention provisions comply with Article 5(3) as interpreted in *Brogan* and *Brannigan*, meaning that the derogation can eventually be withdrawn. One question which will probably be raised eventually in the domestic courts or at Strasbourg will be whether allowing a detention for seven days, even with judicial authorisation, is in accordance with Article 5. Further, it appears that the new arrangements could allow for detention for longer than 48 hours with authorisation only by the police themselves. If, for example, towards the end of 54 hours in detention (a possibility under the TA, as indicated above), the police decided to apply for an extension of detention, they would have the power under s41(5) to continue the detention while the application was being made and then under s41(6) while the hearing was occurring. There is also the highly controversial possibility of continued 12 hourly extensions of detention on review by a superintendent under s41(4); while it is unlikely that s41(4) would be interpreted as allowing much leeway to continue to detain beyond 48 hours, the provision appears to detract from the certainty of the 48-hour deadline. Both these possibilities do not appear to accord with *Brogan* and *Brannigan* since neither provides for any possibility of judicial authorisation of detention. Bearing in mind the wide margin of appreciation allowed in *Brannigan*, a domestic court taking a more activist stance might be prepared to find a breach of Article 5(3) in respect of an s41 detention, depending on its length, in the particular circumstances before it. One clear possibility would be to limit the application of s41(4) in accordance with the government's apparent intention that the new detention regime should comply with Article 5(3) and therefore allow for withdrawal of the derogation.

As indicated in Chapter 5, arrest and detention and, where relevant, treatment within that period, may also be considered under Article 6, whether or not a breach of Article 5 is established.[152] Under Article 6 the Court has developed the concept of the fairness of the trial 'as a whole', allowing consideration of treatment in detention and rendering it unnecessary in appropriate instances to point to specific breaches of implied Article 6(1) rights. In *Saidi* v *France*[153] the Court said that its role was to determine 'whether the proceedings in their entirety . . . were fair'.[154] In *Barbéra, Messegué and Jabardo*[155] the trial taken as a whole could not be said to be fair. This was partly due to features of the treatment of the defendants pre-trial, taken cumulatively. They were held incommunicado for a substantial period of time and when they confessed to the police they did not have legal assistance. Nevertheless, their confessions

[152] See Chapter 5 p202.
[153] (1994) 17 EHRR 251.
[154] At para 43.
[155] A.14 6(2) (1989) 33.

were significant in later questioning by examining judges. The unfair pre-trial treatment clearly had a tendency to render the trial unfair, although it is improbable that such a tendency would have been found without the unfairness at the hearing itself.[156] Nevertheless, the findings in *Barbera* are significant since they emphasize the need to consider the whole criminal process, including any custodial period, in determining fairness. It might be appropriate where the pre-trial custodial treatment, including the manner of questioning, had a cumulatively harsh effect, to stay the prosecution for abuse of process. In other circumstances, exclusion of evidence obtained during or as a result of a course of harsh or adverse treatment might be appropriate in order to satisfy Article 6. These possibilities are discussed further in Chapter 7.[157]

Article 2 of the European Convention allows the use of force which is 'absolutely necessary' in order to arrest. S117 PACE and s114 TA allow for the use of 'reasonable force', if necessary, in the exercise of the powers they provide. This wording could be taken to mean that any force used which was not, objectively speaking, absolutely necessary would be unreasonable, or it might suggest that any force used which appeared, subjectively, necessary at the time would be reasonable. Article 2 suggests that the latter test should be used.[158] Under s3 HRA, it is suggested that the term 'absolutely' should be implied into the domestic provisions. Article 3, which provides a guarantee against torture or inhuman or degrading treatment,[159] may also be relevant where physical force is used in the course of an arrest and detention. In *Ribbitsch* v *Austria*[160] the Court said: 'any recourse to physical force which has not been made strictly necessary by his own conduct diminishes human dignity and is in principle an infringement of the right set forth in Article 3'.[161] Force may only be used where it is strictly required to restrain the detainee and the force used must go no further, in terms of causing injury or humiliation, than is strictly necessary to achieve the purpose of restraint. Thus a strict proportionality test is applied and force outside the limits it sets will infringe Article 3. *A fortiori*, this must be the case under Article 2, where lethal force is used.[162]

[156] There were 'unexpected changes' in the membership of the court, the hearing was brief; most importantly, there was a failure to adduce and discuss evidence orally in the accused's presence.

[157] At pp292–3.

[158] See *Kelly* v *UK* (1985) 8 EHRR 45.

[159] Article 3 treatment may be justifiable where its object is to satisfy the demands of Article 2, the right to life: *Herczegfalfy* v *Austria* A 244 (1992).

[160] (1996) 21 EHRR 573.

[161] At p26. See *Selmouni* v *France* (2000) 29 EHRR 403 for an example of treatment in police custody found to amount to torture.

[162] Article 2 therefore calls into question the recent cases of death due to restraint during arrest. In 'Deaths in Police Custody: Learning the Lessons' Police Research Series Paper 26 (1998) Leigh, Johnson and Ingram, found, in Section 6, 13 cases of death in which police restraint may have been a factor. They found six cases where restraint may have led to 'postural' or 'positional asphyxia', leading to death. In two others, death was due to a neck-hold; in a further two, to force applied with a baton. They viewed these cases

Article 3 treatment may also arise in respect of other aspects of detention. Failure to obtain medical treatment after a forcible arrest was found to infringe Article 3 in *Hurtado* v *Switzerland*.[163] In the *Greek* case[164] the conditions of detention were found to amount to inhuman treatment due to inadequate food, sleeping arrangements, heating and sanitary facilities combined with overcrowding and inadequate provision for external contacts. It was also found that conduct which grossly humiliates may amount to degrading treatment contrary to Article 3. Such treatment may include racially discriminatory and, probably, sexually discriminatory arrests and treatment in detention;[165] it might be found to fall more readily within Article 3 in a non-terrorist context.[166] Where discrimination is a factor, Article 14 would also be engaged.

The substantive criminal law would not be applicable in certain of these instances of Article 3 treatment. Article 3, therefore, provides guarantees against various forms of maltreatment in police detention, which are not currently duplicated in domestic statutory provisions, although the guarantees are limited since Article 3 demands that such maltreatment should be of a high level of severity. In so far as certain conditions of detention are relevant, domestic law currently reflects its guarantees in Code C alone. For example, the conduct of intimate searches is governed by s55 PACE but its provisions are fleshed out in Annex A of Code C. Strip searches, as opposed to intimate searches, are covered only by part B of Annex A to Code C. The use of force to conduct them is authorised by s117 PACE.[167] The provisions governing the conditions of detention mentioned in the *Greek* case arise only in Code C, paras 8 and 9. Provisions in Code C para 8 regarding the use of restraints, including handcuffs, in cells might be viewed as intended to ensure that Article 3 is not infringed. Bearing in mind the quasi-legal status of the Codes, such provisions might be

as having implications for training. *The Butler Report* (1998) also considered a number of deaths in custody cases. In one of these, that of O'Brien, the arrestee, after being handcuffed, was held face down on the ground by at least four officers, one of whom knelt on his back, and one on his legs. The evidence was conflicting, but his family and a bystander stated that he was saying that he could not breathe. The post-mortem found that he had died due to postural asphyxsia and he had bruising to his head, shoulders and right arm. See Chapter 5 p188 in relation to criticism of decisions of the CPS in relation to this case. It is suggested that *prima facie* the force used went well beyond that which was absolutely necessary, and therefore it was not in accord with Article 2.

163 A 280-A (1994) Com Rep.

164 12 YB 1 (1969) Com Rep.

165 *East African Asians* cases 3 EHRR 76 (1973). See also *Lustig-Prean and Beckett* v *UK and Smith and Grady* v *UK* (2000) 29 EHRR 493 which suggested that grossly humiliating, intrusive interrogation could amount to a breach of Article 3 (discussed in Chapter 7 at p292).

166 In *McFeeley* v *UK* 20 DR 44 (1980) intimate body searches in a terrorist context did not give rise to a breach of Article 3 but it has been suggested (see *The Law of the European Convention on Human Rights* (1995) Harris, O'Boyle and Warbrick p83) that this finding might not apply in a non-terrorist context.

167 Clearly, criminal law applicable to indecent assault would not be applicable where the search was properly authorised.

afforded, indirectly, a higher status due to their role in relation to Article 3, under s6 HRA.[168]

Assuming that the treatment arguably falls within Article 3, the burden of proof on the detainee is affected, following the decisions in *Tomasi* v *France*[169] and *Aksoy* v *Turkey*.[170] Once the detainee has shown that he or she was free of the injury or harm in question before arrest the state will then bear the burden of providing a plausible explanation for it which is consistent with the evidence. If it does not do so the domestic court should assume that the injuries in question were caused in the manner alleged by the complainant. It may be noted in this context that allegations of ill-treatment in police custody have recently raised grave concerns.[171]

Article 8 may be viewed as overlapping, to an extent, with Article 3 but it also covers some matters which would not be serious enough to amount to Article 3 treatment.[172] Its guarantee of a right to respect for privacy is subject to a number of exceptions in para 2, including for the prevention of crime. In order to bring Article 8 into play, it must be found that its protection extends to the matter in question – in this context, it would probably be that 'private or family life' is affected. Certain conditions or incidents of detention may fall outside Article 8, such as a failure to provide an interpreter. But a failure to allow a juvenile or a mentally disturbed person to consult privately with a member of his or her family, acting as an appropriate adult, might be viewed as an interference with either private or family life. Strip and intimate searching would probably fall within Article 8 as well as – depending on the circumstances, including the use of force – Article 3.[173] It is notable that the authorisation of a strip search, prior to 1995, had to be by the custody officer but that that requirement is no longer in place under the current Code C provisions.[174]

[168] See Chapter 5 pp195–6.

[169] A 241-A (1992).

[170] Reports 1996-VI, Vol 26, judgment of 8 July 1993. These decisions should also be taken into account where treatment in police custody results in death, engaging Article 2. See Chapter 5 p188.

[171] See the *Report of the European Committee for the Prevention of Torture and Inhuman or degrading treatment or punishment*, based on a visit carried out from 8 to 17 September 1999. See also the *Butler Report* (1998). *Inter alia* the Report covers the case of Derek Treadaway (pp37–38). He alleged that he had suffered ill-treatment, possibly amounting to torture, in police custody, and successfully sought judicial review (31 July 1997) of the decision of the CPS not to prosecute the officers involved. For relevant convention jurisprudence see above p172, note 12.

[172] In the corporal punishment case of *Costello-Roberts* v *UK* (1995) 19 EHRR 112 the Court found that the treatment was not severe enough to fall within Article 3; in the particular circumstances it did not fall within Article 8, but the Court considered that there might be circumstances in which Article 8 could be viewed as affording a wider protection to physical integrity than that which could be viewed as afforded by Article 3.

[173] Violations of both Articles, together with Article 14, were argued for in *Wanyonyi* v *UK* (1999) 27 EHRR 195 in respect of racial abuse and humiliation during strip and intimate searching. The application was declared inadmissible for failure to exhaust domestic remedies.

[174] Code C Annex A Part B.

If a violation of Article 8 was alleged in respect of a strip search it might be found to be in accordance with the law since it is authorised under Code C,[175] to have a legitimate aim (the prevention of crime), but to be disproportionate to the aim pursued and therefore unnecessary in a democratic society, since that element of independence has been removed. If so, the Code provision, which is not itself authorised by incompatible primary legislation as required under s3(2)(c) HRA, could be struck down. Articles 8, 3 and 14 might also be engaged where the interrogation itself was of an especially intrusive nature, particularly where it could also be said to be discriminatory; this possibility is pursued in Chapter 7.

[175] The Codes probably satisfy this requirement. Interpreting 'prescribed by law' in *Sunday Times* v *UK* A30 para 49 (1979) the European Court of Human Rights found: 'the law must be adequately accessible' and 'a norm cannot be regarded as a "law" unless it is formulated with sufficient precision to enable the citizen to regulate his conduct'. In *Rai, Allmond and 'Negotiate Now'* v *UK* 81-A D&R 146 (1995) the Commission said: 'It is compatible with the requirements of foreseeability that terms which are on their face general and unlimited are explained by executive or administrative statements, since it is the provision of sufficiently precise guidance to individuals . . . rather than the source of that guidance which is of relevance' (ibid at p152).

Chapter 7

Criminal Procedure III

POLICE INTERVIEWING

Introduction

In crime control terms the police interview occupies a central position in the criminal justice system; it represents an effective use of resources since if a confession becomes available the criminal process is likely to be accelerated.[1] In particular, since *mens rea* is a requirement of most offences, admissions provide the most readily available means of establishing the state of mind of the suspect at the relevant time. The interview may in effect replace the trial since its results may play a key part in the pre-trial balancing and negotiating process in which the suspect decides whether to plead guilty. Clearly, the stronger the risk of a conviction which would be unaccompanied by a sentence discount the less likely it is that he or she will plead not guilty.[2] If the suspect has confessed or made some admissions he or she may feel that there is no point in pleading not guilty even if the admissions are false, exaggerated or misleading. The interview may also frequently play a part in general criminal intelligence gathering.[3] The crime control advantages of the interview are readily apparent.

From a due process perspective, on the other hand, the police interview is largely unjustifiable since its *raison d'être* is to secure admissions which probably would not otherwise be secured; it therefore undermines the privilege against self-incrimination. This due process norm traditionally underpinned criminal justice practice[4] but it was gradually abandoned until it became accepted in the pre-PACE years that the purpose of the interrogation was to obtain admissions.[5] The precarious position of the

[1] See McConville (1993) RCCJ Research Study No 13 (1993) HMSO; Baldwin (1993) 33 BJ Criminology 325.

[2] See Sanders and Young *Criminal Justice* (1994) p149.

[3] Maguire and Morris RCCJ Research Study No 5 (1992) HMSO.

[4] The 1912 Judges' Rules did not allow police interrogation, although the police could invite and receive voluntary statements.

[5] *Holgate-Mohammed* v *Duke* [1984] 1 AC 437; [1984] 1 All ER 1054.

interview from this perspective explains, it is suggested, why it seemed necessary, when PACE placed police interrogations on a formal basis, to infuse due process elements into them. Such elements are intended to detract from any impression that the confession is involuntary. The police, however, remain the gatekeepers to these safeguards, which tend to run counter to their crime control concerns, and therefore they may not be observed or, more subtly, the weaknesses and loopholes in the interviewing scheme will be discovered and explored.

PACE strongly reflected this uneasy compromise between crime control and due process: the detainee could be detained for the purposes of obtaining a confession under s37(2), but a number of safeguards were created which were influenced by due process concerns to lessen the coerciveness of the interview and to ensure its integrity and reliability so that it could be used as evidence. The extensive and complex rules of Code C which appeared to surround police interviews with a range of safeguards, including access to legal advice, afforded the interview a due process appearance. A number of flaws, however, in due process terms, were built into the scheme when it was first introduced. Most significantly, as Chapter 5 indicated, there were no sanctions for breach of the interviewing rules, including those arising under PACE itself, apart from the possibility of disciplinary action;[6] virtually no guidance was given as to the acceptable limits of 'persuasive' interviewing;[7] there was scope for interviewing away from the police station, thereby evading the most significant safeguards; and there was uncertainty as to when an exchange with police became an interview so as to attract all the safeguards.[8]

The original interviewing scheme under Code C was revised in 1991 and improved by the introduction of tape recording under Code E. That revision, was, it is suggested, concerned wholly with improving the scheme's due process elements, albeit in a manner best described as superficial: the rules became more complex in order to deal with police evasion of them, but their fundamental flaws were hardly addressed. Despite the relationship a number of commentators had observed to exist between coerced confessions and miscarriages of justice,[9] the more far-reaching recommendations made by the 1993 Runciman Royal Commission on Criminal Procedure, which might have continued the improvements undertaken in 1991, were largely ignored.[10] Under the Major government

[6] This possibility became even more remote when s67(8) PACE, rendering breach of the Codes automatically breach of the police disciplinary Code, was repealed in 1994 by the Police and Magistrates' Courts Act 1994 s37 and Schedule 9.

[7] Para 11.3 of Code C merely provides that the interviewing must not be oppressive.

[8] See Fenwick 'Confessions, Recording Rules and Miscarriages of Justice' [1993] Crim LR 174–184.

[9] See C Walker in *Miscarriages of Justice* (1999) p54.

[10] For example, the *Runciman Report* Chap 4 para 23 put forward a recommendation to retain the right to silence, in the context of improved safeguards for suspects, taking into account recommendations intended to lead to improvement in the quality of custodial legal advice. The Report made other proposals for improvement of the interviewing

the disciplinary sanction for breaching the Codes was removed under s37(f) of the Police and Magistrates' Court Act 1994, and the right to silence was curtailed under ss34–37 of the Criminal Justice and Public Order Act 1994 (CJPOA). Largely as a consequence of the changes introduced under the CJPOA, the PACE Codes were revised once again in 1995; this revision, unlike the previous one, appeared to have a dual aim: it seemed to be intended to have some weak due process impact in eradicating loopholes, but it also introduced various provisions in order to give effect to the curtailment of the right to silence. These changes indicated a move away from the rather ineffectual attempts previously undertaken to protect the due process elements in the interviewing process.

Codes C and E were issued in revised versions which came into effect in 1999, but no radical change from the 1995 version was made. The opportunity presented by the 1999 revision of taking forward the improvements made in 1991 was therefore lost, as was the possibility of addressing some of the more fundamental flaws of Code C, in the light of the HRA. The failures to provide any sanction for breach of the Codes, to address the uncertainty as to the status of the Notes, which continue to contain significant protections for due process, to reduce the scope for out-of-station interviews and afford such interviews greater due process protection, or to remove provisions which themselves allow for breaches of the Convention rights, are all continued in the 1999 revision. These flaws, and their implications, are discussed at the relevant points, below.

The interviewing scheme had, from its inception, created a twin-track system under PACE, the counter-terrorist legislation and the Codes; that is, one in which terrorist suspects were exposed to a regime adhering to a lower level of due process than that applicable in respect of 'ordinary' suspects. This regime afforded the coercive elements of the scheme greater rein both formally and informally. Most obviously, as Chapter 6 explains, terrorist suspects could be exposed to a longer period of detention, which allowed greater scope for prolonged pressure during interrogation. The interviewing regime for such suspects was also less protective. The counter-terrorist scheme introduced by New Labour under the Terrorism Act 2000 (TA), its Codes of Practice and the 1999 revision of Codes C and E not only confirms and extends the twin-track system, but applies it to a much wider and more diverse range of suspects. The only concession to due process introduced under the TA is the possible extension of audio-recording, already occurring on a voluntary basis, to interviews with terrorist suspects. As Chapter 5 points out, the acceptance of the primacy of crime control values as underpinning police interviewing, reflected in the changes undertaken in the CJPOA, marked a turning point in criminal justice policies which was unaffected by the change of government in 1997.[11]

scheme including the videoing of a waiver of legal advice (proposal 57) and a special warning to juries regarding uncorroborated confessions (Chap 4 paras 56–87).

[11] At pp179–8.

Out-of-station questioning

Under one version of the classic due process model, protection for suspects' rights should be at its highest, not only when the point of greatest coercion is reached, but when most is at stake during a contact with the police in terms of its likely influence on the ultimate outcome of the investigation. The scheme's inability to meet this obligation remains an enduring characteristic. From this perspective, the position at present reflects the original and inherent defects of the scheme which were confirmed and exacerbated by the changes which took place from the mid-1990s onwards. Street interviewing, possibly originating as part of a 'voluntary' stop and search, remains at quite a high level[12] while the key due process safeguards of access to legal advice, audio-recording and the presence of an 'appropriate adult' continue to be reserved for formal interviews within the police station. The caution which, as suggested below, serves both crime control and due process purposes, can be, and, in most instances should be, used outside the police station, with the result that the suspect is warned of the dangers of failing to speak before the key safeguards can be in place. Due process protection outside the police station is minimal; it consists only of contemporaneous note-taking under caution if an interview is occurring[13] or accurate non-contemporaneous note-taking if the exchange is not an interview.[14] Relevant non-interview exchanges with juveniles and mentally disordered persons may be admissible in evidence although no adult was present. Not only, therefore, is due process virtually abandoned in relation to out-of-station exchanges, but they may also have a structural formative influence on formal interviews and ultimately on the outcome of the process, thereby undermining the protection available for such interviews. Suspects may feel, rightly or wrongly, that they have already prejudiced their position too far during informal exchanges to attempt to retrieve it in a formal taped interview; therefore any confession made in such an interview – or any ill-considered silence – may not be truly voluntary. Thus it is extremely important to determine how far the scheme leaves scope for exchanges to occur before the police station is reached.

Although the meaning of the term 'interview' was clarified under the 1995 revision of Code C, the scheme still seeks to create a somewhat hazy distinction between interviews and exchanges relevant to the offence which are not interviews, under para 11.13, thereby offering some encouragement to police to question outside the station. If questioning is

[12] See D Brown, T Ellis and J Larcombe *Home Office Research Study No 129* HMSO; the study showed that questioning or unsolicited comment occurred outside the station in 24% of cases. The Runciman Royal Commission found that around 10% of interviews took place outside the police station: RCCJ Report Cm 2263 (1993).

[13] Para 11.5 Code C.

[14] Para 11.13 Code C.

occurring, there are grounds to suspect the person of the offence and the questioning relates to the person's involvement or suspect involvement in the offence, the exchange will be an interview under paras 11.1.A and 10.1. In other words, an exchange which relates to the offence may not constitute an interview. There is provision under para 11.2A to adopt any statement or silence which occurred outside the police station in the context of a non-interview once within it, on tape, but no provision that it will be inadmissible if not so adopted. Para 11.1 allows interviewing outside the police station if certain conditions are met. It reads: 'Following a decision to arrest a suspect he must not be interviewed about the relevant offence except at a police station (or other authorised place of detention) unless the consequent delay would be likely: (a) to lead to interference with or harm to evidence connected with an offence or interference with or physical harm to other persons; or (b) to lead to the alerting of other persons suspected of having committed an offence but not yet arrested for it; or (c) to hinder the recovery of property obtained in consequence of the commission of an offence. Interviewing in any of these circumstances should cease once the relevant risk has been averted or the necessary questions have been put in order to attempt to avert that risk'.

At first glance, para 11.1 appears to provide a due process prohibition on interviews outside the police station with a view to ensuring that suspects being interviewed are afforded the safeguards available once they are in it. However, owing to the difference between the levels of suspicion denoted by paras 11.1.A and 11.1 it simultaneously creates leeway which may be advantageous in crime control terms for questioning suspects away from it. The level under para 11.1.A appears to be the lower, giving scope for the argument that the decision to arrest had not yet been made because the level of suspicion was not high enough. This exception implicit in para 11.1 is therefore at least as significant as the express ones. These provisions obscure, it is suggested, the distinction between detention and liberty and create, *de facto*, an uncertain area in which detention for questioning independent of arrest appears to be possible. If a suspect challenges the questioning and asks whether or not he or she is under arrest, officers should arrest him or her and continue questioning at the police station (or in the street under the urgent interviewing provisions), or allow him or her to go free. If the suspect does not challenge it he or she will presumably be deemed to be a volunteer, although the situation, particularly since the caution should now have been given, may be termed a coercive one.

From both a due process and a crime control perspective it would not be appropriate to address the leeway in the scheme for informal interviewing by requiring that, where sufficient suspicion is present, suspects should always be arrested and taken to the police station before any exchange occurs. In crime control terms this might not represent an efficient use of resources since some unnecessary arrests would be made.

In due process terms there are some disadvantages in police station interviewing: the element of detention is coercive and the fact of detention may lead suspects to make admissions in order to leave it. Rather, the due process 'deficit' in street exchanges may be addressed, to an extent, by applying stronger safeguards to such interviewing[15] and, as discussed below, by giving careful consideration, under Article 6, to the admission of such exchanges as evidence.

The curtailed right to silence

There is general academic agreement that, as Sanders and Young put it, 'it is over the right of silence that due process and crime control principles clash most fundamentally'.[16] The right to silence, in the sense of the immunity of an accused person from having adverse inferences drawn from failure to answer questions during police questioning, is central to the due process model. In contrast, adherence to crime control principles logically demands not only that such inferences should be drawn, but that in some or all circumstances, refusal to answer police questions should be an offence in itself, since innocent persons would not thereby be disadvantaged and the burden on the prosecution would be eased. Within the due process camp, retention of the right to silence has been advocated on instrumental and symbolic grounds, while one school of abolitionists departs from a classic crime control stance in arguing for an 'exchange' or trade-off between the PACE suspects' rights and the right to silence.[17] Since the inception of PACE, which adopted the due process stance,[18] there has been a clear movement towards the crime control position, but usually on the basis of 'exchange' rather than 'symbolic' abolitionism.

Drawing adverse inferences from silence

The right to silence was abrogated in 1988 in Northern Ireland in terms of allowing adverse inferences to be drawn from silence at trial.[19] But post-PACE the right was retained for most suspects, including terrorist suspects, in England and Wales until 1994 when it was curtailed or undermined, although not abolished, under the Criminal Justice and Public Order Act 1994 ss34, 36 and 37. The right, in the sense of an immunity from criminal sanctions due to a refusal to answer questions under

15 Using hand-held tape recorders and notifying the suspect of the right of access to legal advice as part of the caution.
16 *Criminal Justice* (1994) p191.
17 See S Greer 'The Right to Silence: A Review of the Current Debate' (1990) 53 MLR 719.
18 The only recognition given to this right in PACE was in Code C, in the wording of the caution, para 10.4.
19 Criminal Evidence (Northern Ireland) Order SI 1988 No 1987 NI 20 1988.

suspicion, still exists as far as the majority of suspects are concerned.[20] The majority of the Runciman Royal Commission agreed with the Phillips Commission in recommending that the right to silence should be retained, although it considered that provision to deal with so-called 'ambush' defences (defences sprung on the prosecution at the last minute by a defendant who has hitherto remained silent as to his or her defence) should be introduced.[21] The Commission's recommendation was based not on a 'symbolic' but on an 'instrumental retentionist' approach;[22] it arose from a concern that otherwise a risk of miscarriages of justice might arise.[23] Given that the Commission was convened in the wake of a number of miscarriages of justice it might have been expected that the government would give these findings some weight. The Home Secretary, however, took what could be termed an exchange abolitionist approach[24] – suspects have greater rights than they did in pre-PACE days and therefore do not need the right to silence. Since curtailment of the right was unlikely to have any effect at all on the crime rate it seems most likely that it was undertaken not in order to gain genuine crime control advantage but in order to give the impression that such advantage might be gained. The conviction rate was unaffected since the change had an impact only on the small number of criminals who are detected and who would otherwise have remained silent. While it may have had some influence on decisions to plead guilty, its main effect has probably been on that tiny percentage of cases which come to court[25] in which the defendant has remained silent and has pleaded not guilty. The academic consensus is that the advantages in terms of crime control are very doubtful, whereas the risk of miscarriages of justice has been increased.[26] At the same time it was acknowledged, prior to curtailment, that 'the reality of the right to silence is much closer [in practice] to the crime control model than it might first appear',[27] partly due to informal inference drawing by juries and magistrates.[28]

[20] See below at pp267–9 for a number of statutory provisions which penalise silence.
[21] RCCJ Report p84 para 2. The proposal found effect in the Criminal Procedure and Investigations Act 1996 which imposes a duty of defence disclosure in most Crown Court cases. Michael Zander, a member of the RCCJ, considered that such disclosure would undermine the presumption of innocence (RCCJ Report *A Note of Dissent* by M Zander p22 paras 8 and 11). It may be found that the provisions of the 1996 Act are not fully in compliance with Article 6(2) of the Convention which guarantees the presumption of innocence. See below at p393.
[22] See S Greer 'The Right to Silence: A Review of the Current Debate' [1990] 53 MLR 719.
[23] Runciman RCCJ Report p55.
[24] Op cit S Greer at p719.
[25] Over 90% of defendants to be tried in Magistrates Courts plead guilty; for Crown Court defendants the figure is 65%.
[26] See Zander *The Police and Criminal Evidence Act 1984* (1995) pp303–323; H Fenwick (1995) Crim LR 132–136; D Jackson (1995) Crim LR 587–601; R Pattenden (1995) Crim LR 602–611.
[27] Sanders and Young (1994) p193.
[28] M Zander and P Henderson *Crown Court Study* RCCJ Research Study No 19 (1993) HMSO.

S34(1) of the Criminal Justice and Public Order Act 1994 provides: 'where . . . evidence is given that the accused . . . (a) on being questioned under caution by a constable trying to discover whether or by whom the offence had been committed, failed to mention any fact relied on in his defence . . . or (b) on being charged . . . or on officially being informed that he might be prosecuted . . . failed to mention any such fact, being a fact which in the circumstances existing at the time the accused could reasonably have been expected to mention when so questioned, charged or informed, . . . ss(2) below applies'. Under s34(2)(d) the court or jury 'in determining whether the accused is guilty of the offence charged may draw such inferences as appear proper'. The difference between ss(1)(a) and (1)(b) is of interest. It is notable that s(1)(b) makes no mention of cautioning or of questioning. It implies that an inference of guilt may be drawn from the failure of the accused to volunteer information. Since it is not confined to the point at which the suspect is charged, it could, theoretically, apply at any point during the arrest and detention. Ss36 and 37 of the 1994 Act provide that adverse inferences may be drawn from a failure to account for possession of substances or objects, or presence at a particular place. Under all these provisions there is still a right to remain silent so long as the accused is prepared to take the risk that so doing may have an adverse impact on his or her defence. The caution under para 10.4 Code C was accordingly revised in 1995 to read: 'You do not have to say anything but it may harm your defence if you do not mention when questioned something which you later rely on in court. Anything you do say may be given in evidence.' In contrast to the old caution, the new one has a dual and contradictory effect: it can no longer be seen simply as a safeguard; it must also be seen as part of the coerciveness inherent in the police interviewing and detention powers. Further special cautions were adopted under paras 10.5A and B of Code C in order to take account, respectively, of the provisions of ss36 and 37 of the 1994 Act.

Ss34, 36 and 37 will be amended by s58 of the Youth Justice and Criminal Evidence Act 1999, when that section comes into force. The amendments will provide that if the defendant was at an authorised place of detention and 'had not been allowed' to consult a solicitor at the time of the failure to mention the fact in question, inferences may not be drawn. This is a very significant change to the interviewing scheme, which was introduced as a direct response to the findings of the European Court of Human Rights in *Murray* v *UK*.[29] The implications of this change are considered in relation to the custodial right of access to legal advice, below.

It is implicit in all three sections that inferences may only be drawn if a sound explanation for the silence is not put forward. Although staying silent carries risks, it may be, depending on the circumstances, less risky

[29] (1996) 22 EHRR 29. See below p282.

than making ill-considered admissions since silence, unlike admissions, must be corroborated.[30] However, as the Runciman Commission pointed out, the caution is likely to put most pressure on vulnerable suspects.[31] The suspect most likely to be unable to evaluate the riskiness of silence is precisely the type of suspect who needs the protection originally afforded by the right. Vulnerable persons interviewed outside the police station may be confused by the caution and without the benefit of legal advice may be pressurised into making inaccurate and ill-considered admissions and perhaps into mentioning matters they have not been questioned about.[32] Thus, although it may be argued that in a number of circumstances it may not be 'proper' for a jury to be directed to draw adverse inferences from silence or that it was not reasonable in the circumstances existing at the time to expect the suspect to speak, this will not benefit the suspect who does in fact speak in response to the new caution. Ironically, it is likely to be the seasoned criminal who understands the operation of s34 CJPOA and may be able to predict that silence may not be a more risky strategy than it was previously, who may not be disadvantaged by the new provisions.

The emerging case-law on s34 CJPOA suggests that the courts are not on the whole taking a restrictive approach, although it has been made clear that where the prosecution does not seek to rely on a silence, the judge should direct the jury positively not to draw inferences.[33] In *Murray* v *DPP*,[34] which was decided on the 1988 Northern Ireland Order, but is clearly applicable to s34, the House of Lords found that silence allows the drawing not only of specific inferences from failure to mention particular facts, but also of the inference that the defendant is guilty. The decision in *Condron and Another*[35] also favoured a broad application of the provisions. The appellants were to be questioned by police at the police station on suspicion of being involved in the supply and possession of heroin. The police surgeon found that they were fit to be interviewed, but their solicitor considered that they were unfit since they were suffering withdrawal symptoms and so advised them not to answer any questions. They relied on that advice during the interview and remained silent. At trial the defence involved reliance on facts which had not been mentioned in the course of the interview and thus potentially fell within s34 CJPOA. The judge held a *voir dire* and rejected argument under s78 that the no-comment interview should be excluded as unfair because they were unfit to be interviewed. Argument that it would be improper to allow

[30] S38(3) CJPOA.
[31] RCCJ Report op cit para 4.50.
[32] It was found in *Nicholson* [1999] Crim LR 61 that if the police have not asked about facts, adverse inferences should not be drawn against the defendant if he or she does not state those facts.
[33] *R* v *McGarry* [1998] 3 All ER 805.
[34] [1994] 1 WLR 1.
[35] [1997] 1 Cr App R 185.

an inference to be drawn under s34 because in making no comment they had only followed the *bona fide* advice of their solicitor was also rejected. The interviews were admitted and the prosecution then argued that they could reasonably have been expected to mention at interview the facts they now relied on in their defence; they were cross-examined on their failure to mention such facts. They gave the explanation that they had relied on the solicitor's advice. In summing up the judge directed the jury that they must determine whether any adverse inferences should be drawn from the failure of the defendants to mention the facts in question during the police interview. The judge did not explain that the inferences could only be drawn if, despite the explanation, the jury concluded that the silence could only sensibly be attributed to the defendants having no satisfactory explanation to give. Thus the jury may have drawn adverse inferences despite accepting the defendants' explanations.

The appellants were convicted and argued on appeal that the jury should not have been directed that they could draw adverse inferences from the refusal to answer questions since they had followed the advice of their solicitor in so refusing. The Court of Appeal took into account an earlier case, *Cowan and Ors*,[36] which concerned the position of defendants failing to testify in court under s35, and applied the principles enunciated to police questioning. The principles were as follows. A jury cannot infer guilt from silence alone (s38(3)) so that the jury should only consider drawing inferences if a *prima facie* case to answer has been made out by the prosecution. Also, the burden of proof remains throughout on the prosecution to prove its case; in effect a silence will be only one factor which can be used to make out the case. Inferences can be drawn if the only sensible explanation of silence was that the suspect had no explanation or none that would stand up to cross-examination. The judge's direction was criticised in that it did not make this clear. The Court then considered the procedure to be followed in relation to s34 where silence is on legal advice. The jury may draw an adverse inference from the failure unless the accused gives the reason for the advice being given. The reason for the advice is legally privileged since it is part of a communication between solicitor and client, but once the client gives evidence of the nature of the advice that will probably amount to a waiver of privilege so that the solicitor and/or client can then be asked about the reasons for the advice in court. The Court found that if an accused gives as the reason for not answering questions in a police interview that he or she has been advised not to do so this assertion without more will not amount to a sufficient reason for not mentioning relevant matters which may later be relied on in defence. The convictions were upheld on the basis of the overwhelming evidence of drug supply, despite the flaw in the summing up.

[36] [1996] QB 373; [1995] 4 All ER 939.

It was made clear in *R* v *Bowden*[37] that explaining the grounds for the advice will amount to a waiver of privilege. Therefore the prosecution can cross-examine the adviser on what was said to the suspect with a view to discovering discrepancies between the grounds put forward at trial and those discussed in the police station. The effect of these two decisions is to place the defendant and adviser in an invidious position. The adviser may be reluctant to advise silence even where there seem to be good reasons for doing so.[38] If the adviser advises silence, it may well appear to the defendant that that in itself is a sound reason for remaining silent. But that reason will not be accepted by a court. The adviser can either refuse to waive legal privilege and accept that adverse inferences will be drawn from the silence, or waive it and hope that the reasons given for the advice will be accepted in order to discourage the drawing of inferences. There may also be other confidential matters which the adviser does not wish to be asked about. It has been pointed out that solicitors may breach their professional Code of Conduct if they act for a client when they may be a material witness in the court case.[39] But if there is an arguably sound reason for advising silence the jury should be directed, following the findings of the Court of Appeal in *Condron*, that if they view the reason as sound, they should not draw adverse inferences.

In *Argent*[40] the Court of Appeal found that when considering whether in the circumstances existing at the time the defendant could reasonably have been expected to mention the fact he now relies on, the court should take into account matters such as the defendant's age, health, experience, mental capacity, sobriety, tiredness, personality and legal advice. It is a matter for the jury to resolve whether, bearing these matters in mind, the defendant could have been expected to mention the fact in question, although the judge may give them guidance. Any restrictive impact of these findings is doubtful; in *R* v *Friend*[41] adverse inferences were drawn under s35 against a defendant aged 14, with a mental age of 9.

Under the Blair government the CJPOA provisions were retained and further provisions curtailing the right to silence in terrorist cases were introduced. S1 of the Criminal Justice (Terrorism and Conspiracy) Act 1998 inserted a new provision, s2A, into the PTA, making further provision for the drawing of inferences from the suspect's silence. These provisions were reproduced in s109 of the Terrorism Act 2000 but applied only to Northern Ireland.[42] S109(2) of the 2000 Act (previously s2A(5) of

[37] (1999) *The Times* 25 February.

[38] See as to the difficulties facing advisers: E Cape 'Advising on Silence' LAG 14 June 1999.

[39] Tregilgas-Davey 'Adverse Inferences and the No-comment Interview' [1997] 141 Solicitors Journal 500. *The Guide to the Professional Conduct of Solicitors* Law Society (7th edn 1996) London para 21.12.

[40] [1997] 2 Cr App R 27; *The Times* 19 December 1996. See K Broome 'An Inference of Guilt' (1997) 141 Solicitors' Journal 202.

[41] [1997] 1 WLR 1433.

[42] Under the transitional provisions of Part VII ss108 and 109 of the TA.

the PTA as inserted) provides that an inference that the suspect belongs to a proscribed organisation may be drawn at trial if the accused fails to mention, on being questioned by a constable under caution and before charge, a fact which is material to the offence and which the suspect could reasonably be expected to mention. Under s109(3) (previously s2A(6)) an inference of guilt may be drawn at trial if the accused failed to mention, on being charged or informed by a constable that the accused might be prosecuted for the offence under s11, a fact which is material to the offence and which he or she could reasonably be expected to mention. Theoretically, s109(3) could apply even before a caution has been given, so long as the provisions in s109 allowing access to legal advice, are satisfied. Presumably, however, if no caution had been given, it could not be said that the accused could reasonably have been expected to mention the information in question.

These provisions are additional to the provision under the CJPOA for drawing adverse inferences from silence and it may be noted that s34 CJPOA is narrower than s109 since it refers only to matters which are later relied on *in defence.* As indicated, case-law on s34 CJPOA already establishes that inferences may only be drawn if a sound explanation for silence is not put forward. Applying this to s109 it would appear that it cannot be inferred that the reason for silence was the need to concoct a false explanation of factors suggesting membership of a proscribed organisation if the real and innocent reason for silence is put forward. Following *Argent* the jury should only consider drawing inferences under s34 if there is a *prima facie* case to answer made out by the prosecution. Under s38(4) the conviction cannot be based on silence alone; the position is the same under the TA, under s109(4). Under s109 the burden of proof remains throughout on the prosecution to prove its case; in effect, a silence will be only one factor which can be used to make out the case. However, s109 leaves open the possibility that the conviction or committal for trial could be based on an inference of guilt from silence together with the opinion of a police officer (admissible in evidence under s108)[43]. Moreover, the possibility may also be open of combining inferences drawn in reliance on ss34, 35, 36 or 37 CJPOA with an inference *or* an opinion under ss108 and 109 TA. Therefore, for example, the possibility is not ruled out of combining silence when questioned as to presence at a particular place (which is, or is near to, a meeting place of a proscribed organisation) with silence on being informed of the possibility of prosecution under s109.

Penalising silence

Prior to the inception of the CJPOA, the right to silence was abolished in certain specific circumstances under a number of provisions which made

[43] See further Chapter 3 pp100–101.

failing to answer questions an offence. The provisions included: s172 of the Road Traffic Act 1988, s2 of the Criminal Justice Act 1987, ss177 and 178 of the Financial Services Act 1986, ss236 and 433 of the Insolvency Act 1986, s437 of the Companies Act 1985, the Banking Act 1987 and the Friendly Societies Act 1992. These provisions, apart from s172 of the RTA, were amended in 1999, as explained below.

While the Conservative governments of 1989–1997 were responsible for the shift towards the crime control position which occurred under these provisions and under the CJPOA 1994, the Blair government was responsible for a further marked shift in that direction. The Terrorism Act 2000 abolished the right to silence – in the sense of making it an offence to refuse to answer questions in defined circumstances – at certain points in the investigation of such cases. The government raised the possibility of creating such an offence in the *Consultation Paper on Terrorism* in 1998. It noted that the recent Criminal Justice (Terrorism and Conspiracy) Act 1998 'extends the provisions by allowing inferences to be drawn in connection with membership of a specified proscribed organisation; but even there that is insufficient in itself to secure a conviction'. The intention was to take this provision further by creating an additional offence of refusing to answer questions, modelled on the power currently given to investigators in a range of cases such as serious fraud investigations, and customs and licensing enquiries. The government recognised that there were what it termed 'serious ECHR constraints on this option'[44] and that in order to circumvent these constraints, the resulting evidence, whether answers or silence, could not be used in a subsequent case against the individual concerned. The government clearly had in mind the case of *Saunders* v *UK*.[45]

These considerations led to the inclusion of paras 13, 14 and 16 in Schedule 5 of the 2000 Act. The provisions relate to terrorism generally, not merely to proscription, but their relatively limited nature indicates the influence the Convention is already having in tempering legislation in attempts to ensure that it is compatible with the Convention. The government clearly did not wish to risk the political embarrassment which it would have incurred had it included provision allowing coerced statements to be included as evidence, provision which would have necessitated issuing with the Act a statement of incompatibility under s19 HRA.

The provisions as they stand are, however, of doubtful compatibility. The requirements of para 13 represent a further infringement of the rights of the suspect, albeit of a relatively limited nature and subject to judicial

[44] *Consultation Paper on Terrorism* (1998) Cm 4178 para 14.3.

[45] (1997) 23 EHRR 313. See below p281.

authorisation. Under para 13 of Schedule 5: 'a constable may apply to a Circuit judge for an order . . . requiring any person specified in the order to provide an explanation of any material – (a) seized in pursuance of a warrant under paragraph 1 or 11, or (b) produced or made available to a constable under paragraph 5'. This does not affect material protected by legal privilege, but under para 13(3) a lawyer may be required to provide the name and address of his or her client. Under para 13(5) para 10 applies to such orders: they will have effect as if they were orders of the Crown Court. Thus a person who refused to comply could incur liability for contempt. But any statement obtained cannot be used in evidence except on a prosecution for an offence under para 14. Para 14(1) provides: 'a person commits an offence if, in purported compliance with an order under paragraph 13, he makes a statement which he knows to be false or misleading in a material particular', or recklessly makes such a statement. This offence is punishable by a maximum prison sentence of two years. Para 16 is even more controversial; it provides a further possibility, untrammelled by judicial intervention, of punishing persons for failing to give explanations, or giving misleading ones. Para 16(1) provides: 'if a police officer of at least the rank of superintendent has reasonable grounds for believing that the case is one of great emergency he may by a written notice signed by him require any person specified in the notice to provide an explanation of any material seized in pursuance of an order under paragraph 15'. Under para 16(3), in contrast to para 13, the suspect will commit an offence carrying a maximum prison term of six months if he or she fails to comply with a notice under the paragraph.

Both paras 13 and 16 allow for the admissibility of coerced statements, although in respect of the para 14 offence only. Thus, courts will have to consider whether admitting such statements in respect of that offence would be compatible with Article 6. Further, the paragraphs do not refer to silences which may be admissible in respect of other offences, as may evidence from the statement against another person. Also the evidence from any statements made, while not directly available to the court, may nevertheless underpin the other prosecution evidence, thereby arguably undermining the right to freedom from self-incrimination (see below)[46].

The transitional provisions applying to Northern Ireland create a further erosion of the right to silence. Under s89(2) TA it is an offence punishable by a fine not to stop when required to do so by an officer; it is also an offence to refuse to answer a question asked during the stop or to answer it inadequately, failing to answer 'to the best of his knowledge and ability'.

46 At pp286–7.

Custodial access to legal advice

Introduction

The due process value of custodial legal advice derives in part from the relationship between access to legal advice and the right to silence. This is a complex relationship,[47] particularly in view of the curtailment of the right to silence under ss34, 36 and 37 of the Criminal Justice and Public Order Act 1994. As indicated above, these provisions place legal advisers in a difficult position and it may be the case that some advisers who might previously have advised silence (or a selective silence) owing to the possibility that the particular client might make false or misleading admissions, now consider that it would be too risky to give such advice owing to the possibility of adverse inference drawing. It was, however, clear, prior to 1994, that advisers did not advise silence routinely.[48] Dixon found in 1991 that solicitors were likely to advise silence at least temporarily if the client was in a confused or emotional state[49] or had been bullied or deceived, or where the police had refused to disclose at least some of the evidence against the client to the adviser.[50]

The presence of an adviser can affect the interview in many other ways, aside from advice as to when and if to remain silent. The adviser can advise on other practical and legal matters and can make representations to the police regarding continued detention, charges and bail. The suspect may feel generally reassured by the presence of a person independent of the police who may be undaunted by the interview process; his or her presence may sometimes be a potent factor discouraging use of improper tactics,[51] and, if an adversarial stance is adopted, may help to alter the balance of power between interviewer and interviewee, thus tending to create a climate in which an unreliable confession is less likely

[47] The relationship is a matter of some controversy; the Home Office Working Group on the Right to Silence (C Division, Home Office, London, 13 July 1989; see 1989 Crim LR 855 for comment) considered that there was a causal relationship between legal advice and silence, but this finding has been doubted by D Dixon: see 'Solicitors, Suspects, Runners, Police' findings reported at [1991] PL 233 at p251. However, the research by A Sanders *et al Advice and Assistance at Police Stations* (1989) found that suspects confess less often when they have advice: 35.8% of those whose solicitor was present at the interrogation confessed as opposed to 59.6% of those who did not receive advice (op cit p136).

[48] See the research undertaken by A Sanders *et al* '*supra* note 47' at p129 which found that out of 24 suspects only 2 were advised to remain silent. D Dixon's findings *supra* note 47 op cit p243 were to the same effect.

[49] See D Dixon 'Common sense, Legal Advice and the Right of Silence' [1991] Public Law 233 at p244.

[50] Op cit p246 and 247.

[51] One of the conclusions of the Sanders research (*supra* note 47) op cit p150 was that suspects who did not receive advice or whose solicitors did not attend the interrogation would have been greatly assisted had the solicitor been present. Two examples are given at pp138 and 139 of forceful or threatening questioning which produced a possibly unreliable confession from an easily intimidated suspect in the absence of a solicitor. This finding received some support from Dixon's study (*supra* note 47).

to be made. Access to legal advice may have, therefore, broadly speaking, an impact in upholding due process which encompasses but goes beyond advising on making 'no-comment' answers. How far it has such an impact in practice is debatable. The impact varies, depending on the contact with the suspect. The Sanders research in 1989 found that telephone advice alone had little impact on suspects: 50% of those who received telephone advice made admissions as opposed to 59.6% of those who received no advice.[52] The research criticised the great variation in practice between advisers, and considered that too many duty solicitors gave telephone advice only, thereby depriving the client of most of the benefits of legal advice.[53] Subsequent research suggests that in 23% of cases when advice is requested telephone advice only continues to be given and only around 12–14% of suspects in police interviews have an adviser present.[54]

Nevertheless, it is still generally agreed that the most significant protection introduced for the first time by PACE[55] for due process is access to legal advice.[56] But this right is far from absolute. Interviews outside the police station continue to be unaffected by it, in the sense that notification of the right is reserved for the police station, thus disadvantaging the inexperienced suspect who is not already aware of it. The very significant reform of notification of legal advice on caution was omitted from all the Code C revisions, including the 1999 one, despite the fact of curtailment of the right to silence and of the strong possibility that questioning accompanied by the risk of drawing adverse inferences from silence without access to legal advice breaches Article 6(1).[57] The right is also subject to a number of formal exceptions, which are broader in terrorist cases, and is dependent on a formal request to exercise it.

[52] Sanders *et al* (1989).

[53] The Sanders research (*supra* note 47) found that only 50% of solicitors attended the police station: 25% gave advice over the telephone and 25% gave no advice. Even attendances at the police station were not always followed by attendance at the interview. A few solicitors merely put the police case to the suspect: op cit p150. It appeared that some advisers who attended the interview disadvantaged the client by seeming to give their imprimatur to improper police behaviour.

[54] D Brown *PACE Ten Years On: A Review of the Research* (HO Research Study 155, 1997) London: HMSO, pp94–95.

[55] The Criminal Law Act 1977 s62 declared a narrow entitlement to have one reasonably named person informed of the arrest. It did not provide that the arrestee must be informed of this right, nor did it provide any sanction for non-compliance by a police officer. That statutory form of this right gave it no greater force than the non-statutory Judges Rules (rules of practice for the guidance of the police: see Practice Note 1984 1 All ER 237, 1 WLR 152). The Judges Rules upheld the right of the suspect/arrestee in the police station to communicate with/consult a solicitor but permitted the withholding of such access 'lest unreasonable delay or hindrance is caused to the process of investigation or the administration of justice'. Any officer, in relation to a person detained for any offence, could deny access to legal advice on these broad grounds; see *Lemsateff* [1977] 1 WLR 812; [1977] 2 All ER 835.

[56] See D Dixon in *Miscarriages of Justice* (1999) p67. The research studies mentioned in this chapter do not question the value of the legal *right* of access, although they do question its quality and the responses of the police.

[57] See further below at pp288–9.

By the late 1990s there was quite a strong academic consensus to the effect that there are two main weaknesses in the legal advice scheme as it stands – the ease of evading its provisions, and the quality of advice given – which mean that the due process protection apparently afforded by this right is not fully available in practice. Ironically, the 'false ideology' propounded by both the police and advisers that 'the trial rather than the police interview is where guilt and innocence is decided'[58] discourages take-up of advice with the result, it is suggested, that the crime control concept of rapidly obtaining admissions (or silences) in order to speed the suspect through the system remains firmly in the ascendant, leading to the continuing fallibility of a certain number of interviews and the marginalisation of the trial.

Quality of advice

Research has found that the *quality* of the advice given is seriously open to question.[59] Research undertaken in 1989 found that many 'legal advisers' were clerks, secretaries and former police officers with no legal education or training in the provision of custodial legal advice. Other recent research echoes these findings as to the quality of advice and suggests that advisers adopt a passive stance in interviews, failing to intervene where intervention is clearly called for.[60] The suggestions that advisers are reluctant to adopt an adversarial stance were given credence by the two post-PACE cases of oppression which arose in respect of tape-recorded interviews with an adviser present.[61] McConville finds: 'Lacking any clear understanding of their role in the process, some advisers simply become part of the machine which confronts the suspect'.[62] The advisers must operate on police territory and may, as Dixon puts it, deal with the resultant pressures by making 'some positive adaptation'.[63] Thus the mere fact that a person termed a 'legal adviser' turns up at the police station and may be present in the interview may have little or no impact in terms

[58] M McConville, A Sanders and E Leng *The Case for the Prosecution* (1991) London: Routledge.

[59] A study conducted for the Royal Commission on Criminal Justice by Jaqueline Hodgson and Mike McConville took place over an eight-month period during which the researchers followed suspects and advisers into 180 interrogations; see 143 NLJ 659. The Runciman Royal Commission proposed that the performance of solicitors should be monitored, and that the police should receive training in the role solicitors are expected to play (proposals 64–69).

[60] 'The Role of Legal Representatives at Police Stations' (1992) HMSO Research Study No 3, summarised at 1993 Crim LR 161. The approach of the research has been criticised: see D Roberts (1993) Crim LR 368 with reply by Baldwin at p371.

[61] *R* v *Paris* (1993) 97 Cr App R 99; *Heron* (1993) judgment of Mitchell J 1 November 1993, unreported.

[62] M McConville and J Hodgson 'Custodial Legal Advice and the Right to Silence' Runciman Royal Commission Study No 13. See also J Baldwin 'Legal Advice at the Police Station' [1993] Crim LR 371.

[63] D Dixon 'Common Sense, Legal Advice and the Right to Silence' [1991] PL 233 at pp236–237.

of evening up the balance of power between suspect and police officer. Indeed, the presence of such a person may be to the *disadvantage* of the suspect since it may offer a reassurance which it does not warrant. In a response to the available research and recommendations of the Runciman Royal Commission[64] the Law Society is undertaking a programme of training with a view to ensuring that clerks or other non-solicitor advisers are accredited in accordance with the Law Society's scheme for accreditation.[65] But the quality of advice, although improving, remains variable: around 26% of those giving custodial legal advice are non-solicitors[66] and where an 'own' as opposed to a duty solicitor gives advice there is no requirement that he or she should have specialist training in this area.

Powers to delay access

PACE and the TA entitle suspects to consult an adviser privately[67] under a publicly funded scheme,[68] to be informed of this right,[69] given, if necessary, the name of the duty solicitor[70] and be permitted to have the solicitor present during questioning.[71] Where the detainee is suspected of a 'serious arrestable offence',[72] however, there are certain saving provisions under s58(8) PACE allowing an officer of at least the rank of superintendent to authorise delay for up to 36 hours,[73] and further powers to interview the suspect without his or her having had legal advice arise under Code C.[74] All these provisions apply to all arrestees,

[64] *Runciman Report* Recommendations 61–8. In response to the McConville study, reported at 143 NLJ 659, the Law Society and Legal Aid Board announced that from October 1993 legal aid would not be available for police station work unless advisers had been through a training course and passed a Law Society test.

[65] See E Sheppherd *Becoming Skilled* (1994) London: Law Society.

[66] D Brown *Home Office Research Study* 155 (1997) London: HMSO p108.

[67] S58(1) PACE: 'A person in police detention shall be entitled, if he so requests, to consult a solicitor privately at any time.' For TA suspects this right also arises under Sched 8 para 7 TA.

[68] See the Legal Aid Act 1988 sch 6.

[69] Code C para 3.1(ii).

[70] Code C Note 6B. The duty solicitor arrangements are governed by the Legal Aid Board Duty Solicitor Arrangements (1994).

[71] Code C para 6.8.

[72] Where s24 and s116 apply.

[73] Under s58(8): 'An officer may only authorise delay where he has reasonable grounds for believing that the exercise of the right... (a) will lead to interference with or harm to evidence connected with a serious arrestable offence or interference with or physical injury to other persons; or (b) will lead to the alerting of other persons suspected of having committed such an offence but not yet arrested for it; or (c) will hinder the recovery of any property obtained as a result of such an offence'. Under s58(8A) delay can also be authorised 'where the serious arrestable offence is a drug trafficking offence and the officer has reasonable grounds for believing (a) that the detained person has benefited from drug trafficking and (b) that the recovery of the value of that person's proceeds of drug trafficking will be hindered by the exercise of the right'.

[74] Code paras 6.5, 6.6 and Annex B. The para 6 provisions are not dependent on the offence in question being a serious arrestable one. A power to proceed with the interview although the suspect has not had advice arises if there are reasonable grounds for believing that

but in terrorist cases there are further exceptions to the general right which arise under Code C: the right can be delayed if a superintendent reasonably believes that communication with an adviser 'will lead to interference with the gathering of information about the commission, preparation, or instigation of acts of terrorism' or make it more difficult 'to prevent an act of terrorism or apprehend and prosecute the perpetrators of any such act'.[75]

Under the Terrorism Act 2000 itself the access can be delayed for up to 48 hours (see Sched 8 para 8(2)) and the grounds for delay mentioned above, with additional ones relating to recovery of the proceeds of crime, are set out in Sched 8 para 8(4). The TA harmonises the arrangements for delay in Northern Ireland with those in England and Wales, in that once access has been granted it will not then be withheld.[76] The arrangements in Scotland under the TA allow for delay under Sched 8 para 16(7) if, under para 17(3), delay is in the interests of the investigation or prevention of crime or in recovering property criminally obtained, or in confiscating the proceeds of an offence, or 'of the apprehension, prosecution or conviction of offenders'. In all three jurisdictions, when a review officer authorises continued detention under Schedule 8 TA the officer must remind the detainee of his or her rights to contact a friend or relative and to consult a solicitor[77] and, if applicable, of the fact of their being delayed. The officer must also consider whether the reason or reasons for which the delay was authorised continue to subsist, and if not, that officer must inform the officer who authorised the delay of his or her opinion. However, there is no provision allowing the review officer to override the view of the officer who originally authorised delay. The TA provisions largely continue the old regime, and therefore do not address the concerns of those who view confessions obtained after 24 hours in detention as inherently fallible,[78] particularly where the detainee has also been held incommunicado.

Under this scheme the power of delay in Scotland is wider and is less dependent than in the other jurisdictions on the interests of preventing or detecting acts of terrorism. This seems to be anomalous given that one of the aims of the TA is to harmonise the position of terrorist suspects

delay would cause harm to persons or serious harm to property, or where a solicitor has agreed to attend, awaiting his or her arrival would cause unreasonable delay to the process of the investigation, or the solicitor is unavailable, or the suspect, having asked for access, changes his or her mind. In the last instance, the reason must be recorded on tape.

[75] Code C Annex B. This applied to detention under the PTA but will apply to the equivalent TA provisions. This provision is likely to appear in the new TA Code.

[76] Under the EPA and its Codes the powers to delay access were broadly the same as under the PTA, but also, once the police had allowed access, further delays could be imposed and there was no right to have advisers present in interviews. This right is not contained in the TA, but may appear in its accompanying Code, when promulgated.

[77] Under para 27. These rights arise under paras 6 and 7 of Schedule 8.

[78] See, for example, C Walker in *Miscarriages of Justice* (1999) p18.

throughout the UK. The changes under the TA also provide further grounds for delay in obtaining access to legal advice, which also apply in relation to a far wider group of persons than those covered by the PTA and EPA since, potentially, a far larger group may become 'terrorist' suspects in future. Within that group are persons who signally fail to fit the stereotype of the 'terrorist' and are therefore more in need of legal advice. The wider possibilities of delaying access under the TA in relation to the terrorist, as opposed to the conventional suspect, are therefore open to question under Article 6, as discussed below.

Informal subversion

Research confirms that the possibility of formally delaying access to legal advice is almost certainly not as significant as the more informal police influence on the notification and delivery of advice and on securing the presence of the adviser.[79] This may be due in part to the determination shown by the Court of Appeal to protect this due process right by restrictive interpretation of the formal exceptions under s58(8) PACE in a key decision.[80] Quite a large body of research suggests that the police continue to prefer to interview suspects who have not had advice and without an adviser present.[81] Notification may be subverted by various methods, most commonly by ensuring that suspects never really take in what is on offer.[82] In 1991 the further requirement to sign the custody record to give effect to the decision not to have advice was included, under para 3.5, but this provision may be subverted,[83] by presenting the requirement for the suspect to 'sign here, here and here' as a mere formality. A further protective requirement was introduced in 1995 under para 3.5A; the suspect should be asked his or her reason for declining legal advice, and this should be noted on the custody record as should the fact that the suspect has declined to speak on the telephone with the duty solicitor after being reminded that he or she can do so. However, the possibility of manipulation of the custody record remains since the whole process of making the record remains in the hands of the custody officer. It has been suggested that a requirement

[79] The research undertaken by A Sanders *et al* '*Advice and Assistance at Police Stations*' (November 1989) put the figure at around 2%. In comparison Brown found that approximately 35% of suspects may have been influenced against advice by the police. The government's Consultation Paper on Terrorism stated that it was not aware of any formal denial in terrorist cases over the last two years in Britain (para 8.31).

[80] *R* v *Samuel* [1988] 2 All ER 135; [1988] 2 WLR 920.

[81] The research undertaken by A Sanders *et al, supra* note 79; D Brown *PACE Ten Years On: A Review of the Research* (Home Office Research Study 155) London: HMSO (1977) p77.

[82] Sanders found that the most popular ploy (used in 42.9% of the instances observed) was to read the rights too quickly, or incomprehensibly or incompletely: op cit p59.

[83] Sanders op cit p48 and p59.

of an own-hand declaration of waiver of advice on the custody record would have represented an effective means of addressing the problem since it would have forced the custody officer to ensure that the suspect understood what was being offered and would have required positive action on the suspect's part to refuse it.[84]

Even where the suspect has requested advice it is possible that the interview will go ahead although he or she has not received it. Under the 1991 revision, once the suspect had changed his or her mind about having advice, the interview could proceed subject to the need to obtain the permission of an officer of the rank of inspector or above. A provision was included in the 1991 Home Office Circular[85] amplifying Code C requiring a note to be made in the custody record of the reason for the suspect's change of heart, and this Circular provision, in the form of a requirement to record the reason for the change of mind and repeat it on tape, became part of para 6.6(d) under the 1995 changes. This provision may allow a court to determine whether the consent *was* based on misleading information, but leaves open the possibility of treating the consent as valid so long as such information was apparently given in good faith.[86]

This discussion suggests that the revisions of Code C in 1991 and 1995 tinkered with the problem of informal subversion of the right but no radical change was undertaken. The 1999 revision signalled an abandonment of attempts to improve the scheme, despite the fact that after 1995 commentators had continued to point out its defects.[87] The fundamental problem is that the process of delivering advice remains in the hands of a body which has an interest in withholding it, while many suspects continue to need disinterested advice regarding the decision whether to have advice.[88] The result is that the introduction of new provisions aimed at curbing informal subversion is unlikely to have much impact and police working practices of subverting the new provisions themselves will tend to develop. It has been found that 'in around 28 per cent of cases prior to the 1991 revisions but in 35 per cent afterwards suspects may have been influenced against seeking advice by the police'.[89] The percentage of suspects who receive advice remains relatively low and the research suggests that this continues to be due in part

[84] Suggested by David Wolchover and Anthony Heaton-Armstrong NLJ 9 March (1990) at pp320–321.

[85] When the 1991 revision of the PACE Codes came into force in April 1991 a Home Office Circular was issued in conjunction with them by F2 Division, Home Office.

[86] See *Hughes* (1988) Crim LR 519 Transcript from LEXIS.

[87] See D Brown *PACE Ten Years on: A Review of the Research* Home Office Research Study 155 (1997) London: HMSO; A Sanders 'Access to Justice in the Police Station: an Elusive Dream?' in *Access to Justice* (1996) London: Blackstone Press.

[88] The Sanders research found that suspects quite often asked officers whether or not they should have advice: op cit p65.

[89] D Brown *et al Changing the Code* (HO Research Study 129 1992) London: HMSO.

to subversion of notification and the responses of the police to requests for advice.[90]

Audio-recording

Once the suspect is inside the police station under arrest or under caution,[91] any interview (i.e. an exchange which falls within para 11.1A Code C) with a person who has been cautioned in respect of an indictable or 'either way' offence[92] should be audio-recorded under Code of Practice E. Initial resistance by the police gave way to a recognition of the advantages of audio-recording which seem to be generally accepted.[93] Audio-recording was not initially used in terrorist cases, under Code E para 3.2, or in cases of espionage under s1 of the Official Secrets Act 1989. This provision was clarified under Note for Guidance 3G of Code E; interviews with those suspected of terrorism solely connected with the affairs of the UK or any part of the UK other than Northern Ireland should be tape recorded. A written contemporaneous record could still be made of interviews which fell within Code E para 3.2. This exemption was included because it was feared that the contents of tapes might become available to terrorist organisations. The Home Office reviewed it in 1990,[94] and although it did not introduce mandatory audio-recording, police in Britain undertook it in terrorist cases on a voluntary basis. Since, under s1 TA, terrorism is defined much more widely to include those suspects covered by Note G, and the problem of Irish terrorism has diminished, the obvious step is to make audio-recording of interviews with terrorist suspects mandatory. Under the original version of the Bill this was accomplished by Schedule 7 para 9 TA which provided for the audio-recording of any interview by a constable of a person detained under section 41 and Schedule 7 TA, once a new Code of Practice had been introduced. This step would not have changed current practice, apart from that in Northern Ireland, but it would have afforded formal recognition to this due process safeguard. The current position is left unclear

[90] D Brown *PACE Ten Years On: A Review of the Research* (Home Office Research Study 155 1997) Lodon: HMSO pp94–95.

[91] Under para 3.4 of Code E (1999 version) once a volunteer becomes a suspect (i.e. at the point when he or she should be cautioned) the rest of the interview should be tape recorded.

[92] Under para 3.1(a) an interview with a person suspected of an offence triable only summarily need not be audio-taped, although under Note 3A it can be recorded at police discretion.

[93] See C Wills, J Mcleod and P Nash *The Tape-recording of Police Interviews with Suspects* 2nd Interim Report, Home Office Research Study No 97 (1988). The study found that police officers and prosecutors generally welcomed taping since it is a faster recording method and renders them less vulnerable to allegations of 'verballing'.

[94] House of Commons *Hansard* Vol 168 col 273, 1 March 1990.

since audio-recording is to be dealt with by a Code of Practice to be issued by the Secretary of State and different provision may be made for different parts of the UK.[95]

Convention requirements under the HRA

As indicated in Chapter 5, criminal proceedings will not provide the only forum in which Article 6 arguments can be raised. Article 6 starts to apply after the suspect has been charged. The term 'charged' has an autonomous Convention meaning and it is necessary 'to look behind the appearances and investigate the realities of the procedure in question'.[96] It has been held by the Commission (only) in *X* v *UK*[97] that 'charged' can cover the point at which a person is arrested, but Strasbourg has not considered the Article 6 due process rights outside the trial context. Certain of the rights considered above, particularly that of access to legal advice, may be viewed as having a value for the suspect which arises irrespective of their influence on the trial.[98] An instance might arise in which the pre-trial process was deeply flawed since a detainee had made admissions after, for example, being refused access to legal advice, questioned aggressively for a long period and racially abused. Under Article 6 there would be a strong argument that the trial would be rendered unfair if the admissions were not excluded from evidence. *Outside* the context of the trial the availability of a remedy in respect of the custodial treatment, apart from a complaint, would be doubtful, assuming that the treatment was not severe enough to fall within Article 3 and the questioning was not viewed as so intrusive as to fall within Article 8.[99] But there might be methods of seeking to rely on Article 6.

Since, as Chapter 2 explains, the HRA requires the courts to construe statutes to be compatible with the Convention rights 'so far as it is possible to do so',[100] and offers a remedy where a public authority violates the Convention rights,[101] it may be argued that while Article 6 only provides guarantees which have value in the context of the *trial*, their significance is such that, interpreting s58 PACE or the right of access to legal advice under Sched 8 para 7 TA, as the domestic embodiments of a right

[95] Schedule 8 para 3(1) and (7).
[96] *Deweer* v *Belgium* A 35 para 44 (1980).
[97] No 8233/78 17 DR 122 (1979).
[98] This 'free-standing' value received recognition under s67(8) PACE (subsequently repealed by s37(f) CJPOA 1994): breach of the Codes was automatically a breach of the Police Disciplinary Code, regardless of the question whether the case came to trial.
[99] See the findings in *Lustig-Prean and Beckett* v *UK* and *Smith and Grady* v *UK* (2000) 29 EHRR 493, below, at p292.
[100] Section 3(1).
[101] Sections 6(1), 7 and 8.

implicit in Article 6, it is clear that a remedy for its breach is required. The central question would be whether Article 6 could be viewed as breached where proceedings were abandoned or discontinued some time after the police interview or where the defendant pleaded guilty. Bearing in mind the fact that the vast majority of instances of police arrest and interviewing do not come to trial, this is a highly significant matter, in due process terms. Not only might the possibility of a tort remedy play some part in deterring police evasion of the due process safeguards, thereby safeguarding the trial process indirectly, but the coercive experience of police interrogation under arrest might be ameliorated if the safeguards are fully adhered to. Moreover, occurrences in police interviews may have a bearing on decisions to plead guilty. The remedy would be for breach of the statutory duty under PACE. Judicial review, based on Article 6 principles, could also be sought of a decision to delay custodial access to legal advice. The HRA may oblige the courts to provide remedies for breach of a number of rights protected by statutory rules, even though they have not so far done so.[102]

A number of Code provisions[103] also cover aspects of rights falling impliedly within Article 6, although clearly it cannot be assumed that breach of such provisions would necessarily amount to a breach of Article 6 in any given instance. For example, Article 6(2) provides for a presumption of innocence which may *inter alia* include an implied requirement that a caution should be administered to suspects before inferences can be drawn from silence.[104] A duty to caution might also be read into Article 6(1). If a suspect sought to sue the police for *inter alia* breach of a Code provision, complaining, for example, that contrary to Code C para 10.1, he was not cautioned, the courts would remain bound by s67(10) of PACE which precludes the possibility of civil liability arising from a breach of a Code provision. Oppressive questioning is also forbidden only under a Code provision, Code C para 11.3. Where such questioning fell short of Article 3 treatment and also fell outside Article 8, Article 6 might be looked to to provide a remedy even outside the trial context. Similarly, PACE itself does not provide that suspects must be fit to be interviewed or that suspects suffering from illness or withdrawal from drugs should not be interviewed or detained. The provision is contained in Code of Practice C paras 9 and 12.3.[105] A suspect who had been detained or

[102] See Sanders 'Rights, Remedies and the Police and Criminal Evidence Act' [1988] Crim LR 802.

[103] Arising under s66 PACE and Schedule 12 para 6(1) TA for England, Scotland and Wales, and s98 TA for Northern Ireland.

[104] This is a requirement under s34 CJPOA, but s34 becomes relevant only when the question of drawing adverse inferences arises at trial.

[105] They provide that no person who is unfit through drink or drugs, to the extent that he or she is unable to appreciate the significance of questions put to him or her and his or her answers, may be questioned about an alleged offence in that condition except in accordance with Annex C (covering urgent interviews with vulnerable suspects including those under the influence of drugs).

interviewed while ill or withdrawing from drugs might also wish to raise these issues under Article 6.

A number of possible courses would be open to a court, assuming that it found a breach of Article 6 which it was prepared to address regardless of the trial process. If it was of sufficient authority[106] it could issue a declaration of incompatibility between s67(10) and Article 6, but since the Convention cannot impliedly repeal incompatible statutory provisions,[107] it could offer no tortious remedy in respect of the breach of paras 10.1 or 11.3, precisely because a breach of a Code provision alone was at issue. Such a declaration might trigger off a 'fast track' amendment to PACE which would repeal or modify s67(10), but the Act makes it clear that a number of such declarations might be made without triggering such an amendment.[108]

The alternative and, it is suggested, more likely course would be to decide the case purely on Article 6 grounds, merely taking the Code provision into account in so doing. Some indications of the possible judicial attitude to the adoption of such a course are apparent from the findings in *R* v *Chief Constable of the RUC ex p Begley*.[109] The House of Lords showed some sympathy with the possibility that there is a common law right to have a solicitor present in police interviews, although they were not prepared to recognise the existence of such a right in the particular legislative context. In the context of PACE the right is enshrined in Code C para 6 which could be regarded as the embodiment of a common law right, recognised also under Article 6. The implication of *Begley* was that had the right in question been recognised, it would have been free standing and possibly would have been underpinned by tortious liability.

It is very clear, however, that Article 6 arguments will most commonly be raised during criminal proceedings; in pre-trial hearings, during the criminal trial and on appeal a number of aspects of police interviewing may be called into question.

Freedom from self-incrimination and the presumption of innocence

Article 6 of the Convention contrasts with Article 14(3) of the International Covenant on Civil and Political Rights and with Article 34(1) of the South African Bill of Rights in that it does not expressly forbid using

[106] Under s4(5) HRA not all courts may make declarations of incompatibility. Broadly speaking, courts of lesser authority than the High Court will be unable to do so. See Chapter 2 p45.

[107] See further Chapter 2 pp42–45.

[108] As indicated in Chapter 2 at p45, a declaration under s4 does *not* automatically trigger off the 'fast track' amending procedure under s10 since under s10(1)(a) an amendment *may* be made if the minister in question 'considers that there are *compelling reasons* for proceeding under this section'.

[109] (1998) HL Publications on the Internet.

compulsion to obtain confessions.[110] The expectation under Article 6(2) that the state bears the burden of establishing guilt impliedly requires that the accused should not be expected to provide involuntary assistance by way of a confession. Thus the presumption of innocence under Article 6(2) is closely linked to the right to freedom from self-incrimination which the Court has found to be covered by the right to a fair hearing under Article 6(1).[111] Article 6(2) further impliedly requires that when carrying out their duties members of a court should not start with the preconceived idea that the accused has committed the offence charged; the burden of proof is on the prosecution, and any doubt should benefit the accused. These matters are at issue when silence under interrogation by law enforcement bodies is penalised by a formal penalty or by drawing adverse inferences from it. The Court has drawn a distinction between these matters, although it recognised in *Murray (John)* v *UK*[112] that they were not entirely distinct since adverse inference-drawing is clearly a form of penalty; it was termed 'indirect compulsion'.

It is possible that curtailment of the right to silence under ss34, 36 or 37 of the CJPOA 1994 may, depending on the particular circumstances of a case, lead to a breach of Article 6 on the basis that it infringes the presumption of innocence under Article 6(2) and the right to freedom from self-incrimination. Consideration of the judgments in *Saunders* v *UK*[113] and *Murray (John)* v *UK* reveals that it is only where a penalty formally attaches to silence, and the interview may then be used in evidence, that a breach of Article 6 is almost bound to be established, but that where adverse inferences can be drawn from the silence at trial a breach may be established, taking into account the question of access to legal advice. *Saunders* v *UK* concerned the sanction for refusing to answer questions in serious fraud investigations under s437 of the Companies Act 1985. Acting under s437 Inspectors of the Department of Trade and Industry had interviewed Saunders regarding allegations of fraud. He was forced to answer the questions put to him and therefore lost his privilege against self-incrimination, which he argued was unfair and amounted to an abuse of process. The interviews were admitted in evidence under s431(5) of the Companies Act and he was convicted.[114] The Strasbourg Court found that the applicant's right to freedom from self-incrimination under Article 6(1) had been infringed owing to the threatened imposition of a penalty for remaining silent and the subsequent admission of the interviews into evidence. This finding was based on the special compulsive

[110] It may be noted that the UN Human Rights Committee has already expressed concerns regarding the compatibility of ss34, 36 and 37 CJPOA with Article 14(3).

[111] *Funke* v *France* (1993) 16 EHRR 297.

[112] (1996) 22 EHRR 29. For comment see R Munday (1996) Crim LR 370.

[113] (1997) 23 EHRR 313; No 19187/91, Com Rep paras 69–75.

[114] His appeal on grounds of abuse of process and on the basis that the interviews should not have been admitted into evidence under s78 was rejected: *R* v *Saunders and Others* [1996] 1 Cr App R 463.

regime applicable to Department of Trade and Industry inspections, but the key issue was the use made of the material obtained in court.

The decision in *Murray (John)* v *UK*[115] may be contrasted with that in *Saunders* since it suggests that, depending on the circumstances of a case, Article 6 takes a different stance towards imposing a formal penalty on silence and drawing adverse inferences from it. Murray was arrested under the Prevention of Terrorism (Temporary Provisions) Act 1989 and taken to a police station. A detective superintendent, pursuant to the Northern Ireland (Emergency Provisions) Act 1987, decided to delay access to a solicitor for 48 hours. While being interviewed Murray repeatedly stated that he had 'nothing to say'. After he had seen his solicitor he stated that he had been advised not to answer the questions. As indicated above, the Criminal Evidence (Northern Ireland) Order 1988 enables a court in any criminal trial to exercise discretion to draw adverse inferences from an accused's failure to mention a fact during police questioning. Such inferences were drawn from Murray's silence in the police interviews once the prosecution had established a *prima facie* case against him, and he was convicted. The Strasbourg Court emphasised that its decision was confined to the particular facts of the case in finding that no breach of Article 6(1) or (2) had occurred where adverse inferences had been drawn at trial from the applicant's refusal to give evidence, taking into account the degree of compulsion exerted on the applicant and the weight of the evidence against him. The Court placed emphasis on the fact that he had been able to remain silent; also, given the strength of the evidence against him, the matter of drawing inferences was one of common sense which could not be regarded as unfair.[116] But, crucially, the Court did find that Articles 6(1) and (3) had been breached by the denial of custodial access to a lawyer for 48 hours since it found that such access was essential where there was a likelihood that adverse inferences would be drawn from silence. In effect, therefore, the Court adopted something close to an exchange abolitionist approach.[117]

The regime under the 1988 Order is, in essentials, the same as that under s34 CJPOA which may therefore be vulnerable to challenge under the HRA. As indicated, the findings in *Murray* were carefully confined to the particular facts of the case, and therefore must be treated with caution. But it is clear that the right to freedom from self-incrimination cannot be viewed as absolute. Drawing adverse inferences from silence in police interviewing does not necessarily breach Article 6(2), but the greater the reliance placed on such inferences at the trial, the greater the likelihood that a breach will occur. The Court said that it would be incompatible with Articles 6(1) and (2) 'to base a conviction solely or mainly on the accused's silence or refusal to answer questions'. Under s38(3) of the

[115] (1996) 22 EHRR 29.
[116] Para 54.
[117] See Greer note 22, above.

CJPOA a conviction cannot be based 'solely' on silence. Articles 6(1) and (2) might therefore be found to be breached in circumstances differing from those applicable in *Murray*, including those in which the evidence against the defendant was less overwhelming. A domestic judge would not satisfy Article 6 if he or she directed a jury that the drawing of adverse inferences could play a major part in a conviction. Further, in *Murray* there was no jury: the case was decided by a 'Diplock' court. Therefore, the evidence was weighed up by a professional who had the expertise to determine how much weight to give to aspects of it, including the 'no-comment' interviews.

Murray makes it clear that drawing adverse inferences from silence when the defendant had not had access to legal advice prior to the failure to reply to questioning will breach Article 6. As indicated above, s58 of the Youth Justice and Criminal Evidence Act addresses that finding. But it need not be assumed, conversely, that Article 6 will necessarily be satisfied where a defendant has had such access prior to that point. Cases such as *Condron* or *Bowden* (above) where the defendants had had legal advice and had acted on it in remaining silent should be considered on their particular facts, in relation to the Article 6 requirements. Such cases differ from *Murray* on the issue of the relationship between silence and legal advice. In *Condron* the defendants acted on legal advice in refusing to answer questions; in *Murray* a breach of Article 6(1) was found on the basis of inference drawing in the absence of legal advice (not on the basis of inference drawing *per se*). In *Condron* the fact of having legal advice was not to the defendants' advantage, possibly the reverse, since in a sense they may have been misled into remaining silent. It is arguable that allowing adverse inferences to be drawn in that context – where the innocent explanation for silence was that it was on legal advice – could in certain circumstances be viewed as a breach of Article 6(1). For example, this might be argued where the adviser had failed to point out that adverse inferences might be drawn despite the advice and/or where the defendant could not be expected – owing to his or her low intelligence, youth or other vulnerability – to decide to speak despite the advice. To hold otherwise might be viewed as undermining the value attached in *Murray* to granting access to legal advice where adverse inferences would be drawn from silence.[118] The principle from *Murray* clearly rests impliedly on the value of such advice, which the domestic decision in *Condron* appears to undermine. The possibility, therefore, arises that even where a suspect has had access to legal advice before taking a decision to remain silent, there may be circumstances, such as those arising in *Condron*, in which the jury should be directed that no adverse inferences should be

[118] It may be noted that such a finding would involve a departure from the current position under UK law as set out in *Condron* [1997] 1 Cr App R 185 and confirmed in *Bowden* (1999) *The Times* 25 February.

drawn, or the interview should be excluded from evidence under s78 if Article 6 is not to be breached.

It was found at Strasbourg that the applicants in *Condron* v *UK*[119] had failed to receive a fair trial under Article 6 on the basis that the Court of Appeal should not have found that the conviction was safe, despite the erroneous direction of the judge to the jury. Since the Court could not know what part the drawing of adverse inferences played in the jury's decision, it should have allowed the appeal. That decision impliedly confirms that juries should be directed that they should not draw adverse inferences where they consider that there was a sound reason for advising silence. The decision affects the role of the Court of Appeal; it does not give guidance on *inter alia* the question when a no-comment interview, based on legal advice, should be excluded from evidence, or as to the reasons which might be viewed as sound for advising a suspect to remain silent.

At present, therefore, the circumstances in which adverse inference drawing will amount to a breach of Article 6 remain uncertain, except in the instance in which access to legal advice is also denied. In that instance, once s58 of the Youth Justice and Criminal Evidence Act 1999 comes into force, no inferences may be drawn from silence. It is notable that s58 does not provide that such a silence will be *inadmissible.* Informal inference drawing, which appeared to occur prior to the introduction of ss34, 36 and 37 of the CJPOA, could therefore still occur. Further, s58 of the 1999 Act does not cover the defendant who has not had legal advice but makes admissions in response to the new caution, or (*prima facie*) the defendant who fails to obtain advice, although no formal denial occurs. These very significant matters are discussed further below.

As *Saunders* v *UK*[120] establishes, the use of formal coercion to obtain statements from persons will clearly be incompatible with Article 6 *if* the statement is then used against him or her in criminal proceedings. In *R* v *Staines; R* v *Morrisey*[121] the Court of Appeal refused, despite the judgment in *Saunders,* to overturn a conviction although the trial judge had refused to exclude evidence under s78 PACE obtained in a similar manner to that adopted in *Saunders.* In the post-HRA era, such a response would not satisfy the duty of the court under s6 HRA or the interpretative obligation of the judiciary under s3. As indicated above, a large number of statutes contain provisions broadly equivalent to the provisions of the Companies Act 1985 which were at issue in *Saunders.* The Attorney-General has issued guidance to prosecutors with a view to ensuring that evidence gained under a number of those provisions should not be used in criminal proceedings. This issue may not therefore arise at present under certain of these statutory provisions – a significant instance in which

[119] Appl No 35718/97. Judgment of 2 May 2000.
[120] (1997) 23 EHRR 313; No 19187/91, Com Rep paras 69–75.
[121] [1997] 2 Cr App R 426.

primary legislation was rendered nugatory even before the HRA was in force. This matter was placed on a statutory basis in s59 and Schedule 3 of the 1999 Act. Schedule 3 lists the statutory provisions mentioned above,[122] apart from s172 of the Road Traffic Act 1988, and provides that the coerced statements will be inadmissible.

Nevertheless, the government appears to envisage that certain very significant statutory provisions allowing for coercion, including a number arising under the Terrorism Act 2000, will be used in the post-HRA era. S172 of the Road Traffic Act 1988 makes it an offence for motorists not to tell police who was driving their vehicle at the time of an alleged offence. The coerced statement can then be used in evidence at trial for the RTA offence in question. The provision clearly contravenes the right against self-incrimination, and this was found to be the case in Scotland in *Brown*[123] during the period of time when the Convention was in force in Scotland, but not in England.[124] The defendant encountered the police officers after parking her car and was suspected of driving while intoxicated; she was asked under s172 to reveal the name of the person driving the car at the relevant time. On pain of the penalty under s172 she did so, revealing that she had been driving, and was convicted of driving while intoxicated, after the coerced statement was admitted into evidence. Her conviction was overturned on appeal due to the finding that s172 contravened Article 6. The ruling of the Edinburgh High Court is of interest since the Court rendered s172, effectively, nugatory. This stance was taken on the basis of the requirements of the Scotland Act which differ from those of s6 HRA since they do not include the possibility envisaged under s6(2)(b) that the authority was 'acting so as to give effect to or enforce those provisions [of incompatible primary legislation]'. Nevertheless Lord Steyn's judgment in *ex p Kebilene*[125] suggests that under the HRA UK courts may avoid convicting defendants under incompatible provisions, by declaring an abuse of process. UK judges may thereby usually avoid issuing declarations of incompatibility in criminal proceedings and in so doing may render a number of legislative provisions nugatory while preserving the notion that Parliamentary sovereignty is unaffected. Taking the contrary stance would not only invite applications to Strasbourg, it would mean that the questions whether a conviction could be obtained and whether one could enjoy fundamental human rights might depend on which side of the border one lived on.[126]

[122] At p268.
[123] (2000) see the *Guardian* News Report 9 February 2000 and (2000) JCIVLIB 193.
[124] The Convention rights were brought into force in Scotland under s57(2) of the Scotland Act 1998.
[125] [1999] 3 WLR 972; see Chapter 3 p107.
[126] Whether this is the case depends on the resolution in Scotland of the difference in this respect between the Scotland Act and the HRA. Possibly the bizarre result will be reached that human rights received greater protection in Scotland *before* the HRA came into force; see further Chapter 2 p42.

Brown and *Saunders* call into question the provisions allowing a limited use of coerced statements in evidence in terrorist investigations under Schedule 5 paras 13 and 16 TA. The possibility of admitting such statements into evidence in order to convict of the offence under para 14 of making a statement which the maker knows to be false or misleading in a material particular, or as to which he or she is reckless, in purported compliance with an order under paragraph 13, may be incompatible with the right against self-incrimination, since a misleading statement might not have been made but for the pressure flowing from the penalties which para 13 and, to a greater extent, para 16 carry.

Perhaps more significantly, Article 6 might be breached in an instance in which a *silence* in response to the threat of penalties under the paragraphs in question was admitted in respect of one of the other offences under Schedule 5, or indeed any other offence. *Brown* and *Saunders* do not expressly address the question whether the admission into evidence of a no-comment interview (as opposed to admissions) in response to formal coercion would breach Article 6. Obviously a situation can be envisaged in which the accused might decide to risk the imposition of the penalty in question. The prosecution might then put forward the interview in evidence for the purpose of drawing adverse inferences from it. On one view, the case for drawing such inferences might be strengthened on the argument that if the accused is prepared to risk the imposition of the penalty in question he or she must have something very significant to hide. But equally it might be argued that a vulnerable defendant who did not have legal advice (as a result of factors other than its formal denial) had made no comment as a defence, uncertain how to deal with the situation; or that the reason for remaining silent was the fear of retaliation from the real perpetrator of the offence. Such situations appear to fall more within the ruling from *Murray* than within that from *Saunders*; therefore the factors identified here as relevant to arguments based on *Murray* would be applicable.

Further, despite the evident attempt in paras 13 and 16 to achieve Convention compliance, bearing *Saunders* in mind, the possibility of incompatibility remains, taking into account the broader implications of fairness in the trial as a whole under Article 6(1). If someone other than the person who had made the coerced statement was on trial and the prosecution wished to admit the statement in evidence, argument could be raised as to the fairness of so doing, bearing in mind the fact that the statement could not be used against its maker.[127] The issue of the fairness

[127] Analogy might be drawn with *Rowe and Davis* v *UK* [2000] 30 EHRR 1, in which statements made by accomplices were used against the accused, although the statements had been extracted on the basis of promise of immunity from prosecution and financial reward. These matters, which did not come to light at the trial, owing to the use of PII certificates, led the Court to find that the accused had not had a fair trial, in breach of Article 6.

of the trial as a whole[128] could also be raised where the statement had influenced the prosecution or enabled the police to obtain evidence, since it could be argued that the statement had had an indirect impact in undermining the right against self-incrimination. Admittedly, there are precedents in current UK law for basing a prosecution on evidence uncovered in reliance on information from statements which are themselves inadmissible.[129] However, each of those precedents will need to be tested against Article 6 standards, taking into account all the circumstances applicable in an individual case.

S89(2) TA, applicable only in Northern Ireland, raises similar issues. S89(2) provides that it is an offence punishable by a fine to refuse to answer a question asked during a stop or to answer it inadequately, failing to answer 'to the best of his knowledge and ability'. Evidence obtained under s89 can be used to convict of the s89 offence itself; further, the TA does not expressly provide that it cannot be used in respect of other TA offences, although in practice it would be unlikely that it would be so used, owing to the incompatibility of so doing with Articles 6(1) and (2).

It may be noted that the PACE Code C provisions, paras 10.1 and 10.5C, which envisage the possibility of coercion under the statutory provisions mentioned, and make provision for it, may also be incompatible with Article 6. Para 10.1 provides that there is no need to caution if information is to be obtained under a 'relevant statutory requirement' while para 10.5C provides that the suspect should be informed of the consequences of failing to cooperate in the interview, regardless of the caution, where a statutory requirement to provide information applies and may render him or her liable to conviction for an offence or arrest. These provisions should therefore have been omitted or modified in the 1999 revision of the Codes. As they stand, the relevant parts of the paragraphs appear to amount to incompatible subordinate legislation which can simply be rendered invalid, if necessary, under the HRA since, although they reflect primary legislation, it cannot be said that such legislation 'prevents the removal of the incompatibility'.[130]

Fairness at trial and legal advice

Article 6(3)(c) provides that everyone charged with a criminal offence has the right to defend themselves through legal assistance of their own choosing. Access to legal advice in pre-trial questioning, as opposed to such access for the purposes of the trial, is not expressly provided for in Article 6. However, it is probable that some protection for such access

[128] The concept of the fairness of the trial taken as a whole was developed in *Barbéra, Messegué and Jabardo* A.14 6(2) (1989) 33.

[129] S76(4) of the Police and Criminal Evidence Act 1984. Impliedly under S9 of the Interception of Communications Act 1985.

[130] See s3(2)(c) HRA.

can be implied into Articles 6(1) and 6(3)(c). Where a violation of Article 6 is claimed in respect of a lack of access to legal advice in pre-trial questioning, a breach of both paras 1 and 3 will be in question. The judgment in *Imbrioscia* v *Switzerland*[131] suggests that if either the accused or his or her lawyer requests that the latter should be present in pre-trial questioning this should be allowed if the answers to questions would be likely to prejudice the defence; the ruling may be applicable to police interviews. As explained above, the Court went further than this in *Murray (John)* v *UK*[132] in finding that Articles 6(1) and (3) had been breached by the denial of custodial access to a lawyer for 48 hours since such access was essential where there was a likelihood that adverse inferences would be drawn from silence. It found that Article 6 would normally require that the accused should be allowed to benefit from the assistance of a lawyer in the initial stages of police interrogation, although that right might be subject to restrictions for good cause. There seems to be no reason in principle to confine this finding to a circumstance where the defendant in fact stayed silent. Rather, as the Court implied, it may be that the suspect who fails to remain silent is most in need of legal advice. Therefore most or all police interviews under caution would seem to be covered by these findings in *Murray* since once the caution has been given it is clear that adverse inferences may be drawn from silence. Thus, a right of access to legal advice in custodial questioning may be implied into Article 6(3)(c) when read with Article 6(1) where the drawing of adverse inferences is a relevant issue. It might appear that such a right is already catered for, under s58 PACE and Sched. 8 para 7 TA. However, the formal and informal loopholes in the access discussed above may not be fully coterminous with the exceptions to this right which may be acceptable under Article 6(1) as interpreted in *Murray*. Moreover, a right to have the adviser present in the interview, as *Murray* appears to require, where adverse inferences might be drawn, arises only under para 6.8 Code C, not under the statutory provisions themselves.

Where access to legal advice has formally been delayed, particularly in the case of terrorist suspects, who can be denied access for up to 48 hours, the grounds for denial will have to be subjected to strict scrutiny. In particular, the good cause for the delay in obtaining advice required by *Murray* may not be satisfied by the grounds for proceeding with the interview although advice has not been obtained under Code C para 6, which includes the vague and broad test: where 'awaiting [the arrival of the solicitor] would cause unreasonable delay to the process of the investigation'. *Murray* also raises questions about the use in evidence of silences and admissions obtained in out-of-station exchanges and interviews prior to the point of notification of the availability of legal advice.

131 (1993) 17 EHRR 441; A 275 (1993).
132 (1996) 22 EHRR 29.

It is suggested that the objections, based on *Murray*, to the use of such exchanges cannot be fully met by the provision of para 11.2A Code C to the effect that any significant silence or statement outside the police station should be put to the suspect at the beginning of an interview at the police station. Such objections relate most obviously to out-of-station *interviews* since the suspect should be under caution and therefore formally aware of the dangers of remaining silent. A silence not under caution would not fall within s34(1)(a) CJPOA and therefore adverse inferences could not be drawn from it. But *Murray* may have an application in the circumstance where a suspect questioned outside the context of an interview (the possibility envisaged by Code C para 13) makes admissions, aware, although not under caution, of the dangers of not speaking. Street interviews or exchanges, of necessity without advice, may have an impact on later interviews even where para 11.2A is adhered to. Further, where the detainee refuses to confirm admissions or silences in an out-of-station interview under this paragraph, nothing in PACE or Code C provides that the admissions or silences are inadmissible. In the light of these comments it is surprising that the revision of Code C in 1999 did not respond to *Murray* by modifying paras 11.1, 11.1A, 11.13 and 3.1 which provide leeway for interviews or exchanges to occur outside the police station without notification that access to legal advice is available in it.

A further significant question is whether Article 6 might be breached where legal advice is not *formally* denied to the defendant for a period of time, as in *Murray*, although he has not in fact received advice before being interviewed. This argument might be raised where a suspect has been influenced by police ploys in failing to obtain advice (whether due to inadequacies in the informing procedure or to direct or more subtle persuasion). The admission of a subsequent interview might be viewed as affecting the fairness of trial, following *Murray*. This argument would be strongest where other adverse factors were also present, including a confession made after 24 hours or more in detention, or where the inexperienced, young, emotionally unstable or educationally sub-normal suspect could not be expected to make his or her own assessment as to the value of having legal advice and was therefore very vulnerable to police suggestions.

If Article 6 is concerned with the objective reliability of the interview in influencing the integrity and fairness of the trial, it can be argued that, unless the defendant made a clear, positive (albeit possibly misguided) decision not to have custodial advice, the admission into evidence of an interview under caution without such advice, whatever the reason for the failure, might affect the fairness of the trial. It is unclear that the fact that a vulnerable defendant (e.g. on the verge of mental handicap) had waived advice, or had received brief telephone advice only, would be relevant where it could be said that the trial, objectively speaking, might be rendered unfair by the admission of the interview. Similar arguments could perhaps also be raised where the adviser attends the station but the advice obtained is clearly inadequate. When the Strasbourg Court spoke of the need for legal advice where adverse inferences were to be drawn from silence, it may be suggested that it had in mind, taking into account the general need for the rights to be genuinely efficacious, not illusory, the notion of sound, adversarial advice.

Clearly there will be uncertainty for a time as to the extent of the application of *Murray* to police interviews without advice, but the central point is clear: under the current domestic provisions there are instances when suspects will be interviewed in the knowledge that adverse inferences may be drawn from silence, but access to legal advice will not be available, although not formally denied. As indicated in Chapter 5, the Court in *Teixeira de Castro* v *Portugal*[133] found that certain pre-trial procedures render a fair trial almost impossible and therefore curb the discretion of the Court in its response.[134] This finding was not made in the context of custodial legal advice but, together with the findings in *Murray*, could be applied to s78 PACE, in support of an argument that the exclusionary discretion embodied under the section may be narrowed almost to vanishing point where no access to legal advice was made available before or during the police interview which is proffered in evidence (possibly even if the lack of access was not due to a clear breach of statutory or Code provisions), although the suspect was aware that adverse inferences might be drawn from silence.[135] There would be a strong argument that such an interview should be excluded from evidence under s78, following *Murray*, since otherwise Article 6 would not appear to be satisfied. Failing to do so would appear to breach the duty of the judiciary under s6 HRA to abide by Article 6 and would arguably also fail to render s78 compatible with Articles 6(1) and 3(c).

An argument similar to this one did not receive much encouragement in one of the early decisions on the HRA, from Scotland.[136] In *Paton* v *Procurator Fiscal*[137] the appellant was to be interviewed about attempted theft and at the police station he indicated that he wanted a solicitor to be informed of his detention. When he was interviewed his solicitor was not present and he was not told that the police had a discretion to allow his solicitor to be present during the interview if he so wished.

[133] (1999) 28 EHHR 101.

[134] At pp200–201.

[135] Under PACE Code C this would include all interviews since, as indicated above, under para 11.1.A the definition of an interview is an exchange regarding involvement in criminal activity which is required to be under caution.

[136] By virtue of s57(2) Scotland Act 1998, a Scottish court is required, *inter alia*, to take into account the various rights enshrined in the Convention. At the time the HRA itself was not fully in force in Scotland.

[137] (1999) Judgment of 24 November 1999.

After caution, the appellant admitted that he was trying to break into the premises in question. When the charges were recited[138] the appellant said that he had been merely passing by when the police chased him. The appellant argued that Articles 6(1) and 6(3)(c) of the Convention had been contravened. The Court took into account the fact that the appellant had not made a request for his solicitor to be present and that neither Scottish law nor the Convention required that in all cases a detained person should be afforded the opportunity to have a solicitor present. The Court found that the question whether a fair trial could be achieved depended not simply upon what happened during the preliminary investigation, but on the whole proceedings, and a number of safeguards were accorded to the accused during the investigation and the trial process; on this basis the appeal was refused and the case was remitted to the sheriff to proceed to trial. These findings do not appear to encourage the notion that certain rights, such as access to custodial legal advice, are of especial Constitutional significance; they encourage a broad brush approach which appears to assume that a breach of suspects' rights may be cured by affording other rights. However, these findings may be based on the lack of a right to have a solicitor present in interview in Scotland and, it is suggested, on a doubtful, minimalist interpretation of Article 6.

It is notable that s109 TA (formerly ss2A(4)(b) and 2A(5)(b) PTA) constitutes a response to the findings in *Murray* similar to that under s58 of the 1999 Act, since consultation with a legal adviser is essential if adverse inferences are to be drawn from silence. These two instances in which Convention compliance has been ensured by Parliament might encourage the courts to consider exclusion of the interview where a suspect who had not had legal advice had remained silent, or to make a finding that no adverse inferences should be drawn from the silence. Apart from the duty of courts under s6, a further route to such a finding would mean interpreting the term 'circumstances' in ss34, 36 and 37 CJPOA strictly to include a failure to have access to legal advice. The phrase 'had not been allowed to consult a solicitor' in s58 of the Youth Justice and Criminal Evidence Act 1999 could also be construed broadly to cover informal denials or even informal encouragement to forgo advice. This would depend on how flexible judges and magistrates are prepared to be in respect of their interpretative obligation under s3 HRA.

It is clear that the courts have the opportunity, if they are prepared to take an activist line in giving a wide interpretation to *Murray*, to curb the

[138] He was charged with attempting to break into premises with intent to steal and, in the alternative, that he was found at premises without lawful authority, the inference being that he might commit theft contrary to s57(1) Civil Government (Scotland) Act 1982.

formally allowed and informally developed police discretion in affording access to legal advice which this chapter has discussed. Eventually Code C may have to be revised to clarify the provisions allowing for delays in access and to require a positive decision to refuse advice. Further moves towards improving the quality of advice may have to be undertaken.

Convention guarantees against unethical interviewing

PACE and the TA make no provisions as regards interviewing techniques, and Code C of PACE hardly touches on this matter, except to forbid oppressive interviewing in para 11.3[139] and to give some very general guidance as to interviewing mentally disordered or handicapped suspects in Code C Note 11B, which is largely repeated in Note E3. No such provisions are duplicated in PACE itself although, as indicated above, oppression is defined under s76(8) as including Article 3 treatment, and under s76(2)(a) a confession obtained by oppression is subject to an absolute exclusionary rule. On its face, the Convention does not bear upon this issue, except in so far as Article 3 covers oppressive interviewing. But, as indicated above, the general requirements of fairness under Article 6 will allow consideration of interviewing techniques as part of the fairness of the criminal process as a whole. Arguments could also be raised regarding unethical, intrusive interviewing techniques under Articles 3, 8 and 14.

It was indicated in Chapter 6 that grossly humiliating treatment may breach Article 3, and this might include very intrusive, prolonged questioning. Where such questioning was accompanied by racist, sexist[140] or homophobic abuse a breach might be found of Article 3 read with Article 14. Article 8 could also be considered where the questioning dealt, for example, with sexual matters. These possibilities were considered in *Lustig-Prean and Beckett* v *UK* and *Smith and Grady* v *UK*[141] in the context of an investigation by service police concerning their homosexuality, but by analogy the findings of the Court would appear to be applicable to police interviewing in certain circumstances. The Court considered the investigations, and in particular the interviews of the applicants, to have been exceptionally intrusive and to constitute especially grave interferences with their private lives, which could not be justified within the meaning of Article 8(2). It considered that treatment grounded upon a predisposed homophobic bias, as in the present case, could, in principle, fall within the scope of Article 3 and that the investigations were undoubtedly distressing and humiliating, but that in the circumstances of the case, the treatment did not reach the minimum level of severity

[139] Code C para 11.3 provides: 'No police officer may try to obtain answers to questions or to elicit a statement by the use of oppression'.
[140] *East African Asians* cases 3 EHRR 76 (1973).
[141] [2000] 29 EHRR 493.

which would bring it within the scope of Article 3. Having found a breach of Article 8, the Court did not go on to consider Article 14 as a separate issue.

The failure to regulate interviewing techniques is a significant gap in the PACE scheme, bearing in mind the established likelihood of a link between coercive questioning and unreliable confessions.[142] Although there has been a movement from such questioning towards so-called ethical techniques,[143] it cannot be assumed that interviewing will not at times verge on the oppressive and abusive. Use of Article 8 as in *Lustig-Prean* may encourage a movement towards ethical interviewing and provide an avenue by which to challenge humiliating, discriminatory questioning. As discussed above, the Race Relations Act 1976, after amendment in 2000, will provide a means of redress in respect of racial abuse or racially discriminatory treatment by police, which will also cover interviewing. But this possibility does not exist in respect of other forms of discriminatory treatment, including treatment which is gender related or homophobic.[144]

Conclusions

This chapter, together with Chapters 5 and 6, has sought to indicate that the New Labour government currently views the due process concerns which influenced PACE as no longer a matter of pressing concern. In 1999 Jack Straw famously found that while the defining cases of the 1980s were the notorious miscarriage of justice cases, the defining case of the late 1990s determining criminal justice policy into 2000 and beyond was the *Stephen Lawrence* case.[145] Thus, the Labour government's current concern is to structure police discretion more greatly in relation to victims; attention has been diverted from structuring it in relation to suspects. The current climate, in 2000, continues to be unfavourable to the introduction of further due process safeguards since the *Lawrence* case and the *McPherson Report*[146] have fuelled media demands for more crime control on the ground that if police discretion is to be trammelled by the

[142] See Justice *Unreliable Evidence? Confessions and the Safety of Convictions* (1994 London).

[143] Home Office Central Planning and Training Unit *The Interviewer's Rule Book* (1992); Home Office Circular 7/1993 'Investigative Interviewing'.

[144] The Sex Discrimination Act 1975 has not been amended in the same way as the Race Relations Act (under the Race Relations (Amendment) Act 2000) and therefore will not cover the actions of public authorities except in the contexts covered by s6 of the Act. At present no statute forbids discriminatory treatment on grounds of sexual orientation. Bearing in mind the 'dualist' impact of international law in the UK this means that Protocol 12 (see Chapter 2 p23) may not provide a remedy for such treatment domestically, even if it is received into domestic law under the HRA.

[145] See *McPherson Report* (1999) Cm 4262-I.

[146] (1999) Cm 4262-I.

need to take racial considerations into account, particularly in stop and search decisions, crime control will be affected.[147] The Terrorism Act 2000 reflects a strong emphasis on crime control values, largely to the exclusion, it is argued, of those of due process.

However, the view that the HRA may allow for a 'reinvigoration of fundamental values' in a criminal justice system which is closer to a state of crisis, as a result of change during the 1990s, appears to be gaining currency.[148] These chapters have sought to demonstrate that, despite unfavourable statutory provisions, particularly those of the Terrorism Act 2000, the Convention offers possibilities of curbing police discretion in the interests of due process values. It allows domestic judges to look much more closely and directly at standards of fairness in the criminal justice system than Strasbourg is prepared to do, owing to the margin of appreciation doctrine. Therefore the inception of the HRA may lead to a return to an emphasis on such values which has not been evident since the early 1990s.

[147] *Daily Telegraph* 19 January 2000: 'Sir William cannot escape responsibility for the two most alarming facts to emerge from last week's figures: the 19% increase in the number of robberies reported last year . . . and the 9.2% reduction in the number of drug reported offences. Both figures are so obviously related to Sir William's crass decision to brand the police as "institutionally racist" that the coincidence cannot be dismissed . . .'. The *Daily Mail* on the same day said that branding the police 'institutionally racist', meant 'the Met police has attempted to redress the balance by reducing the amount of stop and search'.

[148] Walker *Miscarriages of Justice* (1999) p62 (C Walker and K Starmer (eds)).

Chapter 8

Security and Intelligence Services: Evolving Oversight?

Introduction

The Major years saw the creation of a new framework for the security and intelligence agencies and a dramatic break with the tradition of governing them through informal non-statutory mechanisms.[1] After an existence which spanned almost all of the twentieth century it was only in 1994 that the government admitted to the existence of the Secret Intelligence Service (or MI6) and GCHQ, and only in 1989 to the existence of the Security Service (or MI5).[2] The central impetus for change arose from the need to comply with the demands of the European Convention on Human Rights.[3] Once a model for the statutory framework of MI5 had been devised in the form of the Security Service Act 1989, based on the model used for the Interception of Communications Act 1985, also introduced to comply with the Convention, the model was extended to the Secret Intelligence Service and GCHQ in the Intelligence Services Act 1994. At the same time a level of Parliamentary oversight of the agencies was added. Thus the Labour government inherited a particular statutory framework which it built on in the changes made to the agencies' accountability in the Regulation of Investigatory Powers Act 2000. That Act is discussed fully in Chapters 9 and 10, but it will be contended below that

[1] As far as MI5 is concerned, by the unpublished Findlater–Stewart Memorandum and then by the Maxwell–Fyfe Directive published in 1952. Until 1994 MI6 and GCHQ 'maintained [their] existence in legal darkness', (Lustgarten and Leigh 'The Security Service Act 1989' 52 MLR 801 at p802). See also Lustgarten and Leigh *In From the Cold* (1994) *Coda* for discussion of the new statutory framework for MI6 and J Wadham [1994] 57(6) MLR 916. For discussion of aspects of the new position of MI6 see P Davies 'Integrating Intelligence into the Machinery of British Central Government' [2000] 78(1) *Public Administration* 29.

[2] The Secret Service bureau was established in 1909 and became known as MI5 in January 1916.

[3] See *Harman and Hewitt* v *UK* Appl 121175/86; (1989) 14 EHRR 657.

as far as the agencies are concerned it merely represents an extension of the model already available. But, in a manner which will form a central theme in this chapter, that enlarged framework will operate within a changing context which may eventually lead to its modification.

Essentially, two developments are likely to be key to the future of the three agencies post-2000. The first is the introduction of the HRA. It will be argued below that due to the particular model chosen for the statutory framework and the nature of the activities in question, the HRA will be far less likely to have the direct impact it may have in other areas of executive power. But this chapter will seek to show that the issue of compatibility with the ECHR can find certain domestic means of expression. The issue has so far been addressed only in an external sense – at Strasbourg – and the Strasbourg model has provided, in a minimal form, the basis for the current framework. But the issue of compatibility, addressed for the first time domestically, is pertinent now that the HRA is fully in force, and will be especially apposite bearing in mind the changing nature of the work undertaken by the Security Service. The HRA will instil a new government culture of openness and accountability; indeed, there are signs that it is already doing so. The Freedom of Information Act (FoI) may contribute to such a change in culture. It will have no *direct* application at all to the agencies: they are not merely exempt; they are excluded from it. But FoI may have an indirect effect in raising expectations of openness.

The second development concerns the movement of the agencies into new fields of work. Their work changed as the Cold War ended in the early 1990s. In October 1992 responsibility for leading the intelligence effort against Irish republican terrorism was transferred to MI5. But Northern Irish terrorism has greatly diminished due to the peace process[4] which culminated in November 1999 with the establishment of a new cross-party Parliament at Stormont with devolved powers under the Northern Ireland Act 1998. At present the threat is only from tiny splinter groups which oppose the process, and the number of such groups may be diminishing, although their membership may not.[5] On the face of it, it might be expected that the work of the agencies could be reduced.[6] At present MI5 employs 1,900 people compared to 30 officers in 1939 and 850 in 1950.[7] The global figure for the funding of all three agencies for

[4] The *British Irish Agreement reached in the multi-party negotiations* Cm 3883 (1998). On 22 November 1999 Peter Mandelson, Secretary of State for Northern Ireland, said in the House of Commons that the conditions were now in place for the full implementation of the Good Friday Agreement. See further Chapter 3 p66.

[5] Such groups include the Real IRA and the Continuity IRA. Certain of the groups initially opposed to the process also declared a cease-fire before November 1999, but disaffected members of the IRA have joined those groups which remain opposed to it.

[6] This question is raised, but answered negatively, in the Report of the Intelligence and Security Committee for 1997/98 Cm 4073 ppv–vi.

[7] Source: *MI5: The Security Service* 3rd edn (1998) pp35–36.

1997–1998 was £747 million;[8] 25% of the MI5 budget in 1997–1998 related to Northern Irish terrorism.[9] Reduction or redirection of the work of the agencies became necessary in the late 1990s. From 1992 onwards the Security Service played an increasing part in counter-proliferation work.[10] The Major government afforded all three agencies the additional function of assisting the police in the prevention and detection of serious crime; the 1994 Act included this function in respect of MI6 and GCHQ[11] and in 1996 the 1989 Act was amended to include the new function.[12] The Director-General was also afforded a new coordinating function.[13] But given that in 1997–1998 only 2.5% of the budget of MI5 was directed towards the 'serious crime' support, further redirection was needed.

Thus, the Labour government had to address one result of its own, largely successful, effort to institute and promote the peace process. It is unsurprising to find that the redirection, as opposed to the reduction, option was chosen. The obvious response of any large organisation whose function appeared to be about to diminish would be to consider redirection. Any significant reduction in the function of any of the agencies would clearly have had repercussions in terms of quite extensive bureaucratic, structural changes involving employment at various levels, which, apart from other considerations, the managements would be likely to seek to avoid. The choice of the government was reflected in the budgets for the three agencies and, as the government puts it, it has 'set spending plans which will enable the Agencies to face up to the formidable tasks old, new and changing which confront them'.[14] The projected figure for 1999/2000 is £743.2 million for all three services; in 2000/2001 it is £745 million.[15]

The Security Service has had a role in countering terrorist threats since the 1960s. But that role is likely to undergo some redirection in response to the redefinition of terrorism. The justification for the change

[8] The Report of the Intelligence and Security Committee for 1998/9, published November 1999. According to the booklet published in 1998 MI5 had a budget of around £140 million for 1998. The relationship between these two figures is unclear since the three agencies have censored the information provided for the Parliamentary Committee.

[9] Source: *MI5: The Security Service* 3rd edn (1998) p9.

[10] The UK has a duty, under the Nuclear Non-Proliferation Treaty, to act against proliferators: see *MI5: The Security Service* (1998) pp17–18.

[11] Ss1(2)(c) and 3(2)(c) of the 1994 Act respectively.

[12] The Security Service Act 1996 s1(1) and the Police Act 1997 s134(1) amended s1(4) of the 1989 Act. As Chapter 10 indicates at p382, powers of 'intrusive surveillance' by MI6 and GCHQ in relation to this function are curtailed under the Regulation of Investigatory Powers Act 2000 Part II.

[13] The Security Service Act 1996 s1(2) and the Police Act 1997 ss12 and 134(1) amended s1(2)(c) of the 1989 Act.

[14] *The Government Response to the Intelligence and Security Committee's Annual Report* Cm 4089 October 1998 p3 para 1.

[15] *The Intelligence and Security Committee Report* 97–98 Cm 4073 p9. Individual figures for the three services were not published.

was contained in the Labour government's Consultation Paper on the future of anti-terrorism laws published in 1998.[16] The Terrorism Act 2000 was based on the Paper. Terrorism is currently defined in s20 of the Prevention of Terrorism Act 1989 as: 'the use of violence for political ends [including] any use of violence for the purpose of putting the public, or any section of the public in fear'. The government proposed that terrorism should be redefined more broadly. The wider definition appears in s1 of the new Act and, as indicated in Chap 3, it covers the use or threat, for the purpose of advancing a political, religious or ideological cause, of action, designed to influence the government, which involves serious violence against any person or serious damage to property, or serious disruption of an electronic system, or dangers to life, or a serious risk to health or safety of the public or a section of the public'. The Act will also apply wherever terrorist action takes place.[17] Thus the definition now includes 'attacks on computer installations or public utilities'.[18] As far as the government was concerned, redefining terrorism served a dual end. It enabled the current counter-terrorist legislation to be retained and extended, as discussed in Chapter 3. But it also allowed the security services to extend their role in combating terrorism. At present the police will, with some assistance from the Security Service under the 'aiding in the prevention and detection of serious crime' rubric, combat the criminal activities of extremist groups, such as animal rights activists, using the ordinary criminal law and criminal justice system. One view is that by redefining terrorism, the activities of the agencies can be targeted directly against such groups. The agencies need not merely assist the police or the National Criminal Intelligence Service. Since the members of such groups are likely to be redefined as 'terrorists' (whether or not the groups are themselves proscribed)[19] criticism of the use of the agencies against them may be deflected. This suggestion must be advanced with caution since it is possible that these groups could have been targeted in any event under the counter-subversion ground provided by s1(2) of the Security Service Act 1989. However, the counter-subversion work of MI5 is at present negligible.[20] A sudden increase in it in relation to the groups in question might not have appeared to be the most appropriate course.

[16] Home Office and Northern Ireland Office *Legislation against Terrorism. A Consultation Paper* Cm 4178 (1998) London: Stationery Office.

[17] S1(1)(a) provides: '"action" includes action outside the United Kingdom'; under s1(2)(b) 'a reference to any person or to property is a reference to any person, or to property, wherever situated, and (c) a reference to the public includes a reference to the public of a country other than the United Kingdom'.

[18] Ibid para 3.17.

[19] See further Chapter 3.

[20] *MI5: The Security Service* (1998): 'Since the late 1980s . . . the threat from subversive organisations to British Parliamentary democracy has declined and is now insignificant . . . [in] 1997–8 only 0.3% of the Service's resources were allocated to the remnants of this work, predominantly to pay the pensions of retired agents' (p19).

Moreover, the same Consultation Paper proposed that the movement towards extending the counter-terrorism legislation to international terrorism should be taken further[21] so that such terrorism would be included in the definition. Thus the remit of the agencies was greatly broadened when indigenous groups were added. The government and the Parliamentary Committee charged with oversight of the agencies agree in considering that such redirection is fully justified: 'The [Intelligence and Security] Committee acknowledges the continued need for the intelligence and security agencies in a changed but still dangerous world and believes they must be maintained and funded in a sustainable way. The Government reached the same conclusions in the Comprehensive Spending Review'.[22] The Intelligence and Security Committee goes so far as to find that the end of the Cold War provides a *justification* for maintaining spending on the services rather than reducing them: 'the Cold war [was], in its awful way, a form of rigid security system that has now collapsed, and . . . new developments and technology and "globalisation" [have] produced their own dangers'.[23]

But in its Third Report in 1998 the Committee raises concerns regarding the two recent developments indicated here: 'So far from being invented to justify the Agencies' continued existence [new challenges to the Services] are real enough, and the country rightly expects to be protected against them . . . However, the agencies face these tasks in a new environment of greater openness and accountability. They also face them with new technologies available to bring new capacities for the collection of information in many forms, which may pose new challenges to ensuring that the privacy of law-abiding individuals is respected . . . [in times of no grave national threat] public confidence can be very fragile. That is the inevitable consequence of operating within a "ring of secrecy" which prevents a more balanced public view of their activities. The public must therefore be confident that there is adequate independent scrutiny and democratic accountability on their behalf by people within that ring of secrecy. That is the task of this Committee.'[24] These words signal not only a recognition that the model used for the current statutory framework of the services may not be entirely adequate in the changed context, but also that the Committee intends to take a more robust approach to its task, bearing these matters in mind. It may be noted that the tone of this

[21] See further Chapter 3. The scope of many of the PTA's provisions was extended to include international terrorism in 1984. S5 of the Criminal Justice (Terrorism and Conspiracy) Act 1998 makes it a criminal offence to conspire in any act 'or other event' which would also be an offence under the law of a foreign country so long as the offence in question would also be unlawful in the UK. When it comes into force this offence will become part of the Terrorism Act 2000 ss59–61.

[22] *The Government Response to the Intelligence and Security Committee's Annual Report* Cm 4089 October 1998 p3.

[23] The *Report of the Intelligence and Security Committee for 1997/98* Cm 4073 pvi.

[24] Ibid pvii.

introduction differs markedly from that adopted in the Second Report, which makes internal security rather than democratic accountability its central concern.[25] The change of tone appeared to be related to government intransigence regarding David Shayler (see below). The Fourth Report, for 1998/9, also adopted a robust tone.[26] It took particular exception to the continuing refusal of the government to publish a National Audit Office report on the excessive spending of the agencies on refurbishment. The Chairman, Tom King, said: 'The cloak of secrecy has been used to cover up inadequacies and serious lapses in expenditure control.' The Chairman of the Commons Public Accounts Committee endorsed this view on the day the Intelligence Committee's Fourth Report was published.

The Intelligence and Security Committee in both its Third and Fourth Reports is clearly signalling its concern at the probable tension between the continued existence of doubtfully accountable agencies, with an increasing remit, in an age when the expectations of accountability have never been higher. The implication is that the confidence in the balance supposedly struck by the statutory mechanisms between individual rights, especially to privacy,[27] and the demands of secrecy, has never been more fragile, a somewhat ironic finding given the infancy of those mechanisms. The Committee is also demonstrating a recognition of the nature of the emergent but fragile anti-secrecy culture, one that does not view increased secrecy as the means of maintaining public confidence. For example, in the Fourth Report the Committee included the following in para 39: 'In a spirit of greater openness we therefore publish the expenditure totals for each of the agencies . . . in the hope that you will reconsider your concerns over publication'. In fact the totals were censored from the Report.[28] In contrast, the nature of the old culture is neatly and cogently encapsulated in the following comment from the White Paper on the 1989 Official Secrets Act: '[Disclosures by members or former members of the agencies] ought to be criminal . . . because they reduce public confidence in the services' ability and willingness to carry out their essential secret duties effectively and loyally.'[29] The change of culture is clearly indicated both in the fact that Stella Rimmington, the retired head of MI5, intends to publish her memoirs, and in the reception given to this unprecedented move. While it has caused grave concern to Lander, the Director-General of MI5, there has not been a governmental outcry.

While making gestures in the direction of openness and accountability, the statutory mechanisms, including the most recent one, the Regulation of Investigatory Powers Act 2000, are still, this chapter and the next two

[25] The *Report of the Intelligence and Security Committee for 1996* February 1997 Cm 3574 pvi.
[26] Cm 4532, published on 25 November 1999.
[27] See Chapter 9 pp338–9 for discussion of the sense in which this term is being used.
[28] Ibid p16.
[29] *Reform of the Official Secrets Act 1911* Cm 408 (1988) HMSO.

argue, embued with the old culture.[30] Therefore it is questionable whether the more extensive statutory basis for the agencies' activities which is now available will re-establish the public confidence in them which was shaken by the *Spycatcher* episode.[31] *Spycatcher*, written by Peter Wright, a former member of MI5, alleged that MI5 had 'bugged and burgled its way around London', that the Service had tried to destabilise the Labour government of Harold Wilson, and that the Director-General from 1956 to 1965, Roger Hollis, was a Soviet agent.[32] But the prosecution of Richard Tomlinson, the former MI6 officer, in 1998, the attempt to extradite David Shayler, a former MI5 officer, from France in 1998,[33] both for seeking to make public a number of grievances and concerns about the services, together with the concerns raised over MI5 and MI6's handling of the Vasili Mitrokhin affair in 1999[34] and regarding allegations of involvement in the attempt to assassinate Colonel Gadafy, have undermined any public confidence which was established by the statutory developments of 1989 and 1994. The affair undermined the notion of ministerial responsibility for and control of MI5. As one commentator put it: '[MI5] have made intensely political decisions [in authorising the book, *The Mitrokhin Archive*] without informing the politicians . . . who will have to answer for them'.[35] Revelations from former members of the agencies which suggest, as Leigh and Lustgarten put it, that 'a strong right wing bias seems to have influenced the selection of targets',[36] did not cease with the passing of the Security Service Act 1989 and the Intelligence Services Act 1994.[37] There still appears to be a clear mismatch between the comfortable assertions of Home Secretaries and Commissioners that abuse of power by the services is a myth, and the occasional indications from various quarters, emerging with difficulty from the ring of secrecy, that all is not well.

[30] Admittedly, the specifically operational aspects of the work of the security and intelligence services it covers would be secret anywhere in the world. But the tendency to curb the scrutinising role of the ordinary courts discussed in Chapters 9 and 10, especially in relation to the interception of communications, suggests that secrecy remains the dominant value.

[31] See *A-G* v *Times Newspapers Ltd* [1991] 2 All ER 398; [1992] 1 AC 191.

[32] The last two allegations appear to be unreliable, see *MI5: The Security Service* 3rd edn (1998) pp39–40; *The Mitrokhin Archive* (1999) by Vasili Mitrokhin and Christopher Andrew confirmed that the allegation regarding Roger Hollis was untrue.

[33] He was imprisoned in France pending determination of the extradition request which was so that he could face charges under s1 of the Official Secrets Act. France refused to extradite him. Once he returned to the UK in August 2000, he was charged under s1 of the Act.

[34] Mitrokhin was a KGB defector who identified Melita Norwood and others as Soviet agents in *The Mitrokhin Archive.*

[35] Hugo Young in the *Guardian* 14 September 1999.

[36] *The Security Service Act 1989* 52 MLR 801. The targets mentioned include the NCCL (now *Liberty*), CND, obscure Trotskyite organisations and Labour MPs.

[37] In July 1991 a Granada Television documentary 'Defending the Realm' alleged that telexes to the General Secretary of the Scottish Trade Union Congress from trade unions in Eastern Europe were routinely intercepted by GCHQ without warrant and that the information was passed to the Security Service. These allegations formed the basis of the complaint in *Christie* v *UK* 78-A DR E Com HR 119, which is discussed below.

The central theme of this chapter, which reflects certain of the concerns voiced by the Parliamentary Security and Intelligence Committee in 1998 and 1999, is to consider the means whereby a genuine basis can be created for the fostering of public confidence in the services, bearing in mind their increased remit, and the lack of a national crisis. It will be argued that the mechanisms of the 1989 and 1994 statutes will not be able to meet that need; they were put in place at a time when the threat from Irish terrorism was greater but the climate of openness and accountability was less apparent. Therefore their minimalist nature might have been expected to be tolerated, especially as they at least placed the services on a proper basis. In contrast with the past this was a clear first step towards a more appropriate, democratically acceptable model. Nevertheless, concerns as to their efficacy were immediately raised by a number of commentators.[38] In the era of the Human Rights and Freedom of Information Acts – despite the probable marginal direct applicability of the HRA and the complete lack of direct FoI applicability – those mechanisms are likely to appear increasingly inadequate. The Parliamentary Committee has clearly signalled its appreciation of this and its determination to act accordingly. It also appears to have indicated that public confidence can be bolstered by the use of a Parliamentary as opposed to a judicial means of oversight. If it is convinced that such a model can prove effective in the terms it suggests, it is clear, as argued below, that it has some way to go in persuading the government of this and this may be due partly to the fundamental weakness and uncertainty of ministerial responsibility for the agencies. The failure to address this central matter is linked to the failure to attack the assumptions contained in the notion of the 'ring of secrecy'. This refers to the designation of the members of the Committee as subject to s1 of the Official Secrets Act as though they were members of the services. In other words, the Committee implies that, in a sense, improved *internal* regulation (i.e. by those within the ring) is key to improving democratic accountability.

The main contention which will run through this chapter is that ministerial responsibility, Parliamentary oversight and the complaints and checking mechanisms of the Commissioners and Tribunals create only a limited and flawed control of the agencies. It will be contended in Chapter 10 that the changes to the Tribunal system which will occur under the Regulation of Investigatory Powers Act 2000 represent a step in the direction of greater accountability, but are unlikely to have much impact in terms of creating stricter control, since in various respects, including the role of Parliamentary oversight, the new Tribunal system is based on the old model.[39] Without radical structural change to these methods, which

[38] See Lustgarten and Leigh pp438–440; J Wadham 'The Intelligence Services Act 1994' [1994] 57(6) MLR 916 at pp923–925.

[39] See Chapter 10 pp401–408.

will allow some breaching of the ring of secrecy, no real control will be achieved. The HRA may provide some of the impetus for such change.

The framework for the agencies

The functions of MI5 are set out in s1 of the Security Services Act 1989. S1(1) provides: 'the function of the Service shall be the protection of national security and, in particular, its protection against threats from espionage, terrorism and sabotage, from the activities of agents of foreign powers and from actions intended to overthrow or undermine Parliamentary democracy by political, industrial or violent means'. S1(3) adds the function of safeguarding 'the economic well-being of the UK' but only from external threats. The Act was amended to add s1(4) by s1 of the Security Services Act 1996 in order to add to the two existing functions of the Security Service a third function – 'to act in support of the activities of police forces [the National Criminal Intelligence Service (NCIS), the National Crime Squad and other law enforcement agencies in the prevention and detection of serious crime]'. The words in square brackets were added by the Police Act 1997 s134(1), Schedule 9 para 60. As indicated above, the definition of terrorism will be greatly widened under the Terrorism Act 2000. Once this is accomplished, the functions of the Service will have been widened quite significantly since the 1989 Act was passed. The Intelligence Services Act 1994 ss1(2) and 3(2) provides that the function of MI6 and of GCHQ will be exercisable only in the interests of national security with particular reference to the defence and foreign policies of HM government and in the 'interests of the economic well-being of the UK' and 'in support of the prevention and detection of serious crime'. MI6 is empowered under s1(1) to obtain and provide information relating to the actions or intentions of persons outside the British Isles and perform tasks relating to such actions and intentions. Thus MI6 is geared to external rather than internal security, in accordance with its traditional role, but this does not mean that it does not carry out operations on UK soil. Targeted individuals may temporarily come to the UK and information relating to them may be found here.

In order to perform their functions the agencies operate their broad powers under a secrecy and a lack of accountability which would not be acceptable in respect of the police or other law enforcement agencies. But under a model which gave a high priority to oversight and democratic accountability it would be found that the agencies should carry out no function which could be carried out by a service, such as the police, which was more open to scrutiny. A confusion of functions between such services and MI5 is occurring owing to the failure to follow this principle. The police have pointed out that NCIS is a more open and accountable body than MI5 and, further, that there is little point in putting resources into a police intelligence body if MI5 then removes some of its main functions. It does not appear that this principle has been followed, although given the secrecy surrounding the operations of the agencies, it is not possible to come to any conclusion as to the genuine necessity of affording them a serious crime function or of allowing them to investigate the activities of a wider range of groups by designating them 'terrorist'. MI5 is specifically empowered to function against terrorist groups. MI6 and GCHQ can operate against them since part of their function is to further the interests of national security which terrorism is assumed to threaten. Thus, widening the definition of terrorism widens the function of all three agencies.

Warrant procedure

The legal constraints on targets in the UK may be compared with those in Canada and the USA. In the USA warrants are only issued if there is 'probable cause' that the target is a foreign power or agent of a foreign power and collection is for the purpose of obtaining foreign intelligence.[40] In Canada warrants may be issued only if there are 'reasonable grounds' for believing that the warrant is required to investigate a threat to national security.[41] It is apparent that the constraints in these jurisdictions are narrower and, in particular, the serious crime work is not included. The function of the agencies in assisting in preventing or detecting serious crime is likely to form a much smaller percentage of their work than will widening the definition of terrorism. The 1998 MI5 booklet mentions 'arrangements' governing the role of the Service in assisting in serious crime work and the need for a close working relationship with the other agencies in question.[42] The arrangements are not published. Therefore two executive bodies are left to determine, in a barely accountable and 'invisible' manner, the key issue of principle at stake here. Now that the HRA is fully in force this matter will become more pertinent. The accountability of the police will be increased since, as a public authority under s6 HRA, they will be bound by Article 8 of the Convention, which provides that an interference with the respect for private life must be prescribed by law. As Chapters 9 and 10 point out, the police will soon have a legal basis for the use of certain forms of surveillance, under the Regulation of Investigatory Powers Act 2000 (RIPA). But now that the statutory basis has been provided, the police will be more open to challenges in the courts. Although the security and intelligence services are a public authority under s6 HRA, they are unlikely to face such challenges, for the reasons discussed below. Therefore the HRA may be circumvented if an investigation is undertaken by the Security Service, which would be able to use the powers under s5(4) of the 1994 Act and Part II of the

[40] Under the Foreign Intelligence Surveillance Act.
[41] Under the Canadian Security Intelligence Service Act 1984 s2.
[42] Ibid p18.

RIPA, with little fear of judicial proceedings. The relationship between the HRA and these statutory powers is discussed more fully below and in Chapter 10,[43] but it is contended that this suggestion is likely to hold good.

The warrant procedure for all three agencies is governed partly by ss5 and 6 of the Intelligence Services Act 1994 and partly by Part II of the RIPA. Under s5(2) of the 1994 Act the Home Secretary can issue a warrant authorising the 'taking of any such action as is specified in the warrant in respect of any property so specified or in respect of wireless telegraphy so specified'. In other words, members of the agencies can interfere in any way with property so long as it appears that the action would be of 'substantial value' to the agency in carrying out any of its functions. The 1996 Act added subsections 3, 3A and 3B to s5 of the 1994 Act. S5(3) provides that warrants issued to GCHQ and MI6 in respect of their 'serious crime' function 'may not relate to property in the British Islands'. S5(3A) provides that in respect of the Security Service's serious crime work a warrant may not relate to property within the UK unless s3B applies. S3B applies if the conduct in question appears to constitute one or more offences and involves the use of violence, results in substantial gain or is conduct by a large number of persons in pursuit of a common purpose or is an offence for which a person of 21 or over with no previous convictions could be expected to receive a sentence of imprisonment of three years or more. The purpose of the 1996 Act was to allow the Security Service to aid the police in preventing and detecting serious crime, by which the government stated that it meant organised crime. However, the terms of the Act do not limit its application to serious or organised crime. It could be used, for example, against persons engaging in public protest who might well (given the breadth and vagueness of some public order law) commit an offence, such as obstruction of the highway, and who can be said to be acting in pursuit of a common purpose. Thus, a distinction is created between the agencies in terms of what they may do in relation to property, and this is continued in Part II of the RIPA. But clearly all three were able to engage in other activities in relation to persons in the British Islands, whether under warrant or not, so long as, formally speaking, the activities were in accordance with their functions. This position became untenable under the HRA and therefore, in anticipation of its coming into force, such activities were provided with a statutory basis under the RIPA as discussed in Chapters 9 and 10. 'Directed surveillance' and covert 'human intelligence sources' can be used by MI6 and GCHQ, but 'intrusive surveillance', which entails an intrusion onto 'residential premises', can normally be used only by MI5.[44]

It was suggested in debate in Parliament that the 1994 Act should contain a clear set of principles which would govern and structure the

[43] See in particular pp385–390.
[44] P382.

operations of the services in carrying out these statutory functions. It was suggested that they should include the requirements that the more intrusive the technique the higher the authority should be to authorise its use, and that except in emergencies less intrusive techniques should be preferred to more intrusive ones.[45] The government rejected these amendments to the 1994 Act on the ground that they were implicit in s5 of the Act. S5 provides that the Secretary of State should be satisfied that 'what the action seeks to achieve cannot reasonably be achieved by other means'. This imprecise requirement is clearly no substitute for the more detailed set of principles suggested. If a member of the Service wishes to intercept communications on the public telephone system, another level of control is imposed since the procedure under the Interception of Communications Act applies. This is discussed in Chapter 9. The RIPA addressed the anomaly that members of the services could engage in various forms of surveillance in reliance merely on the procedure under the 1994 Act, but that in respect of this particular form, an extra layer of control was added. The individual whose mobile phone conversations are secretly recorded has suffered no less an invasion of privacy than one whose conversations on the system covered by the 1985 Act are recorded. However, although the RIPA extends the controls, it is modelled on the 1985 Act and therefore it is unlikely to provide a significant safeguard for privacy.

The result of s5 is that a private individual can have surveillance devices placed on his or her premises or can be subject to a search of the premises even though engaged in lawful political activity which is not intended to serve any foreign interest. An amendment to the Security Services Bill was put forward that would have exempted such a person from the operation of the legislation, but it was rejected by the government.

The authorisation must be by the Home Secretary, personally, under s6(1) of the 1994 Act, except in the case of emergency warrants which may be authorised by a senior official, with express authorisation from the Home Secretary. The arrangements for intrusive surveillance under the RIPA are similar, as explained in Chapter 10,[46] but no independent authorisation procedure is necessary in respect of the other two forms of surveillance. The s6 warrant procedure begins with a letter from the agency to the Home Office. It is considered in the Warrants Division which may require further information in order to strengthen the application. As Lustgarten and Leigh point out, this process could be viewed as a gulling of their political master by collusion between 'the Security Service and its Whitehall counterpart', or it could be seen as 'conscientious control' over the requests, endowing stronger ones with greater credibility and rejecting weaker ones.[47] Under s5 of the 1994 Act the Home Secretary should

45 HC Standing Committee E col 72 8 March 1994.
46 See p381.
47 *In from the Cold* at p57.

then consider whether it is necessary for the action to be undertaken on the ground that 'it is likely to be of substantial value in assisting the agency in question in carrying out its function, as indicated above'. He must be satisfied that what is sought to be achieved could not be achieved by other means and as to the arrangements for disclosure of information obtained. It is not possible to ascertain how far each of these matters is subjected to serious scrutiny or how far, assuming that they were taken seriously, a Home Secretary would be able to detect weaknesses in the application. Obviously these matters would depend partly on the particular Home Secretary in question. But applications are very rarely rejected and, as Lustgarten and Leigh point out, political considerations as well as legal ones enter into the approval.[48] The warrants are issued for six months initially by the Home Secretary and may be renewed by him or her for that period so long as it is thought necessary for them to continue. There is no overall maximum period and some warrants may therefore be, in effect, permanent. If issued by a senior official the warrant ceases to have effect after two working days.

The warrant procedure has been compared unfavourably with that in other mature democracies. The Canadian Security Intelligence Service may only be granted warrants on the authorisation of a Federal Court judge, thus ensuring a measure of independent oversight. Moreover, the warrant will not be issued unless the facts relied on to justify the belief that a warrant is necessary to investigate a threat to national security are set out in a sworn statement.[49] In the USA the warrants are authorised by special Foreign Intelligence Surveillance Act courts comprising selected Federal judges, although in certain circumstances the Attorney-General can authorise searches or warrants by executive order only. These arrangements present a strong contrast with the UK ones since there is no judicial involvement at all in the UK in the issuing of warrants under either the 1994 or 2000 Acts. Any judicial involvement can occur only after the warrant has been issued. Thus the crucial stage of the procedure is entirely in executive hands – one part of the executive is authorising another to interfere with individual rights. The impact of judicial authorisation must not be overestimated; clearly, some judges may develop a tendency to rubber-stamp requests. But the fact of placing papers before a judge may foster internal scrupulousness in their preparation. Since many persons will have no means of knowing that they have been targeted and therefore will have no ability to make a complaint, judicial involvement at the complaints stage only is of marginal importance. The failure to allow such involvement in the warrant procedure may be viewed as one of the key weaknesses in the scheme. This was one of the matters which the Intelligence and Security Committee in 1998 considered, in comparing the

[48] Ibid p58.

[49] For discussion of the impact of this system in practice see I Leigh [1996] 'Secret proceedings in Canada' 34 Osgoode Hall Law Journal 113.

position in the UK with that in other jurisdictions, but it seemed more concerned with the development of accountability through the complaints mechanisms than through advocating a change in accountability *prior* to issue of the warrants. This may be due to the model it expressed adherence to – that of seeking to ensure accountability within the ring of secrecy.

The system for accountability therefore relies mainly on a level of ministerial control but only as regards activities of the agencies which are under warrant or require Ministerial authorisation under the RIPA. As indicated, a further, judicial level of control is then added which relates only to the warrant procedure. The Commissioner is supposed to provide oversight of the procedure, but only after the event. At present the same Commissioner, Lord Justice Stuart-Smith, operates as Commissioner in respect of all three agencies and will be re-appointed to continue his role as the 'Intelligence Services Commissioner' under s59 RIPA. The oversight is, however, limited. The Commissioner can only oversee the issuance of warrants under ss5 and 6 of the 1994 Act; he or she cannot order that they should be quashed; nor can the Commissioner order an operation against a particular group to cease. The Commissioner cannot address instances in which no warrant was necessary since the procedure in question is not unlawful. The remit of the Commissioner precludes consideration of unauthorised actions since he or she can only consider whether a warrant was properly authorised. If an action does not require a warrant such a question becomes irrelevant. This is also true of actions which are unlawful and unauthorised by warrant, such as burgling a property. In such circumstances a home-owner who realised what had occurred could complain to the Tribunal (see below) and by that means bring the unauthorised action to the attention of the Commissioner. But where the individual does not know what has occurred or for any other reason (such as lack of faith in the complaints procedure) does not complain, unauthorised actions cannot come to the attention of the Commissioner. These two gaps in the Commissioners' remit are very significant. Further, the Commissioner is only concerned with the investigative activities of the services, not with matters such as their use of personal files, although, as indicated below, the Commissioner may look at policy regarding certain files. No independent body is in fact charged with directly investigating such use, which remains entirely without independent regulation.[50]

Now that forms of surveillance falling outside the previous regime have been placed on a statutory basis, under the RIPA, requiring authorisation in order for them to be carried out, the Commissioner's oversight role will be extended under s59(2). In the post-HRA era the Commissioner will also have to apply Convention principles under s6 HRA since he will

[50] The Chief Surveillance Commissioner appointed under the 2000 Act will also have an oversight role in this respect. See Chapter 10 pp383–5.

be bound by them, as a public authority, in carrying out his work.[51] Indeed, except in the very small number of instances of activities of the agencies which result in a complaint to the new Tribunal, he will have the key role in seeking to ensure that the agencies comply with the HRA. An aspect of ensuring such compliance will be the Commissioner's discharge of his oversight role in relation to reviewing the 'exercise and performance by members of the intelligence services of the powers and duties conferred or imposed on them by or under Parts II and III of this Act' (s59(2)(c) RIPA). Prior to the inception of the RIPA it was admitted, tacitly, that unauthorised but lawful actions, such as the use of bugging devices without entrance onto property, occurred without warrant. The HRA of course, reversed the principle that everything that is not unlawful is permitted. As far as public bodies are concerned, all interferences with individual rights now require a lawful basis (under, *inter alia*, the 'in accordance with the law' requirement of Article 8(2)). Thus, now that the HRA is in force the Commissioner should seek to ensure, that actions which should be authorised by warrant or under the RIPA are properly authorised, taking Article 8 of the Convention into account, under s6 HRA. It may be noted that the Commissioner has constantly pointed out that only a small number of warrants are issued.[52] This may support the view that many actions of the agencies were undertaken without warrant and therefore emphasises the significant extension of the Commissioner's oversight role which has occurred.[53] The requirements of Article 8 are discussed below. The RIPA addresses the legality issue but, as Chapters 9 and 10 argue, while it succeeds in providing a statutory basis for actions which currently have no such basis, it does not provide a sound protection for the citizen against abuse of these powers. It is improbable, however, that the Commissioner will be able to do more than seek to ensure that the RIPA is complied with, despite his duty under s6 HRA.

The function which the Commissioner also fulfils, that of checking the issuance of warrants, will also be affected by the HRA. At present the Commissioner applies judicial review principles to this exercise. The Commissioner is not required to do so, but has adopted this approach by analogy with the approach he or she is required to take in respect of complaints regarding interference with property. In other words, the Commissioner is under a self-imposed limitation.[54] Now that the HRA is fully in force the Commissioner should apply the principles a court, bound by s6 HRA, would apply on such an application, to consideration of the

[51] See Chapter 2 pp49–50 regarding the definition of 'public authorities'.

[52] See p3 of the Report for 1998. This point has been made in all the Reports so far.

[53] It is of course not possible to make any judgement as to how many, if any, of these are both unlawful and unauthorised and how many are merely unauthorised. Under the HRA, as argued, there will be no distinction in respect of activities which engage Article 8.

[54] The Commissioner applies 'the principles applied by a court on an application for judicial review': 1989 Act Schedule 1 para 4(1); 1994 Act Schedule 1 para 5(2).

warrant procedure. The part of the Report which deals with the warrant procedure is invariably very brief (usually one page long) and the rubric used is 'Errors'. This word is used to describe serious and unlawful invasions of privacy which might well amount *inter alia* to burglary and to trespass to property and at times an impression of complacency is created: 'I know that any errors are much regretted and very real efforts are made to avoid recurrence'.[55] Where 'errors' are found internal inquiries may be set up and internal procedures may be improved as a result, but the public has to accept, as a matter of faith, that the matter has been resolved and is unlikely to recur. For example, in June 1999 Lord Justice Stuart-Smith found that a Cabinet Minister had exceeded his powers in issuing warrants to an official outside his own department. The warrants allowed MI6 officers to enter, bug and interfere with private property.[56] However, the name of the Cabinet Minister was not disclosed, no criminal charges were brought and there were no indications that disciplinary action resulted. These matters are outside the Commissioner's remit and are entirely within executive hands.

If the Commissioner was to take Article 8 into account in checking warrants, would this make any difference? The probable requirements of Article 8 as regards warrants are discussed below, but possibly they are too broad and imprecise to make much practical difference to the narrow procedure in question. They at least amount to a set of principles which should be allowed, by the Commissioner, to infuse the checking procedure, but given that where errors are found, the Commissioner is prepared to be readily satisfied with assurances that they have been internally rectified and are unlikely to recur, it is unclear that such principles will be able to find any practical expression. They might do so if a Commissioner was appointed who was familiar with Convention principles, including the need to render the rights effective rather than illusory, and was prepared to take a robust and challenging approach to the task.

Creation and use of personal files

The Intelligence and Security Committee has taken a particular interest in the creation and use of personal files stored by the agencies, particularly those on UK citizens. A particular concern was to consider 'the protection for an individual against having information inappropriately or inaccurately gathered, stored and used against their interests'.[57] These files play a significant role in security vetting which affects a wide range of jobs in the UK. It applies to senior staff in a range of government departments, to independent bodies such as the BBC and in the private

[55] Report of the Commissioner for 1998, presented to Parliament June 1999 Cm 4365 p3.
[56] See the *Guardian* 18 June 1999.
[57] The *Report of the Intelligence and Security Committee for 1997/98* Cm 4073 p16 paras 39 and 40.

sector.[58] Security checks will include consideration of information, if any, held on an applicant by MI5.

The Security Service currently holds 250,000 hard copy files on individuals and a further 4,000 are archived on microfiche. Of these 17,500 are currently coded 'green'[59] or active; 13,000 of these relate to UK citizens. The Service is currently reviewing files for destruction by category. The Committee expressed concern that reviewing was restricted to individuals over 55. Thus files may be retained on individuals under that age because they had 20 years ago joined an organisation then classed as subversive, whereas a file would not be opened on a person joining the same organisation today.[60] The Committee found: 'We believe . . . that some form of independent check should be built into the process'.[61] The government's response to this recommendation suggests that secrecy remains the overriding priority: 'The Government does not believe that the process of reviewing files for destruction would be assisted by independent scrutiny'.[62] Clearly, a response of this nature rather negates the purpose of providing the Committee with an oversight role.

The Committee took a somewhat less robust view of the SIS and GCHQ records and data. SIS has 86,000 records, half of which relate to UK citizens. Many of them relate to the staff of the agency and its contacts; 75% of these are closed and some relate back to 1909. Thus it appears to have no destruction policy and of course no independent check that it is not holding files on UK citizens needlessly. The argument for an independent check may not be as pressing as in respect of the Security Service, but it is clearly applicable, especially as internal procedures reveal an unawareness of the abuses which can arise if files are stored for many years without review.

Like SIS, GCHQ does not hold and create personal records in the same way that MI5 does. But its rationale is to hold personal data collected by intercepting communications. GCHQ informed the Committee that such data 'which may arise from collection under warrant *or otherwise* [emphasis added] is a necessary and sometimes key analytical tool'. GCHQ has a lawful basis for interception under s5 of the 1994 Act and under s3(2)(a)(i) of the 1985 Act. But these words imply that GCHQ is currently

58 See First Report from the Select Committee on Defence, Session 1982–3, Positive Vetting Procedures in Her Majesty's Services and the Ministry of Defence HC (182/83) 242 and the Radcliffe Report Cmnd 1681, 1962, Chap 7; I Linn *Application Refused: Employment Vetting by the State* (1990) London; M Hollingsworth and R Norton-Taylor *Blacklist: The Inside Story of Political Vetting* (1988) London. The current vetting guidelines are set out in a statement made at HC Debs Vol 251–766w (15 December 1994).

59 This is part of the 'traffic lighting' process for files: 'green' files are active; 'amber' ones are closed but may have papers added; 'red' ones are closed and retained for research only.

60 Ibid p19 para 47.

61 Ibid p20 para 50.

62 *The Government Response to the Intelligence and Security Committee's Annual Report* Cm 4089 October 1998 p5 para 16.

holding some personal data without a basis of legal authorisation. Since such holding of data is not a criminal offence or civil wrong this practice of GCHQ could not be said to be unlawful until the HRA came fully into force. Assuming that it amounts to an infringement of Article 8, it is now unlawful since it cannot be said to be in accordance with the law. As discussed below, it may well be the case that no avenue other than the complaints mechanism is available to an individual to challenge the holding of his or her personal information which has been obtained unlawfully. In future, such a matter could be brought before the new Tribunal set up under the RIPA; this is discussed in Chapter 10. Without relying on the HRA, the Committee did express some disquiet in 1998 as to the holding of data, collected under warrant or otherwise: 'It is particularly important that the use of such material is kept under close review and that it is destroyed as soon as practicable unless there are clear and continuing operational requirements which will require its own authority'.[63] The last few words appear to signal the Committee's concern that there should be a lawful basis for such holding and use of personal data, especially if it has been acquired without authorisation.

The government responded that all GCHQ interception, use and retention of material is carried out only in accordance with the 1994 and, where appropriate, 1985 Acts and 'these arrangements are subject to continuing scrutiny by the Commissioners' under the two Acts.[64] This response is, it is suggested, disingenuous and misleading; it suggests an attitude not far from contempt for the function of the Committee since it fails to address its central concern. GCHQ had admitted that some unauthorised interception had occurred and that material obtained was retained. If the interception is not under warrant it is unlawful. An individual would normally have no means of knowing that an interception, authorised or unauthorised, had occurred. The RIPA may provide a statutory basis for the retention of some material, accompanied by safeguards, under ss15 and 16, but this matter has been left to be resolved by means of executive arrangements.[65]

One means of allowing a check on the retention and use of personal information would be to allow some access, possibly with use of editing, under the forthcoming Freedom of Information Act to the personal data held by all three agencies. However, the three agencies will all be excluded from the Act. They are also now fully exempt from the obligation to apply the data protection principles under the Data Protection Act 1998, on the basis that the files are held for national security purposes. Under the 1984 Act personal data held on national security grounds was not exempt from the principles, although the agencies did not register under the Act on national security grounds. The protection is therefore

[63] Report of the Committee p21 para 54.
[64] P6 para 19 of the Government Response.
[65] See Chapter 9 p351.

weaker under the 1998 Act, although a person directly affected by the exemption can appeal against the issue of a national security certificate, under s28 of the 1998 Act. Since the agencies, and MI5 in particular, have a role in relation to serious crime, this position is anomalous. As the Data Protection Registrar (now Commissioner) has argued, MI5 should be placed in the same position as the police in relation to this role.[66] The Commissioner has no general statutory remit to obtain access to files for monitoring purposes. But individual cases referred to the Commissioner may raise general issues of file keeping. The position may be compared with that in Canada where the agencies are subject to privacy and access to information legislation, although individuals have no right of access to their files and are not informed that the file exists. An edited version of the file may be made available which will be limited to information already in the public domain. The key point is that the *Commissioners* in Canada have access to the files. In the USA records may only be established and held if they are relevant to the conduct of authorised intelligence operations and they are subject to the Freedom of Information Act. Individuals can ask to see files; they may be given an edited version and the agency can choose neither to confirm nor deny that material has been withheld. These arrangements, qualified as they are, represent an improvement on the complete exclusion of the agencies from the relevant privacy and FoI legislation, as in the UK.

Complaints to the Commissioners and Tribunals

Taking the Interception of Communications Act as a model, the 1989 Act set up a Commissioner under s4 and a Tribunal under s5 as a means of oversight for MI5. The procedure for complaints and composition of the Tribunal are dealt with in Schedules 1 and 2. The 1994 Act adopted the same model for MI6 and GCHQ under ss8, 9 and Schedules 1 and 2, using almost identical wording. The systems of complaint for all three agencies share the same characteristics, which, it will be contended, render them almost irrelevant as a means of providing oversight. These characteristics have at one and the same time attracted universal condemnation from independent commentators and universal approval, not to say complacency, from the executive and from the Commissioner. It has been said: 'A major cause for concern . . . is the failure to confront adequately the need for accountability and review of the Services'.[67] Wadham of

[66] Our Answers: Data Protection and the EU Directive 95/46/EC, The Data Protection Registrar, July 1996. This position was also strongly criticised by Justice in its Report *Under Surveillance: Covert Policing and Human Rights Standards* (1998) p90. For the position of the police under the 1998 Act see Chapter 9 p383.

[67] Ewing and Gearty *Freedom under Thatcher* (1989) p178.

Liberty described the Security Service Tribunal as 'useless'.[68] Gill found: 'this structure . . . has been constructed neither for elegance nor impact'.[69] Lustgarten and Leigh sum up the problem: 'in so far as the government believed that by creating these new structures it would reassure the public that all is well it seriously miscalculated'.[70] In contrast, Jack Straw, the current Home Secretary, wrote in his introduction to the 3rd edition of *The Security Service* (1998): 'the Service is subject to a substantial regime of . . . judicial . . . oversight which ensures that its work is given effective external scrutiny'. The stance of the current Commissioner, who at present oversees all the agencies and has done since the inception of his role, is indicated in various comments scattered across the text below. Apart from the tone of such comments, it is noted that in at least two instances he has interpreted his role even more narrowly than the statutory provisions required. He interpreted his role in checking warrants as subject to judicial review principles, although this is not a statutory requirement,[71] and he has (it appears) on his own initiative adopted a practice of failing to reveal, in his reports, the number of warrants issued to the agencies, although this matter is not covered in either the 1989 or 1994 Acts. He has said that the limitations of the complaints mechanism are the fault of the 'architects' of the statutory provisions,[72] but given his own acquiescence in the limitations of his role this comment is, to an extent, misleading.

A key limitation of the function of the Commissioner and Tribunals is that the statutory provisions have no retrospective effect. Thus complaints may only relate to post-commencement activities. Where enquiries pre-commencement led to the gathering of material, complaint by the individual concerned cannot be made to the Tribunal and the material can continue to be stored. This has been called the gravest defect of the 1989 Act;[73] however, given the inefficacy of the complaints procedure it might now be said that it is not the most significant defect. So far the Tribunal has never ordered that since enquiries which led to the making of a file were unauthorised, the file itself should be destroyed.

No duty is imposed on the agencies to disclose the fact to an individual that an operation has occurred, after it is over. Most individuals will have no means of knowing that it has occurred and therefore will be unlikely to bring a complaint. In contrast, in Germany an individual who has had her phone tapped must be informed of this after the operation is completed unless the investigation would be prejudiced.[74] If an individual

[68] *From the Cold* p439.

[69] P Gill *Policing Politics: Security Intelligence and the Liberal Democratic State* (1994) London at p295.

[70] Op cit p439.

[71] This requirement refers only to complaints regarding warrants, see 1989 Act Schedule 1 para 4; 1994 Act Schedule 1 para 5(2).

[72] Lustgarten and Leigh p438.

[73] Ibid p438.

[74] See *Klass* v *Federal Republic of Germany* (1979) 2 EHRR 214.

brings a speculative complaint to the Tribunal, uncertain whether surveillance or intrusion has occurred, the result may leave him or her none the wiser. The Tribunals only report that the result is unfavourable to the complainant, not whether an operation was indeed taking place, but was viewed as justified. The Tribunals are not permitted to give reasons for their decisions.[75] Service personnel who feel that they have been required to act improperly in bugging or searching a person's property may not disclose the matter. S1 of the Official Secrets Act 1989 prevents members or former members of the security and intelligence services disclosing anything at all about the operation of those services. All such members come under a lifelong duty to keep silent even though their information might reveal a serious abuse of power by the services. These provisions also apply to anyone who is notified that they are subject to the provisions of the section. Similarly, s4(3) of the Act prohibits disclosure of information obtained by, or relating to, the issue of a warrant under the Interception of Communications Act 1985 or the Security Services Act 1989. The 1989 and 1994 Acts provide no avenue for members of the agencies to complain to the Commissioner or Tribunals. Therefore, any disclosure of information to them or to the individual citizen concerned by such members would be a criminal offence under the Official Secrets Act. Thus the persons who would be most aware of an abuse of power are denied this means of either supporting a complaint or enabling the individual concerned to instigate one. They can complain to the Security and Intelligence Services Staff Counsellor, appointed by the Prime Minister in 1987, but the office is, as Lustgarten and Leigh put it, 'a safety-valve for conscience-troubled officials, rather than a form of oversight'.[76] The Reports of the Counsellor for the Prime Minister, Home Secretary and Foreign Secretary are unpublished and therefore there is no means of knowing whether his work has any benefit in terms of terminating unlawful or improper agency activities. It is clear that the Counsellor's role is to prevent such activities achieving any publicity, so that, for example, questions cannot be asked about them in the House of Commons.

Under Schedule 1 para 2 of the 1989 Act the Security Service Tribunal can investigate two types of complaint: that the agency has instituted enquiries about the complainant and, if so, whether it had reasonable grounds for so doing. If the enquiries were due to a person's membership of a category of persons the only question to be asked is whether there were reasonable grounds for believing him or her to be a member of that category, not whether the Service had reasonable grounds for investigating the group in question. Where information has been disclosed to an employer the Tribunal will investigate whether there were reasonable

75 Schedule 1 para 5(3) of the 1989 Act and Schedule 1 para 6 of the 1994 Act.
76 Ibid p430.

grounds for believing the information to be true. No enquiry is to be made into the misleadingness of the information or its factual truth. Nor can the Tribunal consider the reasonableness of the categorisation of a particular group, or part of a group. The final ground for complaint is apparently wide: a person 'may complain to the tribunal if he is aggrieved by anything which he believes the Service has done in relation to him or any property of his'.[77] But the Tribunal cannot investigate a complaint which relates to property and must pass it to the Commissioner who will utilise the principles applied by a Court on an application for judicial review.[78] The provisions under the 1994 Act follow a similar pattern. Under Schedule 1 para 2 of the 1994 Act the Tribunal can investigate two types of complaint: that MI6 or GCHQ has obtained or provided information or performed any other tasks in relation to the actions or intentions of the complainant and, if so, whether applying the principles applied by a Court on an application for judicial review (the agency) had reasonable grounds for so doing. Schedule 1 para 1 contains the same provision as the 1989 Act: a person 'may complain to the tribunal if he is aggrieved by anything which he believes the Intelligence Service or GCHQ has done in relation to him or any property of his'. But the Tribunal cannot investigate a complaint which relates to property and must pass it to the Commissioner who will utilise the principles applied by a Court on an application for judicial review.[79]

The standard of scrutiny in the Tribunals is therefore unlikely to be rigorous: in *Secretary of State for Home Affairs, ex parte Ruddock*[80] (determined prior to the coming into force of the 1985 Act) the question was: whether the decision of the Home Secretary in granting the warrant was 'so outrageous in its defiance of logic or accepted moral standards that no sensible person who applied his mind to the question to be decided could have arrived at it'. Since the Tribunals can merely ask whether the agency had 'reasonable grounds' for its action, they cannot consider the questions whether the action was proportionate to the invasion of privacy and whether the action could have been carried out by the police. The Tribunals sit in secret and the complainant has no right to be informed of the findings of the investigation, only whether it is favourable or unfavourable.

Given these limitations it is unsurprising to find that no complaint has ever been upheld by the Tribunals or Commissioner. Between the introduction of the 1989 Act and the end of 1997 the Tribunal set up under s4 of the 1989 Act investigated 275 complaints; none was upheld.[81] The Reports of the Commissioner are brief and bland in the extreme. For

[77] 1989 Act Schedule 1 para 1; 1994 Act Schedule 1 para 1.
[78] 1989 Act Schedule 1 para 4; 1994 Act Schedule 1 para 3(b).
[79] 1994 Act Schedule 1 para 5(2).
[80] [1987] 1 WLR 1482.
[81] *MI5: The Security Service* 3rd edn (1998) p33.

example, the Report of the Security Services Commissioner presented to Parliament in June 1999[82] covers complaints to both Commissioner and Tribunal in half of one page. It reports that the Tribunal received 28 complaints in 1998 of which 18 were investigated and none were upheld. The other 10 are to be investigated in the following year. The Commissioner received 16 complaints and upheld none.[83] The rest of the material in the Report, which runs to six pages, is largely descriptive, apart from the brief one-page Report on the issuance of warrants, discussed above. The Prime Minister has the power to censor the Report before it is presented to Parliament, a power which is clearly exercised routinely, and this task is made straightforward and convenient for him or her by the Commissioner who has adopted a practice of writing the Report in two parts, the second with the expectation that it will be censored: 'I have again taken the course of writing the report in 2 parts, the confidential Annex containing those parts which you will probably consider should not be published'.[84] In other words, the Commissioner, following the practice of the Interception of Communications Commissioner, is entirely prepared to collude in and facilitate the censorship practice. This detail in itself perhaps suggests that the Commissioner's role has become a comfortable, routinised one which is far from seeking to apply rigorously high standards or from challenging the boundaries of his or her own powers. It may be said, however, that the Commissioner is operating under constraints which appear to render his office a merely tokenistic one. He sits as a full-time judge, has no staff and takes roughly two weeks' leave plus his own free time to carry out his role. He has been appointed to carry out his task in respect of all three agencies, and therefore he is expected to oversee bodies with, as noted, a combined budget of £747 million and a staff of around 5,000.[85] It would be hard to find another organisation in the UK in which a single person was expected to take on a comparable role, while in the USA, Canada and Australia the equivalent bodies have a full-time staff. As Chapters 9 and 10 explain, an Interception of Communications Commissioner as well as a Chief Surveillance Commissioner will be appointed under the RIPA. The remit of the new Commissioners will overlap with that of Lord Justice Stuart-Smith, when he is re-appointed, since it will include some oversight of surveillance undertaken by the agencies.[86]

The stance of the Intelligence and Security Committee in commenting on the oversight system is comparatively rigorous: 'Some see this [no

[82] Report of the Commissioner for 1998, Cm 4365.

[83] Ibid p5.

[84] Report of the Commissioner for 1998, per Lord Justice Stuart-Smith, Cm 4365. The second part was not published.

[85] This is an estimate; the numbers have been censored from the Parliamentary Committee's Report 1998 pp42 and 47.

[86] See pp353–5. For the role of the Chief Surveillance Commissioner, see pp383–5.

complaints upheld] as evidence that the tribunal system does not work. We merely state this as a fact since we have not had access to the material to enable any judgement to be made . . . we lack the ability to investigate directly different aspects of the Agencies' activities . . . we have not had the capability to conduct independent verification ourselves. Without such a capability the Committee cannot make authoritative statements on certain issues.'[87] The Committee recommended that it should be afforded such a capability. As Lustgarten and Leigh put it, reflecting on the response of the Commissioner to the credibility problem arising from the failure to uphold any complaints: 'his view . . . correctly identifies the main problem as flaws in the design of . . . [the 1989 Act] rather than in the competence of the workmen'.[88]

Clearly, discussion of the remedies available if a complaint was upheld is hardly worthwhile since they were never utilised. But it is worth noting that the *appearance* of respect for individual privacy belied by the actuality, which the possibility of complaint on wide grounds represented, was also carried through into the provision of remedies. A number were available, including destruction of the information collected, an order for the cessation of the operation and compensation. But the Tribunal had a complete discretion in awarding the remedies. Even if it or the Commissioner had found in favour of a complainant he or she could have been left remediless. There was no provision that a successful complainant had to receive at least one form of remedy.

It appeared to be almost impossible, in practice, for a member of the public who was dissatisfied with the outcome of the complaints procedure to seek a remedy in the courts. The Tribunals were set up as the only avenue of complaint and under s5(4) of the 1989 Act and s9(4) of the 1994 Act the decisions of the Tribunals, including decisions as to their jurisdiction, were not questionable in any court of law. When the role of the old Tribunals is taken over by the new Tribunal, under the RIPA, discussed in Chapter 10, a similar ouster clause will apply, under s67(8) RIPA. Therefore this limited system, with certain modifications, will continue to provide, in practice, the only remedy.

As the work of the agencies extends into new fields and as greater expectations of accountability are raised, dissatisfaction with the system is likely to rise. When the bodies were set up commentators thought it likely that they would fail to uphold complaints and would not adopt a challenging role.[89] It can now be said with some certainty that these fears

[87] The *Report of the Intelligence and Security Committee for 1997/98* Cm 4073 pp23–25.
[88] Op cit p438.
[89] See for example Ewing and Gearty (1989) p181; Wadham 'The Intelligence Services Act 1994' [1994] 57(6) MLR 916 at p925.

have been realised. The Intelligence and Security Committee pointed out in its 1998 Report that: 'several countries have more extensive forms of independent oversight'; they include Canada, Australia, New Zealand and the USA.[90]

The Reports of the Commissioner and the 1998 MI5 booklet express surprise at certain points that persons should have suspicions that the Security Service might abuse its powers. There are also suggestions that when complaints are made they are mainly from people who have 'paranoid' fears about the Service. As Lustgarten and Leigh put it: 'Some of the complainants are repeaters who, as the Commissioner expressed it informally, are "plain barmy"'.[91] This problem arises in other jurisdictions, but in this one it may be due, at least in part, to the nature of the oversight system. The Commissioner and the documents in question appear to fail to recognise that the framework set up to provide oversight is itself at least part of the reason for suspicion as to the work of the Service. If, for example, persons had to be notified that they had been investigated and if the investigations were more rigorous and transparent, greater confidence would be generated. If persons who are, apparently, not being investigated make complaints, this may partly be due to the uncertainty as to whether an investigation has occurred. The citizen has normally no means of knowing one way or the other. This fact in itself clearly undermines the whole oversight mechanism.

It is possible, since these mechanisms have now been in place for a substantial period and at the time of writing are about to be replaced, to make an evaluation of the efficacy of the Tribunals and Commissioners as a means of providing accountability, in comparison with overseas models. In terms of the available models of accountability, the UK is clearly towards one end of the spectrum – the light touch end – while the USA, Canada and Germany are towards the other. As the Parliamentary Committee pointed out, it is fair to say that public confidence in the system is fragile. The mechanisms in place for providing a measure of accountability inevitably play their part in creating that fragility since, as the Committee pointed out, there is really no means of evaluating the soundness of the claim that the agencies do not abuse their powers. That claim can only be accepted as an act of faith, clearly an unsatisfactory position in a mature democracy.

As indicated, the new Tribunal will replace the current ones and will also take over the Commissioner's complaints' role. This Tribunal is discussed in Chapter 10 since it will cover all state surveillance, including that undertaken by the police and other public authorities. Its

[90] Ibid p24.
[91] Ibid p439.

procedure is still to be determined, by executive order. But it appears to be modelled on the current Security and Intelligence Service Tribunals and therefore it is contended in that chapter that it may be almost equally ineffective. In the post-HRA and FoI era a different climate may be created and this system, unless it develops, is likely to come to seem even more inadequate, especially as the remit of the agencies, and especially of MI5, widens.

As indicated above, the role of the Intelligence Services Commissioner (as he will be known) will change under the RIPA s59 since he will no longer receive complaints. But he will have a statutory duty under s59(3) to assist the new Tribunal in relation to its investigations and determinations. He must, if required to do, give his opinion as to any issue to be determined by the Tribunal. Now that the HRA is fully in force the Commissioner will have to apply Convention principles under s6 HRA since he is bound by them, as a public authority, in carrying out this work.[92] This means that, unless provisions of the 1989, 1994 or 2000 Acts do not allow him to act otherwise, he must decide compatibly with the rights. Article 8 will, of course, be of especial relevance. In assisting the new Tribunal the Commissioner may apply, as it will do, the principles applied by a court on an application for judicial review and therefore should apply the principles a court, bound by s6 HRA, would apply on such an application. In other words, it will not be enough merely to apply *Wednesbury* principles.[93] The principle of proportionality encapsulated under Article 8 should be applied, which should include considering whether the interference with property in question should have been carried out by the police, or other law enforcement bodies, especially where 'serious crime' support was in question. This issue is one of the matters which the Home Secretary should take into account under s5 of the 1994 Act and under the RIPA Part II, in relation to surveillance by the Intelligence Services, as Chapter 10 explains. The question of disproportionality can also be considered even where it is found that the interference could not have been carried out by other means. For example, the period of time for which the warrant was issued might be viewed as disproportionate to its object. Thus, in assisting the new Tribunal in relation to a particular complaint or proceedings, the determination of the Home Secretary regarding proportionality in the particular circumstances would be one of the matters which should be tested directly against Convention standards.

[92] See Chapter 2 pp49–50 regarding the definition of public authorities.

[93] Previously, the Commissioner applied the *Wednesbury* test as follows: he required that the Service make: 'a sufficient factual case to satisfy the Secretary of State . . . that there are grounds for believing that national security interests are involved' for a warrant to be issued (*Security Service Act – Report of the Commissioner for 1990* Cm 1480 (1991) para 12). The application of this very readily satisfied test made it highly unlikely that a warrant would be found to have been issued illegally.

Convention rights under the HRA

Now that the HRA is fully in force, it can be said that the Convention represents a set of principles which may be read into the 1989, 1994 and 2000 Acts so long as no irremediable incompatibility between the statutory provisions and the rights exists.[94] Further, the three agencies in question, the relevant Ministers and the oversight bodies (apart from the Parliamentary Committee)[95] as public authorities are bound by the rights, under s6 HRA. Although, formally speaking, this is the legal position, the means whereby the Convention rights can be enabled to have a real rather than a theoretical impact on the agencies are highly circumscribed. They are discussed below, but although possible methods of bringing the HRA to bear on the agencies in court are considered, it is contended that the main impact of the HRA in this context will be an educative and cultural one: it will provide the openness the Parliamentary Committee currently favours with a clearer basis, and it may have an eventual, incremental impact on the work of the oversight bodies, in terms of the attitude they bring to their work. Most significantly, it may help to provide the impetus for the further evolution of the oversight.

Means of finding domestic expression

There are a number of possible methods of seeking to ensure that the HRA is fully complied with in this context and some of these have already been mentioned. Reliance on court action is very unlikely to be central; rather, a mix of administrative and Parliamentary methods of seeking to ensure compliance may become evident. The new Tribunal will have a duty to comply with the Convention in adjudicating on complaints and the Commissioner will have such a duty, in overseeing not only warrants, but also the discharge of the duties of the Home Secretary and agencies under the RIPA. This has two aspects. These bodies are themselves bound by the Convention; they are also providing oversight of bodies which are themselves so bound. Both aspects should inform their work, as has been indicated above. The new Tribunal will be the only forum in which complaints regarding the work of the agencies can be brought. In practice, it will probably be the only forum – apart from criminal proceedings brought against citizens – in which challenges to operations of the agencies can be mounted. It will have both a complaints and a references jurisdiction, and will operate adversarially, albeit under procedural constraints. Therefore, it represents, at least theoretically, a step forward in terms of creating accountability.

[94] S3 HRA.

[95] Parliament itself is not a public body under s6 and nor is a person exercising function in connection with proceedings in Parliament (s6(3)(b)). It is probable that the Committee is not a public authority under this definition.

The members of the agencies themselves should ensure that in carrying out their work they do not infringe the Convention. In order to achieve this it would appear to be necessary for the management bodies, including the Director-General, to put in place internal reviews which seek to ensure that compliance is achieved, and the Parliamentary Committee should be charged by the Home Secretary with considering Convention compliance as part of its remit and should receive evidence as to the findings of any such review. There is little evidence at present that it considers the compatibility of agency actions with the Convention, although its programme of work for 2000 and beyond will cover the Convention in relation to personal files.[96]

Action in the ordinary courts at the citizen's instigation may be almost entirely ruled out. As indicated above, ouster clauses contained in s5(4) of the 1989 Act and s9(4) of the 1994 Act barred the way to obtaining judicial review of the decisions of the Commissioner and Tribunals. Both were post-*Anisminic*[97] ouster clauses in that they covered decisions of the Tribunals and Commissioner as to their jurisdictions. The new Tribunal will also be protected by such a clause, although there will also be a very narrow right of appeal. The nature of this right and the possibility of circumventing the new ouster clause are discussed in Chapter 10.[98]

It has always been theoretically possible to bring a prosecution or tort action against agency members or to seek judicial review of Ministerial or internal decisions. Any such action in the post-HRA era would have to accord with the Convention. But the possibility of a new tort action against the agencies for breach of Article 8 has largely been precluded by s65 of the RIPA.[99] The use of judicial review in the ordinary courts is similarly circumscribed. As Chap 10 explains, the new Tribunal will probably be viewed as the only forum for action. Prosecution of agents is highly unlikely since no means of referring an investigation to the police is provided in the statutes; further, any risk of revealing secrets would probably be avoided simply by taking a decision not to prosecute. It would also be difficult to acquire evidence owing to the provisions against providing evidence to complainants.

[96] See the Report for 1998–9, Cm 4532 at p36.

[97] *Anisminic Ltd* v *Foreign Compensation Commission* [1969] 2 AC 147. See p407, note 143.

[98] At pp406–7.

[99] Under s6 the Convention rights are binding on public authorities. If the existing law fails to cover actions of such authorities which breach Article 8(1) (such as the use of surveillance devices not involving an entry on to property) new tortious liability would have to be created. The new action or actions would be binding only against public authorities owing to the provision of s6. Such a breach may be justifiable but only *inter alia* if it has a basis in law. The lack of a legal basis led to a finding that the UK had breached Article 8 in *Malone* v *UK* (1984) 7 EHRR 14. Similarly, in *Govell* v *UK* (1997) 4 EHRLR 438 no legal basis was found for police bugging. However, the intention, expressed under s65 of the RIPA, is that against certain public authorities, most notably the police and security and intelligence services, such matters should be considered only by the Tribunal if they fall within s7HRA; see Chapter 10 pp402–4.

Security vetting in the UK, taking into account information held on an applicant by MI5, raises a number of Convention issues. The position of applicants who are dismissed or refused employment as regards obtaining recourse to Industrial Tribunals has recently improved owing to the government response to the findings of the European Court of Human Rights in *Tinnelly* v *UK*.[100] The Court found that a ministerial certificate, stating that the reasons for the failure to employ the applicants were national security ones, effectively blocked the applicants' claim, since the judge could not go behind its terms and consider the claim, and therefore a breach of Article 6 had occurred. As a result of the ruling the law as regards employment hearings in which national security is a factor was changed. S90 of the Northern Ireland Act 1998 provides for the creation of a Tribunal, modelled on the Special Immigration Appeals Tribunal, to review the issue of ministerial certificates in Northern Ireland.[101] Thus the issue of national security will be justiciable. However, the extent to which the evidence can be tested will be questionable. As C White puts it: 'the central difficulty with the type of Tribunal set up by the 1998 Act is that it attempts to create an adversarial forum where one of the parties is severely hampered in presenting his or her case'.[102] This Tribunal provided a model for the new Tribunal to be set up under the RIPA; the discussion of its procedure and its compatibility with the Convention in Chapter 10 are therefore of relevance. The Employment Rights Act 1996 s193 and the Employment Appeals Tribunals Act 1996 s10 were amended[103] so that complaints of unfair dismissal cannot be dismissed on national security grounds unless it is *demonstrated* that the reason for dismissal was on those grounds. All these Tribunals, including the new one in Northern Ireland, are bound by s6 HRA, and therefore their procedure must comply with the Convention, and the Convention points considered below could be raised before them. In Industrial Tribunals, under the previous position, the assertion of national security grounds would have precluded their consideration.

Evidence obtained by members of the agencies on behalf of the prosecution could be challenged during the criminal process. If an individual was charged with a crime and it appeared during the trial that evidence had been obtained against him or her by the agencies, it could be challenged under s78 PACE on various grounds. There might be no authorisation or it might be flawed in some respect. It might become apparent that the information had been obtained unlawfully, under the ordinary criminal or civil law, and under the Convention. As Chapter 5 indicated,

[100] (1999) 27 EHRR 667. For discussion see K McEvoy and C White 'Security Vetting in Northern Ireland' [1998] 61 MLR 341 at pp349–354.

[101] For discussion see C White 'Security Vetting, discrimination and the right to a fair trial' [1999] PL 406–418.

[102] Ibid at p413.

[103] By the Employment Rights Act 1999 Schedule 8. Security and Intelligence members may also have access to Industrial Tribunals, under Schedule 8.

the question of exclusion of evidence in such circumstances will be affected by Article 6 requirements.[104] The broader the role of the agencies, especially MI5, becomes in terrorist and serious crime cases, the more issues as to exclusion of evidence may be of significance. Cases in which security agents give evidence may employ devices, such as screens,[105] *in camera* proceedings,[106] voice scramblers, separate rooms, live video links and/or public interest immunity certificates in order to protect the security of the agents as witnesses and of the information involved. S17 of the Youth Justice and Criminal Evidence Act 1999 (which is not yet in force) allows for the use of screening measures and live video links in respect of intimidated witnesses. S17 would therefore appear to cover security and intelligence agents who had personal reasons to fear reprisal. But it would not cover the use of anonymity for operational reasons. If the use of such devices means that evidence cannot be fully challenged or that arguments under s78 cannot be fully resolved, Article 6 might be breached. Questions of disclosure might also arise[107] as might general issues of fairness. The use of screens and other means of preserving anonymity[108] might have a prejudicial effect on the jury. Issues of exclusion of evidence and of disclosure of evidence are addressed in Chapter 10, but other Convention requirements which may arise in relation to the evidence of security and intelligence agents are considered below.

A further, somewhat remote possibility is that judicial review could be sought of the statutes themselves as failing to ensure compliance with the Convention, by analogy with the decision in *Secretary of State for Employment ex parte EOC.*[109] It was found that the EOC (Equal Opportunities Commission) can seek a declaration in judicial review proceedings to the effect that primary UK legislation is not in accord with EU equality legislation. The House of Lords found that since the EOC had a duty under s53(1) of the Sex Discrimination Act to work for the elimination of discrimination, it was within its remit to try to secure a change in the provisions under consideration; therefore the EOC had a sufficient interest to bring the proceedings and hence *locus standi.* A body standing in a relationship to the agencies equivalent to that of the EOC to UK law would have to be identified. As already pointed out, the Commissioners and the new Tribunal will be bound under the HRA by the Convention rights. Therefore it could be argued that they will have a duty under primary legislation to seek to bring the agencies into compliance with them, and therefore they would have *locus standi* to bring judicial review

[104] See further Chapter 5 pp200–202 and also Chapter 10 pp390–392.
[105] As in the *Matrix Churchill* trial; *R* v *Roberts, Davies and Williams* (1993) unreported; *R* v *Jack (Hugh Thomas)* CA 7 April 1998 unreported.
[106] *Norman* v *Mathews* (1916) 85 LJ 857.
[107] See Chapter 10 p390.
[108] *R* v *Murphy and Maguire* [1990] NI 306.
[109] [1994] All ER 910; [1994] ICR 317.

proceedings against the Home Secretary. Of course, there is little likelihood that these bodies would do so.

A pressure group such as *Liberty* would not be viewed as in a position analogous to the EOC since it was not set up under statute to have a watch-dog role. If a Human Rights Commission is eventually created, as originally promised in the White Paper *Bringing Rights Home*, it would probably have standing by analogy with the *EOC* case and this possibility might then become a more probable and worthwhile one.[110] Obviously in the case of ECHR, as opposed to EC, law, the legislation itself could not be disapplied, but review of aspects of it could lead to a declaration of incompatibility under s4 HRA. The policy of excluding certain matters from the purview of the oversight bodies could be reviewed.

The Intelligence and Security Committee and the Joint Parliamentary Committee on Human Rights have a role in this context although they are not bound by s6. The latter would be expected to consider executive orders in relation to the security and intelligence services made under the 2000 Act, which might be of doubtful compatibility with the Convention. The former could take account of the extent to which Convention principles appeared to find expression in the work of the Commissioner, the new Tribunal and the agencies in general and could operate its review remit accordingly.

Finally, the possibility of further actions at Strasbourg in future cannot be ruled out, probably under Articles 8, 6 or 13, despite the fact that at the present time, as indicated below, the domestic arrangements probably satisfy the Convention requirements in a number of respects. As Chapter 2 points out, decisions of the Commission, taken some years ago and heavily influenced by the margin of appreciation, may not reflect the stance of the Court over the next few years, post-2000. Given the arguments canvassed here, it might be argued that no domestic remedy which must be exhausted, other than that represented by the new Tribunal procedure, exists; such absence would speed up the process of taking a case. In other fields the HRA itself might offer such a remedy which would require exhaustion in the ordinary courts, but in this one that argument is much weaker owing to the provisions of ss65 and 67(8) RIPA.

Convention requirements: potential non-compliance

Since Article 8(1) provides a right to respect for private life, the home and correspondence, it is the Convention Article which is most relevant to the activities of the agencies. Chapter 9 argues for a broad view of what constitutes invasion of privacy, based on the notion of control of personal information.[111] The width of Article 8(1) could be viewed from

[110] See Chapter 2 pp50–51 for discussion of the old standing rules and s11 HRA.
[111] See pp338–9.

a number of aspects. It could be argued that an interference with property was not compatible with such respect. It could also be argued that the provisions of the Acts themselves constitute a continuing invasion of privacy. Fear of the possibility of surveillance might inhibit conversations within the home, for example, thus stultifying the benefits offered by the home and by private life. A straightforward invasion of privacy, such as planting a 'bug' on the premises in question, or entering them in order to remove property, will be likely to amount to an infringement of Article 8.[112] Less obvious invasions will also engage Article 8. In *Harman and Hewitt* v *UK*[113] the European Commission of Human Rights found that secret surveillance by MI5 of two former NCCL officers, Patricia Hewitt and Harriet Harman, had infringed Article 8(1), although they had not been subjected to direct intrusion. The intrusion was termed 'indirect' since information about them obtained from the telephone or mail intercepts of others had been recorded. The argument of the Court in *Klass* that the possibility that a phone had been tapped would represent a continuing invasion of privacy, since conversations would be inhibited, could be utilised, if necessary. It was accepted in *Malone* v *UK*[114] that the tapping of a phone infringed Article 8. It could be argued that where a surveillance device had been placed on property, or where it was strongly suspected that it had been, an invasion of privacy, in terms both of failure to respect private life and, where appropriate, the home, had more clearly occurred than in *Klass* or *Malone*, since while persons might have some wariness in using the public telecommunications system to communicate confidential information, they would expect to have none in making communications in private conversation in their own homes or on other private property. The use made of personal information, including disclosure to others, might also engage Article 8(1). In *MS* v *Sweden*[115] the applicant complained that the use of medical records in respect of a compensation claim had infringed Article 8. The Court found that the disclosure did constitute an interference with the respect for private life, although it was found to be justified under Article 8(2).[116] The findings in *G, H and I* v *UK*[117] implied that the compiling and use of personal files by the Security Service might fall within Article 8, although they also raised questions regarding the onus placed on applicants to establish that they were likely to have been the victims of surveillance, in that instance of positive vetting for civil service posts. *Esbester* v *UK*[118] confirmed that a

[112] See Chapter 10 pp395–6.
[113] Appl 121175/86; (1992) 14 EHRR 657.
[114] (1984) 7 EHRR 14.
[115] (1999) 28 EHRR 313; available from the Court's web-site: www.dhcour.coe.fr.
[116] On the grounds of being necessary in a democratic society to further the economic well-being of the state.
[117] 15 EHRR CD 41.
[118] 18 EHRR CD 72 No 18601/91 Dec 2 April 1993. See also *Harman* v *UK* No 20317/92 (1993) unreported.

security check based on personal information would fall within Article 8. It may be concluded that many, if not almost all, activities of the agencies in obtaining, collecting, using and disclosing personal information are likely to engage Article 8.

Once Article 8(1) is engaged, the question is whether the interference can be justified under para 2. To be justified, state interference with the Article 8 guarantee must first be in accordance with the law. As indicated in Chapter 2, interpreting 'prescribed by law' (treated as an equivalent provision at Strasbourg) Strasbourg has asked first whether the interference has some basis in domestic law and second whether it is of the right 'quality'.[119] In *Huvig* v *France*[120] and in *Kruslin* v *France*[121] the Court said that the requirement of quality means that the law 'should be accessible to the person concerned, who must moreover be able to foresee its consequences for him, and compatible with the rule of law'. The application in *Harman and Hewitt* v *UK*[122] was declared admissible since the activities of MI5 in placing the applicants under surveillance were not in accordance with the law. No sufficient basis in law existed at the time, and the successful application led to the passing of the 1989 Act. Although there is room for argument that certain of the terms used in the 1989, 1994 and 2000 Acts are too imprecise and broad to satisfy the 'in accordance with the law' requirement, it is unlikely that this would be found to be the case in respect of primary legislation in this context, unless the domestic courts are prepared to take a much stricter view of that requirement than that taken at Strasbourg. In *Christie* v *UK*[123] the Security Service and Interception of Communications Acts were both found to meet this requirement and the Commission noted: 'the [Strasbourg] case law establishes that the requirements of foreseeability in the special context of sectors affecting national security cannot be the same as in many other fields'. Nevertheless, in criticising the provisions of the 1996 Act, Peter Duffy and Murray Hunt have argued that it breaches Article 8[124] since it probably does not pass the Convention requirement that an interference with private life should comply with rule of law principles. Executive discretion is so unfettered under the Act that any interference may not be 'in accordance with the law' as interpreted in *Huvig* v *France*[125] and *Kruslin* v *France*.[126] No application from the UK has been made since the passing of the 1996 Act and therefore the 'in accordance with the law' question cannot be regarded as finally settled.

[119] See *Sunday Times* v *UK* A30 para 49 (1979), discussed in Chapter 2 p25.
[120] (1990) 12 EHRR 528 at para 26.
[121] (1990) 12 EHRR 547 at para 27.
[122] Appl 121175/86; (1992) 14 EHRR 657.
[123] 78-A DR E Com HR 119.
[124] See (1997) 1 EHRR 11.
[125] (1990) 12 EHRR 547.
[126] (1990) 12 EHRR 528.

In *Esbester* v *UK*[127], which concerned the alleged supply of information by MI5 regarding the applicant's membership of the Communist Party of Britain and of CND, leading to the revocation of a job offer, the Commission found that the 1989 Act complies with the 'in accordance with the law' requirement since the grounds under s3 were expressed sufficiently precisely. This was a cautious, narrow application of the Convention requirements by the Commission. In *Leander* v *Sweden*,[128] which concerned the holding of information in a secret police register, the Court found that unpublished statements explaining the law could not meet the accessibility requirement. Since, as indicated above, vetting procedures are either unpublished or have not been placed on a statutory basis, it might have been expected that they would fail to meet this requirement. The Commission in *Esbester* seemed to fail to distinguish between the different invasions of privacy created by vetting, and to have failed to look for a satisfactory basis in law in relation to the interference created when the information is supplied. Possibly this is a context in which the Court will eventually allow a narrower margin of appreciation in scrutinising the quality of the domestic basis for vetting more rigorously, bearing in mind its deterrent effects which may undermine freedom of association. Chapter 3 contends that the Court's freedom of association jurisprudence in the context of membership of political groups has recently become somewhat more interventionist.[129] Since security vetting tends to raise issues under both Article 8 and Article 11, it is possible that such a stance may also become more evident under Article 8.

Any residual activities undertaken by the security and intelligence services which at present are not covered by the procedures under the 1994 and 2000 Acts may not be in accordance with the law, assuming that the primary right under Article 8(1) is engaged. For example, at present agents must acquire a warrant if they intend to enter property or interfere with it. They are also bound by the terms of Part 1 of the RIPA; under s1 it is a criminal offence to tap into a public or private telecommunications system without authorisation. But certain surveillance techniques may not be covered by Parts I or II of the RIPA. Until the inception of the HRA use of such techniques was lawful under civil or criminal law in the sense that since no law forbade them they were assumed to be permitted. The Intelligence and Security Committee in its 1998 Report[130] spoke of 'executive and judicial checks that intelligence and security services are obeying the law, in particular on acts which would be unlawful but for express authorisation'.[131] The implied distinction is between acts

[127] 18 EHRR CD 72 No 18601/91 Dec 2 April 1993. See also *Harman* v *UK* No 20317/92 (1993) unreported.
[128] (1987) 9 EHRR 443.
[129] See pp63–64.
[130] Cm 4073.
[131] Ibid p23.

which do not require such authorisation and acts which do. But under the HRA it is unlawful for a public authority to fail to abide by the Convention rights and therefore, as explained below, this distinction between acts which require express authorisation and those which do not will tend to break down. All these activities require a basis in law under the HRA since all or almost all of them represent an infringement of privacy. Following the principle laid down in *Harman and Hewitt* v *UK*[132] it is clear that placing the use of certain surveillance activities on a legal basis, which includes requiring warrant applications, is insufficient if others remain unregulated.

Christie v *UK*[133] concerned an interference, telephone tapping, which requires a warrant if it is not to amount to a criminal offence, as the Commission pointed out. The Interception of Communications Tribunal had investigated and had found no breach in relation to the warrant procedure; this could be taken to mean that no warrant had been issued, a matter outside the jurisdiction of the Tribunal, or that one had been properly issued. The other issue concerned the retention of information collected through the tap by the Security Service. It is unclear, but possible, that had the complaint concerned a procedure which did not require a warrant but which infringed Article 8, its basis in law might have been viewed as insufficient, given that no involvement of the Secretary of State in checking warrants or, under s6 of the 1985 Act, in reviewing the use of resultant material, would have been necessary. This contention must be put forward tentatively since the Commission in *Christie* viewed the terms 'national security' and 'economic well being' as sufficiently precise since they had been explained by 'administrative or executive statements'. It may be that activities which do not at present require authorisation might be said to have a form of legal basis under the statutory provisions if they are carried out in accordance with the stated functions of the agencies in the 1989 and 1994 Acts. But, despite the view expressed in *Christie*, it is suggested that this basis is so exiguous and leaves discretion so unfettered that it may in future be found to fail to satisfy the 'accordance with the law' requirement. The case of *G, H and I* v *UK*[134] raised questions concerning the efficacy of the 1989 Act, although the applications failed. As indicated above, the RIPA 2000 is intended to provide the necessary legal basis. Clearly there may still be activities of the agencies which fall outside it. Further, it is questionable whether the Act itself provides a basis of sufficient quality. This is discussed further in Chapters 9 and 10.

Assuming that an interference is 'in accordance with the law', under the 1989, 1994 or 2000 statutes, it must also, under Article 8(2), have a legitimate aim, be necessary in a democratic society and be applied in a non-discriminatory fashion (Article 14). In cases of invasion of privacy by

[132] Appl 121175/86; (1992) 14 EHRR 657.
[133] 78-A DR E Com HR 119.
[134] 15 EHRR CD 41.

the state Strasbourg's main concerns have been with the requirements of 'in accordance with the law' and 'necessary in a democratic society'. In this context the 'legitimate aim' requirement has always been found to be satisfied. This is unsurprising since the grounds available for interference are so broad. They are: the interests of national security, public safety or the economic well-being of the country, the prevention of disorder or crime, the protection of health or morals, the protection of the rights or freedom of others. The provision against non-discrimination under Article 14 has not been so far a significant issue in the state invasion of privacy jurisprudence. The Court has interpreted 'necessary in a democratic society' as meaning: 'an interference corresponds to a pressing social need and, in particular, that it is proportionate to the legitimate aim pursued'.[135] As explained in Chapter 2, the doctrine of proportionality is strongly linked to the principle of the margin of appreciation. The width of that margin appears to depend partly on the aim of the interference in question and partly on its necessity. In relation to the aim of national security the Court has allowed a very wide margin to the state.

In *Klass* v *Federal Republic of Germany*[136] the European Court of Human Rights found, bearing the margin of appreciation doctrine in mind, that German telephone tapping procedures were in conformity with Article 8 since *inter alia* they provided for compensation in proceedings in the ordinary courts for persons whose phones had been unlawfully tapped. The legality of such interceptions could be challenged in the ordinary courts. No such provision is available under the Security Services Act 1989 or the Intelligence Services Act 1994 in respect of analogous intrusions, although, theoretically, the Tribunals can award compensation, either of their own motion or on a reference from the Commissioner.[137] This system would appear to represent a significantly lower standard of accountability than the West German one in respect of phone tapping and it is at least possible that a breach of Article 8 would have been found in *Klass* had the margin allowed to Germany been narrower. *Leander* v *Sweden*[138] concerned rather similar complaints mechanisms. Information on the applicant was stored on a secret police register for national security purposes and used for employment vetting. This created an interference with Article 8(1) but a wide margin was allowed to the state in choosing the means of protecting national security. The aggregate of remedies available, recourse to an independent Ombudsman and Chancellor of Justice, were found to be sufficient to satisfy Article 13. In *Harman* v *UK*[139] and *Esbester* v *UK*[140] the Commission found that the 1989 Act complied

[135] *Olsson* v *Sweden* A 130 para 67 (1988).
[136] (1979) 2 EHRR 214.
[137] Schedule 1 para 6(1) and para 7(2) of the 1989 Act. Schedule 1 para 8(1)(b) and para 8(2)(b) of the 1994 Act.
[138] (1987) 9 EHRR 443.
[139] (1994) available from the Commission's web-site: dhcommhr.coe.fr.
[140] No 18601/91 Dec 2 April 1993.

with the procedural requirements of Article 8(2), at least in the national security context. In *Christie* v *UK*,[141] in respect of the almost identical mechanisms under the 1985 Act, the Commission found: 'having regard to the wide margin of appreciation in this area' the safeguards provided by the Tribunal and the Commissioner were sufficient in the instant case. These findings need not be taken to mean that the oversight mechanisms provided under the 1989 and 1994 Acts, and now under the 2000 Act, meet Convention requirements. They were made in relation to the particular case, not as abstract comment on such mechanisms in general, and they were heavily influenced by the margin of appreciation, especially wide where national security is in issue. As argued in Chapter 2, that doctrine is not available at national level and this, it is contended, means that it should not influence national decision-makers. An activist domestic judge considering, judicially or extra-judicially (assisting the new Tribunal or as a member of it, or an appeal), whether the domestic complaints or reference provisions meet Strasbourg standards, and untrammelled by the margin of appreciation doctrine, might conclude that the controls built into the UK system under the 1989, 1994 and 2000 Acts are insufficient to prevent abuse. The framework is largely based on scrutiny of the procedure after the event and in a manner which keeps most of its key aspects in the hands of the executive. In this respect it fails to accord with the rule of law since a part of the executive is authorising another part to invade rights; the checking procedure which is then marginally available appears to provide a largely illusory protection and in respect of key aspects of it the only recourse is to the executive again. Arguably, the safeguards would not appear to satisfy Article 8(2). But it is more probable that the judiciary would find that traditional notions of deference in the national security context would yield the same result as the application of the margin of appreciation doctrine.[142] There are signs, however, that at Strasbourg, in its very recent decisions, the Court is becoming less deferential towards claims of national security, although admittedly they have been in the context of Article 6 rather than Article 8, a significant difference due to the qualifications under Article 8.[143] The question whether the new, single Tribunal provides an effective remedy for the citizen, and its compliance with Article 6, is discussed in Chapter 10.[144]

As indicated above, a number of Article 6 issues also arise in criminal proceedings in which the security and intelligence services have played a part, of which only those raised by the anonymity of witnesses are

[141] Also, in *Christie* v *UK* 78-A DR E Com HR 119 the Commission found that the Interception of Communications Act 1985, the model for the 1989 and 1994 Acts, met the 'in accordance with the law' requirement of Article 8(2).

[142] See further Chapter 2 pp30–37.

[143] *Tinnelly* v *UK* (1999) 27 EHRR 249 (discussed above, p00); *McElduff* v *UK* App No 21322/92.

[144] Pp401–413.

addressed at this point. Article 6 envisages a public hearing[145] allowing a confrontation between defendant and witnesses and enabling the defendant to challenge prosecution witnesses.[146] Article 6(3)(d) provides that the accused must be able to 'examine or have examined witnesses against him' under the same conditions as apply to the prosecution in relation to the examination of witnesses. Clearly, measures aimed at anonymity, depending on their extent, will impair the objectives underlying these features of a fair hearing, including the maintenance of confidence under the 'open justice' principle, the ability of the jury to assess the credibility and reliability of witnesses by *inter alia* observing their demeanour and hearing answers to probing questions. In *Van Mechelen* v *Netherlands*[147] the only identification evidence consisted of the statements of anonymous police officers. The hearings took place in two separate rooms connected by sound link, so that the witnesses were never in the same room as the defendants and their lawyers. The anonymity was allowed for fear of reprisals and as a means of preserving the value of the officers in undercover operations. The Court found that Article 6 had been breached. It found that any measures restricting the rights of the defence must be strictly necessary and the least restrictive procedure possible must be adopted. Police officers as agents of the state should be granted anonymity only exceptionally, and not on the basis of preserving their operational value. The defence must be able to question anonymous witnesses in their presence and must be able to assess their demeanour. This was a rigorous approach to upholding standards of procedural justice, which clearly has implications for the giving of evidence by security and intelligence service members. Domestic courts, following *Van Mechelen* under the HRA, would be expected to evaluate the basis on which anonymity was claimed, as far as possible, bearing in mind the Article 2 and other Convention rights of the witnesses and, where it was granted, scrutinise any measures aimed at achieving it, with a view to ensuring their strict proportionality with that aim. These principles would also, clearly, be relevant to claims of public interest immunity. It appears to be implicit in the Court's judgment that certain measures would impair the rights of the defence to such an extent that the evidence in question could not be used since its reliability and the credibility of the witnesses or sources could not be fully assessed. Article 6 may, therefore, curb the tendency of domestic judges to elevate secrecy above fundamental principles of criminal justice.[148]

[145] There are exceptions under Article 6(1) allowing the 'exclusion of press or public in the interests of morals, public order, national security . . . where the interests of juveniles so require . . . protection of private life . . . or to the extent strictly necessary . . . in special circumstances where publicity would prejudice the interests of justice'.

[146] *Unterpinger* v *Austria* (1986) 13 EHRR 175; *Kostovski* v *the Netherlands* (1989) 12 EHRR 434; *Windisch* v *Austria* (1990) A 186; *Doorson* v *the Netherlands* (1996) 22 EHRR 330.

[147] (1998) 25 EHRR 657.

[148] See further R Costigan and P Thomas 'Anonymous Witnesses' [2000] NILQ, forthcoming. The paper deals with anonymous witnesses generally, but covers the use of Security

The Intelligence and Security Committee

The 1989 Act provided for no real form of Parliamentary oversight of the Security Service.[149] But the 1994 Act set up, under s10, the Parliamentary Committee, the Intelligence and Security Committee, to oversee the 'expenditure, administration and policy' of MI5, MI6 and GCHQ.[150] Operational matters were omitted from its remit. Thus for the first time all three services were made, to an extent, accountable to Parliament. The Committee's Report is not, however, presented directly to Parliament but to the Prime Minister who may censor it before presentation on broad grounds – it need not be damaging to national security, merely to the continued discharge of the functions of the services. Appointment to the Committee is by the Prime Minister. Since the Committee is not a Select Committee it has no powers to compel witnesses to appear before it. The members of the Committee have been notified that s1 of the Official Secrets Act will apply to them as though they were members of the services themselves and therefore they will commit a criminal offence if they disclose any information or document they have obtained as a result of their work. They would have no defence that the disclosure revealed a serious abuse of power which could not be otherwise addressed, or that the information was already in the public domain. 'Sensitive' information can be withheld from the Committee by agency heads[151] and non-sensitive information can be withheld by the Secretary of State.[152]

It was clear at its inception that the extent to which the work of the Committee was likely to have a real impact on the agencies depended on its appointees and on the way they interpreted their role. The 1996–7 Report of the Intelligence and Security Committee made no recommendations as to independence at all, in quite strong contrast to the 1997–8 Report which adopted a more adversarial approach. Tom King chaired the Committee over this period of time and appears to be adopting an increasingly robust stance. The 1998 Report signalled a change of direction towards a more rigorous scrutiny, and this continued in the 1999 Report, also under his Chairmanship. At present it may be said that the 1998 and 1999 Reports are the only ones of a number of public documents relating to the agencies which mention the possibility of a different model of oversight from the one already in existence. The other documents (the MI5 and MI6 booklets and the Reports of the Commissioner) merely blandly present findings which show that nothing

Service witnesses. Its general discussion of the dangers of anonymity is highly relevant in this context.

149 See further I Leigh and L Lustgarten 'The Security Services Act 1989' (1989) MLR 801.

150 For discussion of the introduction of the Committee in 1994 see Lustgarten and Leigh *In from the Cold* (1994) *Coda*.

151 Schedule 3 para 3 (2).

152 Schedule 3 para 3 (4).

is amiss, without giving serious consideration to any of the factors which might lead a member of the public to fail to have confidence in such findings.

The 1998 Report was completed after the system had been in place for four years. In its section on oversight it looked especially at the oversight available in other countries, having talked in the past year to counterpart bodies. They found that other countries have 'more extensive forms of "independent" oversight'.[153] One feature of such 'more extensive' models of oversight is the Inspector-General (IG), a full-time appointment who has wide powers of access to operational and other information. The Commissioner for the Security Service has similar powers of access but it is not his function to review operations and the Tribunals only do so in response to a direct complaint. As pointed out above, many members of the public who might have grounds for complaint would not be able to bring one since they would be unaware of the operation. An IG would be able to consider operational abuse of power without depending on a complaint. The Committee did not recommend the introduction of an IG system but it impliedly took the view that further consideration of this possibility should occur. The Committee did point out that it cannot 'investigate directly different aspects of the Agencies' activities' and it found that the Committee's reach should be extended by an additional 'investigative capacity'.[154] It considered that without this capacity it cannot make authoritative statements and needed some reinforcement of authority. This would help in establishing public confidence in the agencies. In its 'Future Programme of Work' it set forth a number of issues to be pursued in 1998 and 1999, including the question whether individuals should have rights in connection with the destruction or otherwise of any file held on them; protections against storage and use, against individuals' interests, of inaccurate information; and the implications of the European Convention. Following this Report additional support was given to the Committee on a non-statutory basis, reflecting its interest in an 'Inspector-General' model of accountability. This is a step forward in those terms, but since no powers are granted, cooperation of the services will be on a consensual basis only.

In the 1998 and 1999 Reports the breakdown of the figures for the funding of the different agencies is concealed by lines of asterisks. In its 1999 Report the Committee had intended to publish the annual figures for each agency in accordance with what it terms 'a greater spirit of openness', but this was thwarted by the agencies. It does report, however, that MI5 spent over £200 million, well over three times the original estimate, refurbishing Thames House, its new headquarters. MI6 spent more than £80 million, four times the original estimate, fitting up its headquarters

[153] P24 para 62.
[154] P25 para 69.

at Vauxhall Cross. It views this overspending as a serious matter that must be addressed. Other, fairly radical suggestions of the Committee are considered above, as is the government's response. Broadly speaking, it seems clear that the Committee is at present determined to take quite a radical view of its role, arguing that it is appropriate at present to do so in accordance with the new climate of openness. Equally, it is not evident that the government is minded to concur fully with this argument; its response is not encouraging, being brief, bland and, on the whole, unreceptive to the recommendations of the Committee. Key indicative phrases included: 'reviewing files for destruction would [not] be assisted by independent scrutiny'.[155]

Conclusions

Jack Straw, the current Home Secretary, wrote in his introduction to the 3rd edition of *The Security Service* (1998): 'I hope that the booklet will help dispel the myth that the Security Service is unaccountable and has no effective oversight. In fact the Service is subject to a substantial regime of Ministerial, Parliamentary, judicial and financial oversight which ensures that its work is given effective external scrutiny'. But the discussion above has revealed serious limitations in the complaints and warrant oversight system, limitations which, it is accepted by the current Commissioner, were built into the system when it was set up. The Intelligence and Security Committee has no means of investigating independently claims made by agency heads, except on a consensual basis; it can merely sum up what it has been told and make recommendations. It is aware that this detracts from its credibility. The Committee, in contrast to the Commissioner, shows a greater awareness of its own inefficacy and has proposed measures to improve it. Inevitably it provides a deeply flawed oversight since it is unlikely to be able to verify claims that the Service has not abused its powers. Equally, it cannot readily verify claims that abuses of power are occurring, some of which result in unsuccessful complaints to the Tribunal. As it points out, it has not yet been able to satisfy those who consider that the Tribunals' record in failing to uphold complaints means that the tribunal system does not work. Therefore its credibility and that of the Service are undermined. In 'heavier touch' models such means of independent verification, albeit under various limitations, are in place. Under the present system none of the available methods can exert any real control and the engagement of the new statutory bodies with the agencies therefore has an air of unreality and impotence about it.

[155] P5 para 16.

This chapter has examined the oversight and accountability system within the context of the tension between the expanding role of the agencies and the limited available means of rendering them accountable. It will end on a divergent note. There are signs of an evolving oversight and a strengthening accountability, taking into account the RIPA changes, particularly the introduction of the new Tribunal, but the mechanisms are still, it is contended, too weak to live up to the expectations currently created in the new era of openness and accountability under the HRA and FoI. At the time when they were put in place the mechanisms were viewed as a radical departure from the old order and all that could be expected of the governments in question. Now, although their inadequacies are apparent, they have provided the model for the mechanisms provided under the RIPA. In the current era the assumptions underlying them look more questionable.

But the introduction of such mechanisms and the extension of a statutory basis for the agencies, under the RIPA, are first steps in a process. It is perhaps no longer likely, now that these first steps have been taken, that the impetus for greater accountability will come from Strasbourg, and the barriers in the way of using the HRA in the domestic courts to create more accountability look almost insurmountable, except, to an extent, in criminal proceedings. It has been suggested that the impetus is most likely to come from pressure from the current oversight mechanisms themselves, especially the Parliamentary Committee, from MPs and from commentators. It is possible that greater accountability will be achieved through the operation of the new Tribunal but, as Chapter 10 argues, its efficacy remains in doubt.

One result may be that the weakness of the ministerial responsibility for the agencies, especially MI5, which was highlighted by the *Mitrokhin affair*, may suffer further exposure. The Constitutional changes currently occurring, including the coming into force of the HRA, may fuel such pressure. In the USA the Constitutional arrangements, including the Bill of Rights, have fostered a culture of openness which has tended to overcome the official predilection for secrecy. Clearly, the UK Constitution differs from that of the USA. But the current changes may be viewed as diminishing the dissimilarities and as moving in this respect towards a US-style governmental culture. The Security and Intelligence Committee has shown some recognition that such a movement is occurring and that as an aspect of it the UK cannot merely continue to operate its mechanisms in an insular fashion, without considering practice elsewhere, and it understands the need for evolutive development of those mechanisms in accordance with the best practice from other jurisdictions. But while the executive holds so much power in this area, such pressure can be disregarded.

The next step will be for the mechanisms themselves to change more radically than they have done already, under the RIPA, which requires the consent of the executive. The Parliamentary Committee clearly sees this as the way forward in the emphasis it places on the evolution of its own role. But how far the government which introduced the HRA and FoI will be receptive to the natural consequences of so doing, in terms of demands for greater openness, is unclear. At present, as the 2000 Act indicates, the New Labour government appears to view arrangements which were put in place in a very different context as, with certain modifications, sufficient and adequate to meet the demands of the current era. The HRA in the domestic setting demands, as this chapter has suggested, more than Strasbourg does; this received some governmental recognition in debate on the Human Rights Bill and this chapter has identified certain movements in the direction of a more rigorous oversight. The RIPA represents, in certain respects, a cautious step in that direction. But at present there is little evidence that this recognition has been fully carried into this profoundly secretive area of executive action.

Chapter 9

A New Framework for State Surveillance I

Introduction

Theoretical perspectives

Since this chapter, and the following one, will focus centrally on the balance found in the UK legislative scheme for state surveillance between individual privacy and various state interests, it is clearly essential that it indicates the sense in which that term will be used. A new definition of privacy will not, however, be attempted; as Wacks has found, 'the voluminous [theoretical] literature on the subject has failed to produce a lucid or consistent meaning of [the] concept'.[1] But within that still unresolved debate there is strong agreement that what may be termed 'informational autonomy' is the core privacy value. The term denotes the individual's interest in controlling the flow of personal information about him- or herself, the interest referred to by the German Supreme Court as 'informational self-determination'.[2] A number of writers, including Wacks,[3] have identified this interest as being the only legitimate concern of a law on privacy. Thus Westin describes privacy as the 'claim of individuals, groups or institutions to determine for themselves when, how, and to what extent information about them is communicated to others'.[4] Arthur Miller's definition is similar: 'the individual's ability to control the circulation of information relating to him'.[5] E. Beardsley has dubbed this the right to 'selective disclosure' – to decide when and how much information about ourselves we will make known to others.[6] It has also

[1] R Wacks 'Introduction' in Wacks (ed) *Privacy* Vol 1 (1993) Aldershot, Hong Kong: Dartmouth pxi.

[2] BGH 19 December 1995 BGHZ 131, 322–346.

[3] *The Protection of Privacy* (1980) London: Blackstones pp10–21.

[4] *Privacy and Freedom* (1967) New York: Athenaeum at p7.

[5] *Assault on Privacy* (1971) Michigan p40.

[6] 'Privacy: Autonomy and Selective Disclosure' in Nomos XIII 54.

been said: 'If I have no control over what is known about me, I am seriously diminished as a person both in my own eyes and in the eyes of those capable of intruding upon me. This dual aspect of respect and self respect is a vital dimension to privacy.'[7] A right to informational autonomy would also protect what Feldman identifies as the value in forming spheres of social interaction and intimacy – for example, work colleagues, friends, family, lovers – which may be seen as essential to human flourishing.[8]

It is instantly apparent that secret state surveillance presents a profound threat to this core value of privacy. It is an instance in which the separation of public and private spheres, as a hallmark of democracy, is most clearly at risk. All the weapons associated with the secret police – telephone tapping, use of sophisticated listening devices and informers – may be deployed with the effect of creating a profound and intensive invasion of privacy. The approach to state surveillance, therefore, consonant with democratic values, would be one which at every point in a legislative scheme when a choice must be made, such as in determining the role of the courts in balancing the demands of privacy against state interests, insisted on adopting provisions which would afford effective rather than theoretical protection to privacy. Such an approach would invariably adopt a nuanced as opposed to an absolutist stance in relation to the protection of the state interests involved. In other words, it would not take positions appropriate only in circumstances where such interests were fully at stake; it would allow for a recognition that greater value could be afforded to individual privacy where the need for protection for such interests was less pressing.

Such an approach would not entail the abandonment of secret surveillance since legitimate state interests, which themselves underpin democracy, are at stake. A state has a duty to protect itself and its democratic ideals which would be at risk if extremist groups could work more freely for its overthrow. But, as Lustgarten and Leigh put it: 'in attempting to protect democracy from threats such as terrorism there is the ever-present risk that . . . that which was to be preserved has been lost'.[9] The approach which succeeds in preserving respect for democracy and for the value of individual privacy, as a hallmark of democracy, while affording respect to state interests, is one which is increasingly reflected in the jurisprudence of the European Court of Human Rights, even taking into account the wide margin of appreciation conceded in this particular area.[10]

[7] Lustgarten and Leigh (1994) p40.
[8] 'Privacy, Dignity, Autonomy: Views of Privacy as a Civil Liberty' 47(2) CLP 42, 51–69. Fried notes that privacy is essential for 'respect, love, friendship and trust' – 'without it they are simply inconceivable' ('Privacy' Yale Law Journal 77 (1968) 477, 483).
[9] Lustgarten and Leigh (1994) p41.
[10] See, for example, the pronouncements of the Court in *Klass* v *FRG* (1985) 7 EHRR 14.

Developments in surveillance and in legislative underpinning

This chapter and the next consider the current UK arrangements for state surveillance in the light of the above comments. In particular, discussion focuses on the principled approach to state surveillance at Strasbourg, informed by the values of the Convention, and examines the means whereby, under the mechanism of the HRA, it may find some expression in domestic law. It may appear ironic that it is necessary to overcome difficulties in finding such means, bearing in mind the recent coming into force of the HRA, but although the current rules governing surveillance were influenced by the Convention, its ability to provide a continuing influence on them remains highly circumscribed in the post-HRA era. This chapter will argue that although the UK is entering a completely new era in terms of both surveillance and human rights, similarities with the old position will still be apparent. The Regulation of Investigatory Powers Act 2000 was introduced partly in response to the HRA. In a bold rejection of the confused and anomalous mixture of statutory, quasi- and non-legal rules which have been the hallmark of UK state surveillance, it will provide the comprehensive statutory basis for surveillance which the Convention requires, and may even exceed Convention requirements, but at the price of curtailing consideration of Convention principles in this context in the ordinary courts.

These two chapters are mainly concerned with aural surveillance – any technical means of enabling a communication from one party to another to be surreptitiously received or recorded for the potential use of state agents. But they also consider some further techniques which *prima facie* infringe informational autonomy. They include telephone and email interception, mail opening, use of listening devices, recording by a wired informant, undercover techniques, use of informants. All these techniques will be regulated in future under the Regulation of Investigatory Powers Act 2000 (RIPA), by far the most comprehensive state surveillance statute ever introduced by a UK government. The RIPA came into force at the end of October 2000; it introduces a new scheme, broadening the functions of the existing legislation and repealing much of the current scheme. The new provisions will therefore be considered in relation to those they have replaced. The new Act continues most of the distinctions previously created between the interception of communications and surveillance by other means. Below, where necessary, the generic term 'state surveillance' will be used to cover both.

State surveillance has been a feature of state activity for centuries.[11] However, the methods available have become increasingly sophisticated. Telephonic interception has been possible for much of the twentieth century, but its incidence and the interception facilities have recently

[11] Foucault, *Discipline and Punish* (Allen Lane 1977).

increased,[12] while 'bugging' equipment has become much more sophisticated in the last 10 years, with the result that it is now very powerful, readily concealable and relatively cheap.[13] The last 20 years have seen an immense and still increasing expansion in the availability and use of a range of highly sophisticated surveillance devices, and state surveillance has become more intensive since Labour came to power in 1997.[14] The recent growth in state use of such devices as part of intelligence-led policing has received encouragement from official studies.[15] The growth in such policing, which involves using covert investigative techniques pro-actively to target suspects, is due, as *Justice* has pointed out, to the need to respond to organised crime, to the availability and efficacy of the new technology, and to the wider use of criminal intelligence due to the growth of national and transnational agencies, including Europol and the National Criminal Intelligence Service,[16] and transnational agreements.[17] The criminal intelligence information obtained can be matched and disseminated with increasing rapidity using the new technology. At the same time, methods of communicating have proliferated, especially the use of email and mobile phones;[18] the widespread use of email via mobile phones is probable within the next few years. The means of protecting communications have also developed, in particular the encryption of emails, raising concerns nationally and internationally regarding the use of the Internet by criminal organisations.

It is very readily apparent that the legislative framework for the interception of communications by state agents which was put in place during the Thatcher and Major years is now out of date. It has failed to keep pace with developments in the communications market place or in policing.[19] This statutory framework was gradually put in place during those years, starting with the Interception of Communications Act 1985, which was followed by the Security Services Act 1989, the Intelligence Services Act 1994 and the Police Act 1997. This legislative scheme was adopted in

[12] *Report of the Commissioner under the Interception of Communications Act* (1998) published June 1999 Cm 4364 at p2 para 13 and p11.

[13] See N Taylor and C Walker 'Bugs in the System' (1966) J.Civ.Lib Vol 1 105.

[14] See figures below at p349.

[15] Audit Commission *Helping with Enquiries* (1993); Home Office *Review of Police Core and Ancillary Tasks* (1995). See S Manwaring-White *The Policing Revolution* (1983); Report of the Commissioner for 1993 Cm 2522; *Security Services Work Against Organised Crime Cm* 3065 1996.

[16] Justice *Under Surveillance* (1998) p7. Walker and Taylor have pointed out that the use of surveillance techniques by police avoids adherence to the PACE interviewing rules and makes it less likely that evidence will be excluded: 'Bugs in the System' (1996) J.Civ.Lib 105 at pp107–108.

[17] See the Memorandum of Understandings on the Lawful Interception of Communications, EU JHA-Council 25 October 1995.

[18] A *Guardian* survey (6 January 2000) found that 24 million handsets were in use at the end of 1999. In 1994 2.5 million people had mobile phones.

[19] See John and Maguire 'Police Surveillance and its Regulation in England and Wales' in S Field and C Pelser (eds) *Invading the Private* (1998) Aldershot: Dartmouth; Uglow 'Covert Surveillance' (1999) Crim LR 287.

response to findings at Strasbourg or domestically to the effect that the previous administrative guidelines governing state surveillance failed to comply with the Convention. The statutes all adopted a similar model in providing highly circumscribed Parliamentary oversight and almost equally circumscribed judicial accountability. An overriding concern was to curb judicial incursion into this area except where judges were acting extra-judicially. In respect of phone tapping this concern was taken to such bizarre lengths in disallowing the direct use of evidence from taps in court, that some prosecutorial advantage was probably sacrificed to it.

At the point when the Blair government came to power, 1997, the legislative schemes underpinning state surveillance, including that under the Police Act 1997, already appeared both inadequate and unprincipled. The legal framework was riddled with gaps and anomalies. This was due in part to the haphazard manner in which the statutory measures were adopted – largely as responses to findings at Strasbourg rather than in a comprehensive, coherent and principled manner. After 1985 and until 1997 the police had statutory authority for telephone tapping, but not for other forms of electronic interception. At one point – between 1989 and 1994 – the Security Service was the only body which had a statutory basis, of sorts, for the use of surveillance devices.[20] Many forms of surveillance, which were as intrusive as those within the 1985 and 1994 statutes, were based only on administrative guidelines. In particular, the use of informers or undercover agents had no sufficient basis in law.[21] The storage, use and dissemination of criminal intelligence information was inconsistently and partially regulated.[22] Thus, the government inherited a patchy, chaotic scheme in 1997 which, it will be argued below, failed to provide sufficient safeguards from abuse of the powers it sanctioned. It was also a scheme which was already becoming increasingly marginalised by the growth in methods of communicating.

The regime relating to the interception of radio pagers and the manner of its adoption provides an example illustrative of the UK response to surveillance. The police relied on the 1985 Act until the activity was stopped on legal advice in 1992. They then relied on the obtaining of production orders in the Crown Court under s9 of PACE. In 1998 it was discovered that this procedure did not provide them with legal authority to intercept pager messages[23] and that in any event the police could not

[20] See Chapter 8 pp303–305.

[21] See further *Under Surveillance: Covert Policing and Human Rights Standards* (1998) London: JUSTICE.

[22] It was partly governed by an ACPO Code of Practice, in the police sector and partly by the Data Protection Act 1984, which is being superseded by the 1998 Act. But, as discussed below, the controls provided are insufficient due to the exemptions under the 1984 Act, continued under the 1998 Act. As Chapter 8 points out (p312) the Security Service is exempt from the 1998 Act owing to its national security function.

[23] At Worcester Crown Court 22 January 1998. The judge, on submissions from Counsel acting as *amicus curiae*, refused to grant an order in relation to a pager message which was not yet in existence. On admissibility, see *R* v *Taylor-Sebori* [1999] 1 All ER 160.

lawfully intercept messages owing to the provision of s5 of the Wireless Telegraph Act 1949.[24] Administrative guidelines were hastily adopted in response. Pending legislation, the Home Office established a non-statutory warranty regime allowing particular officials to authorise pager interception. The guidelines would not have satisfied the in 'accordance with the law' requirement of Article 8, by analogy with the decision in *Malone* v *UK*[25] on similar guidelines. The Home Secretary was not personally involved. The criterion on which warrants were issued was based on the 'serious crime' ground under the 1985 Act, but went further in relation to certain drug supply offences. The ordinary complaints procedure for the police under PACE[26] applied. The Commissioner and Tribunal under the 1985 Act (see below) agreed informally to oversee the procedure.[27] The procedure fell some way short of establishing even the minimal safeguards available under the 1985 Act. Thus this response had all the characteristics which have persistently appeared in government regulation of surveillance: it was non-statutory; it created arbitrary distinctions between state agencies and between forms of interception; the lack of control of the issuance of warrants, even within the executive itself, was striking.

Some, but not all, forms of telephone tapping were covered by the Interception of Communications Act 1985, while police use of some, but not all, other methods of interception were covered by the Police Act 1997. As explained in Chapter 8, when the security and intelligence services deployed surveillance devices they relied on the powers of warrant in the 1994 Act, and in respect of some methods they did not use a specific warrant power since their use was not unlawful. It was clear that that position would become untenable with the introduction of the HRA.[28] The police relied on a limited statutory basis within the 1985 and 1997 Acts rather than on comprehensive powers, and therefore they were open to challenges under the HRA, as explained below, if devices or techniques which fell outside them were used, since no sufficient legal basis was applicable. Thus in this context the police and the security and intelligence services were placed in very different positions, one unfavourable to the police and one which appeared to favour the use, in certain

[24] Under s5 it is an offence to do so other than under the authority of the Secretary of State, or on his or her behalf, or in the course of a person's duties as a 'servant of the Crown'. The police are not Crown servants and therefore would commit an offence if they conducted interceptions. The judgment did not therefore affect the security and intelligence services.

[25] (1984) 7 EHRR 14.

[26] See Chapter 5 pp185–186.

[27] The Commissioner expressed his unease with the situation: 'The interception of pager messages is indistinguishable in principle from the interception of telephone messages. I consider that the new arrangements are acceptable only as a stop gap measure . . . Interception of pager messages . . . should . . . be permitted only with the personal authority of the Secretary of State and with the other safeguards . . . which the Act provides.' Report of the Commissioner under the Interception of Communications Act 1998 published June 1999 Cm 4364 at p5 para 27.

[28] See Chapter 8 p328.

circumstances, of the Security Service, rather than the police, in order to carry out surveillance. The position of the security and intelligence services in relation to technical surveillance was itself anomalous; if agents used the forms of phone tapping which it covered they had to comply with the 1985 Act, but in relation to use of other devices, including other forms of phone tapping, they were subject only to the checks of the Security Services and Intelligence Services Acts.

In response, the Labour government introduced the Regulation of Investigatory Powers Bill 2000[29] with a view to providing a comprehensive statutory scheme for state surveillance, which would meet the requirements of the Convention under the HRA. The RIPA came into force shortly after the HRA came fully into force, in October 2000; the intention was to preclude the possibility that forms of state surveillance might be challenged in the courts as having no, or no sufficient, basis in law, as required under Article 8. (Given the retrospective effect of the HRA under s7(1)(b) such a challenge would not, however, be precluded where evidence from surveillance was relied on in criminal proceedings.) The RIPA places most forms of state surveillance on a statutory basis and therefore operates in tandem with the Police Act 1997. It also extends to most forms of interception, including those outside the current regime, and seeks to deal with the problem of encryption by requiring disclosure of the key to information under s49,[30] rendering refusal punishable under s53, a classic 'reverse onus' clause. It therefore addresses the anomalies identified above, but this chapter will consider whether it is any more adequate at the level of principle than the previous scheme. It is clearly not as vulnerable to challenges under the Convention. Nevertheless, its compatibility with the Convention, largely on substantive rather than procedural grounds, remains in doubt, as discussed below. The JUSTICE Report (1998) influenced its introduction, but while the first of their key recommendations – that there should be an integrated, comprehensive statutory basis for surveillance – has largely been met, it is questionable whether this is true of the second – using a 'coherent set of principles as required by Article 8' to underpin the new scheme.[31]

Under the rhetoric about protecting human rights which was used in Parliament by the Home Secretary in introducing the Bill, 'Human rights' considerations have dominated its drafting',[32] lies an unadmitted concern

[29] It was introduced into the House of Commons on 9 February 2000. The government had previously published a Consultation Paper *Interception of Communications in the UK* Cm 4368 published 22 June 1999. The responses to the Paper are available at: http://www.homeoffice.gov.uk/oicd/conslist2htm.

[30] A s49 notice requires service providers to disclose encryption keys and to keep secret the fact that a key has been disclosed. This provision may lead to adoption of a 'voluntary' key escrow system – a system whereby private encryption keys are deposited with a third party. Such a system would provide protection from prosecution for those who had genuinely lost or deleted their keys. But it clearly has significant privacy implications. See further: Y Akedeniz 'UK Government Policy on Encryption' [1997] WSCL 1.

[31] Ibid, note 21, above; see Recommendation 1 p107.

[32] HC Debs 6 March 2000 col 767.

– to keep scrutiny of such matters out of the ordinary courts. The RIPA achieves that objective in a number of respects, whereas had powers of surveillance remained on a non-statutory basis they would have been vulnerable to challenge under Article 8 of the Convention, once the HRA came fully into force. In certain respects the RIPA realises the worst fears of those who viewed the HRA as likely to lead to a diminution in the protection for liberty in the UK. It has certain features which, it will be suggested, might not have been put before a Commons dominated by Labour MPs had they not been shrouded in human rights rhetoric and accompanied by a statement of their compatibility with the European Convention on Human Rights.[33] While the Liberal Democrats wished to see the scope of the Bill and its tendency to leave power in executive hands reduced, they did not make the point that, although in one sense welcome, the very fact of greater regulation under the model chosen will reduce or exclude judicial scrutiny while confirming the strength of executive power.[34] The journal *Statewatch* attacked the Bill on this basis, calling its title 'deliberately misleading'.[35]

Interception of communications and acquisition of communications data under the RIPA

The statutory framework

Prior to 1985 there was no requirement to follow a particular legal procedure when authorising the tapping of telephones or the interception of mail. The tapping of telephones was neither a civil wrong[36] nor a criminal offence. Interference with mail was a criminal offence under s58 of the Post Office Act 1953, but under s58(1) such interference would not be criminal if authorised by a warrant issued by the Secretary of State. The conditions for issuing warrants for interception of postal or telephonic communications were laid down in administrative rules which had no legal force.[37] Under these rules, the interception could be authorised in order to assist in a criminal investigation, only if the crime was really serious, normal methods had been tried and had failed, and there was good reason for believing that the evidence gained by the interception would

[33] In accordance with s19 HRA. This statement was referred to at a number of points in the Second Reading of the Bill in the Commons in order to allay the concerns of MPs: see, for example, HC Debs 6 March 2000 col 833.

[34] Mr Alan Beith, Deputy Leader of the Liberal Democrats, found that the Bill was welcome in civil liberties terms since it extends the scope of regulation: HC Debs 6 March 2000 col 807.

[35] 'Legitimising Surveillance: the Regulation of Investigatory Powers Bill' (2000) Vol 10(1) 1.

[36] *Malone* v *MPC* (No 2) [1979] Chap 344.

[37] See *Report of the Committee of Privy Councillors* Cmnd 283 1957.

lead to a conviction. If the interception related to security matters it could be authorised only in respect of major subversion, terrorism or espionage, and the matters obtained had to be directly useful to the Security Service in compiling information allowing it to carry out its function of protecting state security.

The Interception of Communications Act 1985 was introduced as a direct result of the ruling in the European Court of Human Rights in *Malone* v *UK*[38] that the existing UK warrant procedure violated the Article 8 guarantee of privacy. The Court held that UK domestic law did not regulate the circumstances in which telephone tapping could be carried out sufficiently clearly or provide any remedy against abuse of the power. This meant that it did not meet the requirement of being 'in accordance with the law' under Article 8(2). The decision therefore required the UK government to introduce legislation to regulate the circumstances in which the power to tap could be used. Since the driving force behind the response of the UK government in the Interception of Communications Act 1985 was the need to provide a statutory basis for interception, it can be termed a largely procedural rather than substantive reform. It was also incomplete. Despite its misleading name the 1985 Act only covered certain limited means of intercepting communications. It did not cover listening devices or all forms of telephone tapping. It covered the interception of only one means of telephonic communication – communication via the public telecommunications system; this covered telephone, fax, telex and any other data transmission on the system, such as email.[39] Given the immense increase in the use of mobile phones,[40] pagers, cordless phones, the potential for email transmission outside the telecommunications system, and the growth of internal telephone systems over recent years, the Act became increasingly marginalised. Marginalisation was likely to increase in the near future since emails are likely to be sent more frequently via mobile phones, using satellites.[41]

In introducing the new, far more comprehensive scheme, therefore, the Labour government sought to bring all forms of interception within it. The Regulation of Investigatory Powers Act 2000, which has repealed the key sections of the 1985 Act,[42] defines the term a 'public telecommunications system', used in s2(1) of the 1985 Act, much more widely to include all such systems which provide or offer a telecommunications service to the public or part of it involving the use of electrical or electro-

[38] (1985) 7 EHRR 14; for comment see (1986) 49 MLR 86.

[39] Prior to the inception of the RIPA the government maintained that some use of email was covered by the 1985 Act where public telephone lines were used.

[40] Mobile to mobile communication would appear to fall outside the Act. Mobile communication which partially uses the telecommunications system (when a system such as Cellnet or Vodaphone sends a signal to the telecommunications system) may be within it.

[41] Possibly without use of a 'server' computer.

[42] Ss1–10, ss11(2)–(5), Schedule 1.

magnetic energy.[43] This definition would cover all the forms of communication, including email, mentioned above, provided by any private company.[44] S2(1) RIPA also covers private telecommunications systems – most obviously those confined to a particular company or body – although its coverage of private systems is limited to those which are attached to the public system directly or indirectly.[45] Its wording appears to be wide enough to cover most forms of telecommunication currently available, apart from entirely self-standing private systems,[46] although not necessarily those which may arise in the near future. Ironically, the point was made in Parliamentary debate that 'the Bill does not recognise the changing technologies'.[47]

In placing interception of the public system on a statutory basis the 1985 Act may have met the 'in accordance with the law' requirement of Article 8(2) in respect of such interceptions, but in so doing it did not fully strike the balance between individual privacy and state interests which was apparent in *Klass* v *FRG*[48] (below) and which, absent the influence of the margin of appreciation doctrine, the Convention may require.[49] The 1985 Act provided very wide grounds under s2(2) on which warrants for the purposes of interception could be authorised by the Secretary of State, and the same grounds appear in the RIPA, with one addition. Under s5(3) a warrant may be issued if necessary '(a) in the interests of national security'; '(b) for the purpose of preventing or detecting serious crime';[50] or '(c) for the purpose of safeguarding the economic well-being of the UK'. In relation to the third ground the information must relate, under s5(5), to 'the acts or intentions of persons outside the British Isles'. This wording almost exactly reproduces that used under s2(4) of the 1985 Act. These grounds are significantly wider than those under the old Home Office guidelines previously relied upon in order to authorise warrants. The last ground falls under sub-para (d): 'in circumstances appearing to the Secretary of State to be equivalent to those in which he would issue a warrant by virtue of paragraph (b), for the purpose of giving effect to the provisions of any international mutual assistance agreement'. This ground relates to Article 16 of the EU Draft Convention on Mutual Assistance in

[43] Under s2(1) 'telecommunications system' covers any system 'which exists (whether wholly or partly in the UK or elsewhere) for the purpose of facilitating the transmission of communications by any means involving the use of electrical or electro-magnetic energy'.

[44] These would include, for example, BT, Orange, Vodaphone. It would also cover other providers of email systems such as Freeserve or Yahoo. However, it is in fact unclear that the technology to intercept emails sent via the Internet is available. Such emails are sent by so-called 'split package' technology: the message is split into a number of different packages, sent by different global routes. If a hundred million messages are sent a day, split into tiny particles, interception of particular messages may be almost impossible.

[45] Its coverage of private systems is a direct response to *Halford* v *UK* [1997] IRLR 471.

[46] Such as intranet systems not connected to any public system.

[47] HC Deb 6 March 2000 col 806.

[48] (1979) 2 EHRR 214.

[49] See *Christie* v *UK* 78-A DR E Com HR 119 (discussed below, p365).

[50] Defined in s81(3).

Criminal Matters.[51] Its purpose is to require satellite operators based in the UK to provide technical assistance to another member state. The discussion below reveals that the safeguards relating to warrants issued on this ground are significantly weaker than those relating to the other three. This is an instance in which the EU's 'Third Pillar' policies relating to law and order and national security have allowed decisions to be taken on matters which may infringe human rights, possibly to the extent of breaching the Convention. Such decisions are taken within 'a framework where the EU's democratic deficit is most prominent'.[52]

S5(2) RIPA, however, contains a stronger proportionality requirement than that contained in s2(3) of the 1985 Act. The Secretary of State 'shall not' issue an interception warrant unless he or she believes that the conduct it authorises 'is proportionate to what is sought to be achieved'. This includes asking, under s5(4), whether the information which it is thought necessary to obtain under the warrant could reasonably be obtained by other means. This question also had to be asked under s2(3). But s5(2) implies that further matters should be considered. For example, where the information *cannot* reasonably be obtained by other means, the proportionality of the particular interception warrant with its objective could still be considered. This might involve considering its contents and duration. Clearly, s5(2) was introduced in an effort to meet the proportionality requirement under Article 8(2), discussed below. Under s7(1) RIPA the warrants must be personally signed by the Secretary of State or, under s7(2), in urgent cases or cases under the fourth ground by 'a senior official' with express authorisation from the Secretary of State. A 'senior official' is defined in s81(1) as 'a member of the Senior Civil Service' and under s81(7) the Secretary of State 'may by order make . . . amendments [to] the definition of "senior official"'. Under the 1985 Act the official had to be 'an official of his Department of or above the rank of Assistant Under Secretary of State'. In this respect the requirements have been relaxed under the RIPA.

This new procedure is based on the model provided by the 1985 Act in that it allows for administrative oversight but maintains executive authorisation of interception; it may therefore be contrasted with that in the USA, where prior judicial authorisation is required,[53] and with that in Denmark where authorisation is by an investigating magistrate.[54] The

[51] The EU Draft Convention on *Mutual Assistance in Criminal Matters* (5202/98-C4-0062/98) was set out in the EU – FBI telecommunications plan adopted by the EU in January 1995. Under ENFOPOL the information required includes email addresses, credit card details, passwords, IP addresses, customer account numbers.

[52] R Norton-Taylor in *Constitutional Reform: The Labour Government's Constitutional Reform Agenda* R Blackburn and R Plant (eds) (1999) p208, Harlow, Essex: Longman. See also *Enhancing Parliamentary Scrutiny of the Third Pillar Select Committee of the European Communities* HL Session 1997–8, 31 July 1997.

[53] *Berger* v *NY* 388 US 41 (1967).

[54] Article 126m Code of Criminal Procedure.

Commissioner, appointed under s8 of the 1985 Act, and reappointed as the new Interception of Communications Commissioner under s57(8) of the RIPA, has a role in overseeing the issuance of warrants, but this is a general review role, which occurs after the event. The possibility of replacing an executive with a judicial mechanism was entirely rejected by the Labour government. In debate on the Bill it received support only from the Liberal Democrats.[55] Judicial involvement only at the complaint stage (see below) is of little significance as a safeguard since many persons will have no means of knowing that tapping is occurring. Nevertheless, prior judicial involvement in authorising warrants cannot be said at present to be a requirement of Article 8.[56]

Under ss4(5) and (6) of the 1985 Act the warrants were issued for an initial period of two months and could be renewed for one month in the case of the police and for six months in the case of the security and intelligence services. Under s9(6) of the RIPA warrants are issued for an initial period of three months if by the Secretary of State and can be renewed for six months if he or she states his or her belief that the grounds under s5(3)(a) or (c) apply. If the other grounds apply the renewal period is three months. If signed by a senior official they can be issued initially for five working days but renewed for three months. In the case of all warrants, particularly those issued in respect of the prevention or detection of serious crime to the police, these are significant increases. The period in respect of the serious crime ground may be compared with that in Denmark, which is four weeks, renewable.[57]

As was the case under the 1985 Act, there is no overall limit on renewals and it is likely to continue to be the case that some warrants will be very long-standing. The number of interception warrants issued is also likely to increase. The Commissioners' Reports only cover the warrants authorised by the Home Office and Scottish Office. These figures show that at the end of 1989 315 warrants were in force and 522 were issued during the year.[58] By 1993 a clear upward trend in the numbers of warrants issued was evident: in 1993 1,005 warrants for telephone tapping and 115 for mail interceptions were issued; 409 warrants were in force at the end of the year.[59] The trend continued: in 1996 1,795 telecommunications warrants were in force or were issued during the year; by 1998 the figure had risen to 2,251.[60] As the Commissioner accepts, these figures do not provide a satisfactory guide as to the number of persons subject to interception

[55] HC Debs 6 March 2000 col 807.

[56] *Klass* v *FRG* (1979) 2 EHRR 214; *Mersch* v *Luxembourg* (1985) 43 D&R 34.

[57] Article 126m Code of Criminal Procedure.

[58] *Report of the Commissioner for 1989* Cm 1063 p2. Similar figures are available for other years; see reports for 1986 (Cm 108) and for 1987 (Cm 351).

[59] See *Report of the Commissioner for 1993* Cm 2522.

[60] The figure for postal interceptions rose from 115 in 1996 to 167 in 1998. Figures from the *Report of the Commissioner under the Interception of Communications Act 1998*, published June 1999 Cm 4364, at p11.

since a single warrant can cover a large organisation. The figures do not cover all the warrants authorised since those authorised by other departments, including the Foreign Office, are viewed as too sensitive.

S8(1) of the new Act suggests that the warrants should be precise; they must specify a person or an address. However, a 'person' can equal 'any organisation and any association or combination of persons'.[61] Once a warrant is obtained all communications to or from the property or 'person' specified must be intercepted, if that is what is required in order to give effect to the warrant.[62] Failure to comply with the warrant is an offence under s11(7) carrying a maximum sentence of two years. Under s11(4) telephone tapping and mail interceptions are conducted by Post Office or 'public telecommunications employees' or by persons controlling or partly controlling private systems wholly or partly in the UK.[63] Under s6(2) the request for the warrant may be made by a number of persons from a non-exhaustive list. They include: the Director-General of the Security Service, the Chief of MI6, the Director of GCHQ, the Director-General of the National Criminal Intelligence Service, the Commissioner of Police of the Metropolis, the Chief Constable of the RUC, Chief Constables in Scotland,[64] the Commissioners of Customs and Excise, the chief of Defence Intelligence, the relevant person for the purposes of any international mutual assistance agreement. The Bill originally also provided: 'or any such other person as the Secretary of State may by order designate'. The government was eventually persuaded to omit the last provision. A number of other such powers are still, however, scattered throughout the Act, as Chapter 10 indicates, meaning that this statute, comprehensive as it is, leaves open a great deal of leeway for significant and more covert extension. On Second Reading of the Bill in the Commons this list was criticised on two grounds. The Conservative Opposition considered that the list was not extensive enough and that, in particular, the Benefits Agency of the DSS[65] and the Inland Revenue[66] should be added to it. The Liberal Democrats, supported by Tom King, Chair of the Intelligence and Security Committee, argued that primary legislation, not a statutory instrument, should be used in order to add bodies to the list.[67]

[61] S81(1) of the RIPA which, with the addition of an 'association', reproduces s10(1) of the 1985 Act.

[62] S11(4).

[63] Bearing in mind the range of companies which are affected and the difficulty of complying, especially in relation to the Internet, a provision regarding practicality was necessary. S11(5) recognises that there may be circumstances under which it is not reasonably practicable to comply with the duty to implement the warrant. The prosecution must prove that it was practicable.

[64] 'Of any police force maintained under or by virtue of section 1 of the Police (Scotland) Act 1967'.

[65] HC Debs 6 March 2000 cols 778 and 831.

[66] HC Debs 6 March 2000 col 821.

[67] HC Debs 6 March 2000 cols 768 and 831.

Ss3 and 4 allow for lawful interception without a warrant. S3(2) covers instances where it is reasonably believed that both parties to the communication have consented to the interception.[68] In such circumstances, the interception must also be authorised within Part II, s26. This provision effects a compromise in relation to so-called 'participant monitoring'. It was pointed out in the leading Canadian authority[69] that the consent of one party does not affect the infringement of privacy suffered by the other.[70] It would not appear to meet the demands of Article 8 to allow such an infringement. But s3(2) does not demand that 'participant monitoring' should be subject to the controls necessary for other interceptions; it is subject only to the lesser controls for 'directed' surveillance, discussed in Chapter 10. S4 covers persons whose communications are intercepted who are believed to be outside the UK, instances where the Secretary of State has made regulations covering the interception for business[71] purposes (s4(2)), and instances in psychiatric hospitals or prisons (within the relevant applicable statutes). These provisions, may raise questions as to their compatibility with the Convention, which are considered below.

S15 provides safeguards regarding the use of the intercepted material. They are intended to limit the persons who can see the material and to ensure that it is destroyed once it is no longer necessary to retain it for the authorised purposes. However, the Act does not state how these objectives are to be achieved; it is left to the Secretary of State to put arrangements into place to secure them. Further, s15 does not apply to material obtained without warrant, under ss3 or 4. Since, as indicated below, personal criminal intelligence information obtained from interceptions and then stored and processed electronically is not subject to the stronger controls under the data protection regime of the 1998 Data Protection Act, it is clear that the controls created under s15 are potentially crucial in protecting this aspect of privacy.

S1 of the 1985 Act dealt with unauthorised interceptions and made it a criminal offence to intercept a postal communication or telecommunication intentionally without authorisation. It did not cover taps outside the public telecommunications system. So, for example, no criminal or even civil wrong was committed by the Chief Constable of Merseyside when a tap on the internal police phone system was used against Alison Halford in order to seek to discredit her and undermine her sex discrimination claim against the police service.[72] The RIPA, which under s1 reproduces the old s1 offence with extensions, also covers interception of private systems, unless they are entirely free standing. However, it

[68] This provision is clearly more protective of privacy than its counterpart under s1(2) of the 1985 Act, which relied on the consent of one party only.
[69] *R* v *Duarte* [1990] 53 CCC (3d) 1.
[70] See also *Smith* v *UK* (1997) EHRLR 277.
[71] 'Business' includes government departments.
[72] See *Halford* v *UK* (1997) www.dhcour.coe.fr.

is subject to an exception under s1(6) which might have been applicable in the *Halford* case. S1(6) provides that conduct is excluded from criminal liability if the interceptor 'is a person with a right to control the operation or the use of the system; or he has the express or implied consent of the [person intercepted]'. S1(3) creates civil liability in relation to unauthorised interception of a private, not a public, system. Possibly in future, therefore, a person in a situation similar to that of Alison Halford might be able to bring a civil action only.

Acquisition and disclosure of communications data

Part I, Chapter II of the RIPA covers the acquisition and disclosure of 'communications data'. This means information regarding communications rather than the communication itself. Such data includes phone metering – the recording of details of the telephone numbers called from a particular phone. Such acquisition has been viewed at Strasbourg (see below) as creating some invasion of privacy but of a less serious nature than the interception of communications. It has therefore been subject to lesser controls, and this regime is continued under the RIPA.

Schedule 2 of the 1985 Act provided that it was an offence for an employee of a telecommunications facility to disclose phone metering details unless in connection with the prevention and detection of crime (not *serious* crime as required in s2(2)(b)), in conjunction with criminal proceedings, under a court order or in the interests of national security. A certificate issued by a Cabinet Minister served as conclusive proof that a request under the national security head was indeed for that purpose. In *Malone* v *UK*[73] the European Court of Human Rights considered that while all the controls necessary in respect of interception need not be in place in respect of metering, certain controls would be necessary in order to satisfy the requirements of Article 8. A statutory basis for disclosure of metering details was provided by inserting a new section 45 into the Telecommunications Act 1984. Disclosure was allowed on the broad grounds of connection with the prevention and detection of crime or in conjunction with criminal proceedings. Disclosure for these purposes was also allowed under the Data Protection Act 1984, and continued under the 1998 Act. Therefore the position as regards metering appeared to be vulnerable under the HRA since it was outside the regime under the 1985 Act. This is the issue addressed by Part I, Chapter II of the 2000 Act.

Under s22(2) the grounds on which such data can be obtained are much wider than those applying to the interception of communications. Those grounds are included, but the other grounds include 'for preventing or detecting crime or of preventing disorder, the interests of public safety; for the purpose of protecting public health; for the purpose of assessing or collecting any tax, duty . . . or other . . . charge payable to a

[73] (1985) 7 EHRR 14.

government department; for the purpose, in an emergency, of preventing death or injury or any damage to a person's physical or mental health, or of mitigating [such] injury or damage' or for any other 'purpose specified for the purposes of this subsection by an order made by the Secretary of State'. It is notable that the grounds go well beyond those provided by Schedule 2 of the 1985 Act. Proportionality must be considered, under s22(5). The authorisation to obtain the data is made by a 'designated person' under s22(1); under s25(2) such persons are 'the individuals holding such offices, ranks or positions with relevant public authorities as are prescribed for the purposes of this subsection by an order made by the Secretary of State'. This order does not need to be approved by Parliament. If a person is designated he or she can then serve a notice on the postal or telecommunications operator under s22(4) to obtain the data (if necessary) and in any event to disclose it. The duty is enforceable in civil proceedings. As indicated below, a person whose privacy has been invaded in the manner indicated will have recourse to the new Tribunal[74] although not to the Commissioner. It is readily apparent that this power has the thinnest of statutory underpinnings. It will be fleshed out by executive order but that course is clearly objectionable. As discussed below, the quality of the law in question is seriously in doubt.

The Commissioner and the Interception of Communications Tribunal

As indicated, the Commissioner had a duty under s8(1)(a) of the 1985 Act, which will continue under s57(2)(a) of the 2000 Act, to keep the warrant procedure under review. He is a senior judge appointed by the Prime Minister on a part-time basis to assist the Tribunal and generally monitor the warrant procedure. Apart from the statutory limitations of his powers, the practical constraints on them have been overwhelming. He had no staff and carried out the checking procedure personally on a part-time basis. Clearly, as he accepts, these constraints precluded consideration of every warrant which was brought to his attention. His powers were very limited. He could not order that warrants should be quashed or that the material obtained should be destroyed; under s8(9) he could merely report a contravention of ss2–5 to the Prime Minister, which had not already been the subject of a Tribunal Report, or a contravention of s6 which covered destruction of material, and he had to prepare an annual Report for the Prime Minister under s8(6). These arrangements were largely continued under the RIPA under ss57[75] and 58 when he became the Interception of Communications Commissioner, although staff may be appointed.

[74] P354, and see Chapter 10 pp401–404.

[75] Under s57(2) 'Subject to subsection (5), the Interception of Communications Commissioner shall keep under review the exercise and performance by the Secretary of State of the powers and duties conferred or imposed on him by or under sections 1 to 11'.

The remit of the Commissioner gave him the opportunity to note that unauthorised tapping had occurred, but only when he was informed of it by the agencies concerned. Where he was so informed, he was told at the same time that the unauthorised action had been recognised, usually 'immediately', and all resultant material destroyed. His view was that these unauthorised actions, namely criminal offences under s1, termed 'errors', were: 'comparatively few in number when considered in the context of the volume and complexity of the operations carried out'.[76] In his annual reports the Commissioner found no instance in which a warrant was issued unjustifiably. Although Crown servants, telecommunications and postal workers were under a duty to provide the Commissioner with the information he required to carry out his task, under s8(3) of the 1985 Act (continued and extended to a wider range of people under the RIPA),[77] he had no effective means of checking that information had not been withheld. He received a list of warrants issued, renewed, modified or cancelled since the last visit, and checked a sample of them. He had no means of knowing whether the list was in fact complete, and unauthorised interception was not, unsurprisingly, recorded on it. If the Commissioner acquires staff to aid him in these tasks, when he carries them out under the RIPA, a greater proportion of warrants may be checked. But these basic limitations affecting his role remain unchanged under the RIPA arrangements. The key reform under the RIPA is to the Tribunal system.

S7 of the 1985 Act established a Tribunal to consider complaints from people who believed that their telephone had been tapped or their mail intercepted. It should be noted that the statutory provisions had no retrospective effect. Thus complaints could relate only to post-commencement activities. The RIPA sets up a new Tribunal, under s65, which, as Chapter 8 indicated, will replace the current one and those set up under the Security Services Act and the Intelligence Services Act. It will also take over the role of Commissioners in hearing complaints under s102 and Schedule 7 of the Police Act 1997, while it will have a new role in considering surveillance undertaken by other public authorities. It will be able to consider some pre-commencement activity, as Chapter 10 explains. Thus, its role extends well beyond that of the old Interceptions of Communications Tribunal. It will therefore have immense significance as the central mechanism protecting citizens against abuse of state surveillance powers. The new Tribunal is discussed fully in Chapter 10.[78]

The old Tribunal set up under the 1985 Act (which consisted of five senior lawyers) had a duty under s7(3) of that Act, on receiving a complaint, to investigate whether a warrant had been issued and, if so, whether

[76] *Report of the Commissioner under the Interception of Communications Act 1998*, published June 1999 Cm 4364, at p10.

[77] S58(1) extends the duty to include police officers, those served with a notice under s22(4) and s49 (see note 30, above) and persons employed by them.

[78] Pp401–413.

it was properly issued – whether there were adequate grounds for issuing it and whether statutory procedures were complied with. Under s7(4) the Tribunal applied 'the principles applicable by a court on an application for judicial review' to this exercise. The Tribunal could only consider the matters referred to in ss2–5 of the 1985 Act concerning the issuance of warrants; it could not consider the questions whether the action was proportionate to the invasion of privacy and whether the action could have been carried out by other means.

The Reports of the Commissioner on the working of the old Tribunal were sometimes exceptionally brief. For example, the Report of the Commissioner presented to Parliament in June 1999[79] covers complaints in one short paragraph. The Report for 1997 covers them in just over one page.[80] The 1998 Report states that the Tribunal received 75 complaints in 1998 of which 72 were investigated and none were upheld. The 1997 Report states that since it was established in 1986 the Tribunal has received 568 complaints and that none have ever been upheld. According to the Report, in only eight of these cases was interception being carried out by a government agency and in each case it was properly authorised. The possibility that in some of the other 560 cases, or in others, unauthorised interception was occurring is seen in the Report as 'very remote' since it would involve a criminal conspiracy between the agency and the Public Telecommunications Operators. It may be noted that the Act did not provide any possibility of recognising that an invasion of privacy could occur owing to the *possibility* that a phone had been tapped. The Court accepted in *Klass* v *Federal Republic of Germany*[81] that this possibility represented a continuing invasion of privacy, since conversations would be inhibited. The Report did not afford recognition to the harm caused by fear of phone tapping in respect of the 560 complainants who were not, apparently, subject to interceptions. Such fear could be addressed by giving further consideration to the possibility of disclosing the fact that an operation had not occurred.[82]

Aspects of the inadequacy of this monitoring system were illustrated in 1990 when Robin Cook raised in the Commons the issue of a tap which had been placed on the phone of one of his constituents.[83] His complaint, in essence, concerned the lack of information available to individuals who suspect that their phones have been tapped. His constituent, a telephone engineer, discovered that his phone had been tapped. As Robin Cook pointed out, it was inconceivable within the terms of the Act that a warrant authorising the tap could properly have been issued. However, it was impossible to discover whether the phone had been tapped without

[79] Cm 4364 at p6 para 30.
[80] Cm 4001 at pp4–6.
[81] (1979) 2 EHRR 214.
[82] See further p364, below.
[83] 24 May 1990, HC Deb Vol 173 cols 443–450.

authorisation. As Robin Cook put it: 'the problem . . . is that the police cannot investigate tapping if it was authorised and the tribunal cannot investigate it if it was not'.[84] He was informed by the Secretary of State that the police 'cannot . . . investigate . . . any interception which may have been authorised'. Had the Tribunal been confronted with an unauthorised tap it would simply have found that no contravention of s5(2) of the Act had occurred. Robin Cook received only a general reply to his concerns, describing merely the function of the Tribunal, from Lord James Douglas-Hamilton who spoke on behalf of the government. This incident suggests that state agents at times bypass the warrant procedure and request unauthorised taps, but there is no means of ascertaining whether this is the case or what its incidence might be. Unsurprisingly, no prosecution of an agent in such circumstances has occurred.

Parliamentary oversight

Under the 1985 Act Parliamentary oversight, such as it was, was limited to interceptions which fell within the statute; it did not include *inter alia* metering. Under the new statute, the oversight is equally limited, but it will cover a far wider range of interceptions. It may cover the acquisition of communications data. If such acquisition is the subject of a favourable determination of the new Tribunal, a report will go to the Prime Minister under s68(5) RIPA *if* the Secretary of State bears some responsibility in the matter. In any event, the Report will not be published to Parliament.

Modelled on the old arrangements, the annual Report of the new Commissioner must be presented to Parliament and published as a Command Paper, under s58(6). The Prime Minister may censor the report under s58(7) if it appears to him that it contains matter 'prejudicial to national security, to the prevention and detection of serious crime or to the economic well-being of the UK'. These grounds are the same as the previous ones under the 1985 Act. A new, broad, one has been added: the matter may be excluded if it appears to be prejudicial to 'the continued discharge of the functions of any public authority whose activities include activities that are subject to review by that Commissioner'. It may be unnecessary, in any event, for the Prime Minister to censor the Report; the practice has been for the Commissioner to designate the part to be withheld.

Thus, Parliamentary oversight will continue to be highly circumscribed since no Committee is directly charged with monitoring state surveillance. Bearing in mind the brevity of the Commissioner's Reports, the opportunity for Parliament to oversee these arrangements is very limited. The example above of Robin Cook's questions in Parliament is illustrative of the impotence of Parliament at present as an oversight mechanism in this context. The Parliamentary oversight is clearly much weaker than

[84] 24 May 1990, HC Deb Vol 173 col 449.

that applicable in Germany, as considered in the *Klass* case (below). The opportunity of enabling the new, comprehensive interceptions statute to reflect notions of openness and accountability to Parliament in the era of the HRA and FoI has been lost.

Convention rights under the HRA

(i) Effects of the HRA

As a 'public authority' under s6 HRA, the new Tribunal has a duty to comply with the Convention in its adjudications. The Interception of Communications Commissioner also has such a duty in discharging his oversight role. The Commissioner should ensure that the agencies he oversees are themselves ensuring Convention compliance. The members of the agencies and telecommunications and postal workers are bound by s6 not to infringe the Convention in carrying out their work. In other words, all the public authorities involved should comply with the requirements of the Convention. But the Tribunal may provide a central means of seeking to ensure that they are in fact doing so. Whether it proves effective in that role will depend on a number of factors, including its own interpretation of those requirements, discussed in Chapter 10.[85]

Parliament is not bound by s6, but in considering the reports of the Commissioner or in debating any issues arising from the operation of the RIPA, it would be expected that the Convention requirements would be strictly borne in mind, especially as a statement of compatibility accompanied the Act. In particular, as the discussion above indicated, at a number of points in the statute matters were left to be resolved by Order of the Home Secretary. They included, as Chapter 10 indicates, such crucial issues as the rules governing the Tribunal procedure, under s69. Parliament will have an opportunity to scrutinise Orders made, for their compliance with the Convention. In the debates on the Bill of 2000 the term the 'margin of appreciation' was never mentioned. The statement of compatibility was not, therefore, challenged on the basis that the provisions of the Bill were arguably compatible with the Convention only because its guarantees had suffered dilution due to the operation of that doctrine, a doctrine inapplicable in domestic law. This is a matter which should be raised in future consideration of any such Orders or in relation to any other relevant matters.

Since courts are bound by s6 HRA and are under the s3 obligation, Article 6 issues could be raised in prosecutions against agency members, police officers, telecommunications or postal workers or other public authorities in respect of the various offences arising from non-cooperation with state interception created under the 2000 Act. Courts may therefore

[85] Pp408–413.

have the opportunity of considering the doubtful compatibility of certain of the 'reverse onus' clauses, particularly that under s53, introduced by the Act, with Article 6(1) and (2). The general compatibility of such clauses is discussed in Chapter 3.[86] Theoretically, prosecution for unauthorised interception under s1 might occur which would also, of course, have to accord with Article 6.

Consideration of the compatibility of intercepts with Articles 8 or 6 in court proceedings appears to be almost entirely precluded by s17 of the RIPA. This rule is clearly arbitrary since evidence deriving from the use of bugging and other surveillance devices can be adduced, as discussed below. Now that interception and other forms of surveillance are covered in one statute the arbitrariness is more readily apparent. S17 is based on s9 of the 1985 Act which provided: 'In any proceedings before any court or tribunal no evidence shall be adduced and no question asked in cross-examination which . . . tends to suggest that an offence under s1 has been or is to be committed by [postal or telecommunications workers or Crown Servants] or that a warrant has been or is to be issued to any of those persons'. S17 provides: 'subject to s18, no evidence shall be adduced, question asked, assertion or disclosure made or other thing done in, for the purposes of or in connection with any legal proceedings which (in any manner) – (a) discloses, in circumstances from which its origin in anything falling within subsection (2) may be inferred, any of the contents of an intercepted communication or any related communications data; or (b) tends (apart from any such disclosure) to suggest that anything falling within subsection (2) has or may have occurred or be going to occur'. S17(2) covers '(a) conduct . . . that was or would be an offence under s1(1) or (2) of this Act or under s1 of the . . . 1985 Act; (b) a breach by the Secretary of State of his duty under section 1(4) of this Act; (c) the issue of an interception warrant or of a warrant under the . . . 1985 Act; (d) the making of an application by any person for an interception warrant, or for a warrant under that Act; (e) the imposition of any requirement on any person to provide assistance with giving effect to an interception warrant'. This is clearly a far more comprehensive clause than s9, although it is subject to certain exceptions under s18, which may allow Convention points to be raised, in accordance with the courts' duty under s6 HRA.

S18(1) provides that s17(1) does not apply in proceedings before the Tribunal or for offences under the RIPA, s1 of the 1985 Act, s4(3)(a) of the Official Secrets Act 1989 and a number of other provisions relating to the secrecy of interceptions. Ss18(4), (6), (7) and (9) provide a number of very significant new exceptions. S18(4) applies *inter alia*[87] where the

[86] See discussion of *ex parte Kebilene* [1999] 3 WLR 972 in Chapter 3 pp102–104, on this issue.

[87] S18(4) also provides that s17(1)(a) does not apply if the interception was lawful by virtue of s1(5)(c) (relating to stored material obtained under another statutory power), or s4(1) (persons believed to be outside UK).

interception was by consent under s3; s18(6) provides that s17(1)(b) does not prevent doing anything which discloses conduct for which a person has been convicted under ss1(1), 11(7), 19 or s1 of the 1985 Act. Under s18(7), s17(1) does not prohibit disclosure of '(a) any information that continues to be available for disclosure' to the prosecution 'for the purpose only of enabling that person to determine what is required of him by his duty to secure [its] fairness' or (b) disclosure to a relevant judge[88] by order of the judge 'to be made to him alone'. Under s18(8) a judge shall not order such a disclosure unless satisfied that 'the exceptional circumstances of the case make the disclosure essential in the interests of justice'. If disclosure is ordered s18(9) allows the judge, in 'exceptional circumstances', to 'direct the prosecution to make any admission of fact . . . that the judge thinks is essential in the interests of justice'. But any such direction must not, under s18(10), contravene s17(1). These provisions are badly drafted, but they suggest that where intercept evidence is still available its disclosure to the judge or to the prosecution may be ordered. It may be noted that the intercept evidence may still be in existence at the time of the trial since it is preserved, for the benefit of the prosecution, under s15(4)(d). Communications data may be adduced in evidence since it is not an intercepted communication as defined in s17(4), so long as it does not suggest that the offences in question have been committed.[89]

S9 of the 1985 Act meant that if an intercept had been used to obtain material, whether unauthorised or not, the information gained would be inadmissible in evidence. But s9 only applied to the forms of interception which the Act covered. S9 was considered in two House of Lords' decisions, which led to a bizarre and anomalous situation. In *Effick*[90] the defendants were prosecuted for conspiracy to supply controlled drugs and police officers obtained part of the evidence against them by means of intercepting and taping their telephone calls. The offence under s1 had not been committed since the calls taped were made on a cordless telephone which was not found to be part of 'a public telecommunications system' as required under s1. The appellants were convicted and appealed on the ground that the intercepted telephone calls should have been ruled inadmissible under s9 of the Interception of Communications Act 1985, or under s78 of the Police and Criminal Evidence Act 1984 (PACE) since they were made without a warrant for interception. The House of

88 *Inter alia* a judge of the High Court or Crown Court. This provision will amend the Criminal Procedure and Investigations Act 1996 s3(4).

89 This position continues that established under the 1985 Act in *Morgans* v *DPP* [1999] 1 WLR 968 in which it was found that s9 of that Act does not preclude a court from receiving evidence of printouts obtained by a logging device.

90 [1994] 3 WLR 583; (1994) 99 Cr App R 312, HL; (1992) 95 Cr App R 427, CA. For criticism of the Court of Appeal decision see Leigh (1992) 142 NLJ 944–945, 976–977; Smith [1992] Crim LR 580. See generally Spencer [1999] CLJ 43.

Lords determined that argument under s9 failed because its provisions were aimed at preventing disclosure of information which tended to suggest that the offence of unauthorised interception (under s1(1) of the 1985 Act) had been committed by specified persons, or that a warrant had been or was to be issued to such persons. These matters were not in issue since the interception was not within the Act. S9 was not intended to render inadmissible evidence obtained which would not reveal such matters. Clear statutory language would have been needed to oust the principle that all logically probative evidence should be admitted. As this was not the case, and as the instance in question did not appear to fall within s9, the evidence was admissible. The submission in respect of s78 of PACE failed because it was not suggested that the police officers had deliberately contravened the 1985 Act. It was found that no unfairness to the defendants had occurred owing to the admission of the evidence, but this begs the question whether the manner in which the evidence was obtained – on no legal basis and by means of a surreptitious act – could lead to unfairness at the trial.

In *Preston*,[91] in contrast, a lawful intercept had occurred and the *defence* wanted disclosure of the evidence derived from it which, it was alleged, might have led to the acquittal of the defendants. In a decision which accepted somewhat reluctantly that the 1985 Act created a scheme designed to elevate the interests of secrecy above individual rights to privacy or to a fair trial, the House of Lords found that s2(2) of the 1985 Act relates to preventing or detecting serious crime, not to prosecuting. It therefore could not relate to defending a criminal charge. Thus the defence had no right to obtain disclosure of the material deriving from the intercepts. Further, since on the proper interpretation of s2(2) read in conjunction with s6(3) destruction of material gained by the intercepts had to be undertaken once the criminal investigation (not the prosecution) was complete, such material would not be available. Any other finding as to the meaning of s2(2) would, Lord Mustill said, mean that s6(3) could not be satisfied. These findings appeared to leave little role for s9. Lord Mustill found that s9 could therefore relate only to the manner of authorising the intercept or to the source of information behind the decision to use an intercept.

The result of this decision was that although telephone tapping could be used as an investigative tool in the criminal process, evidence deriving directly from an intercept would not be admissible and the defence would not be allowed to ask any questions designed to discover whether an intercept was used. Thus, the prosecution might at times be disadvantaged since some probative evidence would not be admissible,[92] but the other

[91] [1993] 4 All ER 638; (1994) 98 Cr App R 405, HL. For discussion see Tomkin (1994) 57 MLR 941.

[92] This factor influenced the Commission in declaring the application from Preston inadmissible: *Preston* v *UK* 2 July 1997 App No 24193/94; available from the Commission's web-site.

side of the coin was that material deriving from the intercept could not be disclosed to the defence even if (as the defence alleged in *Preston*) it might show the innocence of the defendants. One exception, favourable to the prosecution, to the rule deriving from s9, as interpreted in *Preston*, was allowed in *Rasool and Choudhary*.[93] It was determined that where intercepts record consensual evidence it will be admissible. The rule in s9(1)(a) was not found to be sufficient to make consensual material inadmissible; it was found to be irrelevant to the question of admissibility that an offence had been committed in obtaining the evidence. Choudhary's appeal was dismissed while Rasool's was allowed on that ground. Similarly in *R* v *Owen*,[94] the evidence deriving from an intercept was found to be admissible, on the basis that it did not suggest that the offence under s1 had been committed. The defendant, in prison on remand, had admitted the offence with which he was charged in a phone call to his wife. He was deemed to have consented to the interception since notices warning of the likelihood of interception had been posted near telephones in the prison. The defendant claimed that he had not seen any such notice. But it was found that, on the basis that one of the parties had impliedly consented, the admission of the evidence would not suggest that the offence under s1 of the Act had been committed.[95]

The anomalous result of *Effick* and *Preston* was that in one unlawfully obtained evidence, favourable to the prosecution, could be used as part of the prosecution evidence, while in another lawfully obtained evidence could not be used at the behest of the defence. These decisions appear to have influenced the RIPA. Most obviously, the new statute covers most forms of interception so that the argument used in *Effick* regarding cordless phones could not be raised. S18(4), which refers *inter alia* to interceptions without a warrant where one party has consented to the interception (s3), covers the findings from *Rasool* and *Owen*. Significantly, in certain imprecisely defined circumstances, disclosure relating to intercept evidence can be made to the prosecution and, if ordered, to the judge. But the defence may remain unaware of the source of the evidence. The fact that the use of the intercept led to the uncovering of other evidence, which is adduced, might be relevant to any challenge the defence could mount to the evidence. This position may not accord with the equality of arms principle under Article 6 of the Convention since prosecution and defence may not be equally affected by the unavailability of the evidence.[96]

[93] [1997] 4 All ER 439; *The Times* 17 February. Choudhary applied, unsuccessfully, to Strasbourg: see note 123, below. For a further exception, see *Aujla* [1998] 2 Cr App R 16.

[94] [1999] 1 WLR 949.

[95] Since under s1(2) of the Act, interception without warrant but with consent is not an offence.

[96] This could be argued by analogy with the decisions in *Windisch* v *Austria* (1990) 13 EHRR 281 and *Kostovski* v *Netherlands* (1998) 12 EHRR 434.

In circumstances similar to those in *Preston* in which the defence seeks disclosure of the evidence, whether or not it has been disclosed to the prosecution, the defence could make representations to the judge under s18(7)(b), arguing that the term 'exceptional circumstances' must be rendered compatible with Article 6 under s3 HRA, taking into account the requirements of fairness in the particular instance.[97] If the evidence is crucial to the defence, but the judge refuses to make an order, an appeal could be mounted on the basis that the judge had not complied with Article 6. Perhaps the most difficult situation would arise where, as in *Malone*, the defence suspected that an unauthorised intercept had been used. The defence might wish to mount an argument that evidence causally related to such use, rather than directly deriving from it, should be excluded since it would not have been obtained but for the illegality. Such exclusion could be argued for under s78 PACE, interpreted compatibility with Article 6.[98] But ss18(10) and 17(1) appear to stand in the way of obtaining an admission that an unauthorised intercept had been used. Possibly where an activist view of the exclusion of evidence requirement under Article 6 was taken, the only recourse would be to obtain a declaration of incompatibility between those provisions and Article 6(1) under s4 HRA on the basis of unfairness under Article 6(1). However, if it was assumed that no appeal could succeed since those provisions would have to be applied, the defendants might view seeking such a declaration as worthless since it could not provide them individually with any redress. It appears therefore that although ss17 and 18 show signs of seeking to escape from certain of the effects of s9 of the 1985 Act, they nevertheless provide a scheme whose central aim is to preserve the secrecy surrounding interceptions, whether or not the interests of justice are thereby compromised.

Ss17 and 18 are most likely to be relevant in criminal proceedings, but other proceedings are also affected. As discussed below, the route to judicial review of the decisions of the new Tribunal may be barred by the ouster clause contained in s67(8) of the 2000 Act[99] and based on s7(8) of the 1985 Act. S65(2), which provides that the jurisdiction of the new Tribunal is to be 'the only appropriate tribunal' for the purposes of s7(1)(a) of the HRA, also stands in the way of review. S65 is discussed further below[100] and it is suggested that judicial review of executive decisions in the ordinary courts is possible in respect of some surveillance. But in respect of the interception of communications, s17 would also have to be circumvented. Since s18(9) applies to criminal proceedings only,

[97] See Chapter 10 pp393–4. The findings in *Rowe and Davis* v *UK* No 28901/95 20, (2000) 30 EHRR 1, although in a different context, which concerned unfairness arising from the non-disclosure of evidence, would be applicable.

[98] See further Chapter 5 pp200–202.

[99] Replacing s7(8) of the 1985 Act and replacing s91(10) of the 1997 Act in so far as complaints are concerned, and creating a new ouster clause in relation to complaints regarding surveillance by a range of other public authorities.

[100] Chapter 10 pp387–389.

the way to judicial review in the ordinary courts appears to remain barred. The only, faint, possibility seems to be that eventually a declaration of incompatibility under s4 HRA between s17 and Article 6 might be made on appeal from proceedings for permission to seek review.

The possibility of a tort action, including that of a new cause of action based on breach of Article 8, is also probably ruled out on the same grounds. Where the existing law fails to cover interceptions which infringe Article 8 new tortious liability could have been created. Under the 1985 Act the possibility was open of bringing an action once the HRA was fully in force in respect of forms of phone tapping outside the 1985 Act and perhaps in respect of the interception of radio pagers or the use of metering. This position was unsatisfactory and anomalous. But it did leave open the possibility, now probably closed down under Part I RIPA, of raising such matters in the ordinary courts. At present, apart from prosecutions for the offences created by the RIPA, or enforcement of interception in the civil courts, the new Tribunal would probably provide the only judicial forum in which the Convention points discussed below could be raised.

Thus Court action as a method of seeking to ensure that the HRA is fully complied with in this context is highly circumscribed and uncertain. No clear and effective method is currently available, unless the new Tribunal proves to be more effective than its predecessor. Parliamentary oversight is also limited. If the Act is to have any impact it may be most likely to occur through incremental internal change in procedures, rather than through the courts or the complaints mechanisms. It is notable that the inception of court proceedings in relation to interception under Part I RIPA is at present a privilege intended to be accorded only to the state. The role of the judiciary in the ordinary courts in protecting individual citizens, at their instigation, from abuse of state power in conducting interceptions has been almost entirely removed. Instead, the intention is that the courts should be used only to seek to further state ends – as a means of enforcing the use of intercepts. Thus civil or criminal proceedings can be used under ss11(7) and (8) in order to compel private companies to intercept the communications of their customers. At the same time a citizen whose communications appear to have been unlawfully intercepted has no means of challenging the interception in civil proceedings. It is a criminal offence under s19, another classic 'reverse onus' clause, for a telecommunications worker, for example, to inform a member of the public that his or her phone has been tapped under an unlawfully issued warrant. But a member of the public can probably be convicted of a criminal offence, although evidence deriving from an intercept might have led to his or her acquittal.[101] The unsatisfactoriness of this regime leads to the conclusion that modification of Part I RIPA may eventually occur owing to Strasbourg findings.

[101] The evidence would be inadmissible under s17. See also *Preston* note 91, above.

(ii) Convention requirements

As Chapter 8 explains, state interception and surveillance are likely to represent an interference with the Article 8(1) rights to respect for private life, the home and correspondence. The Court found in *Klass*[102] that the possibility that an interception was occurring could infringe Article 8, and this was also accepted in *Malone* v *UK*.[103] In *Klass* the Court said: 'in the mere existence of the legislation itself there is involved, for all those to whom the legislation could be applied, a menace of surveillance; this menace necessarily strikes at freedom of communication between users of the postal and telecommunications services'.[104] Thus the provisions of the 1985 Act, along with other administrative guidelines, such as those governing pager intercepts, can be viewed as representing a continuing invasion of privacy, whether or not in any individual case an intercept had actually been used. The same can be said of Part I RIPA now that it has come into force. As the Court explained in *Halford* v *UK*,[105] under the Convention the issue would be whether, on the particular facts, the essence of the complaint concerned the actual application to her of the measures of surveillance or that her Article 8 rights were menaced by the very existence of the law and practice permitting such measures. *Halford* v *UK* concerned the tapping of the applicant's office telephone by the police at a time when she was bringing a claim of sex discrimination against the police authority in question. The government argued that in using the private internal office system the applicant could not expect to retain her privacy and that an employer should in principle be able to monitor calls made by an employee on the internal system without prior warning or consent.[106] The Court disagreed, finding that calls made from business premises as well as the home may be covered by the notions of 'private life' and 'correspondence' within the meaning of Article 8(1). This stance was also taken in *Kopp* v *Switzerland*.[107] The Court emphasised in that case that the interception of the telephone calls constituted the interference with the right under para 1; the fact that the recordings were not subsequently used was irrelevant. Thus the Court has taken quite a broad approach, strongly protective of informational autonomy, to the meaning of the terms used in Article 8(1), thereby widening their application beyond obviously private spheres, including the home. The use made of material obtained from intercepts, including disclosure to others, may also fall within Article 8(1)[108] as may the obtaining of communications data.[109]

[102] (1979) 2 EHRR 214.
[103] (1984) 7 EHRR 14.
[104] P21 para 41.
[105] App No 20605/92, judgment of the Court: [1997] IRLR 471; (1997) *The Times* 3 July.
[106] Para 43.
[107] 13/1997/797/1000; (1999) 27 EHRR 91 at paras 70–71.
[108] *MS* v *Sweden* (1999) 28 EHRR 313.
[109] *Malone* v *UK* (1985) 7 EHRR 14.

State interference with the Article 8 guarantees must be in accordance with the law, under para 2, if it is to be justified. As discussed in Chapter 2, this requirement covers not only the existence of national law, but its quality. In *Halford* v *UK*[110] the interception of the internal office telephone was clearly not in accordance with the law since domestic law provided no regulation at all of such interception, and therefore the court found a breach of Article 8. Once a basis for a national law is found, it must be asked whether it is 'compatible with the rule of law . . . there must be a measure of legal protection in domestic law against arbitrary interferences by public authorities with [the right to respect for private life under Article 8(1)]. Especially where a power of the executive is exercised in secret, the risks of arbitrariness are evident.'[111] In *Kopp* v *Switzerland*[112] the Court clearly stated that the essential requirements of a national legal basis are those of accessibility and foreseeability so that, in this context, the citizen is sufficiently aware of the circumstances allowing interception. It must be clear as to the 'circumstances in and conditions on which public authorities are empowered to resort to any such secret measures'.[113] In *Christie* v *UK*[114] the 1985 Act was found to meet this requirement in relation to the terms 'national security' and 'economic well being'. The Commission viewed those terms as sufficiently precise since they had been explained by 'administrative or executive statements'. It is notable, however, that this was a decision of the Commission only, that it was influenced by the margin of appreciation doctrine and that it was not made in the context of the 'serious crime' provision under the Act. In *Kruslin* v *France*[115] a basis in law was found but it was not found to be of sufficient quality owing to its imprecision which was found to fail to satisfy the requirement of foreseeability.[116] Similarly, in *Kopp* v *Switzerland*, which was also concerned with crime, not national security, the Court said: 'interception . . . constitutes a particularly serious interference with private life and correspondence and must accordingly be based on a "law" that is particularly precise'.[117] In another case outside the realm of national security or economic well-being, *Valenzuela* v *Spain*,[118] the Court also found that the legal basis available for interception did not satisfy the requirements of foreseeability. In particular the conditions necessary under the Convention to satisfy that requirement, including the nature of the offences which might give rise to an intercept order, were not

[110] App No 20605/92, judgment of the Court: [1997] IRLR 471; (1997) *The Times* 3 July.
[111] *Malone* v *UK* A Vol 82 para 67; 4 EHRR 330. The Court reaffirmed this in *Halford* v *UK*: 'this expression . . . relates to the quality [of domestic law], requiring it to be compatible with the rule of law' (para 49).
[112] 13/1997/797/1000; (1999) 27 EHRR 91 at paras 70–71.
[113] *Halford* v *UK* para 49.
[114] 78-A DR E Com HR 119.
[115] (1990) 12 EHRR 528.
[116] Ibid para 30. See also *Huvig* v *France* (1990) 12 EHRR 528 para 29.
[117] Ibid para 44.
[118] (58/1997/842/1048) (1999) 28 EHRR 483.

included in the relevant provisions.[119] A development towards greater stringency appears to be evident in the jurisprudence, at least within the 'prevention of crime' context.

It is arguable that the 1985 Act did not fully meet the 'in accordance with the law' requirement since *inter alia* the serious crime ground was not defined as *Valenzuela* v *Spain* requires. It is defined in the RIPA, albeit in broad terms.[120] The question whether the RIPA meets this requirement remains open, bearing in mind the possible future development of the Strasbourg jurisprudence on this matter. The grounds under s5(3), including the 'mutual assistance' ground, are clearly ill-defined. The fact that the Act provides for authorisation by executive, rather than judicial warrant, is also relevant to the requirement of foreseeability. In *Kopp* v *Switzerland*, in finding a breach of Article 8 for failure to satisfy that requirement, the Court said: 'it is . . . astonishing that this task should be assigned to an official of the Post Office's legal department, who is a member of the executive, without supervision by an independent judge'.[121]

The provision under s3 of the RIPA allowing for interception with consent on the basis of reasonable belief may be questionable under Article 8, depending on the steps which must be taken in practice to establish the consents, especially in relation to the *recipient* of the communication.[122] Moreover, the authorisation procedure is less demanding than that in relation to interception by warrant and might therefore appear to be out of accord with the requirement of quality. However, at the present time the procedure is in principle in accordance with Article 8. The Court has found that where one party to the conversation has given consent under the equivalent provision of the 1985 Act Article 8 was not breached since citizens would be sufficiently aware of the risk.[123]

The regime under Part I, Chapter II of the 2000 Act governing phone metering might also be viewed as failing the 'in accordance with the law' requirement: it has limited statutory underpinning but provides for a broad range of circumstances in which metering might be carried out, together with safeguards against arbitrariness which are more limited than those in respect of interception. The acceptance in *Christie* that less might be expected of national law in the national security context would not apply where 'ordinary' crime was concerned. If carried out at the request of the security or intelligence services, such acquisition of data would also have a legal basis under the Intelligence Services Act 1994[124] which would

[119] Ibid para 75.

[120] In s81(3).

[121] Ibid at para 46.

[122] See *Lambert* v *France* (1999) 1 EHRLR 123. In *Kruslin* v *France* (1990) 12 EHRR 547 at para 26 it was accepted that although the line of a third party had been tapped, an interference with the applicant's Article 8 rights had occurred, since his conversations on that line had been intercepted and recorded.

[123] *Nadir Choudhary* v *UK* (1999) 1 EHRLR 522.

[124] See further Chapter 8 pp303–306.

also have to be scrutinised, although, taking *Christie* into account, it would probably satisfy this requirement.

As Chapter 2 explains, if an interference is 'in accordance with the law', it must have a legitimate aim and be necessary in a democratic society. The legitimate aims under Article 8(2), indicated in Chapter 8,[125] are very broad and echo those used under s5(3), apart from the fourth one. But since the aim of that ground is to prevent crime this aim would probably be viewed as legitimate. Thus, this requirement appears to be satisfied. But, as noted above, metering may be carried out in relation to any form of crime.[126] The grounds for obtaining data arguably go somewhat beyond those mentioned in Article 8 para 2,[127] and one of them is left entirely open – to be determined at the discretion of the Secretary of State.

The Court has interpreted 'necessary in a democratic society' as meaning: 'an interference corresponds to a pressing social need and, in particular, that it is proportionate to the legitimate aim pursued'.[128] The doctrine of proportionality, as Chapter 2 indicated, is strongly linked to the principle of the margin of appreciation. The width of that margin appears to depend partly on the aim of the interference in question and partly on its necessity. In relation to the aim of national security the Court has allowed a very wide margin to the state. In *Klass* v *Federal Republic of Germany*[129] the European Court of Human Rights found, bearing the margin of appreciation doctrine in mind, that German telephone tapping procedures were in conformity with Article 8 since they contained a number of safeguards. An oversight body, a Parliamentary Board,[130] could consider, on an application from an aggrieved individual or *ex officio*, whether the interception had been authorised and its necessity. There was also quite a substantial degree of Parliamentary scrutiny: the minister in question had to report to a Parliamentary Board and also to give an account of the interceptions ordered to a Commission. The possibility was available of compensation for persons whose phones had been unlawfully tapped and of challenges to interception in proceedings in the ordinary courts, and the individual warrants had to be reviewed by a Commission headed by a person qualified for judicial office.

The Court did not, however, state that these were the minimal safeguards necessary; it said: 'The Court considers that in a field where abuse is so easy in individual cases and could have such harmful consequences for democratic society as a whole, it is in principle desirable to entrust

[125] P330.

[126] S22(2)(b).

[127] But see *MS* v *Sweden* (1999) 28 EHRR 313 para 38 which suggests that 'contributions to government funds' grounds fall within the 'economic well being' exception of Article 8(2).

[128] *Olsson* v *Sweden* A 130 para 67 (1988).

[129] (1979) 2 EHRR 214.

[130] Under Law G10.

supervisory control to a judge. Nevertheless, having regard to the supervisory and other safeguards provided . . . the Court concludes that the exclusion of judicial control does not exceed the limits of what may be deemed necessary in a democratic society. The Parliamentary Board and the . . . Commission are independent of the authorities carrying out the surveillance, and are vested with sufficient powers and competence to exercise an effective and continuous control. Furthermore, the democratic character is reflected in the balanced membership of the Parliamentary Board. The Opposition is reflected on this body and is therefore able to participate in the control of the measures ordered by the . . . Minister'.[131] In *Christie* v *UK*[132] the Commission found: 'having regard to the wide margin of appreciation in this area' the safeguards provided by the Interception of Communications Tribunal and the Commissioner were sufficient in the instant case where the applicant was a trade unionist with links with communist Eastern Europe and his phone was being tapped on the grounds of 'national security' and 'economic well being'. The interception was proportionate to those legitimate aims, on the facts of the case. Similar findings were made, rather readily, by the Commission in *Remmers and Hamer* v *the Netherlands*[133] in the context of serious crime.

Bearing in mind the findings in *Klass*, the findings in *Christie* need not be taken as absolutely conclusive evidence that the oversight mechanisms provided by the 1985 Act, and maintained, with modifications, under the 2000 Act, meet Convention requirements. They were made in relation to the particular case, not as abstract comment on the mechanisms or on the warrant procedure in general, and they were heavily influenced by the margin of appreciation. As argued in Chapter 2, that doctrine is not available at national level and this, it is contended, means that it should not influence national decision-makers, including judges acting judicially or extra-judicially, and other national bodies. The government and the Commissioner have assumed that the decision in *Christie* closes the question as far as the 1985 Act is concerned and as the statement of compatibility accompanying it demonstrates, the government takes this stance in respect of Part I, Chapter I of the RIPA as well. As suggested above, this may not be the case in respect of 'consensual' interception or metering. But in respect of interception under warrant, under the RIPA the issue could be reopened in future, under developments in the Court's jurisprudence, bearing in mind the possibility of changing standards in other member states.

Therefore a national judge (probably sitting in the new Tribunal,[134] not in an ordinary court) would be free to take a more rigorous look at

[131] Ibid p235.
[132] 78-A DR E Com HR 119.
[133] (1999) 27 EHRR CD 168.
[134] Note that Tribunal members, apart from the President, need not be judges (see p402).

the safeguards provided by the RIPA and at the necessity of an interference. The approach taken in practice would depend on the tendency to follow the traditionalist model: it might be found that traditional notions of deference to the executive in this sensitive area would yield the same result as adherence to the margin of appreciation doctrine. But a judge might be prepared to depart from a deferential stance outside the national security context. As indicated above, it is a statutory requirement for the Secretary of State or Senior Official to consider proportionality[135] in issuing a warrant. Therefore the new Tribunal would be expected to consider whether the statutory requirements have been met, taking Strasbourg guidance into account, but adopting a more rigorous scrutiny. The continued lack of judicial authorisation under the RIPA should be considered, when looking at the necessity of an interference, bearing in mind the fact that the other safeguards available, including Parliamentary oversight, are weaker than those in *Klass*.

S17 prevents or curbs access to a court and therefore should be considered under Article 6(1) which has been found to provide a right of access to a court whether or not the domestic legal system allows such access in a particular case.[136] In *Omar* v *France*[137] the Court confirmed that the right of access to a court is not absolute but that limitations must not restrict it to such an extent that the very essence of the right is impaired. Any limitations must pursue a legitimate aim and there must be a reasonable relationship of proportionality between the means employed and the aim sought to be achieved. At present the access is to the new Tribunal under s65, and therefore Article 6 may be satisfied as far as aggrieved citizens are concerned. (If eventually the Tribunal is found at Strasbourg (or possibly domestically, on appeal, as discussed in Chapter 10) to fall outside Article 6 (and/or to fail to satisfy Article 13)[138] this question will arise again since there will be no body within the domestic system before which Convention rights can be raised in any meaningful fashion.) But at present, arguably, the right of access to a court could be raised in *criminal* proceedings in the sense that s17 affects it so greatly that the essence of the right is impaired. In other words, although formally speaking the defendant has had access to a court for the determination of a criminal charge, substantively speaking the access might be rendered, arguably, ineffective if a central issue cannot be raised owing to s17. In effect that issue has been predetermined. This could be argued by analogy with *Tinnelly* v *UK*[139] in which the Court said: 'the right of access cannot be displaced on the *ipse dixit* of the executive'. The analogy would be based

[135] S5(2).
[136] *Golder* v UK A 18 (1975).
[137] (2000) 29 EHRR 210; see also *Tinnelly* v *UK* (1999) 27 EHRR 249 in which it was found that restriction of such access in the national security context impaired the essence of the right.
[138] See below, pp412–413.
[139] (1999) 27 EHRR 249.

on the decision of the police or CPS to proceed with the prosecution although aware of the evidence deriving from an intercept favouring the defendant. S17 appears to allow this to occur. In *Tinnelly* the applicant had obtained access to an Employment Tribunal but the access was meaningless since the proceedings were predetermined by a National Security certificate. This argument must be advanced tentatively, but if correct it would mean that if, for example, an instance such as *Preston* arose in which it was possible that adducing the evidence derived from the intercept would lead to the aquittal of the defendants, it would not be enough to argue that the proceedings as a whole, including any appeal, would be in conformity with Article 6.[140] Therein lies the distinction between the duty of the Strasbourg court and the duty of the domestic one. The judge at first instance would be under a duty to secure such compliance and would have to search for a way of doing so, under s3 HRA. The legitimate aim of s17 should be called into question, following *Omar.* If the use of interception is lawful, and probative evidence is obtained, it would be hard to identify the legitimate purpose of refusing to adduce it directly in court. S18 addresses the question of proportionality to a very limited extent, but the defence would be expected to raise, within Article 6, the question whether the requirements of proportionality (as well as the requirements of equality of arms) can be satisfied by a provision which allows the intercept evidence to be disclosed to the prosecution but not to the defence.

There would also be the possibility of considering whether the new Tribunal meets Convention requirements, in particular those of Article 6. This issue is discussed in Chapter 10[141] since the new Tribunal will deal with all forms of state surveillance, going beyond the interception of communications.

[140] The argument that the trial process, including the appeal, taken as a whole was fair, succeeded in *Preston* v *UK,* note 92 above.

[141] Pp412–413.

Chapter 10

A New Framework for State Surveillance II

Surveillance devices and covert human intelligence sources

Surveillance devices and techniques offer an important weapon to the police and security services in the maintenance of law and order and the protection of national security. However, as the Supreme Court of Canada has said of them: 'one can scarcely imagine a state activity more dangerous to individual privacy than electronic surveillance.'[1] This was also the view of the Younger Committee which listed the range of devices then in use.[2] The use by state bodies of surveillance techniques and 'covert human intelligence sources', and its legal basis, resembles the pattern considered in Chapter 9 in relation to the interception of communications. Despite the development of such techniques and the increased use of them by the police and the security services, they had until recently no or a quasi-legal basis – a position which was possible under a Constitution based on negative liberties since the state, like the ordinary citizen, was, according to a key decision, entitled to do anything which the law did not forbid.[3] They operated until recently outside the realms of Parliamentary, judicial or administrative control. Bearing in mind the power of the state to conduct surveillance, and its intrusiveness, this was an especially anomalous position.

Under administrative guidelines[4] the use of listening devices could be authorised by Chief Constables in order to assist in a criminal investigation, if the crime was really serious, normal methods had been tried and had failed, and there was good reason for believing that the use of such equipment would lead to a conviction. Also the authorising officer had

[1] *Duarte* (1990) 65 DLR (4th) 240.
[2] Report of the Committee on Privacy, Cmnd 5012 1972.
[3] See Megarry VC in *Malone* v *MPC* [1979] Chap 344.
[4] *Guidelines on the Use of Equipment in Police Surveillance Operations* House of Commons Library 19 December 1984.

to weigh the seriousness of the offence against the degree of intrusion necessary. When it became apparent in 1996 that this regime was inadequate, as explained below, since it did not meet the demands of the Convention, the use of some surveillance techniques was placed on a statutory basis in the Police Act 1997. Following the lead of the Interception of Communications Act 1985, it gives an impression of covering the use of surveillance devices by the police, while leaving many areas of their use outside its statutory framework. It does not cover the use of such devices by the security and intelligence services.[5] This regime meant that two layers of control existed in relation to the interception of certain telephonic communications, but one in relation to the use of 'bugging' devices, while many surveillance and information-gathering techniques, including the use of informants, were still outside the statutory regime. Once again the imminence of the HRA, and the effect of Article 8 in particular, was the driving force for change. The unsatisfactory nature of the arrangements was pointed out in the 1998 JUSTICE Report, mentioned in Chapter 9, which argued for integration of surveillance techniques with interception, in one comprehensive statute. Part II of the Regulation of Investigatory Powers Act seeks to address these anomalies. Overlapping with the 1997 Act, most of which it will not repeal, it covers a far wider range of both techniques and public authorities, including the police. It places the use of surveillance by the security and intelligence services on a clearer statutory basis, overlapping with the 1989 and 1994 Acts. It also provides a fuller complaints mechanism, with a view to keeping most scrutiny of surveillance out of the ordinary courts, but nevertheless satisfying the demands of the Convention. In contrast with the position under Part I, it does not create a criminal offence of conducting unauthorised surveillance.

The statutory framework

(i) The Police Act 1997

The House of Lords in *Khan*,[6] confronted with evidence obtained by police bugging involving trespass, recommended legislation, taking into account the fact that the regime governing the use of bugging devices was not on a statutory basis and therefore might not comply with the 'in accordance with the law' requirement under Article 8.[7] Their recommendation was

[5] See Chapter 8.

[6] [1996] 3 All ER 289; [1996] 3 WLR 162; (1996) 146 NLJ 1024, HL; [1995] QB 27, CA.

[7] See the comments of Lord Nolan [1996] 3 WLR 162 at p175 and Lord Slynn at p166. See also the Home Affairs Select Committee 3rd Report for 1994–5, *Organised Crime* HC 18–1, which recommended a statutory basis. It may be noted that *Khan* v *UK* App No 35394/97 was declared admissible at Strasbourg: (1999) 27 EHRR CD 58 and the application was successful (judgment of the Court of 12.5.2000) since at the time there was no sufficient basis in law for the interference with Article 8. See further pp390–2.

one of the factors behind the passing of the Police Act 1997, which therefore represents another instance in which powers posing a grave threat to privacy and other individual rights were governed only by administrative guidelines until it became apparent that such a course could not be justified under the Convention. The Police Act Part III placed the practice under the relevant Home Office guidelines[8] on a statutory basis, with certain changes. It only covers the installation of devices which could have attracted liability under trespass, criminal damage or unlawful interference with wireless telegraphy, under the Wireless Telegraphy Acts 1949 and 1967. Therefore it does not cover 'stand off' devices. Also, it does not cover devices installed with the consent of the person able to give permission in respect of the premises in question.[9] The use of surveillance devices in a range of circumstances therefore falls outside it, as do a range of techniques, in particular the use of informants.[10] Such matters continued to be governed by the Guidelines until Part II of the RIPA (see below) came into force. Part III of the Police Act is largely modelled on the Interception of Communications Act and therefore contains certain similar objectionable features. The basis for allowing the use of bugging is very broad. An authorisation may be issued if the action is expected to be of substantial value in the prevention and detection of serious crime and the objective cannot reasonably be achieved by other means (s 93(2)). Serious crime is defined under s93(4) to include crimes of violence, those involving substantial financial gain, and those involving a large number of people in pursuit of a common purpose.[11] These definitions appear to be significantly wider than those under the old Guidelines. The last possibility could allow bugging to be used against, for example, members of CND or anti-road protesters, if it was expected, *inter alia*, that their activities might infringe s68 of the Criminal Justice and Public Order Act 1994.[12] The 1999 Code of Practice, however, adopted under s101 of the Act, emphasises that the bugging powers must only be used in cases of serious crime such as drug trafficking.

Under s93(5) an authorisation to interfere with property may be issued by the Chief Officer of Police or, if that is not practicable, by an officer of the rank of assistant chief constable of the force in question (s94), if s93(2) applies. The authorisation will be given in writing, except in cases of emergency when it may be given orally by the Chief Officer in

[8] HO Circular to Chief Constables *Guidelines on the use of Technical Equipment in Police Surveillance Operations.*

[9] Under the Guidelines and the Code of Practice, Intrusive Surveillance. One example would be the placing of listening devices in a police station: see *R* v *Bailey and Smith* [1993] Crim LR; *R* v *Musqud Ali* [1966] QB 668.

[10] See *R* v *H* [1987] Crim LR 47 and *R* v *Jelen and Katz* [1990] 90 Cr App R 456. The use of a wired informant may require permission under the HO Circular; Part II of the RIPA – provisions covering covert human sources – now applies.

[11] Or the crime is one for which a person of 21 or over with no previous convictions could reasonably be expected to receive a prison sentence of three or more years.

[12] See Chapter 4 p154.

person (s95(1)). A written authorisation will last for three months, an oral one for 72 hours. Both forms may be renewed in writing for a further three months. The Commissioners appointed under s91(1) must be notified of authorisations as soon as they are made (s96) but this does not prevent the police acting on the authorisation. There is no administrative check under the 1997 Act, as there is under the 1985 one: no minister is involved in the bugging authorisations. Apart from authorisations falling within s97 (below), no other independent prior check is available although special Information Commissioners (to become Surveillance Commissioners under the RIPA Part II) have an oversight role. As has been pointed out in relation to the checking procedure under the 1985 Act, subsequent independent checks are clearly not as effective as prior ones. Again, these arrangements may be compared with those in Denmark, where authorisation of the use of listening devices, wherever placed, and including 'participant monitoring', must be by an investigating magistrate.[13]

As initially drafted, the Bill made no provision for any prior independent scrutiny of the bugging warrants at all, thereby adopting the model used for the 1985 Act, but without even the intervention of Home Office officials. The warrants were to be issued by the Chief Constable of the force in question, continuing the old practice. Michael Howard, the then Home Secretary, considered that exclusion of an independent authorising body was necessary since the police must be able to react instantly to prevent crime. This proposal was severely criticised from various quarters[14] and amendments requiring prior independent approval were put forward by Labour and the Liberal Democrats.[15] The Labour amendment is reflected in s97; prior approval of authorisation is not required in all instances. Under s97(2) such approval by a Commissioner is required where the specified property is believed to be a dwelling, hotel bedroom or office premises. It is also needed where the authorising officer believes that information of a more sensitive nature may be acquired.

The involvement of special Commissioners, even such a limited involvement, may provide a degree of independent oversight and scrutiny, although the Commissioners will probably tend to accept and agree with police representations. Nevertheless, apart from other considerations, the

[13] Article 126 1 and Code of Criminal Procedure.

[14] The criticism came from the pressure group, *Liberty* and from some sections of the press, including sections of the tabloid press. It was argued that other countries accept prior judicial authorisation or bugging warrants and the UK accepts judicial involvement in other aspects of the policing process such as the authorisation of search warrants.

[15] Labour proposed that an Information Commissioner appointed from the judiciary should be involved in checking the warrants, while the Liberal Democrats proposed that a judge acting in his or her capacity as a judge should undertake this role. See Standing Committee F Fifth Sitting, 11 March 1997, cols 131*ff.* The House of Lords accepted both amendments and Michael Howard then reached an agreement with Jack Straw, then the Shadow Home Secretary, that an Information Commissioner appointed from the judiciary should be involved in checking warrants if certain authorisations were in question.

involvement of Commissioners may mean that internal procedures will be tightened up before representations are made. No provision is made under the Act for independent review of the authorisations in the ordinary courts. Nevertheless, under the Labour amendment scrutiny of police practices will be, arguably, somewhat more effective than scrutiny of those of the Security Service, not weaker, as Michael Howard originally proposed. Clearly, this is a more satisfactory situation since the arguments for excluding the judiciary from the process are weaker when matters pertaining to national security are not in question.

Various groups and bodies had put forward pleas for exemption from the provisions of the Bill. These included Catholic priests who were afraid that the confessional would be bugged, doctors and solicitors. S97(2)(b) and the Code of Practice, *Intrusive Surveillance*, adopted under s101 of the Act[16] reflect the concerns of these groups to an extent. Where the action authorised is likely to result in 'any person acquiring knowledge of matters subject to legal privilege, confidential personal information or confidential journalistic material' prior authorisation is required. Under s98 'matters subject to legal privilege' include communications between a professional legal adviser and his or her client connected with the giving of legal advice or relating to legal proceedings. Once approval for an authorisation has been given allowing, for example, for a solicitor's office to be bugged, all conversations between solicitors and clients would be recorded. Under s99 'confidential personal information' includes information relating to a person's physical or mental health or to spiritual counselling. But under s97(3), even where s97 applies, no approval is needed if the authorising officer 'believes that the case is one of urgency'. No requirement that the belief should be based on reasonable grounds is included. However, the 1999 Code of Practice provides that in all but exceptional cases the police must obtain prior approval of the authorisation where s97 applies: the 'urgency' provision must not be used routinely. It may be noted, however, that s101 is to be repealed by the RIPA and this Code will be replaced by a new Code to be issued under s71 of that Act.

The Code of Practice was revised in November 1999.[17] The revision appeared to be intended to limit further the power of intrusive surveillance in relation to the especially sensitive categories of information. Under the Code surveillance operations will be banned in churches or temples where a minister of religion is giving spiritual counselling such as absolution. In order to use bugging equipment in such circumstances, not only will the provisions of the Act have to be complied with, but the police will also have to seek permission from the head of the appropriate church or faith. This provision brings the Church of England and other

[16] It was issued on 27 October 1998.
[17] The revised Code was published by the Home Office on 18 November 1999. As noted, it will be replaced under the RIPA.

churches and faiths into line with the Roman Catholic Church: the sacramental confessional was given added protection under the original Code.

The relationship between the Code of Practice and the statute is significant. The Act grants broad discretionary powers to conduct intrusive surveillance and interfere with property to senior law enforcement officials, but seeks to constrain and structure these powers in two main ways. First, there are general precedent conditions for the exercise of such powers, the most significant being the requirement that the action is likely to be of substantial value in preventing or detecting serious crime. Second, there are specific countervailing provisions intended to protect privacy and confidentiality. In this respect s97 is the key provision, but the Code of Practice, a set of quasi-legal rules, provides a due process underpinning. S97, with its ancillary statutory provisions, together with the Code provisions, could be viewed as providing a detailed domestic scheme satisfying the demands of Article 8. But this view fails to take account of the rule of law implications of placing a number of key protective provisions on a quasi-legislative basis within what Baldwin has termed 'tertiary rules', or government by circular.[18]

In common with many of the Codes accompanying 'state power' legislation discussed in this book,[19] the Code provisions are not on their face discretionary; they are in general phrased in the precise terms of mandatory instructions. Nevertheless, no formal sanction, apart from an internal disciplinary one, is provided for their breach. This is also true of the statutory provisions. However, they cloak otherwise tortious actions with authority, while the mere fact that they are statutory may appear to give them greater weight than the Code provisions in the eyes of those to whom they are directed and of the judiciary. If the provisions were not followed, it would be, theoretically, an internal disciplinary matter and in practice police officers might pay more attention to this than to the theoretical possibility of being sued. But, as Chapter 5 pointed out, the same sanction was used for breach of the PACE Codes and did not appear to be fully effective, taking into account the very few disciplinary charges laid for their breach.[20] Thus, senior law enforcement officials are in effect given at least a partial discretion as to whether to follow the Code rules and thus whether to respect the Article 8 rights which they enshrine.[21]

[18] See R Baldwin *Rules and Government* (1995).

[19] The PACE Codes considered in Chapters 5, 6, 7 were the forerunners of the similar Codes considered in this book, the Codes to be adopted under the Terrorism Act 2000 and the Regulation of Investigatory Powers Act 2000.

[20] See pp174–5.

[21] Ronald Dworkin has argued that if an official's decision whether to comply with a given rule is final and unreviewable, he or she is endowed with a form of discretion (*Taking Rights Seriously* (1977) p69). In practice, decisions taken by police officers in relation to provisions of the Codes of Practice discussed in this book, are in general unlikely to be considered in courts or in police disciplinary proceedings. In a minority of instances, however, such provisions may be considered in relation to exclusion of evidence. Even then, the 'sanction' of such exclusion is unlikely to be used in respect of most forms of non-confession evidence, the form of evidence to which the provisions of the new RIPA

As pointed out in Chapter 5, the concept of a right precludes the idea of an open-ended discretion to infringe it in the pursuit of competing interests.[22]

Unless rigorous, independent review of rule-compliance and a clear remedy for breach is available, the Code rules will remain, in effect, largely discretionary, and the rights protected by them illusory. This is a concern in respect of the statutory provisions, including s97, but it arises *a fortiori* in respect of the Code and will be equally true of the new Code to be introduced under s71 of the RIPA, which will also be accompanied by no clear sanction for its breach (s72(2)).[23] It is suggested below that the new Tribunal system may prove ineffective, and that since no clear Parliamentary or administrative means of seeking to enhance rule-compliance is available, recourse to court-based remedies under the influence of the HRA would be of especial significance in this context if, which is very doubtful, they could find expression.

(ii) The Regulation of Investigatory Powers Act Part II[24]

Part II represents a dramatic incursion of law into a hidden area of executive action. It covers surveillance activities of immense potential to infringe privacy which have been extensively used by a wide range of bodies without any basis in law. For the first time it provides a comprehensive statutory basis for the expanding use of forms of surveillance and of undercover agents or informers.[25] Unlike Part III of the Police Act it covers a very wide range of bodies, including the security and intelligence services. It also covers a much wider range of circumstances. The new framework therefore represents a very significant step forward in terms of openness and accountability since previously there were no requirements of oversight at all in respect of the use of informers[26] or in respect of some of the other forms of surveillance discussed below. Part II therefore introduces regulation for the first time into a previously unregulated

Code are most likely to relate. See, generally, KC Davis *Discretionary Justice* (1980) pp84–88. See also above, p174.

[22] See p173. Dworkin argues that it only makes sense to denote an interest as a right if it will generally win any battle with competing societal considerations: see *Taking Rights Seriously* (1977) p191.

[23] On the model provided by the PACE Codes (adopted for all the Codes mentioned in this book) it will be admissible in evidence under s72(3). It should be taken into account by courts, the new Tribunal and relevant Commissioners under s72(4).

[24] It may be noted that under s46 there are restrictions on Part II authorisations extending to Scotland.

[25] The use of covert surveillance together with other targeting methods, including the use of informers, has expanded rapidly and is seen as immensely useful by the police: see *Policing with Intelligence* HMIC Thematic Inspection Report 1997/9.

[26] In relation to police use of informers there are unpublished, internal ACPO guidelines on the use of certain categories of informers: *Informers who take part in crime* Home Office Circular No 97/1969, now to be found in para 1.92 of Home Office Consolidated Circular on Crime and Kindred Matters No 35/1986. These guidelines are being replaced by a published Code.

area, and in a manner which may, in some respects, exceed the current requirements of the Convention.[27] Therefore the criticisms of the new regime made below must be placed in this context.

Fundamental to the operation of Part II is the distinction it seeks to create between 'directed' and 'intrusive' surveillance under s26. Intrusive surveillance can occur in more limited circumstances and the authorisation requirements are stricter. Under the cumbersome and tortuous definitions provided, 'intrusive surveillance' occurs when a surveillance device or an individual is actually present on residential premises, or in a private vehicle, or it is carried out by such a device in relation to such premises or vehicle without being present on the premises or vehicle. If the device or person is not on the premises or vehicle it is not intrusive surveillance unless 'the device is such that it consistently provides information of the same quality and detail as might be expected to be obtained from a device actually present on the premises or in the vehicle' (s26(5)). 'Residential' is defined in s48(1) as premises used as living accommodation, while 'premises' includes movable structures and land. The definition expressly excludes common areas of residential premises and clearly does not cover office premises (s48(7)(b)). 'Participant monitoring', allowed for under the 1997 Act, will therefore fall partly within the intrusive and partly within the directed or covert human intelligence sources (informers[28] and undercover officers) provisions. Under s26(2) all covert surveillance is directed surveillance if it is not an immediate response and it is undertaken for the purposes of a specific investigation, and in order to obtain private information about a person, even if he is not identified in relation to the investigation.

It appears therefore that some directed surveillance which, as discussed below, can be authorised by the police authorising officers without independent oversight, overlaps with activities requiring approval under s97 of the 1997 Act, thereby undermining the safeguards it provides. For example, 'common areas' could include the hallways of flats. It appears that a surveillance device placed in such an area, so long as it did not operate as efficiently as an 'intrusive' device, would fall within the meaning of 'directed' not 'intrusive' surveillance, while, where police officers wished to employ it, it would also fall within s97. In contrast, a device used to snoop on an office could be present in or outside the office or other non-residential premises so long as s26(2) applies to its purpose.

[27] See *Ludi* v *Switzerland* A 238 (1992), below, at p395.

[28] The criminal justice implications of using informers vary enormously, depending on the category into which a particular informer falls. The JUSTICE Report (1998) p41 usefully categorises informers into four groups: informants who give information to the police in the hope of financial or other benefit; participating informers who provide information about others with whom they are engaged in planning or committing offences; tasked informers – persons who are actively managed by the police to obtain specific information, perhaps involving taking part in committing offences; supergrasses who agree to testify in court against their former criminal associates, usually in the hope of a sentence discount.

Since the regime under the RIPA is less restrictive than that under s97 of the 1997 Act, it would seem that police officers wishing to install a device in such an area would seek to rely on the later Act. In particular, it is notable that the provisions regarding matters subject to legal privilege, confidential personal information and confidential journalistic material are not reproduced in the 2000 Act. Under s30(3) the Secretary of State may impose restrictions on the purposes for which authorisations under ss28 and 29 may be granted. Since all these forms of information could be obtained under authorisations within ss28 and 29, this is the only potential safeguard against using these provisions to undermine s97 of the Police Act, which requires approval of authorisations likely to result in acquiring material falling into these categories.

A further anomaly is created where the interception of communications also amounts to directed surveillance. The possibility that this may occur is recognised under s48(4), which provides that where one party has consented to the interception[29] and no warrant has authorised it, it will count as surveillance. Such an interception, although unauthorised as an interception, will not attract civil or criminal liability due to the provision of s27 which provides that conduct to which Part II applies will be lawful if an authorisation under it applies and the conduct is in accordance with it.

'Directed' surveillance and the use of a covert human intelligence source may be authorised on the same grounds, under ss28 and 29, respectively. The grounds are very similar to those used under s22(2) in respect of the acquisition of communications data (above, Chapter 9). They are far wider than those applying to the interception of communications or under the Police Act Part III. The grounds under s5 of the RIPA are included, expressly or impliedly, but the other grounds include 'for preventing or detecting crime or of preventing disorder, the interests of public safety; for the purpose of protecting public health; for the purpose of assessing or collecting any tax, duty . . . or other . . . charge payable to a government department; or for any other purpose specified for the purposes of this subsection by an order made by the Secretary of State'. This order must be approved by Parliament.

Proportionality requirements are introduced under ss28(2) and 29(2) to the effect that the authorising person must believe that the authorisation or authorised conduct is 'proportionate to what is sought to be achieved by carrying it out'. This might include asking whether the information which it is thought necessary to obtain by these means could reasonably be obtained by other means. Clearly, in common with their equivalents in Part 1, these provisions were introduced in an effort to meet the proportionality requirement under Article 8(2), discussed below. The authorisation is granted by a 'designated person' under ss28 and 29. Under s30 they are 'the individuals holding such offices, ranks or positions with

[29] This refers to s3, discussed, Chapter 9 at p351.

relevant public authorities as are prescribed for the purposes of this subsection by an order' made by the Secretary of State. The Secretary of State can him- or herself be a designated person under s30(2). The 'relevant public authorities' include the police, the security and intelligence services, Customs and Excise, the armed forces, and any other authority to be designated by order of the Secretary of State. Thus the security and intelligence services can undertake directed surveillance or use covert sources on grant of a warrant from a member of the services, with no independent check.

The highly significant question as to the persons within the organisations indicated in s30 entitled to grant the authorisations is therefore left unresolved and entirely in executive hands. The equally significant determination as to the further public authorities which might be added to the list is also placed in the hands of the Home Secretary, although subject to Parliament's approval. In Parliament it was stated that the Department of Health was under consideration for addition. Other bodies, including the Department of Trade and Industry, the Immigration Service and the DSS were mentioned as, it appeared, further possibilities.[30] These bodies appear to use such powers already but unless added to the list would lack a statutory basis for them. These matters would probably not have come to light had the HRA not been enacted, since most, although not all, use of directed surveillance by, for example, the DSS would not have been unlawful: by definition no tort or crime, such as trespass or burglary, would have been committed.[31] However, since it was an inevitable consequence of that Act that such activities would require a legal basis, it might have been expected that a less flimsy and grudging one would have been created. The grounds and the authorisation procedure reflect a questionable assumption that the use of directed surveillance and informants creates a much more insignificant invasion of privacy than intrusive surveillance, just as phone metering is viewed as much less intrusive than interception.

'Intrusive' surveillance, as surveillance invariably involving the creation of existing civil or criminal liability, is treated somewhat differently. Since some surveillance covered by s97 of the Police Act would also amount to intrusive surveillance, any differences between the procedures under the two statutes are significant since, as far as the police are concerned, the less restrictive route is likely to be used.[32] However, the arrangements for intrusive surveillance do not in themselves appear to subvert those

[30] HC Debs 6 March 2000 col 832.

[31] Had such activities been challenged by way of judicial review (for obvious reasons this was unlikely) the authority would have required a legal basis for its actions, although, depending on the context (whether national security or economic well-being or, possibly, prevention of serious crime issues were raised), they might have received a very superficial scrutiny: *R* v *Secretary of State for the Home Dept ex p Ruddock* [1987] 2 All ER 518.

[32] It may be noted that s33(5) provides for 'combined authorisations', where the authorisation combines authorisations given under both the 1997 and 2000 Acts.

under the 1997 Act. Subversion has occurred more subtly, owing to the overlap between *directed* surveillance and s97 of the 1997 Act.

Under s32(3) of the RIPA authorisation of intrusive surveillance is on the same grounds as for the interception of communications and a very similar proportionality requirement is introduced under s32(2). 'Serious crime' is defined in s81(3) in substantially the same terms as in s93(4) of the 1997 Act. Authorisations for such surveillance are granted by the Home Secretary under s41 or, for police or customs officers, by senior authorising officers, who are the highest ranking police officers in Britain.[33] There is also provision for the grant of authorisations in a case of urgency by persons of almost equally high rank, other than the senior authorising officer.[34] The provisions for urgent and non-urgent authorisations under ss33, 34, 35 and 36 mirror those under the Police Act in that, under s35, notice must be given to a 'Surveillance Commissioner' and, under s36, the authorisation will not take effect until it has been approved, except where it is urgent and the grounds for urgency are set out in the notice, in which case the authorisation will take effect from the time of its grant. Under s38 senior authorising officers can appeal to the Chief Surveillance Commissioner against decisions of ordinary Surveillance Commissioners. The Commissioners have responsibility for the destruction of material obtained by surveillance, under s37, but there is no requirement that material no longer needed for proceedings and no longer subject to an authorisation *must* be destroyed.

Under s43 authorisations can be granted or renewed urgently orally by senior authorising officers or in writing by persons authorised to act on their behalf in urgent cases. If, under s43(3)(a), an authorisation is granted or renewed by a person entitled to act only in urgent cases or was renewed by such a person or orally it ceases to take effect after 72 hours. Under s43(3)(b) 'in a case not falling within paragraph (a) in which the authorisation is for the conduct or the use of a covert human intelligence source', the period is 12 months from its grant or last renewal. In a case falling outside s43(3)(a) or (b), it is three months under s43(3)(c).

S42 provides special rules for the intelligence services which overlap with those of s5 of the Intelligence Services Act 1994. Under s42 the security and intelligence services can undertake intrusive surveillance

[33] Under s32(6) they include: the Chief Constable of every police force outside London in England, Scotland and Wales, the Commissioner and Assistant Commissioners of the Metropolitan Police, the Commissioner of Police for the City of London, the Chief Constable and Deputy Chief Constable of the Royal Ulster Constabulary, the Director-Generals of the National Criminal Intelligence and the National Crime Squad, and designated persons. Any person holding the rank of assistant chief constable in that Squad who is designated for the purposes of this paragraph by that Director-General and any customs officer so designated by the Commissioners of Customs and Excise.

[34] Under s34(4) such persons are of a rank almost as high as such officers. In the case of police forces this means a person holding the rank of assistant chief constable or in the case of the Metropolitan or London forces, of commander.

on grant of a warrant. The grounds are those under s32(3). As far as intrusive surveillance is concerned, the function of the services in support of the prevention or detection of serious crime is excluded where the application is by a member of GCHQ or the SIS (under s42(3)). Further, under s42(5) the Security Service cannot act on behalf of the other two services in relation to that ground. This provision seems to preserve the function of the Security Service in relation to that ground as far as intrusive surveillance is concerned, but while the other two services can undertake directed surveillance, use covert sources and intercept communications on that ground, they can undertake intrusive surveillance only on the other two grounds.

S44 provides further special rules for intelligence services authorisations. Under ss44(1) and (2) warrants containing an authorisation for the carrying out of intrusive surveillance under s41 'shall not be issued' or renewed, except 'under the hand of the Secretary of State' unless with express authorisation from him or her in urgent cases, in which case 'the warrant may be issued (but not renewed) under the hand of a senior official'. Under 44(3) a warrant authorising intrusive surveillance issued by such an official, and not renewed under the hand of the Secretary of State, 'shall cease to have effect at the end of the second working day' after its issue. In the case of other such warrants that point will be at the end of the period of six months from the day of issue or renewal. Under s44(5)(a) when an authorisation for the carrying out of directed surveillance is granted by a member of any of the intelligence services and renewed by an instrument 'endorsed under the hand of the person renewing [it] with a statement that the renewal is believed to be necessary on grounds falling within section 32(3)(a) or (c), the authorisation (unless renewed again) shall cease to have effect at the end of the period of six months'.

The distinctions created between forms of surveillance and the resulting distinctions between the restraints imposed on the police and the intelligence services, especially the limit on the powers of GCHQ and SIS in relation to crime, could all be destroyed under the original Bill by provision allowing the Secretary of State to provide for any intrusive surveillance to be treated as directed surveillance. After amendment, s47(1) provides more limited powers for the Secretary of State to extend or modify the authorisation provisions. The Secretary of State can provide for any directed surveillance 'to be treated for the purposes of this Part as instrusive surveillance'. Under s47(2) this power is subject to the negative resolution procedure, but clearly that does not provide the same safeguards as the full Parliamentary process. Under s47 the Secretary of State may also by order 'apply this Part, with such modifications as he thinks fit, to any . . . surveillance that is neither directed nor intrusive'. The power is intended to afford, if necessary, a statutory basis for the use of other powers which may be found to have fallen outside this Act. The compatibility of this basis with the Convention is questionable, partly because, it is suggested, the legal basis for the powers is so uncertain and so dependent on the exercise of executive power. The term 'such modifications' implies that lesser safeguards than those available for directed surveillance might be adopted, a possibility which would be likely to have Article 8 implications. These matters are considered below.

The use and storage of information obtained by surveillance techniques is in general left to be governed by the Code of Practice to be made under s71, although the Surveillance Commissioners also have power, when quashing authorisations of intrusive surveillance under s37, to order the destruction of records. At present storage and retention of police information are governed by a detailed ACPO Code[35] which instructs on the applicability of data protection principles to such information. As indicated in Chapter 8, concerns have been raised regarding record keeping by the Security Service, bearing in mind the fact that it does not have to comply with the Data Protection Act 1998, even in its criminal function.[36] Under the 1998 Act, in relation to personal information, the police do not have to comply with the fair and lawful processing provisions of the first data protection principle,[37] subject access requests, or restrictions on disclosure of personal information, if to do so would be likely to prejudice the prevention and detection of crime or the apprehension and prosecution of offenders. These are not blanket exemptions; they should be considered in their application to individual cases. But it is unclear that careful scrutiny on this basis occurs.[38] The RIPA Code of Practice will therefore be of significance since it could provide much greater clarity and safeguard a significant aspect of privacy. But it is argued that such a significant task should not be undertaken by quasi-legislation.[39]

The oversight role of the Commissioners

The Police Act 1997 set up a complaints system which, apart from the lack of a special Tribunal, strongly resembled that under the 1985 Act, considered in Chapter 9. The similarity was the more striking since the system related to ordinary crime, not necessarily to terrorism or other activities having a potential impact on national security. This model has now been continued under s62 RIPA which adds additional functions to those of the 'Chief Surveillance Commissioner' so that his role mirrors that of the Interceptions of Communications Commissioner. The office of Commissioner under s91 of the 1997 Act is continued but the Commissioners are redesignated 'Surveillance Commissioners' and their complaints role will be removed. Assistant Surveillance Commissioners may

[35] Code of Practice for Data Protection (1995).
[36] See pp312–3.
[37] Except in relation to 'sensitive' data.
[38] See the 1998 JUSTICE report Chap 4 esp at pp92–95.
[39] See Chapter 5 pp174–6 for analogous discussion in relation to the PACE Codes.

be appointed under s63 RIPA to aid the Chief Surveillance Commissioner. Such aid will clearly be needed since he will provide oversight, not only of police surveillance, but also of surveillance carried out by all the persons covered by Part II RIPA. Thus, the oversight role of the Surveillance Commissioners is broader than their role in relation to authorisations, since the latter relates only to the police and customs, while the former covers other public authorities and the Home Secretary's authorising role under s41. Thus, the role of the Surveillance Commissioners overlaps with that of the Intelligence Services Commissioner who has an oversight role which, as Chapter 8 indicated, covers *inter alia*, surveillance carried out by those services.

Under s107 of the Police Act 1997 the Chief Commissioner has reporting duties similar to those of the Intelligence Services Commissioner, described in Chapter 8. (The Commissioner's duty under s106, to report to the Prime Minister if an appeal is allowed and where a finding in favour of a complainant is made by a Commissioner, will be repealed under Schedule 4 of the 2000 Act.) The Commissioner must make an annual report on the discharge of his or her functions. The report must be presented to Parliament and published as a Command Paper. The Prime Minister may exclude matters from the report under s107(4) of the Act if it appears to him that it contains matter 'prejudicial to the prevention and detection of serious crime' or to the discharge of the functions of a police authority, the service authorities for the National Criminal Intelligence Service or the duties of the Commissioner for Customs and Excise.

The 1997 Act provided under s102 that the Commissioners should investigate complaints if they alleged that there had been an interference with property in pursuance of an authorisation under s93(1)(a) or (b). The Commissioners had a duty to investigate whether an authorisation was given under s93 in relation to the alleged interference[40] and, if so, whether it was properly issued: whether there were adequate grounds for issuing the warrant and whether statutory procedures were complied with.[41] The Commissioners could not investigate complaints regarding police use of bugging devices which did not involve an interference with property as defined in s93. Further, the Commissioners' remit, even in relation to such complaints, was narrow. If it was found that no authorisation was given or that the authorisation was properly given they could merely inform the complainant that no determination in his or her favour had been made. The complainant who suspected that his or her property had been bugged was then left not knowing whether in fact bugging was occurring or whether, if it was, it was unauthorised or properly authorised. The complainant was not provided with the information needed in order to pursue a tort action or any other action against the police or customs.[42]

[40] Schedule 7 para 1. Schedule 7 will be repealed under s82 RIPA.
[41] Schedule 7 para 2.
[42] Schedule 7 para 3.

Thus this complaints mechanism resembled that under the 1985 Act in its failure to provide a remedy if an interference with property was unauthorised. If an authorisation was quashed by a Commissioner, destruction of the records of information obtained from the search could be ordered unless they were required for pending criminal or civil proceedings. Thus this power was subject to a broad exception since the records would often be so required.

In addition to the Commissioners (who are senior lawyers) the Chief Commissioner, a senior lawyer, was also appointed by the Prime Minister under s91 of the 1997 Act. As indicated above, under the RIPA the Chief Commissioner will have the role of Chief Surveillance Commissioner.[43] No provision for a Tribunal was made under the 1997 Act. No complaints mechanism at all was provided in respect of surveillance by a number of public authorities. Such surveillance would have had to be considered by the ordinary courts where it fell within an existing tort. Where it did not it could have been challenged by way of judicial review as *ultra vires*. As indicated above, the *oversight* function of the Commissioners will continue, and the RIPA Part II extends it. But their *complaints* function will be taken over by the new Tribunal under RIPA, which, as indicated in Chapters 8 and 9, will provide a single body for the consideration of all types of state surveillance complaints. The reasoning behind this change appears to be that the Commissioner system might not have satisfied s7(1)(a) HRA; citizens might have sought to rely on the Convention to challenge surveillance in ordinary courts. The new Tribunal has jurisdiction under s65 to consider *inter alia* all authorisations under Part II of the RIPA and s93 of the 1997 Act. The procedure and remedies, which are discussed below, are the same as in relation to the interception of communications.

No means of referring evidence of unauthorised interference to the police or DPP is provided in Part II RIPA, although such interference might represent *inter alia* criminal damage.[44] Clearly, given that many of the operations in question are undertaken by the police, this possibility would not be likely to lead to prosecutions. But this fact should be taken into account in terms of the other remedies discussed below.

Convention rights under the HRA

(i) Requirements of the HRA

All the Commissioners should comply with the Convention in relation to their reviewing functions under the 1997 and 2000 Acts. The position is very similar to that in respect of the Interception of Communications

[43] S62 RIPA.

[44] In *R* v *Chief Constable of West Yorkshire Police ex p Govell* (1994, available on LEXIS) the interference clearly did involve criminal damage. The DPP decided not to institute criminal proceedings.

Commissioner since all the Commissioners are bound by the Convention under s6 HRA and are also providing oversight of bodies which are so bound. The Surveillance Commissioners are providing oversight of police officers and other 'public authorities' using surveillance while the Intelligence Services Commissioner is providing oversight of the Services' activities under the RIPA and the Intelligence Services Act. But scrutiny of their oversight function in the ordinary courts appears to be precluded. The 1997 Act contains an ouster clause in s91(10) which is very similar to that contained in the 1985 Act. It provides: 'The decisions of the Chief Commissioner or, subject to ss104 and 106, any other Commissioner (including decisions as to his jurisdiction) shall not be subject to appeal or liable to be questioned in any court'. S106 (as amended by RIPA) deals with appeals by authorising officers against *inter alia* a failure to authorise a bug. S106, which will be repealed, relates to appeals by complainants. The inclusion of 'decisions as to his jurisdiction' was, of course, intended to make the Commissioners' decisions unreviewable. This ouster clause will not be repealed by the 2000 Act but it will no longer relate to the Commissioners' complaints' role, which will be removed under s70(2)(c) of that Act.[45]

There are certain other possible avenues to court action, and in practice they are more likely to be open to the aggrieved individual than the avenues in respect of the interception of communications. The courts are less likely to take a deferential stance in respect of certain of the public authorities in question and towards certain of the broad grounds. They may therefore show a greater willingness to allow the complainant to use the avenues that are, arguably, open. Most significantly, there is no equivalent in the Police Act or Part II of RIPA to s17 in Part I RIPA, which, as indicated in Chapter 9, largely disallows reference to interceptions in any court or tribunal proceedings. Clearly, any such provision would be counter-productive in prosecution terms. But this does mean, depending on the extent of disclosure to the defence (see below), that a defendant may become aware at some point during criminal proceedings that a surveillance operation has occurred,[46] and therefore will be able to take any avenues of redress that may be open, including raising Convention arguments in the trial itself.

The public authorities using forms of surveillance and authorising officers within the authorities are all, by definition,[47] subject to the

[45] Ss106, 107(6) and Schedule 7 of the 1997 Act will be repealed under the RIPA.

[46] It may also be noted that it is not a criminal offence for a police officer to inform someone that an unauthorised operation has occurred since a police officer is not a Crown servant. This is true of other persons within public authorities apart from, in some circumstances, Crown servants who are affected by s4(2) of the Official Secrets Act 1989. S4(2) would probably cover some surveillance operations and is in that respect equivalent to s4(3)(a) regarding the interception of communications. Crown servants who became aware of unauthorised bugging might commit the offence under s4 of the Act if a disclosure was made.

[47] S81(1) provides that 'public authority' has the meaning given it by s6 HRA.

Convention under s6 HRA. The possibility of challenging decisions of such public authorities, as opposed to those of Commissioners, by way of judicial review, might appear to be available. Prosecutions and civil actions against those authorities might also be possible. However, s65 (discussed in full below) may stand in the way of Convention-based actions. Under s65(2) the new Tribunal will be the only appropriate forum for the purposes of s7(1)(a) HRA in relation to certain proceedings. These proceedings are indicated in ss65(3) and (5). In essence, these provisions appear to mean that s65 stands in the way of challenges by way of judicial review or civil actions against the security and intelligence services, or persons acting on their behalf, based on s6 HRA (since s7(1)(a) HRA is intended to provide for the bringing of proceedings where a public authority has acted unlawfully under s6). Ss65(5) and (6) also bar the way to judicial review or civil actions against the police, intelligence services, Customs and Excise, NCIS and the National Crime Squad where conduct has occurred in 'challengeable circumstances' under s65(7) in respect of surveillance under Part II RIPA or s93 of the 1997 Act, and raises Convention issues under s6 HRA. The term 'challengeable circumstances' under s65(7) means that the conduct has authority or purported authority or should have authority.

The availability of civil actions, as opposed to references to the new Tribunal, is therefore affected by the type of surveillance in question. Intrusive surveillance and some directed surveillance, involving entry on property, will be tortious if unauthorised or not properly authorised. Other forms of surveillance may breach Article 8 but may be outside the ambit of the tort of trespass. In either circumstance a complainant might have a remedy under the doctrine of confidence, either alone or in addition to trespass, assuming that some information was obtained and was used in some manner.[48] But in such cases the state body in question would often be able to argue that the public interest defence applied.[49] Any court adjudicating on an action in confidence or trespass in this context would be bound by s6 HRA to ensure that the Convention rights were complied with,[50] but the action would be based on the pre-existing common law, rather than s7(1)(a). This matter raises a fairly difficult issue under s65. As discussed in Chapter 2, the duty of a court, as itself a public authority, in relation to the development of the common law between private parties, does not appear to be an absolute one.[51] But where it is adjudicating on the compliance of another public authority (vertical effect) with the common law, under s6 HRA, the duty would appear to be absolute. This could lead to the development of liability in the common

[48] See H Fenwick and G Phillipson 'Confidence and Privacy: A Re-examination' (1996) 55(3) CLJ 447; see also *Hellewell* [1995] 1 WLR 804.

[49] This defence succeeded in *Hellewell* [1995] 1 WLR 804 in respect of unauthorised police use of a photograph of the defendant, who had been convicted of theft from shops, as part of a shopwatch scheme.

[50] See Chapter 2 pp51 and 58.

[51] See p58.

law depending on whether the defendant was a public authority.[52] S11 HRA would prevent an interpretation of s7(1)(a) which led to a diminution of common law rights. But where s65(2) applied, if the doctrine of confidence or an action in trespass could not be found to cover an invasion of the plaintiff's privacy by means of surveillance carried out by the public authorities falling within s65(6), a tort action in direct reliance on Article 8 would not be open.

However, arguably, s7(1)(a) HRA could be relied upon, in relation to the police, where the challenge in question was not one which the Tribunal could consider, including one concerning the probability rather than the actuality of surveillance, where that probability fell outside the 'challengeable circumstances' as defined in s65(7). In such a circumstance, the plaintiff could seek to bring a civil action based on Article 8 against the suspected public authorities in question, relying on the court's duty under s6. The alternative, which is probably preferable, as Chapter 2 argues,[53] would be to bring such an action by way of judicial review under the rules pre-HRA. Any possibilities of bringing judicial review against the police or intelligence services which existed in the pre-HRA era still exist, due to s11 HRA, so long as such possibilities do not depend on using s7(1)(a) HRA. The ironic possibility arises, in relation to surveillance, that the development of judicial review taking Article 8 into account, as in the pre-HRA era,[54] might be more far reaching and of greater significance than such development in reliance on s7(1)(a), despite the fact that the review would be less intensive.[55]

S65 does not prevent challenges by way of judicial review or civil actions against other relevant public authorities relating to surveillance.[56] But it should be noted that persons engaged in all forms of surveillance under Part II, including covert sources, are exempted from civil liability under s27(2) in respect of conduct 'incidental' to authorised conduct and – in an opaquely worded provision – in relation to conduct to which the warrant or authorisation procedure under a 'relevant' Act[57]

[52] This might occur if the process of infusion of the rights into the common law led to the creation of new torts or at least a stretching of the boundaries of the old ones. See the comments of Sedley LJ in *Redmond-Bate* v *DPP*, discussed in Chapter 4 p144.

[53] It would be preferable because if brought in the 'wrong court' the action would be struck out. It might then be out of time for judicial review purposes. See further Chapter 2 p53.

[54] Either from an activist point of view, by the infusion of the Convention into the common law, which was already occurring (see the findings of the Court of Appeal in *Derbyshire CC* v *Times Newspapers* [1993] AC 534) or from a traditionalist stance, because the Convention yields the same result as common law principle (see *R* v *Lord Chancellor ex p Witham* [1998] QB 575).

[55] See Chapter 2 pp50–51.

[56] This is of significance where, for example, a public authority not yet brought within the RIPA Part II used surveillance without falling within any existing liability, or where this occurred and the public authority, although within the Act, fell outside those listed in s65(6).

[57] The RIPA, s5 of the 1994 Act, Part III of the 1997 Act.

is inapplicable (not capable of being granted) and where it would not reasonably be expected to have been sought. This appears to cover forms of surveillance engaged in by public authorities which have no statutory basis and which, but for s27(2), might attract liability under existing torts or under s7 of the HRA in respect of a breach of Article 8. Since s27(2) could, potentially, prevent a court from discharging its duty under s6 HRA there is a case for suggesting that courts should restrict its ambit by using s3 of the HRA to interpret the term 'reasonably' restrictively.

S66 leaves open the possibility that the remaining jurisdiction of the ordinary courts in relation to surveillance (and, if necessary, to interception) will be partially ousted, by executive order, in providing: 'An order under section 65(2)(d) allocating proceedings to the Tribunal may (a) provide for the Tribunal to exercise jurisdiction in relation to that matter to the exclusion of the jurisdiction of any court or tribunal; but (b) if it does so provide, must contain provision conferring a power on the Tribunal, in the circumstances provided for in the order, to remit the proceedings to the court or tribunal which would have had jurisdiction apart from the order'. In other words, an avenue to court action would be left open if this course was taken in future.

The upshot, then, is that challenges by way of judicial review or tortious actions remain available against some public authorities, whether or not it is argued that the authority has breached s6 HRA. Actions against the police or intelligence services in relation to surveillance operations, based on s6 HRA, would have to surmount the s65 barrier. It is notable that court action was not ruled out expressly under the Security Services Act 1989, the Intelligence Services Act 1994 or the Police Act 1997, although it was under s9 of the 1985 Act. In providing for complaint to be made to the old Tribunal, s5 of the 1989 Act and s9 of the 1994 Act implied that complaint could not be made to a court. The same could be said of the Commissioner mechanism under the 1997 Act. But the provisions did not expressly exclude the jurisdiction of the courts since otherwise the agencies would then have been placed, in effect, above the law. S65 does not expressly exclude the courts' jurisdiction, regarding surveillance by the police and intelligence services, *except in relation to the Convention,* under s6 HRA. Therefore one purpose of the RIPA is to insulate all surveillance undertaken by the intelligence services, and much of that taken by the police, from the effects of the HRA, applied in the ordinary courts, except within prosecutions (due to s7(1)(b) HRA).

S65 is also likely to influence the status of the Surveillance Code to be promulgated under s71. As Chapter 5 suggested, in relation to the PACE Codes, if the provisions of such Codes are found to be coterminous with Convention rights, they may be afforded, indirectly, a higher status than the statute under which they are made affords them.[58] But if s65 bars the

[58] See Chapter 5 pp195–6.

way to the creation of civil liability in respect of breach of Convention rights, or to challenges to such breaches by way of judicial review, that potential avenue to the enhancement of the status of the Surveillance Code will be closed off, as far as a number of key public authorities are concerned. This is a significant matter since the Code is very likely to contain provisions which reflect, *inter alia*, Article 8 guarantees.

The most obvious and useful means of challenging the use of surveillance, especially by the police, will be during the criminal process itself. The issues of exclusion of evidence and of disclosure will be most significant. The duty of disclosure to the defence is restricted under the Criminal Procedure and Investigations Act 1996 and the residual common law rules on the public interest.[59] The fact that an informer or other surveillance technique has been used may not be disclosed on the basis that it is 'sensitive' material. Under that Act the duty of the CPS is to disclose to the defence all material which it considers might undermine the prosecution case, except sensitive material which should not be disclosed in the public interest. The sensitivity of the material need not be based on the need to ensure the personal safety of an informer; it may be based on the need to use the technique or person in question in a future operation. If the prosecutor considers that the material is sensitive an application to a court for a ruling to protect it on grounds of public interest immunity must be made.[60] It can be made *ex parte* with notice to the defence or, in an exceptional case, without notice. In any such application a judge, bound by s6 HRA, would have to consider Article 6 requirements in respect of such disclosure.[61]

Where an interference with property or other means of surveillance either fell outside Part III of the 1997 Act and Part II RIPA, or was unauthorised, or improperly authorised, the leading case of *Khan (Sultan)*[62] on exclusion of evidence would be of relevance, but its findings may need to be looked at afresh in the post-HRA era. In *Khan* a bugging device

[59] S21(2) of the 1996 Act.

[60] See ss3(6) and 7(5).

[61] These guidelines were provided in *Davis, Rowe and Johnson* [1993] 1 WLR 613. Now that the use of public interest immunity in that case has been found to breach Article 6 by the Court (*Rowe and Davis* v *UK*; App no 28901/95, [1999] Crim LR 410; judgment of the Court 16.2.00, (2000) 30 EHRR 1) they will have to be re-examined. The domestic courts will have the opportunity of doing so now that the HRA is fully in force. The findings in the same context in *Fitt and Jasper* v *UK* (1999) EHRLR 430 will be relevant. The Court said that in those instances, the judge had been able to consider the sensitive material in question and therefore was able to conduct a balancing act between fairness to the defence and to the prosecution. On that basis no breach of Article 6 was found. The *Davis, Rowe and Johnson* guidelines may be compared with those adopted in other countries, particularly those used in Denmark after the *Van Traa Inquiry Report* (an inquiry which is generally viewed as an especially useful guide to the use of such methods in modern policing) into the use of covert methods, including particularly the use of informers and undercover officers. The new Danish law adopted in response sought to ensure that the trial judge or defence would not be subject to complete non-disclosure of evidence and of investigative methods.

[62] [1996] 3 All ER 289; (1996) 146 NLJ 1024, HL; [1995] QB 27, CA.

had been secretly installed on the outside of a house which *Khan* was visiting. The case against him rested solely on the tape recording obtained. The defence argued, *inter alia*, that the recording was inadmissible as evidence because the police had no statutory authority to place listening devices on private property and that therefore such placement was a trespass, and, further, that admission of the recording would breach Article 8. The House of Lords agreed with the Court of Appeal that the evidence was admissible, relying on the decision in *Sang*[63] to the effect that improperly obtained evidence other than 'involuntary' confessions is admissible in a criminal trial subject to a narrow discretion under s78 PACE to exclude it.[64]

This decision clearly did not mean in itself that even where there is no statutory authority allowing them to do so, the police have a right to commit forms of trespass, including entering property without the consent of the owner. In such instances, as in *Khan* itself, a civil action for trespass would arise. Thus this decision did not in itself violate the principle from *Entinck* v *Carrington*.[65] Nevertheless, it obviously offered some encouragement to the police to continue to breach the law of trespass when it appears to them to be expedient to do so. No caveat was entered in the Lords to the effect that a very clear and serious breach of the civil law would or might render evidence thereby obtained inadmissible.

It is quite possible that the judiciary will continue the *Khan* approach to exclusion of evidence in the post-HRA era. In coming to their decision, the Lords relied on an exclusion of evidence case at Strasbourg, *Schenk* v *Switzerland*,[66] where a very wide margin of appreciation had been allowed. As argued in Chapter 2, the activist approach assumes judicial acknowledgement that domestic courts cannot rely upon the margin of appreciation, which should include refusing to apply the margin of appreciation aspects of decisions. In other words, Strasbourg decisions influenced by the doctrine should not be straightforwardly relied upon to 'water down' Convention rights. The decision in *Schenk* is a case in point; it merely confirms that admitting evidence obtained owing to a breach of Article 8 is within the margin of appreciation allowed to the national courts. But if a court, taking a traditionalist stance under the HRA, while rejecting the margin of appreciation doctrine, finds that the common law yields the same result as the Convention jurisprudence, it would perceive no duty to depart from established principle. It might find that the action of officers in interfering with property or the use of an informer had breached not only the RIPA or 1997 Act, but also Article 8 (see below), but go on to find that such breaches would not necessitate excluding any evidence gained. This would be in accordance with the stance

[63] [1980] AC 402; [1979] 2 All ER 1222, HL.
[64] See further Chapter 5 pp202–207, esp note 193.
[65] (1765) 19 St Tr 1030, as to the need for a legal basis for state infringement of property rights.
[66] (1988) 13 EHRR 242.

taken in *Khan* since illegality in terms of trespass to property was not found to necessitate exclusion of evidence. Alternatively, a court might find no breach of Article 8 and therefore the argument for exclusion of the evidence obtained would rest on common law principle as expounded in *Khan* and on the right to a fair trial under Article 6(1).[67] On the other hand, a more activist court might be prepared to consider what the outcome in *Schenk* might have been had no margin of appreciation been conceded to the state. It might be prepared to give greater weight to a breach of Article 8, since otherwise obtaining redress for breach of the fundamental rights it reflects would be – in practice – problematic, owing to the use of the comprehensive ouster clause and the other difficulties facing complainants.

(ii) Requirements of the Convention

The use of surveillance devices by the police and other public authorities is clearly a matter which may engage with a number of Convention Articles, most obviously Articles 8 and 6. Article 6 will clearly be relevant to the question of the admissibility of surreptitiously obtained evidence[68] including the evidence of informers and undercover officers. The use of the evidence of informers clearly raises issues of fairness under Article 6. Its key requirements in respect of exclusion of evidence are discussed in Chapter 5,[69] but it is suggested here that four main issues, specific to surveillance, arise. First, where evidence was obtained by means falling outside the statutory regime created by Part II RIPA or Part III of the 1997 Act, and without incurring pre-existing liability, it would be found that no sufficient basis in law was available for the interference, assuming that, in the circumstances, Article 8(1) was engaged (see below). Its obtaining would be unlawful under s6 HRA, although it would not have been before the HRA came into force.[70] Second, if in the circumstances the statutory basis applied but the surveillance was unauthorised or improperly authorised, the public authority in question would then have breached both s6 HRA and the provisions in question themselves. Third,

[67] See further Chapter 5 pp200–207.

[68] In *Khan* v *UK* App No 35394/97 (1999) 27 EHRR CD58, judgment of the Court of 12.5.00, the Court merely found that, at the time, the interference with the Article 8 guarantee had no basis in law. This breach was *not* found to necessitate exclusion of the evidence obtained and therefore no breach of Article 6 was found. See above, pp200–7.

[69] See pp200–203. The use of an undercover officer in the *Colin Stagg* case (see news reports 15.9.94) might provide an example in which a breach of Article 6 would be likely to be found.

[70] It may be noted that underlying this statement is a paradox at the heart of the HRA. If redress for breach of the duty under s6 is (absent existing remedies), apart from exclusion of evidence, only available in judicial review proceedings, it could be argued that nothing has changed since a person in the position of *Khan* could have brought judicial review proceedings against the police authority in question and might have succeeded since the action would probably have been accounted *ultra vires*. In that sense, although the House of Lords did not consider this, the action was unlawful in the pre-HRA era.

a court might consider that although the statutory provisions had been complied with, a breach of Article 8 had nevertheless occurred. Again this possibility is contemplated below. The court would not, it is suggested, need to issue a declaration of incompatibility under s4 HRA (assuming that it was able to do so). It would simply need to go on to consider whether to admit the evidence in question, in accordance with the requirements of s78 PACE and Article 6. Fourth, a court might find that proper authorisation had been given and no breach of Article 8 had occurred, but unfairness would arise under Article 6(1) owing to the admission of the evidence. This might be most likely to arise in respect of informant evidence, especially the evidence of 'participant' informants. In such instances questions as to the reliability of the evidence are likely to arise,[71] as well as questions of disclosure. The use of evidence obtained by undercover work raises issues of entrapment.[72]

Disclosure of evidence, especially pertinent in respect of surveillance, raises separate issues under Article 6. The fair hearing requirement of Article 6(1) has been found to connote equality between prosecution and defence,[73] ('equality of arms') and the changes brought about under the Criminal Procedure and Investigations Act 1996 may not accord fully with this requirement.[74] That Act preserved the use of public interest immunity following the guidelines provided in *R* v *Davis, Rowe and Johnson*.[75] Now that its use in that case has been found to breach Article 6 by the Court[76] the guidelines will have to be re-examined under the HRA. Witness anonymity appears to be out of accord with the first limb of para 6(3)(d) – the right to cross-examine witnesses. This right would seem to be specific and unambiguous in its guarantee. In principle, limitations which prevent the defence challenging the credibility of a witness cannot be reconciled with the Article 6 guarantees.[77] However, the Strasbourg case-law has left a discretion to the national court[78] as to the interpretation of para 6(3)(d) and so has deprived this right of some of its effect. The position appears to be that the rights of witnesses to life, liberty and security, which fall within the Convention, should be balanced against the rights of the defendant. Measures should be available to test the evidence,

[71] In such instances consideration will be given to the fairness of the trial as a whole (*Edwards* v *UK* (1992) 15 EHRR 417); see further Chapter 5 p200. This stance was reiterated in *Webb* v *UK* App No 33186/96, a case which concerned participating informers.

[72] See Chapter 5 pp200–201.

[73] Judgment of 27 June 1968 *Neumeister* A.8 (1968) p43.

[74] See J Niblett *Disclosure in Criminal Procedure* (1997); S Sharpe 'Disclosure, Immunity and Fair Trials' (1999) Journal of Criminal Law 67.

[75] [1993] 1 WLR 613.

[76] *Rowe and Davis* v *UK*; App No 28901/95 [1999] Crim LR 410; judgment of the Court of 16 February 2000 (2000) 30 EHRR 1.

[77] *Kostovski* v *Netherlands* (1989) 12 EHRR 434; *Windisch* v *Austria* (1990) 13 EHRR 281. See Chapter 8 pp323–4 for further discussion.

[78] See, for example, *Asch* v *Austria* (1990) Case 30/1990/221/283; *Liefveld* v *the Netherlands* [1995] 18 EHRR CD 103.

while recognising the need to protect the witness.[79] The balance may tip more towards the defence where the witnesses are undercover officers.[80]

The question whether Article 8 has been breached would be relevant to the issue of admissibility of evidence under Article 6, but would also be a free-standing enquiry in relation to particular interferences with property, other uses of surveillance devices and use of information. A preliminary question in any proceedings, including proceedings before the Tribunal set up under the RIPA, might concern the status of the individual in question as a victim, where he or she was uncertain whether surveillance had occurred. The Court put forward the following reason in *Klass* v *Federal Republic of Germany*[81] for regarding the applicants as 'victims' under Article 25 despite the fact that they were uncertain whether or not their phones had been tapped: '[normally] an applicant cannot challenge a law *in abstracto*... the position is different [when] owing to the secrecy of the measures objected to, he cannot point to any concrete measure specifically affecting him'. Thus the existence of legislation permitting secret measures, which may include the 2000 and 1997 Acts, may allow a person to claim to be the victim of a breach of Article 8. Given that the standing provisions in the HRA are the same as those under the Convention,[82] this finding would aid the claim of such a person in the ordinary courts, although in order to proceed with it that person would have to show a 'reasonable likelihood' that surveillance had occurred.[83] The remit of the new Tribunal under s65, discussed below, might not allow it to consider such a claim, unless it interprets its jurisdiction more widely.

Assuming that there was a reasonable likelihood that surveillance had occurred, a key question for the new Tribunal or court would be whether in the particular circumstances it fell within Article 8(1). The extent to which Article 8 provides protection from surveillance outside the home or other living accommodation might be considered. The limited regime of Part III of the Police Act reflects a perception that only certain places can be adjudged 'private' and that therefore a statutory regime is not necessary in respect of some forms of bugging device, especially where no interference with property is entailed. Its singling out of certain places and categories of information for special protection under s97 implied a failure to contemplate a broad test of a reasonable expectation of privacy.[84] Part II RIPA takes a similar stance but makes a somewhat more

[79] See *Doorson* v *Netherlands* (1996) 22 EHRR 330.

[80] *Van Mechelen* v *Netherlands* [1998] EHRLR 517, cf *Verdam* v *Netherlands* (1999) 28 EHRR CD 161.

[81] (1979) 2 EHRR 214.

[82] See Chapter 2 p50.

[83] *G, H and I* v *UK* 15 EHRR CD 41.

[84] It may be noted that in its 1998 Report Justice recommended a test of a reasonable expectation of privacy and considered that authorisation only from a senior police officer would be adequate where such an expectation was absent (Recommendation 2). This test, which is argued for below, is not adopted under the 2000 Act; 'directed surveillance'

sophisticated attempt to engage with a notion of degrees of privacy in creating distinctions between the three forms of surveillance. Under a crude distinction between public and private places – a distinction which appears to be implicit in both the 1997 and 2000 Acts – surveillance in public or semi-public places would fall outside Article 8.

The principles at stake are similar to those discussed in Chapter 9 in relation to interception: all these forms of surveillance interfere with informational autonomy. But while it is now clearly settled in the Strasbourg jurisprudence that in most circumstances interception (at least in the form of telephone tapping) creates an interference with Article 8 guarantees, this cannot be said with equal certainty of all the diverse forms of surveillance covered by Part II of the RIPA or Part III of the 1997 Act. In the context of Article 8 it has been said: 'The Court has not perceived the rights in Article 8 in wholly negative terms – the right to be left alone. Instead it has acknowledged that states must ensure . . . the effective enjoyment of liberty.'[85] This comment implies not only that the right to be left alone in a physical sense by state authorities is in the core of Article 8, but that more insidious methods of curtailing the enjoyment of liberty also infringe it. Effective enjoyment of liberty cannot occur when persons fear that they are under surveillance: 'The state [has an obligation] to respect private life by controlling the activities of its agents [in collecting personal information]'.[86] Chapter 8 indicated that interference with property for surveillance purposes by the security and intelligence services has been found to fall within Article 8.[87] Collection and use of information derived from covert investigative techniques may do so unless the applicant is already involved in criminal activity.[88] The acquiring of information represents one form of invasion of informational autonomy; further invasions may occur owing to the storage and dissemination of the information. In a number of cases Strasbourg has found that the collection of information about an individual by the state without his or her consent will, in principle, interfere with the right to respect for private life[89] and it has contemplated the possibility that compiling and retaining the information will also do so.[90] The use of listening devices has been found to create an interference with the Article 8(1) guarantee.[91] Systematic or even

or covert sources might gather information in circumstances in which there was such an expectation.

[85] Harris, O'Boyle and Warbrick p303.

[86] Ibid at p310.

[87] See p326.

[88] *Ludi* v *Switzerland* A 238 (1992).

[89] See *Murray* v *UK* A 300 paras 84, 85 (1994); *McVeigh* v *UK* 25 DR 15 at p49 (1981).

[90] See *G, H and I* v *UK* 15 EHRR CD41 (application of first and third applicants failed on the basis that they had not shown sufficient likelihood that such compiling or retention had occurred).

[91] See *Govell* v *UK* (1997) 4 EHRLR 438; *Khan* v *UK* App No 35394/97 (declared admissible 20 April 1999) (1999) 27 EHRR CD 58; judgment of the Court 12.5.00.

indirect targeting of an individual is also very likely to involve such an interference.[92]

The Strasbourg case-law suggests that where an interference occurs in a more obviously 'private' place, an infringement of the primary right will be found. The extent to which, outside such places, an invasion of privacy might be found in respect of surveillance is a matter which is subject to a developing jurisprudence at Strasbourg and nationally. An individual may expect to retain a degree of privacy in a semi-public environment, such as a restaurant,[93] gymnasium,[94] solicitor's office, pub, shop[95] or business premises.[96] Strasbourg has been prepared to extend the notion of private space beyond obvious places such as the home; as Harris, O'Boyle and Warbrick put it: 'it is not enough just for the individual to be himself: he must be able to a substantial degree to keep to himself what he is and what he does . . . the idea of private space need not be confined to those areas where the person has some exclusive rights of occupancy'.[97] In this respect the Strasbourg approach may be developing in a direction which will take it away from the current UK statutory approach: 'the expanding understanding of private life set out in the *Niemitz* case indicates that a formal public/private distinction about the nature of the location will not always be decisive'.[98] This identifiable general trend suggests that this is another instance in which the emphasis should be on the evolutive nature of the Convention[99] rather than on the outcome of particular applications to the Commission, such as that in *X* v *United Kingdom*.[100] The Commission found that the actions of the police in taking and filing photographs without consent of a woman arrested for taking part in a demonstration disclosed no *prima facie* breach of Article 8. The reasoning was unclear, but a central factor appeared to be the public and voluntary nature of her activities. The decision has been viewed as out of line with the trend of Article 8 jurisprudence: 'In the opinion of some scholars, the . . . decision

[92] *Harman and Hewitt* v *UK* (1991) 14 EHRR 657.

[93] A situation considered in a decision of the German Supreme Court: BGH 19 December 1995 BGHZ 131 pp322–346.

[94] The location where surreptitious photographs were taken of the former Princess of Wales, in *HRH Princess of Wales* v *MGN Newspapers Limited and Ors* [1993] Transcript, Association of Official Shorthandwriters Ltd, 8 November 1993.

[95] See *Dixons* case CA (unrep 20 May 2000).

[96] See note 98, below.

[97] *Law of the European Convention on Human Rights* p309.

[98] Harris, O'Boyle and Warbrick p309. *Niemitz* v *FRG* A 251-B (1992) concerned office premises, making it clear that rights to respect for privacy are not dependent on an interest in property.

[99] The Convention must be given an 'evolutive' interpretation (*Johnstone* v *Ireland* A 112 para 53 (1986)) which takes account of current standards in European society (*Tyrer* v *UK* A 26 para 31 (1978)). These would be expected to include the presence of privacy laws across Europe.

[100] (1973) Appl 5877/72 16 YBCHE 328.

may well be an outdated aberration in the case law of the Strasbourg organs'.[101]

The approach in other jurisdictions may indicate the direction in which the Strasbourg jurisprudence is likely to develop. The German Supreme Court[102] refused to follow the approach of the Appeal Court that privacy 'stopped at the doorstep' and that therefore no action lay for invasion of privacy in respect of events which had taken place outside the home or other clearly private spaces. The approach indicated was that one may still be entitled to respect for privacy in semi-public places if, as the court put it, it is clear by reference to 'objective criteria' that one wishes to be 'left alone' so that one can, 'relying on the fact of seclusion, act in a way that [one] would not have done . . . in public'. In other words, the interest in privacy was clearly distinguished from property interests. The Canadian Criminal Code also reflects such a stance.[103] Thus it may be argued that public/private distinctions based on location are too simplistic and that a test of a reasonable expectation of privacy or, more broadly still, of *control* of private information would be more satisfactory.[104] On the basis of such a test, if, for example, one person engages in a whispered exchange with another in an almost empty street, and this exchange is recorded by means of a listening device, it is contended that an invasion of privacy has occurred which may fall within Article 8(1). The main concern of this Chapter and the last is with the interception of communications and forms of aural rather than visual surveillance, but it may be noted in passing that this test might bring some use of CCTV within Article 8(1).[105]

As Lustgarten and Leigh observe: 'An atmosphere in which people practise self-censorship . . . is stultifying and fearful . . . Citizens should be

[101] L A Bygrave 'Data Protection Pursuant to the Right to Privacy in Human Rights Treaties' [1999] 6(3) IJLIT 247, 265. Bygrave notes: 'there are good grounds for holding that it ought to be accorded little weight in present and future interpretation of article 8'. In spite of these comments, however, Bygrave concedes that in the later decision of *Friedl* v *Austria* (1995) A 305B (not treated by the Court on the merits due to friendly settlement), 'the Commission laid weight upon the same . . . kind of factors as those mentioned in *X* v *United Kingdom*' (*ibid* at p266). See also *Stewart-Brady* v *UK* (1999) 27 EHRR 284 in which a claim of an interference with Article 8 rights due to the taking of a photograph was declared inadmissible (although these findings were made in the context of positive state obligations and there was a conflict with Article 10).

[102] BGH 19 December 1995 BGHZ 131 pp322–346.

[103] S487.01(4).

[104] The Press Complaints Commission's Code of Practice defines 'private places [as] public or private property where there is a reasonable expectation of privacy'. Such a test was recommended by the Irish Law Reform Commission: *Privacy, Surveillance and Interception* (1996) Consultation Paper.

[105] S163 of the Criminal Justice and Public Order Act 1994 clarifies the power of local authorities to install closed circuit cameras for surveillance purposes. See *R* v *Brentwood Council ex p Peck*, [1998] CMLR 697, now in the Strasbourg system. For further discussion see *Surveillance, CCTV and Social Control* C Norris, J Moran and G Armstrong (eds) (1999). It may be that the fact of capturing the image of a person on CCTV may not, in the circumstances, in itself constitute an invasion of privacy, but that the use of the information later on may do so. See further JUSTICE *Covert Surveillance* (1998) p31.

able to assume that unless there are overwhelming reasons to the contrary, their thoughts and feelings will be communicated only to those to whom they choose to utter them.'[106] These comments clearly apply equally to conversations in the street, in a vehicle, in pubs, in hotel rooms. Obviously there may be circumstances in which it is impossible to speak without expecting to be overheard, as in a crowded train. But in other circumstances this expectation would depend entirely on the circumstances. In a reasonably quiet street it would be viewed as socially and probably morally unacceptable to approach two persons speaking quietly together with the obvious intention of eaves-dropping on their conversation, since the two would have a reasonable expectation of enjoying a degree of privacy. It follows, therefore, that the issue as to whether the respect for private life has been infringed by the secret recording of a communication should be resolved not by reliance on fine distinctions regarding the degrees of 'privacy' to be associated with different locations, but according to the intentions and reasonable expectations of at least one of the parties to it.[107] In other words, a shift in the meaning of 'privacy' would have to occur, one which appears to be in accordance with the notion of informational autonomy as the core privacy value and with changing perception of privacy at Strasbourg. Therefore, there is a sound argument that the use of surveillance devices or covert sources in most circumstances may lead to findings that an interference with the primary right under Article 8 has occurred.

Once it is established that such an interference has occurred, it cannot be justified if it is not in accordance with the law. Until the 1997 Act and then the Regulation of Investigatory Powers Act 2000 Part II were introduced, the use of various techniques, including the use of informers or undercover agents, had no sufficient basis in law.[108] Such a basis is now established but it is questionable whether it is of sufficient quality.[109] The regimes governing the forms of surveillance show dissimilarities, especially between 'intrusive surveillance' and the other two forms. The position regarding the use of such surveillance is broadly the same as that discussed in Chapter 9, in relation to interception, under Part I, Chapter I of RIPA, since the provisions are equally foreseeable and accessible. The same may be said of the regime under s97 of the 1997 Act.[110]

[106] *In From the Cold* p40.

[107] This proposition finds support from the position in the USA. The US Supreme Court has found: 'the Fourth Amendment protects people not places'; the significant issue was not the location of the covert device, but the existence of a reasonable expectation that privacy would be protected (*Katz* v *US* 389 US 347, 351–353 (1967)).

[108] See above, note 4. See further *Under Surveillance: Covert Policing and Human Rights Standards* (1998) London: JUSTICE Chap 7.

[109] As indicated in Chapter 2, Article 8 may not be satisfied merely on the ground that interferences with privacy have a basis in primary legislation. See p25.

[110] In *Christie* v *UK* 78-A DR E Com HR 119 the Commission found that the Interception of Communications Act met the 'in accordance with the law' requirement of Article 8(2), taking into account a wide margin of appreciation allowed in relation to national security and economic well-being.

Bearing in mind the strictness of these requirements in this context, discussed in Chapter 9,[111] it is unclear that the requirement as to quality would be found to be satisfied in respect of certain of these provisions. This may be said in relation to the use of some directed surveillance, of listening devices within the 1997 Act, but outside s97, and in respect of some use of covert human sources. Similar points can be made about the use of undercover officers. As indicated above, ss28, 29 and 30 allow the Secretary of State, by order, to make provision regarding 'designated persons', further grounds, and for allowing further bodies to engage in directed surveillance or use covert sources, on the very broad grounds under ss28 and 29. The extent to which, in all these instances, power is placed in executive hands so that it might be exercised in an unpredictable fashion calls into question the quality of the law, even accepting that in some, but not all, of these instances there is a lesser invasion of privacy, calling for less precision.[112] The accessibility of the law would also be questionable, bearing in mind the opportunities for its extension by executive order, albeit with the approval of Parliament. In respect of all these provisions the means of keeping a check on their arbitrary use is in doubt owing to the failure to include any independent check at all on authorisations of directed surveillance and the use of covert human sources, outside the public authority in question.[113] No judicial or administrative check is necessary, in contrast to the provisions for intrusive surveillance and interception.

Assuming that an interference with the Article 8(1) guarantee occurs, which is found, in the particular circumstances which confront a court or the Tribunal to be in accordance with the law, it must be shown that it had a legitimate aim. The 'legitimate aim' requirement would probably be readily satisfied in respect of intrusive surveillance and under the 1997 Act since the grounds justifying interference under Article 8(2) correspond with the three grounds under s32(3) of the 2000 Act and with the 'serious crime' ground under the 1997 Act. There may be room for argument that certain of the grounds for the other two forms of surveillance within the 2000 Act, under s28(3) and s29(3), are less clearly within para 2 since they cover *inter alia* the purpose of collecting any contribution due to a government department. However, they would probably fall within the 'economic well being' exception.[114] The possibility is left open of including other grounds, by order of the Secretary of State. Any such further grounds would also have to fall within the para 2 aims. So far, under Article 8(2), the state has always satisfied the legitimate aim requirement.

[111] See pp365–6.
[112] This may be argued by analogy with the findings in *Malone* v *UK* 4 EHRR 330 regarding phone metering; see Chapter 9, p352.
[113] In *Leander* v *Sweden* (1987) 9 EHRR 433 the Court said 'in view of the risk that a system of secret surveillance poses . . . the court must be satisfied that there exist adequate and effective guarantees against abuse' (para 60).
[114] *MS* v *Sweden* (1999) 28 EHRR 313 para 38.

It must further be shown that the interference 'corresponds to a pressing social need and, in particular, that it is proportionate to the legitimate aim pursued'.[115] As explained in Chapter 2, the doctrine of proportionality is strongly linked to the principle of the margin of appreciation. In relation to the aim of national security the Court has allowed a very wide margin to the state[116] but it is less wide in relation to the prevention of crime and arguably also in respect of the other grounds. In any event the margin of appreciation should be irrelevant in domestic decisions. In terms of the outcomes of applications, Strasbourg has not provided clear guidance on the question of when a pressing social need would be discerned in this context.[117] But some analogous jurisprudence is available. As indicated above, it was found in *Klass* v *FRG*[118] that judicial or administrative authority for warrants would provide a degree of independent oversight. While the arrangements for intrusive surveillance under the 2000 Act or under s97 of the 1997 Act may meet this requirement, those under s93 or for directed surveillance and covert sources might fail to do so since no independent administrative or judicial check is available. The general principles espoused at Strasbourg may also be indicative. If it is accepted that informational autonomy lies in the 'core' of Article 8, as a value which a democratic society should respect,[119] interferences with it by a public authority should receive the strictest scrutiny. Such scrutiny would be of the arrangements for authorisation and their application in the particular instance. Even where the authorisation process itself was found to satisfy Article 8(2), a particular authorisation might be found to allow an interference disproportionate to the legitimate aim pursued. The use of tasked informers – those recruited and managed by police in order to provide information on suspected criminals – would not be viewed, depending on the circumstances, as analogous to the use of a participating informer – one who comes forward in order to volunteer information in the hope of gain. The two groups tend to raise very different issues of privacy. In relation to the first, especially where surveillance devices, such as 'wiring' the informer, are used, police officers (or other state agents) actively manage a prolonged invasion of privacy. Therefore it is questionable whether the same regime is appropriate in relation to both groups. Measures which might be found to be proportionate to the aim pursued might

[115] *Olsson* v *Sweden* A 130 para 67 (1988).

[116] *Leander* v *Sweden* (1987) 9 EHRR 433.

[117] As indicated in relation to the interception of communications, the key cases discussed in this book tend to divide into two groups: those in which the interference has no basis in law (*Malone* v *UK* (1985) 7 EHRR 14) and those in which the interference has such a basis and the safeguards available, particularly in the context of national security, are sufficient, taking the margin of appreciation into account (*Christie* v *UK* 78-A DR E Com HR 119). See further Chapter 8 p329.

[118] (1979) 2 EHRR 214.

[119] *Kjeldsen* v *Denmark* (1976) 1 EHRR 711, 731; see also the comments of the Court in *Socialist Party* v *Turkey* (1999) 27 EHRR 51, paras 41, 47, 50 as to the need for pluralism in a democracy.

be satisfactory in the one circumstance, but not the other. Issues of proportionality might also arise where a listening device placed outside a house provided information of only a marginally lower quality than would be provided were it on the premises.

The difficulty lies, as indicated above, in finding a means of affording expression to these principles. This ought to be the central role of the new Tribunal.

The new Tribunal

It may be noted initially that in practice applications to the Tribunal will not be frequent since, as noted above, an individual has normally no means of knowing that an interception or surveillance has occurred; in contrast to the position in Germany[120] or Denmark,[121] the police and the other state agencies have no duty to inform the individual of the interception, after it is over. This position is contrary to the recommendation of the Data Protection Working Party for the European Commission which said in May 1999 that a 'person under surveillance [should] be informed of this as soon as possible'.[122] An individual will therefore normally be able to bring complaints or proceedings to the new Tribunal only if he or she has become aware of the surveillance due to criminal proceedings. S17 will normally prevent this occurring in respect of interception. Police officers or other state agents who are aware that improperly authorised or unauthorised interception is occurring have no means of complaining to the new Tribunal or the Commissioners.[123] S4(3) of the Official Secrets Act 1989, as amended by the 2000 Act,[124] is also available to punish such disclosures. A further limitation is placed on complaints relating to interceptions. S67(5) provides that unless the Tribunal in the circumstances considers it 'equitable' to do so such complaints will not be considered if made more than one year after the conduct in question took place. Otherwise, conduct under s65(5) can be considered whenever it occurred. Thus, pre-commencement surveillance can be brought before the Tribunal.

Membership and jurisdiction

Schedule 3 governs the membership of the new Tribunal. Members, who are appointed for five years, by the Lord Chancellor on behalf of the

[120] See *Klass* v *Federal Republic of Germany* (1979) 2 EHRR 214. Germany's new 'bugging' law contains this requirement.

[121] Para 788 Criminal Procedure Code.

[122] See *Statewatch* (1999) Vol 9 Nos 3 and 4. The UK is the only member state to have entered a derogation to Principle 2(2) of the Council of Europe Recommendation on the use of data in the police sector R(87)15.

[123] Under s19(4) of the RIPA any such disclosure would be an offence punishable on indictment by a maximum term of five years' imprisonment: s19(4)(a).

[124] Schedule 4 para 5.

Queen,[125] must have held 'high judicial office' or have a 10-year general qualification within the meaning of s71 of the Courts and Legal Services Act 1990; in Scotland and Northern Ireland they must be practitioners of at least 10 years' standing. Thus they need not be judges, although the President must be a judge. The Schedule leaves open the questions whether the Tribunal will be a part-time body and whether it will have administrative officers.[126] Its members will be remunerated by the Secretary of State, but can be removed from office only on an address to the Queen by both Houses of Parliament under Schedule 3 para 1(5). These arrangements afford the Tribunal a measure of independence from the executive, which is considered below in the context of the Convention.

The jurisdiction of the new Tribunal is *prima facie* less circumscribed than that of the old one under the 1985 Act. It can consider surveillance as well as interceptions, and unlike the old Tribunal it can investigate complaints regarding interceptions outside the 'public telecommunications' system. The old Tribunal's remit, even in relation to persons complaining about a suspected tap of a phone within that system, was narrow since it could not consider unauthorised interceptions. Thus the new complaints' provisions address the anomaly that the subject of an unauthorised interception was in one sense in a worse position than the subject of an improperly authorised one.

Under s65(2) the new Tribunal will have three main functions and a potential fourth one. First, challenges to surveillance on Convention grounds by certain bodies or to interception by all bodies must be brought within it. In the words of the subsection: 'it will be the only appropriate tribunal for the purposes of section 7 of the Human Rights Act 1998 in relation to any proceedings under subsection (1)(a) of that section (proceedings for actions incompatible with Convention rights) which fall within subsection 3 of this section'. Under s65(3) they are proceedings against any of the intelligence services . . . or 'against any other person in respect of any conduct, or proposed conduct, by or on behalf of any of those services' . . . or 'relating to the taking place in any challengeable circumstances of any conduct falling within subsection (5)'. S65(5) applies to 'conduct . . . (whenever it occurred) by or on behalf of any of the intelligence services; in connection with the interception of communications in the course of their transmission by means of a postal service or telecommunication system'; conduct to which Chapter II of Part I or Part II applies; 'the giving of a notice under section 49[127] or any disclosure or use of a key to protected information; any entry on or interference with property or any interference with wireless telegraphy'. S65(6) introduces a significant limitation in providing: 'for the purposes only of subsection (3)', conduct to which Part II applies, an entry on or interference

[125] S65(1) and Schedule 3 para 5.
[126] Under para 5(1) officers may be appointed by the Secretary of State.
[127] A notice requiring disclosure of an email encryption code: see p344 above.

with property or an interference with wireless telegraphy is not conduct falling within subsection (5) 'unless it is conduct by or on behalf of a person holding any office, rank or position with (a) any of the intelligence services; (b) any of Her Majesty's forces; (c) any police force; (d) the National Criminal Intelligence Service; (e) the National Crime Squad; or (f) the Commissioners of Customs and Excise'. In other words, as indicated above, the intention is that surveillance by these bodies can be challenged only in the Tribunal where it is argued that they have breached a Convention right.

Second, the Tribunal is the appropriate forum for complaints if, under s65(4), 'it is a complaint by a person who is aggrieved by any conduct falling within subsection (5) which he believes to have taken place in relation to him, to any of his property, to any communications sent by or to him, or intended for him, or to his use of any postal service, telecommunications service or telecommunication system; and to have taken place in challengeable circumstances or to have been carried out by or on behalf of any of the intelligence services'. Ss65(7) and (8) apply in relation to both ss65(3) and (4). S65(7) defines 'challengeable circumstances' as conduct which '(a) takes place with the authority, or purported authority, of anything falling within subsection (8); or (b) the circumstances are such that (whether or not there is such authority) it would not have been appropriate for the conduct to take place without it, or at least without proper consideration having been given to whether such authority should be sought'. Thus, in its complaints, and 'proceedings' jurisdiction the Tribunal can consider unauthorised interception. In relation to complaints the term used under s67(3)(b) is 'investigate the authority' which does not appear to confine the Tribunal, bearing in mind the meaning of 'challengeable circumstances', to merely considering whether the authority (if it exists) was properly given. S65(8) covers: interception warrants under the Acts of 1985 or 2000, an authorisation or notice under Chapter II, Part I or an authorisation under Part II of the 2000 Act, a permission of the Secretary of State under Schedule 2 (relating to powers to obtain data protected by encryption), a s49 notice given with such a permission, or an authorisation under s93 of the Police Act 1997.

Third, the Tribunal has jurisdiction (s65(2)(c)) to determine a reference to it by a person that he or she has suffered detriment as a consequence 'of any prohibition or restriction' under s17 (the exclusion of evidence section) on his or her relying on any matter in, or for the purposes of, civil proceedings. It is notable that no means is provided of seeking redress for detriment arising when evidence is excluded in *criminal* proceedings.[128] Finally, under s65(2)(d) the Secretary of State can also, by order, allocate other proceedings to the Tribunal but a draft of

[128] See *R* v *Preston* [1993] 4 All ER 638 (above, Chap 9 p360) in which the appellants probably suffered detriment due to the exclusion of evidence derived from phone tapping under the predecessor of s17, s9 of the 1985 Act.

the order must have been approved by a resolution of each House of Parliament.[129]

Procedure

The new Tribunal has, in appearance, a court-like function as well as being a mechanism for hearing complaints. It is modelled on the Special Immigration Appeals Commission (SIAC)[130] which in turn provided the model for the new Tribunal set up under the Northern Ireland Act 1998.[131] Its jurisdiction, as regards 'proceedings', may be exercised in a more adversarial fashion than its complaints' jurisdiction although this will depend on its own interpretation of its role. Possibly it was thought that a complaints jurisdiction only might not satisfy the HRA and Convention, bearing in mind the lack of access to a court under the RIPA (see below), although it is arguable that at present the provision of a Tribunal on this model exceeds the Convention requirements.[132] The procedure for determining 'proceedings' may be the same as that for hearing complaints;[133] until the nature of those proceedings becomes clear it will not be possible to judge whether much has been gained in terms of protection for the individual. Since the new Tribunal is, in appearance, more like a court, it may more readily engage Article 6, whereas the old Tribunal procedure might not have done so. In other words, it may satisfy Article 6 requirements as to access to a court and may go beyond what is currently required in this particular context. But this means that if Article 6 is engaged, its procedural requirements must be met. The implications of this possibility are discussed below.

The old Tribunal sat in secret and the complainant had no right to be present or to have a legal representative present. It is unclear whether the new Tribunal will follow these practices since the manner in which it exercises its jurisdiction is to be determined, under s69, by rules made by the Secretary of State (subject to the Parliamentary resolution procedure). These rules may 'prescribe the forms of hearing or consideration to be adopted by the Tribunal in relation to particular proceedings, complaints or references (including a form that requires any proceedings brought before the Tribunal to be disposed of as if they were a complaint or

[129] S66(3).

[130] Set up under s1 of the Special Immigration Appeals Act 1997 in response to the findings in *Chahal* v *UK* (1997) 23 EHRR 413.

[131] Under s90. See also Chapter 3 pp94–5.

[132] At present it cannot be said that the Convention requires access to a tribunal or court in respect of grievances caused by surveillance so long as the aggregate of remedies can be viewed as effective: *Leander* v *Sweden* (1987) 9 EHRR 433. On the other hand since in respect of interceptions, the right of access to a court is so impaired, by s17 RIPA, Article 6 might have been found in future to be infringed: see *Tinnelly* v *UK* (1999) 27 EHRR 249.

[133] See s69(2)(f).

reference made to the Tribunal), prescribe the practice . . . to be followed . . . (including, where applicable, the mode and burden of proof and the admissibility of evidence)'. They may also allow for hearings in 'the absence of any person (including the person bringing the proceedings or making the complaint or reference and any legal representative of his)'. No provision is expressly made for security clearance for Counsel on the model provided by the SIAC. It appears possible that the determinations of the new Tribunal will be as secretive as those of the old and the position of the complainant equally weak. The difficulty with Tribunals of this nature is that they may seek to give the appearance of adversarial proceedings, but the limitations under which they operate, which limit the opportunities of the defence to challenge evidence, tend to detract from the benefits of such proceedings.[134]

In its 'proceedings' under s65(2)(a), and in considering complaints under s65(2)(b),[135] uses 'the principles applicable by a court on an application for judicial review'. Under the HRA it should therefore apply the principles a court, bound by s6 HRA, would apply on such an application. It follows that the proportionality requirements under RIPA should be strictly scrutinised. The problem is, as Chapter 2 indicated, that the procedure may be unsuitable as a means of conducting such scrutiny owing to its inefficacy in a fact-finding role.[136] The new Tribunal, like the old one, will merely report its conclusion; it cannot report the reason for the decision.[137] If it finds that no warrant or authorisation exists and that apparently no surveillance or interception is occurring, or that proper authorisation occurred, it will merely inform the complainant that the complaint has not been upheld. The complainant who suspects, for example, that his or her phone or emails are being tapped is then left not knowing whether in fact tapping is occurring. But if the complaint is upheld he or she will know that tapping was occurring but unauthorised. This is, at least theoretically, an improvement on the old position since the fact that a complaint was not upheld could mean that unauthorised tapping was occurring. For example, on 6 December 1991 Alison Halford complained to the Interception of Communications Tribunal in respect of the suspected tapping of her home and office telephones.[138] From the circumstances it appeared that tapping was probably occurring. She was informed on 21 February 1992, without any reason given, that the complaint had not been upheld: no contravention of ss2–5 of the Act had

[134] See Chapter 3 pp94–5; C Walker *The Prevention of Terrorism* (1986) p82; he advocates an inquisitorial system for such Tribunals; see also C White [1999] PL at p413, discussing the new Tribunal set up under the Northern Ireland Act 1998.

[135] S67(2) and S67(3)(c), respectively.

[136] P54. See Leigh and Lustgarten 'Making Rights Real: The Courts, Remedies and the Human Rights Act' [1999] CLJ 509.

[137] S68(4) of the 2000 Act. This matter was covered by s7(4)(1) and Schedule 1 para 4(2) of the 1985 Act.

[138] See the facts of the case in the European Court of Human Rights, below.

been found. The Tribunal later confirmed by letter that it could not specify whether any interception had in fact taken place. She was left in ignorance as to whether an intercept had indeed been authorised, whether one was in place, although unauthorised, or whether no interception was occurring.[139] Had it been authorised it is inconceivable, bearing in mind the circumstances, for it to have been authorised properly.

The remedial powers of the new Tribunal will be similar to those of the old.[140] Under s67(7), 'the Tribunal . . . shall have power to make any such award of compensation or other order as they think fit; [subject to the power of the Secretary of State to make rules under section 69] and . . . may make an order quashing or cancelling any warrant or authorisation; and an order requiring the destruction of any records of information which has been obtained in exercise of any power conferred by a warrant or authorisation; or is held by any public authority in relation to any person' (subject to s69 orders). Thus the award of remedies continues to be discretionary; the successful complainant or applicant could be left remediless. The Tribunal will not have the power to make a declaration of incompatibility. If the new Tribunal finds in favour of an applicant, a report would not automatically go to the Prime Minister under s68(5); it would do so only *if* the Secretary of State bore some responsibility in the matter.

Recourse to the courts from the Tribunal

At present the RIPA seeks to make it impossible for a member of the public who is dissatisfied with the outcome of the Tribunal procedure to seek a remedy in the courts. The Act, like the 1985, 1989, 1994 and 1997 Acts, contains a post-*Anisminic* ouster clause. S67(8) provides: 'Except to such extent as the Secretary of State may by order otherwise provide, determinations, awards, orders and other decisions of the Tribunal

[139] Lord Nolan, the current Commissioner, has defended the failure to inform complainants as to whether an intercept has occurred on this basis: 'If the tribunal were able to tell a complainant that he or she had not been the subject of legitimate interception, silence or any equivocal answer on another occasion might be interpreted as an implication that interception had taken place. Furthermore a positive answer would allow criminals or terrorists to know whether they were subject to interception or not' (Report of the Commissioner under the Interception of Communications Act 1998 published June 1999 Cm 4364, at p2 para 13 and p11). One answer to this might be that if, out of 568 complaints made up until 1997, only 8 interceptions were in fact occurring, not many positive answers would have to be given. Criminals who took evasive action for fear of interception would usually merely be taking extra precautions. Currently, the secrecy of the procedure, and the fact that a failure to uphold a complaint does not mean that no interception is occurring, means that someone with something to hide, who suspected interception, would be likely to take evasive action in any event. In other words, the secrecy under the 1985 and 2000 schemes may be counter-productive. Over-estimation of the extent of interception might well mean that a criminal whose communications were not being intercepted might take evasive action, which would defeat the purpose of interception if it was subsequently put in place.

[140] Under s7(5) of the 1985 Act the Tribunal could order quashing of the warrant, destruction of material obtained and payment of compensation to the victim.

(including decisions as to whether they have jurisdiction) shall not be subject to appeal or be liable to be questioned in any court'. This leaves open the possibility that a Tribunal or other body might be established to hear appeals.[141] Under s67(9) the Secretary of State is under a *duty* to establish such a body to hear appeals relating to the exercise of the Tribunal's jurisdiction under s65(2)(c) or (d), but not, significantly, in relation to the broader and much more important jurisdiction under s65(2)(a) or (b). The upshot is, at present, that the citizen who wishes to challenge a finding as to interception rather than surveillance outside the Tribunal must surmount two barriers as indicated in Chapter 9. A citizen seeking to challenge a Tribunal decision in respect of surveillance would not be affected by s17 but would have to circumvent s67(8).

Under s3 HRA it is conceivable that s67(8) could be interpreted in an application for leave under Order 53[142] in accordance with the Convention in such a way as to allow review. The argument for seeking to circumvent s67(8) would depend upon the extent to which the Tribunal appeared to meet Convention requirements, considered below. The courts have not so far circumvented such post-*Anisminic*[143] clauses. It could be argued that the wording of s67(8) cannot be intended to be taken literally. If it was to be so taken a Tribunal which decided that it had jurisdiction to determine egg quotas would be able legally to do so. Therefore there must be some ambiguity in the words, since it must be possible to depart somewhat from their literal meaning. This helps to allow s3 HRA to bite. In seeking to fulfil its duty under s6 HRA, a court might be prepared to read into s67(8) after 'court' the words 'unless in the circumstances Article 6 would not be satisfied' or 'an effective remedy would be unlikely thereby to be assured'.[144] The possibility of thus considering Article 13 is open owing to the *Pepper* v *Hart* statement of the Lord Chancellor to the effect that although it was omitted from the rights protected by the HRA, the courts and other public authorities may be able to view acceptance of the need to allow an effective remedy under Article 13 as an aspect of the intention behind the Act.[145] Or, the courts could rely on *Anisminic* itself in seeking to satisfy s6 HRA, in that since the word 'decision' is used in relation to Tribunal findings themselves, and in relation to its jurisdiction, the argument is open that any decision tainted by an error of law is a nullity; and therefore the ouster clause cannot bite on it.

[141] S67(8) by an Order of the Secretary of State.

[142] Of the Rules of the Supreme Court Act 1981 s31.

[143] In *Anisminic* v *Foreign Compensation Commission* [1969] 2 AC 147 the House of Lords refused to accept that the jurisdiction of the courts was entirely ousted on the basis that the Commission had acted outside its powers. Therefore it had not made a determination; it had made a purported determination – that is, a nullity. The ouster clause under the RIPA seeks to avoid this possibility since it provides that the jurisdiction of the Tribunal cannot be questioned in any court.

[144] This would clearly be an activist approach: see Chapter 2 pp37–39 and 43.

[145] See Hansard HL 18 November 1997 col 477, Hansard HC 20 May 1998 col 980.

Since the Tribunal can determine its own jurisdiction under s67(8) and it is bound by s6 HRA, argument could also be raised before it that, at least in respect of the circumstances of certain claims, it does not provide a fair hearing under Article 6, due *inter alia* to Orders made under s69, and that therefore its duty under s6 requires it to declare that its jurisdiction does not cover such claims. If the Tribunal is unreceptive to such claims, which is, of course, likely, they may eventually have to be raised at Strasbourg.

Convention rights

The Tribunal is bound by all the rights, including Article 6, under s6 HRA, but Article 6 will apply only if the Tribunal hearings are within its field of application. The issue as to the compliance of the old Tribunals (under the 1985, 1989 and 1994 Acts) with Article 6 was not raised in the Strasbourg cases considered in Chapters 8 and 9, presumably because it was thought that its guarantees did not apply. The proceedings or determination of complaints or references of the new Tribunal might be viewed as the 'determination of civil rights and obligations' under Article 6(1). The term 'civil' has, however, been taken to mean that these are rights in private rather than public law,[146] although a clear distinction between rights in private as opposed to public law is not apparent in its recent jurisprudence: 'Recent jurisprudence by which more and more rights and obligations have been brought within Article 6, is not easy to explain in terms of any distinction between private and public law which is found in European national law'.[147] In its proceedings it will be likely to enquire into breaches of Article 8, which represents a right binding on public authorities, including the agencies, under s6 HRA. At Strasbourg that in itself would not be sufficient to engage Article 6, while domestically, the guarantees may be viewed as operating in public law only, in which case Article 6 would not apply. On the other hand, certain of the rights claimed are private law rights since where authorisation is not given existing tortious liability may arise.[148] But other claims only concern 'rights' in the sense that Article 8 has been breached and it is binding against public authorities. The role of the Tribunal under s7(1)(a) HRA as providing a remedy against public authorities suggests, as a matter of domestic law, that it need not satisfy Article 6, as does the fact that under s67 it must apply the principles applied by a court on an application for judicial review in relation to that role. These factors suggest that it cannot be viewed as determining private rights, depending on the sense in which such rights are viewed as 'private'.[149] The term 'civil', however, has

[146] *Ringeisen* v *Austria* A 13 para 94 (1971).
[147] Harris, O'Boyle and Warbrick (1995) at pp174–175.
[148] See *Golder* v *UK* A 18 (1975).
[149] See Chapter 2 for discussion of the public law/private law issues; p53.

an autonomous Convention meaning and therefore cannot merely be assigned the meaning of 'private' as understood in UK administrative law. Whether a breach of the RIPA, which gives rise to liability only under Article 8, could be viewed as a matter of private law is debatable, although Strasbourg may be moving towards a position in which 'all those rights which are individual rights under the national legal system and fall into the sphere of general freedom . . . must be seen as civil rights'.[150] Where it could be argued that breach of the RIPA did *not* give rise to liability under Article 8,[151] which may be the case in relation to some use of covert human sources, this question would be even more problematic.[152]

In this respect a distinction may need to be drawn between the Tribunal's 'proceedings', complaints and reference jurisdiction, the first perhaps being most likely to engage Article 6, bearing in mind the likelihood that the complaints jurisdiction of the old Tribunal fell outside Article 6. However, it could also be argued that in relation to both complaints or 'proceedings' there is a dispute between state and applicant. Its reference jurisdiction relates to civil proceedings and therefore may also be viewed as a dispute regarding a civil right. In *Tinnelly* v *UK*[153] the Court found that a clearly defined statutory right aimed at freedom from discrimination should be viewed as a civil right. Under the RIPA public authorities must satisfy the statute before using surveillance, in a manner that answers to the Article 8 rights of those under surveillance. In this sense Article 6 may apply, although the point cannot be regarded as settled. The better view is, it is contended, that the Tribunal is bound by Article 6, at least in relation to its 'proceedings' and reference jurisdiction, in which it is acting in a more judicial manner. It has potentially a pivotal role in upholding Convention rights in the face of the most significant assertions of state power. It would therefore be contrary to its role, as indicated under the RIPA, to find that it itself was not bound by the key due process guarantee. From a domestic standpoint it would be anomalous in the extreme if it were not so bound, bearing in mind its role in satisfying s7(1)(a) HRA in respect of the obligations of a wide range of bodies, including, in particular, the police, under the RIPA. (Whether it falls within Article 6 will be a matter which, initially, will be raised before the Tribunal itself. If it considers that it is adjudicating on a public law matter, and is therefore outside Article 6, the matter will no doubt be raised at Strasbourg eventually.)

Assuming that the Tribunal is covered by Article 6(1) or, under the development of the Strasbourg jurisprudence, may be found more clearly

[150] *Bentham* v *UK* B 80 para 10 (1983), dissenting opinions of Mr Melchior and Mr Frowen.

[151] See above, pp395–398, for discussion as to invasions of privacy which are likely to engage Article 8.

[152] But see *Fayed* v *UK* (1994) 18 EHRR 393 in which it was found that although, strictly speaking, there was no legal basis for the action and so no dispute to trigger Article 6, Article 6 applied to blanket immunities preventing access to a court.

[153] (1999) 27 EHRR 249.

to be so covered in future, it is hard to see that it is likely to provide a fair hearing for the applicant, bearing in mind the procedure it may follow, indicated above, since the complainant or applicant may be in such a weak position before it. As Chapter 5 indicated, since Art 6(3) contains *minimum* guarantees the para 1 protection of a fair hearing goes beyond para 3.[154] In investigating a fair hearing the domestic authorities are not confined to the para 3 guarantees; they can consider further requirements of fairness. If consideration is given to the procedures in question it is apparent that, apart from any of the other requirements of fairness, the minimal safeguards of Article 6(3) may not be satisfied, depending on the nature of the Orders regarding its procedure issued by the Secretary of State. In particular, as indicated above, the power to make rules limiting or preventing cross-examination, or excluding the applicant[155] or his or her legal representative, or limiting disclosure of evidence may not comply with Articles 6(1) or (3).[156] Clearly, the applicant or his or her legal representative could seek to raise argument before the Tribunal that it must, as a public authority, seek to comply with Article 6 in so far as it has leeway to do so under the Orders in question. The Tribunal will apply the principles of judicial review in its adjudications, which will include considering proportionality, since it is bound by s6 HRA, and Article 8(2) requires such consideration. The problem will be, as Chapter 2 indicated, that in order to consider proportionality the Tribunal may need to evaluate a number of factual matters. But it may be bound, as indicated, by subordinate legislation and may have no discretion as to requiring cross-examination or disclosure of documents. Thus, the procedural limitations under which it will be likely to operate may place even greater difficulties in its path in considering issues of proportionality than there would be in an ordinary court, in judicial review proceedings. If it therefore operated a very 'light touch' review, based in effect on *Wednesbury* unreasonableness, it would fail to satisfy the demands of Article 13, as recently interpreted at Strasbourg,[157] and therefore *a fortiori* it would not satisfy Article 6.

Following *Tinnelly*, if it is argued that documents or sources cannot be disclosed on grounds of national security or the prevention of crime, under Article 8(2), the applicant could argue that the Article 6 requirements override such a claim. The success of such an argument would

[154] See pp184–185.

[155] See, on this point, *Zana* v *Turkey* (1999) 27 EHRR 667, in which, in the context of terrorism, the applicant was not allowed to be present at the trial; a breach of Article 6 was found on this basis.

[156] See further Chapter 5 p207.

[157] *Smith and Grady* v *UK* (2000) 29 EHRR 493. The domestic court found that the continuance of the ban on homosexuals in the armed forces was not beyond the range of responses which was open to a reasonable decision-maker. The Strasbourg Court considered that the threshold at which the domestic court could find the policy irrational was set so high that it effectively precluded consideration of the proportionality of the ban with the aim in view. Therefore judicial review was not found to satisfy the requirements of Article 13.

depend upon the particular circumstances of a claim and in particular the ground under the RIPA in question since, as the Court found in *Tinnelly*, proportionality should be found between the infringement of the rights of the claimant and the aim in question. Where the aim concerns, for example, one of the 'economic' grounds founding directed surveillance or covert human sources under the RIPA the claim of the state would be less pressing and the question of proportionality should be more intensively scrutinised. If this was impossible owing to the procedural constraints, the applicant could claim that the Tribunal should consider whether its duty under s6 HRA requires it to disapply the subordinate legislation in question, and conduct, in such circumstances, a more intensive inquiry. This possibility would be open to it since s6(2)(b) HRA does not apply in respect of subordinate legislation, while it cannot be said that s69 RIPA, which only provides that the Secretary of State *may* make the Orders in question, *requires* the Tribunal to depart from Article 6. In this context the impartiality and independence requirements of Article 6(1) could also be considered. It is suggested that the appointments procedure for the Tribunal probably complies with the Article 6 requirements in these respects,[158] but that it is debatable whether this is the case in relation to the possibilities provided for under the Act for executive instruction as to the procedure.[159] These considerations would fuel the argument for disapplication of the Orders in question.

In respect of the national security ground under the RIPA, the Tribunal may take the view that it cannot consider the documents in question or other relevant matters in order to make a finding as to proportionality. In *Balfour* v *Foreign and Commonwealth Office*[160] the court found that once an actual or potential risk to national security had been demonstrated by a public interest immunity certificate, the court should not exercise its right to inspect the documents. This view of national security as the exclusive domain of the executive was not adhered to in the robust approach taken to the concept in the context of deportation by the Special Immigration Appeals Commission (on which the new Tribunal is partially modelled) in the case of *Shafiq ur Rehman*.[161] However, the Court of Appeal overturned its ruling, finding that the threat to national security was for the government to determine and that it should be broadly defined to include the possibility of future threats, including those to the UK's 'allies'.[162]

158 See *Campbell and Fell* v *UK* A 80 (1984). Whether this view would be taken in this context would depend on the view taken of the role of the Lord Chancellor – whether he could be viewed as sufficiently independent of the executive.

159 *Sramek* v *Austria* A 84 (1984). One of the central questions, which cannot yet be answered, will be the practice adopted: *Campbell and Fell* v *UK* A 80 (1984). See also the findings on impartiality in the context of military discipline – *Findlay* v *UK* (1997) 24 EHRR 221; *Hood* v *UK* judgment of 25 February 1997.

160 [1994] 2 All ER 588.

161 (1999) unreported.

162 See News Reports 24 May 2000.

These findings are not fully in accordance with the findings of the Strasbourg Court in *Tinnelly* or in *Chahal* v *UK*.[163] Both, particularly *Tinnelly*, took the view that the threat to national security should be demonstrated. Where Article 13, as opposed to Article 6, was in question, as in *Chahal*, the requirements thereby placed on the state would be weaker since Article 13 must be read with Article 8(2).[164] But where Article 6 is engaged, as indicated, the requirements would be stricter. The Tribunal may be placed in the difficult position of choosing between the domestic and the Strasbourg jurisprudence as to the stance it should take in respect of assertions of national security considerations. If so, the way would be open, under s3 HRA, to depart from the former.

As indicated above, it could also be argued before the Tribunal (or, if necessary, at Strasbourg) that it ought to provide an effective remedy under Article 13. It should play a part in providing an aggregate of remedies which, combined, would provide such a remedy[165] but the other potential remedies, such as raising complaints with an MP, are too ineffective to make much contribution. In *Harman and Hewitt* v *UK*[166] a breach of Article 13 was found on the basis of the lack of an effective remedy. The 1989 Act was precisely intended to address this failure by creating the oversight mechanisms. In *Christie* v *UK*,[167] the Commission avoided the question whether the Interception of Communications Tribunal had provided an effective remedy since it found that the applicant did not have an 'arguable case' and that therefore Article 13 was inapplicable.[168] However, it found that it did provide such a remedy 'in principle'.[169] Judicial review proceedings have been found at Strasbourg to satisfy Article 13,[170] although, as indicated above, they may no longer do so. The Tribunal's inability to give reasons or to take a binding decision may not render it ineffective.[171] In *Govell* v *UK*,[172] the use of a bugging device was the subject of an unsuccessful police complaint. The Commission found that the police investigative system did not meet the requisite standards of independence under Article 13 since *inter alia* the Home Secretary appointed and remunerated members of the Police Complaints

163 (1997) 23 EHRR 413 (in the context of Article 13).

164 *Leander* v *Sweden* (1987) 9 EHRR 433.

165 Ibid.

166 Appl 121175/86; (1989) 14 EHRR 657.

167 Also, in *Christie* v *UK* 78-A DR E Com HR 119 the Commission found that the Interception of Communications Act 1985, the model for the 1989 and 1994 Acts, met the 'in accordance with the law' requirement of Article 8(2).

168 Similarly, in *Halford* v *UK*, in respect of alleged tapping of the applicant's home phone, which was within the 1985 Act, the Court avoided this question in relation to the old Tribunal since it found that the applicant did not have an 'arguable case' and that therefore Article 13 was inapplicable.

169 See also *Esbester* v *UK* (1993) 1860/91; affirmed in *Mathews* v *UK* (1997) EHRLR 187.

170 *Soering* v *UK* A 161 (1989). See also *Esbester* v *UK* 18 EHRR CD 72, on this point. Cf *Smith and Grady* v *UK* (note 157, above).

171 *Esbester* v *UK* 18 EHRR CD 72.

172 (1997) 4 EHRLR 438.

Authority and had a guiding role in determining the withdrawal of charges. In *Chahal* v *UK* the Advisory Panel on deportation decisions was not found to satisfy Article 13 since it failed to offer sufficient safeguards for Article 13 purposes. The Court said that the remedy offered should be 'as effective as it can be' given the need, in the context in question, to rely on secret sources. In relation to the new Tribunal it might be argued that the Orders made by the Secretary of State may reduce its efficacy to the point where it no longer satisfies Article 13. While the Tribunal's adjudications may appear adversarial in a superficial sense, the position of the applicant may be so weakened by the procedural limitations under which it operates that it cannot be said to be effective. The role of the Home Secretary in relation to remuneration would also be relevant. The point at which independence would be said to be lost is not at present fully settled in the Strasbourg jurisprudence.

Unless a means of appeal from the Tribunal is created in relation to its jurisdiction under s65(2)(a) there will be no clear independent domestic means of determining whether the Tribunal offers an effective remedy and whether it should abide by Article 6. Article 6 does not require that a court to which to appeal should be available. But it could be argued that Article 6 itself requires that the question of its own field of application should be able to be raised before an independent body.[173] While the Strasbourg jurisprudence would probably not support such an argument at present, it could be argued – somewhat less boldly – that Article 6 requires that the question whether a particular body provides an effective remedy under Article 13 should be able to be raised before an independent body and not merely in the disputed body itself. In principle this is a strong argument, bearing in mind the fact that the new Tribunal will be, in most circumstances arising under the RIPA, the only forum in which citizens will be able to raise the issue of violation of Article 8 rights. The mere fact that a body termed a 'Tribunal' has been created should not obscure the possibility that it may have a merely cosmetic effect. Had a body been created which appeared to have even less credibility, such as a Panel of Advisers or Commission, or a body required to accept National Security certificates, the guarantee under Article 6 of access to a court[174] or, under Article 13, of providing an effective remedy, might have been found at Strasbourg to have been violated[175] and the domestic expectation would have been that this would eventually be the case. But the formal appearance of the new Tribunal may be belied by the nature of its proceedings which may mean that, substantively, it is as ineffective as such bodies would have been.

[173] See Van Dijk and Van Hoof *Theory and Practice of the European Convention on Human Rights* 3rd edn (1998).

[174] Such a guarantee has been implied into Article 6(1): see *Omar* v *France* (2000) 29 EHRR 210.

[175] As in *Tinnelly* (1999) 27 EHRR 249 and *Chahal* (1997) 23 EHRR 413 respectively.

Conclusions

The central value which is revealed by consideration of both the old and the new surveillance arrangements is secrecy, in the protection of state interests. The value of individual privacy is consistently and readily overcome, at almost every point in the arrangements at which a choice was made. The HRA had aroused the expectation, not only that a new comprehensive statutory basis would be introduced, but that it would be underpinned by Convention principles.[176] While the introduction of such a basis is clearly a significant step forward in terms of protection of individual rights, there is little feeling that the provisions are nuanced in such a way as to recognise such principles where the stated aims of the legislation are less at stake. The complaint of Alison Halford to the Interception of Communications Tribunal provides a salutary example which could recur under the new scheme, notwithstanding the broader statutory basis it provides for interception. The justification for failing to specify whether an interception had in fact taken place takes no account at all of the invasion of privacy suffered by figures, such as Halford, who are left with no means of knowing whether interception had occurred or was occurring. When, in the circumstances, the justification for the level of secrecy is weak it can nevertheless warrant profound damage to individual privacy.

Further striking examples of the failure of the new scheme to adopt a graduated approach are found in ss65(2) and 17 of the 2000 Act, which afford a disproportionate value to secrecy while treating rights to respect for privacy and to a fair trial with something very like contempt. The ouster clause in s67(8) reflects a similar approach. Apart from the possibility that the Secretary of State might provide otherwise, in unspecified circumstances,[177] little attempt is made to adopt a principled approach to the Tribunal procedure, one allowing final recourse to a court under certain circumstances and with, if necessary, appropriate safeguards such as hearing some evidence in camera. The presence of these provisions creates a scheme which seeks to rule out consideration of the interception of communications and of much surveillance in the ordinary courts. Indeed, probably the most striking feature of the new Act is the determination evinced under it to prevent citizens invoking Convention rights in the ordinary courts against state bodies in respect of the profound threat to privacy represented by state surveillance. The development of Convention jurisprudence in the ordinary courts in relation to such techniques has largely been prevented, before it had a chance to begin. Antinomy is therefore revealed, it is contended, between the values underlying the RIPA and those underlying the HRA, despite their introduction by the same government.

[176] This was the expectation of the JUSTICE Report (1998), see note 108 above.
[177] S67(8).

A comparison between the Acts of 1985 and 2000 is perhaps indicative of the nature of the current era. The 1985 Act revealed itself, at first glance, as a naked assertion of state power, which paid only the most cursory attention to the value of privacy. At the same time it created an inefficient, non-comprehensive scheme, leaving open many unregulated loopholes for potential future exploration in the courts or at Strasbourg. In contrast, the 2000 Act takes a more open, rights-conscious approach in providing far more comprehensive provisions. At the same time it is far more complex, almost a caricature of tortuous drafting. But its determination to protect state power is not only equally, if not immediately, evident; it is more insidious, since despite its length and reach, the scheme is riddled with avenues to the broadening of such power, to be explored by the executive outside the full Parliamentary process.

The democratic values enshrined in the Convention demand that citizens in the democracy should be able to feel confident that secret surveillance by the state is undertaken for appropriate ends, by proportionate means and with respect for privacy. The RIPA pays lip-service to proportionality while largely emasculating methods of scrutinising it. It is apparent that a statutory scheme which hides the operations it empowers largely from scrutiny, and which, for the most part, places power in the hands of the executive, while shrouding the citizen's complaints' mechanisms in secrecy, fails to reflect those democratic values. In the current climate of openness and accountability more secrecy militates against confidence rather than, as was assumed under the old tradition, bolstering it. It is possible that the assertions of the Interception of Communications Commissioner and the government to the effect that propriety and respect for individual privacy is observed in state surveillance are factually correct, but the available means of verification are unlikely to be capable of convincing the public that this is the case.

It might have been expected that in introducing a new and comprehensive surveillance statute, the New Labour government would have discarded the old model used for the 1985 and 1997 Acts, and adopted instead a model reflecting rule of law principles which would have been in harmony with the values underlying its proposed FoI legislation and the HRA. In particular, the very meagre level of Parliamentary oversight evident in the current state surveillance schemes required reconsideration with such principles in mind. Had these expectations been realised it would have been possible to view the legislative scheme underpinning state surveillance as consonant with the central aim of the Convention, the promotion of democratic values.[178] The new Act has, however, largely taken the old statutory model as a basis, creating a scheme which is

[178] *Kjeldsen* v *Denmark* (1976) 1 EHRR 711, 731; see also the comments of the Court in *Socialist Party* v *Turkey* (1998) Case 20/1997/804/1007 (1999) 27 EHRR 51 as to the need for pluralism in a democracy.

incapable of affording full recognition to such values, including respect for the core privacy value of informational autonomy. The hallmark of the new scheme is its tendency to insulate itself from the infusion of Convention values applied in the ordinary courts, thereby perpetuating the failures to protect privacy endemic under the previous one, which the HRA might have addressed. Having taken a form which reflects a minimal version of the Convention, the new scheme has then sought to stifle its own future development under a more dynamic and protective interpretation.

Chapter 11

Conclusions

This book was written at the beginning of the post-HRA era. Therefore any conclusions must be provisional, as must comments on the civil liberties record of New Labour. Nevertheless, themes and trends can be identified since the New Labour years have already seen a revolution in civil liberties terms. The HRA was introduced and then followed by the creation of the most extensive statutory framework for coercive uses of state power ever put in place in such a short period of time by a UK government. It was necessary to have that framework in place since otherwise certain coercive uses of state powers would not have been in accordance with the law under the Convention. A central theme of this book has concerned the interaction between the new framework and the Convention under the HRA. It should now be clear that the new scheme constitutes at one and the same time a response to the Convention and, potentially, a means of undermining it since, in a number of respects, the scheme impedes reliance on its guarantees, both formally and substantively. It has been argued that although the HRA indicates adherence to liberal principles, they fail to find expression in the new scheme. While the rights to respect for privacy, to a fair trial, to liberty of the person and to the freedoms of expression, association and assembly are afforded domestic protection under the HRA, the new scheme undermines them to such an extent that they are likely to become illusory or largely ineffective in a number of the contexts it covers. The counter-terrorist provisions in particular fail to afford expression to the Dworkinian notion of using rights in order to safeguard minorities from majoritarian intolerance.

Central themes

The HRA provides the impetus for Constitutional change based on the Convention principles of legality, necessity, proportionality, recognised as Constitutional principles across the world. The irony is that the two main statutes which have constituted the first major legislative response to the HRA have not, this book has argued, fully met those principles. A basis in law has been created, thus recognising the principle of legality, although its quality is questionable in some respects. But the principles of necessity and proportionality have been recognised in a grudging and minimal fashion. Further, the partial insulation of the provisions, and their use in practice, from scrutiny under the HRA in the ordinary courts means that a domestic Convention jurisprudence, which might have enhanced such recognition, has been stifled. In effect, one strand of the rule of law is reflected in the attempt to minimise adherence to a further strand, since the bodies set up in place of the ordinary courts may show less rigour and transparency in their proceedings.

A recurring theme, therefore, has been the curtailment of the role of the ordinary courts in protecting citizens' liberties under the new scheme. The government which introduced the HRA has sought to utilise its provisions in order to aid in such curtailment, in certain key respects. S7 HRA is utilised to delineate the areas of legal challenge placed outside, or largely outside, the courts' purview. The proscription provisions considered in Chapter 3 will tend to keep challenges under s7 HRA to proscription decisions out of the ordinary courts under the Terrorism Act 2000. Under the Regulation of Investigatory Powers Act 2000 the attempt is made to keep challenges to state surveillance, under s7, which would have arisen due to the provisions of Article 8, out of the courts and to confine them to a new Tribunal, which will be subject to executive direction as to its procedure, determined upon outside the full Parliamentary process. The Proscribed Organisations Appeals Commission is of a similar nature, although the direction will come from the Lord Chancellor, rather than the Home Secretary. The legislation makes it apparent that these two new bodies, central to the new framework, will be likely to deliver lower standards of procedural justice than those available in a court. (Clearly, they may, on occasion in practice, take a more activist stance, but this does not appear to be the intention underlying the legislation.) The judiciary continues to be excluded from the authorisation process for the exercise of powers of stop and search, of surveillance and of the security and intelligence services. In this respect the new scheme is clearly based on the model for state surveillance, counter-terrorism and special police powers established under the Conservative governments of the 1980s and 1990s.

In so far as the courts have a role, mainly in criminal proceedings, it is circumscribed owing to the prevalence in the scheme of very broadly drawn offences, frequently requiring no proof of *mens rea* and based on presumptions of guilt. If the accused chooses to call no evidence he or she can be found guilty of serious offences on the basis of minimal evidence. As Chapter 9 argues, the scheme manipulates the role of the courts: while efforts – very serious ones in the case of the interception of communications – are made to keep the citizen out of the ordinary courts in attempting to ameliorate the effects of the scheme by relying on Convention rights, the state at the same time claims the right to use the courts in order to enforce onerous duties on citizens, including the duty to inform on their fellows or to intercept the communications of work colleagues or customers, at the request of the state. Citizens are to be turned into a nation of spies and informers, on pain of imprisonment.

The check represented by Parliament, especially in reliance on the Convention guarantees, has also, it has been argued, been undermined. A hallmark of the new scheme is the marginalisation and manipulation of Parliament. Again the HRA itself has been utilised to this end. The Terrorism and the Regulation of Investigatory Powers Bills put before Parliament were incomplete; they were riddled with clauses allowing for the extension of a number of powers, by executive order, and the gaps were frequently found in the most crucial, potentially rights-infringing areas. The use of executive order, subject to the negative resolution procedure, to fill them means that full scrutiny is avoided. Further, at a number of points in debate the HRA was used as a smoke screen, as a means of persuading MPs that Convention safeguards were available, while at the same time including ouster clauses or provision steering actions away from the courts, so that the safeguards could hardly be used. In other words, the HRA was used to afford this draconian legislation a misleading appearance of rectitude. Both these Bills were accompanied by statements of their compatibility with the Convention and such compatibility was referred to at certain points in debate with a view to quieting unease with the provisions. The legal advice founding the statements was not revealed. It appeared from the Parliamentary debates that the statements were based only on a better than 51% chance of achieving compatibility.[1] The Convention provisions were therefore afforded the most minimal interpretation possible in order to put forward the statements. Political argument was disabled on the basis of a very doubtful standard of human rights. In this sense fears that the HRA would obscure human rights rather than enhance them are being realised.[2]

The failure to set up Parliamentary Committees or to afford new powers to the existing ones, in the arenas covered by the new legislation, is part of the same trend. No Committee is directly charged with the scrutiny of state surveillance, despite the new, extremely extensive powers which have been introduced. The model of the Interceptions of Communication Act 1985, which made provision for a very meagre level of Parliamentary scrutiny, was adopted wholesale for the new scheme. The introduction of new, permanent counter-terrorist legislation, and abolition of the previous scheme of annual review and renewal, create further marginalisation of Parliament's role at the most crucial and controversial interface between liberty and state power.

[1] See in particular HC Debs March 2000 col 368.

[2] See Gearty 'Terrorism and human rights: a case study in impending legal realities' 19(3) LS 367 at 379.

New Labour's civil libertarian ideology

One of the central concerns of this book, then, has been to chart and analyse New Labour's tendency towards illiberality. It has suggested that, judged on the basis of its surveillance and counter-terrorist schemes, the central arenas of state power, the civil liberties agenda of the government is little more liberal than that of the last one. If, in social and economic terms, the 'Third Way' is between neo-liberalism and redistributive social democracy,[3] it is suggested that in civil liberties terms it has elements both of Thatcherite authoritarianism and liberal normativism. While the HRA provides scope for arguing that the 'Third Way' embraces fundamental liberal rights-based assumptions, such an analysis would not take account, it is argued, of the new 'state power' scheme introduced under the New Labour government and examined in this book.

The Blair government is prepared to follow trends already put in place by the Conservative governments of 1989–1997 and to introduce legislation, such as the Regulation of Investigatory Powers Act 2000, which not only bears all the hallmarks of its predecessor's legislation, but introduces new illiberal ones of its own. Unlike the Thatcher government which, as Dworkin has argued, appeared to have little understanding of human rights values, viewing them as a commodity which could readily be discarded, the Blair government shows understanding of such values. But it is also pursuing a populist crime control agenda which was foreshadowed in its Opposition stance under Blair. Two parallel and contradictory trends emerge: a determination to introduce illiberal legislation based on illiberal populist policies, but an awareness of the human rights context, created by the HRA, within which such legislation must take effect. To an extent New Labour appears to wish to have a sound human rights record, as indicated by the strong aduration of s3 of the HRA. But it also wants to appear 'tough on crime'. The inherent conflicts created have sought resolution in a tortuous fashion as Chapters 3, 6 and 9, in particular, indicated. But their consequences which, while ironical, are clearly intended, are to undermine and marginalise the impact of the Convention under the HRA. While certain avenues to the use of the ordinary courts have been closed off, the responsibility, within the criminal process, for finding a means of reconciling the illiberal, populist measures of the new 'state power' scheme with the Convention guarantees, has largely been handed to the judges. If they display liberality in discharging it the government will not appear to be implicated. In civil libertarian terms, then, there is no 'Third Way' since at present New Labour's civil liberties and human rights stance is too incoherent and inconsistent to emerge as an ideology.

[3] Giddens *The Third Way* (1998) Polity Press. In the social and economic context it has been argued that the 'Third Way' is too eclectic to constitute a coherent ideology: M Freeden 'The ideology of New Labour' [1999] *Political Quarterly* 42–51.

The model used for the two main New Labour Bills discussed in this book is not new; it is largely based on the Thatcherite model for such legislation. Both have strong parallels with the previous legislation they replace. The Prevention of Terrorism Act was first passed under a Labour government in 1974, but its later accretions were added under both Thatcher and Major. The addition of 'international terrorism' and the application of certain of the terrorist offences to the new groups foreshadowed the far wider application undertaken under New Labour. The Interception of Communications Act strongly foreshadowed its later, far more comprehensive successor. It largely prevented consideration of interception in the ordinary courts and set up an administrative body to hear complaints, none of which, as Chapter 9 pointed out, were ever upheld in the 15 years of its existence. The introduction of the 1985 Act paralleled that of the RIPA since it was also a response to the Convention, which used the creation of a statutory basis for the regulation of phone tapping as a means of precluding the development of any domestic jurisprudence on the subject or the use of Convention principles in so doing. It also maintained the exclusion of the judiciary from the authorisation process. In short, it used legislative regulation as a means of protecting executive power. The only jurisprudence on telephone tapping has developed in criminal proceedings, due to the anomaly of s9, and its result has always been to favour the prosecution, even where standards of criminal justice might thereby be compromised.

Thus the new 'state power' legislation merely continues and extends the illiberal characteristics of its predecessors. The new aspect is the HRA and the need to circumvent it. In order to do so, while issuing statements of compatibility, the government has adopted what this book has termed a minimalist approach. This means basing the legislation on Strasbourg decisions, such as *Esbester* or *Christie*,[4] which were strongly influenced by the doctrine of the margin of appreciation, and then encapsulating a minimalist interpretation even of those decisions in the legislation. In other words, the narrowest possible interpretation of the Convention jurisprudence has been adopted.

Although the HRA has, this book contends, been used in the new scheme as part of a cynical manipulation of Parliament, New Labour must be given credit for passing it, for putting obstacles in its own way. The Thatcher government, as it stated in its election manifestos, would not have done so. Nor would the Conservatives under Major, had they taken office in 1997. Since the Conservative Party in Opposition under Hague supported the two key measures introduced by New Labour, only decrying their insufficiently draconian aspects, it can be assumed that it would eventually have introduced legislation that looked rather similar, possibly in response to successful applications to Strasbourg, had it been in office.

[4] See Chapter 8 pp330–331 and Chapter 9 p365.

Any such legislation would probably have been less comprehensive since it would not have been introduced under the impetus of the HRA, and most significantly, that Act would not have been available to act as a check on its effects in practice. But the attempts to curb the influence of the Convention in its own two major Bills suggest that while, in contrast, the New Labour ideology encompasses a commitment to an ideal of liberty, it is an ideal which is viewed as requiring control and limitation and which is centrally determined. The notion of plural and diverse views of liberty and of the best means of protecting it seems to be a foreign one. Hence Blair's hostile outburst at the Labour Conference in September 1999 condemning 'libertarian nonsense masquerading as freedom'.[5]

Parliament as the guardian of liberty in the post-HRA era

Traditionally, under the UK Constitution, Parliament is supposed to fulfil its role as the guardian of individual liberty. The doctrine of Parliamentary sovereignty is supposed to be accompanied by an acceptance of this responsibility. In practice, as Chapter 1 indicated, these notions are flawed. In reality, the doctrine hands immense power to the executive, while Parliament's ability to curb that power is greatly weakened by the large majorities which the voting system delivers.

But this traditional analysis of the weakness of democracy, as recognised under the UK Constitution, in protecting liberty, must give way to a different one at the present time. New Labour can get draconian legislation passed, not only because of its large majority, which it has not had to rely on in relation to the two major Bills discussed in this book, but because the main Opposition Party unites with it in favouring such legislation. Both new Bills were supported by the Conservative Party in Opposition, but some criticisms were advanced, to the effect that the legislation was not draconian enough. One of the main criticisms from the Conservative Opposition of the Terrorism Bill was that it did not reintroduce internment, throughout the UK.[6] The RIPA was attacked by the Shadow Home Secretary, Anne Widdecombe, on the basis that it did not afford the DSS powers to apply for authorisation of intrusive surveillance.[7] Both major parties believe that they are satisfying populist crime control views in relation to the new legislation. Indeed, in mid-2000 Hague adopted a position on criminal justice policy which was, at least in terms of the rhetoric adopted, to the right of the Labour government, on the basis that creating such a distinction on this particular issue, even if it was only an

[5] Noted in *The Economist* 2 October 1999.
[6] See Chapter 3 p68.
[7] HC Debs 6 March 2000, col 778, and see Chapter 9 p350, Chapter 10 p380.

apparent one, would improve Conservativ
parties may be right in perceiving electoral a
inal justice policies. It is clearly possible that pa
such policies in the debased and impoverished term
and would vote accordingly.[9] Current Parliamentar
reflects a failure of democracy, but it is not the failure
during the Thatcher years, when the Labour Opposition
to ameliorate draconian legislation, but was unable to do so
of the large Conservative majority.

As Chapter 1 argued, there is at present a continuing Parliam
consensus in rights-based terms post-2000 as revealed by debate on th
two major Bills. That consensus predated the current Parliament bu
became clearer during it. It gives every sign that it is likely both to endure and to become more marked, in the sense that both parties may seek to outdo each other in adopting an anti-liberal stance. Clearly, the House of Lords may continue the activist stance it has adopted, identified in Chapter 1, since its partial reform. It played a significant role in ameliorating some of the worst features of the new schemes, including narrowing down the extraordinarily wide definition of terrorism put forward by the government in the original Terrorism Bill. It will have a continuing role in relation to the new scheme since gap-filling executive orders under it will be put before the Lords, under the negative resolution procedure. It may well play a highly significant part in improving the new legislation. But it is hard to read the Commons' debates on those two New Labour Bills without re-evaluating any subsisting notion that democracy can be relied upon to protect individual rights.

Thus, the argument for reforming the voting system for the Westminster Parliament to bring it into line with all the other UK voting systems, and for strengthening the scrutinising powers of Parliamentary bodies, including in particular the Security and Intelligence Committee, are as pertinent now as they were during the Thatcher and Major years. But until and if real curbs on the power of the executive are created, it is not realistic, in the current populist era, to expect Parliament to play a key role in ameliorating executive power in the contexts covered by this book.

[8] In mid-2000 Hague launched a number of attacks on the 'liberal establishment' which improved his popularity rating according to private polling for the Conservative party. As Ed Vaizey observes, it is more difficult to draw a distinction between the two parties on other issues (see the *Guardian* 24 May 2000). By appearing especially 'tough on crime' Hague is following the model espoused by Michael Howard and seeking to appeal to populist notions of crime control.

[9] This possibility was suggested by the improvement in Conservative poll ratings on this issue in mid-2000, in contradistinction to the failure to improve on others such as health or education, suggesting that the improvement was not due to a general rise in Conservative popularity but to the approval accorded to Hague's criminal justice policies by parts of the electorate. This suggestion must, however, be advanced with caution since further polling over a longer period of time would be needed to substantiate it.

d other bodies, in particular
erforming such a role.

ontinue to view the allocation of any
a dangerous step and therefore consider
berties should be left to Parliament.[10] It is
es not take full account of the impact of Bills
dictions or of the dismal record of Parliament
wards, particularly its supine acceptance, at a time
was in being, of the extension of terrorist offences
ted range of groups. Contrary to such a view, it is con-
notion of antinomy between the role of Parliament and
judiciary in the post-HRA era is flawed. The relationship between the courts and Parliament as twin guardians of liberty has become, at least theoretically, a closer one due to the provision for making a declaration of incompatibility under the HRA. The courts are able to inform Parliament that it has breached the Convention and, although the executive retains crucial decision-making powers at key points in the process for responding, it also accords a significant measure of power to Parliament.

Much more significantly, the central aspiration of the Convention is to protect democratic values, including respect for the rule of law, and to provide the means whereby participation in the democratic process may occur, in substantive terms. If freedom of expression and of the media is curbed, such participation is curtailed, as Chapters 3 and 4 pointed out. In so far as minorities are excluded from the political process, the Convention guarantees may be instrumental in helping to afford them a voice, as Chapter 4 argued. The strong support of the Convention for political expression will tend to foster pluralism and tolerance. Alternative viewpoints may obtain a hearing. The populist backlash against the 'liberal establishment', currently evident, may be reversed or, at least, tempered. The net result of the infusion of Convention principles into domestic law would be, it is argued, to support rather than undermine the democratic process. In a more direct sense the judiciary has the opportunity of providing a corrective to ill-considered and draconian criminal measures and more generally to police responses to populist demands. The judiciary has the opportunity of relying upon the Convention standards of criminal procedure in order to protect the rights within that process of those who are vulnerable owing to lack of education, youth, class, mental illness, race, origin – of those, in other words, who have been the subject of

[10] See J Griffiths 'The Brave New World of Sir John Laws' [2000] 63(2) MLR 159.

the notorious miscarriage of justice cases of the past, the overwhelming majority of which have been terrorist cases.

This book has indicated possible judicial approaches to the Convention. It may well be that what has been termed 'traditionalism' will merge into activism as decisions under the HRA are handed down. It may be that the Convention will subtly infuse itself into the common law so that it energises judicial decision-making which was steering in a rights-based direction in any event, and affords it greater credibility. Weaknesses of the common law may be addressed under a robust interpretation of the Convention. Although the traditionalist approach had its origins in the Diceyan notion of protection for liberties, rather than rights, aspects of that approach, especially as regards notions of legality, still have relevance to the domestic development of the Convention jurisprudence. The minimalist will, however, remain, it is argued, out of step with the new development. If a minimalist approach takes hold in the House of Lords, its record may come to be viewed as similar to that of the Supreme Court of Canada which commentators agree in viewing as timorous and unflattering.[11] The Supreme Court has failed to take a bold and innovative approach, one which could be viewed as showing the way forward for other such courts throughout the world. If the House of Lords follows suit domestic litigants might be denied rights which would be accorded to them in higher courts in other jurisdictions. But the adoption of an activist stance, a strong reliance on Convention principles, whether or not expressed in Convention outcomes, possibly as a development from a traditionalist one, would provide a firm basis for the expectation expressed that the judiciary will raise human rights standards under the HRA. If such a stance is not adopted, if the traditionalist approach is followed in seeking to absorb rather than develop Convention values, on the basis that they have already found expression in the common law, then expectations that the judiciary can play a key part in defending central democratic principles in the coming years are likely to prove misplaced. Activism would mean affording full weight to freedom of expression in public protest cases, considering exclusion of evidence obtained in breach of a Convention right, questioning claims of public interest immunity, refusing to accept presumptions against defendants, requiring some evidence where claims of a threat to national security are put forward. In other words, the infusion of Convention principles would counter the tendency of the judiciary, discerned by a number of commentators, to fail in crucial instances to protect the rights of the weak.

Dawn Oliver has argued that what has been termed the 'ethical aimlessness' of the common law – its lack of a sense of clear moral direction – means that because the judges have no coherent common conception

[11] See D Beatty 'The Canadian Charter of Rights: Lessons and Laments' [1997] 60(4) MLR 487.

of how the law should develop, they have not framed any set of 'guiding principles or priorities where civil and political rights clash with public interests'.[12] As David Feldman argues, the Convention provides such a set of principles. His argument is that the judiciary has the opportunity of infusing substantive value into an 'almost entirely procedural' Constitution which has been said to be suffering from a 'deep malaise' since 'few of the values of our society find expression in constitutional form'.[13] But, as Chapter 2 contends, it is arguable that this process can occur in a manner which is procedurally constrained, in the sense that neutral principles of formal justice should structure judicial decision-making so that the realisation of the ideological goals of particular judges is strongly curbed.[14] Although in certain key fields, as this book argues, the avenues by which the judiciary might take an activist approach have been wholly or partially closed off, it has also sought to identify the means by which, even in such fields, that approach can find expression.

The challenges ahead

The Convention, then, as interpreted in a robust and creative fashion by the judiciary, has the potential to preserve and enhance the underpinnings of the democracy for the future. In this sense the rights afforded further effect under the HRA show more respect for democratic principles than would the retention of the untrammelled power of the majority of the day.[15] But the responsibility for this enterprise also lies outside the judiciary. This book has considered a wide variety of methods of seeking to ensure that the Convention rights are given genuine efficacy, in particular by the public authorities who are bound by s6 HRA. The failure of the democratic process to protect individual rights mentioned above is not intended to imply that the enterprise of providing such protection should be abandoned or that academic attention should be withdrawn from it. Rather, that process must be used in order to press for the measures of social and economic rights without which the rights granted have value only in a formal sense. A recognition of its weaknesses in this

[12] 'A Bill of Rights for the UK' in *Government in the United Kingdom* (1991) p151.

[13] D Feldman 'The Human Rights Act and Constitutional Principles' (1999) 2 LS 165.

[14] See further Sir John Laws in 'The Good Constitution: Morals and Rights' [1996] PL 624. Laws' basic argument is that the Kantian imperative of respect for others' moral autonomy is what underlies Western liberalism and that the notion of rights, properly understood, is there only to police infringements of this respect, and does not in itself imply any confrontational stance towards others. On the contrary, Laws argues, such an attitude of respect provides the basic preconditions without which civil society cannot flourish.

[15] Such a view is of course endorsed by a number of legal philosophers and civil libertarians. See Dworkin, *A Bill of Rights for Britain* (1990); the view also clearly underpins his general political philosophy, see for example 'Liberalism' in *A Matter of Principle* (1985). See also Hart *Law Liberty and Morality* (1963), and Lester *Democracy and Individual Rights* (1968).

respect is beginning to be evident in the ongoing extensions of the Convention itself. It appears to be moving away from first generation civil rights and towards second generation social and economic rights, as indicated, albeit somewhat tentatively, in its later Protocols. The latest one, the 12th Protocol, has a concern which reaches well beyond civil rights since its protection extends to freedom from discrimination in the social and economic sphere.

Most significantly, the manipulation of Parliament[16] discussed in this book under the Human Rights Act – the tendency to mislead it into believing that statements of compatibility denote a satisfactory process of human rights auditing – may be tempered in future. Activist decisions of the judiciary, a general, educative, rise in rights consciousness and, more specifically, in understanding of the Convention system and concepts, combined with the impact of the work of the Joint Parliamentary Committee on Human Rights, may eventually curb the illiberal governmental and Parliamentary tendencies discussed above and indicated throughout this book.

These are aspirations for the future. In the immediate term, as this book has argued, the infusion of substantive values into domestic law in reliance on the guarantees and the Strasbourg principles may have to occur despite New Labour executive decisions and its centrepiece state power scheme, not as a result of them. The challenge is to move beyond the view that a statutory basis for the exercise of a number of investigatory powers is sufficient. It is to demand the infusion of Convention values into that basis. In the past, under the Thatcher government, when encroachment on liberties took place in hidden areas of the executive, unforeseeably and inaccessibly, on the ground that the state was in the same position as the ordinary citizen in being able to do that which the law did not forbid, the achievement of a statutory basis for the exercise of a number of such powers was a hardly realisable aspiration. That era is over and the New Labour government deserves credit for putting an end to it in the Regulation of Investigatory Powers Act. But not only has there been a failure to satisfy the expectation that a new statutory basis for the exercise of state power adopted as a result of the HRA would fully reflect Convention principles, there has been an attempt to prevent its development in the ordinary courts by reliance on such principles. There has also been a movement towards the extension of state power aimed at the suppression of dissent in the Terrorism Act 2000, contrary, as Chapter 3 argued, to the underlying Convention principles. In a number of aspects of both schemes rule of law principles have not been adhered to, as Chapters 5, 6 and 7, in particular, argued. Thus, while the contribution, in the HRA, of the New Labour government to liberty in the UK must be recognised, the struggle which lies ahead in order to make the enterprise successful must also be acknowledged.

[16] See in particular Chapter 1, pp3–4 and Chapter 2, p44.

Index